AFRICA'S HIDDEN HISTORIES

AFRICA'S HIDDEN HISTORIES

EVERYDAY LITERACY AND
MAKING THE SELF

Edited by Karin Barber

INDIANA UNIVERSITY PRESS
BLOOMINGTON AND INDIANAPOLIS

This book is a publication of

Indiana University Press
601 North Morton Street
Bloomington, IN 47404-3797 USA

http://iupress.indiana.edu

Telephone orders   800-842-6796
Fax orders   812-855-7931
Orders by e-mail   iuporder@indiana.edu

© 2006 by Indiana University Press

The paper used in this publication meets the minimum
requirements of American National Standard for
Information Sciences—Permanence of Paper for
Printed Library Materials, ANSI Z39.48-1984.

Manufactured in the United States of America

Library of Congress Cataloging-in-Publication Data

Africa's hidden histories : everyday literacy and making
the self / edited by Karin Barber.
        p. cm. — (African expressive cultures)
    Includes index.
    ISBN 0–253–34729–7 (cloth : alk. paper) —ISBN
0–253–21843–8 (pbk. : alk. paper)   1. Literacy—
Social aspects—Africa.   2. Educational anthropology—
Africa.   3. Letter writing—Africa.   4. Africa—
History—1884–1960.   I. Barber, Karin.   II. Series.
    LC158.A2A3995 2006
        302.2'244096—dc22   2005030257
    1 2 3 4 5 11 10 09 08 07 06

CONTENTS

Acknowledgments

This book began as a series of seminars on the theme of "social histories of reading and writing in Africa." Funded by the Economic and Social Research Council of the UK, the two-year program of meetings brought together historians, anthropologists and literary scholars from five institutions: the University of Birmingham, Cambridge University, Oxford University, the University of the Witwatersrand, and the University of Natal-Durban. We are grateful to the ESRC for making this possible. The meetings were informal and involved the delighted perusal and discussion of what we came to think of as "tin-trunk texts": letters, diaries, obituary notices, pamphlets, and other things that people across Africa often keep in boxes hidden under their beds. These texts represent obscure but important uses of literacy, often overlooked in favor of the more visible, public writings of political and educational elites. The exploration of this "hidden history" led us to a broader inquiry into the role of literacy in the lives of ordinary people—clerks, teachers, catechists, school pupils, local healers, entrepreneurs, and others—and to an exploration of local reading circles and debating societies.

As the program unfolded, more people became drawn in, prompting us to expand the final meeting into a small international conference. Several of the conference participants subsequently became contributors to this volume. For additional funding for the conference, we are grateful to the Royal African Society, the African Studies Association of the UK, the British Academy, and the National Research Foundation of South Africa.

This volume, then, arose from collaboration and discussion sustained over several years, and it is in a real sense the outcome of a collective practical as well as intellectual effort. Members of the group took it in turns to help convene the meetings, rotating between Birmingham, Cambridge, and Oxford. Especially vital was the contribution of Stephanie Newell, who co-convened the final conference and whose enthusiasm and perspicacity were a driving force behind the whole project. Three of the original group did not offer papers for this volume but played an important role in the seminar: Ato Quayson and John Lonsdale at Cambridge and Gavin Williams at Oxford. Our thanks to them for their stimulating participation.

We would also like to thank the Kenya National Archives for permission to reproduce the letters discussed in Lynn Thomas's chapter.

AFRICA'S HIDDEN HISTORIES

INTRODUCTION: HIDDEN INNOVATORS IN AFRICA

Karin Barber

The Proliferation of Written Texts in Colonial Africa

Colonial Africa saw an explosion of writing and print, produced and circulated not only by the highly educated and publicly visible figures that dominate political histories of Africa but also by non-elites or obscure aspirants to elite status. Waged laborers, clerks, village headmasters, traders, and artisans read, wrote, and hoarded texts of many kinds. Local, small-scale print production became a part of social life. In coastal West Africa in particular, pamphlets and booklets were run off on artisanal presses by entrepreneurs who were sometimes also the editors and even the authors of the texts they printed. Tracts, obituary notices, tales and histories, guides to the interpretation of dreams, advice on choosing a spouse, and elaborate church programs all rolled off these small presses in response to local demand. Handwritten documents were if anything even more remarkably profuse. Letters became an established feature of family and business life, especially crucial in those areas of Southern Africa that were dominated by massive and systematic labor migration. Professional letter-writing—with pen or typewriter—became one of the new occupations of the colonial era. Diaries and notebooks became an adjunct of literate people's self-management, and self-documentation was sometimes taken to extraordinary lengths.

Some individuals engaged in marathon feats of writing. Louisa Mvemve, a woman herbalist working on the Reef and in the Eastern Cape in South Africa from about 1914 to the 1930s, wrote hundreds of letters—often chatty, personal, and heartfelt letters—to the impassive officials of the Native Affairs Department (Catherine Burns, this volume).[1] Boakye Yiadom, a Ghanaian schoolmaster and catechist, kept a diary and personal memoir over a period of nearly sixty years, documenting, among a great variety of other things, the complex negotiations he conducted with his seventeen wives and fiancées

1

(Stephan Miescher, this volume). Akinpẹlu Obiṣẹsan, an Ibadan trader and local politician, made almost daily additions to his diary between 1920 and 1960, leaving an archive of seventy-two boxes of papers which have barely begun to be explored for the light they shed on the culture and consciousness of colonial Nigeria (Ruth Watson, this volume). Henry Muoria, a Kikuyu and Kenyan nationalist, not only wrote prolifically on politics, history, and household management, but, aided by his wife Judith, published a weekly Kikuyu newspaper in the very teeth of the Emergency (Bodil Folke Frederiksen, this volume). And more obscure people than these surface through the texts they produced and preserved: a Kenyan schoolgirl and schoolboy whose vivid and elaborate letters to each other became evidence in the paternity case that resulted from their romance (Lynn Thomas, this volume); the young men who served as scribes in the Nazarite church of Isaiah Shembe, producing and copying the community's idiosyncratic sacred texts (Liz Gunner, this volume); the humble and sometimes only partially literate circle of people attached to the Ekukhanyeni mission station in Natal who created a virtual community through individual and collaborative letter-writing (Vukile Khumalo, this volume); the Ghanaians who became expert at a new genre, the biographical obituary notice distributed at the funerals of their kin (T. C. McCaskie, this volume).

Such printed and handwritten texts were often preserved for many years, to be brought out from time to time and read over, alone or to company. People all over Africa kept precious documents in tin trunks under their beds—or in a suitcase (Audrey Gadzekpo, this volume), plastic bags (Van Onselen 1993), or a glass-fronted cabinet (Stephan Miescher, this volume), reminiscent of the bookcases favored by British working-class autodidacts of the same period (Rose 2001). This hoarding of texts, often taking place over a lifetime, provokes inquiries not just into the nature of the texts themselves but into the habits and dispositions surrounding them. What we appear to be witnessing is a kind of local, do-it-yourself archiving, the purpose and effects of which we want to explore further.

The writing of texts was connected to regimes of reading, originally learned in school but often expanded through attendance at church Bible groups and social literary clubs or by diligent private study. The question is not only what people read but how they read. Forms of sociality were built around reading, which was seen as an edifying and civilizational activity. Schools' literary and debating societies may have been the model for the many "reading circles" which flourished widely, particularly in coastal West Africa. The activities of school literary societies and adult cultural organizations in

South Africa fed into debating and speech-making, and thus eventually into national political discourse (Isabel Hofmeyr, this volume; Bhekizizwe Peterson, this volume). Reading circles also fostered creative writing when participants turned to the production of popular novellas (Stephanie Newell, this volume). And in all these cases, the activities of reading circles were also closely bound up with the local press, which functioned as a showcase and sounding board for their activities.

These people were innovators. They had urgent reasons for engaging in such marathons of personal textual production, for accumulating and preserving private collections of texts, and for inventing new spaces in which to cultivate the practices of literacy. In some cases there was clearly a desire to find forms in which to express the ideas and emotions—whether political critique or personal love—emerging in new social circumstances. In others there must have been an ambition to memorialize and make a mark that transcended time. One can see also a desire to assemble and investigate a personal self and to create a repository of values, the crystallized tokens and products of "civilization," "progress," "enlightenment," and "modernity." In all cases, these individuals—who were often socially precarious and culturally isolated in their textual pursuits—were pioneers, working out new forms of creative expression.

Tin-Trunk Texts as a Field of Inquiry

This project, then, is focused on three themes: the profusion of innovative individual writing and enterprising efforts in local, small-scale print publication by non-elites in the colonial period; the propensity to collect and "archive" such texts; and the significance attached to reading, especially as a mode of collective and individual betterment. What we seem to be looking at is not isolated examples of the uses of literacy scattered across the continent but the history of a remarkably consistent and widespread efflorescence—a social phenomenon happening all over colonial Anglophone Africa at the same time and with comparable features.[2]

We have here a zone of activity which has been systematically overlooked in favor of more salient and more official styles of reading and writing by academic and political elites. If brought into view, it could reveal the underside, or the obverse, of the better-known face of social and political history in Africa. In particular, it could show how innovations in textual forms and in associated institutions such as reading circles by these obscure literati were linked to the imagining of new kinds of personhood, new ways of being social, and new ways of relating to the world of officialdom. In some cases—as in the Asante obituaries discussed by McCaskie—their inventions caught on and became an important new vehicle for individual, family, and class competition and (at least for a time) for subversive political comment. In others, as in the literary inventions of the Oṣogbo schoolmaster S. A. Adenle (Barber, this volume), they had no imitators and their innovative works simply disappeared from view. But the failures and isolated one-off inventions are no less revealing than the self-reproducing successes. As Khumalo demonstrates in his study of the Ekukhanyeni circle of Zulu-language letter-writers, the strands of cultural and political history that were *not* taken up by the narrative of mainstream nationalist historiography are as significant as those that were. Taken together, they cast light upon both the openness and the limits of personal and collective cultural innovation in colonial Africa. And the exploration of this, in turn, casts light forward onto contemporary expressive cultures. The continuity is well brought out both in McCaskie's account of the changes in the Asante obituary genre—from its invention in 1932 to its popularization and brief politicization in the 1940s to its eclipse by video in the late 1990s—and in Graham Furniss's discussion of the parallel history of the Hausa poetry circle of northern Nigeria, which proved an extraordinarily resilient institution. Dating back at least to the 1804 jihad, when Islamic intellectuals convened to debate politics and poetry, it became highly significant in the 1930s and 1940s as a forum where nationalist and regional concerns were articulated and where the early versions of the political parties that have since dominated northern Nigeria took shape. Most recently, it has been redeployed to produce and disseminate Hausa-language romantic novellas and then to make dramatic versions of them on video (Graham Furniss, this volume). To understand present-day expressive genres and the institutions within which they are produced, then, it is necessary to look back to the era in which they were formed and underwent their greatest development.

If tin-trunk literacy can be envisaged as a field defined by its very obscurity, we could go on to ask what these tin-trunk literati have in common, apart from their relative invisibility and their propensity to create innovations in text, genre, and institutional form. The prolific producers and consumers of texts documented in these pages range from Mrs. Mercy Ffoulkes-Crabbe (née Quartey-Papafio)—born into one old elite Gold Coast family and married into another—to migrant laborers in South Africa whose letters were often written not as embellishments to civilization but in the desperate hope of survival (Breckenridge, this volume). Mrs. Ffoulkes-Crabbe took literacy and its benefits for granted and believed its civilizing influence should be spread; the migrant workers used it sparingly and strategically under a regime where literacy was experienced as an instrument of oppression more than a means of liberation. Between the educated elite and the manual laborer, however, there are all the people who assiduously cultivated literacy without feeling fully entitled to the status with which it was associated. In this middle zone, tin-trunk literacy involved a fervent regard for the capacity of reading and writing to enhance personal and social existence and create a particular kind of civilized and civic community. One senses in the most prolific of these writers an exhilaration about the very possibility of writing and the power it brings with it. But inseparable from this hope is a persistent anxiety. Only a tiny fraction of those who attended primary school in colonial Anglophone Africa had the chance to go on to secondary, let alone tertiary, institutions. Most of the readers and writers in this book were people whose schooling, though it set them apart from the illiterate majority, did not progress much beyond primary school. (Breckenridge points out the immense and understudied cultural impact of this new class of primary school leavers.) Literacy embodied aspiration, and aspiration was founded upon lack—a sense of personal inadequacy associated with an education perceived as incomplete. A poignant moment in Obiṣẹsan's diary is when, after many doubts and revisions, he submits an article to *The Lagos Weekly Record* and waits anxiously to see whether or not it will be published. It is not, and he comments regretfully "I am still thirsty to know deep the English language. I see that my knowledge of the precious language is very weak." And the aspirations of the pregnant Kenyan schoolgirl "Sara" were more cruelly rebuffed. Her letters were a desperate attempt to convince college-going "Thomas" that she was sufficiently civilized to be his wife, but her mistakes in grammar and in attitude only attracted an outpouring of epistolary contempt from him.

It was not only the level of formal schooling that determined status. Literacy was a vector rather than a fixed attribute of particular social classes or segments of society. As an avenue to status change and a key mode of social and personal self-positioning, it involved dedicated and unremitting individual effort. Some primary school leavers might make little use of their ability to read and write beyond inscribing the odd birth or death date on the wall or reading the occasional letter. Others might carefully cultivate it, read newspapers, buy self-help books from overseas, join a literary circle, keep a diary, and even write romances or collect and publish proverbs and other items of "cultural heritage." By doing these things, they would lay claim to membership of a social world defined precisely by this culture of literacy. These social worlds could be long-established spheres defined by an old literate elite, as in the

Lagos and Gold Coast colonies, but in other cases they were themselves novel and fragile creations that required assiduous maintenance. In the latter category were the "youngmen's" often-ephemeral reading groups in Ghana (Newell, this volume) and the epistolary circle at Ekukhanyeni mission station, which was composed of royal exiles, "preachers, wagon makers, migrant workers, scholars and prison inmates" and the bishop's daughter Harriette, who learned to write fluent Zulu (Khumalo, this volume): a heterogeneous collection of participants which was constituted as a new, virtual, transnational community only through the act of letter-writing itself. Neither individual nor collective status in these new communities of readers and writers was ever wholly secure. It depended on the shifting mutual evaluations of others and on their own, often unstable, social and financial means. The writings of the tin-trunk literati thus reveal something of the complexity and contingency of social orientations and affiliations in colonial Africa.[3] A recurring theme is these individuals' precariousness and their sense of isolation, even when they were at the center of extended families or business networks.

The unease engendered by this sense of educational and socioeconomic fragility was mirrored by another source of anxiety, for projects of personal self-betterment through literacy were hemmed in by the documentary state. British colonial regimes made extensive use of documentary forms of domination (Hawkins 2002). Local government was everywhere conducted largely through letters (often unwelcome) from the district officer or other colonial officer. At the level of everyday personal experiences, the greatest contrasts in forms and modes of tin-trunk literacy across sub-Saharan Africa may correlate with the intensity and pervasiveness of the colonial documentary regime—ranging from full-blown pass laws in South Africa through the *kipande* system in Kenya to the lesser nuisance of tax receipts and radio licenses in West Africa. What they had in common, though, was that people everywhere experienced some form of documentary bullying—even those people who felt themselves to have benefited most from the status and employment opened up to them by schooling. If the most common strategy was to try to get the better of it by mastering the language and techniques of officialdom, another response appears to have been to try to limit contact with schools and literacy to a functional useful minimum, as with the Southern African labor migrants discussed by Keith Breckenridge.[4] However, officialdom did not necessarily remain an external framework to be adopted or resisted; more ambiguous, intimate relationships are evidenced in these case studies. The unease stemming from an aspirational sense of lack was thus compounded by an uneasy relationship to the documentary regime itself. A doubly anxious yet nonetheless fervent aspiration may have been what stimulated some of the people discussed in this volume to take textual production to the extraordinary lengths they did.

The formation of this broad category of aspirational readers and writers, finally, is a coherent historical phenomenon in the sense that all over sub-Saharan Anglophone Africa it was the product of similar social, political, and economic innovations. Among these were the clerkly class created to serve colonial government and commerce; the British missionary and government schools with their particular disciplines and syllabi; the church and its emphasis (which was greater among Protestant denominations) on individual contemplation of sacred texts and popular literacy as a civilizing influence; and the rise of self-help institutions in an era when development goals were preached but the material means for development were sparse. At the same time, the different forms these institutions took and the varying impact they had in different social and historical contexts means that there is scope in future for a focused comparative study, which could trace in detail the ways in which different institutional, economic, and political histories are imprinted in the fine grain of personal texts.

To this extent, tin-trunk literacy can be thought of as a field—and a field which opens onto questions of intense interest to Africanist scholars today. It provides extraordinary access to the way personal writing was involved in the constitution of new kinds of self-representation and personhood—along lines quite different from the classic model of the formation of subjectivity in Enlightenment Europe. It gives close-up, internal views of local ideals of civic virtue and the formation of local publics—through newspapers and book publishing but also through reading circles and debates. It discloses the point of contact between the documentary colonial state and the daily lives of ordinary people who both subverted and internalized official procedures and discourses. And finally, it is a site where cultural innovation can be observed at close quarters, allowing us to witness new genres in formation and with them new conceptions of social being.

Diaries and Letters in the Constitution of the Self

The new genres of the letter and the diary were largely, though perhaps not exclusively,[5] modeled on European prototypes—missionary journals and government and commercial correspondence. They inevitably suggest comparisons with eighteenth-century Europe, where an astonishing efflorescence of personal writing has been interpreted as being intimately connected with the emergence of new conceptions of the self (Taylor 1989). There is something intuitively convincing about the proposition that the newly expanded genres of personal letter, diary, autobiography, and sentimental novel helped to constitute new forms of consciousness rather than just providing new outlets to something that was already there (cf. Stone 1977). Writing about the self produces "a separation between the self as object and the self as subject" (Freccero 1986, 17). Writing intimate letters launches one's own private thoughts across time and space in a concrete, externalized form which both sender and recipient can scrutinize. Diaries, to an even greater degree, present the self to the self, as if one were looking into one's own eyes. This makes possible new forms of self-examination—but also new styles of self-projection and self-dramatization.

In eighteenth-century Europe, it has been suggested, letters and diaries played a part in constituting subjects as "private" people who, on that basis, could come together to form a "public sphere" to defend their interests vis-à-vis the state (Habermas 1962/1992). And from a perspective influenced more by Bourdieu than by Habermas, Brewer suggests that diaries and journals "recorded both a public cultural repertoire and a cultured private self, and [that] the conversation between these two was what mattered" (Brewer 1997, 111). One only has to look at the journal of Anna Larpent (Brewer 1997, 56–61) or the letters of the Lennox sisters (Tillyard 1995) to see how profuse, detailed, and confident was this cultivation of sensibility, this sociable interiority.

Did the diary, the letter, and the autobiography play a comparable role in the colonies? Dipesh Chakrabarty has suggested that in India, the plethora of genres of personal writing produced since the middle of the nineteenth century were devoted to public affairs or the affairs of the extended family and "seldom yield pictures of an endlessly interiorised subject" (1992, 9). There was a public sphere but no private sphere at its heart. In colonial Africa, the fragility and cultural insecurity of the thin stratum of literates—dominated by a heavy-handed bureaucratic colonial state while dependent on proximity to it for their status—meant that the new practices of personal writing were more lonely and more visibly self-conflictual than the comfortable and sociable self-investigation of the bourgeoisie of the European Enlightenment. The contributions to this volume suggest that the genres of the diary and the letter were indeed involved in the constitution of new kinds of self and self-consciousness—but in ways that provoke an expansion and rethinking of existing, predominantly Enlightenment-based, models of relations between writing and subjectivity.

The central issue of the nature of the private is strikingly raised by the

cases of shared authorship and shared reception described by Keith Breckenridge and Vukile Khumalo. Though founded on personal emotion and intimacy, letters written by migrant workers and by the adherents of the
Ekukhanyeni mission were often collective and cooperative rather than purely
individual. People helped each other write and read private letters, and among
the migrant workers groups of male friends would gather at weekends to
coauthor love letters to the girls at home (Breckenridge 2000). But in neither
case did this mean that the individual was submerged in the collective, for the
letter genre also made possible the composition of intensely private expres-
sions of emotion. The sense of betrayal voiced by Magema Fuze when one of
his private letters was opened by the Natal colonial government (Khumalo,
this volume), the warning by a Kgatla migrant worker to his lover to hide or
destroy his intimate and erotic love letter (Breckenridge, this volume)—these
reveal a sense of personal privacy that needed protecting. The genre of the letter, then, simultaneously opens new areas for communicative collaboration
and provides new modes of interaction in a privacy that borders on secrecy.

Both private and public domains were constituted under the shadow of
colonial officialdom. All the letter-writers and diarists presented in this volume engaged in one way or another with the colonial state—by writing directly to colonial officials, by establishing an alternative epistolary network, by
using a diary to keep meticulous records of official information, by writing
love letters with one eye on their possible future use as legal evidence, by
recording their own public achievements and civic contributions (perhaps
with a view to being appropriately obituarized in due course), or by participating in the constitution of an exacting religious community, enclosed within
the state but reversing some of its key values. In their interstitial and insecure
social location, they were in urgent need of aids to management and self-
management; they were vulnerable to official bureaucracy but also hoped to
harness it to their own ends. Their uses of writing suggest an attempt to co-
opt official language and procedures to stabilize their personal lives—to make
arrangements stick and hold other people accountable. In doing so, they were
also assembling and consolidating selves. But these selves were in many cases
not constituted in the manner described by Charles Taylor (1989) as autonomous agents founded upon an individual interiority and subjectivity.
Often, instead, what we find is a form of exteriorization and projection, or a
text that goes behind the scenes rather than into the interior of personhood.
The ways in which this was done were closely linked to innovation in, and experimentation with, the genres of writing they used.

Social insecurity stimulated prodigious feats of textual production. Akinpẹlu Obiṣẹsan, though an influential figure in Ibadan politics and eventually an OBE as well as a town chief (Williams 1993), was frequently in debt or in difficulties and dependent on wealthier traders to bail him out. He used his assiduous diary-keeping to record his hopes of future prosperity, and perhaps will it into being.

Akasease Kofi Boakye Yiadom, the writer of a detailed autobiographical journal maintained over sixty years, was a *krakye*, of the small clerkly class, belonging neither to the old Ghanaian royal and chiefly families nor to the ranks of established and highly educated coastal professionals. He worked as a schoolmaster-catechist in small rural towns all his life, and Miescher suggests that "My Own Life" was intended as a monument to substitute for the house he could not afford to build. This diary was doubtless partly inspired by the local Presbyterian church with its roots in the Basel Mission's Pietist tradition, for like other Protestant missions it set great store by the personal journal as a tool for self-examination and spiritual growth. But Boakye Yiadom combined this with the models of the practical reference work and encyclopedia. He recorded local historical and cultural information and painstakingly transcribed all kinds of official details where they were relevant to himself, from the methods for calculating average attendance in school to the exact results of an eye test, carefully tabulated, and the numbers of all his lottery tickets, as well as all the transactions he entered into with his wives, "girl-fiancées," "fiancées-conceived," "fiancée-wives," and family members. This use of official record-keeping was clearly intended to be useful in managing his practical affairs, but it went beyond this. When he signed himself, in a stern memo to himself within the diary, as "School Teacher (Reg. No 970/44)," "Group Scoutmaster (Reg. No 41160/46)," and "Ex-Service Brigade Signaller (G. C. 19944/40)," it was as if he sought to fix and buttress his self-conception as a responsible citizen in order to make a private resolution stick. It is as if officialdom here is drawn inside to become the carapace of the self. And Miescher shows that rather than functioning as an aid to spiritual introspection, the diary projected and orchestrated a shifting multiple self and was at least as much a script for the performance of a persona as it was an exploration of interiority. His writings "reflect the multitude of Boakye Yiadom selves and alliances" as the diarist, over the course of his life, "moved in and out of various social contexts with competing expectations of him as an adult man." In the diary, he prepared behind the scenes for a public performance of his self. The diary provided him with a launchpad for "readings" of his life-narrative to his family, readings which involved the oral performance, in Twi, of what he had written in English. He told Miescher "I do loudly read my old diaries to my wife, children, grandchildren and the householders to their amusement, laughter and sorrow, knowing and studying my progress, backwardness or retrogression in life; so that they too may be aware of themselves in their living." In projecting his diarized persona to his family, Boakye Yiadom was offering not his interiority or private consciousness but himself and his experiences as an example. And examples are by definition transferable and thus communal: he hopes that by holding himself up to them, the other members of his family "may be aware of *themselves* in their living."

Another diarist who was deeply influenced by Protestant church texts was Lazarus Maphumulo, one of the scribes of the Nazarite church in Natal. Here we see someone working within an extremely rigid communal framework who nonetheless experiments with forms of writing and discovers for himself a new style. The radically independent Nazarite church in Natal drew heavily for its doctrine and ritual on Zulu oral traditions but was nonetheless deeply entranced with writing and influenced by the Wesleyan church to which its founder, Isaiah Shembe, had originally belonged. Literate members of the predominantly illiterate community were called upon to transcribe and copy the hymns, testimonies, and laws that made up the religious patrimony of Isaiah Shembe and his successors. The church maintained powerful control over individuals' uses of texts, treating both these and the spiritual experiences that inspired them as communal property. Liz Gunner shows how Lazarus wrestled with the problems of format and personal expression. His own diary is initially an impersonal collection of hymns and third-person accounts of significant events, laid out in numbered verses like the Bible. But at a certain point, the diary restarts in continuous prose, and eventually the writer breaks through from the third person into the pronoun "I," as if only this personal witness could do justice to the miraculous event being described.

Louisa Mvemve is perhaps the most remarkable inventor represented in this volume. A black South African woman of little formal education, she described herself in her letters as a "civilised person, native healer, public benefactor and loyal subject of the Crown." She had periods of prosperity when she owned land and cultivated a white clientele. In these periods she pioneered medical treatments that combined traditional and western healing methods, established a herbarium, sought patents for her own medicines, and even wrote and published a pamphlet of advice to women. But her life was one of sharp reversals, and she also had periods of debt, difficulty with the authorities, and even imprisonment. Though she impressed the Native Affairs Department (NAD) officials with her vivacity and fluency in face-to-face encounters, she depended on amanuenses to write her letters, well aware that poorly written English would cause her to lose face. Like Boakye Yi-adom's diary, her letters clearly had an immediate practical purpose. They were a means to "navigate the twisting channels of bureaucracy" and, as a weapon in her "battles to win admiration, respect, legality and financial success" (Burns, this volume), a way of carving out a position for herself as "a new kind of medical broker" and a proclamation of her success in that very undertaking. Her stream of missives to NAD officials asked for advice about patents, informed the officials of her ongoing legal problems, and complained about mistreatment and harassment but above all affirmed her remarkable successes as a healer. Her very epistolary excess, however, suggests a project that included but also went beyond the immediately instrumental and involved an ingenious kind of projection of the self into official space, a deposition of an enduring personal monument. For though the officials' responses to her letters were restrained and, over the years, progressively less sympathetic, she kept writing—and writing voluminously. She recounted her daily preoccupations with a degree of detail that made her letters almost like a diary. "Sir, Permit me to explain fully to you my troubles . . ." "Just a line. Awful sorry to trouble you but I fill that I must show you this . . ." As Burns remarks, we have here "a most exciting possibility: a woman who reckoned on the preservation of her documentation well beyond her lifespan." Like Boakye Yiadom—but resourcefully co-opting official personnel rather than just official rubrics—she may have been archiving herself (Breckenridge 1999; Burns 1996).

These case studies show how individuals and communities adopted the established textual genres of diary and letter and refashioned them to express new forms of social being. They evoke forms of personal publicity and collective privacy, modes of projection, distribution, multiplication and storage of lives and personalities for which we still need to develop a vocabulary.

Reading Cultures, Publics, and the Press

The explosion of personal writing was matched by an intense and sociable interest in reading. In West African coastal cities, young men with a year or two of post-primary education set up "reading circles" which were associated with self-edification and the acquisition of civilization. An advertisement in the Lagos *Comet* in 1940 announced that "the Sonian Reading Circle caters for youth eager for self-improvement," while a young man posted to a provincial town lamented, in the next issue, the lack of any such amenities there: "Every man one meets in the street with despair written deep on his face exclaims what a boring life this is. . . . There is a Reading Circle here I understand but this has decayed to an undistinguished heap of ruin."

Though these clubs' recreational dimension was important, even more significant was their function as a seedbed of nascent civil society. Stephanie Newell's chapter shows that the young members of literary clubs in the Gold Coast took themselves seriously as potential representatives and guides of their unlettered fellows and as a point of articulation between the colonial authorities and the "native" population. In effect, their aim was to make their intermediate position pivotal. The same civic consciousness and sense of public responsibility, bound up with a strong sense of the participants' class position, seems to be characteristic of literary and debating societies in South Africa, both in the boarding school discussed by Isabel Hofmeyr and in the Bantu Men's Social Centre established in Johannesburg in 1929 discussed by Bhekizizwe Peterson.

The young men's civic role took shape in several ways. In the practical organization of the associations—with their regular meetings, their rules and regulations, their elected officers, their minutes and reports—the participants were not simply practicing the techniques of government in preparation for a future role (though this was certainly one of the things they were doing), they were also actively participating in the constitution of civil society on the ground. Furthermore, the content of their discussions often bore upon matters of public and civic concern. The "youngmen" in the Gold Coast associations avoided explicitly political topics, and the students at Lovedale were discouraged by staff from broaching them. Despite these precautions, both managed to discuss themes such as "Self-government," "Is the Gold Coast a nation?," and "Should Socialism be adopted?" And finally, as Peterson shows for the Bantu Men's Social Club, the very pursuit of "civilization" and "enlightenment" embodied an implicit claim to political equality. By constituting themselves as fully civilized, the black intermediate classes demonstrated that they were eligible to participate politically. It was no accident that civic aspirations revolved around reading circles and the discussion of literary classics, for literature was held to be the principal repository of civilized values. In adopting this elevated view of literature, Peterson argues, the early black South African intelligentsia were responding to a discourse of racist exclusion that went back at least to the eighteenth century but was still very much alive in the twentieth century: a discourse based on the premise that Africans had no literature and therefore no culture. It was for this reason that the Bantu Men's Social Club, like other early nationalist groups across Africa, made it an urgent priority to study and create literary texts.

In the reading circles of the Gold Coast, the pursuit of "civilization" may at times have been taken to comical extremes, as when a club member at Dunkwa was told that "there is no excuse whatsoever" for a member of any club to appear in anything but a three-piece suit (Newell, this volume). This kind of behavior certainly attracted the ridicule of almost everyone: the young men's unlettered age-mates,[6] the more-secure and better-educated elite,[7] and the British authorities who from Lugard onward appeared horrified by results of their own educational policies. But the resonance of the reading circles' activities in the wider population should not therefore be overlooked. If it is true that "civil society" in Mamdani's strictly legalistic terms was minuscule and segregated from the mass of the population in all colonial African states (Mamdani 1996), this does not mean that civil society as a broader organizing idea was lacking in influence. On the contrary, the self-improving and "civilizing" activities of reading circles and debating clubs provided a focus of political aspiration and expectation for the wider community. In 1938, for example, the cocoa farmers of the Gold Coast, having embarked on a "hold-up" to resist the British firms' commercial monopoly, lambasted the literary circles in the pages of the *African Morning Post* for failing to take the lead in the ensuing public debate (Newell, this volume).

In South Africa, the contradictions inherent in the position of aspiring literates were greatly intensified by the distinctive features of that country's history: the massive rapid expropriation of African farmland, which by the end of the nineteenth century had dispossessed much of the progressive landed African middle class as well as subsistence farmers; the formation of a large and restless industrial working class; missionization to saturation point; and intrusive regimentation and segregation using written documents as a punitive and disciplinary instrument. School education in itself was not a guarantee of social status, and the smaller landholders were as likely to go down in the world as up, becoming migrant laborers to supplement their shrinking incomes (Bundy 1979; Guy 1979; La Hausse de Lalouvière 2000). The "ambiguities of dependence" (Marks 1987) in this situation seem much starker than they were for the Nigerian and Gold Coast colonial clerkly class, for whom land expropriation was not an issue and for whom school education remained a passport to a certain level of salary and status until well after independence.

These political and economic differences lie behind the differences in form, structure, and aim of the reading circles in the two contexts. In the Gold Coast, young men initiated numerous small and short-lived reading circles for themselves, made up their own rules, and ran them without outside support or interference. Though Ghanaians chafed under colonial restrictions and inequitable terms of trade, they looked forward to fuller political participation, wider educational opportunities, and imminent independence. The reading circles expressed this optimism, confidently affirming the value of both English and indigenous civilization. In South Africa, by contrast, the Bantu Men's Social Centre was established and controlled by liberal whites with a library supplied by a major American philanthropist. It was a large, long-lasting, and heavily regulated institution. With deepening racial segregation foreshadowing the policy of "separate development," both indigenous culture and "civilization" itself were open to question.

In their constitution of a civil society, both the Ghanaian and the South African institutions reached out to the press. Newspapers were a vital adjunct of their activities. The literary societies used the local press as a notice board, a gazette, and almost as an antechamber opening their in-camera discussions to a larger public. The press could also constitute a kind of reading circle in its own right.

There is an enormous literature on the role of the press in the establishment of the public sphere and national identity. But what may be worth adding, especially with regard to Ghana, Nigeria, and Kenya, is the significance of artisanal entrepreneurial small presses, often run as solo operations, and the heterogeneous, participatory, dialogic nature of the African-language texts they published. In Nigeria and Ghana, what we may be looking at is not so much a "print culture" as a "printing culture," where people could take their handwritten texts to the local printer and get them typeset and run off in a matter of days. Such publications were produced for a local audience, not a national one; sometimes their distribution was confined to the participants in a single localized event.

In colonial Kenya, where the first generation of literati appeared on the scene more than half a century later than in West and South Africa and were instantly involved in radical anticolonial politics, there was no culture of reading circles. But the press functioned as a kind of extended debating chamber. Lonsdale has written about the way the early Kikuyu nationalists constituted a new sense of ethical community through print (Lonsdale 1996, 2002). One of the most active of the early Kikuyu writers and small publishers was Henry Muoria, who wrote popular self-help books, historical works, and political pamphlets and who also founded and ran a popular Kikuyu-language newspaper called *Mumenyereri* (Bodil Frederiksen, this volume). Like his contemporary Gakaara wa Wanjau (Pugliese 1995), Muoria took correspondence courses in journalism, saw writing and publishing as a business, and succeeded in making a living from it for several years before the Emergency supervened. The entrepreneurial flair that Muoria brought to the business was typical of small publishing outfits elsewhere in Africa up till today: he wrote in order to publish, published in order to sell what he wrote, oversaw the entire operation from writing to distribution, and used family labor rather than waged employees.

The enterprise depended not only on the inputs of Muoria's wife Judith—who gathered material for the paper and coauthored one of his first book publications—but also on those of a large number of readers and "correspondents" who made contributions to *Mumenyereri* that ranged from a one-off letter to a regular column. This collaborative mode of assembling the text resulted in a loose, heterogeneous, and participatory texture. It was a forum for debate, created in reaction to the attempts of the Kenyan government to use print media in English and Swahili to spread progovernment propaganda while censoring and monitoring the Kikuyu press. According to Frederiksen, the government's attempts at popular communication were largely ignored while *Mumenyereri* sold rapidly and was read by far more people than actually bought it. What this suggests is that the local press's mode of constituting an imagined community depended not so much on its simultaneity and uniformity (Anderson 1983) as on its hybrid, porous, and responsive character. Rather than becoming conscious of themselves as members of one collectivity through the awareness that all other addressees of the paper were simultaneously reading the same text, it seems more likely that people were *drawn into* a Kikuyu and Kenyan collectivity by contributing elements to, and taking elements from, an ongoing conversation mediated through the press. And the government censors understood only too well the threat this kind of collaborative and interactive mode of communication posed: *Mumenyereri*'s mixing of genres and openness to all kinds of input from unauthorized sources alarmed the government press officer greatly.

Thus, if print helped make possible the constitution of an African civil society, it is important to consider the role of struggling self-made men, solo operators, one-off ventures, and the do-it-yourself ethos in this endeavor. Even in South Africa, where the press was most heavily controlled, centralized, and official, there seem to have been opportunities for individuals to broadcast their opinions and projects through the medium of print: Paul La Hausse's brilliant study (La Hausse de Lalouvière 2000) shows how Petros Lamula, a downwardly mobile cleric in early-twentieth-century Natal who was sacked by his Norwegian mission employers, pursued his political projects through the publication of streams of pamphlets, fliers, and books, often combining this with live lectures and debates so that each would stimulate uptake of the other. The experience of marginalization, repression, and loss of status produced in Lamula and people like him "an attachment to documents verging on papyrophilia" (ibid., 266). To understand the character of the early forms of civil society in Africa we need to attend to the fact that the sphere of print was relatively hospitable to solo entrepreneurs, innovators, and eccentric prophetic figures whose interventions sometimes helped form a communal political and moral identity—as in the case of Muoria—but which were also very likely to be forgotten in subsequent historical accounts.

There are links not only between reading circles and the local press but also between the local press and the tin trunk. In the case of the Ghanaian headmistress Mrs. Mercy Ffoulkes-Crabbe, it was a secret link. Mrs. Ffoulkes-Crabbe wrote a memoir in notebooks which she kept in a suitcase under her bed; she never showed it to anyone and no one suspected its existence until more than a quarter of a century after her death. Though kept so private, to the point of secrecy, this memoir is written in a formal and entirely public and impersonal style, as if for publication. Mrs. Ffoulkes-Crabbe refers to herself consistently in the third person and mentions only public events and achievements. Personal emotions are carefully excluded; it seems to be an autobiography without subjectivity. At the same time, Mrs. Ffoulkes-Crabbe was contributing an anonymous weekly column to the *Gold Coast Times* under the byline "Gloria." This lively column seems to reveal more than the private memoir. It is as if the anonymity of the newspaper persona provided a mask from behind which she could speak more freely than in the text written in her own name. The secret of the column's real authorship, too, was never revealed during her lifetime. This fascinating story may give us a glimpse of what was at stake for women writers. Though Mrs. Ffoulkes-Crabbe was a well-educated professional, her gender may have put her in an uncomfortable position at the edge of the public sphere, comparable in some ways with the position of lower-status men.

The genre of the letter lies at the center of both domains—the sphere of public print and the sphere of personal writing—and yokes them together. The local press could not have survived without letters. Muoria's dependence on readers' letters and his numerous "correspondents" who framed their contributions in epistolary form was typical of vernacular newspapers across Africa. Popular fiction, often closely associated with the popular press, gave the letter a singular and potent function. The novelette *When the Heart Decides,* by the Ghanaian writer E. K. Mickson, "revolves around a dossier of Lucy's love-letters, each of which is read aloud by three other characters"

(Newell 2000, 104). In Gakaara wa Wanjau's Kikuyu novella *Ũhoro wa Ũgũrani* (Marriage Procedures), it is the young woman's suicide letter that tells the truth, reveals all, explains all, and testifies to the genuineness of her love (Pugliese 1995). The text generally regarded as the first Yoruba novel is an entirely epistolary work, purporting to be a series of letters to the editor of a Yoruba weekly from a former Lagos prostitute recounting her sinful past. Conversely, personal letters such as those of the Kenyan students "Thomas" and "Sara" were infused with idioms derived from their reading of detective stories and Swahili newspapers, "combin[ing] introspection with the projection of public personas, and intimacy with instrumental desires to document" (Thomas, this volume). The prevalence of the letter in the popular imagination and its pervasiveness in the actual conduct of life show how the public and private spheres are joined through the creative development of those new genres of writing poised on the interface between the two.

Genre and Cultural Innovation

The writers and readers discussed in this volume, then, were cultural innovators who redeployed old genres or invented new ones. In the process they often took up a critical stance in relation to their lived ideational worlds.

This happened, first of all, through the sheer fact of writing. Tin-trunk literacy was a hazy zone where oral and written genres existed in particularly close rapport. Letters and diaries were often composed in the style of a speaking voice, to be read aloud to family or confidants. The very desire to trap significant utterances and events in the lapidary forms of letters, diary entries, obituaries, and dates inscribed in Bibles and on walls can be seen to be in continuity with the fixing and memorializing strategies of many African oral genres. Studies of "entextualization" in oral genres (see Silverstein and Urban 1996) show that the will to fix text so that it transcends time precedes the adoption of writing. The amateur writings of the tin-trunk literati may in some cases be using new and expanded means to fulfill the function of praise poetry and family histories, laying down markers that recall the distinctiveness of personal and collective lives. Personal writing, then, could be seen as entering a field predisposed toward its reception, enabling an efflorescence of memorializing unprecedented in its scope, for now all kinds of things, idiosyncratic as well as communal, could be permanently lodged within reach of recuperation.

But writing also made possible a new relationship to oral culture, which was indispensable to people who were still embroiled in that culture but who, as converts and partial scholars, had also developed some reservations about it. Writing, that is, made possible unprecedented feats of cultural editing. For writing, and especially print, offers a license and an instigation to refashion what is being written down in ways that authorize the legitimate, excise the illegitimate, and permanently inscribe that act of separation. Oral traditions are of course themselves being continually revised and reinvented from within, but writing brought a different order of revision and reinvention, for it gave unprecedented opportunities for either sanitizing or expelling elements of the oral lifeworld. Writing, and especially print, puts the writer into a relation of partial detachment from the traditions s/he inhabits, setting her or him over against them in the act of writing them. Early converts, especially those of a cultural-nationalist orientation, often pioneered such exercises in "writing tradition." John Lonsdale has shown how the first authors of printed history in Kikuyu, the Christian *athomi,* or "readers," simplified and indeed suppressed the complexities of oral traditions in order to convene a pan-Kikuyu print public. He quotes a passage from Stanley Gathigira's 1935 book on Kikuyu customs which made the practice of cultural editing quite explicit by inviting readers to participate in the operation: "No tribe on earth has all good or all bad customs. Thus I have written all these, for every Kikuyu to choose what to propagate and what to abandon" (Lonsdale 2002, 240). By engaging in continuous and prolific lifelong acts of inscription, they were refashioning and sanitizing their oral traditions from within, but as if from outside—and this was because of the urgent need to deal with the uncertainties arising from their intermediate position between the "enlightened" educational elite and representatives of colonial authority on the one hand and their own less-literate home communities on the other. In attempting to address these two audiences at once, the need for editing must have been intense.

An example of both these possibilities—the continuation of the oral impulse to consolidate text in lapidary form and the use of writing to adopt a selective editorial stance in relation to tradition—can be seen vividly in the Ghanaian obituaries discussed by Tom McCaskie. The genre of the printed obituary can be traced back to the famous official pamphlet published at the instigation of the colonial authorities for the one-year custom following the death of the Asantehene Agyeman Prempeh in 1931. But this obituary, and to an even greater extent the printed obituaries of less-illustrious people that followed in its wake, was positioned in a ceremonial space previously occupied exclusively by an oral genre, the funeral oration that blended spoken encomium with recitation of *apae* praise poetry. The written obituary in a sense continued and brought to its fullest realization the oral genre's aspiration to create an enduring memorial to the dead. "Funeral things," including "printed, mimeographed, photocopied, or handwritten 'death notices'; valedictions; genealogies; biographies; burial programs; church notices; signed photographs; sympathy and visiting cards; and sometimes even inscribed commemorative plates" functioned as "mnemonics of death," as McCaskie puts it. Unlike oral praises, they could be preserved for decades in the tin trunk without material change. But like the *apae,* when they were brought out, their meaning could be fully constituted only by rich oral contextualization in the form of narratives, reminiscences, and genealogical explanations. The continued contiguity and interaction of oral and written memorial forms made possible a pointed and ongoing debate about what was appropriate to include in an obituary and what was not—witness the dispute between Chief Kwame Frimpon's daughter and nephew over what aspect of his life should be emphasized at his funeral in 1937. Writing an obituary text put the writers in the position of consciously scrutinizing the form and contents before publication. The sources examined by McCaskie give unusual insight into the formation, efflorescence, and eclipse of a written genre and its continued cohabitation with oral practices and repertoires.

In other cases, a new genre may not be taken up and may simply disappear from the record. Nonetheless, it may provide a rare glimpse into what people at the time saw as textual possibilities that existed or could be created. Such is the case with S. A. Adenle, the schoolmaster-trader who invented a strange didactic poetic-narrative genre in Yoruba and—having become the *ọba* of his town—reprinted his two pamphlets in vast quantities, but to little avail: most copies remained unsold and his wives "used them for firewood" (Barber, this volume). This example points to a problem for historiography. In what sense do the lonely, isolated, one-off inventions of tin-trunk literates constitute a history? Clearly such writers had models and shared cultural influences—in Adenle's case, as in that of most of his contemporaries, the Bible, the hymnbook, the school reader, and possibly *The Pilgrim's Progress* as well as edifying vernacular texts. Nonetheless, Adenle's text has no clear antecedent or successor and it was not generated in a responsive environment, unlike the work of Adenle's contemporaries in Lagos and Ibadan, which was shaped by a lively critical and participatory written culture. The image of Adenle shutting himself into his room to write, suspected by his wives of communing with spirits, and distressed by the "large intellectual gap" between himself and his people brings home the fact that tin-trunk literati could be pioneers operating, in some respects at least, in a vacuum. It was a vacuum which spelled freedom to invent but also a dizzying absence of points of reference.

Almost the opposite of the lonely inventor is the institutional continuity of the poetry circle or literary society in Hausaland. Graham Furniss's chapter brings to the fore the important point that genres are often underpinned and made possible by particular institutional forms. These forms can persist as a recognizable framework of generative activity for a very long time—in this case, for more than two centuries. The Hausa version of the reading circle and debating club not only antedated colonial rule by nearly a hundred years but also outlasted it and is still flourishing today. However, as Furniss clearly demonstrates, this institutional form was not simply a given; it was a creation that was constantly being redefined and recreated. In the early nineteenth century, the Islamic reform movement revolved around the intense intellectual activity of groups set up to debate the nature, norms, and prospects of Islamic society. In the early colonial era, reading and discussion circles were a feature of early northern opposition to colonial rule. After independence, in the 1970s, poetry circles played a significant role in fostering literary production and assigning status to the poets. Today, clubs and literary circles mediate the production and consumption of a new popular genre, the romantic Hausa-language novelette. When the video craze arrived, the same institutional form was adapted to produce and disseminate Hausa drama videos. Here we see an institution so tenacious and so influential that a history of civil society in Northern Nigeria could probably be written by tracing its successive incarnations: it would be a history of creative conservation and deep-rooted innovation.

The aim of this project, then, is not the reconstruction of a sealed-off compartment of colonial history but the probing of a past that is still living, in the sense that its potentials—those taken up and those still latent—are with us today.

NOTES

1. Similarly, Kenneth Mdala, a clerk in Malawi, "kept up a voluminous correspondence (all typewritten) from the late 1920s to the early 1940s with the British colonial administrators in Nyasaland." It was a one-sided correspondence, for a 50-page exposition would produce a one-line reply saying that his observations had been noted. But Mdala was undeterred and kept up a flow of disquisitions on all kinds of subjects—especially his own version of clan and dynastic history of the Yao, which he diligently researched (Vaughan 2000).
2. Whether it was also present in Francophone and Lusophone African colonies is an

important question which could be taken up in future research. A starting point would be studies of autobiographical writing in Francophone African countries: see Lüsebrink (1996); Westermann (1943).

3. Chartier (1995) suggests that instead of mapping literacy and other cultural practices onto an existing social structure, we could start from reading habits and ask what social affinities they suggest. These may bracket or crosscut class divisions or suggest subsets of self-assigned commonality/identity. This approach is likely to be particularly useful for fluid situations of rapid social change where, as among African populations under colonial rule, social hierarchy was sustained by entrenched cultural distinctions only to a very limited extent.

4. Derek Peterson, in his discussion of views of literacy, education, and bureaucracy among insurgent Kikuyu in colonial Kenya, stresses their role as practical and political tools that were deliberately acquired for specific ends rather than as repositories of cultural value: "Their strategy of education diagnosed British learning not as a vehicle of enlightenment but as a set of techniques to be practised and learned" in order to make claims on the state or, later, to set up a forest counterstate (Peterson 2003, 92–93). See also Peterson's excellent book on translation, bookkeeping, and the work of the imagination in colonial Kenya (2004).

5. Islamic literacy in Arabic influenced new genres of personal writing in some areas of Africa. The Fulbe ruler Hamman Yaji, for example, began keeping his diary in Arabic at a time when he was still engaged in slave-raiding among subject populations and did not yet have regular contacts with the French, German, and British officials who successively claimed authority over his emirate (Vaughan and Kirk-Greene 1995). On Islamic genres of personal writing in Northern Nigeria, see also Reichmuth (1996).

6. "*Alakọwe to di tai mọrun, Ebi o kilọ fun*" (The literate person with a tie round his neck / Hunger has not yet warned him), mocked the popular Yoruba song. Ghanaian concert party and Yoruba popular theater had a good line in lampooning the affectations of the clerkly class.

7. See for example Kobina Sekyi's *The Blinkards,* a lampoon of Ghanaians who aspired to English civilization. Sekyi himself was a British-trained lawyer with full command of English conventions of expression and behavior.

REFERENCES

Anderson, Benedict. 1983. *Imagined Communities: Reflections on the Origin and Spread of Nationalism.* London: Verso.

Breckenridge, Keith. 1999. "Orality, Literacy and the Archive in the Making of Kas Maine." In *Oral Literature and Performance in Southern Africa,* ed. Duncan Brown, 138–147. Oxford: James Currey; Athens: Ohio University Press.

———. 2000. "Love Letters and Amanuenses: Beginning the Cultural History of the Working Class Private Sphere in Southern Africa, 1900–1933." *Journal of Southern African Studies* 26, no. 2: 337–348.

Brewer, John. 1997. *The Pleasures of the Imagination: English Culture in the Eighteenth Century.* London: HarperCollins.

Bundy, Colin. 1979. *The Rise and Fall of the South African Peasantry.* London: Heinemann Educational.

Burns, Catherine. 1996. "Louisa Mvemve: A Woman's Advice to the Public on the Cure of Various Diseases." *KRONOS: Journal of Cape History* 23: 103–134.

Chakrabarty, Dipesh. 1992. "Postcoloniality and the Artifice of History: Who Speaks for 'Indian' Pasts?" *Representations* 37 (Winter): 1–26.

Chartier, Roger. 1995. *Forms and Meanings: Texts, Performances, and Audiences from Codex to Computer.* Philadelphia: University of Pennsylvania Press.

Freccero, John. 1986. "Autobiography and Narrative." In *Reconstructing Individualism: Autonomy, Individuality, and the Self in Western Thought,* ed. Thomas C. Heller, Morton Sosna, and David E. Wellbery, 16–29. Stanford, Calif.: Stanford University Press.

Guy, Jeff. 1979. *The Destruction of the Zulu Kingdom: The Civil War in Zululand, 1879–1884.* Pietermaritzburg: University of Natal Press.

Habermas, Jürgen. 1962/1992. *The Structural Transformation of the Public Sphere.* Trans. Thomas Burger with Frederick Lawrence. Cambridge, Mass.: MIT Press.

Hawkins, Sean. 2002. *Writing and Colonialism in Northern Ghana: The Encounter between the LoDagaa and "the World on Paper."* Toronto: University of Toronto Press.

La Hausse de Lalouvière, Paul. 2000. *Restless Identities: Signatures of Nationalism, Zulu Ethnicity and History in the Lives of Petros Lamula (c.1881–1948) and Lymon Maling (1889–c.1936).* Pietermaritzburg: University of Natal Press.

Lonsdale, John. 1996. "'Listen while I read': The Orality of Christian Literacy in the Young Kenyatta's Making of the Kikuyu." In *Ethnicity in Africa: Roots, Meanings and Implications,* ed. Louise de la Gorgendière, Kenneth King, and Sarah Vaughan, 17–53. Edinburgh: Centre of African Studies, University of Edinburgh.

———. 2002. "Contests of Time: Kikuyu Historiography, Old and New." In *A Place in the World: New Local Historiographies from Africa and South Asia,* ed. Axel Harneit-Sievers, 201–254. Leiden: Brill.

Lüsebrink, Hans-Jürgen. 1996. "Du journal de voyage au témoignage—autobiographies fragmentaires d'auteurs africains dans la presse ouest-africaine à l'époque coloniale (1916–1950)." In *Genres autobiographiques en Afrique/Autobiographical Genres in Africa,* ed. János Riesz and Ulla Schild, 83–100. Berlin: Dietrich Reimer Verlag.

Mamdani, Mahmood. 1996. *Citizen and Subject: Contemporary Africa and the Legacy of Late Colonialism.* Princeton, N.J.: Princeton University Press.

Marks, Shula. 1987. *The Ambiguities of Dependence in South Africa: Class, Nationalism, and the State in Twentieth-Century Natal.* Baltimore: Johns Hopkins University Press.

Newell, Stephanie. 2000. *Ghanaian Popular Fiction: "Thrilling Discoveries in Conjugal Life" & Other Tales.* London: James Currey.

———. 2002. *Literary Culture in Colonial Ghana: "How to Play the Game of Life."* Manchester: Manchester University Press.

Peterson, Derek. 2003. "Writing in Revolution: Independent Schooling and Mau Mau in Nyeri." In *Mau Mau and Nationhood,* ed. J. M. Lonsdale and Atieno Odhiambo, 76–96. London: James Currey.

———. 2004. *Creative Writing: Translation, Bookkeeping, and the Work of the Imagination in Colonial Kenya.* Portsmouth, N.H.: Heinemann.

Pugliese, Cristiana. 1995. *Author, Publisher and Gikuyu Nationalist: The Life and Writings of Gakaara wa Wanjau.* Bayreuth: Eckhard Breitinger, Bayreuth University, in cooperation with Institut français de recherche en Afrique.

Reichmuth, Stefan. 1996. "Autobiographical Writing and Islamic Consciousness in the Arabic Literature of Nigeria." In *Genres autobiographiques en Afrique* (Autobiographical Genres in Africa), ed. Jànos Riesz and Ulla Schild, 179–189. Berlin: Dietrich Reimer Verlag.

Rose, Jonathan. 2001. *The Intellectual Life of the British Working Classes.* New Haven and London: Yale University Press.

Sekyi, Kobina. 1974. *The Blinkards.* London: Heinemann Educational.

Silverstein, Michael, and Greg Urban, eds. 1996. *Natural Histories of Discourse.* Chicago: Chicago University Press.

Stone, Lawrence. 1977. *The Family, Sex, and Marriage in England, 1500–1800.* London: Weidenfeld and Nicolson.

Taylor, Charles. 1989. *Sources of the Self: The Making of the Modern Identity.* Cambridge, Mass.: Harvard University Press.

Tillyard, Stella. 1995. *Aristocrats: Caroline, Emily, Louisa, and Sarah Lennox, 1740–1832.* London: Vintage.

Van Onselen, Charles. 1993. "The Reconstruction of a Rural Life from Oral Testimony: Critical Notes on the Methodology Employed in the Study of a Black South African Sharecropper." *Journal of Peasant Studies* 20 (April): 494–514.

Vaughan, James H., and Anthony H. M. Kirk-Greene, eds. 1995. *The Diary of Hamman Yaji: Chronicle of a West African Muslim Ruler.* Bloomington: Indiana University Press.

Vaughan, Megan. 2000. "Diary." *London Review of Books,* November 16, 32–33.

Westermann, D. 1943. *Autobiographies d'Africains.* Trans. L. Homburger. Paris: Payot.

Williams, Gavin. 1993. "Garveyism, Akinpelu Obisesan, and His Contemporaries: Ibadan, 1920–22." In *Legitimacy and the State in Twentieth-Century Africa,* ed. Terence Ranger and Olufemi Vaughan, 112–132. London: Macmillan.

PART ONE

Diaries, Letters, and the Constitution of the Self

"MY OWN LIFE": A. K. BOAKYE YIADOM'S AUTOBIOGRAPHY— THE WRITING AND SUBJECTIVITY OF A GHANAIAN TEACHER-CATECHIST

1

Stephan F. Miescher

> *Wo yɛ huuhuu a, wobɛbɔ ka; na wo yɛ dwaeɛ nso a, wo behu amane.*
> If you bluff, you will fall into debt; if you are arrogant, you will suffer.
> —*A. K. Boakye Yiadom*

When I visited the nonagenarian Akasease Kofi Boakye Yiadom, a retired teacher-catechist, he led me to a corner of a courtyard building in the old Christian settlement of Abetifi. In this Kwawu town, part of Ghana's matrilineal Akan area, Boakye Yiadom lives in a modest one-room home that he used to share with his late wife, Susana Akosua Ansomaah. Usually he entertains on his veranda. But once, when talking about writing, he led me into their room. There I was struck by a wooden closet with glass doors standing prominently in the small space. This closet is full of papers, books, notebooks, and old magazines and journals, neatly stacked and protected from the tropical humidity. Enhancing the importance of this piece of furniture, a large color reproduction of Jesus Christ hovers behind the closet. Jesus is reaching out his hand, providing divine protection for this shrine to literacy (see fig. 1.1).[1]

Writing and, to a lesser degree, reading are crucial for Boakye Yiadom's subjectivity. Over the last seventy years, he has filled dozens of notebooks and frequently engaged in active correspondence. Some notebooks are autobiographical, others contain collections of proverbs, herbal medicines, or draft sermons. Boakye Yiadom has also created a remarkable personal archive: his own writings are kept in the glass cabinet; letters, receipts, and pamphlets, organized in folders, are stored in the Key Bar Soap box on top (Yiadom 2000a,

Figure 1.1. A. K. Boakye Yiadom in front of his "shrine to literacy."

2000b). But literacy has been more than a pastime. Since leaving school in 1935, Boakye Yiadom has used his writing skills to support himself and his dependants, earning an income as a teacher, an occupation that was interrupted by short periods of clerical employment. Because of his limited educational credentials, his career did not go beyond the position of a primary school headteacher. To improve his economic situation, especially in retirement, he has been planting cocoa in his second hometown, the village of Kurofa, Asante-Akyem, where his mother had remarried in 1927.

Boakye Yiadom considers himself a *krakye* (clerk); in his youth, he joined the group of clerks, teachers, store managers, accountants, and ministers, which was small at the time. This social group, loosely defined here as *akrakyefoↄ*, shared not only the skills of literacy but also the experience of western education (at least to Standard VII), forms of gendered behavior, specific clothes and material needs, and the expectation of regular salaried income (Miescher 2003, 2005). In the context of colonial Ghana, particularly during the 1930s and 1940s, *akrakyefoↄ* were members of intermediary classes that experienced a double form of social exclusion. Most of them were neither part of older and established chiefly elites, who as "traditional" rulers were in charge of local administration under indirect rule, nor did they belong to the highly educated and financially secure intelligentsia, the lawyer-merchant class, who controlled an increasing number of African-owned newspapers and gathered in exclusive social clubs in cities while waiting to inherit the colonial state. Still, *akrakyefoɔ* had political, social, and cultural aspirations. Many hoped for a share of political power and sought to be part of a modern world. Scholars have identified *akrakyefoɔ* as "the ordinary salariat: the clerks of government offices, commercial houses and school teachers," products of educational reforms of the 1920s who were "creatures of colonial urbanisation" with unfixed lifestyles and allegiances but "were anxious for self-improvement" (Agovi 1990, 10). By the 1950s, their fortunes had improved: rallying for the nationalist cause, many joined mass parties such as Kwame Nkrumah's Convention People's Party (CPP) and gained at least some political power (Austin 1964; Allman 1993). Yet this larger characterization, which implies a trajectory of increased status and political clout particularly after self-rule and independence, was not fully the experience of village schoolteachers such as Boakye Yiadom. His existence never became urban, nor was he swept away by the nationalist fever. Rather he maintained for much of his life a marginal and rather ordinary position—with one important exception. Writing became a way to document, comment, and at times even challenge the constraints of his predicament.

Boakye Yiadom's shrine to literacy is not uncommon for a *krakye* of his generation. During my visits and interviews with retired teachers born in the first two decades of the twentieth century, I frequently saw cabinets with books and papers in formal sitting rooms. For example, Rev. E. K. O. Asante (1911–1997) of Abetifi began acquiring a small library on anthropological, historical, and theological subjects while in training college. Displaying his collection of books underlined his literacy—his "bookish" knowledge—and marked him as member of the *akrakyefoɔ*.[2] Another former teacher and retired education officer, B. E. Ofori (1909–1995) of Akropong, acquired books, especially English literature, for classroom use. When I asked him about his reading habits as a young man, Ofori recalled Shakespeare. When I inquired about newspapers, his memory became more animated. He quickly named important Gold Coast newspapers of the 1940s and 1950s, commenting that he regularly bought the *Accra Evening News,* published by Nkrumah's CPP. His son, who was present during the conversation, interjected that some of the newspapers had been saved; only after some pleading did the father release one (Ofori 1993a, 1993b). Unlike Asante and Ofori, Boakye Yiadom's reading habits involved fewer literary and scholarly texts. Rather, his cabinet contains school readers, religious tracts, self-help books, volumes on scouting, and a few political pamphlets. Receipts and correspondence document his membership in book clubs. In 1961, he purchased *Boys' and Girls' Encyclopedia* for eleven shillings and tenpence and *Universal Doctor* for nineteen shillings and eightpence from Lennards mail order in Bristol, England. Two years later, he subscribed to free issues of *Israel News* and joined the Accra Book Club, which distributed Soviet periodicals in English, till he fell behind with payments in 1965.[3] Later, religious titles and marital advice books dominated, such as *Happiness for Husband and Wife,* which he ordered for six cedis. In 1972, the Ghana Bible Research Centre shipped titles advertised in the *Christian Messenger* for one cedi thirty pesewa: *The Bible and Politics* and *The Bible and Sex.* Stationed in village schools, Boakye Yiadom never had the opportunity to participate in literary clubs (cf. Newell 2002).

Between Asante, Ofori, and Boakye Yiadom, there are important differences that marked more than the content and location of their book cabinets. These differences were a direct motivation for Boakye Yiadom's own writing. Asante and Ofori had relatives close to local power structures. Ofori's father and Asante's uncle were elders at the palaces of Abetifi and Akropong. They had the opportunity to continue their education early in life by attending training college immediately after receiving the Standard VII certificate. This allowed them to ascend the social ladder and acquire some wealth by becoming pastors and education officers who replaced Europeans as school inspectors following Ghana's self-rule in 1951. Thus, in retirement, Asante's book cabinet was not placed, as was Boakye Yiadom's, next to his bed in a cramped one-room home but occupied a more prestigious location in his parlor. For Boakye Yiadom, writing became an expression of his aspirations. Writing was his vehicle for seeking social prestige denied to him because of his lack of income, education, and family connections.

Among Boakye Yiadom's notebooks, there is a two-volume autobiography entitled "Autobiography: My Own Life" (MOL), which is mostly written in diary format and in English with a few sections in Twi (n.d.a). The following discussion explores the content, meaning, and personal significance of MOL. It looks at the text's principal personae and explores Boakye Yiadom's motives, models, and intended audience. Since MOL mainly follows a diary format, I first address diary-writing.

Writing Diaries

Boakye Yiadom began keeping a diary at the age of 21 while enrolled in the Presbyterian boys' middle boarding school at Abetifi. In a letter he explained that "there were a few students who started writing diaries," mentioning six of his classmates (1995). During the interwar period, only a small minority attended school, even in educational centers such as Abetifi. Boakye Yiadom, who enrolled at the age of 16 in 1926, was the first in his family to be sent to this prestigious boys' boarding school, where he received the Standard VII certificate in 1935, making him part of the *akrakyefoɔ*.[4] Among literate members of the Presbyterian Church, diary-writing was not uncommon. Two men of Boakye Yiadom's generation whom I interviewed joined this mission church in their youth and kept diaries for at least part of their lives. E. K. Addo (1904–1998), a former Abetifi trader, acquired literacy by hiring private tutors. Among his papers, there are two volumes of diaries from the 1930s recording his business activities, travels, and church visits. The aforementioned B. E. Ofori used his scheduling books for personal entries when he worked as an education officer: he mainly recorded his travels and expenses, although there are scattered references to family and friends.[5]

Why did diaries become popular among men exposed to the Presbyterian church early in the twentieth century? This church, which was in charge of most schools in Akuapem and Kwawu, had evolved out of the Basel Mission, a Swiss and German organization. In the 1840s, the Basel Mission opened a permanent station in Akropong, Akuapem, and thirty years later, it opened one in Abetifi.[6] The Basel Mission was strongly influenced by Pietism, a reform movement within the Lutheran church of Württemberg that advocated a personal relationship with God and emphasized the importance of regular introspection. Keeping a diary was part of an educated Pietist lifestyle. As early as the seventeenth and eighteenth centuries, the founders of Lutheran Pietism—Philipp Jacob Spener (1635–1705) and August Hermann Francke (1663–1727)—promoted the habit of searching one's heart and deeds, communicating directly with God, by creating a personal record of one's life in the form of a diary.[7] Basel missionaries, who were instructed to keep a diary during training, continued this practice. They were required by the home board to write quarterly and annual reports that reflected on their daily activities and revealed their inner lives. These reports presented a summary of their diaries.[8]

With the opening of outstations, which were staffed by African teacher-catechists and (later) ordained pastors, Basel missionaries demanded that those in charge maintain station diaries. In one of them, printed in day format, the opening page notified its users that it was a "diary into which the keeper has to enter shortly, exactly and truly what he has done during every day."[9] In the 1900 volume of a small outstation in the Odumase-Krobo district, the teacher-catechist wrote about launching a school, interviewing candidates for baptismal classes, asking the chief for more schoolboys, and receiving visits by the supervising missionary.[10] Following the expulsion of the Basel Mission during World War I, this practice continued within the reorganized structures of the Presbyterian Church, under the guidance of the Scottish Mission. In the 1935–1936 volume of Abetifi, the local pastor recorded information about the congregation's deaths and births, his journeys to outstations, and arbitrations he was involved in.[11] Yet unlike those kept by missionaries, these diaries were free of introspection and intimate details of the keeper's life. Rather, they served as an official logbook that provided information for the station's chronicle, which was usually a separate tome. The diary also permitted church authorities to monitor the conduct of a pastor or catechist.[12]

Boakye Yiadom and his age-mates were exposed to the notion of diary-keeping by their Presbyterian teachers and pastors, who had been trained by Basel missionaries. At the boarding school, religious instruction emphasized introspection in the form of daily prayers and establishing a personal relationship with the Christian God. Reflecting on his school days, Boakye Yiadom noted his interest in Christianity; in those days he was hoping to become a minister (1993). Yet in his autobiography MOL, which is structured like a diary, Boakye Yiadom did more than merely emulate Pietist practice; he adapted this genre to serve his own purpose.

Organization of "My Own Life"

MOL consists of two worn notebooks that show signs of frequent use. The 123 pages of the first volume cover the years up to 1964; the second, more detailed, deals on 192 pages with twenty-four years (see fig. 1.2). Both are written in script in black or blue ink. The first volume opens with a section presenting a chronological narrative of the first thirty-six years of Boakye Yiadom's life. This section, which is probably based on earlier notes, was modeled on Presbyterian (auto)biographies. Boakye Yiadom was familiar with this genre—biographical narratives were presented during Presbyterian funeral services. Moreover, in another notebook, he listed biographies of African mission pioneers from the nineteenth century, among them Rev.

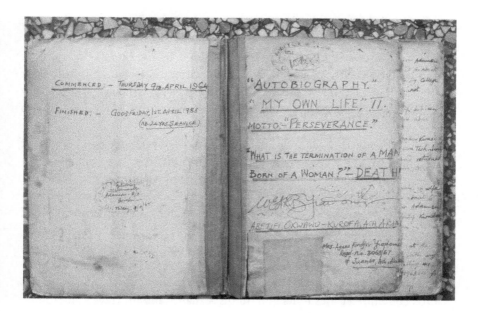

Figure 1.2. The opening pages of the second volume of "Autobiography: My Own Life."

Peter Hall's autobiography.[13] Like Hall, Boakye Yiadom begins with his birth and his parents' names. Then he immediately sketches his educational path from junior to senior (middle) school until passing "the big Examination" of the Standard VII certificate. The narrative mentions his teachers and their transfers and acknowledges their influence: "Mr. Asimang was one of the most learned English teachers I have ever surveyed on the globe of this world and my English essays and speaking depend fully upon his teaching" (n.d.a, 1:8–9). In 1935, after leaving the boarding school and entering the "Life of the World" (10), Boakye Yiadom recorded his first employment as cocoa-weighing clerk, which was followed by military service in 1940. He included a description of the circumstances leading to the birth of his first seven children, four of whom died in infancy, and his relations to their mothers, two of whom he married. The dramatic high point is the year 1945, when he and his first Christian wife, Alice Mansah Safoaah, lost their one-year-old daughter in Kumawu. Within the next ten days, Safoaah prematurely delivered a second child who died and passed away herself. In great detail he noted the extensive funeral celebrations. The opening narrative ends with a long list of witchcraft activities the mother of his seventh child confessed to, recorded, unlike the rest of the volume, in Twi (26–31). Starting in June 1946, the volumes of MOL are organized in diary format: mostly brief entries with precise dates, usually at least once a week, although at times they are less frequent; sometimes there are interruptions from several months to over a year.[14]

MOL documents the migrations Boakye Yiadom undertook because of his literacy, in which he sought teaching positions in village schools across southern Ghana and clerical work in commercial towns such as Nsawam, Nkawkaw, and Koforidua. In 1950, he enrolled in a Presbyterian training college in order to reach the status of a certified teacher, after which he pursued a one-year catechist course in Abetifi. Beginning in 1952, he had several positions as headteacher of rural Presbyterian primary schools while serving as catechist in villages of Asante-Akyem, Brong-Ahafo, Kwawu, and Akyem-Abuakwa until his retirement in 1978.[15] The remaining discussion addresses MOL's content—entries in relation to his sexuality and his travels and to historical events—and examines its audience.

Wives and Concubines

A central feature in MOL is Boakye Yiadom's entries about his relations with his wives and concubines. There is a striking discrepancy in different presentations of his married life. Initially in our conversations, and in the short autobiography he wrote for the Presbyterian congregations of Abetifi and Kurofa, he mentioned only two wives, those with whom he entered a Christian marriage—one, as mentioned, died in childbirth in 1945; the other, Susana Akosua Ansomaah, passed away in 1999 (1993, n.d.b). However, MOL contains accounts of seventeen women, with whom he had fathered twenty-seven children. Although many of these relationships were never formalized beyond initial negotiations with relatives, Boakye Yiadom did enter customary marriages with about half of his children's mothers, and with five of them, their marriage was blessed by a Christian church.[16] He periodically listed his children and their mothers, most extensively on a table in volume two (n.d.a, 2:74–77; see fig. 1.3).[17] Meticulously, he recorded expenses related to these relationships and documented any changes in the organization of their arrangements such as presenting gifts or performing customary and Christian marriage rites. He noted conflicts and mediation, listing witnesses,

Figure 1.3. Records of A. K. Boakye Yiadom's family in MOL (n.d.a., 2:74–77).

agreements, and pacification fines. The entries show both the processual character of his marriages and the complex and polygynous networks he maintained.[18] To demonstrate MOL's logbook character, as well as the fluidity of his relations with wives and concubines, I provide a close look at the years 1954 to 1961.

In 1954, Boakye Yiadom's wife, Yaa Adomako of Aduamoa, with whom he had entered a customary and Christian marriage, left him. Before they formally divorced over two years later, Boakye Yiadom looked for a new wife.[19] He started relationships with several women; with three of them—Sophia Yankeraa, Akua Adu, and Agnes Adwoa Fodwoo[20]—he also entered marriage negotiations. In November 1955, he reported the birth of his thirteenth child; his "fiancée," Sophia Yankeraa, was the mother. The baby, named George Kwabena Agya Fah, was Yankeraa's ninth child. In conversation, he explained that they had met in 1954 while he was stationed in her hometown of Juansa, Asante-Akyem (1994). In August 1956, he wrote about a visit to Hweehwee Market, Kwawu, to discuss with his wɔfa (maternal uncle) Kwabena Opong and his wife the possibility of a cross-cousin marriage with their daughter Akua Adu.[21] Marriage was promised when Akua Adu passed her Standard VII examination. Listing the witnesses, Boakye Yiadom noted that "up to that time," he had spent fourteen pounds, nineteen shillings, and ninepence (n.d.a, 1:86). The next entry deals again with Sophia Yankeraa, referring to her as "fiancée-wife," who had her first menses "exactly" eleven months after the birth of their child George (87). Interested in fertility and procreation, Boakye Yiadom frequently recorded the menstrual cycles of women close to him. In November, the other "dear fiancée," Akua Adu, arrived with her mother at Kurofa, where Boakye Yiadom had relocated. A few days later, Akua Adu left for a town nearby to complete schooling; he recorded his assistance in securing her employment as "pupil teacher" (89). In this endeavor, he could rely on his position as headteacher, aided by rapid expansion of primary education under self-rule in the 1950s (McWilliam and Kwamenah-Poh 1975). The relationship with Akua Adu took an unexpected turn in February 1957, when she returned to her Kwawu hometown accompanied by her brother "without [Boakye Yiadom's] knowledge"—so far he had spent "about £34 4/10d" on her (90). This was not the final word. In June, he noted that "the proposed marriage" with his "fiancée" Sophia Yankeraa had been "totally dissolved or cancelled." Instead, Akua Adu "was officially given" to him by her father, his younger wɔfa. Boakye Yiadom presented the customary "official stamp," tiri nsa, in the form of half a bottle of whisky and two bottles of soda in front of his wɔfa, other lineage members, and the bride's mother. This event brought the negotiation "very near marriage" (91–92).

In February 1957, there is an entry about a third woman. Boakye Yiadom recorded that his "fiancée-conceived" and "may be future wife," Mary Adwoa Mansah, had arrived in Kurofa from her Abetifi hometown (93). According to customary practice, Adwoa Mansah stayed with him for the final months of her pregnancy.[22] In early October, she returned for delivery to Abetifi. He recognized the child by naming him after his senior *wɔfa*, Emanuel Kwadwo Opong, who had co-financed his schooling with the other *wɔfa*. Yet Boakye Yiadom did not further formalize his relationship with Adwoa Mansah.

In January 1958, which is emphasized with a red star, there is an entry about a fourth woman, his "girl-fiancée," Agnes Adwoa Fodwoo of Juansa. Fodwoo's parents declared Boakye Yiadom her "permanent care-taker" in the presence of her father's elder sister, her brothers and sisters, and three witnesses: the Abetifi trader Kwame Baah, teacher Bosampem of Bompata, and Boakye Yiadom's mother, Afua Ntoriwah. Again, MOL kept track of financial obligations. Her parents paid school fees while Boakye Yiadom, "as the proposed husband," provided schoolbooks, dresses, and other school material for the next two years, "after which the necessary marriage customs would be settled." These were the young woman's commitments.

[The] girl, *Agnes Adwoa Fodwoo*, agreed to be honest and abide by the rules of her parents and myself to finish School without any disappointment [such as] to bring or create any trouble for the refunding of all amount spent on her. (96–97)

Boakye Yiadom used his literacy and the pages of MOL to prepare himself with ample documentation for a possible complaint against Agnes Fodwoo's parents.[23] Should she break the agreement, he could recover his expenses. Concluding negotiations, Boakye Yiadom presented half a bottle of schnapps "as the official stamp on the promised 'fiancée' palaver" (97).

In February 1958, Sophia Yankeraa, whom he now referred to as "wife," had another child. Keeping up the statistics, Boakye Yiadom classified the child as her tenth and his fourteenth (should be fifteenth), named Longage Amma Ankomaa Antieh after his great-grandmother. Over the next five months, entries deal with his troubled relationship with Yankeraa. Five weeks after the birth, he noted a "preliminary divorcement [termination] of marriage," although no official marriage had been arranged. Mediation was initiated by the Presbyterian congregation at Juansa. In May 1958, the case was "amicably settled" by the Agogo district pastor and presbyters (church elders) from the congregations at Juansa. Boakye Yiadom joyfully commented that finally their "permanent, Christian and native Customary Marriage was lovely and jointly performed at Juansa." Writing about this "grand day," he listed representatives of his wife's lineage and her father's family as well his own. He paid a seven-shilling registration fee and had additional expenses of almost ten pounds.[24] Marital troubles continued. After "exactly 3 months [of] marriage," they were divorced, which was swiftly followed by reconciliation in January 1959. He "pacified" Sophia Yankeraa with three pounds because of his marital agreement with Agnes Fodwoo (101–103). During the same month, another concubine, Adwoa Bemmah, delivered his sixteenth child, named after his younger uncle, Kwabena Opong. There is no word about marriage negotiations with her.

MOL provides a record of how Boakye Yiadom coordinated visits of wives and concubines to avoid troubles.[25] In February 1959, right after his transfer to Adidwan outside Mampong-Asante, Sophia Yankeraa left to visit Juansa. Five days later, concubine Adwoa Mansah arrived from Abetifi before leaving "for good" in June. After merely five days, following Mansah's departure, Yankeraa returned. Yankeraa and Boakye Yiadom's togetherness did not last. Within seven weeks, she was again on her way to Juansa, this time pregnant and leaving "without the consent" of her husband and the local presbyters. Mentioning his position as teacher-catechist, Boakye Yiadom indicated how these marital difficulties undermined his status.[26] Yankeraa came back with her "younger father" for another round of mediation, which was presented to the Adidwan Presbyterian Session and settled "amicably." Boakye Yiadom supplied drinks to "clear the case" (105). Four months later, in March 1960, Yankeraa delivered her eleventh child, his seventeenth, named Solomon Kwadwo Nkansa after his late stepfather, the Kurofa chief (108).

In the course of his dispute with Sophia Yankeraa, Boakye Yiadom also recorded the evolution of his relationship with his younger fiancée, Agnes Fodwoo. In November 1959, she arrived from her Juansa hometown for a three-day visit. During Christmas break, he traveled to Juansa with an entourage of three friends to complete the customary marriage rites. They returned together to Adidwan, and Boakye Yiadom wrote that Agnes Fodwoo now stayed "permanently with me as wife." In February 1960, he was "provoked" when he learned about her "private 'Boy Friend' by name George." After hitting her three times, Boakye Yiadom expressed deep regrets, appealing to divine assistance never to lose his temper again and hurt his "own wife" (107). In this rare moment of introspection, his writing resembles the Pietist model.

While Boakye Yiadom experienced difficulties with church officials because of his extramarital affairs in the 1940s, his complex arrangements with Sophia Yankeraa, Agnes Adwoa Fodwoo, and other concubines in the late 1950s did not cause reactions by the Presbyterian Church, at least not any recorded in MOL. Perhaps the marriage with Sophia Yankeraa was no longer considered valid. Further, due to changes in educational policies under self-rule, the Presbyterian Church was less effective in enforcing its rules among teachers (Smith 1966). In an interview, Boakye Yiadom declared that during the 1950s, education officers were more interested in his classroom performance than in his marital life. Boakye Yiadom sought to prevent situations in which more than one woman stayed with him.

> I did not marry them all at once! They [the different women he was involved with] . . . were not married all at once staying at my house. (1994)

He no longer recalled that some marriages had overlapped. Instead, he evoked Presbyterian norms of monogamy, at least serial monogamy. Therefore, he preferred to mention only two of his Christian wives in his shorter, more polished autobiography, "My Life History" (n.d.b). Yet according to MOL entries, relationships with different women coexisted but could be concealed from church officials who did not condone them.[27] In September 1960, Boakye Yiadom transferred to a new station in Adamsu, Brong-Ahafo, accompanied only by Agnes Fodwoo and four "House Boys" (n.d.a, 1:110). Four months later, he finally divorced his senior wife, Sophia Yankeraa. This cleared the way for entering an official marriage with Agnes Adwoa Fodwoo according to "Native Customary Law and in respect of the Presbyterian Church of Ghana" (see fig. 1.4). He reported expenses of ten pounds, six shillings, and sixpence (112–113). In January 1961, Fodwoo delivered her first child, Fathia Anna Abena Afrah, "named after Dr. Kwame Nkrumah's wife and my grandmother-in-law."[28]

Travelogue

There is surprisingly little information about Boakye Yiadom's career as a teacher-catechist, which spanned more than three decades in the MOL volumes. While he noted his transfers, there are few remarks about his classroom teaching. Instead, he wrote about his frequent travels, including comments on the means of transportation, the names of his drivers, travel costs, and the purposes of the journeys. When he purchased a "doubled Iron Bed" for the

Figure 1.4. Entries in
MOL—note the asterisk in
the margin, highlighting
Boakye Yiadom's divorce
(1:112).

sum of twenty pounds at the SCOA (Société Commerciale de L'Ouest
Africain) store in Asante-Mampong, this acquisition was "carried by a lorry
known as 'LOVE ALL', *'Boafo yɛ na'*" and was driven by Kwasi Donkoh "free
of charge" (110). During vacations, he visited relatives and friends, attending
to his obligations as son, nephew, *wɔfa*, husband, father, and friend and fellow
teacher of other *akrakyefoɔ*. A close reading about these journeys allows a reconstruction of his social networks, which encompassed *abusua* (matrilineage)
members in his hometowns of Abetifi and Kurofa, wives and concubines and
their relatives, and selected friends and their wives and children. These passages show how knots were tied, loosened, and rearranged over the course of
his life. An excerpt from 1964 documents his mobility and recording style
(n.d.a, 2:9–12):

OCT. 26   *MONDAY* at 2.30 p.m. my younger brother, Adu Kwasi of
           Kurofa arrived at Adamsu on visit and for special request of £3
           loan to add to his £7 in making £10 to find work for his son,
           Kwadwo Nkansah now at Tamale in search of either Teaching or
           Agricultural work.

OCT. 31   *SAT'DAY*—My younger bro., Adu Kwasi left Adamsu with £1 loan for Kurofa.—Paid to bro. Ksi Ampomah.

This episode shows Boakye Yiadom's responsibility toward *abusua* members. As a salaried man he was expected to assist his kin, regardless of his other financial commitments.

NOV. 2   *MONDAY*—I left Adamsu for Abetifi with my son, Agya Fah and met Adu Kwasi in Kumasi who took Agya Fah for Juansa while I went straight to Abetifi, reached there at about 6.30 p.m.

On his way to Abetifi, Boakye Yiadom dropped off his nine-year-old son to be reunited with his mother, Sophia Yankeraa, at their hometown.

NOV. 3   *TUESDAY*—At Abetifi.

*NOV. 4   *W'DAY*—Left Abetifi for Pepease with my dear darling, Susana Akosua Ansomaah of Abetifi Presbyt. Church-Salem, my younger father, Kwabena Somuah of Akasease, Yaw Fosuhene, driver of Akasease now in Accra, [blank] Asante, my nephew and Kwadwo Bosh my elder bro-in-law to Susana to see Susana's father for all marriage customary rites of £1 1/-"Behume", £5 8s and a full bottle of Schnapps @ £2 2/-; Abetifi Presby Church Box Marriage Fee of 10/6d; Women's Fellowship 10/6d, Transport Abetifi/Pepease and back 10/-; Palm Wine 4/-and chop 4/- all totalling £10 10/-.

N.B.   1. My wife's real father=*Daniel Kwabena Korateng Afrim* of Pepease
2. My wife's real mother=*Felicia Akosua Akyeaah* of Abetifi, Khu

The asterisk (in red ink) signals the importance of this event. Boakye Yiadom was formalizing his relationship with his second wife, who had recently given birth to his twenty-first child, her eighth (n.d.a, 2:7). Emphasizing Susana Ansomaah's Presbyterian credentials, he noted her origins in Abetifi Christian Quarters. He intended to fill the blank space (before Asante) with a name. Such blanks are frequent in MOL, since he kept revising the text. The marriage payments testify to Ansomaah's connections with the Presbyterian church. To what extent all participants were aware that she had become the co-wife of Agnes Fodwoo is not clear. According to Akan custom, his second marriage was not an unusual thing, but church officials would have frowned.

NOV. 5   *THURSDAY*—Left Abetifi for Kurofa.
NOV. 6   *FRIDAY*—At Kurofa

NOV. 7   *SAT'DAY*—Attended both Funeral obsequies of Nana Kwame Afram, Late-Omanhene of Juansa's 40 days celebration who died on Friday 25/9/64 at Kumasi Central Hospital (GEE) and buried at Juansa on Monday 29th inst. at Ahenfie and Nana [blank] Tiwaah, Op. Kofi Kɔkɔɔ's mother at Juansa who also died on [blank space of several lines]

Throughout his life, Boakye Yiadom maintained close relationships in Kurofa, his second hometown. He might have used the day to inspect his uncle's cocoa farm, in which he had participated since 1935. The visit focused on funeral celebrations for the late chief of Juansa,[29] his teaching station in 1954 and the hometown of his wives Sophia Yankeraa and Agnes Fodwoo and four of his children. He never filled the blank space reserved for elaborating on the second funeral.

NOV. 8   *SUNDAY*—After Service at Kurofa I arrived at Agogo per Juansa to see my dear wife, Agnes Adwoa Fordjor Yiadom at the Presbyt. Women's Tr. Trg. College at the premises of Mr. Nyarko-Mensah of Kurofa, an English/Geography Tutor at the College and returned to Patriensa to see Mr. K. O. Frimpong, the Headteacher of Patriensa United Middle School transferred from Adamsu in Sept 1964 and returned to Kurofa via Juansa. Gave wife 10/- and 2/- to her 2 friends who met me there.

This entry documents how he supported his other's wife professional ambitions to be trained as a teacher at the Agogo Presbyterian women's college. He provided Fodwoo with financial support and her (female) friends with cash gifts. To secure a private meeting place, he relied on his teachers' network. When he returned home, he added a stop to greet Frimpong, a former colleague.

NOV. 9   *MONDAY*—Returned from Kurofa for Adamsu to resume duty—reached at 7.35 p.m.

NOV. 16   *MONDAY*—Susana Akosua Ansomaah, my beloved darling arrived Adamsu from Abetifi Presbytn. Mission-"Salem" with my new born baby, Felicia Abena Frempomaah born on Tuesday, 8/9/64 at Abetifi, and Comfort Yaa Ayaw, Susana's own daughter at 7.35 p.m.

The last two entries show Boakye Yiadom back at his station with characteristically little information about his work as headteacher and catechist; more important was the arrival of the new wife with their child and a child of her previous marriage.

Chronicle

In addition to entries about Boakye Yiadom's travels and his relationships with wives, concubines, and their children, the two MOL volumes include references to occurrences outside his immediate life. This unique chronicle reveals more about the author's subjectivity. For example, the end of World War II is not mentioned, nor do political events of the 1950s receive much space, although Boakye Yiadom, an active CPP member, participated as polling assistant in elections and worked for the 1960 census.[30] In lieu of commenting about Nkrumah's political triumphs, Boakye Yiadom singled out the former's attainment of fatherhood to first mention his name. The entry is highlighted with "STOP" and six exclamation marks, all in red ink:

> On this remarkable W'Day, March 18, 1959, Dr. Kwame Nkrumah now 49 yrs born in 1910 [blank] the 1st Prime Minister of Ghana (Gold Coast) and his wife, an Egyptian woman, Madam Fathia now aged 28 yrs. born in 1931 brought forth their "First" baby son Kwaku Nkrumah at the Govt. House Osu Accra (Christiansborg) at 6.20 p.m. May God bless and give both the child and parents everlasting life and a healthy condition. (n.d.a, 1:104)

Foregrounding this event reveals the importance of fatherhood in Boakye Yiadom's understanding of (adult) masculinity. Similar to a critique expressed by CPP opponents, Boakye Yiadom did not consider Nkrumah a "real man," much less an elder, until he had fathered a child.[31] In the 1960s, political events were reported more frequently, such as the third anniversary of independence and the proclamation of Ghana Republic, both in 1960 (106–107). The 1966 coup ousting Nkrumah received a heading of "STOP" four times and three asterisks—which he recorded as "2nd Ghana Revolution" (the first being independence). The one against Busia in 1972 received just one asterisk despite Boakye Yiadom's membership in the Progress Party (n.d.a, 2:35, 155). The later coups are not mentioned.

Boakye Yiadom was more attentive to local histories. He listed twenty "Ashanti Kings" (n.d.a, 1:49) and updated the table after the enstoolment of Opoku Ware II in 1970. One entry tells the story of a nineteenth-century loan of 200 pounds by his ancestor Nana Kwasi Ampoma to the Abetifi chief, as narrated by his grandmother Adwoa Antie (73–78). He also recorded her involuntary migration to Abetifi and listed her descendants (56–60). Further, he incorporated passages about Kwawu customs and compiled appellations for animals, *mmran* (50). In conversation, he explained his passion for recording. Although as a Presbyterian catechist he was supposed to maintain distance from non-Christian Akan rituals, he did not always comply. In 1954, a renowned ɔbosomfo (diviner) came to Juansa. He was eager to witness the performance:

> If I go and see that it is true, well, I can sometimes write it down, write in my notes. That on this or that date, that man came into the town, and he was a great magician, and that he was catching something like an egg or fowls or buckets, anything abstract from the air.

"Then," he added, "I put it down, just to tell my children."[32] Boakye Yiadom acted as chronicler. What he perceived as special events received an entry in books like MOL to be preserved for posterity and to leave a record for his children, this text's principal audience.

Audience

The MOL volumes provide a bridge between literacy and orality. They were written to be read in private and in public. When I asked about the audience for diaries like MOL, Boakye Yiadom gave a simple but complex answer:

> I do loudly read my old diaries to [be heard by] my wife, children, grandchildren and the householders to their amusement, laughter and sorrow, knowing and studying my progress, backwardness or retrogression in life; so that they too may be aware of themselves in their living. (1995)

Boakye Yiadom has regularly *performed* excerpts from his writings like MOL. Since some "householders" were not fluent in English, he needed to translate into Twi. The condensed MOL text was far removed from a verbatim script. Entries merely served as a reservoir of key words that triggered stories of past events. He generated a coherent narrative only while offering an oral presentation of MOL for the edification of his audience. In this way the stored information left the confined boundaries of literacy and reentered the realm of orality. By interjecting comments and questions, even extending the narrative, the audience helped to relocate the fixed written text about the past into the open oral present.[33] This use of Boakye Yiadom's autobiographical writing is remarkable, since MOL entries detail private transactions and personal matters which people usually do not reveal to others, particularly not to juniors and dependants. Thus, Boakye Yiadom was engaged in two projects. One focused on the conventional model of learning from example, his public renditions of MOL. The other dealt with acts of storing up, secreting almost, the very things that normally are not shared—not because they are revealing and emotionally intimate but because they are a behind-the-scenes mechanism of his public persona. Boakye Yiadom's detailed accounts of his dealings with his wives and concubines were not just a record of the past but a script for the future, in that he kept track of negotiations and arrangements, thereby preparing his next moves.[34]

Boakye Yiadom's performance resembles the Akan practice of story-telling, *anansesɛm* (spider stories), recalled by him and others of his age group as an important leisure-time activity in their childhood (Kyei 2001; Miescher 2005). The tales feature the trickster figure Kwaku Ananse, who is portrayed as full of wit, eloquent, selfish, and lazy. Ananse seeks to enrich himself at the expense of others. Although clever in gaining an advantage, in the end Ananse usually gets entangled in his own web. Most tales close with a moral statement that express norms and reaffirm the social order. Since *anansesɛm* plots were known to the audience, the skillful performer excelled by adding personal interpretations and embellishments. *Anansesɛm* were oral entertainment that taught youngsters about values and appropriate behavior (Yankah 1983). Obviously Boakye Yiadom is not Kwaku Ananse, and the MOL volumes do not seek to reproduce *anansesɛm*. They are a collection of personal experiences interspliced with passages about local history. Nevertheless, if we examine Boakye Yiadom's practice of narrating MOL excerpts for the "amusement" of his audience, we need to look for inspirations in the local oral arts.[35]

When he presented MOL's content to an audience assembled in his courtyard, Boakye Yiadom did not follow a model inherent in (auto)biographical accounts of the pioneers of the Basel Mission and Presbyterian Church. MOL, with the exception of the opening section and a few recorded local histories, is not narrative. Nor does this text copy the genre of the personal diary as stipulated by a Pietist understanding of introspective writing in search of communication with God. Rather, Boakye Yiadom has been creating a hybrid form that draws on (auto)biography, station diary, and chronicle while featuring his personal innovations. The incorporation of visual marks (see figs. 1.3 and 1.4), the red asterisk, the use of uppercase "STOP," and bundles of exclamation marks serve as signposts, stage directions to adapt the MOL material for public performance. Boakye Yiadom has been experimenting with a form of writing that makes possible a transformation through the use of genres appropriate and familiar to his environment. His characterization of the public reading as evoking "laughter and sorrow, knowing and studying about progress, backwardness or retrogression in life" has moral overtones. The tales spun from MOL may engage with Kwaku Ananse, with the message of *anansesɛm*. Commenting on his son's reading, Boakye Yiadom noted:

> What I did what was right he should continue. What I did and I wrote in this book that is not good, he should not do so. That is why I wrote my life; I want to give it to my children to see how [their] father was. (2000a)

Yet Boakye Yiadom has also created more-successful and more-linear accounts of his life, based on biographical data listed as "particulars" in MOL's final pages (n.d.a 2:189–191). In his shorter autobiography, "My Life History" (n.d.b), and in correspondence presenting his life to Kwame Nkrumah or more recently to Presbyterian officials when seeking ordination, he narrated a heroic tale of a man who has overcome the odds of life, who has achieved, thanks to his education and Christian faith, the position of a teacher-catechist.[36]

Conclusion

Throughout his life, Boakye Yiadom had a compulsion to write. "Autobiography: My Own Life" reflects the multitude of his selves and alliances. He constructed different masculine identities, defining himself as teacher-catechist, devout Presbyterian, father, husband, *wɔfase* (nephew), son, and *wɔfa*. For decades he moved in and out of various social contexts with competing expectations. As a Presbyterian headteacher and catechist he was expected to present a model Christian family life. While working as a salaried migrant, he tried to maintain a presence in the lineage affairs of his hometowns and fulfill obligations by helping with loans and at funerals. MOL provides rich evidence of these conflicting loyalties. It documents his struggle to overcome with "perseverance"—the text's motto (see fig. 1.2)—his life's constraints, to do the right thing as a man, and to become a respected elder (Miescher 2001).

When Boakye Yiadom left school in 1935, there were few men and women with a similar education in colonial Ghana. At that time, *akrakyefoɔ* sought employment, status, and material possessions based not on their birth and family connections but on their educational qualifications. But by the end of Boakye Yiadom's life, literacy and the position of a teacher-catechist were no longer unusual. As a social group, *akrakyefoɔ* had become ordinary. Moreover, because Boakye Yiadom entered training college late, he did not have the opportunity to climb the social ladder during the Africanization of the education service or to be ordained as a Presbyterian minister. Still, his writing remains an expression of his aspirations in terms of class and status; it reflects his attempts to reconstruct his selves through specific self-presentations. He sought to join those public figures—Presbyterian pioneers and politicians—who produced autobiographies. He did not write the MOL volumes merely for personal record-keeping or as a mnemonic device for settling disputes and for telling good stories. He noted that they should serve "as future references to be *read* over and over again to know about my life by my children and children's children (the great grandchildren)" (1995, emphasis added).

In Kwawu, as in other Akan societies, twentieth-century bigmen—traders, cocoa farmers, chiefs, and politicians—constructed impressive buildings to demonstrate their accomplishments and preserve their legacy (van der Geest 1998). Since Boakye Yiadom did not erect such a monument, he hopes that his writing will outlive his physical mortality, thereby creating a form of afterlife. Among Akan people, there is the practice of evoking names of important ancestors during libations; the most elaborate ones are performed by the ɔkyeame, the chief's spokesperson (Yankah 1995). Not being close to the royal lineage, and as a Presbyterian teacher-catechist, Boakye Yiadom cannot expect his name to be mentioned in such prayers. Rather, because he has provided his children and their children with the record of MOL, there is a chance that their silent reading or their public performance will preserve his memory. Finally, it appears that Boakye Yiadom's motivation in giving me access to his writings, in speaking with me extensively, reflects his desire to invite others to learn from his life. This is also his hope—that this chapter's intended reader will do the same.

NOTES

1. I am very grateful to A. K. Boakye Yiadom for his friendship and willingness to share his personal papers with me. Thanks also to Kwame Fosu for assistance in translating some of Boakye Yiadom's Twi texts. Research for this chapter was supported by the Wenner-Gren Foundation, the John D. and Catherine T. MacArthur Foundation, the Janggen-Pöhn Stiftung, Northwestern University, Bryn Mawr College, and the University of California, Santa Barbara.

2. On his reading habits, see Asante 1993a, 1993b.

3. Boakye Yiadom ordered titles such as the weekly magazine *International Affairs* or the monthly publications *Soviet Union, Moscow News, Soviet Woman, New Times, Culture & Life, Soviet Literature, Soviet Film,* and *Sports in the U.S.S.R.*

4. According to the 1931 census, 4 percent of Abetifi's population had received at

least a Standard IV education; in 1948, this figure had climbed to 13 percent (Gold Coast 1932, 1950).

5. I am grateful to the sons of E. K. Addo and B. E. Ofori, Ofori Atta Addo and J. Opari Kwame Asa-Ofori, for providing me access to their late fathers' papers. In July 2000, during a conference at Pembroke College, Cambridge, where this material was presented, Audrey Gadzekpo (University of Ghana) commented that her grandfather, a storekeeper like Addo, had regularly kept a diary. Gadzekpo recalled him explaining that "he *had* to keep a diary," since this was what a *krakye* did.

6. For the Basel Mission's activities in Akropong, see Middleton 1983; for Kwawu, see Nkansa-Kyeremateng 1976 and Miescher 2005; see Smith 1966.

7. For the development of Pietism in Württemberg, see Lehmann 1969; for the importance of (auto)biographical writing in Pietism, see Schmidt 1972.

8. Some diaries were deposited at the Basel Mission Archive, Basel, Switzerland (hereafter BMA); see personal files, Brüder-Verzeichnis and Schwesternverzeichnis. On a personal note: the practice of diary-writing is very familiar to me. I was born into a Swiss family influenced by Pietism that had ties to the Basel Mission, and many of my older relatives kept diaries. I started one at the age of 11.

9. Waosidu (?) Diary, Odumase-Krobo district, Presbyterian Church Archives, Accra (hereafter PCA), 10/1.

10. Ibid.

11. Abetifi Diary, PCA, 10/6.

12. For a similar practice of keeping diaries and journals among CMS (Church Missionary Society) missionaries and its African assistants in nineteenth-century Yorubaland, see Peel 2000.

13. They are part of the Pioneer Series, published by the Presbyterian Church: Hall 1965, Martinson 1965, Keteku 1965a and 1965b, and Debrunner 1965.

14. For example, there are no entries between November 17, 1950, and August 26, 1951 (Yiadom n.d.a, 1:66–67) or from August 20, 1954 (reporting the birth of a child) till November 15, 1955 (noting the birth of another child; ibid., 84).

15. Each change of employment is carefully recorded in MOL; all his stations of employment are also chronologically listed in Boakye Yiadom's other autobiography (n.d.b), which was written after 1978.

16. Yiadom 1994, 2000a, 2001.

17. It is not clear whether this table includes the births of *all* his children. During conversation, we noticed that one son who did not live had been omitted. Boakye Yiadom (2000) added him as 11b (see fig. 1.3). Another daughter appears to be missing as well.

18. Cf. Allman and Tashjian's observations about "marriage as a process" (2000, 58).

19. Boakye Yiadom divorced Adomako in August 1956 and the procedure was finalized before her father in January 1957. Since she had left "without reasonable ground," Boakye Yiadom was granted five shillings as compensation (Yiadom n.d.a, 1:89).

20. Yankeraa is also spelled Yankera or Yankeraah; Fodwoo is also spelled Fodwɔɔh or Fordjor.

21. The practice of cross-cousin marriage used to be common in Akan societies; see Rattray 1927; Fortes 1950; and Bleek 1975.

22. In Kwawu, men were expected to stay with their pregnant wives or concubines, support them, and continue sexual intercourse for the pregnancy to mature. See cases brought to the Native Tribunal of the Adontenhene, Abetifi, such as *Atta Kwabena v. Ama*

Aframea, June 20, 1940, Kwawu Traditional Council, Mpraeso (hereafter KTC), 3:380, 382–388.

23. Since the 1940s, Kwawu litigants have increasingly used written documents as evidence to strengthen their cases brought to Native Tribunals. See Miescher 1997.

24. The expenses were: "Agya Nyameguan £2; Agya Ayɛyɛdeɛ 2/-; Ena Ayɛyɛdeɛ 10/6; Abusuafoɔ Mmaa 13/-; Abusuafoɔ Mmarima 21/-; nea ɔde ɔbaa no kyɛ 4/-; Local Church 10/6; Singing Band 4/-; Women class 4/-; Choristers 4/-; *Ti* Aseda 2 Bottles Schnapps @ 30/-, ca.=£3" (Yiadom n.d.a, 1:99–101).

25. According to the Kwabena Atia laws (a set of customary marriage rules), when a husband "happens to intermix himself between his two wives . . . , and a case through jealousy arises between the women, the man is responsible." Cited in Native Tribunal of the Adontenhene, Abetifi, *Kisiwaah v. Kwasi Mununu,* June 21, 1937, KTC, 2:280, 296–308.

26. Concerning Presbyterian marriage norms, see Presbyterian Church of the Gold Coast, *Regulations Practice and Procedure,* revised 1929, BMA, D-9.1c 13d.

27. As a Presbyterian teacher-catechist in a village, Boakye Yiadom had a public position. Local church elders would have admonished him for not following rules, even during a time period when education officers were becoming less interested in a teacher's married life; see Miescher 2003.

28. This patriotic act was acknowledged: the regional commissioner presented the child with twenty shillings (Yiadom n.d.a, 1:114). Boakye Yiadom had written a personal letter to the Osagyefo on March 20, 1961; Boakye Yiadom papers, Abetifi.

29. Whose death was recorded on September 25, 1964 (Yiadom n.d.a, 2:7).

30. Among his papers, there are documents about the 1954 elections and the original "Kurofa Register of Voters" for 1957; MOL records his work as an "Enumerator for Atonsuagya and its 15 villages" for the 1960 census (Yiadom n.d.a, 2:109).

31. A political paper by the Asante Youth Organization from the early 1950s noted that "[Nkrumah] has failed to marry in order to bear children to increase the population of the country [of which] he is Prime Minister contrary to custom"; quoted in Allman 1993, 35. For understandings of masculinity, see Miescher 2005.

32. Yiadom 1994. In a different notebook, he recorded the celebration of the 1994 *afahye* festival in Kwawu.

33. For interrelations between literacy and orality in colonial Africa, see Hofmeyr 1994.

34. I am thankful to Karin Barber for clarifying my thinking about the larger implications of Boakye Yiadom's performance of MOL.

35. For the connections between *anansesɛm* and the style, presentation, and techniques in Ghanaian popular theater, see Cole 2001.

36. See Boakye Yiadom to Osagyefo, March 20, 1961, and various letters to church officials among his papers.

REFERENCES

Agovi, Kofi. 1990. "The Origins of Literary Theatre in Colonial Ghana, 1920–1957." *Institute of African Studies Research Review,* n.s., 6, no. 1: 1–23.

Allman, Jean M. 1993. *The Quills of the Porcupine: Asante Nationalism in an Emergent Ghana.* Madison: University of Wisconsin Press.

_____. and Victoria Tashjian. 2000. *"I Will Not Eat Stone": A Women's History of Colonial Asante*. Portsmouth, N.H.: Heinemann.

Asante, E. K. O. 1993a. Interview with the author. Abetifi, January 26.

_____. 1993b. Interview with the author. Abetifi, May 18.

Austin, Dennis. 1964. *Politics in Ghana, 1946–1960*. London: Oxford University Press.

Bleek, Wolf. 1975. *Marriage, Inheritance, and Witchcraft: A Case Study of a Rural Ghanaian Family*. Leiden: Afrika-Studiecentrum.

Cole, Catherine M. 2001. *Ghana's Concert Party Theatre*. Bloomington: Indiana University Press.

Debrunner, Hans W. 1965. *The Story of Sampson Opong*. Accra: Waterville.

Fortes, Meyer. 1950. "Kinship and Marriage among the Ashanti." In *African Systems of Kinship and Marriage*, ed. A. Radcliffe-Brown and D. Forde, 252–284. London: Oxford University Press.

Gold Coast. 1932. *The Gold Coast Census, 1931: Appendices, Containing Comparative Returns and General Statistics of the 1931 Census*. Accra: Government Printer

_____. 1950. *Census of Population, 1948*. London: Crown Agents.

Hall, Peter. 1965. *Autobiography of Peter Hall*. Accra: Waterville.

Hofmeyr, Isabel. 1994. *"We Spend Our Years as a Tale That Is Told": Oral Historical Narrative in a South African Chiefdom*. Portsmouth, N.H.: Heinemann.

Keteku, H. J. 1965a. *Biography of Rev. Nathanael Victor Asare*. Accra: Waterville.

_____. 1965b. *The Reverends Theophilus Opoku and David Asante*. Accra: Waterville.

Kyei, T. E. 2001. *Our Days Dwindle: Memories of My Childhood Days in Asante*. Portsmouth, N.H.: Heinemann.

Lehmann, Hartmut. 1969. *Pietismus und weltliche Ordnung in Württemberg*. Stuttgart: Kohlhammer.

Martinson, A. P. A. 1965. *Biography of Rev. Benjamin A. Martinson, 1870–1929*. Accra: Waterville.

McWilliam, H. O., and M. A. Kwamenah-Poh. 1975. *The Development of Education in Ghana*. London: Longman.

Middleton, John. 1983. "One Hundred and Fifty Years of Christianity in a Ghanaian Town." *Africa* 53, no. 3: 2–19.

Miescher, Stephan F. 1997. "Of Documents and Litigants: Disputes on Inheritance in Abetifi—A Town of Colonial Ghana." *Journal of Legal Pluralism and Unofficial Law* 39: 81–119.

_____. 2001. "The Life Histories of Boakye Yiadom (Akasease Kofi of Abetifi, Kwawu): Exploring the Subjectivity and 'Voices' of a Teacher-Catechist in Colonial Ghana." In *African Words, African Voices*, ed. L. White, S. F. Miescher, and D. W. Cohen, 162–193. Bloomington: Indiana University Press.

_____. 2003. "The Making of Presbyterian Teachers: Masculinities and Programs of Education in Colonial Ghana." In *Men and Masculinities in Modern Africa*, ed. L. A. Lindsay and S. F. Miescher, 89–108. Portsmouth, N.H.: Heinemann.

_____. 2005. *Making Men in Ghana*. Bloomington: Indiana University Press.

Newell, Stephanie. 2002. *Literary Culture in Colonial Ghana: "How to Play the Game of Life."* Bloomington: Indiana University Press.

Nkansa-Kyeremateng, Kofi. 1976. *One Hundred Years of the Presbyterian Church in Kwahu*. Accra: Presbyterian Press.

Ofori, B. E. 1993a. Interview with the author. Akropong, January 5.

————. 1993b. Interview with the author. Akropong, October 31.

Peel, J. D. Y. 2000. *Religious Encounter and the Making of the Yoruba.* Bloomington: Indiana University Press.

Rattray, R. S. 1927. *Religion and Art in Ashanti.* Oxford: Clarendon.

Schmidt, Martin. 1972. *Pietismus.* Stuttgart: Kohlhammer.

Smith, Noel. 1966. *The Presbyterian Church of Ghana, 1835–1960.* Accra: Ghana University Press.

van der Geest, Sjaak. 1998. "*Yebisa wo Fie:* Growing Old and Building a House in the Akan Culture of Ghana." *Journal of Cross-Cultural Gerontology* 13, no. 4: 333–359.

Yankah, Kwesi. 1983. *The Akan Trickster Cycle: Myth or Folklore?* Bloomington: African Studies Program, Indiana University.

————. 1995. *Speaking for the Chief: Ɔkyeame and the Politics of Akan Royal Oratory.* Bloomington: Indiana University Press.

Yiadom, A. K. Boakye 1993. Interview with the author. Abetifi, June 27.

————. 1994. Interview with the author. Abetifi, November 15.

————. 1995. Letter to the author. Abetifi, March 1.

————. 2000a. Interview with the author. Abetifi, August 12.

————. 2000b. Interview with the author. Abetifi, September 2.

————. 2001. Interview with the author. Abetifi, August 26.

————. n.d.a. "Autobiography: My Own Life." 2 vols.

————. n.d.b. "My Life History: The Autobiography of Akasease Kofi Boakye Yiadom."

"WHAT IS OUR INTELLIGENCE, OUR SCHOOL GOING AND OUR READING OF BOOKS WITHOUT GETTING MONEY?" AKINPẸLU OBIṢẸSAN AND HIS DIARY

2

Ruth Watson

In 1914, at the age of 25, Akinpẹlu Obiṣẹsan bought himself a diary. For the next six years he wrote in it sporadically. He recorded births and deaths in his extended family and within his circle of friends.[1] He also referred to family disagreements and problems with maintaining control over his family's extensive cocoa farms.[2] He noted some significant events in Ibadan, the large Yoruba city where he lived. *Balogun* Ọla died "miserably and violently," he wrote in 1917, a victim of the incessant conspiracies among Ibadan chiefs.[3] The following year he described the "raging influenza epidemic" and commented that "men and women are dying like flies."[4] On a few occasions he wrote about more personal matters, noting in one instance that his wife Ayọka had her menstrual period early.[5]

Obiṣẹsan bought his second diary in 1920. It is unclear what specifically motivated his increased diligence from February of that year, but we must appreciate the length of time it was sustained. For the next forty years, Akinpẹlu Obiṣẹsan kept a daily account of his life, and he chose to write it English, even though he was also literate in his mother tongue of Yoruba. By 1922, he had so much to write in his diary entries that he reduced his handwriting to a minuscule size (see fig. 2.2). He kept this up until the end of 1960, leaving us with a legacy of forty diary volumes, each with an entry for nearly every single day. The final diary recorded that he was in poor health and it seems that this

Figure 2.1. Frontispiece, 1921 Diary. Obiṣesan purchased diary books manufactured for the South African
market. His favorite was Quarto Series no. 33, which
offered a "week in opening," though he sometimes
bought Octavo Series no. 100, which offered "one day
on page" and Folio Series no. 31, which offered a "week
in opening" in the foolscap size. Courtesy the University
of Ibadan Library.

was the reason he stopped his diary-keeping, a few years before he died in
1963.

The diaries fill just eight of the seventy-two boxes that constitute the
Chief Akinpẹlu Obiṣesan Papers, which are deposited with the Kenneth Dike
Library at the University of Ibadan. The remaining boxes contain documents
relating to Obiṣesan's leading role in organizations such as the Ibadan Cocoa
Cooperative Marketing Union, the Association of Nigerian Cooperative Ex-
porters, and the Nigerian Cocoa Marketing Board. In addition, private correspondence and papers concerned with Ibadan politics and land disputes
form an important part of the archive. As such, the Obiṣesan Papers are a veritable treasure trove of tin-trunk literacy. That we have access today to this
unique source is due to the care of Lapade Obiṣesan, who gave his father's tin
trunks to the University of Ibadan in 1965.

Although a few scholars have consulted the Obiṣesan Papers, they have
used the collection only as a source of information for predefined research
topics (Falola 1989; Williams 1993; Watson 2003). Its existence as a personal
archive is simply taken for granted. Yet the survival of these private papers is
not a historical accident. Their sheer scope and their particular form—diaries
and private correspondence in addition to official documents—reveal the
local do-it-yourself archiving that characterizes the people and the tin-trunk
literacy this book is about. As such, we need to ask: What motivated Akinpẹlu
Obiṣesan to write so assiduously? Why did he then hoard his textual creations? The obvious place to look for clues to answer these questions is the
diary itself, which Obiṣesan used to reflect on the role of literacy in his life.

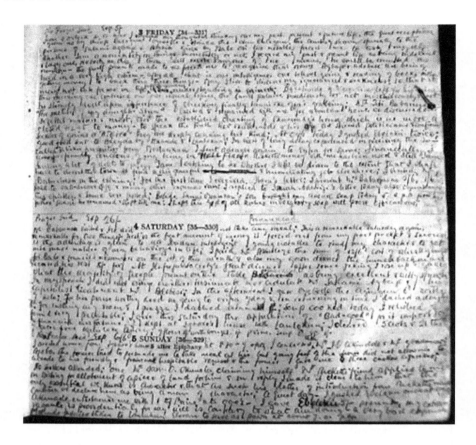

Figure 2.2. Diary entries, February 3–5, 1922. Courtesy the University of Ibadan Library.

Even during the early period of his diary-keeping before 1920, when his entries were somewhat patchy, Obiṣẹsan used his diary for an intensely personal activity. He wrote down accounts of his dreams. These accounts were brief and formalistic but were explicit about his aspirations. Thus, in May 1914 he self-consciously recorded: "Thy dream foretells poverty in youth, but in thy old age thou wilt have riches," while the following month he asserted "Thy dream signifies much society and the introduction to many excellent friends."[6]

It is in one of these "dream narratives," recorded in his first diary but dated 1918, that Obiṣẹsan asserts his "literate subconscious." Having described himself as engaged in beating back evil spirits and seeing a vision of one of his mothers-in-law and his mother very early in the morning, he concluded the narrative by stating:

> To my surprise a written letter appeared before me in which I was warned not to keep bad company—this is the third time that God is speaking to me by asking me what he wants me to do in writing.[7]

What are we to make of Obiṣẹsan's assertion that God "speaks" to him "in writing"? I argue that it is evidence of what Karin Barber has identified as "a fervent regard for the capacity of literacy to enhance personal and social existence."[8] That Obiṣẹsan had a dream in which he had a vision of a letter from God appearing before him shows the extent to which he believed in the empowering potential of reading and writing. Indeed, not only did he see the letter in the dream, he actually *read* it and could thus report on its instruction "not to keep bad company."

Clearly, Obiṣẹsan had a far more sophisticated conceptualization of literacy than that implied by those who focus on the "silencing" effects of writing in English in colonial contexts.[9] Obiṣẹsan was far from "silenced." He embraced literacy in English wholeheartedly and not only dreamed about a written text but also wrote out an English-language narrative of his dream. By doing this he unwittingly blurred distinctions between oral and written genres, since he expressed the empowerment of literacy in terms of orality. That is, his act of reading translated the subconscious written text into an oral one and enabled him to have a sense that God was "speaking" to him. In this way, he created his own peculiar genre of personal commentary which requires further explanation.

This chapter investigates the first few years of Obiṣẹsan's diary-keeping. It initially examines his early life and the influence of a mission education on his orientation to literacy. Next, it considers the extent to which his diary can be read as a coherent narrative. The final part of the chapter explores how Obiṣẹsan's diary-writing projected him into an emergent literary world. That is, although keeping a diary would seem to be concerned with writing more than reading, Obiṣẹsan's diary enabled him to assert his literacy skills in a much wider sense. Such action helped him constitute his respectability and confirm his status as a Christian gentleman in colonial Ibadan. He did this in defiance of the British authorities, who were at that time dismissive of educated Africans and sought to exclude them from the administration of the Nigerian colonial state. Obiṣẹsan remained perplexed, however, about why the status of being literate was not necessarily associated with material wealth.

Akinpẹlu Obiṣẹsan's Early Life

Akinpẹlu Obiṣẹsan was born in Ibadan about 1889. He was the son of an elephant-hunter, Obiṣẹsan Aperin, and a slave woman. Aperin had risen to a prominent position in Ibadan toward the end of the nineteenth century, when he was one of a group of hunters stationed on the southeast fringes of the city that defended it against Ijẹbu invaders. As recognition for his services, Aperin gained the chieftaincy title of *Agbakin* in 1893. Shortly afterward he was a signatory to the Ibadan Agreement, which marked the formal commencement of British colonial rule in Ibadan.

Very little is known of Akinpẹlu Obiṣẹsan's mother except that she was a slave woman whom Aperin took as his wife. However, her low status made Obiṣẹsan's position as a chief's son somewhat marginal. This possibly influenced the decision to send him to Arẹmọ mission school in 1896, which was run by the Church Missionary Society (CMS). Two years later, Obiṣẹsan moved to Ọyọ and continued his education under the guardianship of Rev. (later Bishop) Melville Jones at the CMS Training College.

In 1905, Obiṣẹsan was articled to work in the Ibadan office of the British Resident, and he subsequently joined the Lagos Railway as a clerk. By 1912 he had become a stationmaster, but he resigned the following year and then returned to Ibadan.[10] In 1914, Obiṣẹsan began managing his family land, which had been claimed by his father, Aperin, in the 1880s. During the decade that followed, Aperin and his family gradually transformed the vast tract of forest into a cocoa-growing district.

By the early colonial period, the Aperin family land was both productive and valuable, but ownership of it was contested and subject to land claims. Obiṣẹsan was thus appointed by his older, illiterate brothers as the family secretary, and his main task was to lobby colonial officials to support his family's claim to the land. He was also needed to make written submissions and statements to the colonial courts in order to assert the Aperin family's right to allocate land to tenants. Simultaneously, Obiṣẹsan sought to defend the cocoa farms against people he called "trespassers," the tenants of rival claimants to the land.[11]

Since Obiṣẹsan purchased his first diary in the year that he became the family secretary, we could speculate that he began writing it as a way of keeping records. Much of the first diary is filled with lists of births and deaths in his extended family and short reports on incidents related to the family land. However, the diary soon became much more than simple reports on his family duties. Since this occupation did not provide sufficient income for his needs, Obiṣẹsan continued to work for mercantile firms such as Patterson Zochonis and Miller Brothers from 1913 onward. He sought to make his fortune as a produce trader, selling mainly cocoa and palm kernels. However, it is evident from his diary entries that he was quite unsuccessful. As he himself admitted, this was partly because he was too involved in matters relating to the family land to give sufficient attention to business.[12]

Nevertheless, Williams has suggested that the reasons for Obiṣẹsan's lack of success in trade must go beyond his obsession with family politics, especially since his early career is similar to that of many educated Christians in Ibadan. Men such as I. B. Akinyẹle and J. O. Abọdẹrin also left government service in the second decade of the twentieth century to try their luck with the European trading firms. Some even succeeded in setting themselves up independently for a brief time, directly shipping produce abroad without employing middlemen. They had the advantage of literacy in English, which possibly made it easier to establish ties with English-speaking managers in the mercantile firms. These relationships were vital if they were to obtain sufficient credit to buy produce.

But crucially, Williams argues, the educated Christians engaged in trade "in order to finance the lifestyle which they believed appropriate to a Christian gentleman. For the prominent Muslim traders, trading was a way of life" (Williams 1993, 114). By the 1920s, three such men—Salami Agbaje, Adebisi Giwa, and Fọlarin Ṣolaja—were evidently wealthier than any of their Christian counterparts. When Obiṣẹsan tried to establish himself in trading, it was to them that he looked for help. As we shall see, he used his diary to comment on his continuing financial insecurity, revealing an intriguing tension between his ambition to be a Christian "literary man" and a desire to be "dazzling in riches." First, however, we must explore why being Christian and being literate in English were so closely associated in colonial Ibadan.

"Book-People" in Nineteenth-Century Yorubaland

Obiṣẹsan's experience of mission education, particularly in Yorubaland, influenced his orientation to literacy in important ways. Most fundamentally, it exposed him to models of reading and writing which shaped his belief in the power of literacy and perhaps even introduced him to the discipline of diary-keeping. The relationship between Yoruba missionaries and literacy has

Figure 2.3. Picture of
Akinpẹlu Obiṣẹsan in *The
Yoruba News,* May 4, 1943.
Reprinted from *The Yoruba
News.* Courtesy the Nigerian
National Archives, Ibadan.

The Hon'ble Akinpelu Obisesan

been examined by Peel, who argues that early Yoruba understandings of the power of Christianity "focused on its character as a religion of the Book." Thus, for example, the name by which Christians were most commonly known was *onibuku,* or "book-people" (Peel 2000, 223).

Henry Townsend, the head of the first Yoruba CMS mission station (established in Abẹokuta during 1846) himself fostered the Christian mission's association with written texts. Townsend had a special enthusiasm for printing, and he set up a press to produce service sheets and hymn pamphlets. In 1859, he published the first edition of Nigeria's first newspaper, *Iwe Irohin* (News Sheet). Peel suggests that although Townsend did not explicitly articulate it, he perhaps sought to encourage individual self-reflection through reading, a quality integral to evangelical sensibility (131).

Books and reading were thus central to the CMS Yoruba Mission. So too was a specific form of writing. For most of the nineteenth century, all CMS agents were expected to write journals, of which extracts were sent to the London headquarters. African agents of the mission composed the largest proportion of these journals, and a small number of them also kept private diaries, among whom was Daniel Olubi. An early Yoruba Christian convert, Olubi succeeded the German David Hinderer as head of the Ibadan mission in 1869, just seventeen years after its establishment.

Olubi was the first local Yoruba person (as opposed to a repatriate from Sierra Leone) to assume charge of a mission station and the first to be ordained a priest. It was Olubi who initially taught Obiṣẹsan when he began his education in 1896. In this way, Obiṣẹsan was introduced to a missionary community of readers and writers who were significant in mediating relations between the British and Yoruba rulers in the late nineteenth century. During the 1870s and 1880s, these African agents were the lifeline of the CMS Yoruba Mission, since a combination of factors caused the European personnel to retreat to the British territory of Lagos (141).

By the 1890s, however, the CMS had abandoned the idea of African self-government of the church and the Yoruba Mission had adopted a colonial model. Mission districts were to be headed by Europeans, who were to superintend the work of African evangelists or pastors working at the local level (151). Despite this change, Olubi and many of his contemporaries remained highly influential through their continuing roles in mission education and local politics. They trained and influenced the aspirations of young men such as Obiṣẹsan and the Akinyẹle brothers, Alexander and Isaac, who later became prominent figures in the religious and political life of colonial Ibadan (Watson 2003, 97–100). Both these men also kept personal diaries in English, although only Alexander Akinyẹle's has survived.[13] Indeed, Peel has argued that Christian missionaries had a pervasive influence on Yoruba cultural and intellectual life throughout the twentieth century and helped to bring the ethnic category of "Yoruba" into existence (Peel 1989). He contends that the CMS journals written by the early Yoruba missionaries such as Olubi were "not just their literary apprenticeship. They were the first works of the modern Yoruba intelligentsia" (Peel 2000, 11).

One of Obiṣẹsan's aims in writing his diary was to identify himself as a member of this Yoruba intelligentsia. He commented on reading and writing as tools of self-improvement and sought to become a member of an emerging literary circle in colonial Ibadan whose origins were in the nineteenth-century Yoruba missionary community. He once remarked that in comparison to

Abẹokuta with its longer history of mission endeavor, Ibadan was inferior "judging from [the] educational point of view" and he feared the city would "not rise until it [had] learnt how to educate its sons & daughters."[14] Taking his own duties in this regard very seriously, he reported in April 1920 that he had flogged his daughter and two of his sons for playing truant.[15]

This dedication to educating his children set Obiṣẹsan apart from his household, as did the self-conscious act of diary-writing, which most of his family probably could not understand.[16] All the same, although his reputation as an educated man was central to his self-identity, Obiṣẹsan frequently used his diary to confess insecurity about his English language literacy. In this context, his diary was simultaneously a goal, a discipline by which to reach that goal, and a forum to express frustration at not having achieved it.

Narrative and Diary-Writing

In his analysis of the CMS journals as composed texts, Peel cautions that his project does not necessitate the abandonment of a historical and anthropological inquiry "for some post-modernist literary project where nothing exists beyond the text, of which an infinite number of 'readings' is possible" (Peel 2000, 14). The relationship between writing and living remains crucial, he asserts. Nevertheless, a focus on this relationship takes us beyond an emphasis on the world the text represents to a closer interest in the world the text itself forms. Peel's distinction neatly reveals the somewhat one-sided analysis that characterizes most research based on the Obiṣẹsan diaries. The few scholars who have used his diaries have usually consulted them as a primary source for the political and socioeconomic history of colonial Ibadan. That is, they have focused on the world represented by the diaries. The way the diary entries also serve to *create* a social world that Obiṣẹsan inhabits has not been closely studied.

For this project a useful starting point is the analytical framework Peel developed in his comparison of the CMS journals with the private diary of Robert Oyebọde (which Oyebọde kept in 1877 when he was an Ibadan schoolteacher). The main contrast between the journals and the diary, Peel suggests, is that the journals are narratives written for others to read whereas Oyebọde's diary is a chronicle that lacks an overall narrative. As such, the diary is not completely intelligible since it is entirely self-addressed. Both the journals and the diary share to some extent a daily-entry format, but the diary entries have a prosaic quality compared to the sometimes-dramatic accounts of religious encounter in the journals.

As a chronicle, events in Oyebọde's diary are recorded as they occur, day by day, with no attempt to impose a longer-term meaning. This is characteristic of Obiṣẹsan's diary too, where events are simply jotted down in a disjointed and abbreviated way without punctuation, so that individual entries are not always comprehensible. For example, consider these three entries from Obiṣẹsan's first week of dedicated diary-writing in February 1920, where he detailed happenings related to his family land and the disputed Ibadan-Ijẹbu boundary. He seems to have taken his diary with him on a short trip away from Ibadan, giving some indication of his commitment to keeping it:

14 Saturday
At Abẹku [a village under the jurisdiction of the Aperin family]. The Jẹbus a mass of them arrived at about 2'oclk & in the evening owing to incompetent handlings of things by Mr Lapage—it was deemed expedient that I should go home to see Mr Grier & Rosedale [senior British colonial officers] & left Abeku at 6.30pm.
15 Sunday
First—I left Inuodi at about 11am & arrived Ibadan—people surprised to see me returned so quick & immediately left for Residency [the office of colonial administration in Ibadan] to see Mr Rosedale [the Ibadan District Officer] but did not see him & I left there for Akanbi Akinloye's [a friend] house to see him if I can get his motor car to take me to Oyọ [the seat of colonial government]. Entertained me with beer . . . failed owing to Akinloye's driver illness.
16 Monday
At Ibadan. In the morning left for Residency at first Mr Rosedale seemed to be indisposed to receive me & the A.D.O.'s letter but I tried & explained things to him, after 5 minutes he dealt with my matter & became disposed to me—he instructed Subaru & his colleagues to deliver—message to the Balẹ [Ibadan's head chief] to send one principal chief to Ibadan-Jẹbu border where Mr Lapage to represent the dignity of Ibadan—but on our way to Bale's as we reached the Residency Hospital we saw Mr Grier [the Acting Resident] on his car coming from Oyọ who ordered us back to DO's [District Officer's] & he took over the matter to hands himself & he wrote us a letter & charged us to take it to Mr Lapage.[17]

For Peel, the diary format makes narratives of all but the shortest time span difficult to achieve. However, in these few days of entries from Obiṣẹsan's diary, we can identify a developing narrative about his dealings in family land matters, particularly his meetings with colonial officials. Much of his activity on Monday, February 16, centered on him receiving and delivering letters from one official to another. All of these letters would have been written in English since this was the language of the colonial state—thus we see how important English-language literacy was to Obiṣẹsan's task of managing the family land. At the same time, Obiṣẹsan built his social world through his diary-writing, detailing whom he visited and who entertained him and the news of deaths among his acquaintances and family.[18]

The use of a diary to construct long-term social relationships is another feature Peel identifies in Oyebọde's diary. In this case, Peel suggests:

> The diary seems intended less as a representation than as an instrument of his life, a mnemonic aid to the continuous narrative self-monitoring that effective human lives require and which, perhaps, evangelicalism especially imposes on its adherents. (Peel 2000, 15)

Similarly, in his study of the life histories of Boakye Yiadom, Stephan Miescher argues that the Ghanaian teacher-catechist used the two volumes of his autobiography (written in diary form) as a mnemonic device. However, unlike Peel, he suggests that Yiadom was not so much concerned with "narrative self-monitoring" as with "preserving moments of his life for an explicit audience of his wife and children, other close relatives and friends" (Miescher 2001, 165). At the same time, Boakye Yiadom also made notes on private inner experiences in his autobiography, recounting dreams, prayers, and pledges to himself, in much the same way as Obịṣẹsan did.

We can recognize parallels with Obịṣẹsan's diary here, since it is clear that Obịṣẹsan kept his diary as a "life-record" to help define his self-development. Consequently, although some entries are partially or completely incoherent, it would be misleading to assert that there is no narrative structure to the diary at all. Above all, it is made coherent through Obịṣẹsan's continual return to a narrative of self-reflection, which is focused on his aspirations for economic and social success.

Thus, like Boakye Yiadom, Obịṣẹsan used his diary to imagine himself as an example in comparison to others. However, rather than publicly narrating his writing, Obịṣẹsan's example was self-referential. It seems that Obịṣẹsan did not read out his diary to his family members, instead he re-read it to himself. Sometimes he made annotations on his entries; at other times it appears that he edited entries or added them later.[19] Being illiterate, most members of Obịṣẹsan's household would not have been able to read his diary even if he had let them see it. Thus, his keeping of it was most likely a private activity.

It is significant that Obịṣẹsan frequently articulated his aspirations in religious terms, making reference to his destiny being "in God's hands." Indeed, from May 1920 his diary entries began with the underlined statement "Prayer offered" or, more rarely, "No prayer offered."[20] On one occasion he wrote that he "became completely depressed" after his wife Atunwa miscarried, noting "I offered no prayer owing to perplexity of mind and unsound health."[21] In Jan-

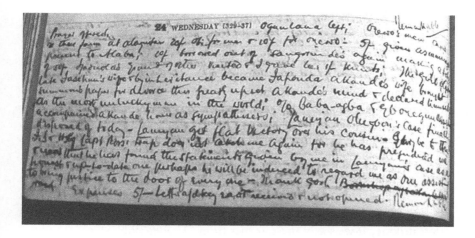

Figure 2.4. Diary entry, October 16, 1929. Courtesy the University of
Ibadan Library.

uary 1924 he invoked God more explicitly when he wrote, "Those who doubt
the wonder of God let them read my diary back from Sept. of 1923 to the
present date & they will learn how to seek God."[22] Obiṣẹsan referred here to
the fact that while in September 1923 he was heavily in debt, by January 1924
he was in a better economic position.

This narrative of self-reflection can already be identified at the end of
Obiṣẹsan's first year of regular diary-keeping. For example, he used his last
diary entry for 1920 to examine developments in his life during the previous
year:

> Glory be to the father, the son and the Holy Ghost; at the beginning of this clos-
> ing year I commanded a great sum of money but as it is now closing I could not
> boast of having few pounds with me; my wife Atunwa miscarried in the month
> of May; & God replaced the misfortune with joy when Larewaju gave birth to a
> male child in July; in my business I have had many misfortune, I have been
> cheated by my own people through their selfishness forgetting that if I take away
> my hands in the family affairs everything will collapse & the misfortune which
> dreaded before will revive again. Fadairo, Ogunlana & Bolarinwa [Obiṣẹsan's
> brothers] have asserted me a great deal, I may also mention Abodunrin [another
> brother] but truly speaking if he had rendered any assistance at all it is nothing
> but "*owu ni ofi se eni owu*" ["he used cotton to offer an 'extra' on a cotton pur-
> chase"—an aphorism, meaning, in this instance, that Abọdunrin used a fraction
> of what he had gained from Obiṣẹsan to make a donation back to him[23]]. He

made fortune at my expense afterwards found him to be the most perfidious, mischievous, extremely selfish man. However, I thank God—I have done all was required of me to assist others to master all their difficulties, but who will reciprocate me is the agitating question of the day.[24]

By mid-January 1921 Obisẹsan lamented that his situation had worsened, remarking that: "I am now in great poverty unequalled in the annals of history of my life, latter part of 1917 excepted."[25]

The narrative of Obisẹsan's diary developed in this form for the next four decades, as he used his entries to critically assess his success or otherwise in life. His entries became more standardized—for example, from June 1920 he recorded his daily expenses in addition to his note on whether or not he said a prayer.[26] The conscious and candid nature of Obisẹsan's self-assessment is often striking, as we see in these entries from October 1929:

I am in a state of penury; my condition comparatively speaking is worst than the one of 1921 when Adedeji Olugbode robbed me of all the money I had; then I had no large number of dependants and family to hang their ~~livings~~ responsibility around my shoulders; I was popular but my needs & my aspirations & ambitions were small and limited. Now I spend over £20 a month & my income of £30–£40 hitherto suddenly dropped to £7. Is there exists now today at Ibadan any man of my rank & standing whose path is more blighted and thorny than this?[27]

A few days later Obisẹsan viewed his life even more dramatically:

I am in two cross roads, one leads to failure, shame, contempt and disgrace & the other leads to prosperity, happiness and joy. The road of the former is broad and metalised [tarred] but the latter is narrow & thorny & one finds numerous reptiles that are vigilant to bite any traveller to death if he does not possess the requisite quality to tread the line & what it is? It is a great invocation to the almighty God. I am a debtor & consequently I am regarded as a nuisance by my employers: what to do I cannot say. I have not been very thrifty as I ought to do & in fact I laid foundation of a house to cost £1000 when my aggregate income is £10 per month & I want the building to complete in a very short time. Oh! Ah! Ah! Chee! Chee! Eh![28]

As is clear from these entries, Obisẹsan's narrative of self-reflection was dominantly focused on his wish to be rich. However, he did not conceive "wealth" in purely economic terms. His aspiration for material wealth went hand in hand with concerns about his "rank and standing" in colonial Ibadan society. His perception of respectability was closely tied up with a belief in the cultural value of reading and writing in English. With this in mind, let us explore the literary world revealed through Obisẹsan's diary.

Literary Men and Indirect Rule in Colonial Ibadan

Colonial administration in Ibadan during the 1920s was characterized by the indirect-rule policies of Resident Captain Ross. From 1912, Ross sought to establish the judicial and political supremacy of Ọyọ over Ibadan and made Ibadan chiefs subject to the suzerainty of the *Alaafin* (Atanda 1973). Associated with this was the policy, explicitly stated by Governor Lugard in his *Political Memoranda* (1919), that educated Africans should be excluded from positions in the local administration.[29] Summing up the era as "a great blot," local historian Isaac Akinyẹle wrote sarcastically of Ross: "The Great 'Ọga' Master hated the educated civilised men and usually termed them 'Lagido,' a monkey; he caused the chiefs also to hate them and he did practically nothing for the school during his time" (Akinyẹle 1946, 85). "The school" was the Ibadan Government School, which was opened as a secular institution in 1906 to educate the sons of Ibadan chiefs but was crippled by poor attendance rates (Watson 2003, 77).

It was partly in response to these circumstances that in 1914 a group of educated Christian men established a cultural organization called the Ẹgbẹ Agba–o–tan (Association of "Elders Still Exist"). As the second generation of mission-educated Ibadan men, its members considered themselves custodians of the past and thus granted themselves "elder status," although most of them were barely middle-aged (Adeboye 2004, 200). A few of them were related to the literate community of the nineteenth-century CMS Yoruba Mission through direct family connections.[30]

Initially a secret society influenced by freemasonry, the Ẹgbẹ Agba–o–tan sought to "institute researches into all Yoruba Religions, Customs, Philosophy, Medical Knowledge, Arts, Sciences, Manufactures, Poetical Cultures, Political and National Histories."[31] It established a publication committee that issued two history books in the Yoruba language and can in some ways be described as an elite literary club. Obiṣẹsan was its secretary by 1920, and once he began his dedicated diary-keeping, he often mentioned its activities.[32] On July 13, he noted that a bookshop in Lagos had ordered 200 copies of *Iwe Itan Ibadan* and 100 copies of *Iwe Itan Ọyọ*, the two books published by the society. He had visited Isaac Akinyẹle that day, where he "had the privilege of reading Ibadan Treaty" and was particularly pleased to see his father's name as a signatory.[33]

By the 1920s, the Ẹgbẹ Agba–o–tan sought political influence, particularly an advisory role in the colonial administration. To that end, Obiṣẹsan was part of a delegation that met Resident Captain Ross on June 24, 1920, but that achieved nothing.[34] Three years on, Obiṣẹsan still lamented "the plan of the present day political officers to keep educated and enlightened young-sters in subjection [and to] repress and set chiefs against them."[35]

Hence it is important to realize that at the time Obiṣẹsan began keeping his diary regularly, the British authorities had little interest in either recogniz-ing or using his literacy skills. This contrasted with the situation two decades earlier, when mission-educated assistants had been appointed to the Ibadan Council (Jenkins 1967, 220).[36] Nevertheless, Obiṣẹsan was not deterred. Ig-noring the lack of career opportunities in the local colonial administration, he doggedly invested in his reading and writing pursuits and instead looked for recognition in a developing literary scene in Ibadan. All the same, his diary entries make clear that he spent the vast majority of his time negotiating fam-ily affairs.

In early March 1920, Obiṣẹsan complained of a lack of money and diffi-culties in getting workers to come and clear his cocoa.[37] After "writing letters all about" on March 1, he agreed the price of 70/- per cwt (1 cwt = 50 kg) with one Mr. Martins.[38] The produce was weighed up on March 12 and Obiṣẹsan earned the princely sum of £148.12.6.[39] Three days later, as soon as he had collected the money owed to him, Obiṣẹsan spent it on his reading and writing interests. He visited a bookshop and bought "two diary books" and then purchased the *Africa and Orient Review* from his friend Daniel Ọbasa.[40]

Produce traders such as Obiṣẹsan were enjoying prosperous times in Ibadan during early 1920. The price of cocoa had shot up—it was £70 a ton when Obiṣẹsan sold his produce in March and it later rose to £80 per ton. However, by the end of the season the price had crashed to £28, and in 1921 it fell further to £15 per ton. Williams has argued that it was these volatile trade conditions, combined with the discrimination of indirect rule, which led Obiṣẹsan and his contemporaries to be influenced by the ideas of Marcus Garvey. As he describes it, for a brief period between the end of 1920 and early 1922, "Garveyism came to Ibadan in a journal [but] not in person" (Williams 1993, 125). This journal was *Negro World*, and Obiṣẹsan first read it on December 23, 1920, declaring it "very inspiring, instructive, amusing & interesting."[41] For Obiṣẹsan and his friends, the suggestion that African traders should establish independent banks, shipping lines, and businesses spoke directly to their concerns (Williams 1993, 112).

Williams has explored this episode, which coincided with local attempts to establish an Ibadan branch of the National Congress of British West Africa (NCBWA). However, Obiṣẹsan and his associates became more focused on setting up a parochial political organization, which emerged in 1921 as the

Ibadan Native Aboriginal Society (INAS). Associated with this was a plan to publish a newspaper, the *Ibadan Weekly Review*. Salami Agbaje, the city's wealthiest African trader, donated his printing press, which had arrived in Ibadan a year earlier.[42] Praising Agbaje's generosity, Obiṣẹsan remarked he would "one day be called the King of intelligent natives."[43]

Obiṣẹsan was elected to be editor of the *Ibadan Weekly Review*, but a letter he wrote to a friend acquainted with Ernest Ikoli (editor of the *Lagos Weekly Record*) reveals that he was very insecure about taking this on. This letter also disclosed Obiṣẹsan's view of his place within Ibadan's literate community:

> Since 1919 I have been waging a social battle & I know it will gratify you to know that I have been successful in my campaign. Now we have a printing press & this is what I have been hankering to get. . . . I have been appointed to be Editor . . . the wearer of the shoe is the only one who knows where it pinches. As a sagacious man I appeal to your conscience to give your opinion of me without any fear, favour or prejudice, I could see that I am being over-rated by Ibadan public—I know my knowledge of English language is shallow—believe me my friend I will not take the appointment until I hear from you.[44]

His panic was unfounded, as it turned out, because internal divisions in the newspaper's managerial committee caused the venture to collapse.[45] An Ibadan-based newspaper did not materialize until January 1924, by which time it was called *The Yoruba News*. Obiṣẹsan's journalistic prospects had since waned, and his friend Daniel Ọbasa became its editor and proprietor.[46]

The irony of Obiṣẹsan's anxiety is that his diary reveals him to be a highly literate man who wrote English in an often elaborately erudite way. One might think his letter expressed false modesty were it not for his many admissions of self-doubt about his English-language abilities in his diary entries. His diary thus reveals his determined effort to improve his English-language literacy, not only through the daily discipline of writing his entries but also through recording his participation in an emerging colonial reading community. For example, on March 18, 1920, he sent £4 to the secretary of the Negro Literary Society to cover eight membership subscriptions. He did not comment on its activities or who the other members were, although a month later he recorded that its name had changed to the "Young African League."[47]

Obiṣẹsan was also an avid newspaper reader, often discussing his reading with his peers. On one occasion he recorded that he "lectured them about the Egypto-British Govt. agitation article in Africa & Orient Review & some of our own internal political troubles and the indifference between ourselves."[48] A few days later he noted his enjoyment of an article in the *Weekly Dispatch*.[49] Indeed, it seems he regularly read four newspapers (*Africa and Orient Review*,

Weekly Dispatch, The Lagos Weekly Record, and *The Times of Nigeria*) as well as the magazine *West Africa*.

All this reading seems to have inspired him to try writing for the Lagos newspapers more than a year before he considered the editorship of the doomed *Ibadan Weekly Review*. Throughout April and May 1920 he commented in his diary about this, writing on April 1 that he "busied up to compose articles of general interest to be published."[50] On April 15 he was occupied with "writing of interest reviewing the administration of our late Gov. Gnl. F.D. Lugard" and was busy with this "from morning to night" a week later.[51] On this day, he explicitly stated why such activity was important to him: "My purpose at present is known to God only but I hope to become a literary man with perseverance in study and reading."[52]

Obiṣẹsan's understanding of the value of literacy thus had clear links with the nineteenth-century evangelical sensibility of self-directed private study. Indeed, his statement is strikingly similar to Henry Townsend's declaration that he published *Iwe Irohin* so as to encourage "the practice of seeking instruction and information by reading" (Peel 2000, 131). Nevertheless, Obiṣẹsan also aspired to a more secular cultural status, which he associated with being "a literary man." On April 25 he wrote: "My thirst to learn is becoming severe & my desire is to know things generally to the utmost God can give."[53]

Obiṣẹsan completed his piece about Lugard the next day, but on April 27 he read the *Times of Nigeria* and decided that the article was not finished after all.[54] Two days later he commented "Re my articles—my mind is unsteady up & down like a balance but continued still writing and inserting correction."[55] On April 30 he added three illustrations, but it seems he regained confidence only on May 6, when in a dream he "had assurance from the spirit friend to write my article on Sir Frederick Lugard and that no evil will come thither."[56]

The same day, Obiṣẹsan also commented on the death of Baba Ojoo, who, like him, was a produce trader. Baba Ojoo had seen little reward for his hard work, he declared, and instead had "laboured for others to reap."[57] Since Obiṣẹsan was himself struggling to make ends meet, he reflected on this as "a lesson for others," obviously including himself. It appears that the worry continued to prey on his mind a few days later when he wrote: "Still feeling sorrow for my poor condition—all around the time, young men are dazzling in riches whilst I remain poor." He suggested this was because in the past six years he had "devoted my entire time to the progress of my people." Although he judged himself successful in managing his family affairs, he was obviously troubled by his limited monetary reward.[58]

Despite these concerns, Obiṣẹsan continued his unpaid work on his article and gave it to one Mr. Okunyiga (who seems to have been his son Ojo's schoolteacher) for "correction" on May 8. The following week he received Mr. Okunyiga's book *How to Speak English Well* and afterward noted that the corrected article had been returned. It appears that he was disappointed, since he concluded his diary entry that day by regretting: "I am still thirsty to know deep the English language. I see that my knowledge of the precious language is very weak."[59] Determined nonetheless to persevere, he bought foolscap paper the next day and finished writing out the article neatly.

Some time later he discussed his article with Mr. Ricketts, a mercantile agent, who subsequently sent it back with his written comments.[60] The next day, Obiṣẹsan continued to combine socializing with his literary activities. On a visit to Rev. Dada he took the trouble to send a messenger back to his house to bring the article for Rev. Dada and his gentlemen friend to read. "Both praised me very highly," wrote Obiṣẹsan, satisfied that two senior members of the educated Christian community had recognized his literacy skills.[61] Finally, on May 27, he sent the article for publication in the *Lagos Weekly Record*.[62]

He did not mention it again for over three weeks, perhaps because he was very preoccupied with a personal financial crisis. However, when he bought his newspapers on June 19, he declared that he had lost hope of seeing his article published, since it had not yet appeared.[63] After this setback, Obiṣẹsan suspended his efforts to publish in the Lagos press, at least for the short term. However, he was obviously pleased when he received a book on the "art of English writing" by Mr. Okunyiga, along with a "commentary and complimentary letter" some days later.[64]

Diary Writing, Self-Realization, and Honor

In addition to reflecting on his English-language literacy, Obiṣẹsan used his diary to comment on his economic situation. He was perpetually in financial difficulties because his expenditure nearly always exceeded the limited sums he earned as a produce trader. For example, his daily record of spending and income in his 1921 diary revealed that his expenditure for the year was over £79, while he made only £32.[65] The high cocoa prices of early 1920 meant he was better off that year, but despite the significant payment he had received for his cocoa in March, on June 9, 1920, Obiṣẹsan reported: "I wake up this day in poverty—no penny I could boast of in my hand."

He managed to borrow sixpence from his wife to buy some breakfast and with threepence remaining he went to Elekuro market. This was one of the main markets frequented by produce buyers and mercantile agents:

> At Elekuro I was greatly honoured by the scalemen there & in every side due respect was given to me—after spending about 30 minutes I left Elekuro market for Bamgbade's house to visit the late Dunwade's children—& was honourably received with the usual prestige respect—Bamgbade the head of the house gave me 6 knuts [kola nuts]; a plentiful supply of meat & agidi & 2 gl pwine [2 gallons of palm wine] with kolas in abundance. In recognition of this I gave the mourners 10/- being the burial present which they greatly valued.

Although Obiṣẹsan did not explicitly admit that he obtained credit from the "scalemen" (so called because they used scales to weigh up produce), it seems clear that his reference to being "greatly honoured" was a way of saying that he had been given money. He gave away some of this cash almost immediately, so as to acknowledge the recognition shown to him in Bamgbade's household. Thus, having begun his day impoverished, he summed up: "This day is a very enjoyable day, full of joy and merriment."[66]

In this way, Obiṣẹsan used his diary as a tool of self-realization, proving to himself that his peers respected him. He confided in it to reassure himself that even if he was not as affluent as he wanted to be, he nonetheless enjoyed a certain status in his household and the wider Ibadan community. This reputation was vitally important to him, since it was the basis on which he obtained loans from other family members and acquaintances. Consequently, he generally tried to hide the severity of his financial problems from his social circle. A few days before his visit to Elekuro market he acknowledged that he was very poor but consoled himself by writing that "others don't know this."[67] On June 10, he remarked that "on all sides people are continued honouring me, every moment my soul enlightenment is becoming greater."[68] The next day he was still in a "state of poverty," but in the afternoon he managed to borrow £2 from Fọlarin Ṣọlaja, one of Ibadan's three leading Muslim traders.

That same day, Obiṣẹsan's friend Mr. Laluwoye visited and they discussed "the these days Olowos." Describing his friend as a "thoughtful man," Obiṣẹsan remarked that Mr. Laluwoye had advised him that it was "useless to aim to be rich." Instead, he had suggested that Obiṣẹsan should find contentment in a moderate lifestyle.[69] All the same, Obiṣẹsan felt unable to go to church that week, since he had promised more than £5 to the organ fund, which he did not have. He could not go without it, he wrote, since that would be "a disgrace."[70]

The term *olowo* designated "money-men" who, like Fọlarin Ṣọlaja, were invariably wealthy Muslim traders. According to Ibadan political discourse, the term *olowo* differentiated such "nouveau riche" men from the *olola*. These were men who held chieftaincy titles, which ascribed honor, or *ola*. As Barber defines it, "What underlies *ola* is the notion of recognition, of being acknowledged as superior and of attracting admirers and supporters as a result" (1991, 203). In this sense, especially when he was short of money, Obiṣẹsan used his diary to attribute *ola* to himself. The more precarious his financial position became, the more his diary entries mentioned people respecting and honoring him.

By June 18, Obiṣẹsan wrote with relief that his poverty was "greatly lessened" after he received a £5 payment from Mr. Ricketts and another £3 from his cousin Motosho.[71] Yet only a week on, he lamented, "poverty again come, I crummed a few pence."[72] In the days that followed, Obiṣẹsan began the cycle of borrowing against his reputation all over again and, just as before, he dutifully recorded who honored him and where and when they did so.[73] It is as if he sought to make up for his lack of money by reaffirming his self-worth in writing.

As time went on, however, Obiṣẹsan questioned why the status of being literate and the status of being affluent did not necessarily go together. For example, on July 2, 1920, after writing up the minutes of a recent Ẹgbẹ Agba-o-tan meeting, he reflected: "I thank God the knowledge of English language which I am daily seeking is being given liberally. I could see that there is improvement." That same day, he also wrote of having no money, which he attributed to bad luck and the fact that creditors were pressuring him to settle his debts. "I am somewhat depressed & perplexed," he admitted. "Anxiety fill[s] my mind. I hope it will not keep long."[74]

A year and a half later, this puzzlement had turned to ambivalence about the value of literacy. The day after he had visited two of Ibadan's most senior chiefs in the company of the city's wealthiest African traders (Salami Agbaje and Adebisi Giwa), Obiṣẹsan remarked that financially, he was in "hell fire." He asked himself whether he was a "nonentity" and suggested that his past and present life "had been lazy and indolent." He continued:

> Nobody in this town will revere anyone of no means, he would be counted as no-man—the great presents made to us forced me to recognise that Messrs Agbaje and Adebisi are being held in very high esteem—after all what is our intelligence, our school going and reading of books without getting money to back these three things—May I live to discover my ignorance and weakness, so that it may not late for me in life before gaining understanding.[75]

Thus, despite his efforts to honor himself in his private diary entries, Obiṣ-ẹsan was forced to concede that in public, material wealth brought greater recognition.

Conclusion

"What is our intelligence, our school going and our reading of books without getting money?" Obiṣẹsan's rhetorical question is one that many young academics today also ask of themselves. By way of conclusion, let me offer an answer.

Obiṣẹsan was just four years old when his father signed the 1893 Ibadan Agreement, which incorporated his birthplace, Ibadan, into the British Empire. By the time he began his dedicated diary-keeping in 1920, he was living in a colonial society. This society was less than a generation old, and the place of young men such as Obiṣẹsan within it was uncertain. Obiṣẹsan did not have the established Christian pedigree of his friends the Akinyẹle brothers, who came from one of the older Christian compounds in the town.[76] Nor did he have the recognized authority of *Mogaji* Ogunjọbi, who was the head of *ile* Aperin, his own family compound. Nevertheless, he possessed a skill that was vital to his family's effort to maintain authority over their land in the face of an increasingly bureaucratic colonial state. This skill was literacy in English.

A mission education had exposed Obiṣẹsan to the idea of reading and writing as tools of self-edification and possibly had introduced him to the discipline of keeping a diary. He clearly regarded education in general and literacy in English in particular as having intrinsic value. This is unsurprising to some extent, because his occupation as the family secretary proved the utility of his particular expertise. On the other hand, his literacy skills were not sought by the colonial state, which in 1920s Ibadan purposely excluded educated Africans. Obiṣẹsan resented this, but in spite of the policy of indirect rule, he was not deterred from investing in his literary interests. He sometimes found his skills useful in his work as a produce trader, since he could write to mercantile agents and set prices directly with them. Even so, Ibadan's most prosperous African traders were not literate in English and Obiṣẹsan was painfully aware that they made much more profit in business than he did.

Thus, Obiṣẹsan's commitment to literacy in English was not just pragmatic, it was fundamental to his self-identity and public reputation. He did not seek it for his career; instead, he sought a successful career to support, among other things, his literate lifestyle. As a Christian Yoruba gentleman in colonial Ibadan, his social world was defined by a culture of literacy. Showing his dedication to this style of life, apart from his daily activity of writing his diary, which certainly set him apart within his household, Obiṣẹsan read newspapers avidly and discussed them with his friends, he wrote his own newspaper articles and showed drafts to others to read, he joined Lagos-based literary societies and corresponded with them, he attended meetings of the Ẹgbẹ Agba–o–tan and served as its secretary, and he wrote innumerable letters to colonial officials.

One of the difficulties with Obiṣẹsan's diary, however, is that he never explained precisely *why* literacy in English was culturally valuable to him. He simply asserted that it was and fretted that his knowledge of the language was "weak" and "shallow." Thus, he declared his aspiration to be "a literary man," as if the importance of this status was self-explanatory. Two years on, he wondered whether the esteem of being literary was sufficient "without getting money." All the same, he did not give up his diary-writing after this realization—he continued the next day and every day after that for another thirty-two years. By doing so, he created an immensely rich narrative of his life, which even he seems to have enjoyed re-reading from time to time.

Thus, ultimately, it is within Obiṣẹsan's self-reflective and self-referential life-narrative that we find an answer to his question. Through the activity of writing about the day's events, assessing his financial and emotional state of being, and then reflecting on these two things in relation to his aspirations, Obiṣẹsan used literacy to understand the multiple identities of being a colonial subject. In this way, he realized himself, the world around him, and his place within it.

NOTES

Thanks to Gavin Williams for introducing me to Akinpẹlu Obiṣẹsan and for generously giving me his extensive notes on the diaries. Seminar audiences in Oxford and Birkbeck made useful suggestions on earlier drafts of the chapter, particularly Hilary Sapire and Naoko Shimazu. I am grateful to Wayne Dooling, who provided an essential critical reading, and Karin Barber, who has been endlessly patient. This chapter is dedicated to J. D. Y. Peel in recognition of his inspiring contributions to Yoruba history.

1. Akinpẹlu Obiṣẹsan Papers, Box N: 1914–19 Diary (hereafter OP/N: 1914–19), Kenneth Dike Library (hereafter KDL), University of Ibadan. See for example entries for January 5, 6, 12, 22, 26, 27.

2. OP/N: 1914–19, April 16.

3. OP/N: 1914–19, entry on April 28, dated August 29, 1917.

4. OP/N: 1914–19, entry on October 31, dated October 31, 1918. See also entry on May 7.

5. OP/N: 1914–19, entry on January 5, dated June 13, 1916.

6. OP/N: 1914–19, entries on May 25 and June 2, date uncertain.

7. OP/N: 1914–19, entry on October 19, dated November 3, 1918.

8. See the introduction to this volume.

9. For example, Ashcroft, Griffiths, and Tiffin 1989. For a critique of this literature, see Barber 1995.

10. For a brief biography of Obișesan, see *The Yoruba News,* May 4, 1943, Nigerian National Archives (hereafter NNA), Ibadan.

11. OP/55: 1920, March 1.

12. OP/55: 1920, May 10.

13. The Bishop Akinyele papers are also held in the Kenneth Dike Library, University of Ibadan. Isaac Akinyele's diary was referred to in many interviews I did, but it seems to have been lost.

14. OP/55: 1920, October 3.

15. OP/55: 1920, April 29.

16. I am indebted to Dr. Olufunkẹ Adeboye for making this point.

17. OP/55: 1920, February 14–16. Obișesan's use of Yoruba orthography is inconsistent. I have followed his style here.

18. OP/55: 1920, February 12–13.

19. For example, see OP/55: 1920, November 24. Here Obișesan annotated "Remarkable" in a different color pen than the original entry, suggesting that he re-read it at a later date. See figures 2.3 and 2.4.

20. OP/55: 1920, May 10.

21. OP/55: 1920, June 1.

22. OP/55: 1923, January 16.

23. I am grateful to the late Chief Adebayọ Ogundijọ of Ọbafẹmi Awolọwọ University for furnishing this explanation.

24. OP/55: 1920, December 31.

25. OP/55: 1921, January 17.

26. OP/55: 1920, June 11.

27. Obișesan crossed out the word "livings" in his entry, revealing his tendency to correct his entries on re-reading. OP/47: 1929, October 16.

28. OP/47: 1929, October 23.

29. Memo 9, Paragraph 45, Lugard 1919. For a study of the experience of clerks in Northern Nigeria during the same period, see Mason 1993.

30. For example, founding members Alexander and Isaac Akinyele were nephews of Rev. Oyebọde, the keeper of the private diary discussed earlier. Rev. Okusẹinde, who was the chairman, was a brother-in-law of Rev. Samuel Johnson, who was head of Ibadan's Arẹmọ mission station before becoming pastor of Ọyọ and completing his monumental *History of the Yorubas.*

31. Bishop Akinyele Papers, Box 44: *Constitution, Rules and Regulations of Ẹgbẹ Agba-o-tan* (Ibadan, 1914), KDL.

32. OP/55: 1920, April 5 and 9; June 15, 18, 22, 24, 25, 28; July 1, 2, 3, 9, 13; August 2.

33. OP/55: 1920, July 13.

34. OP/55: 1920, June 24.
35. OP/55: 1923, December 4.
36. The high point of political cooperation between colonial officials and educated Africans in Ibadan was the period under Resident Ward-Price (immediately after Ross's tenure), from 1931 until 1936. See Watson 2003, 123–129.
37. OP/55: 1920, March 1.
38. OP/55: 1920, March 1 and 10.
39. OP/55: 1920, March 12.
40. OP/55: 1920, March 15.
41. OP/55: 1920, December 23.
42. Obiṣẹsan reported that Agbaje's printing press had been delivered on June 15, 1920; he and other Ẹgbẹ Agba–o–tan members discussed it a week later. It appears they wanted to use it for some undisclosed enterprise, because on July 1 Obiṣẹsan reported that Rev. Akinyẹle had declared Agbaje "would not give up his press." There was no mention of the press again until June 1921. OP/55: 1920, June 15 and 22; June 22; July 1.
43. OP/55: 1921, June 17.
44. OP/P: Letter Book, 1921–23, Obiṣẹsan to Ọnọjọbi, October 21, 1921.
45. OP/55: 1921, December 26.
46. *The Yoruba News,* January 15, 1924, NNA, Ibadan.
47. OP/55: 1920, March 18 and April 22. Another group Obiṣẹsan mentioned is the African Progress Society (July 1, July 7).
48. OP/55: 1920, March 19.
49. OP/55: 1920, March 22.
50. OP/55: 1920, April 1.
51. OP/55: 1920, April 15.
52. OP/55: 1920, April 23.
53. OP/55: 1920, April 25.
54. OP/55: 1920, April 26–27.
55. OP/55: 1920, April 29.
56. OP/55: 1920, April 30 and May 6.
57. OP/55: 1920, May 6.
58. OP/55: 1920, May 10.
59. OP/55: 1920, May 8, May 12, and May 13.
60. OP/55: 1920, May 18–19.
61. OP/55: 1920, May 20.
62. OP/55: 1920, May 27.
63. OP/55: 1920, June 19.
64. OP/55: 1920, June 27.
65. OP/55: 1921 diary. Gavin Williams calculated this figure from Obiṣẹsan's records of his spending and the cocoa proceeds in his diary entries.
66. OP/55: 1920, June 9.
67. OP/55: 1920, June 6.
68. OP/55: 1920, June 10.
69. OP/55: 1920, June 11.
70. OP/55: 1920, June 13.
71. OP/55: 1920, June 18.
72. OP/55: 1920, June 25.

73. OP/55: 1920, July 6, 8, 18, and 20.
74. OP/55: 1920, July 2.
75. OP/53: 1922, February 3. See also figure 2.2.
76. For an account of the foundation of the Akinyẹle compound at Alafara in Ibadan, see Peel 2000, 273–274.

BIBLIOGRAPHY

Adeboye, O. A. 2004. "'Elders Still Exist': Socio-Cultural Groups and Political Participation in Colonial Ibadan." In *Indigenous Political Structures and Governance in Nigeria,* ed. O. Vaughan, 197–234. Ibadan: Bookcraft.

Akinyẹle, I. B. 1946. *The Outlines of Ibadan History.* Lagos: Alebiosu Printing Press.

Ashcroft, B., G. Griffiths, and H. Tiffin, eds. 1989. *The Empire Writes Back: Theory and Practice in Post-Colonial Literatures.* London: Routledge.

Atanda, J. A. 1973. *The New Ọyọ Empire: Indirect Rule and Change in Western Nigeria, 1894–1934.* Harlow: Longman.

Barber, K. 1991. *I Could Speak Until Tomorrow: Oriki, Women and the Past in a Yoruba Town.* Edinburgh: Edinburgh University Press for the International African Institute.

———. 1995. "African Language Literature and Postcolonial Criticism." *Research in African Literatures* 26, no. 4: 3–30.

Darnton, R. 1991. "History of Reading." In *New Perspectives on Historical Writing,* ed. P. Burke, 140–167. Cambridge: Polity Press.

Falola, T. 1989. *Politics and Economy in Ibadan, 1893–1945.* Lagos: Modelor.

Jenkins, G. 1967. "Government and Politics in Ibadan." In *The City of Ibadan,* ed. P. C. Lloyd, A. L. Mabogunjẹ, and B. Awẹ, 213–233. Cambridge: Cambridge University Press.

Lugard, F. J. D. 1919. *Political Memoranda: Revision of Instructions to Political Officers on Subjects Chiefly Political & Administrative, 1913–1918.* London: Waterlow.

Mason, M. 1993. "The History of Mr. Johnson: Progress and Protest in Northern Nigeria, 1900–1921." *Canadian Journal of African Studies* 27, no. 2: 196–217.

Miescher, S. F. 2001. "The Life Histories of Boakye Yiadom (Akasease Kofi of Abetifi, Kwawu): Exploring the Subjectivity and 'Voices' of a Teacher-Catechist in Colonial Ghana." In *African Words, African Voices: Critical Practices in Oral History,* ed. L. White, S. F. Miescher, and D. W. Cohen, 162–193. Bloomington: Indiana University Press.

Newell, S. 2002. *Literary Culture in Colonial Ghana: "How to Play the Game of Life."* Manchester: Manchester University Press.

Peel, J. D. Y. 1989. "The Cultural Work of Yoruba Ethnogenesis." In *History and Ethnicity,* ed. E. Tonkin, M. McDonald, and M. Chapman, 198–215. London: Routledge.

———. 2000. *Religious Encounter and the Making of the Yoruba.* Bloomington: Indiana University Press.

Rudolph, S. H., L. I. Rudolph, and M. S. Kanota, eds. 2002. *Reversing the Gaze: Amar Singh's Diary, A Colonial Subject's Narrative of Imperial India.* Boulder, Colo.: Westview Press.

Watson, R. 2003. *"Civil Disorder is the Disease of Ibadan": Chieftaincy and Civic Culture in a Yoruba City.* Oxford: James Currey.

Williams, G. 1993. "Garveyism, Akinpẹlu Obiṣẹsan and his Contemporaries: Ibadan, 1920–22." In *Legitimacy and the State in Twentieth-Century Africa: Essays in Honour of A. H. M. Kirk-Greene,* ed. T. Ranger and O. Vaughan, 112–132. London: Macmillan.

Zachernuk, P. S. 2000. *Colonial Subjects: An African Intelligentsia and Atlantic Ideas.* Charlottesville: University Press of Virginia.

THE LETTERS OF
LOUISA MVEMVE

Catherine Burns

3

It is with great pleasure that I Peter Zwana husband of Johanna Zwana do hereby publicly certify that my wife gave birth to a daughter on the third of August 1913. I took my wife in 1908 and since then I have not had a single child alive.... I had given up all hope of getting her cured I intended to part from her and give her up as a bad job when on a sudden I met a girl that I thoroughly knew from home. I found her with a baby where-as I knew that she was also suffering from not having children. So I asked her how she got the baby. She therefore explained to me and advised me to see Louisa Mvemve. I went straight to Louisa Mvemve.... She accepted my case and took my wife and gave her a thorough course of her herbal treatment. I have no power to express my gratitude for her remedies work wonders. Moreover now as I am writing this my wife gave birth to a daughter healthy and strong as well as the mother. I never knew that amongst our race there was one who could do such wonders its marvellous.[1]

Introduction: A Most Prolific Correspondent

Who was Louisa Mvemve? One simple answer was provided by A. L. Barrett of the Native Affairs Department (NAD) of South Africa in a note to the secretary for the justice department when he forwarded files related to her "herbal cures": "This woman is one of our most prolific correspondents."[2] Another view is provided by Peter Zwana, whose letter of testimony written in 1915 from the town of Benoni, east of the conurbation of Johannesburg, marveled at the effective herbal treatment his wife, Johanna Zwana, received from Louisa Mvemve. This letter is one among dozens of similar such letters of testimony about Louisa Mvemve stored today in the Central Archive Depot in Pretoria. From the eve of World War I to the 1930s, Louisa Mvemve made sure that these letters of testimony (both originals and handwritten facsimiles) reached the offices of the secretary of native affairs as well as various magistrates, health officials, and patenting officials as part of her effort to consolidate her tenuous position as a herbalist, women's health expert, and healer in the greater Johannesburg area. For eighteen years, Louisa Mvemve initiated and maintained a detailed and voluminous series of communications with officials and representatives from virtually every level of central and state government in the land.[3] Tracing letters about and by her, through layers of files in disconnected local and central state departments, has forced me to reconsider many of my presumptions about the capacities and powers of a woman born into a landless Xhosa-speaking family in a settler colony and her journeys to a segregated and hostile urban space after the birth of the Union to make a living, create a reputation, and secure a dignified life. The letters of testimony written on her behalf, letters of complaint authored by her, copies of her own pamphlets, legal appeals, and personal notes in the Central Archive Depot and municipal and local archives reveal that she was a skilled publicist and communicator. She wrote some of the letters in her own hand but began to use customized rubber stamps and letterhead paper and the assistance of skilled amanuenses along the way to becoming the prolific correspondent described by Barrett in 1931. Over the years, Louisa Mvemve's successes and tribulations framed her engagement with different layers of authority. The extant record of her activities and thoughts is varied, uneven, and complex. The written records of her life show that for certain periods she was able to navigate the twisting channels of bureaucracy with astonishing aplomb, and she achieved at least some of her ends. But over time Louisa Mvemve's economic circumstances and personal judgments were unequal to the massive obstacles she faced in her battles to win admiration, respect, legality, and financial success.

During World War I, Louisa Mvemve wrote to the governor-general of South Africa to tell him who she wanted to become. From at least the time of this letter, which was written in May 1914, until the early 1930s, she embarked upon a series of ambitious and daring attempts to "be granted the might of a medical man to examine the people who wants to be cured by my herb and Root Mixtures."[4] In other letters Louisa Mvemve described herself variously as a midwife, a healer, an herbalist,[5] a diagnostician, and an innovator of cures.[6] She also testified that she stored the curative practices of past generations and that this was crucial in the nursing skill of her maternal grandmother and the medical knowledge of her maternal grandfather.[7] At the same time, Louisa Mvemve clearly viewed herself as in the company of scientists: willing to have her methods tested and "proved."[8] While she was respectful of western biomedicine (indeed, she often praised doctors and medical institutions for their work among "her people" and mused about starting her own "nursing home"[9]), she nevertheless saw herself as able to provide cures when "Doctors had given up the case."[10] It is clear from the records of a 1916 court case in Benoni that Louisa Mvemve had established a workshop for bottling and preparing herbs, and by 1930 she had a mature herbarium and an extensive workshop on her property in Hastings Avenue, Brakpan.

Although Louisa Mvemve wanted to keep many of the "recipes" for her remedies secret and did see at least some of her talent as preordained in her ancestry and the circumstances of her birth, she explicitly explained herself and pleaded her case through discourses of good healing, Christianity, and civilization, and she repudiated what she termed witchcraft and dangerous practices.[11] She sought out, commissioned, and, on occasion, won the company of many certified physicians and chemists. She also aroused the admiration and curiosity of scientists, administrators, chiefs, and elders as well as a spectrum of ordinary women and men across the four provinces of the Union of South Africa and beyond the borders of the country (in Bechuanaland, Basotholand, and the Rhodesias).[12]

Her ambitions, both grand and modest, were thwarted by the early 1930s. A series of legal trials and associated negative newspaper publicity provide some details of this period in her life; only a handful of her own letters survive from this period. Thereafter a much thinner set of letters and papers follow her journey back to her Eastern Cape roots, where the textual trail about her life ends. There are many stories to be told about how and to what extent she succeeded or failed to meet her own ambitions. They cannot all be sketched, let alone analyzed, here. Instead, Louisa Mvemve's writings, and her medical and healing inventiveness documented in them, are the focus of this chapter.[13] The extant documents she generated (both ones she wrote and responses and interventions written by legal, bureaucratic, and medical officials) and the range of life experiences to which they testify provide a glimpse of the complexity of the life of an extraordinary, independent and talented woman.

The Archives of Louisa Mvemve

Louisa Mvemve's lifespan bore witness to the shift from British colonial rule to white settler government, from a world of African peasant communities competing on the frontier lands of the Eastern Cape to the migration of men and women north into the city of gold. Louisa Mvemve's letters and papers reveal that she was at times debt-ridden or imprisoned and ill-treated in city jails. But she was willing to travel vast distances to set up dealer networks for her cures in rural parts of the Transkei, Eastern Cape, Transvaal, and even Lesotho, and for a successful period after the war she tasted the life of a property-owner of some means. She held land in the periurban areas on the eastern edge of Johannesburg in municipalities that would became known as the East Rand, such as Benoni and Brakpan. In these moneyed periods of her life, Louisa Mvemve aspired to the world of respectability and wrote letters about herself which projected an image of Victorian womanhood. In these periods her conspicuous attempts to win friends and influence among white clients and her often-patronizing and objectifying references to working-class and rural black men and women reveal her ambivalent position as an aspirant person. Her personal statements indicate that she saw herself as distinct from her black working-class peers because of her talents and capacities. Yet she was neither formally educated nor did she have the support of either a royal or a professional patriarch, and thus she was not guaranteed any place among the ranks of the Union's small black elite. Thus Louisa Mvemve was a complex person in her day, and the ambiguities of her self-representation, her audience, and her reception provide a central thread throughout the remains of her documented narrative.[14] Her story is an unusual and vital, if partial, biography of an African woman living through, and making her mark upon, a period of great turbulence. The 1920s and 1930s saw the increasing systematization of oppressive laws and practices that directly affected the lives of black South Africans, especially black women. Despite this, Louisa Mvemve moved in the space of five years from laboring as a domestic servant to employing scribes, messengers, and domestic workers of her own. However, her class mobility was not unequivocal or permanent. She suffered complete financial ruin on several occasions, and as we lose sight of her in the early 1930s, her chances for a continued hold on a comfortable existence seemed doubtful.

These experiences and the "archive of communications" occasioned by her activities over two decades offer a nuanced insight into a much broader arena than this chapter can address. But two subjects it will address lie right at the heart of this largely self-constructed archive. First, these letters and documents are about her effectiveness as a healer. Unlike the testimonies, autobiographies, accounts, papers, and reports of many other health administrators, medical missionaries, doctors, and nurses, the recorded history of Louisa Mvemve was generated and written by an unlicensed black South African woman healer. Second, and against the grain of historically tuned expectations, her written words and opinions were written with this conceit as their basis: my addressee will preserve these letters and papers because I am a human of worth and my letters and papers are also worth taking seriously.

Preservation and Audience

We know that her letters and patents were read by government officials, physicians, lawyers, and her patients. We know this because the extant archive she generated was commented upon, written over (often in cryptic penciled-in notes), referred to in other letters, and even copied out or quoted in yet other letters and court records. Even a small proportion of the daily verbal communications she enjoyed with these networks of people have proved thus far untraceable.[15] We can imagine, though, based on officials' references to her demeanor mentioned in asides in their letters, that like her letters, her verbal communications bore the same imprint of a quality of self-possession and attention to public address that is quite idiosyncratic in relation to similar bodies of letters found in state archival material from the same period.[16] Louisa Mvemve's self-consciousness—revealed especially in her correspondence concerning several court cases—proffers evidence of a most exciting possibility: here was a woman who reckoned on the preservation of her documentation well beyond her lifespan. Once again most unusually, in these records, if not in her day-to-day life, her words take up more than equal space with those of white male officials. Here her particular experiences of male-dominated medical guilds and the skepticism of newspaper reporters, police officers, and government officials concerning the capabilities and intelligence of women are recorded. The intention and voice of Louisa Mvemve are at least as powerful in the letters as the intention and voice of the officials and institutions she addressed.

Healing Powers

To develop a case for the efficacy of her healing arts, Louisa Mvemve reckoned on drawing together a number of authenticating traditions. She wanted her cures "tested" and written up by experts. She wanted to patent them. She wanted to receive a state license to practice, though this was impossible in law for a woman of her background outside of Natal. She wanted to assert and document her links to indigenous medical skills and metaphysical powers. And she used various kinds and forms of address and analysis and reportage to achieve this end, attempting to draw authenticity for her particular herbal skills from her rural and Xhosa background. She stressed as well that her gender lent a special authenticity to her treatments for women for their menstrual needs (including pills and treatments "for irregularities"), her empathy for couples unable to conceive and her reputation as a fertility restorer, her "marvellous" midwifery skills, and her treatments for venereal disease for both men and women. In certain circumstances this opened the way for special comradeship with other women, including white women, on the basis of her healing mission and her personal experiences of, and ideas about, motherhood.[17] Mvemve's claim to respectable womanhood could not filter their way through the same channels as the handful of women who were "noted" in the barometer of bourgeois acceptance, the *African Yearly Register*, published in 1931 by T. D. Mweli Skota, wherein nurses and teachers were afforded some recognition. Thus, clearly Louisa Mvemve's status derived partly from her position as a healer of note, a role she saw in some measure as an inheritance from her grandparents. The role of healers in various Xhosa-speaking societies at the time would have prepared her and her patients to see her work as high status, but it was also a social position that was largely self-engineered. She did not want to create a niche for herself as a nurse or western doctor or as a diviner or traditional healer or as a mere hawker of goods: she wanted to carve for herself no less than the role of a new kind of medical broker. But Louisa Mvemve embarked on this journey to fashion a new craft from the skills of her ancestors and the techniques of western biomedicine at just the time when the medical academy in South Africa was beginning to close its ranks, centralize its authority, and undermine the expertise of a host of independent practitioners such as midwives and herbalists.[18]

A new Health Act was finally passed into law in 1928, a few years after a battery of new Urban Acts that were specifically directed against both the increasingly permanent settlements of Africans in cities and one of the most threatening features of this migration: independent African women. During the 1920s, the work that many urban black women carved out for themselves as beer brewers and sex workers became the subject of sustained debate among officials within the NAD and among municipal authorities and notable African men and women.[19] Documented in the pages of Louisa Mvemve's correspondence is a powerful history of her reactions over time to the changes in legislation and official attitudes toward black South Africans, especially women in urban areas. We also glimpse a personal view of her experience of changes in laws that affected rights of citizenship, movement and occupation, access to tenure and property, the hiring and occupation of space, and access to local and central institutions such as courts, police authorities, and transport. We see, especially toward the end of the archive in the early 1930s, that the odds, which were stacked so heavily against an African woman herbalist who provided treatment for whites and blacks and lived and worked and grew herbs in a "white" area, were insurmountable. Measured in these terms, she lost her battle and was forced to retreat to the Eastern Cape.

Literacy, Communication, and Representation

The archives of Louisa Mvemve consist of a collection of hundreds of letters as well as telegrams, notes, court documents, testimonials, and advertising booklets spread across the boxes and files of several departments of the central state, housed today in the Central Archive Depot, Pretoria. Communications with her engaged the energies of dozens of state officials because of her compelling and unusual requests, her insistent questioning and solicitation of advice, and the correspondence necessitated by her tireless zeal in lodging complaints and reporting unfair treatment. She constantly disrupted official explanations by falling outside anticipated categories. Louisa Mvemve laid claim to traditional cures and knowledge and yet she employed chemists and doctors to work for her and patented and packaged her herbs as modern medicines. The NAD was unable to pin her down regionally either: she moved between rural districts in the Eastern Cape and Transkei as well as through the urban smog of burgeoning reef towns such as Benoni. Louisa Mvemve's recorded narrative provides vivid evidence of the increasingly systematized operations of the central state while it simultaneously furnishes a corollary to the panoptical vision offered by Michel Foucault. She may not have vanquished the objectifying mechanisms of officialdom, but she found ways to work within, manipulate, and at times disrupt various systems of rules and procedures to great effect.

In her attempt to gain the ear of authorities, Louisa Mvemve drew upon a discourse that was very familiar to a woman coming of age in the late-nineteenth-century Eastern Cape, namely the appeal to patriarchal protectors. She never mentioned a male partner until late in the correspondence when she termed herself a "poor widow," and yet her status as an independent woman has to be set alongside her calls on Lord Buxton as her "father and protector" and her establishment of powerful relationships of patronage with NAD officials such as Edward Barrett and Edward Dower and physicians such as Dr. Kerr Muir and Dr. Scott. Her most prolific communications were with the various secretaries and their assistants in the NAD and the Office of the Governor-General of South Africa.[20] Louisa Mvemve also made contact with, and sparked inquiries from, officials of the Department of Inland Revenue, the Department of Lands, the Department of Justice, the Office of the

Attorney General, and the Office of the Secretary of the Interior; various sections of the South African police; the native commissioners; officials of several municipalities, including Johannesburg, Benoni, and Brakpan; and the magistrates and commissioners of Grahamstown, Kingwilliamstown, Pietermaritzburg, Witzieshoek, Peddie, Alice, Umtata, and Butterworth. She made clear references in several letters to her acceptance by and good relations with rural-based chiefs and noted occasions when such leadership figures made journeys to her home for special cures and treatments.[21]

Mvemve's communications occurred against the backdrop of substantial changes in policy and methods of administration within the Native Affairs Department itself. Her personalized correspondence began at a time when Dower and Barrett, who had experience administrating the Transkeian Territories, were attempting to run an embattled department that was overshadowed by the Departments of Labour and Justice and was fragmented along the regional lines bequeathed to it at the time of Union. Saul Dubow has detailed some of the tensions and debates between the NAD and the Smuts government which led to the forced resignation of Edward Barrett in 1923. After his demise, a tightly systematized department came alive under the tutelage of the new Secretary for Native Affairs, Major J. F. Herbst and a corps of energetic officials who were more sympathetic toward the increasingly segregationalist ideals of the central state. Less time was devoted to maintaining the detailed correspondence with Louisa Mvemve that Barrett had achieved, although it must be noted that the Native Affairs Department and its officials continued to expend energy on Louisa Mvemve's inquiries and continued to represent her sympathetically to officials from other departments beyond their brief. For example, toward the end of the correspondence, in January 1931, and in the midst of Louisa's final trial, A. L. Barrett (who was not connected to Edward) wrote to the public prosecutor in Grahamstown:

> Louisa Mvemve has been known to this Department for many years as a Native herbalist. She is believed to be a well-meaning person, and, in so far as this Department is aware, there is nothing against her character.[22]

This statement leaned heavily on the side of Mvemve, as the department by his time had files of letters in which white chemists and other correspondents had complained of her unscrupulousness and inefficiency and three court actions had been made against her activities. It would seem that even at this late stage, the vivacity of her personality and a sense of perhaps nostalgic responsibility moved even younger and committed officials. Finally, and this is most crucial, the NAD recognized that without the services of people such as Louisa Mvemve, most black urban dwellers would have had few alternatives in sickness and physical need. The same week in January 1931 that Barrett wrote this testimonial, D. L. Smit (the head of the NAD) met with officials from the health departments of Johannesburg and Pretoria to discuss the dire shortages of black nurses and the overcrowded hospital facilities for black men and women across the region.

Louisa Mvemve's extant correspondence makes wide use of different technologies of communication. She would often begin a letter by reminding the NAD official, or Buxton, of a previous communication or interview with them, thus personalizing the relationship and implying continued contact. To create and sustain the form of a dialogue, she would usually close by soliciting advice, even at the end of letters which opened "Just a line to let you know," and she usually received a letter of acknowledgement to even her most personal and rambling letters. She would often add weight to her letters by including originals or copies of testimonials from patients or letters of thanks, and every few months she would ensure that the governor-general's office and the NAD at least received copies of her latest brochures and pamphlets. When she was involved in court action, she would make use of telephones and telegrams, especially when she called on the NAD to provide her with copies of letters she had received from them in the past that she had either mislaid or could not get access to quickly enough. When she was anxious about being observed by officials in a district, her correspondence would read almost as a diary of her daily events as a way to use their offices as her own body of evidence. On several occasions, she mentioned moving her "box of letters" around with her during her frequent trips, and on two occasions she lost most of her correspondence. However, she seemed to realize early on that she could rely upon the record-keeping of the NAD in particular, and thus in certain ways it functioned as her own archive. She made frequent trips to Pretoria to interview and question NAD officials, and when she was in the Eastern Cape and Transkei, she made certain to present her case in person to local magistrates.[23]

Examination of at least three different handwriting styles in her corpus of letters reveals that Louisa Mvemve employed at least two "scribes" on some kind of permanent basis, perhaps dictating letters to them. However, her ability to recall details of previous correspondence; her spidery but distinctive signature (which appeared on the odd document from 1914–1932); her obvious command of fluent oral English, evidenced by the court records; and her representation by Edward Barrett as "a highly educated woman" in his first four

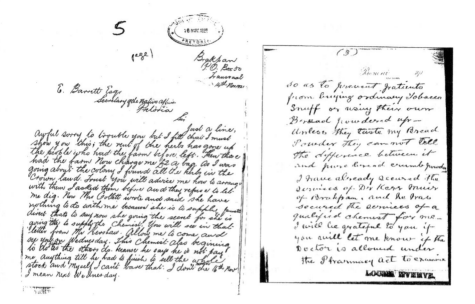

Figure 3.1. Two letters from Louisa Mvemve, showing how the quality of the amanuenses she employed fluctuated with her fortunes. Left: letter to E. Barrett, November 14, 1921. Right: letter to Mr. Koch (Patents Office), July 8, 1920. Courtesy the National Archives Department of South Africa, Pretoria.

years of contact with her suggest that she was at least to some degree literate in English. It would seem that in an attempt to fix the authenticity of her documents and officialize her correspondence, she wrote, whenever she had supplies, on paper printed with her address and "Tiger Trade Mark" on the letterhead, and she signed most of her correspondence with a purple-inked stamp that was very similar to those the NAD used.

Her decision to use a tiger's head as her "logo," particularly as tigers are not considered by animal scientists to be indigenous to Southern Africa, calls for further research into Victorian and early-twentieth-century representations of healing, tigers, and the patented branding of health and beauty products in British colonies and metropolitan centres.[24] The official history of the leading brand "Tiger Balm" claims that it was only after 1926 that the Rangoon-originating medication gained worldwide popularity—and Louisa Mvemve found the logo useful for her remedies long before this product en-

LOUISA MVEMVE'S

Herbal Remedies.

Tiger Remedies
COMPANY,
P.O. BOX 50,
BRAKPAN,
TRANSVAAL.

Bread Powder Herb.

The Guaranteed harmless and Effective Remedy
for removing every Impurity of the Blood and
all morbid conditions of the body.

DIRECTIONS.

Place the contents of enclosed packet in about half a cupful of milk ; mix well and take first thing in the morning on an empty stomach ; half an hour afterwards drink some hot mutton broth or Beef tea. Keep on with this nourishment until the powder stops acting.

Persons very weak and debilitated may begin with a teaspoonful and increase the dose as the patient recovers health and strength.

Special directions for Children will be given upon application.

Price : TEN SHILLINGS PER PACKET.

Figure 3.2. Louisa Mvemve's Tiger Remedies logo and advertisement.
Courtesy the National Archives Department of South Africa, Pretoria.

tered the diaspora.[25] In Nelson Mandela's autobiography he mentions that the subject of the existence of tigers in South Africa was the focus of frequent and even heated dispute among Robben Island political prisoners over a period of some years. Xhosa has a separate word for "tiger" and "leopard" ("tiger" in isiXhosa is "*ingwe*" and "leopard" is "*ihlosi*"). Mandela and others doubted that a specific word would exist if there had indeed been no tigers in the region (Mandela 1994, 415–416). Many European and especially British products in the later nineteenth century were branded with tiger logos,[26] and today one of South Africa's best-selling cereal products, Tiger Oats, uses this logo to great effect.[27] Beyond these enticing generalities it is difficult to pinpoint Louisa Mvemve's specific sources of inspiration for this logo, but several letters of testimony written by second-language English-writers about her work refer to Louisa Mvemve's "Tiger Remedies" as if the word "Tiger" is a word meaning "powerful" or "efficacious."

Her logo also helped her to authenticate her written communication even when she herself did not pen a letter. But it was not just because of the volume of her correspondence that she called upon amanuenses. A close analysis of her letters for the year 1916 shows her in a very strong financial position at the start and then, after a trial, in great financial difficulties. Her loss of resources resulted also in her reliance on her own hand, and the quality of her English interventions as well as the penmanship of her presentations declined. Louisa Mvemve's command of spoken English was never in question, and when she could pay for and obtain the service of scribes fluent in English, she maintained the image of a highly educated woman. However, as soon as she left Benoni, in 1916, she relied on less-able scribes, and the tone of her letters (although still as confident as ever) was not matched by their erudition. Clearly her case suffered accordingly in the minds of officials. Soon Edward Barrett realized that she was employing others as her correspondents and began to see her in a different light. After a particularly poorly expressed set of letters concerning her dispute with chemists and magistrates in Grahamstown at a time when her finances were at a low ebb, E. Barrett, perhaps forgetting the years in which he viewed her as a "civilised and educated woman," wrote:

> I strongly advise you to accept some offer of employment in the ordinary course and to give up your present manner of life. You claim to have effected many remarkable cures, and for aught I know you may have done so but you are an ignorant almost illiterate woman and the difficulties against which you are contending are too great for you. As your sincere well-wisher, this is the best and kindest advice I can offer you. I am enclosing the letters you wished me to return.[28]

Louisa Mvemve did not take his advice or respond to this patronizing and probably hurtful letter. Five months passed before she called on the NAD again, and when she did, she made certain that her scribe was very skilled.[29] The clearest examples of the link between her financial security and her access to scribes who were literate in English occur when she was traveling around small towns such as Kingwilliamstown and Grahamstown between 1919 and 1931. Her financial affairs and litigation were the cause of much correspondence in the 1920s, when she attempted to sue chemists and agents for moneys she felt she was owed. During this period, and before she returned to Brakpan and engaged the able services of J. Gumede (whether as a scribe or lawyer is not certain), she battled to express her case lucidly. On occasion, however, she was able to find an eloquent interlocutor, as in her letter to Prime Minister Hertzog in 1930 and in her statement about her life and activities to the native sub-commissioner in Benoni in the same month, when she stated, with her previous confidence:

> I am a Native woman Herbalist. I began my work as a herbalist in the Transvaal in 1915, and my affairs are well known in the Native Affairs Department, Pretoria. . . . I am a Linguist. I speak English and Afrikaans besides my language.[30]

"I could trace myself if anyone wants to know. . . ."[31]

As I have indicated, the bulk of what we know of Louisa Mvemve's biography is scattered throughout various layers of recorded commentary, offered mainly by her but also by people such as the Kerr Muir family as well as newspaper reports of the day. What is clear is that she could and did draw on layers of identity to represent herself in particular circumstances and that her correspondence provides a possibly unparalleled opportunity to read and analyze a black Southern African woman's complex, situational, and unfolding sense of self.[32] In letters about her by white senior central and local state bureaucrats she was often referred to as a "Fingo" woman, although she herself did not use this designation in any extant letters or documents.[33] This description of her by others in authority as "Fingo" (or Mfengu, a more-recent Africanized term) implied an ambiguous identity at the time.[34] Historical and anthropological opinions on Eastern Cape history from the 1920–1940 period as well as commonly expressed sentiments in white newspapers of the day spoke of the "Fingo" people as having originated from a group of refugees that was dispossessed as a result of the upheavals set in motion by the rise of the Zulu Kingdom in Natal in the 1820s. In this narrative, the "Fingo" were regarded as both debtors to the British, who were their saviors, and as allies against more-hostile Xhosa-speaking groups in the region and thus were rewarded with access to land and cattle, albeit through forms of bondage or apprenticeship to white farmers and officials. By the early twentieth century, Fingos were first-language Xhosa-speakers. Despite this, researchers such as Monica Hunter continued to set them apart from their Xhosa, Pondo, Bhaca, Hlubi, and Thembu neighbors, pointing out that although extensive inter-family connections existed with Fingos by that period, there was a remaining sense of their greater affiliation with whites and at times a sense of their greater exposure to western education and Christianity. In this context it is relevant that Louisa Mvemve was viewed as a Fingo, with all that connoted, by several magistrates in the Eastern Cape and by the officials of the NAD who had trained in the Transkei.[35] Born in the Eastern Cape, in a coastal region near Port Alfred, Louisa Mvemve grew up in daily contact with white farmers from an early age and had access to a large family network that at some point extended into Grahamstown. It would seem that Louisa Mvemve had the opportunity to draw on a wide range of experiences, histories, and types of education. Perhaps one of the key ingredients in her extraordinary success as a herbalist and a personality of note was an ability to seize and draw upon her rich heritage and context.

The issue of her identity came to the fore after treatment she suffered at the hands of a clerk in a small Eastern Cape railway hamlet, probably during a visit there for fresh herbal products referred to in other letters from the period. In early 1919, an infuriated and indignant Louisa Mvemve complained to the secretary of native affairs, E. Barrett, and to Mr. Tippett of South African Railways and Harbours about the treatment she had received from a clerk at Komgha station. She revealed something of her past, and of her self-perception, in this angry missive:

> Well I must say according to the language that was used by the clerk at Komgha to me; I was never a red kafir I never wore red blankets I have never used kafir mats for matress and I have never used stones for my pillows either, I myself was born to the farm near Port Alfred, the farm was Mr Maclock's I could trace myself if anyone wants to know where I was brought up. My mother was working for Mrs Maclocks, and my father was also a servant of the Magistrate in Sailem When I was nine years old I went out to work to play with baby I was getting a shilling a month, and my food and clothes. The lady I was working for was Mrs Webber. When I explain this I mean I can prove I was never a red kafir as he calls me and also my grand father never seen him with Red blankets, and my grand mother is still alive.[36]

In this letter she "traces" herself by claims of proximity and of distance. She distances herself from "*amabomvu*" or "red" Xhosa speakers (signposting the common terminology of mission-educated Xhosa speakers as well as whites of the day) and associates herself by reference to waged-labor relationships to settler families on farms as a child. She refers to both her father (and through her father to the magistrate of a small regional town) and her grandfather (who never wore "red blankets") but as subsidiary aspects of her status. At this very time the South African Native National Congress, led by people such as Solomon Plaatje and John Dube (Willan 1985), was appealing to the Union government to allow so-called civilized natives (such as themselves) access to a better class of train compartment than "raw natives." This was before the flowering of a more-radical trend in the organization, and Louisa Mvemve's outrage probably refers to being forced to move off the platform and being forced to share space at the station and on the train with rural migrants who shared neither her dress nor her class. This position contrasts notably with her statements in 1914 to the governor-general, when she assured him she could get donations for the war fund from ordinary people skilled in regional crafts because of her excellent relationships with locals from the region. Perhaps Louisa Mvemve strategized consciously about the naming of families in the letter, specifically anticipating the route her letter would take to at least two audiences—although the letter is addressed to the secretary of native affairs, Louisa Mvemve would probably have known that the official was likely to send a copy on to the railway officials in the Eastern Cape, which is in fact what transpired. Local white railway officials, she may have reckoned, would be impressed by the local white families named and feel shamed by this as well as by the fact that the letter she wrote had been sent on to them by officials in Pretoria for response. Sadly, no record of the Eastern Cape railway officials' responses to these communications could be traced. I am making informed speculations about her intentions. But it is an enticing example of her use of personal and professional references, name-dropping, citations of laws or quotations, variations of personal address, and manipulation of the methods of bureaucratic lines of authority embedded in state practice.

In the remaining corpus of her letters, wherein she often refers to employers and to people she had assisted in her capacity as a healer in the Eastern Cape, the Maclock family is not mentioned again. But in much earlier correspondence from April 1916, when Louisa Mvemve applied through the NAD to the Department of Lands for permission to have access to Crown Lands to dig for her herbs, one of the farms she named was that of the Webbers, who were also named in her railway complaint.[37] Information from the Cory Library for Historical Research in Grahamstown turned up a reference to the Webbers as running a farm with herbal crops. It is possible that Louisa Mvemve gleaned some of her knowledge of planting and tending herbs and of their medicinal properties in her youth working as a baby-minder for the Webber family or that she referred to them in letters to the Department of Lands to authenticate her herbal knowledge. Her aim was to underscore both her commercial herb-growing and her Xhosa indigenous herbal knowledge. She also refers to the Webbers in later letters to substantiate her claims that she worked for wages as a child-minder and nurse, and letters to women and about curing children featured as an important part of her recorded work. She writes of one more white family, the Kerr Muirs, for whom she did occasional housework. Her paid work at their East Rand home near a mine in Benoni for a few years from 1905 is substantiated in letters of reference that Dr. Kerr Muir, a mining doctor, wrote on her behalf, but without her knowledge, to the secretary of the Public Health Department of the Union.[38] She remained in contact with them until the death of Dr. Kerr Muir in 1927, when, according to her, she received a bequest in his will.[39]

The example of a former domestic servant referring to her previous employees to provide character testimonies seems part of a world of paid waged female labor redolent with European and particularly British contexts. At the end of World War I, as Van Onselen, Cock, and others have shown, relatively few African women in either the Eastern Cape or Natal had ever worked as paid domestic laborers. In the letters where Louisa Mvemve draws on these youthful experiences, she represents herself, at several key moments, as a working-class Victorian woman who was proud to be "born under the British flag."[40] Even her English Christian name rings with Victorian sensibilities, and in none of her letters does she or anyone else call her by any other first name. However, just as she represented herself as a progressive and Christian woman, she could also draw powerfully on aspects of her heritage that reflected her family's skills and pride in an arena outside the settings of the mission, the settler farm, or the school. In 1916, anxious to contribute to the war effort, she contacted Lady Buxton through the offices of Lord Buxton, the governor-general, and offered to raise money for the governor-general's fund by collecting "curios." It would seem that Louisa Mvemve did not dash around the Eastern Cape (from Cape Town to Grahamstown to Peddie to Alice to Umtata and back to Grahamstown) solely for altruistic reasons: she always took the opportunity to mention her medicines and herbal cures to the women from whom she solicited articles and curios. She nevertheless was zealous enough in her collecting activities to please the Buxtons and install herself in their memories, at least for a few years. She provided for their faulty memories when in correspondence to the governor-general in the late 1920s and in 1931 she reminded him of curios she had collected during the Great War, "which had even been sold in Europe." Her excited letter to Lady Buxton of November 1916 provides a different glimpse into her concept of ethnic identity and selfhood:

> Just a few lines to let Madam know I am in Graham's Town. I met my coloured friends and explained to them about the "curios" which we want to sell for the Governor-General's Fund. They were surprised for they hadn't heard of it before. All the same they took my word and started at once to gather curios . . . we have already Baskets, Kaffir Mats, Fancy Sticks, I'm sending you a sample for a present, Basket and Basket Cups made by my own Mother The things will be sent first week in January. I am going to Fort Peddie next week I wrote to the women there they are also preparing to send things. From Peddie I am going to Transkei. I wrote to the different chiefs and asked them to explain everything to the women what to make, Skins, Karosses, Clay Cups, Mats, Door Mats, Walking Sticks. . . . I must tell you Madam that some women would like to bring their presents themselves so as to bring them safely. They fear to have them broken. Others would like Her Excellency to see how they crush and grind their food. I dont want to praise my Nation but Madam will see some wonderful things. Better than what came from Basutoland . . . I'll gather samples of things made by different tribes. . . . Besides what the Kaffirs, Fingoes, and Amaxosas will send.[41]

This letter, in which Louisa Mvemve "praised her Nation," underscores again her ability to maintain a complex vision of her self-identity and her determination to refuse any one categorization for herself or her work. It is not clear what her own family and household thought of her work or how they participated in her projects. In the remainder of her records, all other references to her son, her two brothers,[42] and her other children relate to her medicinal work,[43] and it is to this that we will now turn.[44]

"I am a Native woman Herbalist"

During the 1920s efforts were made to regulate the healing and herbal practices of indigenous and immigrant unlicensed healers. However, there were ways and means for herbalists to continue their trade, especially before the passing of the 1928 legislation. Healers often used the press and handbills as a new means of drawing together a clientele for their cures and remedies. At almost exactly the time that Louisa Mvemve began her battle to gain recognition, deciding early on to use printed pamphlets to her advantage, it was dawning on the officials in the NAD that the issue of the "Natal exception" (which allowed chiefs and, through their advice, magistrates, to grant certain "Zulu medicine men and women" licenses to practice but no other black South Africans) was going to become an administrative thorn. When Dower and Barrett were in office, they avoided pursuing herbalists whose practices did not come within the ambit of the law, although their department and the Offices of the Governor-General and the Attorney General attempted to create legislation which would better control "witchcraft." Almost without exception, the debate at the time was framed as one between two opposing and contradictory discourses and bodies of knowledge and practice: western biomedicine and a primitive cosmology of cures.[45] Even in the early decades of this century this debate, formulated by health officials such as Minister of Health James Alexander Mitchell, ignored the vast range of patent medicines and chemists' and hawkers' "tonics, devices and regimes" which were obtainable legally and at a price through registered druggists as well as via the mail-order companies such as W. R. Pimm & Co., whose large illustrated advertisements in the major English papers and in *Imvo Zabantsundu Zomzantsi Afrika*, *Ilanga lase Natal*, *Abantu Batho*, and *Umteteli Wa Bantu* attracted wide attention.[46] Newspapers at the time also gave space to discussions of the quackery of western-trained physicians, and many officials in the Department of Native Affairs privately voiced their suspicion about the viability of fully eradicating "traditional healers," not only because of the paucity of other options but also because of the tenuous efficacy of western techniques in the treatment of many conditions and maladies. Applicants to the NAD for licenses increasingly called upon another group of professionals—advocates and attorneys—to speak in support of the rights of herbalists. About a third of all applications throughout the 1920s to the late 1950s were accompanied by "lawyer's letters." Of course it would be fair to assume that many of these letters were motivated by the lucrative fees lawyers earned by writing them, and many of Louisa Mvemve's experiences with lawyers underscore this assumption. The aspirations, successes, and ambitions of Louisa Mvemve as a herbalist and chemist belied the simple categorizations that state medical officials put forward during her lifetime. Thus, when Louisa Mvemve applied in writing for the first time for a license to practice as a herbalist, legislation already existed to forestall her. However, built into her request was the option of "selling through others," so it is possible that she had already done some informal investigating before she petitioned the NAD and Lord Buxton. After asking to be "granted the might of a medical man to examine the people who wants to be cured," she continued:

> There is a large number of Europeans and Natives who have approached me asking me to give them my Herb Mixture for cures of Cancer, Leprosy, Rheumatism, Paralytic, Sterile As I know where the roots and herbs are obtainable in the District. . . . P.S I enclose the addresses of chemists which I am about to supply with the Herbal Mixture to avoid crush because the people they all rush to where they hear of me. LM[47]

The phrase "buy now to avoid the crush" was used in newspaper and billboard advertising at this time and Louisa Mvemve's use of it in the postscript to the letter above suggests that she saw it as a useful phrase to capture both the urgency of her situation and the value of her product.

This letter met with a polite but terse reply and no comment about the enclosed herbal mixture, which was probably presented in one of her packaged white or brown powder mixtures; one only needed to add water or milk and boil to reconstitute an infusion. Louisa Mvemve, as with other correspondents with the Departments of Land and Public Health, used the postal system to move seeds and pieces of plants, dried chemical preparations, and even sponge-encased semi-liquids inside or with letters.[48] After receiving no substantial help from the governor-general, Louisa Mvemve decided to interview officials in the NAD about the matter in Pretoria in April of the following year, after she had moved back up to the Reef. It must have been quite a meeting! Her first written communication to the secretary for the NAD, on April

15, 1915, referred to this meeting (which took place earlier on the same day the letter was written and posted) and passed on the name of her reference (Dr. Kerr Muir). The letter also enclosed an eight-page professionally printed booklet on her herbal remedies and three letters of testimony from satisfied patients.[49] These precious and rare documents, which are collected and stored in no other place I can find, are worth a close read.

Louisa Mvemve's extraordinary booklet, entitled *A Woman's Advice: A Woman's Advice to the Public on the Cure of Various Diseases,* included detailed descriptions of how to take her herbal mixtures, how and when to bathe and eat and sleep, and how to bandage wounds and apply compresses. In this way it predated first aid manuals and booklets which the Department of Health and the Red Cross brought out a decade later.[50] The booklet is interesting too in its adoption of the tone of a morality tale, evoking the imagery of biblical stories prepared for children. In her classic study of advice to women and working-class mothers in England in the 1890 to 1920 period, Anna Davin collected many of the health, hygiene, and sanitation pamphlets circulating through missionary, school, and local health authorities (Davin 1979). Her analysis of these texts and their intended impact dovetails with the work by Julia Grant and Katherine Arnup on advice books for women and mothers in Canada and the United States at the same time (Grant 1998, Arnup 1994). In South Africa, these small books and pamphlets circulated through cheap publications often reprinted by churches. African women and men were the targets of some of this health advice, and health and hygiene advice pamphlets were a staple of missionary presses such as Lovedale. Jeff Guy has recently written on the creation of simple and didactic texts by teachers such as Dr. R. J. Mann in Natal in the late nineteenth century that was based on British antecedents and was available in Zulu and Xhosa as well as English (Guy 2003). Elaine Katz (1994) and Randall Packard (1989) have written about the beginnings of first aid and health booklets for miners—first directed at white working-class miners and then at black and Chinese men—on the South African gold fields at the same time. In these booklets, there are also suggestions of the influences of simple adventure novellas. The advice pamphlets for miners contain didactic health messages wrapped up in narratives of young men arriving in cities for the first time, encountering gangsters and other dangers as they try to do an honest day's work. The public health literature for men and for white South African women, like their counterparts in Europe and in other settler colonies, contained many domestic health pamphlets which would often contain narratives that purported to be of real experiences as well as heroic tales of survival and sage advice. The existence of books from the United States in Eastern Cape libraries at the time, such as Catharine E. Beecher's *Treatise on Domestic Economy*, from the 1840s, Harriet Beecher Stowe's *The American Woman's Home*, first published in 1869, and Louisa May Alcott's *Little Women*, suggests that Eastern Cape literate women may have imbibed, whether or not they digested in full, many of the same messages as their western counterparts. Did Louisa Mvemve read these books and pamphlets? Did she read versions of *Little Women* as she worked in Eastern Cape nurseries and kitchens in the late nineteenth century? Perhaps her sense of destiny (which she underscored in the text) was captured by the combination of her first name and her choice of the heading "The Little Woman's Advice" when she organized the material in her pamphlet. Shula Marks was able to show that even as late as the 1940s, the protagonist in her study of three South African women's interrelated lives, who was born in the Eastern Cape in the 1930s, was an avid reader of the Louisa May Alcott books (Marks 1987).

Louisa Mvemve chose for the professional publication of her own pamphlet the same agency which produced the medical texts of Eustace H. Cluver—who ended the decade as the secretary for public health. His widely read and cited medical texts, such as *Medical and Health Legislation in the Union of South Africa*, were published by the Central News Agency in Johannesburg in the 1940s and again in the 1950s. Louisa Mvemve tried to sue the Central News Agency in the late 1920s for failing to publish the required amount of texts, and records of the lawsuit ended up in court documents although no judgment was made in the case. Despite being set and printed in a rather conventional manner, the expression and punctuation are idiosyncratic. It is unfortunate that there is no indication of who, if anyone, helped with its preparation or execution. But the most important section of the pamphlet, headed by a distinctive title, focused on conception and birthing advice for women. In this section, "The Little Woman's Advice," Louisa Mvemve offered help to "the woman who wants children." After describing the herbal remedy and how to take it and ways to comport oneself during pregnancy in order "to ensure safe passage of the child," her tone shifts. Here Mvemve's concern seems to be with both persuading skeptical potential clients as well as entertaining with a narrative involving trials, advice from secret family sources, and magical resolutions.[51]

Reflecting on the possible inspirations for this story and the manner in which it is recounted suggests that missionary texts, medical pamphlets, and school set works—core texts set for national examinations—far from exhaust the possible repertoire of literature that was familiar to its author, Louisa Mvemve. Recent research conducted into the power and resonance of Eastern Cape oral and narrative traditions has suggested that historically women played a crucial role as local experts in the fields of medical and historical knowledge. In a collection of oral texts recorded in the late 1960s, Harold Scheub translated from Xhosa into English a series of interlaced narratives told and performed by an elderly woman from the Transkei region of the Eastern Cape, Nongenile Zenani, who was probably born in the last years of the nineteenth century (Scheub 1992). Nongenile Zenani was considered a particularly talented explicator of *intsomi,* a repertory of local historical narratives, mythical tales, motifs, and stories. Her renditions and enactments of gestation and birthing and death stories and her specialist's knowledge as a herbalist and healer provide an interesting parallel to Louisa Mvemve's narratives in her pamphlet from 1915. The descriptions of herbal fluid medications and tied waist ropes in Louisa Mvemve's story are mirrored in uncanny ways in the conception and pregnancy tales of Nongenile Zenani fifty years later. Interviews of present-day herbalists and midwives in the Transkei region yielded evidence that a corpus of knowledge and practice around pregnancy and birth survives into the 1990s.[52] As with the additions and developments initiated by Louisa Mvemve in the early decades of the century, practitioners in the last decades of the twentieth century have welded together techniques, recipes, and exegeses from a variety of local sources as well as experiences of hospital and clinic care, school teachings, and Christian cosmology into their own corpus of knowledge.[53]

In 1915, when A. L. Barrett, the secretary of the NAD, received Louisa Mvemve's application to practice as a herbalist and "women's healer" along with her pamphlet, envelopes with her bread powders, and copies of testimonials from her patients, he was evidently impressed with the plethora of materials before him as well as with the presence of Mvemve herself. She had by this time established some connections in the eastern part of the city, particularly in Benoni and Brakpan, which were increasingly connected to the urban center by railway lines. As soon as he received her initial materials from Benoni, Barrett wrote to her "reference," Dr. Kerr Muir:

> I have been approached by a Native woman, Louisa Mvemve, who has, or claims to have, a knowledge of a number of herbs possessing healing properties. The list of diseases she claims to cure is so formidable as to almost take one's breath away but the woman's manner and appearance, and her anxiety to submit her cures to analysis seem to remove her very far from the impostor class. She evidently has faith in the efficacy of some of her remedies as do also a number of others, both

European and Native, whose letters she is able to produce. You are aware of the difficulties in the way of according any measure of recognition or assistance to persons of this class and I should be much obliged if you would favour me with any information in your possession regarding this woman.[54]

Kerr Muir's reply began by describing his and his wife's relationship with Louisa Mvemve, indicating that she had worked for them intermittently in about 1905 and 1906. This evidence suggests the possibility that she could have learned certain medical terminology and practices such as the manner of dealing with patients common to a western-trained physician, the names and diagnosis of certain ailments, and the conventions of dealing with and ordering from chemists through her connection to this physician and his family. His letter also revealed his anxiety that he should not be seen to be agreeing to Louisa Mvemve's scheme to involve him in the examination of her patients. In fact, it would seem that in the early 1920s he did see a number of her patients, although on what terms it is not clear. He commented:

> Recently she turned up at my house with a proposal that I should see her patients and merely diagnose their diseases. I was to get £1 per patient and she calculated that there would be about 30 per day. So she obviously has a good practice. Of course I refused to have anything to do with the matter. My wife however advised her to see someone in authority in the Native Affairs Department. . . . My opinion about this woman is that she is a very able person and has evidently faith in the efficacy of her remedies. I believe that in some cases she does good to her patients; in many cases of course she can do no possible good. I am aware that the Medical Council is averse from allowing unqualified persons to practice, but I have for long been of the opinion that natives should be allowed to consult natives, in whom they may have faith, although such may not be qualified legally. Often all-faith in one's medical advisor is a powerful factor in effecting a cure.[55]

Here Kerr Muir evinced a position that was open-minded for his day, suggesting that many sorts of "medical advisors" relied on the faith of their patients. He also described Louisa Mvemve's work using medical terminology rather than the language of "quackery." In one respect he followed a well-worn script: he believed her activities were acceptable if she practiced "among natives." A great fear of doctors in Natal and along the Reef in particular at the time was that their own coffers were being reduced by the energetic activities of "armies of herbalists." Many of the more-progressive supporters of the Natal Native Code's licensing provisions argued their case on the basis of native custom and faith, but nowhere have I found recognition among the medical fraternity of the fact that white South Africans, both in rural dorps and trading posts and in the cities along the coast and on the Reef, visited herbalists and believed there was efficacy to their cures.[56]

Following these communications, Barrett set into motion a series of inquiries and elicited recommendations on Louisa Mvemve's behalf from the commissioner of patents, who was attached to the Office of the Attorney General. He also obtained advice for Louisa from the patent company of D. M. Kirsch and put her into contact with their agents. After months of discussing legal options with Barrett, Louisa Mvemve decided to patent certain of her remedies (at some expense and inconvenience, as she had to repeat the process in each province) and to take out a patent on her trademark, which she decided within days would be a tiger's head. This was despite the fact (which she found out to her dismay) that far from "securing" her secrets, the patenting process demanded that she reveal the exact ingredients of her remedies, and thus although the copyright would protect her own packages and bottles from being copied and enable her to begin a vigorous advertising campaign and win customers and patients on the basis of her trademarked Tiger's Head cures, she could not prevent others from attempting the same process.[57] Nor could she ensure that people paid her for her services and advice.

After writing to Barrett at the end of 1915 about her success in obtaining the services of a chemist through the help of Kerr Muir, Louisa Mvemve asked if the NAD could help her recoup moneys owed to her by "800 natives including native ministers." Barrett replied with a barely concealed warning about her even reporting such "debts":

> I fear that I cannot advise you in regard to the recovery of debts which you state are owing to you. For any other than a registered medical practitioner to undertake the cure of diseases for remuneration would constitute a contravention of the Medical, Dental and Pharmacy Ordinance of 1904, nor would a binding contract result.[58]

But Louisa Mvemve could not contain her activities to the realm of supplying chemists with herbs. Despite warnings, harassment, three major court cases, and many instances of civil litigation, she never gave up her calling to minister to her patients, offer advice, and diagnose, however much she attempted to cover her tracks with the use of chemists' shops and helpful doctors. From the late teens to the late 1920s, testimonials from women in particular to the NAD and to Louisa Mvemve, who then sent them onto the NAD, offer thanks for help with difficult births, a child with polio, a sickly child, a child who would not eat. Photographs of toddlers with grateful notes attached containing questions about new problems and ailments testify to her continuing, if increasingly fragile, practice.[59]

On January 17, 1916, calamity struck Louisa Mvemve's medical practice. A Greek man died while in her care, and within a few days, a charge of culpable homicide was brought against her.[60] Before ten days had passed however, she had marshaled all the support structures at her disposal, calling for evidence, backing, and help from friends around the country, especially in Grahamstown, where she first developed her reputation as a healer. From these friends she received dozens of letters of support, including a petition signed by supporters. She was able to prove her innocence in the face of the manslaughter charges, but she was fined £35 on a charge of contravening the 1914 and 1915 medical ordinances. She was able to convince the court that she was "trying to do some kindness to this dead man." Her letters during and shortly after the trial were directed at protecting her reputation and seeking help from NAD officials and officials in the Justice Department as she fought to have her bail returned to her in full and retain access to her residence and her herbal farm. She wrote:

> It is necessary for me to reside at my present residence so as to be able to manufacture my Herbal Remedies in the building a few yards away from my residence, also to interview intending patients both Europeans and Natives. It is quite impossible for me to do so at the Location. As I am a Public Benefactor by curing so many people, I consider that I should be exempted from the law compelling natives and coloured people to reside in the locations who are not BONA FIDE servants of Europeans.[61]

Even in the midst of a trial for murder, she maintained her confidence and demanded recognition. Her faith in the remedies of litigation and the justice obtainable through law was perhaps born in these two cases, and throughout the 1920s, she brought civil suits against her debtors, principally chemists, winning many of them, though at great cost. She seemed to grow wary of certain magistracies, keeping her distance after losing petitions for licenses. In July 1920, she wrote to Lord Buxton:

> I found out the Law of Kingwilliamstown is not for Natives as I am a Native Woman nothing could be done for me.[62]

And in the same letter, in which she complained about the unscrupulousness of the lawyer she had hired, who had demanded a £40 deposit before he would take up her appeal, she commented;

> This reminds me of slaving time, which our Queen Victoria done away with if a Native Woman or Native Boy, if they were put on the market to be sold, they had no one to stop, til our Queen Victoria stopped it.

These setbacks and disappointments were matched by successes, and Louisa Mvemve continued to chart them by sending copies of testimony and letters of thanks to the new set of officials in the offices of the NAD.

However, two legislative turning points in the 1920s irrevocably altered the terms under which Mvemve—and many other entrepreneurial urban Africans—could maneuver, namely the passage of the 1923 Urban Areas Act and the 1928 Medical, Dental and Pharmacy Act. The passage of the former act resulted in her eventual expulsion from Brakpan, and indeed the Reef, and the consequences of the latter, especially the new clauses restricting the work of uncertified midwives and reinforcing prohibitions on herbalists, resulted in her retreat to a severely circumscribed practice in Grahamstown.

After a period in the Eastern Cape in the 1920s, Mvemve quickly reestablished herself on a farm in Hastings Road, Brakpan, where within a short time she had cultivated a large herbarium, which was sought out by such experts in pharmacology as Professor Watt from the University of the Witwatersrand. Her success and her notoriety were directly related to the actions she faced in her battle for legitimacy. She could not remain unnoticed in the white-designated areas of Hastings Road for long. Yet the passage of the 1923 Urban Areas Act and its attendant amendments did not translate immediately into action by municipal authorities, as writers such as Eales (1987) and Bonner (1990) have demonstrated. But by the early 1930s, local governments such as Benoni and Brakpan had begun a process of devising influx measures, permit systems and tighter pass controls to regulate their black townships, enforce segregation more fully, and control access to housing and employment (Cohen 1982; Sapire 1989).

After a series of complaints by that ubiquitous but anonymous force in South African social history, "members of the public," and reports by the chief sanitary inspector of Brakpan, Louisa Mvemve was ordered to quit her rented property and abandon her famous herb garden.[63] Interventions for a stay of time from the NAD, which again received her case with some sympathy, were to little avail. Served with her quit orders by Chief Inspector Botha in January 1930, she eventually left Brakpan in late April or May of that year. For the last few months she had to ride into and out of the town daily, sleeping in Johannesburg, where she found a place in Jeppe, two blocks from the Fairview property of the Helping Hand Club for Native Women.[64] She had to retain her rail warrants as proof that she had not slept the night in the town she had called her home off and on for six years.

Not willing to take these new and very serious threats lying down, Louisa Mvemve crafted a response. In a series of erudite letters, she appealed to the governor-general once again, reminding him of all she had done for his office. Next she petitioned Prime Minister Hertzog directly, informing him in her letter of her many cures for "Dutch people," her ability to speak Afrikaans, and the justice of her claims for fair treatment after paying taxes and license fees for nearly twenty years. She appealed to Hertzog:

> I could not be ordered to leave the town as I had business, unlike other natives. . . . I have lived in Towns all my life and never in a Location. When I was ordered to go and live in the Location I was surprised. I lost no time. I called on the Authorities and protested, but I was told that it is Segregation Law that is driving me to the Location. . . . I held some rights long before the birth of the Native Urban Areas Act of 1923.[65]

These appeals were of no avail. Instead, within months of forced departure from the Rand, Louisa Mvemve faced legal action again. By this time the 1928 act was being more forcibly applied in urban centers across South Africa, and her work had reached the ears of authorities, even in distant Cape Town.

In early 1928 Louisa Mvemve, now back in Grahamstown, again applied to the governor-general for a license to sell medicine, this time in the Transkeian territories. She stated that her requests had been poorly received by the chief magistrate at Umtata and she requested the governor's intervention; the response was merely an acknowledgement letter.[66] Clearly agitated by her treatment, she approached the magistrate of Butterworth, who received her "in a civil way." Her long-standing Eastern Cape chemist partner, Mr. Carnegie, apparently had warned her about the reason behind the rudeness of the Umtata chief magistrate:

> [H]e must have mistook me for an American woman, the Magistrate in Umtata. As there was little trouble here before with the natives, trying to form colleges, saying they are instructed by Americas. Well, I am not in with those natives doing that although they are my nation. As I was born under the British Flag, I don't remember nothing, what the America did for them. So I do not want to be included with any of those people what are working against the law.[67]

Both Louisa Mvemve's concern to present herself as a loyal subject and her references to rumors of American influences point to the tensions and political context of the late 1920s as expressed through the prophetic Israelite and separatist Africanist movements of the Eastern Cape, chiefly signaled—in the existing and growing historiography on the subject—by the figure of Wellington Buthelezi.[68] Soon after this she faced one last case; she was arrested and charged for acting beyond the law as an unlicensed midwife to a woman, Mrs.

Khol, who was described as suffering from "womb cancer" in court documents. In this, the last case against Mvemve for which records have been located, Louisa Mvemve testified on her own behalf, and her evidence, along with inconsistencies in the prosecution's case, resulted in a verdict of not guilty after several weeks of deliberation. The language of the law was ambiguous and the state could not prove harmful intent on Mvemve's part. Once again she had maneuvered around the provisions of very restrictive legislation, but it would seem that even the remarkable Mvemve was unable to withstand the attacks of those who made and enforced segregation law and the onslaught of the increasingly professional South African medical academy.[69]

Conclusion

Louisa Mvemve's writings reveal a powerful and often ambiguous story of a woman making her way through her healing practice and constantly writing about herself and her work. She and her networks of helpers, detractors, and patients are long dead, but many of the letters and texts she wrote are still accessible and communicate with fresh power to an early-twenty-first-century audience. Her advice pamphlet and her letters and petitions gave powerful expression to her aspirations and her struggles to succeed as well as her interest in posterity and the view of her life and work that people in the future would take. Her letters reveal her to have been, among many other identities, an aspirant petit-bourgeois woman who often repudiated her connections to other people of color in her determination to be respected and sought after. On the other hand, her ambitions did not blind her to the plight of poor black women and men or to that of working-class whites in Reef towns in the 1920s and in the rural hamlets and towns throughout the Eastern Cape and Transkei. Her letters communicated her pride in her historical and cultural bequest from her Xhosa-speaking grandparents and she embraced all African ethnicities in South Africa as part of her "Nation." Against all odds she developed and maintained relationships with, among others, the Thimbler family of Grahamstown, the Kerr Muir family of Brakpan, and her extensive networks of black women and men supporters throughout South Africa and beyond (for example, Chief David Molapo of Lesotho).

Her letters were part of a huge communication bridge she created over time and space. Through personal visits and consultations but also through letters she laid girders connecting herself to other readers and writers, including working-class white women and men, that went beyond attempts at class mobility. The records she left and those officials wrote about her show that

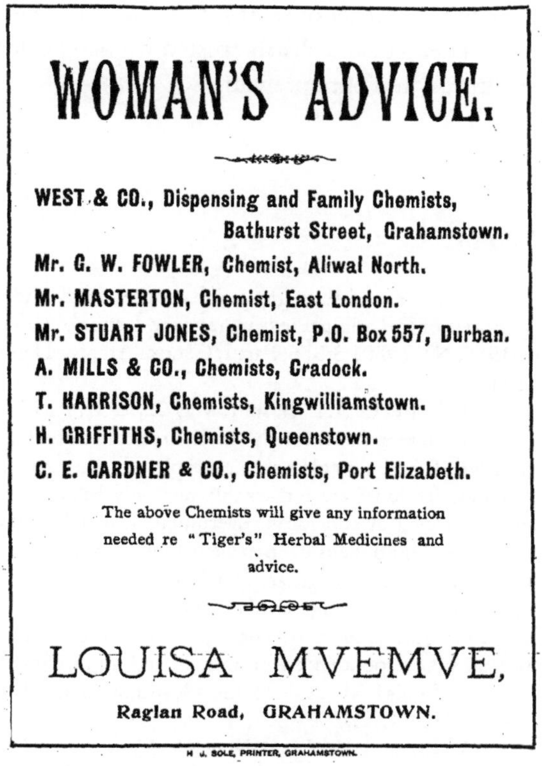

Figure 3.3. Louisa Mvemve's
Woman's Advice pamphlet.
Courtesy the National
Archives Department of
South Africa, Pretoria.

WOMAN'S ADVICE.

WEST & CO., Dispensing and Family Chemists,
Bathurst Street, Grahamstown.

Mr. G. W. FOWLER, Chemist, Aliwal North.

Mr. MASTERTON, Chemist, East London.

Mr. STUART JONES, Chemist, P.O. Box 557, Durban.

A. MILLS & CO., Chemists, Cradock.

T. HARRISON, Chemists, Kingwilliamstown.

H. GRIFFITHS, Chemists, Queenstown.

C. E. GARDNER & CO., Chemists, Port Elizabeth.

The above Chemists will give any information
needed re "Tiger's" Herbal Medicines and
advice.

LOUISA MVEMVE,

Raglan Road, GRAHAMSTOWN.

H. J. SOLE, PRINTER, GRAHAMSTOWN.

she charged high prices for her remedies but often gave free advice and supplied herbs without hope of repayment to people in whom she took an interest. In her work as a midwife in Johannesburg and the East Rand towns she
provided a service and a level of expertise not easily available to any women of
color. She was not, unlike the black women who would train as midwives after
1928, a school-educated woman. Indeed, she had worked as a domestic servant in her youth and early adulthood. However, in some of her letters we can
read that at times she aspired to the gentility of a Victorian woman in her
self-representation. Her chutzpah, humor, tenacity, and confidence ring
through to a contemporary reader and insist that she was successful in at least
one ambition: she left a remarkable record of some aspects of her life. Today
her archive and the personal qualities still living in its boxes and files animate
our understanding of debates around medicine and healing, literacy and au-

thority, the impact of segregation, and the day-to-day difficulties of an ambitious, talented, and clearly trusted woman healer, diagnostician, midwife, horticulturist, and entrepreneur.

NOTES

1. Here, and throughout the chapter, I have not altered the spelling, expression, or grammar of the original text in any way. Letter of Peter Zwana, Benoni Location, August 6, 1915, NTS 9301 3/376, Part I, Central Archive Depot, Pretoria, South Africa (hereafter CAD).

2. Letter of A. L. Barrett, May 22, 1931, JUS 576 01 418/81, CAD.

3. In searches through the files relating to herbalists in the Central State Archives, I have not found a single other example of such repeated or prolific communication. Her "communications" are remarkable not only because they extend across so many departments of central and local government (involving hundreds of letters, many notes and telegrams, and dozens of interviews) but also because the staff of the Native Affairs Department (NAD) recognized her as most prolific, and unusually so. Finally, and crucially, although I have found letters from a handful of women herbalists to the NAD, the governor-general, and attorney general in the period after the 1940s, nearly all of the herbalist correspondence is from men and no case involves more than a few letters.

4. Louisa Mvemve to the Governor-General, Lord Buxton, May 13, 1914, GG 1109 48/504, CAD.

5. *Woman's Advice: A Woman's Advice to the Public on the Cure of Various Diseases* (Central News Agency, n.d.), NTS 3901 3/376 Part I, 1915, CAD.

6. In November 1916, Mvemve informed Lord Buxton: "I intend opening a factory in Graham's Town to make my medicines to supply the Chemists in different towns." See Louise Mvemve to Governor-General, November 21, 1916, February 23, 1916, and January 15, 1930, NTS 9301 3/376, CAD.

7. See *Woman's Advice*, 5. After describing the manner and circumstances of her own birth and her grandfather's intervention, she states: "These herbs were all my grandfather's secrets; they will cure all manner of diseases."

8. She also made numerous attempts to get certified physicians "of the government's choice" to examine leprosy patients she claimed to have healed (June 7, 1915, and August 15, 1915, NTS 9301 3/376, CAD). The *Cape Times* of March 12, 1931, reported the examination of her herbs by doctors and indicated that tests of these were undertaken at the Kleinfontein Hospital.

9. Mvemve mentions this several times, but her most extensive comments can be found in letters from Kingwilliamstown in February 1919. She claimed that her "European" clients wanted her to open a nursing home for Europeans in the town. February 20, 1919, NTS 9303 3/376, CAD. In 1928, in correspondence with the governor-general she again cited the need to open a nursing home for her "European" patients, this time in Brakpan; January 10, 1930, GG 3/4864, CAD.

10. Throughout the records Mvemve continually testifies to having taken on pa-

tients, especially cancer patients, that other doctors had given up on. One example is January 30, 1931, JUS 576 01 418/31, CAD.

11. This is most explicitly stated in a four-page letter Mvemve wrote to the secretary of the NAD (May 24, 1916, NTS 9301 3/376, CAD) and in a letter to Lord Buxton on the subject of her healing powers (May 31, 1916, JUS 231 01 3/98/16/1, CAD).

12. Mvemve won the friendship of Dr. Kerr Muir and his wife in her Benoni days and the partnership of Dr. Scott of Grahamstown in the 1920s. She also maintained tempestuous relationships with chemists such as Mr. Miller, Mr. Carnegie, and Mrs. Neal. Examples of her letters of testimony from patients and letters containing references to people she cured occur throughout the files. For one example of letters of reference (sent in by black and white women and men) from Grahamstown, Benoni, Van Ryn, Port Elizabeth, Pretoria, Somerset East, Brakpan, Beggers Bush, Uitenhage, and Roodepoort, see February 2, 1916, GG 919/01 33/67, CAD.

13. Another view of her life from the perspective of health and medical history is in Burns (1996). Parts of the opening arguments of that paper are summarized here. Thanks to *KRONOS* for permission.

14. See the brief examination of her self-representation below.

15. Attempts to trace and interview descendants or people who remember anything about her through newspapers and local radio stations or networks of Mvemves in the current Eastern Cape and Gauteng have so far proved fruitless.

16. A fine example of historical reconstruction based on the letters that passed between three South African women is Marks (1987).

17. See letters of testimony written to Mvemve, particularly those from 1916 contained in GG 919/01 33/677, CAD, and the letter and photograph from the Du Preez family, January 10, 1930, NTS 9301 3/376, CAD.

18. In the 1920s, debates around maternal health and welfare led to the creation of new legislation that sharply circumscribed the activities of family and local midwives. However, the lack of training facilities for certified black midwives and the absence of any maternity homes for black women jeopardized the enforcement of the new laws. In 1928, the same year a new health act was passed, an act that was directed at herbalists and independent healers, a group of philanthropists in Johannesburg opened the Bridgman Memorial Hospital for black women and embarked on a program to train black midwives. But it was not until the late 1930s that the local state was able to offer black city-dwellers any alternatives to uncertified midwives.

19. See Eales (1987); Bonner (1990); and Kuzwayo (1987).

20. For a detailed analysis see Dubow (1989, 1986).

21. Mvemve cultivated relationships with three important chiefs: Menzime of Grahamstown, David Molapo of Basutoland, and Mopedi of Witzieshoek. She helped them with personal cures and assisted in the birth of Menzime's grandson.

22. January 27, 1931, NTS 9301 3/376, CAD.

23. Isabel Hofmeyr (1994) has offered suggestive insights into the relationship between forms of communication and political authority.

24. Any overview book on animals in Southern Africa makes this clear. Recently a controversy has raged over the introduction of five Chinese tigers to the Karoo; see "Releasing Tigers," available online at http://www.lairweb.org.nz/tiger/release10.html. The eventual aim is the release of the tigers into a 300-square-kilometer area that has been secured by the group "Save China's Tigers" in the Free State.

25. The official Tiger Balm website claims that the Rangoon-based family who developed and marketed the balm transformed a home-produced salve into a global brand. See "History of Tiger Balm," available on line at http://www.tigerbalm.co.uk/intro.html.

26. After the 1850s, tiger brands became a staple of Orientalist and Indian images. See the famous cartoon in *Punch* in 1857 by John Tenniel, "The British lion's vengeance on the Bengal tiger." Available online at http://www.victorianweb.org/periodicals/punch/53.html.

27. Tiger Brands, which owns this and other best-selling brands, is expanding internationally, including into an Eastern and Southeast Asian market. See http://www.tiger brands.com.

28. E. Barrett did not impress his views on others in his department. Throughout the 1920s (after he had resigned from the NAD), Louisa Mvemve received warm testimonials from the other officials. July 20, 1920, NTS 9301 3/376, CAD.

29. Louisa Mvemve sent a most erudite letter following NAD inquiries on her behalf in January 1921. January 25, 1921, NTS 9303 3/376, CAD.

30. The letters to Prime Minister Hertzog and the native sub-commissioner of Benoni were both in connection with her imminent removal from Brakpan. January 10, 1930, and January 15, 1930, respectively, NTS 9301 3/376, CAD.

31. December 1, 1919, NTS 9301 3/376, CAD.

32. We can now compare Louisa Mvemve's writing with that of her peers in the long-awaited collection of late-nineteenth- and early-twentieth-century Southern African literate women's texts published in Daymond, Driver, and Meintjes (2002). The section on Louisa Mvemve is a reproduction of her health pamphlet for women with my introduction to the primary text. The collection also brings to print many oral performances, reflections, and analyses by women from the region.

33. She also spoke of "natives" as "her people" and of herself as a "native herbalist"; see November 21, 1916, GG 145 01 3/2232/1, CAD.

34. See the summary of Fingo/Mfengu history provided by Les Switzer (1993).

35. The studies of the Mayers and of Hammond-Tooke, among others, have continued to explain the Mfengu in similar terms. However, a recent reworking of this "mfecane-based" thesis is under way in the work of the historian Julian Cobbing and his graduate students at Rhodes University in Grahamstown, and although not many new answers have been forthcoming from the work of people such as Alan Webster, the entire edifice of documentary evidence upon which the narrative rested for so long has been vigorously questioned (Webster 1991). See also Hunter (1936); Mayer and Mayer (1961); Hammond-Tooke (1962); Moyer (1976); Cock (1990).

36. December 1, 1919, pp. 1–2, NTS 9301 3/376, CAD. In this letter Louisa Mvemve also indicates that she and her family were School, or Christian, people, rather than Red—or ochre—people (*amaBomvu*).

37. April 28, 1916, May 27, 1916, and July 12, 1916, NTS 9301 3/367, CAD.

38. Dr. Kerr Muir to E. Barrett, NAD, May 25, 1915, NTS 9301 3/376, CAD.

39. Louisa Mvemve to the Native Sub-Commissioner of Benoni, March 12, 1927, NTS 9301 3/376, CAD.

40. July 17, 1928, GG 3/4834, CAD.

41. November 21, 1916, GG 145 01 3/2232/1, CAD.

42. April 17, 1916, NTS 9301 3/376, CAD.

43. The only references to her son speak of him working on a herb farm in Orange

Grove and her attempts to move him to Mrs. Kerr Muir's care instead, "as he is still under age." December 24, 1917, NTS 9301 3/376, CAD.

44. One possible clue to the view black men and women could have had of Louisa Mvemve is the reference to her in a 1917 "Grahamstown riots" Report. In a section titled "Native Unrest: Grahamstown," issued from the office of the deputy commissioner of police of that town, a reference was made to a "Louisa Mvemve": "During the early hours of the morning, the natives again forcibly prevented male and female servants from proceeding to their work. One native woman, Louisa Mvemve, who insisted on going to her work when stopped by a native picket, was assaulted, badly knocked about, and seriously injured." April 28, 1917, SAP 34 6/498/17, CAD. Many thanks to K. S. T. Shear for this reference.

45. This entire formulation was gravely at fault, and nothing like a closed system existed on either side of the divide. See Young (1981) and Comaroff (1981). The only contemporary commentary that I have found, which "complicated" the concept of logical and thought systems within indigenous medical crafts, is that of J. D. Krige, who argued that the framework of criteria, categories of thought, and explanatory principles of Bantu health practices bore a great resemblance to those of biomedicine; both used observation, physical and chemical knowledge, and theories of causation. He focused his analysis of difference on available technologies and pointed out the religious thought embedded in the practice of many medical missions. Krige also reminded readers of the short history that western biomedicine could claim and its own wellsprings in the traditions of Judeo-Christianity and European cosmological ideas (Krige 1944).

46. Mitchell played a key role here, as did other members of the Public Health Administration, such as Gale. In Natal, a sometimes-tense relationship between the official watchdogs of the medical profession and magistrates lasted until the 1940s, as the magistrates were vigorously lobbied by local chiefs to continue issuing licenses to herbalists and "medicine men."

47. April 13, 1914, GG 1109 48/504, CAD.

48. Although these products were often received with annoyance, correspondence from the 1920s shows that there were occasions when even the Department of Native Affairs called for magistrates and missionaries in rural areas to send in these products because they related to animal sicknesses or remedies for human illnesses.

49. *A Woman's Advice to the Public on the Cure of Various Diseases.* In NTS 3901 3/376, Part I 1915, CAD.

50. E. H. Cluver, *Physiology and Hygiene* and *Public Health in South Africa,* both published in Johannesburg by the Central News Agency in the 1920s and the latter again in the 1930s and 1940s.

51. It should be clear to the reader at this point that this chapter is not an attempt to substantiate Louisa Mvemve's powers as a herbalist or to call western biomedicine into question. I have attempted to track down some of the more common cures she described and have found this one mentioned in J. Watt and M. Breyer-Brandwijk's study (1932), created from the *agapanthus umbellatus* plant. It would seem from Watt and from the testimony of Frank Brownlee, magistrate of Butterworth, that this pregnancy aid was widely used across the Transkei and Eastern Cape. See also the 1927 report in NTS 27/400 7750, CAD.

52. Author's interviews with Mamtolo Dubazana, Isiyaya, August 22, 1992, and Nora Mdlamza, Mount Frere, October 17, 1992. Thanks to Nokhatazeka Mzayifani (translator) and Nontobeko Luqola (transcriber).

53. Author's interview with Mamtolo Dubazana, Isiyaya, August 22, 1992. A detailed examination of the legacy of nineteenth- and early-twentieth-century medical practices in the late twentieth century, and the transmission of knowledge and skill to younger chosen specialists, awaits further research. I intend to make some of these questions the basis of a future research project.

54. Barrett to Kerr Muir, April 20, 1915, NTS 9301 3/376, CAD.

55. Kerr Muir to Barrett, May 25, 1915, NTS 9301 3/376, CAD.

56. This is well documented in works such as Hellman (1948); Phillips (1938); and Longmore (1959).

57. Letters between April 15, 1915 and September 17, 1915, NTS 9301 3/376, CAD.

58. Mvemve to Barrett, April 12, 1915 and Barrett to Mvemve, December 8, 1915, NTS 9303 3/376, CAD.

59. Mvemve to Barrett, April 15, 1915 and September 17, 1927, NTS 9301 3/376, CAD.

60. There are some telling and rich passages in her written testimony to NAD and the governor-general concerning this case. Mvemve was represented at her best by her scribes, legal assistants, and advisors, and when she appeared in court she evidently impressed reporters from the *Star* and *Rand Daily Mail* with her command of English and her unusual and powerful responses to cross-questioning. See the letters, court records, telegrams, police reports, and testimonials in January 27, 1916 to June 1916, NTS 9301 3/376, GG 919/01 33 676 and 377, GG 920/01 33/712, and JUS 231 01 3/98/16/1. All in CAD.

61. February 23, 1916, p. 2, NTS 9301 3/376, CAD.

62. July 8, 1920, NTS 9301 3/376, CAD.

63. This paragraph is taken from evidence in documents dated January 8, 1930 to April 26, 1930 in NTS 9301 3/376, CAD.

64. This hostel for black city women was started in 1919.

65. January 15, 1930, NTS 9301 3/376, CAD.

66. June 21, 1928, GG 207 3/4864, CAD.

67. July 17, 1928, GG 207 3/4864, CAD.

68. Some of the best writing on this subject includes Beinart and Bundy (1987); Edgar (1982); Bradford (1987); and Sundkler (1961).

69. January 27, 1931 and JUS 576 01 418/31: December 8, 1930 to July 9, 1931, NTS 9301 3/376, CAD.

REFERENCES

Arnup, Katherine. 1994. *Education for Motherhood: Advice for Mothers.* Toronto: University of Toronto Press.

Beinart, W., and C. Bundy. 1987. *Hidden Struggles in Rural South Africa: Politics and Popular Movements in the Transkei and Eastern Cape, 1890–1930.* Johannesburg: Ravan Press.

Bonner, P. 1990. "'Desirable or Undesirable Basotho Women?' Liquor, Prostitution and the Migration of Basotho Women to the Rand, 1920–1945." In *Women and Gender in Southern Africa to 1943,* ed. C. Walker. Cape Town: David Philip.

Bradford, H. 1987. *A Taste of Freedom: The ICU in Rural South Africa, 1924–1930.* New Haven: Yale University Press.

Burns, Catherine. 1996. "Louisa Mvemve: A Woman's Advice to the Public on the Cure of Various Diseases." *KRONOS: Journal of Cape History* 23: 108–134.

Cock, J. 1990. "Domestic Service and Education for Domesticity: The Incorporation of Xhosa Women into Colonial Society." In *Women and Gender in Southern Africa to 1945,* ed. C. Walker. Cape Town: David Philip.

Cohen, J. 1982. "A Pledge for Better Times: The Local State and the Ghetto, Benoni, 1930–1938." Honors dissertation, University of the Witwatersrand.

Comaroff, J. 1981. "Healing and Cultural Transformation." *Journal of Social Science and Medicine* 15 (B): 367–378.

Davin, Anna. 1978. "Imperialism and Motherhood." *History Workshop Journal* 5: 9–65.

Daymond, M., Dorothy Driver, and Sheila Meintjes, eds. 2002. *Women Writing Africa.* Vol. 1, *The Southern Region.* New York: Feminist Press.

Dubow, S. 1986. "Holding 'A Just Balance between White and Black': The Native Affairs Department in South Africa c. 1920–33." *Journal of Southern African Studies* 12, no. 2: 217–239.

———. 1989. *Racial Segregation and the Origins of Apartheid in South Africa, 1919–1936.* London: Macmillan.

Eales, K. 1987. "Patriarchs, Passes and Privilege: Johannesburg's African Middle Classes and the Question of Night Passes for African Women," in *Holding Their Ground: Class, Locality and Culture in 19th and 20th Century South Africa,* ed. Philip Bonner, Isabel Hofmeyr, Deborah James, and Tom Lodge. Johannesburg: Witwatersrand University Press.

Edgar, R. 1982. "The Prophet Motive: Enoch Mgijima, the Israelites and the Background to the Bulhoek Massacre." *Journal of Southern African Studies* 15, no. 3: 401–422.

Grant, Julia. 1998. *Raising Baby by the Book: The Education of American Mothers.* New Haven and London: Yale University Press.

Guy, Jeff. 2004. "IMIFANEKISO: Photographic Portraits from Mid-Nineteenth Century Natal: The Work of Dr. R. J. Mann." Paper presented to WISER seminar series, University of the Witwatersrand. Available online at wiserweb.wits.ac.za.

Hammond-Tooke, W. D. 1962. *Bhaca Society.* London: Oxford University Press.

Hellman, E. 1948. *Rooiyard: A Sociological Study of an Urban Native Slumyard.* Cape Town and London: Oxford University Press.

Hofmeyr, Isabel. 1994. *"We Spend Our Years as a Tale That Is Told": Oral Historical Narrative in a South African Chiefdom.* Johannesburg: Witwatersrand University Press.

Hunter, M. 1936. *Reaction to Conquest: Effects of Contact with Europeans on the Pondo.* London: Oxford University Press.

Katz, Elaine. 1994. *The White Death: Silicosis on the Witwatersrand Gold Mines, 1886 to 1910.* Johannesburg: University of Witwatersrand Press.

Krige, J. D. 1944. "The Magical Thought-Pattern of the Bantu in Relation to Health Services." *African Studies* 3: 1–13.

Kuzwayo, E. 1987. *Call Me Woman.* San Francisco: Aunt Lute Books.

Longmore, L. 1959. *The Dispossessed.* London: Jonathan Cape.

Mandela, N. 1994. *Long Walk to Freedom.* Randburg: Macdonald Purnell.

Marks, Shula, ed. 1987. *Not Either an Experimental Doll: The Separate Worlds of Three South African Women.* Pietermaritzburg: University of Natal Press.

Mayer, P., and I. Mayer. 1961. *Townsmen or Tribesmen*. London: Oxford University Press.

Moyer, R. A. 1976. "A History of the Mfengu of the Eastern Cape 1815–1865." Ph.D. diss., London University.

Packard, Randall. 1989. *White Plague, Black Labour: Tuberculosis and the Political Economy of Health and Disease in South Africa*. Berkeley: California.

Phillips, R. 1938. *The Bantu in the City*. London: Oxford University Press.

Sapire, H. 1989. "African Urbanisation and Struggles against Municipal Control in Brakpan, 1920–1958." Ph.D. diss., University of the Witwatersrand.

Scheub, H. 1992. *The World and the Word: Tales and Observations from the Xhosa Oral Tradition: Nongenile Masithathu Zenani*. Madison: University of Wisconsin Press.

Sundkler, B. 1961. *Bantu Prophets in South Africa*. Oxford: Oxford University Press.

Switzer, L. 1993. *Power and Resistance in an African Society: The Ciskei Xhosa and the Making of South Africa*. Madison: University of Wisconsin Press.

Watt, J., and M. Breyer-Brandwijk. 1932. *The Medicinal and Poisonous Plants of Southern Africa*. Edinburgh: Livingstone.

Webster, A. 1991. "Unmasking the Fingo: The War of 1835 Revisited." Paper given at a conference entitled "The 'Mfecane' Aftermath." University of the Witwatersrand.

Willan, Brian. 1985. *Sol Plaatje: South African Nationalist, 1876–1932*. London: Heinemann.

Young, A. 1981. "The Creation of Medical Knowledge: Some Problems in Interpretation." *Journal of Social Science and Medicine* 15 (B): 379–386.

EKUKHANYENI LETTER-WRITERS: A HISTORICAL INQUIRY INTO EPISTOLARY NETWORK(S) AND POLITICAL IMAGINATION IN KWAZULU-NATAL, SOUTH AFRICA

Vukile Khumalo

4

Introduction

On April 5, 1906, Pixley ka Isaka Seme, a law student at Columbia University in the United States, delivered an award-winning speech entitled "The Regeneration of Africa."[1] Through the speech Seme sought to reinsert Africa and what he saw as its ancient but changing civilizations into a new world of science, commerce, and the production of knowledge in general. For Seme, who would later become one of the founders of the South African Native National Congress (SANNC) and much later its president (see Rive and Couzens 1992), something new was emerging in the continent of Africa. In his speech he invited the audience to "cast [their] eyes south of the Desert of Sahara." And, he continued, "If you could go with me to the oppressed Congos and ask, what does it mean, that now, for liberty, they fight like men and die like martyrs." From the Congo he took the audience to Bechuanaland and Abyssinia and then, "oh," he exclaimed, "if you could read the letters that come to us from Zululand." Partly because of what written communication made possible, Seme felt strongly that this mode of communication that people in Africa had established among themselves and with others beyond their regional boundaries represented a "new order of things that belong[ed] to this new and powerful period" (Seme 1913, 438). And partly because of these international and transcontinental linkages, Seme argued in the language of his time, Africans had come to "learn that knowledge is power" (ibid., 439).

As Seme read the speech and announced a "new order of things" in front of a university audience, much was happening in the hills and valleys of his homeland: a "rebellion" was under way in Natal and Zululand.[2] Was this a coincidence? This uprising took place four years after the Anglo-Boer War and it inaugurated the end of an era of chiefs, the "Bambatha rebellion" of 1906.[3] Bent on balancing the books, the Natal government imposed a poll tax on all adult men. This imposition (combined with the impact of the effects of the "natural disasters") triggered the start of the upheavals that the Natal government dubbed "the Bambatha rebellion." While the Natal government managed to suppress the uprising, for colonial officials around South Africa it raised a possibility of a large-scale disturbance. And for this reason, the "rebellion" had a direct impact on the outcome of the National Convention of 1908 that divided South Africa into four provinces. As is now well documented in the South African historiography, not all South Africans took part in the National Convention; women and African men were excluded. While Natal was reluctant to join the Union, it could not afford to stand alone for fear of still another uprising. As negotiations for a Union of South Africa took place, some South Africans, including the ones who sent letters to Seme, held their own conversations about the possible political future of South Africa. Their conventions took place in a parliament without walls—an epistolary network. Indeed, those who could not directly be engaged in these political activities that saw the formation of the SANNC set out to write histories for future generations—for posterity.[4] The letters carry the thoughts of people who could not participate directly in the formation of the Union of South Africa but were very much involved in the shaping of South Africa's destiny in the twentieth century through writing from a distance.

While Seme's speech identifies the spirit of the period, it does not explore the content of this "new order of things," nor does it tell us how this order unfolded. Perhaps these concerns never occurred to Seme almost a century ago. But most important, what Seme hints at in his paper is a less-explored area in South African nationalist historiography; that is, the body of literature that deals with African politics before union. In this literature, one of the celebrated and binding traditions is the search for the origins and evolution of African nationalism and political consciousness.[5] This tradition, which is in part a resistance tradition, sees African protest politics at the turn of the twentieth century as a road that led to the formation of the South African Native National Congress in 1912 (Odendaal 1984). In trying to analyze the political developments in South African politics and their impact on social and political life, scholars of nationalism in particular have been quick to herald the dawn of African nationalism and political consciousness. But a close look at the development of African politics in nineteenth-century South Africa reveals that the process was not as straightforward as the literature would have us believe. Much of this historiography has been caught up in the teleology of the nationalist narrative, and its linear reading of the developments in African nationalism neglects the complexity and convoluted nature of African politics before Union. It also overlooks the fact that the decisions people made were contingent upon local, regional, and imperial factors and, most important, they relied upon the epistolary moment.

This chapter argues that through the practice of letter-writing, the writers (a category that included preachers, wagon-makers, migrant workers, scholars, and prison inmates) built a network of letter-writers and -readers who shared similar thoughts and dreams. Having mastered the technology of letter-writing, they sought to conquer space through ink and were able to establish connections that did not rely on physical, face-to-face proximity. I suggest that this was a network because the writers were connected by the medium of the letter. This network was not just a line of communication, it was an environment in which these letter-writers lived, acted, and shared their thoughts. As time went on, the network shaped what I call here a *sphere*; that is, an imaginary environment where the letter-writers felt free to converse among themselves about issues that affected their lives. Such an environment was akin to what the writers called an *ibandla*.[6] The total number of participants was quite small, but the significance of this epistolary network went beyond its impact on the actual letter-writers and -readers, affecting political negotiations with the Zulu royal family, missions, a nascent literate African opposition, and other interested parties.[7]

Drawing upon diverse and existing forms of correspondence and institutions such as *ibandla* and using the infrastructure of the postal office and the very practice of writing, these writers engaged the political discourse of the Natal colonial state. Employing their masterly control of the conventions of letter-writing, they commented, reflected upon, and articulated their views on social, political, intellectual, and economic situations in the colony. This chapter begins to map the terrain that had an enormous influence on the ideas of these letter-writers.

Ekukhanyeni as a Political Sphere

At the turn of the twentieth century, on a hillock five miles east of the colonial capital, Pietermaritzburg, and two miles southeast of the Valley of a Thousand Hills in the Natal midlands stood Ekukhanyeni mission station.[8] With the support of the colonial government and African chiefs, the Anglican bishop William John Colenso had established this mission station in 1856, two years after his arrival in Natal and a decade after the establishment of the colony.[9] He arrived at a time when Sir George Grey, the governor of Cape Colony, was in Natal making plans to grant land to the missionaries to build mission stations (Peires 1989). The Natal government granted missionaries land under the Deed of Grant of 1856, which gave mission boards of different denominations powers to control their lands. The character of the mission stations reflected the interests of various mission societies. Some missionaries emphasized the evangelical aspect of their mission while others, such as the American Board Mission, encouraged individual land tenure (Bridgman n.d.).

Because of the concentration of missionaries in one area between 1850 and 1900, Natal was one of the most heavily evangelized regions of the globe. In his book *Preachers, Peasants and Politics in Southern Africa,* Etherington suggests that "no other quarter of nineteenth-century Africa was so thickly invested with Christian evangelists. The Secretary of the American Board of Commissioners for Foreign Missions estimated in 1880 that the number of missionaries in Natal was proportionately greater than in any other community on the globe two or three times over" (Etherington 1978, 5). By the turn of the century in Natal alone there were 40,000 communicants and 100,000 adherents to Christianity (Marks 1970, 52). Most of the converts lived in mission reserves, and they occupied about 175,000 acres of land.

What distinguished Ekukhanyeni from these other mission stations was the extent of its involvement in the politics of the colony of Natal. This does not imply that the other mission societies did not participate in politics; the difference is that between 1850 and 1900, they participated in a way that did not challenge the colonial state. For instance, because of its marginal political position in a British colony, the American Board Mission took a generation to rethink its position in the colony and begin to challenge the policies of the Natal government. In contrast, the Ekukhanyeni mission station was entangled in political and legal debates with the colonial government within less than a decade of its founding. Bishop Colenso's actions against the government were in part influenced by his close relationships with the men and women who worked with him at the mission station—William Ngidi, Jonathan Ngidi, Magema Fuze, and many others. The political involvement of the station began after the brutal destruction of the Hlubi chiefdom.[10] The mission station "protested against the manner in which Natal put down the alleged rebellion of Langalibalele and his Hlubi people in 1873" (Guy 1979, 89). The Bishopstowe faction, as they became known, saw the incident as a miscarriage of justice and sought to expose the brutality of the Shepstone system.[11] From 1873 onward, Colenso denounced "Shepstone and his regime as rotten to the very core" (Etherington 1978, 42).

The next clash between Bishopstowe and the colonial government took place during the events leading to the British invasion of the Zulu kingdom in 1879. The invasion resulted in the Battle of Isandlwana on January 23, 1879, when the Zulu army defeated the British army. However, six months later, on July 4, 1879, the British came back with reinforcements and defeated the Zulu army at the Battle of Ulundi. The view from Ekukhanyeni came through William Ngidi, who decried the repercussions of the invasion. He said:

> I quite hope that now you know that the Zulus are set at loggerheads by the cunning of white men, who want to eat up their land. My heart is very full of grief, I cannot find words to express it, for this splendid old Zulu people.[12]

This was a political position from Ekukhanyeni which was unlike that of other mission stations. The sustained political position that Ekukhanyeni took demonstrated the political life the station enjoyed. It was a place for debate and political discussion. One of the issues discussed at the mission was the capture and exile to Cape Town of the Zulu king, Cetshwayo. After a period of imprisonment in the Castle, he was sent to England to meet Queen Victoria. He returned three years later, when the country was plunged into a civil war between the Usuthu, a section loyal to him, and Hamu-Zibhebhu section, which had broken ties with the Zulu king. Cetshwayo died in February 1884, less than a year after Colenso. Ekukhanyeni was the only mission station openly against the invasion.

However, the existing body of literature that covers these political developments has not fully explored how ideas like those of Ngidi developed or how a sphere of critical political debate in a colonial situation was nurtured. What were the mechanisms by which these ideas were exchanged? The letters provide an unusual view of the backstage communication among the Ekukhanyeni letter-writers and, most important, what sustained their political opinion. The vibrant discussion among the letter-writers contributed to the vigor of these political engagements with both the colonial and the imperial governments in late-nineteenth-century colonial Natal.

The authors of the letters were part of the developments after the civil war. They sought to expose the Natal colonial government's injustices and inconsistencies in dealing with members of the Usuthu.[13] In 1888, Dinuzulu, the heir to the Zulu throne, was charged with inciting the civil war. The Natal colonial government removed him from Zululand, and he was exiled to St. Helena with some of his supporters, commonly known as the Usuthu.[14] What had been for sixty years an independent kingdom (some call it an empire) was divided into thirteen magisterial districts (Kunene 1979). The Natal colonial government deposed Usuthu chiefs and installed chiefs that had been loyal to it during the invasion. I suggest that in their engagements with the colonial and imperial structures, this network of letter-writers specifically imagined a future of new British-Zulu relations where the two political systems would coexist productively. It was this imagination that shaped their conversations in the letters.

Ekukhanyeni as a Literary Sphere

Established in 1855, Ekukhanyeni was one of the most influential educational institutions in Natal before the turn of the century. It was founded to provide education to "African boys, especially the sons of chiefs and headmen" (Brookes and Webb 1965, 106). At its commencement, the school offered training in agriculture, carpentry, and construction as well as religious lessons. The first year the school opened, it enrolled nineteen boys. The next year the center registered thirty-three students. In 1859, there were forty-two students studying at the institution (ibid.).

Between 1860 and 1880, Ekukhanyeni became an important alternative center of intellectual life in Natal. Through its mission press, the center established itself as one of the leading mission publishers in the colony and beyond. In four years, the Ekukhanyeni Press published a Zulu-English dictionary, a Zulu grammar, and a translation of St. Matthew's Gospel. In less than ten years, the Mission Press published a number of significant books in both isiZulu and English. Major publications included a translated version of the "New Testament and the books of Genesis, Exodus and I and II Samuel in the Old Testament, Zulu liturgy, a tract on the Decalogue and Zulu readers in Geography, Geology, History and Astronomy, as well as sundry Grammars and general Readers" (ibid., 105). The translation of biblical texts alerted Bishop Colenso to questions of truth about the Bible. His co-translator,

William Ngidi, sparked his questioning of the Bible as a truth. While translating the story of the flood, Ngidi asked:

> Is all that true? Do you really believe that all this happened thus,—that all the
> beasts, and birds, and creeping things, upon the earth, large and small, from hot
> countries and cold, came thus in pairs, and entered into the ark with Noah? And
> did Noah gather food for them all for the beasts and birds of prey, as well as the
> rest? (Rees 1958, 69)

Colenso asked himself "shall a man speak lies in the Name of the Lord? I dare
not do so."[15] The questions that Ngidi posed led Colenso to enter contemporary debates in the field of biblical criticism (Brookes and Webb 1965, 107).
Soon after Colenso, Ngidi, and others completed a translation of the book of
Genesis, Bishop Colenso published a book which led to his excommunication
from the Anglican church. The book was entitled *The Pentateuch and the Book
of Joshua Critically Examined* (J. W. Colenso 1970). Published in 1862, it became one of the most controversial literary works in the field of biblical scholarship in its time.

The policies of the various missions regarding education varied, and so did
the early reactions of local chiefs, some of whom seized the opportunity to employ missionaries as scribes and emissaries, others of whom tried to keep them
at arm's length, preferring to acquire literacy, insofar as they needed it, from
government schools. What is clear, however, is that the demand for, and provision of, schooling grew enormously in the last quarter of the nineteenth century. In 1885, there were 64 schools in Natal; by 1901, this figure had more
than tripled to 196. But a second, less welcome, change was in the nature of the
curriculum. After 1893, when the Natal colonial government was granted
greater autonomy, the broad and varied curriculum (which reached advanced
levels in a range of "literary" subjects such as Latin, Greek, music, German,
history, and geography and also offered useful practical instruction) was nar-
rowed down to basic literacy and numeracy in English and Zulu. This change
in government education policy was partly a response to the demands of local
sugar-planters, who had no use for educated natives, who were described by
newspaper editorials as "lazy good for nothing." This shift dismayed the earlier
generation of educated, progressive middle-class Africans (the *amakholwa*),
who publicly championed the "civilization" that only an advanced education
could bring. As Solomon Khumalo put it in an interview published in the
Inkanyiso Yase Natali newspaper:

> Natives generally would like to see their children educated. Of course, when I say
> "educated" I mean educated in the true sense of the word. . . . In Natal . . . they

only oblige aspirants to read Fourth Royal reader, to have sufficient acquaintance with the elementary rules of arithmetic, a smattering of the English language, and well—that's about all.[16]

He deplored the poor educational background of the native teachers, proposing that the only solution was to get "teachers right out from England. . . . We shall then have a proper education." This project never materialized.

But what is significant for our purposes in this chapter is that Ekukhanyeni letter-writing was taking place in a context of rapid educational expansion, when the *kholwa* were highly conscious of the desirability of schooling and yet aware of the oppressive colonial uses to which it was being put and when various different models of the curriculum were being supported by different parties, among them the colonial government, the different brands of missionaries, and the *kholwa* themselves.

The letter-writers, or *kholwa*, in general wanted their children to be able to take part in this network as able contributors of ideas. The discussions on education and the role of the imperial center were discussed through letters, and Ekukhanyeni served as the central institution for these writers. The vibrant theological, political, and intellectual life at the mission station affected its students. It was these discussions that shaped the later generation of writers that were connected to Ekukhanyeni and its wider social networks.

Creating a Network: Ekukhanyeni Letter-Writers and the Practice of Letter-Writing

Letter-writing was one of the major forms of communication among the *kholwa* during the second half of the nineteenth century in Natal. Letter-writing was an integral part of the social lives of the Ekukhanyeni Christians, and it was this medium of communication that enabled the imagining of a network whose members' lives found their expression in the letters. The extent and reach of this network ignored boundaries. It involved men and women living in the villages, towns, and cities of Natal, Zululand, Eastern Cape, Cape Town, Johannesburg, St. Helena, Great Britain, and the United States. Between 1860 and 1910, the corpus of Ekukhanyeni letters shows that the mission station was an important center or reference point for most writers. What attracted disparate groups of people to Ekukhanyeni was its intellectual environment and promise. As other spaces for free discourse became circumscribed, writers found audiences at Ekukhanyeni who were prepared to listen, respond to, and engage with their concerns. Because of the nature of the composition of mission-station communities and the fact that

Ekukhanyeni did not emphasize denominational politics, letters came from different regions of Southern Africa written in various languages, but chiefly in isiZulu, English, and isiXhosa. The choice of language depended on the outcome the writer wanted to achieve. Writers used isiXhosa and isiZulu for friendly conversations. Writers who thought that writing in their language would help them become enlightened and also preserve the language from extinction or being corrupted by the English language particularly used isiZulu.[17] Indeed, writing in isiZulu helped some pass on codes that were not easily discernable by the authorities. For instance, the exiled members of the Usuthu in St. Helena could talk about the Anglo-Zulu War of 1879 as *impi Yabelungu* (English war). Writers in isiZulu newspapers could seek to revive the ancient idea of *ibandla* to elicit support, solidarity, and comradeship; thus, they asked all writers to warm themselves in the society of men (*bothe ibandla*). English was used in most cases when one wanted to lay a complaint to colonial authorities. But as time went on, writers soon realized that English was a resource that enabled them to forge wider transcontinental linkages with people in Britain.

For us to understand the epistolary relations these writers created, we have to appreciate the importance they attached to writing and reading. These two practices constituted a significant part of their lives. To these letter-writers, writing was like constituting a sphere, an imagined sphere free of the harsh realities of colonial life. The letter constituted a space for discussion and dreaming. Letter-writers valued those who knew how to write and encouraged the novice.

One of Harriette Colenso's letters to the members of the Usuthu shows the significance they attached to the technology of writing. Harriette Colenso was the eldest daughter of Bishop John Colenso. Born in Nortfold, England, in 1847 (Marks 1963, 403), she came to Natal in 1855, when she was 8 years old. In 1862, she returned to England with her father and studied at Winnington School in Cheshire until 1865 (H. Colenso 1893, vii). After her studies in Britain, she came back to Natal, where she resumed her isiZulu lessons. By the early 1880s, she was a fluent isiZulu-speaker and -writer. She wrote most of her letters after 1880 in isiZulu and was a valued member of this network. They gave her an affectionate name: *nkosazana* (daughter). Harriette Colenso wrote:

> To the Zulu chiefs, Ndabuko and Tshingana
> The letters which Dinuzulu writes give us great satisfaction, as does his desire for learning. Truly both his father and mine would be pleased with him, and in time to come he will be of help to the Zulu people. I am going to write to him soon.[18]

The letter gives an insight into a sense of togetherness this network of letter-writers had developed. Harriette Colenso's use of "us" is telling. The letter was not just for her; it was for everyone at Ekukhanyeni, and they took delight at seeing Dinuzulu—the Zulu king who was imprisoned at St Helena—learning the conventions of letter-writing.

Indirect authorship of letters was a common practice. Some of the members of this network asked other skilled letter-writers to write for them. Rev. Moses Sibisi's letter to Ekukhanyeni demonstrates this practice. Sibisi asked Magema Fuze to write for him.[19] It was not that Sibisi could not write. He wrote many letters himself, but because this letter was sensitive, he had to get someone who was skilful in writing to write the letter. The letter was entitled, *"Indaba ka Ayliff Gcwensa* or The story of Ayliff Gcwensa."* Ayliff Gcwensa was a preacher, but after he expelled his wife from his house, he was ordered by the trustees of the Church of England in Natal—in which Moses Sibisi was a catechist—to stop conducting his services until he allowed his wife to return home. Because of the nature of Gcwensa's case, Sibisi asked Fuze to write for him.[20] Sibisi concluded the letter:

Namhlanje sesizwa esekipha uKoza, owafakwa yithi kuleyondlu, sathi kayipathe, afundise lapho. Kuloba mina otume uFuze ukuba angilobele.	Today we hear that he [Gcwensa] has removed Koza from the house, [Koza] whom we had put in charge of it, so that he can teach in it. I have asked Fuze to write for me.
	Rev. M. Sibisi.[21]

The practice of asking skilled letter-writers to write letters also comes out in one of the letters that R. Twala wrote to Harriette Colenso. Twala talked about the common practice among the letter-writers of getting people who knew the conventions of letter-writing to write for the beginners. Twala wrote:

Siza ungincede uthumele leyo ncwadi eyabhalwa nguMarwick nokubonga; waze wena wathi ayifanele (ngani). Bengifuna neCopy yayo: nje abantu abangakwazi uku-loba bayabhalelwa: nje kufunwe amazwi amahle.	Please send the thank you letter that Marwick wrote, you even said it was not appropriate (why). I want a copy of the letter, people who do not know how to write, find people to write for them. The important thing is to look for good or beautiful words.[22]

Having become part of the community of letter-writers and -readers and being able to write was not enough. The ultimate goal was to perfect one's skills by mastering the conventions of letter-writing. Twala stressed that "people who do not know how to write, find people to write for them," but said that was not sufficient: "The important thing is to look for good or beautiful words." Twala's letter suggests that writing gave these writers pleasure and fun. And looking for beautiful words was in itself a search for excellence, perfection, and discovery.[23]

The network was also used as a space for experiments. Writers wrote in different styles to each other and asked for reactions. Most writers experimented in playing with philosophical ideas about the impossibility of knowing or understanding. Mbuzeni's letter to the exiles at St. Helena demonstrates how writers used this sphere clearly. He wrote:

> If only I knew how to do so in writing I should wish to make inquiry into your bodily health, but, indeed, as scholars, we are only feeling our way; for one day one fancies—now I begin to understand—whereas in fact he does not at all see the real intention of what is written or painted. Just as one who sees the sun from its rising to its setting, and cannot say that he does not see the shine but dazzled.[24]

Mbuzeni's letter and many other letters suggest that the rules governing this epistolary network encouraged horizontal relationships and reciprocal responsibilities. The letter that Nceke Mthimkhulu wrote to Mubi Nondenisa supports this view. On March 28, 1887, Mthimkhulu wrote:

> Mr Bubi Nondenisa
> My friend, I wish to ask you if you do not receive my letters. My reason for asking is because I do not get any from you now. I am constantly writing but receive no reply. I am at a loss what to do.
> Nceke Mthimkhulu
> Cape Town[25]

Receiving a letter placed a responsibility on the recipient to respond. This also suggests that the content of the letters contained issues that the writers thought to be of great importance and deserving of attention.

Through the different styles of letter-writing these writers employed one gets insight into their social status. Chief among these styles is a certain kind of writing employed by the prison inmates. These writers had learned a particular style which allowed them to articulate their grievances. This was a style geared to lure someone's sympathies.

The writing paper they used was standard prison letterhead that identified the prison in which the inmates lived. An examination of these letters also shows the constraints this prison stationery imposed on the writers. It had very clearly designated margins. This shows some sort of order and perhaps discipline that the standardized letterhead imposed on the inmates. For instance, the letter that Mayatana Cele wrote to Ekukhanyeni shows constraint not only upon the inmate but also on the recipient of the letter. The formal writing paper had instructions that the writer should follow. These were the instructions:

> *Instructions to sender of reply.* When replying the address must give full name and number exactly as above. Letters may be written in English, Dutch, German, French, Zulu, Sesetho or Sixosa. Letters in any other language may be delayed or even returned. Money must not be enclosed in Prisoners Letters, but sent to the Superintendent of the Prison. Letters to Prisoners must bear ordinary postage. Unpaid letters are liable to be returned.[26]

The prison letters stand in sharp contrast to the letters that went back and forth between the letter-writers outside the purview of the colonial state. Some of these letter-writers used scrap paper to convey their message to their friends. Most of the letters are neither dated nor signed. This shows that a degree of intimacy existed between the individuals who wrote the letters. It also demonstrates the frequency with which they talked to each other through letters. The style of these writers did not follow any rigid way of writing. The salutations in most of the letters are in the body of the letter. And sometimes there is no formal conclusion. The typical ending is *"Yimina omaziyo"*; that is, "I am—the one you know."[27]

The sense of freedom the writers had had an impact on the extent to which they discussed personal issues in the letters. The letters might as well have been public; they were intended for all readers residing at the mission station. These letters are indeed telling in what they say about the people at the mission station. Ekukhanyeni was a place where people discussed issues openly.[28] At the mission station lived people who spent most of their time reading, writing, and talking about each other's personal concerns, especially household matters. This was also a network composed of migrants, who found in this network of letter-writers a proper place to leave messages for their families. One such migrant was A. Gilbert, who wrote a letter to his father through the mission station:

Dear Baba.	Dear father
Nginazisa ukuthi sengikhona lapha eTransvaal. Ngahlangana nabakithi uManyayiza, uFrance, uMzuza, uNgatizana. Nabanyeke abaningi. Ngicela ukuba ungifakele amehlo kuMtwana Baba, naku Nkosazana nakubalobokazi.	I would like to inform you that I am now here in Transvaal. I have met my homeboys Mnyayiza, France, Mzuza and Ngatizana and many others. Please father; look after my child, my daughter and my wives.[29]

124

The style of handwriting people used in their letters tells much about the writers and their network. When the writers wrote to a novice, they wrote in big cursive writing. This was probably intended to enable the new reader to read and become part of the network of readers. Nondela's letter to Fundi demonstrates this point quite clearly:

> I am getting a big man now and someday perhaps will come and play with you again as we did once. I think Miss Colenso will read this to you and perhaps you can so I write it large.

Nondela wrote this letter while he was in England. In the letter he informed Fundi "about the fire which I had not long ago, all my things were burnt that was up in Scotland."[30] One can get a picture of Fundi still in the process of learning how to read, so that Nondela had to "write it large." In case he could not read it, Miss Colenso was available to read the letter to him.

As I have stated above, most letters were read in public. If a writer wanted a letter to be private, he or she needed to insist that a particular letter was directed specifically to a certain person. For if that was not specified, everybody could gain access to people's "private matters." In one case Harriette Colenso had to specify that one of the *leaves* in her letter to the chiefs at St. Helena was directed particularly to Mubi Mtuli kaNondenisa, alias Bubi.[31] Harriette Colenso wrote:

Ehe, Mubi amazwana ezindaba niyakuwafumana encwadini leyo engibalobele namuhla abantwana. Lelikhasana liyakuqonda wena nje wedwa.	Ehe, Mubi you will get snippet of the news in the letter that I have sent to the princes today. However, this leaf will go direct to you, alone.[32]

Mubi Nondenisa was one of the skilled letter-writers. As time went on, he became a very close friend of Colenso. Mubi was born in the mid-1840s along the south coast. He was a student at Ekukhanyeni from 1856 to 1861. Toward the end of 1860s he was a teacher, an interpreter, and a prolific letter-writer. He worked as secretary to King Dinuzulu in St. Helena.[33]

Through the letter Harriette Colenso wrote to Nondenisa, one gets an insight not only into how letters were read but also how letter-writing enabled the carving of space for letter-writers to circulate news about political developments in England, Southern Africa, and the United States. In this letter, Harriette Colenso talked about the political developments regarding the case of the Zulu chiefs in the Colonial Office in London and the Jameson Raid that had taken place at the Witwatersrand and how it was received in London. The language she used to refer to the English raiders is very strong. She condemned their action:

| *AmaBunu avumile-ke ukuba icala lilethwe Englande, nezoni ziyeza kaloko, AmaBunu azidedela. AmaNgisi kodwa aseJohannesburg ababehlangene nalendaba asetilongweni njalo.* | The Boers reluctantly agreed to allow their [the English sinners'] trial to take place in England. The sinners have been allowed by the Boers to come here [England]. Some of the English people who participated in this [raid] are still imprisoned in Johannesburg.[34] |

Like that of most writers, Harriette's language in this letter draws from the biblical vocabulary. She refers to English participants in the raid as sinners.

A Reading Network

One of the things that connected these readers was the sharing of information. If one of them had read something of interest in a book or newspaper, he or she shared it with others. Through this they managed to create a network of readers who had a common language and some consensus about the issues they discussed. But the ideas they shared were not givens; they constructed them as their connections developed. This construction or production of ideas about themselves and the society they imagined was shaped to a large degree by the kinds of books and newspapers that they read. As one reads the letters, one gets a strong sense of the importance of books and therefore of reading. The letter-writers demanded books—not just any books, but specific kinds of books. Mbili Sinoti's letter shows the profound importance they attached to the books they read.[35] He wrote:

> Please sir I beg you that you should be able to send me some of those books you have. A Visit to the Zulu King translation glossary and Grammatical Notes. Incwadi yomuhla uBishop WaseNatal ehambela KwaZulu and some of other books English—Zulu Gramma best one please. If you get them send me those I ask for them please. If you have not got that please send me two-shilling English-Zulu Dictionary that is all I close.
>> I remain your humble servant
>> Mbili Sinoti
>> C/o Public School.[36]

The emphasis is on *A Visit to the Zulu King* and *Grammatical Notes*. Colenso wrote the former after his first visit to the Zulu king, Mpande, in 1859. As with most of Colenso's books, William Ngidi, a partner whom he acknowledged, assisted him in this work. The book was published in both English and isiZulu. It contained a very detailed account of the visit to the king by Magema Magwaza, Ndiyana, and William Ngidi, who recorded what they encountered on their way. The striking difference between this book and other writings at the time is that it avoids the nineteenth-century stereotypes that became characteristic of most missionary accounts. In the end of the book, the visit to the king remains a dignified endeavor, almost a pilgrimage (Colenso 1901).

It was not just Mbili Sinoti who was passionate about books. Mahlathini Gumede's letter echoes similar sentiments. Gumede spoke not only for himself but also for "all young Zulus," as he called them, who read books. From Johannesburg, Gumede wrote to Harriette Colenso:

> Dear Madam, I am very glad to find this present opportunity to write to you and acknowledge you that those books you have sent me have reached me safely and I am grateful for these little books for they are of great importance to me and many of my friends like them very much indeed. So they are welcomed by all young Zulus.[37]

Books "are of great importance," said Gumede, expressing his delight at receiving them.[38]

How were these books read or interpreted? What interpretations did readers prefer over others? It is difficult to answer these questions at this stage, but one can speculate that reactions to some of these books were debated through letters. And letter-writers had some sort of consensus about which books were good to read and circulate. Gumede said the books "are welcomed by all young Zulus." The implication of this assertion is profound; the obvious point to begin with is what Gumede's understanding of "all young Zulus" was. What does this statement tell us about the readers who were included or excluded in this network of letter-writers? Did they have to be imagined or imagine themselves as Zulus? During this time Zulu "identity" was gaining momentum among Africans in Natal and especially among English women. Harriette Colenso called herself a Zulu and Miss Susie Tyler, the daughter of Rev. Josiah Tyler—an American missionary who went to live in Zululand in 1859—introduced herself to the students at the Hampton Institute in Virginia in the United States as a Zulu. She said, "I was born amongst the Zulus, and so I call myself a Zulu."[39]

Not only books but also newspapers were shared. The letter-writers notified each other about the interesting latest news. Twala asked Harriette Colenso to read the newspaper *Ilanga* lase Natal, especially an article by one Johannes:

> Have you read (Abantu Johannes—a native) the newspaper about you? Please see the 26th "*Ilanga*."[40]

Making sure that they were abreast of the contemporary situation was one of the ways they maintained their connection. Letters were an efficient way of circulating news.

The influence of the network the Ekukhanyeni letter-writers established between 1890 and 1900 is hard to assess. But as campaigners against the unfair laws of the Natal colonial government, they were well known not only in South Africa but also in England and the United States. L. T. Mallet's letter to Harriette Colenso sheds light on the extent of their influence. Mallet asked Colenso to give lectures on the subject of the Zulus. Mallet wrote:

> You will probably not remember me at all; but I had the pleasure of meeting you at dinner at Mr Woolcott Browne's in Rochester Terrace, and also elsewhere to trouble you in order to ask whether you would be able and willing to deliver to the N. Reus Women's Liberal Association lectures on the subject of the Zulus, their rights and wrongs? I do not know when you are leaving England, but if you are staying over this winter, and would lecture on the first Thursday in the month for us, at any time after November we should be most grateful.[41]

Shula Marks has written about Harriette Colenso's campaign in England (Marks 1963). Colenso was a leading campaigner in London for the release of the Zulu chiefs who were imprisoned in St. Helena. However, what has not been stressed is the extent to which her activities were linked to a broader network of friends or letter-writers. The broader implications of this friendship and the knowledge they produced in their personal correspondence deserve close consideration, especially the ideas about their position in the colony and their voices. A letter written by Elka M. Cele offers some insights on the extent of this network:

> I am sending you duplicates of the two receipts from Seme of which you asked. Mr Dube is here and sends his greetings and good whishes for your noble work for the Zulu people. He is proceeding to Natal tomorrow.[42]

Cele's letter shows the extent of the network and the individuals involved; Seme and Dube were well-known political figures at the time.[43]

Re-Figuring Power Relations

The political language of the state was one of the sites where the letter-writers contested with the colonial state. A letter written by Magema Fuze shows the depth of the political discussion among these letter-writers. Fuze, alias Magema Magwaza, was born around 1848 near Table Mountain east of Pietermaritzburg. He came to Ekukhanyeni in 1856 and received his formal education at the Ekukhanyeni mission center during its formative years. During the years he spent at the school, he perfected his reading and writing skills in English and isiZulu. In the late 1860s, he was working as a compositor for the Ekukhanyeni Press. In 1889, Fuze was tutor to Dinuzulu in Zululand. And in 1890, he taught typesetting at St Alban's College in Pietermaritzburg. By 1896 he was secretary to King Dinuzulu and his uncles, who had been "found guilty of treason towards the government of the colony of Zululand" and were exiled to St. Helena (Wright 1998, 2). It was also during this time that he started writing his book entitled *Abantu Abamnyama Nalapho Bavela Khona* (The Black People and Whence They Came). Fuze had difficulty publishing his book and was later to receive help from his friends, including Mr. N. J. N. Masuku of Edendale. The book was published in 1922 and was later translated into English by Lugg and edited by T. R. Cope in 1978 (Fuze 1979). But Fuze did not live long enough to respond to critics of his book, for he died soon after it was published. His contemporaries noted that Fuze lived his last years in a "humble tenement in a back street of Pietermaritzburg" (Wright 1998, 2). Like his friends Mubi Nondenisa, Mahlathini Gumede, and Miss Giles, there is little trace of him in most of the vast historical literature on South Africa.

The letter I have selected shows a very clear understanding of his rights as an individual citizen vis-à-vis the colonial state. Such a clear sense of one's rights as a "colonial subject" comes out in other letters that Fuze and his fellow letter-writers wrote, and they sought to engage the colonial government while laying claim to a connection to the empire. Below is the final version of the letter that appears in draft in figure 4.1, which Fuze wrote to "His Excellency, Governor of St. Helena and Her Majesty's Resident Commissioner at Eshowe in Zululand, Sir M. Clarke."

> Francis Plain, 5th Oct. 1896
> To H.E. the government of St. H.—the Castle.
> Sir
> I beg to inform His Excellency that I merely received (for the first time) Miss C's letters of the last mail from England, and was so shocking to find it quite open after seven days detention.
> 2). I may as well explain to His excellency that at my first arrival into this Island I was told not to interfere with the Guardian's work of the Zulus, but just keep on writing all what is necessary for translation, and forward it to the Guardian for translation, and that my own letters will go forth and back because I am not a prisoner; and for this reason therefore I had always bought stamps and posted my own letters. But I understand that my letter referred to was opened for purpose of getting English translation from Zulu.

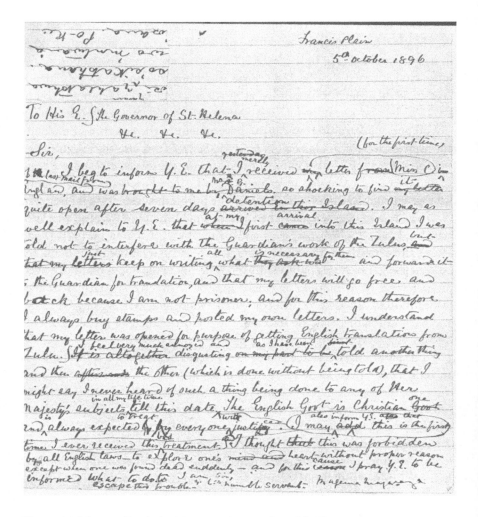

Figure 4.1. Magema Fuze's draft letter to the governor of St. Helena, 1896.
Courtesy the Campbell Collections of the University of KwaZulu-Natal.

3). I feel very much hurtful and disgusted as I have been told another thing
and then the . . . (which is being done without being informed of), that I might
say I never heard of such a deed being done to any of H. M's subjects in all my
life time till this date.

4). I may also inform His Excellency that this is the first time I have received this bad treatment. The English government is Christian one with justice.
And is always expected to treat everyone with justice. And I thought this was
forbidden by all English laws—to explore [someone's] heart without proper rea-

son I expect when one was found dead suddenly. And for this case, I pray His Excellency to advice me what to do to escape this trouble.

I am, Sir, Y.E.

Magema Magwaza

Oct. 6th I took in the above letter personally to His Excellency, who kindly told me that it was the Natal government's intention that my letters should be opened, and advised me to write to the government of Natal on the subject.

Should Natal government thinks good and make its mind to do all justice toward me as well as to other bodies in accordance to all civilized and Christian rules set apart for our use, I pray your Honor let my letters be not opened without my [leave].

I have the honour to be

Sir

Your Honour's most obedient Servant

(Signed) Magema Magwaza

Eshowe

Being able to write and read enabled him and other writers to contest the control of the colonial state. The conversations moved from petitions in the street of Pietermaritzburg and under the pine trees in front of the Natal native administration offices to one-to-one official correspondence with colonial administrators. This was a novel form of political engagement with the state. By analyzing the political grammar of the colonial state, for instance such notions as "English law" and the "Christian state," Fuze attempted to come to grips with the language the colonial state used and the ways in which it affected his everyday life. But this required a very thorough knowledge of the conventions of official prose and petitioning and the discipline of converting one's emotional feelings into written words and sentences. Fuze found a way around this by first drafting the letter. The draft letter shows that he wanted to retain some of his emotion in the message. For instance, in line three of the draft he deleted "arrived in this Island" and put in "detention" instead. This was meant to emphasize the physicality and force in withholding the letter from him for seven days. But Fuze did not end here when he edited and reworked the letter. In line eleven he deleted "It is altogether disgusting" and replaced it with "I feel very much annoyed and disgusted."

The ideas of justice and Christianity run through the letter. For Fuze, a Christian state was just, and as a citizen he expected respect from the colonial state which he did not get. In the second letter he wrote to "His Honor, Sir Clark—the Majesty's Resident Commissioner, Eshowe, Zululand," on October 15, 1896, Fuze concluded by insisting that "should Natal government think good and make its mind to do all justice toward me as well as to other bodies in accordance to all civilized and Christian rules set apart for our use."[44] Here Fuze is drawing from the current discourse and using it to lay claim to colonial privileges.

The letter-writing medium enabled Fuze and this network of writers to carve a space for themselves as individual Christian upholders of justice. It was in this space that they imagined a world of fair treatment in contrast to the one in which they lived. However, even this space was monitored. Letters were opened. For Fuze this constituted an invasion of his private space. The letter he received from his friend Harriette Colenso was a "heart." As Fuze wrote:

> I thought this was forbidden by all English laws—to explore someone's heart without proper reason I expect when one was found dead suddenly.[45]

The metaphor of the heart is striking, not only because it clearly expresses Fuze's attachment to letters but also because it expresses ideas about privacy, confidentiality, and a strong sense of self. The metaphor is powerful and it demonstrates the profound significance he attached to the conversations he had with his friends, especially Harriette Colenso. The violation or invasion of his private space was tantamount to meaning that he was dead. He wrote "I feel very much hurtful and disgusted as I have been told another thing."[46] This language is very strong and is intended to be directed to someone in power. This implies that he was convinced and conscious of his right to privacy.

After this "trouble," as Fuze calls it, on November 26, 1896, he asked Miss A. Werner and other friends to address his letters to Miss M. Burchill, Ruperts Valley, St. Helena.[47] This not only demonstrates the extent of the epistolary network but also the fact that it involved many individuals who were prepared to help each other and keep the connections and conversations alive.

Fuze's letter is similar to Mubi Nondenisa's letter that talked about justice. For Nondenisa justice was at the center of their engagement with the colonial state. One of the issues that provided these letter-writers an opportunity to engage the colonial state was the case of the Usuthu. When the letter-writers realized that the cases against the chiefs could not receive a fair trial in the colony, they sought to take the cases to the metropole, England. According to Nondenisa, they expected a settlement to come from London. Writing to Miss K. Giles in Pietermaritzburg,[48] Nondenisa expressed his opinion on the matter:

> We are all well here, even the chiefs, who still asks us "when Miss Colenso be here?" and this is to fulfil justice done by the inkosazana (Miss Colenso). They

and all of us expect for the settlement of their case in England, daily as many ru-mours of newspapers and Zulus in the Reserve (amambuka) speak everything they wish of them.[49] Also we long to see our people at home, as it is nearly a year since we parted them.[50]

However, for them to be able to take the cases effectively to London, they had to deal with the language of the colonial state. In this case they had to change the status of "prisoner" that the colonial state attached to the Zulu chiefs. This involved forging a relationship between Zulu and English royal houses. The letter-writers seized on the death of the Duke of Clarence in the English royal house as an opportune time to forge a link between the Zulu king and the English queen. They asked the chiefs at St. Helena to send a let-ter of condolence through Harriette Colenso to the English royal house ex-pressing warm sympathies. The letter was accepted. The queen of England re-sponded in "the proper way." The response to the two Zulu chiefs, Ndabuko and Tshingana, was as follows:

> Marlborough House
>   Sir Francis Knollys is desired to convey through Miss Colenso to the Zulu chiefs Cetshwayo's brothers at St. Helena the sincere thanks of the Prince and Princess of Wales for the warm sympathy they have expressed on the occasion of their Royal Highnesses' great bereavement. Sir Francis Knollys is further desired to thank them for the photograph which accompanied Miss Colenso's letter and enclosure.
>   The Queen's words of acceptance, Her Secretary says, have been sent to you in the proper way, by the hand of Secretary of State for the Colonies.
>   4th April 1892[51]

The queen's acknowledgment of the chiefs' letter of condolence was not enough; they insisted that "beside our thanks we would be very thankful to come to England, so that we may see you with our eyes."[52] So pronounced was the St. Helena–based letter-writers' wish to visit England that in bidding farewell to Harriette, who was departing on one of her countless visits to London to present the chiefs' case, Dinuzulu melodramatically wrote: "We watch longingly the path of the sunset by which you went. That is path which we desire for ourselves." When the chiefs returned to Zululand without hav-ing been allowed to visit England, they could only say:

> We trust you to make it clear to the Queen that we are setting off without the least satisfaction or rejoicing over our very return to Zululand, for that we have hoped so greatly that we should go and see the Queen and her Indunas [head-men] and her glory.[53]

VUKILE KHUMALO

Rosemary Hall
Saint Helena
October 29ᵗʰ 1891.

Miss Colenso.

Kuwe Nkosazana.

Ngyabuza ukuba mavadi yetu wayitola na? Sezwa izwi elavela ku Rulumente lokuti lomuntu esimfunayo ukutunga izicoco angeze ngoba kutiwa kungaciteka imali eningi ukumwelisa umuntu ukupata lomsebezi wodwa. Sezwa kutiwa ukuba izinto zonke ezidingekayo ukusebenza lomsebenzi ziyakutunywa abasi Natal. Po? Siyawutola pi umuntu kuleizwi lase Sentiliwa ukutungana? Ukona mi ofundileyo na? Ngoba natiti akwaziwa bantu bonke kupela abapati balomsebezi. Sclhlupekile kakulu; sesesaba nokupumanga pandhle. Sicela ukuba usi nike izwi ukuba senzanjani na, Pisa, Nkosazana ngokusipendula masinyane. Sisize nokusincengela ukuba sundol' umuntu.

Tina esingowako
Undabuko notshingwa.

Siyakonza indaba kuwe, nendhlu yonke yakini Siyakonza sonke, tina indhlu yakiti. Sisapila kahle tina. Nina nisapila na?

134

Rosemary Hall
Saint Helena
October 29th, 1891

Miss Colenso
These [words] to you, Daughter [of Bishop Colenso],

We are asking whether our letter ever found you? We had heard an announcement [order] from the governor [of Natal and Zululand] saying that the person
desired by us to do our head-rings cannot be allowed to come because, it said,
too much money would be spent in bringing over a person to attend to that
matter only. But it is ordered that all the materials required for the head-rings
shall be sent to us by the Natal people, but without the person to use them. But
what is the use of that? Where in this island of St Helena can we find a person
who knows how to make a head-ring? Is there anyone here who has an idea how
to do it? Even in our own land, and amongst our own people, it is only those
specially charged with this business who know how to do it. Our trouble is great
in as much as we are ashamed to go out into the light of day. We therefore beg
of you to give us advice as to what course we should follow in this plight. Help
us, Madam, by a speedy answer, aid us and entreat for us that we may receive the
person we desire.

We are yours,
Ndabuko and Shingana

We commend all our matters to you and yours. We desire respectful remem-
brance, all of us and yours. We are in good bodily health, and you? Is it well with
you all?

Figure 4.2. Letter from Ndabuko and Shingana (on St. Helena) to Harriette
Colenso (in London), 1891 (left); with translation by Vukile Khumalo
(above). Courtesy the Campbell Collections of the University of KwaZulu-
Natal.

While letters traveled back and forth between London and St. Helena, Natal-
based writers were sending their letters to the Ekukhanyeni mission station,
inquiring about the cases against the chiefs. Some of the letter-writers wanted
to visit Dinuzulu and Usuthu in St. Helena. Thembelina Dlamini was among
the letter-writers who asked to be allowed to visit "her king." She wrote:

Please Mss H.E. Colenso I would be glad when you let me [go] see my king.[54]

The request perhaps does not deserve as much attention as her reference to Dinuzulu as "my king." After the destruction of the Zulu kingdom, the status of the son of Cetshwayo, the last independent Zulu king, was lowered to a chief of a small village in Zululand. Thembelina's choice of the word "king" to refer to Dinuzulu is telling. To what extent this reflected the view of this community of letter-writers is an open question. Mahlathini Gumede expressed similar views. He ended a letter to Harriette Colenso by asking for news about Dinuzulu, the son of the late king. Mahlathini wrote:

> Dear Madam before I end my letter I pray you if possible to let me hear a word about the Martyr of our nation the son of our late King.

These two writers' conscious choice of words is revealing of their understanding of the meaning attached to the two words "chief" and "king." In their search for "beautiful words," as Twala has stated, it seems that they came to realize that Dinuzulu was not a "chief," as the colonial state called him, but a "king." And for Gumede he was a "Martyr of our nation." Gumede put the "M" for martyr in capital letters. This shows a deep level of understanding of how language, especially the political language of the colonial state, worked.

In doing this, Fuze, Thembelina Dlamini, Mahlathini Gumede were trying to grapple with words and the language of the colonial state. Analyzing their use of terms such as "chief" or "king" provides some ways of getting to know how they understood the official discourse of the state and sought to construct their own new discourse about themselves. The imperial connection and the contemporary discourse of the civilizing mission enabled these writers to make sense of the world in which they lived.

The Letter as a Sphere for Political Conversations

The space these letter-writers created also served as a sphere for debate and the exchange of political ideas. Since most of the spaces for public opinion were not free or were under the control of the colonial state, the imaginary world created by the letter offered them a space to dream aloud. Fuze's letter illustrates this point clearly. He wrote this letter after Dinuzulu had been allowed back to Zululand in 1902. Fuze wrote to the Zulu king:[55]

> You should fight for that which is yours by right as all people do . . . [but] now our only resource is to fight in a lawful way as do all wise nations under the sun. Indeed, I say this to you because I fear that if you are quiet and do nothing we shall find out that you are left alone and all the Zulu nation scattered from you by cunning and alienated from you so that you shall have no place of refuge and be in want of all things.[56]

136

Through letter-writing the writers were able to ink into existence a new world where they were able to devise political strategies. The Ekukhanyeni letter-writers also used the letter to warn their co-writers of certain political dangers. Harriette Colenso asked Fuze to write to Jabez to alert him of an imminent danger.

Wetu Jabez, Ngithunya unkosazana kuwe ukuba ngikwazise ukuthi ikona ingozi embi opakati kwayo wena, nakuba wena kodwa awazi lutho ngayo. Ngalokho iti inkosazana kimi angikulobele loko, utshetshe ukhawuleze ufike kuyo, ngoba yona iyakulinda ukuba ikululeke ngokwamandla ayo.

Uyabona-ke, ngikutshelile, fika lapha masinyane, nawesekuyakuba kuwe lokho kokuzilibazisa, uyazi futhi ukuthi inkosazana iyakutanda, aitandi ukuba uwe pansi ngengozi enjalo, inxa yona seikuzwile okubi okuthile okuphethe wena kabi, njengoba nawe uyazi.

Ngingowakho Omaziyo
Magema Magwaza.

My contemporary Jabez, Nkosazana has asked me to warn you about a danger that might befall you, you don't know about it. She asked me to inform you about it. She said, please hurry and come to see her. She wants to advise you about what she knows.

You see, I have told you. Come here quickly, if you delay that is up to you. You know that Nkosazana loves you. She does not like to see you fall into danger when she has heard about it, as you know.

I am yours—you know.
Magema Magwaza (Fuze)[57]

Numerous letters to John Dube, Harriette Colenso, and other Ekukhanyeni-based letter-writers asked about the political situation in the colony, and some letter-writers offered ways of dealing with their political predicament. One of the letter-writers even suggested that they should buy land in Zululand since they had no significant political control unless they were landowners. Abraham D. Zulu wrote to Ekukhanyeni about his displeasure at how he lived in Melmoth. In the letter he proposed that they should buy land where they could live together.

Nami angisalithandi lelizwe nakho imali yami iyincosana kodwa ngingamthola u £100 pawunde. Ngiyaphela lapho Zulu
Yimina Owakho
Abraham D. Zulu.

I do not like this land anymore, although I have little money I can raise £100. I end there, Zulu.
I am yours
Abraham D. Zulu
Melmoth[58]

The proposed land was to be in the north of Zululand at KwaNobamba. But this, of course, was a suggestion. It does not appear that the writers followed it through. This letter should be seen in the context of how they saw circumstances and possibilities and made certain choices.

Conclusion

Epistolary activities centered on Ekukhanyeni altered the position of the mission station in nineteenth-century KwaZulu-Natal. For letter-writers, the mission station was a central institution where they held intellectual conversations through letters, and, indeed, for some of the writers Ekukhanyeni was the "heart of the land or nation."[59] The writers' conversations about the practice of letter-writing, education, their ideas about the queen, English law, Christian justice, and the range of choices available to them at that time provide a fresh perspective on how they saw circumstances, recorded their thoughts or political imagination, and fashioned their lives. These conversations were made possible by the nature of the epistolary network these writers created, a network based on a strong culture of letter-writing that helped transform these writers' sense of affiliation to each other. And the governing conventions of this network encouraged horizontal relationships, epistolary reciprocity, and experimentation.

The vibrant conversations the writers held among themselves through letters helped them engage with colonial and imperial discourses. The letters the chiefs wrote to Queen Victoria and the role of Harriette Colenso (and others in London) in sending them through appropriate channels suggest that these writers had a good understanding of how the imperial system worked. Fuze's letter illustrates the fact that he depended on his fellow writers, and his invocation of his right as a free person suggests that this network had certain ideas about the limits of state power. According to Fuze and his friends, the fact that the state "explored" his letter went against their expectations of how a Christian state should treat its citizens. These letter-writers felt that the state should treat everyone with justice. As I demonstrate elsewhere, the reach of the network influenced how people responded to power.[60] Ekukhanyeni provided those who had grievances or wanted to influence colonial politics with resources to write their petitions to government.

NOTES

1. This presentation won the first prize at the Curtis Medal Orations.
2. For detailed studies on the "rebellion," see Marks (1970) and Carton (2000).
3. Dlomo (2001).
4. See chapter 2 of Khumalo (2004).
5. See Roux (1954) and Walshe (1971). According to Walshe, the origins and evolu-

tion of African political consciousness can be divided into three phases: 1) early African participation; 2) formation of political attitudes; and 3) formation of the African National Congress in 1912. Jabulani "Mzala" Nxumalo had just begun to launch a critique of the South African historiography when he died. For this reason, his conclusions celebrate the resistance paradigm. See his paper "The National Question in the Writing of South African History: A Critical Survey of Some Major Tendencies" (n.d.).

6. In the nineteenth century, *ibandla* meant several things. In the first sense it could mean "all the men, young and old, in one place, whether only two or three or a large band, or the whole body; hence, company." In the second sense, *ibandla* meant a "tribal council, assembly, strength of a kraal or tribe." When missionary activities took foot in Natal and Zululand, *ibandla* acquired a new meaning, which I refer to here as a third sense, that of a "company of believers or church."

7. These writers left behind more than 3,000 letters, which are housed at Pietermaritzburg Archives Repository; Rhodes House in Oxford; Killie Campbell Library at the University of Natal, Durban; and the Don Africana Library in Durban.

8. "*Ekukhanyeni*" means "at the place of enlightenment."

9. The defeat of the Voortrekkers at Khongela in the early 1840s meant the end of the Republic of Natalia and the occupation of Natal by the British in 1842. This British settlement had far-reaching consequences for Natal and the independent Zulu kingdom to the north. See Brookes and Webb (1965).

10. Magema Fuze and other Ekukhanyeni mission station students were involved in an inquiry into what the colonial government did to this chiefdom in the early 1870s.

11. Theophilus Shepstone was the secretary of native affairs in the Colony of Natal from 1847 to 1875. See Hamilton (1998). Bishopstowe was the name of the bishop's house and farmlands. As time went on, the name Bishopstowe was associated with these letter-writers.

12. William Ngidi, April 1, 1883, cited in Guy (1979, 69 and 1997, 241).

13. Usuthu was a section of the community in Zululand that remained loyal to the Zulu king, Cetshwayo.

14. St. Helena is in the South Atlantic Ocean.

15. Rees (1959, 69). The debate between Colenso and Ngidi became well known in South Africa and Britain. As British Minister Disraeli commented in 1879 after the Anglo-Zulu war: "A wonderful people the Zulus! They beat our generals, they convert our bishops, and they write finis to a French dynasty." See Brookes and Webb (1965, 107–108).

16. *The Star* (Johannesburg), December 6, 1895, SNA 1/1/212, Pietermaritzburg Archives Repository.

17. Tambuza, "*Ulimi* / Language / Tongue," *Inkanyiso Yase Natali,* November 1, 1889.

18. Harriette Colenso to Ndabuko and Tshingana, Pietermaritzburg Archives Repository (hereafter Colenso Collection), A204, Box 67. All their fathers had died ten years previously. She wrote this letter in 1894, when she was in London.

19. Moses Sibisi's letter to Ekukhanyeni, Colenso Collection, A204, Box 67. Rev. Moses Sibisi was a senior preacher in the Anglican church.

20. According to the letter Fuze and Sibisi wrote, Gcwensa had a dispute with his wife. She had asked him not to come home at night. However, Gcwensa never stopped doing that, and at some point he asked his wife to leave. She thereupon reported him to the trustees. The trustees stopped him from preaching until he allowed his wife to return

home. Ayliff Gcwensa told the trustees to take his wife because, according to him, the church elders had taken his wife. Colenso Collection, A204, Box 67.

21. Sibisi wrote this letter to Ekukhanyeni explaining the behavior of Ayliff Gcwensa to the mission station. The letter does not mention its recipient.

22. R. Twala to Harriette Colenso, n.d., Colenso Collection, A204, Box 71. Rev. Twala was a Wesleyan preacher based in Pretoria. He participated in the funeral arrangements for King Dinuzulu.

23. Here I face a basic question of what happened when these letter-writers searched for beautiful words and entered into a situation or realm where everything—figuratively speaking—was possible.

24. Mbuzeni's letter to the exiles at St. Helena, September 1891, Colenso Collection, Box 67.

25. Nceke Mthimkhulu to Mubi Nondenisa, March 28, 1887, SNA, 1/1/78–1/1/79, Pietermaritzburg Archives Repository.

26. Mayatana Cele to Ekukhanyeni, n.d., Colenso Collection, Box 71. Mayatana Cele wrote this letter when he was imprisoned at Number 2, De Beers Convict Station, Kimberley.

27. This is the ending of most letters.

28. This suggests that at this mission station there were public performances or gatherings of people reading letters.

29. A. Gilbert to his father, n.d., Colenso Collection, Box 69.

30. Nondela Colenso's letter to Fundi Zulu, n.d., Colenso Collection, Box 67.

31. "Leaf" is a direct translation from isiZulu. It means "a page."

32. Harriette Colenso to Mubi Nondenisa, February 1896 (?), Colenso Collection, Box 67. When Harriette wrote this letter, Mubi was at St. Helena; when he received the letter, he was making his preparation to return to Natal.

33. Mubi Nondenisa played a significant role by investigating the case and looking for witnesses during the trial of the Usuthu. During his travels in Zululand, Nondenisa wrote a diary that has yet to be published in its original form. It is the most detailed account of the repercussions of the invasion of Zululand and the civil war that followed thereafter. The author allowed the victims of the civil war, who were mostly women, to tell their eyewitness accounts of what had happened. In a nutshell, the Nondenisa diary demonstrates the power of narrative as a form of catharsis.

34. Harriette Colenso to Mubi Nondenisa, January 24, 1896, Colenso Collection, Box 67.

35. I have yet to discover the recipient of this letter.

36. *Incwadi yomuhla uBishop WaseNatal ehambela KwaZulu* (The Book about the Bishop of Natal's Visit to Zululand).

37. Mahlathini Gumede to Harriette Colenso, n.d., Colenso Collection, Box 71. Gumede wrote this letter when he was in Johannesburg.

38. Mahlathini Gumede to Harriette Colenso, n.d., Colenso Collection, Box 67.

39. *Southern Workman and Hampton School Record* 23, January 1894, 213.

40. John Langalibalele Dube founded *Ilanga lase Natal* in 1900. The newspaper is still in existence today.

41. L. T. Mallet to Harriette Colenso, September 16,——, Colenso Collection, Box 71. Mallet wrote this letter when Harriette was in England campaigning for the release of Dinuzulu and members of the Usuthu.

42. Elka M. Cele to Harriette Colenso, n.d., Colenso Collection, Box 71.

43. Pixley Seme studied at Colombia University (United States), Oxford, and the Inner Temple and was one of the founders of the South African Native National Congress (SANNC), which became the African National Congress in 1912. By the turn of the century, he had established his law practice in Johannesburg. John Langalibalele Dube was the son of Rev. James Dube, a minister at the Inanda part of the American Zulu Mission. John Dube studied at Adams College (later changed to Amanzimtoti Institute) and Oberlin College in the United States. He became the first president of the SANNC. This network was also in part a political network through which they shared ideas about their political futures and that of South Africa.

44. Letter to Sir M. Clarke, October 15, 1896, 90/1/11, Killie Campbell Africana Library, Durban, South Africa (hereafter KC).

45. Letter to Sir M. Clarke, 90/1/11, October 5, 1896, KC.

46. Magema Fuze to Harriette Colenso, 90/1/11, October 5, 1896, KC.

47. Magema Fuze to Miss A. Werner and friends, 90/1/11, November 26, 1896, KC.

48. At this stage I do not have much information on Miss Giles; I only know that she was one of the letter-writers based in Pietermaritzburg.

49. "*Amambuka*" means "traitors."

50. Mubi Nondenisa to Miss K. Giles, October 18, 1889, Colenso Collection, Box 67. Nondenisa wrote this letter when he was at Eshowe during his long stay in Zululand.

51. Colonial Office to the Zulu chiefs in St. Helena, April 4, 1892, Colenso Collection, Box 67.

52. Dinuzulu kaCetshwayo to Miss Colenso, Maldivia, St. Helena, April 22, 1895, Colenso Collection, Box 71.

53. Dinuzulu, Ndabuko, and Shingana to Harriette Colenso, November 26, 1896, Colenso Collection, Box 71.

54. Thembelina Dlamini to Harriette Colenso, n.d., Colenso Collection, Box 71. The letter is written in isiZulu but this last sentence is in English.

55. I use the word "king" because the letter-writers preferred it over "chief."

56. A.G.O. 1/7/53, letter written by Magema Fuze, quoted in Marks (1970, 114).

57. Magema Magwaza to Jabez, February 13, 1885, Colenso Collection, Box 71. Fuze wrote this letter on behalf of Harriette Colenso to Jabez, their friend.

58. Abraham D. Zulu to Ekukhanyeni, n.d., Colenso Collection, Box 71.

59. Ipepa to Hlanga, September 1, 1903.

60. Khumalo 2003.

REFERENCES

Bridgman, F. B. N.d. "A Statement Regarding the Obstructive Policy of the Government toward Christian Work amongst Natives," A/608, American Board Mission Files, Pietermaritzburg State Archives.

Brookes, Edgar H., and Colin de B. Webb. 1965. *A History of Natal.* Pietermaritzburg: University of Natal.

Carton, Benedict. 2000. *Blood from Your Children: The Colonial Origins of Generational Conflict in South Africa.* Charlottesville: University Press of Virginia.

Colenso, Harriette. 1893. *Cases of Six Usutu (Other Than the Exiles at St. Helena): Punished for Having Taken Part in the Disturbances of 1888.* London: Arthur Bonner.

Colenso, John William. 1901. *Three Native Accounts of the Visit of the Bishop of Natal in September and October, 1859, to Umpande, King of the Zulus.* 3rd ed. Pietermaritzburg and Durban: Vause, Slater, & C.

———. 1970. *The Pentateuch and Book of Joshua Critically Examined.* London: Longman, Green and Co.

Dlomo, Albert. 2001. Interview with Vukile Khumalo and Muzi Hadebe, April 19, Durban, South Africa.

Etherington, Norman. 1978. *Preachers, Peasants and Politics in Southeast Africa, 1835–1880.* London: Royal Historical Society.

Fuze, Magema. 1979. *The Black People and Whence They Came: A Zulu View.* Pietermaritzburg: University of Natal Press.

Guy, Jeff. 1979. *The Destruction of the Zulu Kingdom: The Civil War in Zululand, 1879–1884.*

———. 1997. "Class, Imperialism and Literary Criticism: William Ngidi, John Colenso and Matthew Arnold." *Journal of Southern African Studies* 23, no. 2: 219–241.

Hamilton, Carolyn. 1998. *Terrific Majesty: The Powers of Shaka Zulu and the Limits of Historical Invention.* Massachusetts: Harvard University Press.

Inkanyiso Yase Natali (Durban), November 1, 1889.

Khumalo, Vukile. 2003. "The Class of 1856 and the Politics of Cultural Production(s) in the Emergence of Ekukhanyeni, 1855–1910." In *The Eye of the Storm: Bishop John William Colenso and the Crisis of Biblical Inspiration,* ed. Jonathan Draper. London: T & T Clark International.

———. 2004. "Epistolary Networks and The Politics of Cultural Production in KwaZulu-Natal, 1860–1910." Ph.D. diss., University of Michigan, Ann Arbor.

Kunene, Mazisi. 1979. *Emperor Shaka the Great: A Zulu Epic.* London: Heinemann.

Marks, Shula. 1963. "Harriette Colenso and the Zulus, 1874–1913." *Journal of African History* 4, no. 3: 403–411.

———. 1970. *Reluctant Rebellion: The 1906–1908 Disturbances in Natal.* Oxford: Clarendon Press.

The Natal Witness (Pietermaritzburg), December 17, 1998, 2.

Nxumalo, Jabulani ["Mzala"]. N.d. "The National Question in the Writing of South African History: A Critical Survey of Some Major Tendencies." Available online at http://dpp.open.ac.uk/pdfs/wp22.pdf.

Odendaal, Andre. 1984. *Black Politics in South Africa to 1912.* Totowa: Barnes and Noble.

Peires, Jeff B. 1989. *The Dead Will Arise: Nongqawuse and the Great Xhosa Cattle-Killing Movement of 1856–7.* Johannesburg: Ravan Press.

Rees, Wyn, ed. 1958. *Colenso Letters from Natal.* Pietermaritzburg: Shuter and Shooter.

Rive, Richard, and Tim Couzens. 1992. *Seme: The Founder of the ANC.* New York: Africa World Press.

Roux, E. 1954. *Time Longer Than Rope.* Madison: University of Madison.

Seme, Pixley. 1913. "The Regeneration of Africa." In *The African Abroad on His Evolution in Western Civilization: Tracing His Development under Caucasian Milieu,* ed. William H. Ferris. New Haven: Tuttle, Morehouse & Taylor.

The Star (Pietermaritzburg), December 6, 1895.

Walshe, Peter. 1971. *The Rise of African Nationalism in South Africa: The African National Congress 1912–1952.* Berkeley: University of California Press.

Wright, John. 1998. "The History of Isizulu," *Natal Witness,* December 17.

REASONS FOR WRITING: AFRICAN WORKING-CLASS LETTER-WRITING IN EARLY-TWENTIETH-CENTURY SOUTH AFRICA

Keith Breckenridge

5

Contemporary South African intellectuals who have gone in search of an explanation for our current president's enigmatic personality have tended to focus on an episode from his childhood. As a very young man, Thabo Mbeki acted as an amanuensis in his parents' cooperative store in the village of Mbewuleni, in the impoverished labor reserve of the Idutywa district in the southern Transkei. The store, like many others in the rural areas of South Africa, served as a post office and as a "place where you would come for advice if you did not understand the world." In the late 1940s, the future president found himself, at the tender age of 7, "reading and writing for the adults of his community." In the view of some of the most astute commentators, this exposure to the agonizing intimacies of working-class life recorded in the not-private letters of the rural poor "aged him beyond his years" and equipped the young Mbeki with a reservoir of untempered anger at the effects of colonial rule and institutional racism (Gevisser 1999; Sparks 2003; Asmal 1999).

I have written elsewhere about the unusual form of lettered private sphere that emerged among migrant workers in twentieth-century South Africa (Breckenridge 2000). I made the point that the popular conception of widespread "functional illiteracy" as a national failure has tended to downplay the success of letter-based forms of household communication and the power of a certain kind of patriarchal family politics over the field of literacy. Conservative heads of households, often themselves active or former migrant workers, have actively and deliberately cultivated a radically constrained form of literacy among their children, specifically organized around the mastery of the writing of the vernacular letter. The combination of an anemic state-sponsored educational system, the absence of on-the-job literacy training, and the efforts of many conservative patriarchs to limit the effects of schooling on their children have placed amanuenses at the center of household politics for the rural poor. Collaborative forms of literary intimacy—drawing on the writing skills of known and unknown individuals, groups of peers, expert letter-writers, and even children—have had unusually powerful effects on the makings of the private sphere among twentieth-century migrant workers in South Africa.

In this chapter I want to go over some of the same ground to consider a set of questions closer to the general project of this anthology. It has been the better part of a century since Isaac Schapera tried to persuade South African social scientists to take African letter-writing seriously (Schapera 1933). Letters, he observed, offered an unmatched opportunity for inquisitive social scientists to explore the hidden world of African consciousness; they were "among the most valuable evidence of what the people feel and say to one another in private." Sadly, Schapera's efforts were not taken very seriously. Yet more unfortunately, very few of the actual letters themselves have survived.

With the evidence that I do have, most of which is indirect, I want to show that letter-writing was a common feature of working-class life before the Second World War and then attempt to find answers to three relatively straightforward questions: Who wrote? Why did they write? What did they write? And in the background I want to consider what we could call the minimum conditions for lettered correspondence. Why was letter-writing common among Xhosa-speakers in the early 1900s but only noticeable a generation later among workers from southern Mozambique?

The Historical Sociology of Letters

We know that letter-writing, and especially the composition of love letters, was enthusiastically adopted by the converts on the missions in the Eastern Cape and Natal in the second half of the nineteenth century.[1] An obvious analytical question emerges from this enthusiastic correspondence: Did writing define a new class, separated and alienated from the broader mass of peasants in the late nineteenth and early twentieth centuries? Putting aside, for the moment, the implications of the Mayers' work on the distinction between "Red" and "School" ideologies among the isiXhosa-speaking people, there are very good grounds for seeing writing as a definitive marker of class.

Possession of the skill of writing, and want of this skill, is a mundane part of the way in which rural workers think about their own identities. One of the most traditional of all the men I interviewed in the early 1990s, Ngil-ambi Sohlathi, a Xhosa-speaking migrant born soon after the turn of the century, made a very clear distinction between the manual jobs underground which all "cause damage to one's blood" and the work of the clerks, the *amabhalana*, literally the ones who cause writing. "The clerks are the better ones, because they work sitting down like this here." In an effort to get his aged uncle to differentiate forms of work underground, my host and assistant, Jones Mzayifani (who attended three years of school) responded: "Educated people can't be like us, the uneducated people, who don't know anything" (Sohlathi 1992). In an important sense, then, writing did define a distinct social class. And the inability to write certainly does the same work in contemporary South Africa.

Yet the evidence that unschooled migrants wrote is overwhelming. As early as the first decade of this century, A. M. Mostert, an independent recruiter for the mines on the West Rand, for example, provided paper, envelopes, and postage to the Xhosa workers in his compounds. "I find that the boys are very fond of writing these letters," he told the committee drafting the 1912 Native Labour Regulation Bill, "and write more than 4,000 a month." (His compounds housed about 8,000 workers.) The early-twentieth-century archives are full of evidence of officials and chiefs being "hindered by letters" written by, or on behalf of, Xhosa workers employed on the gold mines.[2] Officials and employers at this time perceived Cape workers as more educated, more aware of their "rights," and particularly likely to make use of the postal system to defeat the operations of Lord Milner's elaborate system of pass controls.[3] In this sense, at least, Xhosa workers were the first to make use of letter-writing as a tool for managing the exigencies of migrancy. Of course, they had the advantage of a large-scale system of government-supported and self-funded mission schools dating back to the 1860s (Switzer 1993).

Reasons for Writing

For this first generation of letter-writers, household management, especially between husbands and wives and mothers and sons, was the most important reason for writing letters. Many of the letters that Isaac Schapera published in *Married Life in an African Tribe* dealt with the microeconomic predicament Tswana workers faced in the Depression years. One such set was composed by a man at Crown Mines to his wife in the Kgatla Reserve. His letters are remarkable for their preoccupation with the minute calculus of household economics. Here is one fairly typical example:

First receive my letter. I greet you and ask how you are. I have got a sore shoulder, I don't use its hand. All this time I have not been writing to you because I heard you say that you were going to the cattle-post. Now just lately R_____ came here and told me that you are still at home. I let you know that I sent a shawl with S_____ when he left here to go home; I don't know whether he has given it to you. I have heard your word when you say that a plough is also needed. My wife, there you have spoken the truth; but I don't know whether we can manage in one year all the things that we lack, for I am still thinking that when I come home I must bring with me some shillings with which we can help ourselves. And now the winter is coming, and it is going to be cold; there are no good blankets for the night. I will try to send you a blanket, because I have stopped using one of the blankets, the white which was already getting old. (Schapera 1941, 145)

From the early years of the twentieth century into the present, migrants, and those they left behind, have used letters as a forum to negotiate the most pressing issues of economic need and investment in the rural household. Letters served as one of the few tools those who remained at home might use to extract resources from the small wage workers received in the towns.

For those for whom writing was not an easy task, survival was more commonly the motivation for sending a letter. Collected during the famine of the Depression years, Schapera's letters speak repeatedly of bitter poverty and the complete dependence of parents, wives, and children on the wage-earners in the city. A widowed mother writing to her son working in Johannesburg revealed the interior of financial extremity, the humiliation of betrayal by some children, and a searing demand for empathy.

I greet you and ask how you are living. I am sick, my child, I have nothing to say except starvation. You have left me in loneliness. The starvation is very, very serious. I beg you to send me just one bag of corn, so that I can help my child who is at the cattle-post. . . . The whole day, my child, we sit at the store hoping to get a little corn (as relief rations) but we come back empty. I don't know what to do, but you must know that I depend upon you, and put all my hopes in you. You must "carry" us, as you usually do. Other men are striving for themselves, but M_____ does not care for anything; he looks to me, but I have nothing for him. Do not let the eyes of the people look at me (with scorn). You complain that I do not write to you, but you know that I have nothing with which to buy stamps. That is all I can tell you. Many greetings, my child. (Schapera 1941, 152)

The letters Schapera includes in *Married Life* reveal more eloquently than almost any other source the terrible ordeal migrant families faced in the Depression years. But it is also clear from other later sources that African families in the countryside faced a continuous subsistence crisis after 1933. It was this ongoing economic catastrophe that prompted many of them to write, always appealing for resources from their children and husbands in the town.

During the Second World War, government censors were charged with monitoring the flow of letters to and from African workers on the gold mines and other strategic institutions, such as the Durban harbor, for evidence of subversion or sabotage. To their constantly expressed exasperation, the censors were required to read all letters that crossed the Mozambican border, a much smaller set from known activists, and a sample of other letters to and from local African workers. It is abundantly clear from these reports that African workers tended to avoid the political issues that prompted the state to open their letters in the first place. Indeed, many workers clearly understood that their letters were being monitored. "The other day I received a letter which appeared to have been opened and closed again," one of the Maluleke sons noted to his father, "You must never at any time dare write anything about the war, because you will cause us to be arrested, that is hot being discussed it is prohibited. You may die and we also die, it does not matter, I have heard all you have said about starvation."[4] The terse accounting of this surveillance suggests that for many rural people the primary reason for writing to their loved ones in town after 1933 was that their own survival was at risk.

In the censors' reports on the body of African letters, there is one constant and familiar refrain. "I have received your letter," Mrs. Lubisi of the Nazarene Mission in Acornhoek wrote to her son, "but what I would like to tell you my son is that we are dying of hunger here at home."[5] The same phrases appear again and again in these letters: "Whether the rain comes we have no seed," and "Please render us your aid."[6] Wives addressing their husbands described mothers-in-law fainting "owing to starvation" and, for good measure, threatened their husbands' prized livestock at home: "Even the pig which was given to you will have to be slaughtered because now the pigs will be taxed and I have no money and if you want it, send the money for paying the tax."[7] For those trapped within the collapsed labor-reserve economies after the Depression, letters served as the most powerful available mechanism to ensure that their migrant relatives did not "forget us at home."

Migrants had other reasons to write, not least of which was the need to invoke the aid of their relatives in their dealings with an intrusive and coercive state. From the start of the century, indeed from the moment the documentary state was brought into being by the Milner administration, migrants used letters to soften and circumvent the banal force of the state's documentary regime. Schapera included letters that sought to comply with the operations of the state's elaborate paper requirements without comment.

> I also let you know that I always forget about my tax-receipt. You must ask M_____ [her brother] to send it. If you can go to Mosanteng [where he formerly lived in Mochudi], get me a little yellow paper, it is (a pass) for work, it is in the big yellow book, and put into your letter. I want to get this paper because I want to show it to people when I look for work. (Schapera 1941, 144)

Many other records, especially in the archives of the Witwatersrand pass commissioner, noted the common practice of requesting rural relatives to send labor passports, using new names or aliases, that would allow urban workers to break their current contracts. Occasionally the practice worked in the opposite direction, with urban workers sending illegally obtained passes to their rural friends: "I am herewith enclosing a blank special pass which you are required to fill in all the necessary words."[8]

The documentary state that emerged in South Africa in the first half of the last century was obsessed with written documents as arbiters of authority. It is not really a surprise, then, that the best biographies of African men and women in this period show an imperative toward the construction of personal archives as a means of protection against the capricious activities of white landlords, supervisors, and state officials (Burns 1996; Van Onselen 1996). Of course, the strength of these biographies is derived in large measure from the richness of these personal archives (Breckenridge 1997). Yet there is little to suggest that the determined preservation of personal and official documents by people such as Kas Maine in the Western Transvaal or Louisa Mvemve in the Eastern Cape and the East Rand was unusual behavior. If the documentary state taught one lesson, it was that even the most insignificant piece of paper might make the difference between success and catastrophe.

Love Letters

Many of the letters written across the gulf of migrancy were motivated by the kinds of crises that Walter Benjamin called the "state of emergency" of the oppressed (1968, 257). And it is these letters that people have in mind when they speak of the searing effects of Thabo Mbeki's work as a youthful amanuensis. But many other letters were written with more pleasurable ends in mind. One of the primary reasons for writing letters—especially for South African workers—was desire.

Over the course of the Second World War, the government censor's reports on the character of local African letters commented repeatedly on the significance of courtship in the overall volume of letters. A report written by the Durban censor at the end of 1942 described "the younger educated class of both sexes" as the principal source of "a considerable volume" of love letters, of which "some in English employ extravagant terms."[9] Two years later the reports described a "considerable correspondence" between the "younger class of student Natives of both sexes of the love-letter type." The same report observed that "most of the letters" from workers in Durban were addressed to "women, wives and sweethearts."[10] The most revealing comment on the content of these letters came in an earlier report that complained, in prim Victorian tones, of a "certain amount of slackness of morals in some of the Native Schools."[11]

Schapera found letters during his research that are eloquent testimony to the poetic abilities of their writers. Indeed the most powerful of these letters, written to his wife by a young man in Johannesburg, offers a metaphysical celebration of bodily desire (and commodity fetishism) that seems to echo the young John Donne:

> I still think of how we loved each other; I think of how you behaved to me, my wife; I did not lack anything that belonged to you. All things I did not buy, but I just got them, together with your body; you were too good for me, and you were very, very sweet, more than any sweet things that I have ever had. We fitted each other beautifully. There was nothing wrong; you carried me well; I was not too heavy for you, nor too light, just as you were not too heavy for me nor too light; and our "bloods" liked each other so much in our bodies. (Schapera 1941, 46; see also Schapera 1933, 24)

This is letter-writing as pure affect, identical to the "intimate sphere of the conjugal family" that played such an important part in the history of European privacy and western political culture (Habermas 1989, 48). But there were also clearly some very important differences among the love-letters working-class South Africans wrote in the early twentieth century.

It is, I think, important to remember that in the 1930s the compounds of the Witwatersrand gold mines housed some 300,000 young African men, many of them single and energetically in search of appropriate wives. In the early 1990s, I began looking for old migrants who could recall life on the mines between the Great Depression and the beginnings of apartheid. Some of these men remembered a startling practice in the mine compounds of collectively writing love letters. Lahlekile Mphephanduku worked briefly on the mines in the later 1930s and then spent most of his adult life working for Reef municipalities. To his own and general hilarity he explained to Vukile Khumalo and myself the art of writing love letters in the compounds.

> During Sundays and Saturdays we used to go out of our rooms and lie down on the lawn. Then we would write letters to the girls at home, yes. A person would mention his girlfriend—and others would follow, and others would be sitting

and writing letters [here]. After that we would say, "On Monday these letters must go to the Post Office," yes. It must be clear when November comes whether this girl rejects us or not.

VK: I see.

Lahlekile Mphephanduku: Then we would stay and wait for the letter [he] had sent. When the letter arrives we would gather again to hear what the girl says. Awu! she rejects [us], she says; she wants to see [us] face to face.

VK: Ha! Then what do you do?

Lahlekile Mphephanduku: [But] the one who is fortunate [among us] receives good news, the girl accepts his request. Then we would go home.

While we should interpret this joint authorship as a kind of play, it does also bear the distinct imprint of Mpondo peer organizations. For the girls receiving the letters at home would also "write together" in response to love letters from the mines (Mphephanduku 1996).

The point here is not simply that migrants made use of collective authorship because of their illiteracy. They appear, on the contrary, to have chosen to make use of skilled letter-writers, even when they were able to write themselves. David Sogoni, for example, is a well-educated man by the standards of his peers, and he certainly spent enough time at school to write a letter comfortably. At the mines, however, he stayed with his older brothers in "one room at the mine," and the process of courting by letter he describes seems to have required the skills of more than a single individual. "Yes," he answered in reply to the question of whether or not he wrote letters,

we talked with a lady at home. We would call someone who was able to write, and come together to share opinions. And talked to a lady there. Each one of us would come with a plan. . . . Ha! Once the lady responds favourably you would leave your job and go home to your new girlfriend. (Sogoni 1996)

The very form of eloquence described here seems to have demanded the efforts of more than a single individual.

Yet letters, even those between young lovers, were not always celebrations of desire. The evidence from Schapera's fieldwork and the extracts from the government censors irrefutably show that even the most intimate correspondence often dealt with the pain of betrayal and abandonment, made only more intense by the prolonged absences of migrant employment. And almost every one of the letters in these collections combines a detailed consideration of the microeconomics of household reproduction and communal subsistence with an affective interest in personal relations with kin and lovers. If ever evidence was needed of the intrinsically secular, and material, preoccupation of working-class South Africans, it can be found in their private letters.

Necessary Conditions

I want now to address a problem that has concerned me throughout this discussion: What were the sociological requirements for large-scale working-class letter-writing? What were the regional, institutional, or intellectual preconditions for large-scale migrant letter-writing? The censors' records from the two world wars allow us to build an answer. During the First World War, the government censor monitored the flow of letters across the Mozambican border, and in these reports there is no mention of a significant flow of African letters.[12] By the 1940s, the position was very different.

The censor in Durban complained throughout the second war of the "heavy" volume of letters moving between Durban and Mozambique. These letters were overwhelmingly addressed to, or sent from, the workers on the sugar estates of Natal and Zululand. A scattering were written in Portuguese, about one-fifth in isiZulu or one of the cognate isiNguni dialects, and the remainder—the vast majority—in one of the unrelated Mozambican languages. The variety of these dialects and the real scarcity of official competence in these "seven or eight" different languages presented the censor with what he modestly described as "considerable difficulty."[13]

During the 1940s, many of the sugar estates in Natal and Zululand relied on illicitly recruited workers, and this bedevils the task of calculating the total number of Mozambican workers in the region. A decade earlier, Mozambican migrants made up about half of the total workforce of some 20,000 at work on the Zululand sugar fields (Jeeves 1997, 118; Lincoln 1997, 143). By the 1940s this number may have declined in the face of competitive recruitment from other industries. My best estimate is that there were between 5,000 and 10,000 Mozambican workers on the Natal and Zululand sugar fields during the war.

We have much better statistics on the flow of their letters. In the week after November 16, 1942, for example, the censor reported that his office had examined "360 inward and 469 outward" letters from the Mozambican workers on the farms, and the other reports document a steady flow of some 2,000 outward and 1,500 inward letters every month of the war. These letters were clearly written by individuals who were new to letter-writing. The censor complained that the messages were mostly "written by illiterates and very difficult to decipher."[14] A year later he had not changed his mind. "They write badly," he complained in January 1943; they "split up words into syllables, which makes it very difficult to connect them to their context."[15]

So what changed between 1918 and 1939 that might explain the development of working-class letter-writing, however ungrammatical? In short, basic primary education. Before 1920 there was practically no education in Mozambique, where ninety Catholic schools taught fewer than 7,000 pupils. After the introduction of state support for the Catholic schools, the numbers of Mozambicans at school grew dramatically over the course of the 1930s, and by the start of the war, nearly 60,000 pupils were at school and about a quarter of these were girls. This educational infrastructure was still perfunctory; it was preoccupied with teaching trades and Portuguese literacy (Sheldon 1998, 606). Nonetheless, it was sufficient to foster the development of popular letter-writing among the unfortunate men and women who took up badly paid jobs on the Zululand sugar fields. This is remarkable testimony—if anyone still needs it—to the effectiveness of the most basic primary education.

Conclusions

In this study, and in others, I have tried to make the point that South African migrant workers were significantly more literate than is often allowed by our historiography and much of our contemporary social policy. Yet, as the now-famous anecdotes from Thabo Mbeki's youthful biography suggest, there is little to celebrate in this popular letter-writing correspondence. After the Depression, South African migrants were often shaped by, and preoccupied with, an array of personal economic constraints and requirements under conditions of terrible scarcity, and their letters very often give the sense of being written near the point of death. We can see this quite clearly from the content of the letters examined here. From the mournful complaints of the dying, abandoned mother that "other men are striving for themselves" to the excruciating domestic arithmetic between husbands and wives, letters provided a medium for (and insight into) the development of a new kind of *homo economicus in extremis*. But survival was not the only reason for writing. Migrants also wrote to give poetic expression to their love and their desire. These intensely intimate, and celebratory, accounts stand in juxtaposition with the pedantic conservatism of *ukuhlonipha* (the elaborate rules for demonstrating respect in Nguni societies). Finally, of course, I think that migrants wrote because they had been taught, either directly in their own schooling or indirectly through the education and literacy of their peers, that letters could address the key problems of subsistence and desire better than any other mechanism. They had few meaningful options, but the letter seems, nonetheless, to have served them very well.

NOTES

1. See "Obscene Letter Sent through Post to Native of Impolweni Mission Station, Complaint from Reverend J. A. S. Scott, 1895," December 15, 1897, PMG 46, GPO3/1895, Pietermaritzburg Archives Repository. See also Coka 1963 and Khumalo in this volume.

2. See "Complaint re the Treatment of Native Labourers Employed on the Mines of the Witwatersrand," B. E. Kwezana Mabandla, Lower Chumie, to Secretary for Native Affairs, Cape Town, May 8, 1905, TAD SNA 273, 1561/05, National Archive Repository (hereafter NAR).

3. See Transvaal Cd. 1906 2819, Further Correspondence relating to Labour in the Transvaal Mines (In continuation of [Cd. 2788] January 1906), February 1906, British Parliamentary Papers.

4. Anonymous, c/o The Power Station, Jeppe St., Johannesburg, Room 2, to Mapaia Maluleke, c/o Ngala Ltd., Mapai, via Zoekmekaar, November 12, 1942, Censorship of Letters, Naturelle Sake, 9658, 541/500, NAR.

5. Mrs. Lubisi, Nazarene Mission, Acornhoek, to Mr. D. Lubisi, P.O. Box 13, Room 277, State Mines No. 4, Brakpan, October 22, 1943, Censorship of Letters, NTS 9658, 541/500, NAR.

6. Various Natives in the Union of S.A, November 3, 1932, Censorship of Letters, NTS 9658, 541/500, NAR.

7. Miss Azaria Mukosi, Cottondale, to Filemon Mukosi, State Mine No. 4, Brakpan, November 1, 1943, Censorship of Letters, NTS 9658, 541/500, NAR.

8. William Kamoshaba, P.O. Box 440, Pretoria, to Francis Manyama, P.O. Modjaji, via Duivels Kloof, January 12, 1943, Censorship of Letters, NTS 9658, 541/500, NAR.

9. Office of the Deputy Chief Censor, Durban, December 4, 1942, Censorship of Letters, NTS 9658, 541/500, NAR.

10. Office of the Deputy Chief Censor, Durban, January 5, 1944, Censorship of Letters, NTS 9658, 541/500, NAR.

11. Office of the Deputy Chief Censor, Durban, to Currently Unknown, November 4, 1943, Censorship of Letters, NTS 9658, 541/500, NAR.

12. Censorship of correspondence passing through the Union to Portuguese East Africa: Reports of Chief Censor, 1915–1917, War 1914–1915, Mozambique, Governor-General 644, 9/77/8, NAR.

13. Office of the Deputy Chief Censor, Durban, January 6, 1943, Censorship of Letters, NTS 9658, 541/500, NAR.

14. Office of the Deputy Chief Censor, Durban, December 4, 1942, Censorship of Letters, NTS 9658, 541/500, NAR.

15. Office of the Deputy Chief Censor, Durban, January 6, 1943, Censorship of Letters, NTS 9658, 541/500, NAR.

REFERENCES

Asmal, Kader. 1999. "Statement in the National Assembly by the Minister of Education, Professor Kader Asmal, MP, on the Occasion of International Literacy Day." September 8. Available online at http://www.info.gov.za.

Benjamin, Walter. 1968. *Illuminations: Essays and Reflections.* Ed. Hannah Arendt. New York: Schocken Books.

Breckenridge, Keith. 1997. "Orality, Literacy and the Archive in the Making of Kas Maine." *Journal of Natal and Zulu History* 17: 120–130.

———. 2000. "Love Letters and Amanuenses: Beginning the Cultural History of the Working Class Private Sphere in Southern Africa, 1900–1933." *Journal of Southern African Studies* 26 (June): 337–348.

Burns, Catherine. 1996. "Louisa Mvemve: A Woman's Advice to the Public on the Cure of Various Diseases." *KRONOS: Journal of Cape History* 23: 108–134.

Coka, Gilbert. 1963. "The Story of Gilbert Coka of the Zulu Tribe of Natal, South Africa." In *Ten Africans,* ed. Margery Perham. Evanston: Northwestern University Press, 273–322.

Gevisser, Mark. 1999. "Insight." *Sunday Times,* (Johannesburg), May 16.

Habermas, Jürgen. 1989. *The Structural Transformation of the Public Sphere.* Cambridge: Polity Press.

Jeeves, Alan. 1997. "Migrant Workers and Epidemic Malaria on the South African Sugar Estates, 1906–1948." In *White Farms, Black Labour: The State and Agrarian Change in Southern Africa, 1910–1950,* ed. Alan Jeeves and Jonathan Crush, 114–136. Pietermaritzburg: University of Natal Press.

Lincoln, David. 1997. "Plantation Agriculture, Mozambican Workers and Employers' Rivalry in Zululand, 1918–1948." In *White Farms, Black Labour: The State and Agrarian Change in Southern Africa, 1910–1950,* ed. Alan Jeeves and Jonathan Crush, 137–146. Pietermaritzburg: University of Natal Press.

Mphephanduku, Lahlekile. 1996. Interview by Vukile Khumalo and Keith Breckenridge. Isiyaya, Eastern Cape, October 19.

Schapera, Isaac. 1933. "The Native as Letter Writer." *The Critic: A South African Quarterly Journal* 2 (September): 20–28.

———. 1941. *Married Life in an African Tribe.* New York: Sheridan House.

Sheldon, Kathleen. 1998 " 'I studied with the nuns, learning to make blouses': Gender Ideology and Colonial Education in Mozambique." *International Journal of African Historical Studies* 31, no. 13: 595–625.

Sogoni, David. 1996. Interview by Vukile Khumalo and Keith Breckenridge. Isiyaya, Eastern Cape, October 19.

Sohlathi, Ngilambi. 1992. Interview by Jones Mzayifani and Keith Breckenridge. Siyaya, Eastern Cape, October 17.

Sparks, Allister. 2003. "Child of the Struggle." *Natal Witness,* June 13.

Switzer, Les. 1993. *Power and Resistance in an African Society.* Madison: University of Wisconsin Press.

Van Onselen, Charles. 1996. *The Seed Is Mine: The Life of Kas Maine, a South African Sharecropper, 1894–1985.* Cape Town: David Philip.

KEEPING A DIARY OF VISIONS: LAZARUS PHELALASEKHAYA MAPHUMULO AND THE EDENDALE CONGREGATION OF AMANAZARETHA

6

Liz Gunner

How does one begin to keep a diary when no one has ever suggested the possibility? What cultural models assist the keeping of a "diary" or "journal" especially if these concepts do not, as yet, exist in your mother tongue? And how do these activities join with the wider currents of epistemic change, with the violence that punctuated twentieth-century South Africa? These questions inform this chapter and I lay out some answers, or tentative conclusions. The notebook of Lazarus Phelalasekhaya (House Cockroach) Maphumulo, a member of Isaiah Shembe's Nazareth Church at its Edendale temple, is the map from which I read; the script moves from decorative squiggles to a firm boxlike hand and then to a broader, more flowing, muscular lettering, and it takes us through the years of his life as a black subject, a scribe, a devout believer—a point of consciousness in the vibrant yet agonistic world of his time and place. I try to reconstruct a part, at least, of his reading and writing life and understand its wider significance in the history of "the word." Besides using the text of his diary to do this, I was able, with the help of Phumulani Ngubane, a member of the church, to visit the Edendale Temple of Enhlanhleni and speak to elderly members, in particular Mrs. Mathonsi, Mrs. Made, and Mrs. Seme, who remembered Lazarus, or "Phela" (Cockroach), the affectionate nickname Isaiah gave him by which he was widely known.

In the period 1926 to the early 1930s, the Nazareth Baptist Church was made up of a small band of scattered followers who would meet at their central holy village of Ekuphakameni (near Durban) for the annual July festival and for the January pilgrimage to the holy mountain of Nhlangakazi at Ndwedwe, in the Valley of a Thousand Hills region north of Durban. They were led by a magnetic prophet, Isaiah Shembe, founder of the church, who was viewed with suspicion by both the main mission churches and the state and was on more than one occasion summoned to appear before magistrates or state officials. One such time was in Pietermaritzburg in 1929. However, in the later period of the mid-1930s and early 1940s, under the leadership of Isaiah's son, Johannes Galilee, a graduate of the University College of Fort Hare in the Eastern Cape, the church grew enormously both numerically and in terms of its organizational structures. It was always a church of narratives, dreams, and prophecies, many of which were recorded by Isaiah Shembe and his young amanuenses. Writing was always an important part of church life, and the documents gathered by the founder were selectively used by his successor to print the first published combined hymn and prayer book—and that was when Maphumulo's and other congregants' earlier notebooks were put aside and, on the instructions of the new leader, Johannes Galilee Shembe, became part of the church's archive at Ekuphakameni. It was also, from its beginning, a church of healing—a factor viewed with great irritation by the more rationalist *amakholwa*, the Christians of the mainstream churches.

The written text on which this chapter focuses was largely fashioned in the small locality known as Siyamu within the community of Edendale, in what was at the time the province of Natal. Edendale was an African freehold area on the fringes of the town of Pietermaritzburg, the capital and administrative center of the province. The town, with its core of the white colonial elite, was in many ways insular and conservative. Its white citizens, largely intent on excluding Africans from anything but a laboring class, had already, by the 1920s, engaged in fierce controversy over how African worldviews could be accommodated within Christianity (Meintjes 1988). Bishop Colenso, based at Bishopstowe on the northeastern outskirts of Pietermaritzburg, had lost his Anglican bishopric over the question of accepting African polygamists as members of the Christian communion (Guy 1983). The championing of King Dinuzulu and the royal house during and after the Bambatha rebellion of 1906 by Colenso's daughter Harriette and her sister Frances had led only to increasing control of their movements and isolation from the conservative settler community. The Colensos and their African allies and supporters held an enlightened position on race, equality, and the understanding and negotiation of diverse cultural models, but their views were violently rejected by the ruling white elite (Meintjes 1988; Guy 2002). In Edendale itself, by the 1920s, when the political disabilities, economic restrictions, and social problems of the past forty years had all whittled away past securities, a sense of Christian dignity, or what in isiZulu would be called *isithunzi*, still remained. Historian Sheila Meintjes describes it like this:

> Edendale held its reputation as a respectable, Christian village. No non-Christian ventured into the village improperly clad. Concertina players did not walk through the streets playing their music, as they did in the hills and dales of the neighbouring Swartkop location. If there were festivities in the village, there was no stamping of feet, *ukusina*, as amongst "the people outside," instead the more-genteel shuffle, *ukutamba*, was associated with dancing at Edendale. (Meintjes 1988, 69)

Writing One's Place in the World

Testimony to the importance black subjects placed on writing and on securing a place and a voice in the public sphere through print comes from the case of Magema Fuze. As early in the century as 1905 the remarkable Fuze, who was the pupil of Bishop Colenso as well as his mentor in Zulu language and culture and was also a printer and tutor to King Dinuzulu, had finished his ambitious history of the Zulu, *Abantu Abamnyama Nalapho Bavela Khona* (The Black People and Whence They Came). It was, however, seventeen years before it found its way into print; it was published in 1922, with the financial support of the wealthy Masuku family of Edendale and Harriette Colenso (La Hausse 2002, 100, 118). The chapter by Vukile Khumalo in this volume gives a vivid sense of how Fuze's writing and working life was intimately joined to the town and its contested discourses on culture, Christianity, and civil society. Fuze was part of the strong network of *amakholwa* letter-writers associated with the Colenso sisters and with Ekukhanyeni, the Colenso home at Bishopstowe. Later in his life, after King Dinuzulu's return from exile, Fuze was the king's secretary when he was in Eshowe. The writer and journalist R. R. R. Dhlomo, who had spent his early years in Siyamu, close to the school of that name in Edendale, published his first novel in 1928. Called *An African Tragedy*, it outlined the dangers of urban life in Johannesburg; the main character, Robert Zulu, moved from peaceful Siyamu to the mining city and thereafter spiraled into a life of depravity and a violent death. Dhlomo juxtaposed Johannesburg with idyllic Edendale, a formulation more suited to his moral fiction than to the realities of life in Siyamu.

Edendale had its own modern cultural energies and tensions, which filtered into even the sequestered community of the AmaNazaretha, as Lazarus's journal reveals. His pained reference near the end of his notebook (written in the early 1940s) to "the singing of lewd songs" by the distinctly restive young girls of the community allows the modern reader an insider's glimpse into the multiple layering of black culture at the time. As Christopher Ballantine points out in his fine study of black urban music in the 1920s to 1940s, *Marabi Nights* (1993), vaudeville, the *tsaba tsaba* dance, and jazz were all flourishing in the 1930s and 1940s. The riotous music of the backyard slums, known as *marabi*, was also likely to have penetrated Edendale as land was split up into ever-smaller units and economic and social pressures intensified. Equally, concerts and musical events in Pietermaritzburg in the late 1930s, such as the "Sensational Musical Burlesque" which was billed for April 8, 1938, at the Berg Street Native Recreation Hall and the farewell fundraiser in August 1938 before William Mseleku left to study music in Manchester give a sense of a thriving black music scene which drew creatively on western and African music traditions.[1]

Lazarus Maphumulo's notebook, which never found its way into print, can nevertheless be "read" as part of a varied and finely articulated map of black writing. Moments in his journal suggest the diversity of cultural and religious choices available to those who lived in and near the city, offering a view of a close-knit religious community responding with discomfort to a mix of the sacred and the profane. Other points of his writing demonstrate huge angst and even a kind of holy terror as Lazarus faced perplexing symptoms of psychosocial disorders in his fellow church members and found himself drawn in, not as a copyist but as an actor, recorder, and interpreter. Lazarus was, in an important sense, a writer of his time. Clearly, different forms of writing had a place in the hybrid world of colonial Pietermaritzburg and its surrounding African townships in the 1920s, 1930s, and 1940s. The isiZulu version of John Bunyan's *Pilgrim's Progress* would also have circulated, and Isabel Hofmeyr makes a tantalizing point concerning "a complex understanding of literacy and spiritual authority" when she refers to the dreams and visions of heaven by members of African independent churches such as the AmaNazaretha. She mentions that Isaiah Shembe was known as the Zulu Holder of the Keys at the Gate of Heaven. There is here, she suggests, a "family resemblance" to the final scene of *The Pilgrim's Progress*. "What might Bunyan's book tell us about literacy and heaven?" she asks (Hofmeyr 2004, 139–140). Besides the broadsheets of hymns and concert advertisements and the newspapers, Bibles, and popular novels read by black and white readers, handwritten records circulated by the 1920s and 1930s among the small but influential African Initiated Church known as the AmaNazaretha. Their leader, Isaiah Shembe, was one of the many notable Africans to be summoned to Pietermaritzburg in 1929 and again in 1932 as part of the Native Economic Commission, where he was interviewed by Carl Faye and closely questioned about the church's land holdings, his "wealth," and his level of literacy (Union of South Africa 1932; Papini 1999). Although Shembe told Faye that he could not write and had never had any formal schooling, the written word had always been hugely significant in his ministry. The power of writing and the importance of literacy was indeed taken as a given by Shembe. This was perhaps due partly to his early exposure to the Protestant emphasis on the written "word" through his Wesleyan contacts. Also his friendship at the turn of the century with the dynamic and indefatigable Rev. William Leshega of Boksburg, initially a Baptist and then a minister of the African Native Baptist Church, was surely influential (Gunner 2000).

The Importance of the Scribes

Members of the AmaNazaretha church, with its headquarters at the holy village of Ekuphakameni at Inanda, some fifteen miles from Durban, obtained their own printed hymn and prayer book only in 1940. Before then, assiduous scribes—young women and a few young men, some with only a basic primary education—copied down hymns, prayers, the account of his early life and calling, and his letters and sermons. In the first instance they were copied into a small number of large notebooks, the official books of the church, one of which is believed to have been buried with the prophet at his request (Dube 1936). The material in the church's official records was, however, not cut off from its receptors. Like the "word" of the holy scriptures being cast into the world, such material was sent into the congregation of the church to become part of the ongoing process of shared memorialization. Thus, before the 1940 printing of the hymn and prayer book, which was undertaken by the founder-prophet's educated son, Johannes Galilee Shembe, church members who could write or who had access to a scribe were encouraged to have their own notebooks. There they recorded the growing number of hymns composed by their leader, other significant testimonies, sermons, and even copies of Shembe's letters. There was, it seems, a fevered need to hold the written word and its physical, spiritual, as well as magical power. In the first instance this meant using the growing number of hymns in an orderly way at the church's services. These services were held in the "temples," the sacred spaces on the land Shembe had acquired for the church and for the often-homeless church members (most particularly women) in different parts of Natal and Zululand.[2] The numbered hymns themselves also became available as reference points for plotting memory and visions. The community did not have easy access to a culture suffused with literacy and reading. Nevertheless they forced their own inclusion through their focus on the domain of the sacred in their writing (Gee 1996, 84).

Beyond the writing of the hymns, Lazarus Maphumulo's notebook demonstrates the scope of choice about what one wrote in one's personal notebook or "Book of the Laws of Ekuphakameni," as his book is entitled. Church members kept their own personal archives in addition to records of the hymns in the church's liturgy. Very few people had Bibles then, Phumulani Ngubane and I were told in an interview with Mrs. Made of Nhlazatshe, Edendale, so the handwritten notebooks served as part of one's imprint of the sacred. The hymns, carefully written down by Lazarus (in the case of the Edendale community) or by one of the other young scribes, would be carried to services and on occasional preaching expeditions to neighboring districts. These books seemed to acquire their own iconic status. Yet they may also have become, for those who could write, the vehicles for writing the self, for making a history for oneself and one's community that incorporated both spiritual and secular elements.

Lazarus Maphumulo's notebook was not kept in a plastic bag like the documents of Kas Maine (Van Onselen 1996). Instead, he may have kept it with him to use as a hymnbook for services and as the place where he copied for himself the widely available accounts of the founder-prophet's early life and the other items of interest that had been recorded in the large "Church Book," a form of archive the leader himself had assembled. Perhaps because the printed hymnbook was produced in 1940, Lazarus's notebook thereafter became more of a diary or journal where he could record moments and events that were in some ways remarkable but also more closely related to himself and not necessarily emblematic incidents marking the wider trajectory of church history. As the notebook lengthens, it is his, Lazarus Phelalasekhaya's, vision and sense of his own place in the community of Ideni that begins to engross him. He begins to struggle too, with genre, with questions of addressivity: Is the latter part of his journal for himself alone or is it meant to be read aloud, as earlier shared testimonies might be? Moments in the journal suggest an inner struggle to understand; other moments where he throws in a comment such as, "And what do you make of that, you wretched fellow?" suggest that he hoped to communicate forcibly with a skeptical audience, the Wesleyans of Edendale, perhaps.

This sense of uncertainty about his own position is matched by an element of newness in what begins to be recorded. Problems creep in as Phela (as he refers to himself in the latter part of the notebook) wrestles with questions of narrative and dialogue, with representing verbatim accounts of members of the congregation in the grip of spirit possession. He has the problem of how to make the wildly incoherent, swift passage of events into a readable whole. This, one can see quite clearly, is a very different task from that of being a serene, if perhaps harassed, copyist of hymns. It is likely that in the early 1940s (the last entry in Lazarus's notebook is July 1942), this energetic writer, copyist, and church dancer of note[3] handed in his notebook, as did many other members of the church, to the leader, Johannes Galilee, son of Isaiah Shembe. It then became part of the church's greater archive, and it was assumed that members would all use the new printed hymnal and prayer book. There must have been a central storage point at the holy village of Ekuphakameni for all these rich treasures of church and personal records. There Lazarus's book lay, perhaps referred to, perhaps not. His book, as I have written elsewhere, was one of three loaned to me in late February 1987 at Ekuphakameni by the "dissident" leader, the late Rev. Londa Shembe, son of Johannes Galilee, who features so strongly in Lazarus's notebook, and grandson of Isaiah (Gunner 2002). Londa Shembe handed the writings to me at a time of acute social and political instability and turmoil. In early 1987, Inanda was still smoldering in the aftermath of the attacks on Indian families in the area some six months before, and the province of Natal and the fragmented Bantustan of KwaZulu were engulfed in violence. Londa himself was assassinated in April 1989.[4]

A Writing Journey

This chapter, then, explores the movement of Lazarus Maphumulo's "Book of the Laws of Ekuphakameni" as a journey from public to private space. Lazarus is at first an official scribe, copying down for the congregation at Ideni the hymns composed by Isaiah Shembe, some of the major prayers, and other key narratives. He then becomes a more private writer, journal-keeper, and reader. In this second capacity Maphumulo is able to record, largely for himself, some of the extraordinary events that gripped the lives of the believers who were members of the small AmaNazaretha congregation at Edendale. Their "temple"—and the land on which the community was based—was known simply as Ideni, or Minischool, possibly after the Christian chief of Edendale of the period, Stephanus Mini. Ideni, the land bought by Isaiah Shembe from the wealthy kholwa Msimang family, was near Siyamu and near the section of Edendale known as Caluza, after the musically gifted land-owning family of that name. One of their members, the musician Reuben Caluza, was the composer of catchy popular songs mostly in the

African American–derived genre which became known in South Africa as "iRagtime." It may well have been his songs that were sung so freely by the young girls of the congregation to Lazarus's great disapproval—a point that we see emerging toward the end of his journal.[5]

There are thus two kinds of writing in operation in the notebook of Lazarus Phelalasekhaya Maphumulo. On the one hand, there is an engagement in an official discourse. This is carried out by the newly formed church and its prophet-leader, who was respected, mistrusted, and feared not only by the state but also by the clergy of the missionary churches (Gunner 2002). It is part of the African appropriation of the Bible or, more broadly, of the religious discourse of the Bible, a form of re-membering by a new congregation of African believers (West 1999). On the other hand, there is a tentative exploration of more personal writing.

Mrs. Made could remember "Phela" (Cockroach) well. He was so much in demand as a scribe for hymns for church members' personal copies that it is possible that he may have had little time for his own hymn entries. Also, he traveled a fair amount, sometimes being away from his own congregation of Ideni for long stretches but always returning to base and to his home at nearby Mphumuzo. It may have been difficult for him to nurture his own choices about what he wished to select as truly worthy of recording from the multitude of visions, dreams, and extraordinary events, the vernacular of the sacred. Nevertheless, Phela's narratives of the struggles and successes of the Edendale congregation provide the modern reader with some understanding of how the fairly unknown terrain of writing and reading may have been important to an individual who was negotiating novel modes of expression and for whom writing and reading were certainly of great value but also problematic. His script opens up questions and leaves narratives unfinished. He has trouble deciding on what form to use and most often sets his prose accounts in verses, like the scriptures. His language is very flat, and he has little if any command of illocutionary features such as speechmarks, exclamation marks, and syntax division. The change from public scribe to personal recorder seems to perplex him; he moves cautiously into using the first person for events in which he is involved. In this reluctance to engage formally with "I," the self, he is like the animated narrator Meshack Hadebe, who had his own story to tell of the church's history and the conversion of his family. In the remarkable family autobiography of the journey from Lesotho to Durban in search of the unknown prophet (who turns out to be Isaiah Shembe), Hadebe refers to himself in a similarly distanced way (Hadebe 1934; Gunner 2002). Phela seems to fear the "I" voice, preferring the security of the communal. The stories which contain the name Phela and thus indicate that these are events in which he personally took part come toward the end of the journal. How does the notebook chart this journey from scribe to struggling narrator? What templates of memory are being shaped? Did the latter parts of the journal allow access to "deleted" church material, officially erased memories? The latter part of Phela's journal is technically a failure, but it is a key pointer to areas of experience that were rarely documented because of their sheer linguistic, discursive inaccessibility.

The Winding Road of the Text

Lazarus's notebook begins with the laying out of sixty-four of the church's hymns, all composed by Isaiah Shembe. At first these are separated from each other by carefully ruled decorative lines, suggesting, perhaps, the same pulsating reverence for their text as that alluded to by the copyists of medieval texts who illuminated their scripts with elaborate lettering and figures (Olson 1994, 93–94). However, the pressure of time begins to intervene. After the sixth hymn, Lazarus leaves aside the elaborate lines and simply sets out the hymns' sequential numbers. Hymn number 6 refers to the gates of Ekuphakameni as a metonym for the gates of heaven, and in its opening it uses the device of direct address and personification so familiar in the oral genre of *izibongo* (praise poetry):

> Greetings Phakama
> Greetings Judea
> Where have you sent our brothers
> Who were sent to you . . .
> Gates of Phakama
> Lift us up let us enter
> We have overcome our weaknesses
> Just as others have.
> Come O come
> We are going to the place on high
> May the one who is coming be praised
> At Ekuphakameni.
> Jehovah do not leave
> That high place
> Ring it around Lord
> On all four sides.
> (Maphumulo 1942, 5, my translation)

Hymn 23, carefully copied like those before and after it, mentions the psychological sickness known as *amandiki*. We will encounter another mention to this as part of the traumatic and difficult events Lazarus grapples with later in his notebook. Here, however, relatively near the beginning of the notebook, the neatly written hymn gives a sense of formal wholeness, of both tension and containedness, trouble and surety, set in the richly poetic imagery of the soul which often gave Shembe's compositions their startling quality:

> Lord I am the dust of ancient times
> I was stolen from the world
> I was thrust into a new hope
> Which is my soul
> I was not [then] given the dirt
> Which I have with me today
> The *amandiki* and the *amandawu*
> Sickness is there, brought by foreign nations . . .
> Lord I love you
> Lord remove all my sickness
> That is in my working hours
> And in my soul.
> (Maphumulo 1942, 16, my translation)

After the copying of 64 hymns Lazarus renumbers his pages from 1 and turns to a new topic or section of his book, giving it the title "The Book of Zinzilini, of Beautiful Laws."[6] All the entries in this section seem to have been copied from the large "Church Book": there are short prayers composed by Isaiah, the set of rules for dealing with errant ministers, letters asking for money due. He also copied the widely circulated account of Shembe's early life and his visionary calling, and next to this, an account copied possibly from a contemporary newspaper or pamphlet of a visit by an interested and enthusiastic visitor, a Mrs. Wells, to the village of Ekuphakameni and the prophet Shembe during one of the annual July meetings. The description covers the orderliness of the community; the healing of the sick, with mention made of an Indian man who had been on the verge of death and was healed of tuberculosis; the gowns of white worn by church members; and their dancing. It ends:

14
    After we had been talking to Shembe for a short while we heard a great hubbub and the sound of "Bayede" and the Nyuswa Chief was being greeted ceremonially. People such as he treat Shembe with the greatest respect and have endorsed his esteemed position.
15
    Those who were dancing were clothed beautifully with garments that came to their knees; and they wore fillets of white on their head and carried umbrellas, and the onlookers were ululating.

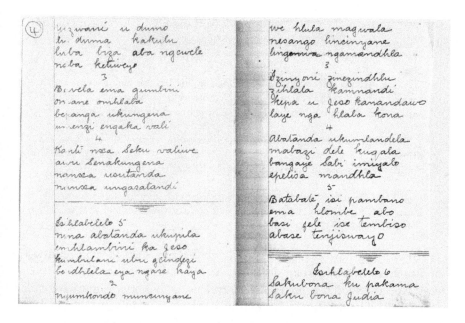

Figure 6.1. A page from Lazarus Maphumulo's notebook.

16
    All the hymns have been composed by Shembe. We watched them dancing for two-and-a-half hours.
    (Maphumulo 1942, 42–44, my translation)

Following this eulogistic account by an interested outsider, which Lazarus set out like biblical script in verse form, he copies for his book one of the most extraordinary and influential of Shembe's sermons, given in December 1929 at the Zululand church center of Judea near Gingindlovu: that of the dead child brought to life. This includes the journey of the child much later as a youth to Johannesburg seeking work; his second death, this time in Johannesburg; his mother's search for him; and his second miraculous return to life (Maphumulo 1942, 39–61). Again he sets it in verses, as if attempting to create the high gravitas of holy scripture. The language of the sermon quivers with the visionary dream, with angels in starry forms who touch life back into the four-days-dead child, and it is followed, as the child grows to maturity, by a realist, if cryptic, account of the horrors of black working life in the city of gold at the time. The account of the first return to life is as follows:

> 29
> The woman slept with the corpse and as she lay, she had a vision and it seemed to her that stars came in and circled the walls, coming close to and then surrounding the infant. Next a voice came from one of the stars and it said,
> 30
> "Where is the infant's death?" Another voice answered, "His mother's drunk it."
> "In that case," asked another voice, "how can he die?"
> 31
> Then the infant turned over, the house expanded and the stars sang saying, "Awake with us. We will bring light to your midday, your eyes and your spirit."[7]
> (Maphumulo 1942, 53, my translation)

By copying down as well as constantly hearing such sermons and testimonies, Lazarus was perhaps learning the idiom of the visionary and revelatory text—the speech genre of the marvelous, as Bakhtin might have called it.[8] Lazarus then selects for his entries the laws of marriage and advice for those marrying in the church, followed by "The Prophecy of Shembe on April 1923," then Shembe's prayer at Ekuphakameni on March 18, 1931, followed

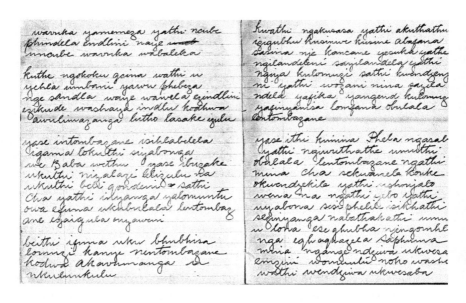

Figure 6.2. A page from Lazarus Maphumulo's notebook.

by maxims headed "Shembe's words of wisdom." The penultimate entries in his carefully numbered pages, in verse format, all concern varieties of healing: first of all a record of Isaiah Shembe enabling a woman who had long been barren to bear children; his healing of a crippled child; his revival of the dead infant of an Indian couple at Empangeni who had begged Shembe for his help; and finally his curing of the barrenness of another Indian woman. It must be emphasized that there were devout Indian members of Shembe's church during Isaiah's lifetime. Mrs. Harry Jokum was one such; Shembe cured her of barrenness. In an interview in 1987, Mr. Jokum emphasized that members of Shembe's church guarded the houses of Indian followers in Cato Manor in 1949 during the Indian-African riots. Finally, Lazarus's numbered pages stop at page 101, after nine verses of a long prayer asking that "the steward of the Lord" be protected from the perils sent by his enemies both black and white and that Ukuphakama (the village of Ekuphakameni) be kept safe from harm.

The Chronicler and Woman Troubles

We must assume that there is some kind of break in the notebook at this point, which is marked by the abrupt ending of the numbered pages; possibly Lazarus put his notebook aside for a period. Possibly the break came with the change of leadership—the death of Isaiah in May 1935 and the succession of Johannes Galilee, who saw to the systematizing of the prayer and hymnbook and its printing and distribution to church members. Whatever the reason, the remaining pages in the book mark the shift to writing that is markedly different. The numbered pages are gone; so too are the verses, although material is still set out in blocks resembling separate verses. There is another change: the focus of events is now very much on a particular place and group of people, the congregation of Ideni, the Nazarite center on the edges of the town of Pietermaritzburg, which Zulu-speakers still commonly refer to as "eThawini." Can we assume that Lazarus is from this point on regarding himself partly as a chronicler for his own church community and partly as a chronicler for himself?

Lazarus's journal provides an insight into what he regarded as important and the struggles of such a community in its imagining of itself. What is clear is the role of script in this writing of the community into the world of the 1930s and early 1940s. And we see the enduring importance of the Bible as a model for script. The Bible itself and newsprint are likely to have been the major sources of reading material for those who aspired to literacy or who were to some degree literate. The writing and reading—aloud perhaps—of journals such as Lazarus Phela's were a part of the way people who were on the very edges of settler society were moving away from an older worldview. They were remaking their environment and redefining themselves both culturally and in terms of a new religious pluralism (Werbner 1985, 257). Lazarus's diary, moving as it does into the early 1940s, covers in its latter pages the early era of the church's second leader (1935–1976), Johannes Galilee, a man of both the scripted and performative word and, as we hear from the journal, a man of extraordinary powers.

We could say that through writing, Lazarus turned both to the constitution of his own congregation and to himself and the further making of his own consciousness. Yet although the writing of entries from the large "Church Book" or from fellow members' books may have provided a kind of apprenticeship, the question of what to select and how to record it presented another series of challenges. A set of troubling circumstances relating to the life of his congregation drove Phela to return to his journal. It was specifically the problematic behavior of the young women at Ideni in the late 1930s or very early 1940s that turned him back to his book and his pen. Hymn 23, quoted above, with its mention of the "*amandiki* and the *amandawu* / Sickness . . . brought by foreign nations" is a sign that in the time of Isaiah Shembe such an illness existed and must have caused anxiety among the congregation.[9] The hymn pleads, "Lord I love you . . . remove all my sickness / That is in my working hours / And in my soul" (Maphumulo 1942, 16, my translation). For Phela, some twenty years later, something similar seems to have afflicted those he knew and worshipped with. But what kind of "sickness" was it?

The name *amandiki* was used in the last decade of the nineteenth century to describe women in Zululand "who were banding together and travelling without permission through the countryside. Making a nuisance of themselves, the women danced and sang, held healing ceremonies, and then aggressively demanded gifts and sacrifices" (Parle and Flint forthcoming, 2). The sickness was described by bemused onlookers, often homestead heads or colonial officials, as a kind of mania. By the victims themselves it was not seen as madness but as an illness, a form of spirit possession they called *indiki* which had come from the north (ibid.). While accounts of both its precise manifestations and its causes vary (sometimes the possessing spirits were male ancestors rather than alien spirits), it seems to have been linked with times of acute social stress, often "triggered by the sharpening of patriarchal authority" (Edgar and Sapire 2000, 49), and to have afflicted women most of all, frequently young women.[10] Another form of spirit possession that manifested it-self in the same period with symptoms of "violent aggression, hysteria or threat of suicide" was known as *ufufunyane*. Harriette Ngubane has argued for a direct link between both these forms of spirit possession and the harsh social conditions that were part of the experience of Zulu migrants and urban im-migrants to South African cities in the first two decades of the twentieth cen-tury (Ngubane 1977, 147, in Edgar and Sapire 2000, 50). Both *indiki* and *ufu-funyane* were perhaps linked to the trauma of intense social change and to attempts to highlight and break free from suffocating forms of authority, and they were treated in various ways by society. Jail or the mental asylum was the fate of some sufferers. In other cases, victims could be cured by a diviner (*isan-goma*), by a self-styled healer, or by healing within one of the prophetic churches, such as the AmaNazaretha.[11] The trancelike state of spirit posses-sion may have continued to remain on the margins of the acceptable; al-though linked slightly to the state of *ukuthwasa*, the experience of being called to be a diviner, it remains an area of ambivalence between illness, mad-ness, resistance, and clairvoyance.[12] Unlike the presence of, for instance, the *bori* cult among the Hausa, which is marginal but institutionalized, spirit pos-session in Zulu culture seems to have no clear place.[13]

Phela Maphumulo, turning again to his notebook, which had become his journal, does not himself use either term (*indiki* or *ufufunyane*) to describe the strange and disruptive behavior of the young girls or young women of the congregation of Ideni. However, one of those who is herself caught in some form of possession does mention them, if only to deny the affliction. Phela begins by turning to the case of Thembani Shangase. Not all young women, it seems, were happy with the church decision (well established by the time Jo-hannes Galilee Shembe took over in 1935) that the practice of worship through dancing should involve an adoption of dress style associated with tra-dition rather than with the modern world of western clothes. The semiotics of dress may have been a particular issue in a place such as Edendale, where many of the land-owning *amakholwa* were Wesleyans. As mentioned earlier, Sheila Meintjes notes that even in the 1920s, with the old securities gone, Edendale was seen as a "Christian village." No wonder, perhaps, that the young Thembani Shangase resisted the Nazarite dress code for the occasions of dancing for God. Phela reports it as follows, though it seems that he was not actually an eyewitness from the start:

Thembani Shangase did not take note of the Lord's laws and couldn't care less. She didn't like it at all when the Lord said that the people of The Thorn-Bush-that-Ensnared[14] should dress according to tradition. She said she among others was not in favor of this heathen habit. The Lord [also] laid down a rule that every person who was a member of the Nazarite church should not buy anything from Msikatshani's [lit. Grasscutter's] store.

She went straight off and bought things there.

Well, after a while she fell really ill, and began to waste away.

(Maphumulo 1942, new page 1, unnumbered; my translation)

Johannes Galilee then preaches that if she dies she will be "given up" (the Zulu word Phela uses is *lahlwa*, lit. lost) but that as this happens her spirit will enter another young girl and if she in turn dies it will enter yet another one. The girl does indeed, after a time, die, and, Phela continues, "she took possession of Ida Nokuphila Mkhize, one of the young girls of Ideni." At this point Phela begins to describe the unfolding event in which he is one of the main actors. He uses the first person and not the distancing third person. The account here has a flat sober quality that must have differed enormously from the living moment. Phela, a little overwhelmed and clearly inexpert in the complex task of writing up such drama, does the best he can:

I wanted to experience that extraordinary thing that had never happened before.

Indeed on that very day I took hold of the cloth that was used for praying over those who were afflicted. I wanted to experience this extraordinary wondrous happening for myself. I really held on tight so that the spirit of the Lord would come.

Indeed it [Thembani's spirit] came forth [in Ida] and said: "Ha! I know that you wanted to hear me speak. You see me. I'm not sick neither am I a demon, neither have I *jufunyane* hysteria, and I haven't got *amandiki* either.

It said, "I am Thembani Shangase; I've died because I was given up by the Lord.

That very Johannes Shembe," she said, "Heaven is his.

Me, he threw away, with the church dues I'd given." As she spoke she picked bits up from the ground, she said, "Here's my church dues from the girls' offering, here's my support money, here's my money for the [holy] mountain.

"You gave me up with all my offerings." And she got out and jumped up above the house and grabbed the grass thatching and began to eat it.

We grabbed hold of her and she said, "Let me eat grass and the seeds of trees because I broke his law, because I bought seed bread and ate it and didn't care a bit about him.

"But today I am warning you that he is indeed the only Lord."

Then she began to sing the song that says, "My sins are more numerous than the hairs on my head. Who will rid me of this heavy load?"

[Hymn 62]

Phela then brings himself directly back into the narrative, as speaker to an imaginary audience made up of both believers and unbelievers: "And you,

MaZulu, I ask you, which is the Lord who has opened the gate that was closed so that s/he that was on the other side is on the other side, and s/he that is there, is there, and he has opened the gate so that the dead can preach to those who are still on earth in this world of ours that we have today? Luke 16-24-25-26-27-28-29-30-31." And at that point Phela simply closes off the narrative of what he has called "a wondrous event" (isimangaliso), draws two straight short lines under it, and moves to his next "wonder" (isimanga). But note what the Luke reference is—surely one that Phela (Lazarus), as it involves his namesake, knew particularly well. The rich man looks up at the beggar covered with sores, who in life lay at his gate but is now in the bosom of Abraham, and says, "Father Abraham have mercy on me and send Lazarus that he may dip his fingers in water and cool my tongue, for I am tormented in this flame" (Luke 16: 24). In the New Testament version, Abraham refuses to let Lazarus speak from the gates of heaven to the rich man's brothers in the world to warn them of the dangers of their profligate life. Yet here, Phela implies, through the dead girl possessing the spirit of the living, the voice of warning passes from the dead to those on earth. The difference is, of course, that the rebellious spirit of Thembani Shangase is hardly likely to be in Abraham's bosom as she speaks. The emphasis of the story that was so loved by the radical Protestants of Bunyan's time, with its strong social message of the redemption of poverty in the next world, is replaced by one that stresses obedience at all costs.[15]

The account that follows the narrative of Thembani Shangase again takes up the strand of anxiety over unruly girls and sets it alongside a visionary moment that celebrates Shembe's power in the presence of a competing church. The visionary moment is one that Phela is comfortable with recording; it is after all the genre of the marvelous with which he is entirely familiar. Dissidence is more difficult. Two short entries refer to a brush with the Wesleyan congregation and show the tensions between a prophetic healing church such as Shembe's and one from the mainstream Protestant tradition. Isaiah Shembe had himself at one time in his early life attended the Wesleyan church and he had an abiding love for its hymns; his own church's relations with the Wesleyans seem to have been at times close, yet strained (Gunner 2002, 17–18, 53). The entries in Phela's journal that touch on relations with the Wesleyans bring to the fore points of social and organizational strain both between the churches and within each church. And they are described alongside the ongoing trouble with the girls. Under the heading "A Happening at Shembe's place in Pietermaritzburg, at Edendale" and set out in the form of short verses, he reports the following:

> The Lord Shembe, Johannes Galilee Shembe left his famous home of Ekuphakameni, the house of God. He made his way to Edendale, to baptize there.
>
> After he had done so, he said that he wanted the sick to be prayed for.

The last statement refers to the disturbance among the young girls (*amantombazane*) of the congregation. One young woman could not pray, and the only conclusion the preacher and deaconess of the congregation could come to was that if that particular "form of death" showed itself again among the girls, they would be beaten.[16] The account of the first invitation by the Wesleyans then follows:

> On another day a letter of invitation came from the preacher of the Wesleyans, inviting us Nazarites to take the service. We agreed because he had stipulated that we should all go.
>
> We tried by all means to stop the young girls going to the service because we didn't want things to go wrong, but it didn't work out like that, and we went with the girls. We worshipped[17] the whole night and things went perfectly fine.
>
> But in the early morning as all the formal ceremony was over, the girls made the most awful noise. They broke the windows and the door, rushed out of the house and ran off.
>
> The Wesleyans made fun of us and said, "Where's your witness from your God?" They shouted at us and said, "Bring them to us so we can pray for them in the name of the Lord Jesus and not Shembe the deceiver."
>
> Oh we were so disappointed but what could we do? Well we said we just must stick to our own day of worship [the Saturday Sabbath] and we felt sure that before the next week was out the Lord would resolve things for us even if he didn't come in person. We all implored our Lord to help us and then in the afternoon we left, feeling much better.

The next verse continues:

> On another day, a Sunday, a lady called us to take the [Wesleyan] service, and the girls followed behind us. We took the service and present was the very well known lady who was a member of the Wesleyan congregation and who had invited the whole Nazarite congregation, a Mrs. Cele.
>
> Well, as we spoke about how the Almighty God was revealed to us and to our children, that wife of Mr. Cele had a revelation.
>
> She saw a person who [suddenly] appeared, but all you saw was his legs, standing in the midst of the congregation. She didn't see his face but when she looked at the feet of that person she saw that they were exceedingly beautiful and then as she was still gazing at the feet she saw that there were eyes on his toes and they were gazing at her. She noticed to her complete amazement that there seemed to be people in that man's feet, looking straight at her. Her spirit yearned for the preaching to stop because she was so afraid. The service was quickly brought to a close. And then the person vanished.

Phela makes no further mention of the Wesleyans, and the implication is that the vision that so disturbed the member of the Wesleyan congregation was a manifestation of Shembe's power, presented as an alternate center of visionary and religious truth. This can be viewed as a part of "the argument of images" the Nazarite church was engaged in (Fernandez 1978; Werbner 1985, 256) as it wrestled with broader ideas of displacement and what Werbner has called "a decentring of reality." But the problem of the girls is still present and is linked perhaps to broader movements of social distress that manifested themselves both outside and within the small church community. Phela has this to represent as well; he is compelled, it seems, to follow it through even if he is not sure where it is taking him.

If the matter of the competing claims to the sacred was, at least for a while, laid to rest by the power of the vision of eyes in the toes, the matter of the troublesome girls still needed resolution. They did not, it seems, interfere with Mrs. Cele's vision, but they soon feature again in Phela's records as he wrestles with his medium and tries to give an account of these surprising events. The question of writing and reading and its relation to cultural models and to the ideologies embedded in those models is one that James Gee has alerted us to (Gee 1996). As Phela noted the "marvelous" events of church life as they erupted around him, he was surely wrestling with exactly how best to record them. He uses his pen and ink to write down the kind of event that at some moments would have been entirely familiar to mystics such as St. John of the Cross (the eyes in the feet, for instance) but were also part of the broad, if culturally ambivalent, repertoire of Southern African religious experience, namely spirit possession and the idea of the spirit medium; Nongqawuse of the Xhosa cattle-killing of 1853 is another such example. It seems to have been the young girls of the congregation who were, in the eyes of those in authority, the most problematic and disruptive and it is their behavior that causes Phela to write no longer as a relatively serene copyist but as a chronicler of more-enigmatic and more-troubling behavior which was not so easy to place on record. Phela attempts to catch precisely what happened—like a careful ethnographer—and at the same time he writes as one intimately involved and needing to record its bewildering unfolding. His problem is compounded by his unwillingness to use, or lack of knowledge of, the setting out of dialogue, the metaframes of language. He tracks and records the actions of the girl Beauty, who becomes possessed by—it seems—the spirit of the absent Shembe and who takes command of a chaotic situation which the local pastor and deaconess are unable to handle. It is an event in which Phela himself becomes a reluctant player. A few extracts follow; for clarity I have added punctuation and conventional line breaks for different speakers, without, I hope, misreading Phela's original. The deaconess, MaNdlovu, has just called the two girls who are "sick" and one of the sick girls responds:

> She said, "Do you see me?"
> They said, "We see you."
> She said, "Who am I?"
> They said, "You're Beauty."
> She said, "I'm not her. That's Beauty. Do you want to know what that noise was all about? It's I, Lord Shembe coming from KwaZulu. I will stop that awful noise of the morning of March 1941 at 10 a.m., and the demons."
> She went into the house and said, "Call Phela."
> I went.
> She said, "Do you see me?" [Beauty then reaffirms that Shembe is speaking through her and Phela writes, "We were amazed." He continues:]
> The next day at nine she said, "The sick girls must be brought." She said, "Take them to the Lord's house, the small one." The girls went in and after a moment she could be heard crying and she went there. We followed. She came and stood next to the door. She said, "Today's the day. Come out! Run away, like you did before." The girls cried but kept inside. She said to us and Simelane [one of Phela's church companions], "You see. I will tell them to come out but don't follow them."
> What was amazing was that as the girls called out, "Shembe's killing us," there was no Shembe there, it was only the girl [Beauty] whom they saw.[18]

In the account that follows, the possessed girl, Beauty, becomes increasingly authoritative, and the bemused attenders, one of whom is Phela, meekly obey her as she faces the seemingly demented girls and gives her orders. The sickness seems to abate and rise again, and Phela describes the following day:

> She said once more that the girls should be brought again; she prayed for them and the sickness came back and they cried lying on the ground. She got them all lying down in the same place.
> Then she said to [the deaconess] MaNdlovu. "Take your cloth and put it over the girls." She put it over them and the cloth became cold. The demons covered themselves with it. [Again Beauty asserts her authority:] "Why, Deaconess, are the demons covering themselves with your cloth?" [Phela continues:]
> We all thought this was absolutely amazing. Then she said her scarf should be taken and held out a little. The demons cried. Then she said to us, "Fellows do you really belong to Nhlalisuthi [the men's church regiment based on the idea of the Zulu military regiment]?"
> We said, "Yes."
> She said, "Take off your jackets, put them on the sick people." We did that and the demons said, "Shembe's killing us!"
> (Maphumulo 1942, 108, my translation)

At this point Phela wishes to introduce more information and provide another slant on the problem of the rebellious and "demon filled" girls who are themselves being treated by a "sick" girl who is possessed by Johannes Galilee Shembe himself. He has, he confesses, been having problems with the girls of the congregation whom he has caught singing "lewd love songs" (*ngi-wafinyanise ehlabelela amagama amahumusha*), a fact which both they and their mothers vehemently deny when he questions them about it. The older women who support their daughters, and not him, say, "You're back, and you're going to cause trouble and we've been perfectly happy without you" (Maphumulo 1942, 108, my translation). What happens next in Phela's narrative—because it has become a narrative—vindicates him entirely:

> Then the girl [Beauty who is possessed] called the girls and said "I'll lead you." She said, "Each one of you will sing a lewd song. Each one will sing her own."
>
> She raised her hands and whistled and there was a great noise and each sang the song she liked. One and all behaved as if they had gone quite mad. They were all dancing as fitted these lewd songs. We were amazed because they'd just denied it all to me, and so had their mothers. But God even showed them dancing.
>
> The Almighty made it quite clear that the mothers had been dancing too. [He continues] When we told the girls all that had happened they were ashamed. (Maphumulo 1942, 109, my translation)

Phela then leaves the account of Beauty, who had for a short time become a figure of authority through whom the absent leader spoke. He leaves the rebellious girls, who seem (at least for a time) cured of their "demons," and moves on to a case of suspected witchcraft. How did the church community continue to cope with these discourses of both sickness and rebellion? And how were they recorded elsewhere? Or were they simply excised so that what we have left are the discourses of the marvelous and the discourse of dreams? Do women of the AmaNazaretha dream now instead of showing the sickness of *ufufunyane* or *amandiki*? Did Phela touch on a deeper question of what a culture records of itself and what it prefers to leave on the untidy and messy margins of its records of memory because they are simply too difficult to integrate? And how, now, in the present times of huge stress evoked through the pandemic of AIDS and HIV in the region, are such sicknesses as *ufufunyane* given a space, recorded, dealt with?

One of the final records in the journal section deals with Phela's own difficulties with church discipline because his mother had allowed nonmembers to move onto church land, and after that statement, nothing. That last entry concerning admission points to the larger question of inclusion and exclusion within a culture: in the Edendale of the early 1940s, and specifically at Ideni, what place was there for psychic or psychological unease in the wider discourse of the self? If the marvelous and the extraordinary manifested themselves, certain forms of expression may have been acceptable—the landscape of visions, of dreams—but not others (Muller 1999). Did rebellious sentiments have no place? By what means did an African church that was moving between discourses and technologies of the modern and the traditional attempt to hold its community together? What if its members manifested signs of acute stress linked to deeper social agony or to pleasures? It may have been acceptable for women to express the forbidden within dreams but not through the wildness of spirit possession, a form never completely integrated into Zulu patterns of belief and social action. The notebook that becomes the journal of Lazarus Phelalasekhaya gives this reader an astonished glimpse into the not-so-tenuous connections between a past era of cross-cultural uncertainty and the difficult present. Only the words on the pages which he has left for us give the modern reader this small, opaque window of connectivity.

NOTES

1. I would like to thank both Pippa Stein and Ben Carton for pointing me in the direction of sociolinguistic and historical references I would otherwise have missed and for our discussions as this chapter evolved. Thanks also to Kai Easton for comments on the chapter. My thanks also to Dolly Simelane and to Wiseman Masango for helping me puzzle out answers to Lazarus's text and for discussion on the many difficult questions the text raises. The late Phumulani Ngubane was a wonderfully courteous and knowledgeable helper; I miss him very much. Mrs. Mathonsi and Mrs. Made from Enhlanhleni Temple at Edendale were more than generous with their memories of Phelalasekhaya (House Cockroach), as they affectionately knew him. My thanks also to Karin Barber, who was as insightful and illuminating as ever in her comments on early drafts.

The programs and handbills of 1938 are under Caluza 4/3/44 in the City of Pietermaritzburg Minute Papers, Pietermaritzburg Archives Repository. My thanks to Ben Carton for directing me to them.

2. Liz Gunner and the late Phumulani Ngubane, interview with Mrs. Made (MaNgidi), Nhlazatshe, Edendale, November 15, 2000. Mrs. Mathonsi, who was present at the interview, mentioned that at Ideni there were houses for the widows who lived there and for their sons.

3. As we were informed by Mrs. Mathonsi of Enhlanhleni Temple, Edendale, during the interview of November 15, 2000.

4. For analysis of the civil war in Natal, see Kentridge (1991); Greenstein (2003); and Jeffrey (1997).

5. See Ballantine (1993) for a rich description of the black popular music of the time.

6. "Zinzilini" seems to have been a name, a little like the Hebrew "Yahweh," that Shembe used for the great power of the universe, God.

7. Lazarus does not put any speech marks in; I have added them for the reader's convenience.

8. See Bakhtin (1987).

9. The first dated hymn in the hymnal is Number 126, marked as composed at Judea in June 24, 1926 (Shembe 1940, 101). So it is likely that Number 23 was closer to 1920; Johannes Galilee remarks in his preface to the hymnal and prayer book that his father "wrote" very little between 1914 and 1919 but did so prolifically after that (Shembe 1940).

10. For other accounts of *amandiki* and related illnesses, see Ngubane (1975, 1977); Harries (1994); Edgar and Sapire (2000). See also Marks (1987) for an illuminating account of psychological stress and its consequences in the life of one woman. Carton (2000) gives a clear account of the stresses and strains on Zulu women of different ages in the late nineteenth century as the pattern of homestead life was assaulted by colonial taxation, urban migration, and the conflicting demands and expectations of them. See especially chapter 3, "Disobedient Daughters and Discontented Wives: Competition and Alliance between White and African Patriarchs." For contemporary work in psychiatric illness and cross-cultural hermeneutics, see (*inter alia*) Ellis (2003). My thanks to Simone Honikman for pointing me to this article.

11. Edgar and Sapire (2000, 51) refer to a renowned healer of *ufufunyane* called Qobo Dlamini who practiced in Estcourt.

12. See the rare account by Lee (1969, 129–156).

13. See the brief account in Furniss (1996, 92–95).

14. One of Isaiah Shembe's praise names which would have passed into the composite praise poem for himself and his son, Johannes Galilee, and by which I often heard him affectionately called. *Ugagane* is a small thorn tree common in the Natal Midlands.

15. My thanks to Isabel Hofmeyr for pointing this out.

16. According to Dolly Simelane, beating was and still is one of the accepted methods of treating someone who seems to be suffering from *ufufunyane*. Personal communication, May 18, 2003.

17. The isiZulu word is *sebenza*, which I have translated as "worship."

18. The translation is difficult and I cannot translate the whole section. It reads as follows in isiZulu and with Phela's punctuation: *okusimangaliso ukuthi uma ekhala athi Safa uShembe abamboni bathi intombazane abasamboni nangebizi elikhanyayo na.*

REFERENCES

Bakhtin, M. M. 1987. *Speech Genres and Other Late Essays.* Trans. Vern McGee, ed. Caryl Emerson and Michael Holquist. Austin: University of Texas.

Ballantine, Christopher. 1993. *Marabi Nights. Early South African Jazz and Vaudeville.* Johannesburg: Ravan.

Carton, Benedict. 2000. *Blood from Your Children: The Colonial Origins of Generational Conflict in South Africa.* Pietermaritzburg: University of Natal Press.

Dhlomo, R.R.R. 1928. *An African Tragedy.* Tyume: Lovedale Press.

Dube, John L. 1936. *uShembe.* Pietermaritzburg: Shuter and Shooter.

Edgar, Robert, and Hilary Sapire. 2000. *African Apocalypse. The Story of Nontetha Nkwenkwe, a Twentieth-Century South African Prophet.* Johannesburg: Witwatersrand University Press.

Ellis, Chris. 2003. "Cross-Cultural Aspects of Depression." *South African Medical Journal* 93, no. 5: 342–345.

Fernandez, James. 1978. "African Religious Movements." *Annual Review of Anthropology* 7: 195–234.

Furniss, Graham. 1996. *Poetry, Prose, and Popular Culture in Hausa.* Edinburgh: Edinburgh University Press for International African Library.

Fuze, Magema. 1922. *Abantu Abamnyama Nalapho Bavela Ngakhona.* Pietermaritzburg: City Printing Works. Published as *The Black People and Whence They Came.* Trans. H. C. Lugg and A. T. Cope. Pietermaritzburg: University of Natal Press, 1979.

Gee, James. 1996. *Social Linguistics and Literacies: Ideology in Discourse.* 2nd ed. London: Falmer Press.

Greenstein, Ran, ed. 2003. *The Role of Political Violence in South Africa's Democratisation.* Johannesburg: Community Agency for Social Enquiry.

Gunner, Elizabeth. 2000. "Hidden Stories and the Light of the New Day: A Zulu Manuscript and Its Place in South African Writing Now." *Research in African Literatures* 31, no. 2 (Summer): 1–16.

———, ed. and trans. 2002a. *The Man of Heaven and the Beautiful Ones of God: Writings from a South African Church.* Leiden: Brill.

———. 2002b. "Dislocation, Memory and Modernity: The Prophet Isiah Shembe and the Search for Voice and Space." In *African Modernities,* ed. Jan-Georg Deutsch, Peter Probst, and Heike Schmidt, 67–84. Oxford: James Currey.

Guy, Jeff. 1983. *The Heretic: A Study of the Life of John William Colenso, 1814–1883.* Johannesburg: Ravan Press.

———. 2002. *The View Across the River: Harriette Colenso and the Zulu Struggle against Imperialism.* Charlottesville: University of Virginia Press; Oxford: James Currey; Cape Town: David Philip.

Hadebe, Meshack. 1934. "The Testimony of Meshack Hadebe." Unpublished manuscript. Photocopy in Shembe manuscript collection. MS380453, Archives, School of Oriental and African Studies, London. Original in Ekuphakameni Archive, Inanda, Durban. English and isiZulu versions are in Gunner 2002a.

Harries, Patrick. 1994. *Work, Culture and Identity: Migrant Labourers in Mozambique and South Africa circa 1860–1910.* Johannesburg: Witwatersrand University Press.

Hofmeyr, Isabel. 2004. *The Portable Bunyan: A Transnational History of* The Pilgrim's Progress. Johannesburg: Wits University Press; Princeton: Princeton University Press.

Jeffrey, Anthea. 1997. *The Natal Story: Sixteen Years of Conflict.* Johannesburg: Institute of Race Relations.

Kentridge, Matthew. 1991. *The Unofficial War.* Cape Town: David Philip.

La Hausse de Lalouvière, Paul. 2002. *Restless Identities: Signatures of Nationalism, Zulu Ethnicity and History in the Lives of Petros Lamula (c. 1881–1948) and Lymon Maling (1889–c. 1936).* Pietermaritzburg : University of Natal Press.

Lee, S. G. 1969. "Spirit Possession among the Zulu." In *Spirit Mediumship and Society in Africa,* ed. J. Beattie and J. Middleton, 128–156. London: Routledge and Kegan Paul.

Maphumulo, Lazarus. 1942. "Lazarus Maphumulo's Notebook." Unpublished manuscript. Photocopy in Shembe manuscript collection. MS380455, Archives, School of Oriental and African Studies, London. Original in Ekuphakameni Archive, Inanda, Durban. Excerpts in English and isiZulu in Gunner 2002a.

Marks, Shula, ed. 1987. *Not Either an Experimental Doll: The Separate Worlds of Three South African Women*. London: Women's Press.

Meintjes, Sheila. 1988. "Edendale 1851–1930. Farmers to Townspeople: Market to Labour Reserve." In *Pietermaritzburg, 1838–1988: A New Portrait of an African City*, ed. John Laband and Robert Haswell, 66–69. Pietermaritzburg: University of Natal Press.

Muller, Carol. 1997. "'Written into the Book of Life': Nazarite Women's Performance Transcribed as Spiritual Text in Ibandla lamaNazaretha." *Research in African Literatures* 28, no. 1: 3–14.

———. 1999. *Rituals of Fertility and the Sacrifice of Desire: Nazarite Women's Performance in South Africa*. Chicago: University of Chicago Press.

Ngubane, Harriet. 1975. "The Place of Spirit Possession in Zulu Cosmology." In *Religion and Social Change in Southern Africa: Anthropological Essays in Honour of Monica Wilson*, ed. Michael Whysson and Martin West, 48–57. Cape Town: David Philip.

———. 1977. *Body and Mind in Zulu Medicine*. London: Academic Press.

Olson, David. 1994. *The World on Paper: The Conceptual and Cognitive Implications of Writing and Reading*. Cambridge: Cambridge University Press.

Papini, Robert. 1999. "Carl Faye's Transcript of Isaiah Shembe's Testimony of His Early Life and Calling." *Journal of Religion in Africa* 29, no. 3: 243–284.

Parle, Julie, and Karen Flint. Forthcoming. "Healers, Witchcraft and Madness." In *Being Zulu: Contesting Identities Past and Present*, ed. Benedict Carton, James Laband, and Jabulani Sithole. Pietermaritzburg: University of KwaZulu-Natal Press.

Shembe, Johannes Galilee (and Isaiah). 1940. *Izihlabelelo zaManazaretha*. Durban: Elite Printers.

Union of South Africa. 1932. *Report on the Native Economic Commission, 1930–1932*. Pretoria: Government Printing Press.

Werbner, R. 1985. "The Argument of Images: From Zion to the Wilderness in African Churches." In *Theoretical Explorations in African Religion*, ed. W. Van Binsbergen and M. Schoffeleers, 165–182. London: Routledge.

Van Onselen, Charles. 1996. *The Seed Is Mine: The Life of Kas Maine, a South African Sharecropper, 1894–1985*. Cape Town: David Philip.

West, Gerald. 1999. *The Academy of the Poor: Towards a Dialogical Reading of the Bible*. Sheffield: Academic Press.

SCHOOLGIRL PREGNANCIES, LETTER-WRITING, AND "MODERN" PERSONS IN LATE COLONIAL EAST AFRICA

Lynn M. Thomas

7

In August 1960, Sara Wangari, a Kikuyu schoolgirl in colonial Kenya, wrote a letter to Thomas Mwangi, a Kikuyu student at Makerere College in Uganda, asking him to accept responsibility for her pregnancy. Sara opened her English-language letter by referring to their previous correspondence and describing her emotional distress.

> I think you have received the letter I sent you a few days a go, I needed the reply badly but I have not seen it yet. I wrote it in a very bad way but I did not mean it, the reason for it is that, your letter was very harsh and yet you had not known anything by then and I was so hurt to learn that you were not cincere to me, and you had of a pleasure of a few minutes which brought me tears without end.

She explained that as the pregnancy was now "too big," she had been compelled to drop out of school and had informed her parents of the situation. Sara noted that while in the past "very rich men" and others "with high education" had pursued her, she had only ever loved Thomas. Responding to previous statements or insinuations by Thomas that she was "a girl without any understanding," Sara reminded him that she was just about to complete Standard VII and that she had planned—prior to her pregnancy—to attend high school or teachers' training college. She insisted that in addition to "high education," she had "the rest which are needed in this modern days." With these words, Sara suggested that she was a worthy partner for a college student.

Thomas's response was scathing. He began,

> Instead of thanking you for your recent letter I find I was rather easy to tell you how very amused to see that you thought you could hook me and yet go

through with it. Sorry baby you are UTTERLY mistaken. Your threats and advertisements completely failed to move me an inch!

You must have thought that I am one of these idiotic lads to be told to wallow a thing and then do so like a docile child. But you forget that I know more of you than you guess!

Very absurd that you are going to have a baby. You don't know whether the baby is alive or dead. You must be in a precarious condition [Sara]. And a little surprise for you just before I go on: How is the Mjaluo? I mean the father of your unborn child?

You were a virgin. Never went out late, never had boy-friends and yet there's the Luo! Well, don't think that I'm to ridicule you but it surprises me to see how guilty the whole world is.

You better stop cheating yourself because you'll only end in disaster.

Thomas went on to dismiss Sara's claim to being a "modern lady." Accusing Sara of trying to "hook" him through trickery, he wrote the last portion of his letter in the form of a detective story.[1]

I found Sara and Thomas's letters in a court case file deposited at the Kenya National Archives. Sara's father submitted the pair of letters as evidence in a civil suit he brought against Thomas in December 1960. As Thomas refused to accept responsibility for the pregnancy, Sara's father sued him under the Kikuyu customary law of pregnancy compensation. After hearing testimony from Sara's father, Sara, and Thomas and reviewing the two letters, a Nairobi court ordered Thomas to pay Sara's father 680 Kenya shillings (Ksh.).

In this chapter, I use Sara and Thomas's exchange to explore the role that letters and letter-writing played in schoolgirl pregnancy disputes in late-colonial East Africa. The first part of this chapter places schoolgirl pregnancies in historical perspective by examining how premarital pregnancies emerged as an acute dilemma for school-going young women and men in mid-twentieth-century central Kenya and how this dilemma related to ongoing colonial debates over female initiation. Protestant missionaries' opposition to female "circumcision," or excision, heightened some parents' fear that sending daughters to mission schools made them sexually and reproductively vulnerable. When schoolgirl pregnancies occurred, young people and their parents often viewed them as foiling plans to build better and more prosperous lives. Letters became an important, though often contested, form of evidence in the pregnancy-compensation civil suits that ensued when a young man refused to accept responsibility for a premarital pregnancy.

With these historical contexts established, I then return to a consideration of Sara's and Thomas letters. Their exchange suggests how young people in late-colonial East Africa debated notions of the "modern" and how their notions were often linked to cultural forms encountered in schools and elaborated outside their boundaries. School-taught practices of reading and writing figure prominently in how Sara and Thomas represented themselves as "modern" persons. Through their letters, Sara and Thomas also deployed practices of reading and writing to construct forms of personal publicity and collective privacy. These hybrid forms defy the notion that the rise of literacy and print cultures neatly correlates with the construction of discrete public and private realms. Rather, Sara and Thomas's letters suggest how the reading and writing of letters, detective stories, and Swahili newspapers could combine introspection with the projection of public personas and intimacy with instrumental desires to document.

Schoolgirls' Reputations, Gendered Mobility, and Generational Authority

From the earliest years of colonial rule, central Kenyans feared that schooling for girls would promote promiscuity and confound reproduction. When Protestant missionaries first opened schools for girls in the early 1900s, some central Kenyan parents worried that by sending their daughters to school, they might ruin their reputations. As John Lonsdale has argued, parents were nervous about "their daughters' adolescent transition to full sexuality occur[ing] in the ritual seclusion of school, subject to foreigners" (1992, 392). By moving outside the immediate purview of their families, schoolgirls might pursue inappropriate relations or be preyed upon by powerful men, most notably teachers.[2] This association between schooling and unrestrained sexuality lingered in central Kehya even as female school attendance increased. My own research on the history of colonial maternity services in Meru (Thomas 2003, 66–71), an area on the northeastern slopes of Mt. Kenya, reveals that one of the greatest obstacles to recruiting schoolgirls for colonial midwifery work was parents' fear that a training stint in Nairobi would render their daughters "loose" women.

Central Kenyan concerns about schooling for girls were closely tied to colonial debates surrounding female initiation. These debates culminated in the "female circumcision controversy" of 1928–1931, when Protestant missionaries attempted to pressure the colonial government to ban excision. Many black church members and the Kikuyu Central Association (a leading black political organization) responded to this effort by denouncing it and leaving mission churches and schools to found independent ones. Schoolgirls stood at the center of this controversy. Protestant missionaries hoped that by securing a legal prohibition on excision, they would be able to protect adolescent schoolgirls from abandoning their studies and voluntarily or forcibly undergoing the "indecent" and "barbaric" practice of female initiation. By attacking a practice that many central Kenyans viewed as curbing excessive female desire, however, Protestant missionaries only strengthened local suspicions that their schools contributed to undisciplined sexuality (Lonsdale 1992, 380–397; Thomas 2003, 110–115).

Reproductive predicaments faced by some of the first schoolgirls to renounce excision only confirmed such suspicions. For example, in 1939, Dr. Clive Irvine of the Presbyterian mission station at Chogoria wrote a letter to the Meru district commissioner, drawing attention to the "increase in immorality between men and unmarried girls." Irvine described the cases of two schoolgirls (one of whom was the "head girl") who had become pregnant; in each case, the man held responsible for the pregnancy—an ex-elder of the church and a young man training to become a medical assistant—refused to follow "native custom" and marry the girl. Irvine blamed such "immorality" on schooling that "quickens all the sensibilities and gives rise to increased sex desire" and causes girls to "get themselves up attractively." Unwilling to cast his fervent opposition to excision in a negative light, Irvine admitted only in passing that these cases were "complicated by the fact that [the girls] . . . were uncircumcised."[3] The district commissioner, H. E. Lambert, who had long been critical of Protestant missionaries' campaigns to end female initiation, viewed the situation very differently. Lambert pointed to the girls' uninitiated status as the crux of the problem. He stated that men were not marrying the pregnant schoolgirls because they were not initiated.[4] The men, or perhaps their female kin, could not accept incorporating an uninitiated girl into their households. By drawing girls outside of their parents' immediate purview or encouraging them to renounce female initiation, schooling could tarnish sexual reputations and leave unmarried mothers in its wake.

By the post–World War II period, schooling had become part of being upwardly mobile in much of the region. Parents used hard-earned cash to pay their children's school fees. They viewed schooling as crucial to providing their children with the knowledge and skills necessary to succeed in a colonial and, later, postcolonial world. School education, the logic went, enabled young people, particularly men, to obtain employment as clerks, teachers, hospital personnel, and government officials. From these comfortable salaried positions, they could accumulate wealth by developing family farms, purchasing land, and owning businesses. Young women and their parents hoped that schooling would lead to lucrative employment and/or marriage to a successful man. Black Kenyans embraced schooling as the key to acquiring and maintaining prosperity during the 1960s, and primary school enrollments increased from just over 1 million in 1964 to 1.4 million in 1970, while secondary school enrollments increased more than threefold, reaching over 126,000 (Kitching 1980, 309–311, 438–455; Leys 1975, 191, 201–204; Maxon 1995, 126–132). It was within this context of parents and young people investing considerable resources in school education and expecting high returns that schoolgirl pregnancies became such a compelling issue.

School officials normally responded to pregnant schoolgirls by expelling them. Schoolboys accused of involvement in such pregnancies usually remained in school. In cases in which the accused boy or man refused to marry the young woman or was deemed an unsuitable marriage choice, the young woman's father or guardian could sue for pregnancy compensation under customary law. In 1960s central Kenya, a successful suit meant that the boy or man paid the young woman's father or guardian around 700 Kenya shillings (Cotran 1968, 18, 40–42). Some plaintiffs interpreted this compensation as a partial repayment of school fees. In two of the fifty-seven pregnancy compensation cases I examined from 1950s and 1960s Meru, fathers specifically stated that their suits were an effort to recoup money spent on their daughters' schooling.[5] In Kenya and elsewhere in Africa, such premarital pregnancy litigation, while it was not limited to cases involving schoolgirls, became closely identified with them (Penwill 1951, 73–75; Vellenga 1974; Bledsoe and Cohen 1993, 107–108; Puja and Kassimoto 1994).

Some contemporaries blamed schooling for young men's reluctance to accept responsibility for such pregnancies. In an interview my research assistant Richard Kirimi and I conducted in 1995, Naaman M'Mwirichia, a teacher and school supervisor in Meru during the 1930s and 1940s and later a headman, explained the problem as the product of young men's experiences attending schools and working for wages, often far from home. According to M'Mwirichia, "Young men started parting with old men. If you're from Makerere [the college in Uganda] or if you're from Nairobi Hospital or you're from Great Britain or you're from America, when you come it's difficult to see a person who is older than you and to stay with him and ask him about customary ways."[6] M'Mwirichia's words are eloquent testimony to the changing generational relations that challenged the ability of elders to compel young men to marry those whom they had helped to make pregnant. According to M'Mwirichia, young men who had attended school and worked far away viewed themselves as sophisticates, no longer bound by the knowledge and advice of their elders.

One colonial development that had a direct bearing on premarital pregnancy litigation was schoolboys' skepticism of local oaths. In her semi-autobiographical account of growing up in central Kenya during the 1940s and 1950s, Charity Waciuma (1969, 40–41) described how local tribunals required any accused young man who denied responsibility for a premarital pregnancy to take an oath to prove his innocence. The oath involved the young man presenting a goat to the elders, slaughtering and roasting it, and eating a portion of its heart while declaring "If I be responsible in this matter may the judgement of God strike me down." According to the logic of the oath, if nothing unfortunate occurred in the next week, the man was vindicated. Waciuma explained that as "younger educated men did not believe in the oaths and did not fear their power," they would take them regardless of whether they were responsible or not. Such skepticism probably also enabled some young men to disregard the Christian, Muslim, or "pagan" oaths (depending on their declared faith) administered in colonial and postcolonial courts. In causing young men to dismiss oaths and elders' advice, schooling weakened previous methods of holding young men responsible for the consequences of their sexual relations. As we will see, such changing generational relations also informed the letters and, in some instances, the forgeries that were submitted as evidence in pregnancy-compensation cases.

In their own defense, schoolboys and teachers often claimed that the reason they were the targets of so many pregnancy-compensation suits was not because they, compared with their age-mates, were more irresponsible but because they were the "best catches." According to this perspective, when it came time for a young woman to identify who was responsible for her pregnancy, she paid more attention to which of her lovers had the brightest future than to who was actually responsible. For instance, prior to appearing in court, one defendant wrote a letter stating that the plaintiff's daughter "wanted to be married by a teacher, that's what made her say that the pregnancy she has is mine."[7] Moreover, interviewees who had been the "victims" of pregnancy-compensation litigation claimed that women specifically enticed them or singled them out from a number of lovers because they were secondary school students with promising futures and, in one case, from a wealthy family.[8]

By promoting the Christian ideal of monogamy, schooling also changed how young men approached marriage. In their study of premarital pregnancy in 1970s Botswana, John L. Comaroff and Simon Roberts argued that the rise of such litigation was due to "the spread of monogamy within a society organ-ised in terms of the assumption of polygyny." According to Comaroff and Roberts (1977), premarital pregnancy cases were part of a new pattern of se-rial monogamy that had emerged to replace polygyny. In central Kenya, schoolboys who planned on monogamous marriages may have been more dis-criminating about who and when they married than age-mates who viewed polygyny as a possibility. In a 1942 memo circulated to other missionaries in East Africa, E. Carey Francis, the principal of Alliance High School (the first and most prestigious Protestant secondary school in Kenya) explained such decisions as one of the dilemmas posed by Christian monogamy. He wrote that while with polygyny, "it is fairly easy to choose a cook cum labourer cum producer of children who can be sacked if inefficient," under monogamy "it is far harder to choose a helpmeet 'till death do us part.'"[9] Although Francis overdrew the distinction between marital decisions under polygyny and monogamy, caricaturing the former as a loveless relationship, he was right to suggest that an expectation of monogamy cast courtship and marriage in a new light.

Many school-educated young men expected their only wife to be school-educated as well. In one pregnancy-compensation case, a young woman testi-fied that the defendant refused to marry her because she "was not educated."[10] Other considerations related to the prosperity that schooling was supposed to bring. A letter written by Stephen Anampiu in 1957–1958 to his former teacher W. H. Laughton in Meru suggests how for an upwardly mobile man, the decision to marry entailed careful financial planning. Anampiu wrote, "I am no longer the Stephen who used to be suspicious of getting married. For next year my love and my coffee will support a family. My pay [salary] will support my professional standard and I hope I will then be a man!"[11] In order for Anampiu to be the sort of father, husband, and "man" who could provide smart clothing, good housing, and small luxuries for himself and his family, he needed to have a coffee farm as well as a salaried position. An early marriage could have delayed or even spoiled Anampiu's attainment of financial well-being.

Intertwined issues of generational authority, class mobility, and marriage animated schoolgirl pregnancy cases. By disobeying elders and refusing re-sponsibility for such pregnancies, school-educated young men sought to pre-serve their marriage options and avoid assuming the financial burden of a family too soon. Compared to their female counterparts, school-educated men were far less eager to marry in early adulthood. Whereas young pregnant women often seemed to have viewed marriage as a means to turn an embarrassing situation into a more respectable and promising one, school-educated men frequently viewed such marriages as creating problems that could perhaps be evaded altogether.

Pregnancy-Compensation Litigation and Letter-Writing

Letters became a part of pregnancy-compensation cases when plaintiffs, defendants, and witnesses made reference to them in their testimonies or submitted them as evidence in court. Nearly all of the letters, which were written in Meru or English, followed a form taught in schools.[12] They contained a return address and date in the upper-right-hand corner, a salutation below on the left-hand side, body paragraphs, and a closing remark centered at the bottom and followed by a signature. Young women often used letters to notify men of their pregnancies and to ascertain whether or not they would accept responsibility. In her testimony before the court, one woman explained how she sent a letter of notification. As translated from Meru and paraphrased in the English case record, her testimony reads as follows: "On the 30th of July 1963 I had sexual intercourse with the Defendant and then got conceived. I then notified the Defendant by the letter."[13]

Letters of notification that specified the date on which conception occurred could prove decisive in the court's efforts to determine whether the defendant or someone else was the father of the child. For instance, in another case, a defendant used an English-language letter of notification sent to him in November 1963 to demonstrate that he was not the father of the child. The relevant section of the woman's letter read:

> This month [November 1963] I am so worried about myself. We are nearing the end of it and I have not received my period yet. I receive it at the same dates every month but this month they have missed. That I think is one of the signs of pregnant.
>
> Now please forgive me for being so rude to you telling you things which does not concern any male.

This excerpt suggests how letters could be used to communicate practical information about delicate matters. As the baby was not born until the following October—eleven months after the time that they had had sex, the court found that the defendant was not liable for the pregnancy.[14] In some cases, it appears that the point of exchanging letters was, in fact, to record competing claims about sex and conception dates before the birth of the child. For instance, one young woman stated in court that she had asked the defendant to "write a paper" specifying when they had had sex. She explained that though he "refused" to write his paper, she had written hers, indicating that November 13, 1965, was the day that they had had sex and she had conceived.[15] This case and others like it suggest how letters exchanged during pregnancies were often written with an eye toward impending litigation. In such cases, seemingly private letters functioned like other documents, including receipts, contracts, and wills, that could be enlisted in legal disputes.

In a 1964 case, a young man argued that a letter he had written to the plaintiff stood as "*kiama*." Within premarital pregnancy disputes, *kiama* referred to a group of two or three respected older men from the woman's clan representing both generational sets of *kiruka* and *ntiba*. Once a woman's family learned of her premarital pregnancy, her father or brother was required to send a *kiama* to the home of the man suspected of being responsible for the pregnancy. The *kiama* was charged with informing the man's family of the pregnancy and ascertaining whether marriage would follow or compensation would be paid. Sending a *kiama* was crucial for subsequent pregnancy-compensation proceedings. African courts interpreted a *kiama*'s involvement as evidence of the male guardian's good-faith efforts to resolve the dispute through customary channels. They automatically dismissed cases in which a *kiama* was never sent or not sent until after the child was born.[16] This 1964 case reveals how one man, in an interesting, albeit unsuccessful, effort, sought to imbue a letter with the communicative capacities and cultural authority of a group of respected male elders.[17]

Court officials often viewed even vaguely worded letters from defendants as evidence of paternity. For instance, in one case, court officials interpreted a Meru-language letter written by the defendant requesting the young woman to come and discuss the pregnancy as proof that he was responsible.[18] As a man from Meru who had been involved in such cases explained in an interview that I conducted in 1995, love letters were powerful tools for proving that the defendant and the young woman "were not just friends."[19] Defendants had a difficult time in court distancing themselves from such letters. In another case, a plaintiff submitted as evidence a Meru-language letter written by the defendant to the plaintiff's daughter stating, "I know that those things are mine" (*Nimbiji ati mantu jau ni jakwa*). In his defense, the defendant insisted that this statement was not an admission of responsibility for the pregnancy but an effort to "screen" the young woman's sincerity. With this explanation, the defendant suggested that letters could not always be read at face value as writers might be using them to elicit rather than to convey truths.

Court officials rejected this subtle logic as a lie and ordered the defendant to pay compensation.[20]

This example suggests how letters could become contested forms of evidence within pregnancy-compensation cases. As Isabel Hofmeyr has argued, in contexts of limited literacy, the written word often appears more impermanent than durable and trustworthy (1993, 65–66). Compared to oral testimony, written documents were just as likely to be products of deceit and trickery. A 1967 pregnancy-compensation case from Meru involving a Standard VII schoolgirl named Jennifer and secondary schoolboy named Francis reveals how court officials could be quite skeptical of letters. In that case, Francis, the defendant, testified that he had had sexual intercourse with Jennifer in March and May 1966 and that in June 1966 Jennifer wrote him a letter informing him that she was pregnant as a result of their May encounter. Francis claimed that he then drafted, and both he and Jennifer signed, an agreement stating that he would accept responsibility if the child was born nine months from May. Francis stated that when the child was born in October 1966, just five months later, he knew the child was not his. Francis submitted as evidence this agreement along with three love letters allegedly written by Jennifer. Before the Court, however, Jennifer denied that she had ever signed such an agreement or written such letters, including one with the opening epithet of "dearest innermost super guy." She pointed out that the letters and agreement were signed Joyce, rather than Jennifer, Kinanu.

In its ruling in favor of Jennifer's father, the court dismissed the letters and the agreement as forgeries perpetrated by Francis and two friends. Officials stated that the "standardized and fluent English" in which the letters were written could never have been produced by someone like Jennifer, who had only achieved a Standard VII education. The court also noted that nowhere on Jennifer's school certificates did her name appear as Joyce.[21]

Other court records too contained suspicions or accusations of forgery. In a case from 1966, court officials rejected as evidence three letters (two in Meru, one in English) submitted by the plaintiff and allegedly written by the defendant on the grounds that their authenticity could not be verified as the plaintiff had not provided "other examples of handwriting to compare."[22] While the use of handwriting samples may have been a routine procedure when court officials considered letters, no other judgments that I examined made specific mention of it. In other instances, court officials ignored accusations of forgery. In a case from 1965, the plaintiff's daughter and her female amanuensis argued that a letter submitted by the defendant and allegedly written by the two of them was a fake as their original letter had been written on a different date and with a different kind of pen. The court officials, however, accepted the letter as authentic and ruled in the defendant's favor.[23]

In addition to forgery, other factors rendered letters as potentially fragile forms of evidence. Letters could disappear entirely. Young women stated that letters containing defendants' admissions of paternity were lost or were "washed by the children with the clothes."[24] While letters provided litigants and witnesses in pregnancy-compensation cases with another form of evidence upon which to rest their positions, it was not a form that was inherently more stable or persuasive than oral testimony.

In spite of this fragility, letters frequently became focal points in premarital pregnancy disputes because of the social positions and ambitions of the school-educated young women and men who were so often involved in these cases. Letters were a performance of young peoples' school-educated status. They enabled a form of personal publicity through which young people could project their school-educated personas to potential spouses and, perhaps later, to parents and court officials. At stake in many of these cases was whether or not the young woman was a suitable match for a secondary school student, a teacher, or some other school-educated and salaried man. By writing a letter in Meru or, better yet, in English and in the form taught at school, young women sought to demonstrate that they were suitably well educated and would make worthy wives.

At a more practical level, letters appeared to enable discreet communication between two people who might be working or attending school at a distance. Many of the sexual encounters that resulted in conception seem to have occurred during the holidays when salaried workers and students returned to their home areas. Letters enabled young women and men to communicate about their relationship and the pregnancy once they had returned to their offices and schools located all over the district, as indicated by the return addresses.[25] Letters appeared to offer confidentiality and intimacy. In some cases, letters announcing pregnancies, specifying conception and projected birth dates, and arranging face-to-face meetings were also love letters. They included romantic declarations such as the statement that no one is "your friend more than I am" (*mucoore waku nkuru ki yakwa*), "you know how much I love you," and "your picture still remains in such a deep corner of my heart" as well as the intimate closing phrase "I am yours" (*Nini waku*).[26]

Yet letters, like those that wound up in pregnancy-compensation-case records, rarely circulated just between two people. Rather, they constituted a form of collective privacy through which young people sought to sort out personal matters with either the immediate or future assistance or intervention of others in mind. References to the involvement of friends or an amanuensis suggest how letter-writing itself, as in the case of the South African mineworkers examined by Keith Breckenridge, could be a joint venture. Letters announcing pregnancies and specifying sex and conception dates were often written with an eye to being read or heard by parents, elders, and court officials, not just a boyfriend or a girlfriend. Moreover, letters sent to school addresses might easily be opened and read by school staff, who often sought to regulate students' morality by screening and, if necessary, censoring their mail. For instance, a letter submitted in one pregnancy-compensation case mentioned that the sister principal at a Catholic girls' school opened letters, read them, and then resealed them "with glue."[27] Such censorship as well as the fear of litigation might have been what prompted a few letter-writers to substitute "As usual" for their return addresses or leave their letters unsigned. Presumably, in these cases, the intended letter-reader knew the writer's identity; as one letter specified, "There is no need for me to write my name because the letter explains the writer."[28] Young people conceived their letters about the seemingly intimate subject of schoolgirl pregnancies with particular publics in mind. Rather than being a confidential correspondence between two young people seeking to sort out their own personal problems, these letters were embedded in webs of peer, familial, and institutional relations and could easily be put to instrumental ends.

Letters between a Pregnant Schoolgirl and a Makerere Student

The exchange that opened this chapter between Sara and Thomas illustrates well how such letters helped construct forms of personal publicity and collective privacy. Sara and Thomas's exchange also highlights how such letters could become forums through which young people debated what made someone a suitable, specifically "modern," spouse and, in turn, how such conceptions of persons and selves were tied to specific practices of writing and reading.

Sara's father presented the two English-language letters—one written by Sara on August 25, 1960, and the other written by Thomas on September 2, 1960—as evidence in his pregnancy-compensation suit filed in a Nairobi court in December of that year. Sara's father learned of her pregnancy in July when, according to Sara's testimony, she sent a woman, perhaps an aunt or family friend, to inform him of it. Sara's father testified that once he learned of the pregnancy, he asked her to write to Thomas to see if he was willing to marry her. He informed the court that Thomas was a "friend" of his with whom he had worked in the same office before Thomas had left for Makerere. When questioned by court officials as to why he himself did not write the letter to Thomas, Sara's father explained, "It was not right for me to write him while he was far away from here. I wanted to know from him through my daughter." This response, alongside of Sara's mention of her woman-messenger, suggests how letters could fit together with long-standing protocols about how best to communicate delicate (notably sexual, reproductive, and marital) matters between genders and across generations. Sara, perhaps at her father's insistence, made either a hand or carbon copy of the letter that she sent to Thomas on August 25th. It was this copy that Sara's father submitted as evidence in his suit.[29]

In her two-page letter, Sara described the sorrow and hardship she was suffering because of the pregnancy and Thomas's refusal to accept responsibility. She stated that Thomas's "pleasure of a few minutes" had brought "tears without end" and that her pregnancy had compelled her to withdraw from school before being expelled. She explained that her relationship with Thomas had only been motivated by love: "I tell you Thomas if I ment to make love with people I could have made it with very rich men and even with high education as you have. But I had and still have no love for them even." Defending herself as a suitable spouse for a college student, Sara wrote,

> You think I am a girl without any understanding at all, all I have missed is high education but the rest which are needed in this modern days I know and I need not be taught by my husband or anybody else. Even I would not like to have a husband who have not a real understanding of this days.

After stating that she was "not ready to get married" even though she still loved Thomas, she specified that crucial point of fact in such cases—the date of conception: "you know you are the only man who did it on the 17th April, the first time you had me." Sara closed her letter, insisting on a response, "Please inform me of your coming as soon as possible!!! 'Prepare your talks to dady.' I remain sad. Yours Sara."

Thomas's four-page rebuttal was biting. He opened his letter by stating that he was "amused" to see that Sara still thought that she could "hook" him. While Thomas never denied having had sex with Sara, he argued that she had a Luo boyfriend (with a car) and that that boyfriend was the one responsible for the pregnancy. Thomas explained that the letter that Sara was reading was the carbon copy of an original that he would soon send to her father, who would then be ashamed of her and her "Luo child." By insulting Sara and insisting that she had another boyfriend of a different—notably uncircumcising—ethnicity, Thomas sought to embarrass Sara and make clear that he would never admit responsibility for her pregnancy. Thomas began the last page of his letter by asking Sara if she was "interested in detective stories" and then providing her with one.

> 1. Background. Boys jilting a girl because she's desperate in life and she has no plans.
>
> 2. She hangs around and gets in a jam. She don't know what to do.
>
> 3. Waits for a pick-up. Students come home.
>
> 4. Tries to hook a graduate but he's too cunning.
>
> 5. Waits for a week! She sees a happy-go-lucky & throws the dice. And you know what happens, even before they meet she's so pregnant that even the CHROMOSOMES on the face and loss of appetite and menstruation period show clearly she's worried to death.
>
> This is not a fairy story. It can be true. Very true even in 20th century and when the child was born, it was too soon!

Sara was presumably the "desperate" girl and Thomas the "happy-go-lucky" who would be vindicated once Sara's baby was born "too soon," less than nine months after their encounter. Through this detective story, Thomas embellished his letter with a literary flourish and restated his determination not to accept responsibility for Sara's pregnancy.

Thomas's letter also referenced another form of popular writing—newspapers. By 1960, premarital pregnancy had become a favorite topic in Kenya's Swahili papers. The Swahili press became an important part of colonial popular culture in the post–World War II period when newspapers, initially started by the government to stem anticolonial sentiment, were turned into profitable commercial ventures (Abuoga and Mutere 1988, 13–24). *Baraza*, *Taifa Weekly*, and *Taifa Leo* regularly featured pieces on pregnancy-compensation litigation on the letters-to-the-editor page and in sections devoted to court reporting. These letters and articles often provided entertaining descriptions of courtroom testimony and titillating descriptions of the intimate relations that preceded the pregnancies. With a combined weekly circulation in 1964 of 180,000 and with copies often being passed among people with some reading it aloud, these three Swahili newspapers spread news about premarital pregnancies to a significant portion of Kenya's 9 million citizens (Soja 1968, 40–43).[30] In his letter to Sara, Thomas wrote "Once it's in the courts, it won't help going to the papers and that will not only kill you but ruin your family." Thomas closed his letter by claiming that he himself would not be daunted by a court appearance: "You forgot I can face *anybody* and at any time. Law follows its course!!!!" With these harsh words and grave predictions, Thomas sought to project a public persona that would deter Sara's father from filing a pregnancy-compensation suit and convince Sara that her testimony would be no match for his own.

Perhaps more hurtful to Sara than Thomas's denial of responsibility and efforts to intimidate was his elaboration of why she was not a "modern lady."

> I was horror struck to see you advertise yourself that you are a "modern lady." You don't go to pictures, you don't have high heeled shoes, you don't wear lipstick, you don't shampoo your hair, you don't have "fashion" pins, not even know how to dance. And you say you're very modern. Trying to imply that you would do for me. Who on earth told you I was going to marry and in that case you? Damn it all!!

According to Thomas, being "modern" was not simply about schooling; a "lady" worthy of a college student also needed to wear high heels and hairpins, use cosmetics, enjoy movies, and know how to dance. Moreover, like the "old" Stephen Anampiu, Thomas expressed suspicions about marriage altogether. He wrote that while he was still undecided as to whether he would marry or not, his career plans made it clear to him that he "shouldn't bother about marriage" until he was "29 or 30 years old." Thomas insisted that Sara's less-than-modern appearance and pastimes together with his own career demands made their marriage an ill-suited prospect.

By the time this case appeared in a court, Sara's attitude toward Thomas had decidedly soured. When asked in court by her father if she would be willing to marry Thomas, she responded "no." Compared to his literary persona, Thomas's courtroom personality (as reflected in the case record) was less blustery and haughty; it was, no doubt, easier to be abusive and disrespectful in a letter to a schoolgirl, even one carbon-copied to her father, than in a face-to-face meeting with elders and court officials. Thomas admitted having had sex with Sara without ever "lov[ing] her for marriage." He never mentioned the Luo boyfriend or anyone else who might be responsible for the pregnancy. Instead, Thomas rested his defense on the claim that he had used a "penis-durex" (condom) on all but their first occasion together. After hearing the evidence, the court officials rejected this defense as unconvincing and ordered Thomas to pay Sara's father pregnancy compensation.

"Modern" Persons and Late-Colonial Practices of Reading and Writing

Over the past decade or so, "modernity" has become a ubiquitous topic of discussion within African studies and beyond. In these discussions, many scholars have challenged the notion of a singular modernity, arguing instead that it should be understood as having alternative (Appadurai 1991; Comaroff and Comaroff 1993; Chakrabarty 1993; Barlow 1997; Gupta 1997; Rofel 1999), multiple (Eisenstadt 2000), vernacular (Donham 1999), or parallel (Larkin 1997) forms. By posing various forms of modernity, this scholarship seeks to refute the claims of 1950s modernization theory that predicted that "all industrial societies would one day converge" around a common set of values and institutions first developed in Europe (Graubard 2000, vi). The scholarship on alternative, multiple, vernacular, and parallel modernities, however, has been plagued by a reluctance to specify what these different forms of modernity hold in common. When scholars have sought to specify the common links between these forms, they have often dealt in abstractions, pointing to the introduction of new notions of human agency and individuality, new conceptions of time and historical change, or, and perhaps most relevant to the concerns of this volume, the construction of distinct private and public spheres.

Historical sources such as Sara and Thomas's letters suggest another—more concrete—method for approaching the study of modernity. These letters together with the history of schoolgirl pregnancies embody East African debates over the "modern." Notions of the "modern" had popular appeal in the late-colonial period because journalists, politicians, and parents attributed new practices and apparent trends to its impact. Within these discussions, few other social ills were as frequently framed as a result of the onslaught of the "modern" and the "breakdown of tradition" as schoolgirl pregnancies.

Sara and Thomas's letters suggest, however, that the young people involved in such cases were less concerned with the deleterious effects of the "modern" than with its definition. At the heart of their epistolary dispute was the question of what made a person "modern." Perhaps what is most striking about their definitions of the "modern" is the centrality of schooling and the practices of reading and writing that extended from it. As was the case with the letters from the Meru pregnancy-compensation cases, Sara and Thomas's English-language letters were a form of personal publicity through which they projected their school-educated status. In light of Thomas's previous insinuations or remarks that Sara was a "girl without any understanding," Sara may have been particularly interested in demonstrating her proficiency in letter-writing and English. Moreover, Sara specifically declared in her letter that it was her seven years of schooling that provided her with ample preparation for "this modern days." Thomas's sense of himself as an accomplished person who deserved a "modern lady" if and when he chose to marry was most likely rooted in his position as a student at Makerere College, the premier institution of higher learning in late-colonial East Africa. Nonetheless, when it came to "lad[ies]," at least, Thomas insisted that schooling alone did not make them "modern"; rather, the female "modern" was defined through her use of cosmetics, her knowledge of fashion, and her enjoyment of movies and dances, popular cultural practices and forms that might be encountered in school but could be elaborated only outside its boundaries.

Despite Thomas's insistence that being "modern" could not be reduced to being school educated, his letter repeatedly returns to practices of reading and writing. Particularly noteworthy is his reference to two literary forms of popular culture: detective stories and newspapers. Through writing the final page of his letter as a detective story, Thomas demonstrated his familiarity with a "modern" literary genre and, once again, sought to intimidate Sara into dropping her accusations against him. While conveying the didactic message that trickery will not succeed, Thomas portrayed himself as a "happy-go-lucky" and Sara as a desperate girl who ultimately would be humiliated and proved a liar. Stephanie Newell (2000, 2002) and others in this volume have argued that such reworking of imported genres for the purpose of moral instruction is one of the defining features of African popular writing. With Thomas's letter, we have an example of a reader in late-colonial East Africa engaging the literary form of detective stories as a model for his own writing and as a means to both teach and threaten. A desire to instill fear in Sara and to deter her father from filing a suit against him similarly animated Thomas's reference to Swahili newspapers' coverage of pregnancy-compensation cases. Such coverage turned pregnancy-compensation cases from the concern of court officials and the families involved to a form of news and entertainment for all those with access to Swahili papers. By publicizing these cases, Swahili papers widened the circle of those included in the collective privacy of schoolgirl pregnancy disputes. Thomas's evocation of detective stories and Swahili newspapers illuminates how readers and writers could turn popular literary forms to a wide variety of ends, including those of instruction, intimidation, and humiliation.

Sara and Thomas's epistolary dispute over what made a person "modern" demonstrates how young people in late-colonial East Africa engaged and participated in imperial and transnational discussions of the "modern." Both the content and form of their exchange—English-language letters written with an eye toward impending pregnancy-compensation litigation—suggests that the history of the "modern" in Africa and elsewhere does not lie in the wholesale adoption of new conceptions of the individual or historical change, or in the creation of a sharp divide between the public and the private.[31] Rather, Sara and Thomas's letters reveal "modern" persons using practices of reading and writing to construct hybrid forms of personal publicity and collective privacy, forms that could help them negotiate the rapidly shifting terrain of gender relations, generational authority, and class mobility. Through their letters, the young people involved in these cases sought to forge public personas and webs of social support that would enable them to either mitigate or evade altogether the dilemmas posed by schoolgirl pregnancies.

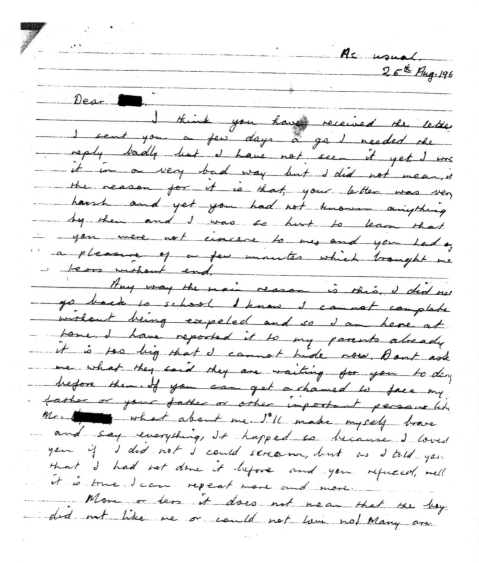

Figure 7.1. Sara's letter to Thomas. Courtesy the Kenya National Archives.

writing to know who is that brave boy who won me because they have tried and fail many are sorry to see that they have misse me all the more. I tell you ████████ if I we to make love with people I could have mad it with very rich men and even with high Education as you have. But I had and sti have no love for them even.

You think I am a girl without any understanding at all, all I have missed is high education but the rest which are needed in this morden days I know and I need not be taught by my husband or anybody else. I've would not like to have a husband who have not a real understanding of this days, so don't full me. You know my father very well, he mean, me to do K.A.P.E. so as to go to high school or to the teachers training, but it is all finished I can not continue, Its you who have done it and aga you want to say not.

I am not ready to get married and I don't w it to so soon although I am like this.

I want to speak to you about this before we — called, if I dont get married to you as I love and you have conceived me I am not in this world then. Please it is better if you say "Yes" than decay, you knew you are the oly mand who did it on the "17th April. the very first time you had me. Please inform me of your coming as soon as possible!!! Prepare your talks to dady, I remain sad
Yours
████████

199

(Page 1)

Sept 2 1960

████ !

Instead of thanking you for your recent letter I find it was rather easy to tell you how very amused to see that you thought you could hook me and yet go through with it. Sorry baby you are UTTERLY mistaken. Your threats and advertisements completely failed to move me an inch!
You must have thought that I am one of these idiotic lads to be told to wallow a thing and then do so like a docile child. But you forget that I know more of you than you guess!
"Very absurd that you are going to have a baby. You don't know whether the baby is alive or dead. You must be in a precarious condition ████.
And a little surprise for you just before I go on: How is the Mjaluo? I mean the father of your unborn child?
You were a virgin. Never went out late, never had boy-friends and yet there's the Luo! Well, don't think that I'm to ridicule you but it surprises me to see how guilty the whole world is.
You better stop cheating yourself because you'll only end in disaster.

You must have been completely out of your senses — that is crazy — to try and lay the whole thing on me. You also tried to threaten me by saying that you didn't think I could

stand facing your father or my father for
that matter. You will notice I am sending
you a carbon copy of a letter. Because the
original goes to your father after one
week!! He must come to know
that if you ███████ try to defame
my name, you'll end up in court.
And I don't mean maybe. You said
that if I deny about this baby,
you'd die. You better hang
yourself right away because if you
don't your father will be ashamed of you
and your Luo child.
        Can't you stop for one minute and
reason out like any normal woman that
people don't go on marrying after
knowing one another for a fortnight?
You only saw me when your father
sent me home to bring eggs, & meat.
Queer! You think I've been blind
to see how you went out of your
way to make my acquaintance; like
the days you delayed to go to school.
I was horror struck to see you
advertise yourself that you are a
"modern lady". You don't go to pictures,
you don't have high heeled shoes, you
don't wear lipstick, you don't shampoo
your hair, you don't have "fashion" pins,
not even know how to dance. And you
say you're very modern. Trying to
imply that you would do for me.
Who on earth told you I was going to marry
and in that case you? Damn it all!!

(3)

I'm wondering whether you'll afford to face m when I come — when I bring this letter to yo father — and speak as boldly as you seem to be. Because I would like to warn you to be very careful. It will be proved beyond ~~measure~~ that, ~~you're~~ not the innocent girl you pretended to be but a rotten skunk full of rotten ideas. Once it's in the courts, it won't help going to the papers and that will not only kill you but ruin your family. Perhaps you never knew that the medical profession has put it clearly before me that I shouldn't bother about marriage till I'm 29 or 30 years old. Reason being it would be ~~useless~~ to marry before then. You either take it or you don't. But if I'm to marry, one thing is dead certain, not ~~you~~! You don't have a thing. Even ~~shape~~!

I don't know whether you are crying just now but I'm immensely amused to see you all in a tangle and then sending a letter this way on 1/9/60 saying "it is too big."

Well... I think now I better stop and I feel it is clear — as clear as water — that you realise I know all about you and your rotten tricks and your Luo boy-friend.

Wish ~~you~~ happy time with him.

Will be seeing you with your baby!

My salaams to all at home and, don't forget to go to church!!

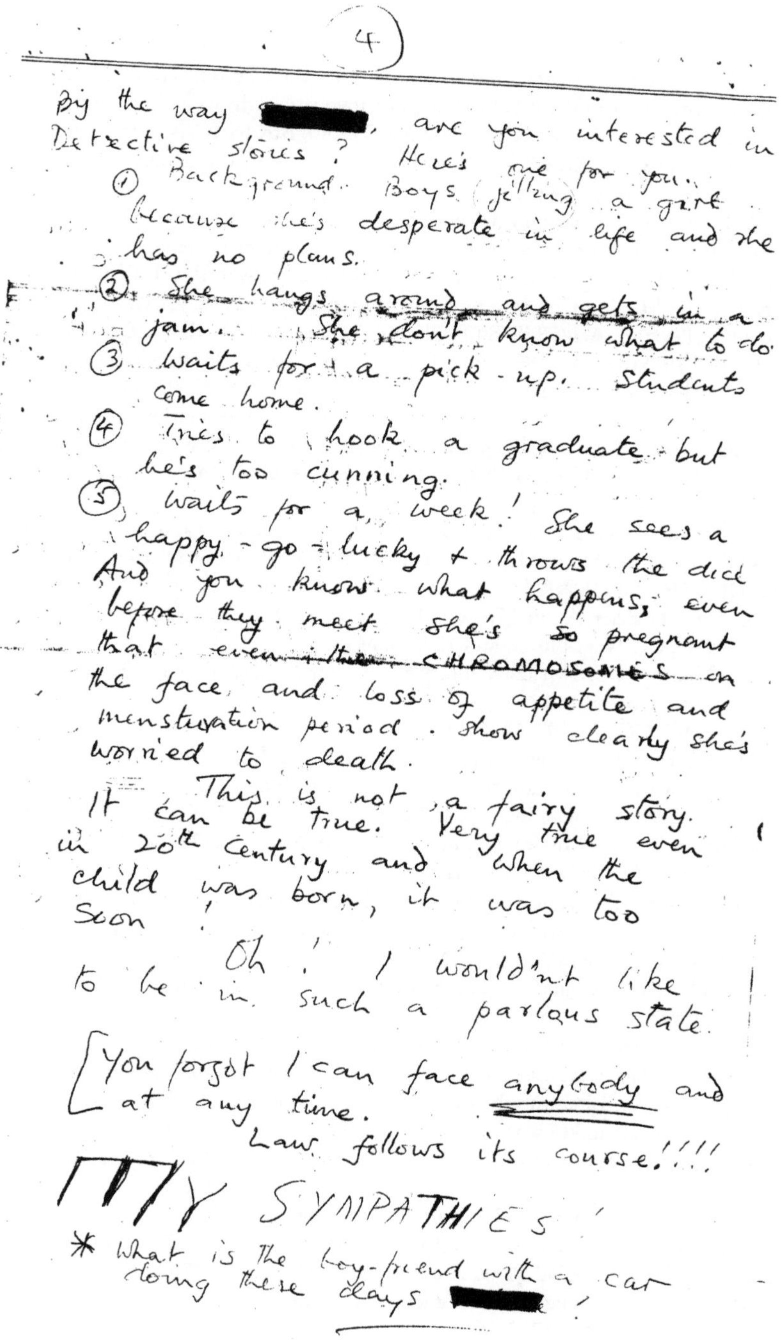

By the way ███████, are you interested in Detective stories? Here's one for you.

① Background. Boys jilting a girl because she's desperate in life and she has no plans.

② She hangs around and gets in a jam. She don't know what to do.

③ Waits for a pick-up. Students come home.

④ Tries to hook a graduate but he's too cunning.

⑤ Waits for a week! She sees a happy-go-lucky & throws the die. And you know what happens; even before they meet she's so pregnant that even the CHROMOSOMES on the face and loss of appetite and menstruation period. Show clearly she's worried to death.

This is not a fairy story. It can be true. Very true even in 20th Century and When the child was born, it was too soon!

Oh! I would'nt like to be in such a parlous state.

[You forgot I can face anybody and at any time.

Law follows its course!!!!

MY SYMPATHIES!

* What is the boy-friend with a car doing these days ███████ !

Figure 7.2. Thomas's letter to Sara. Courtesy the Kenya National Archives.

NOTES

1. These names are pseudonyms. Throughout the chapter, various details have been changed to protect the identity of the litigants involved in the case. These letters were submitted as evidence in Nairobi Civil Case No. 353/60, Box RMC/Nairobi/1960–63, Kenya National Archives (hereafter KNA). The two letters, with the names deleted, are reproduced at the end of this chapter.

2. In a range of twentieth-century African contexts, missionaries, parents, and young people complained of male teachers taking advantage of female students. See Donald M. McFarlan (former missionary in Nigeria), Glasgow, to Rev. J. W. C. Dougall, Secretary, Foreign Mission Committee, Edinburgh, March 1, 1943, African Foreign Mission Council Collection, Acc/7548/B404 National Library of Scotland, Edinburgh; Penwill (1951, 74–75); Mbembe (1992, 23); Rogo, Bohmer, and Ombaka (1999, S61); Mager (1999, 138–139, 203); Niehaus (2000); Summers (2002, 7–8, 47, 98, 112n8, 194n18). For pregnancy-compensation cases from 1960s Meru that involved fathers suing their daughters' teachers, see Kinoru African Court records (hereafter KAC), Civil Case (hereafter CC) Nos. 517/66, 443/66, 397/64, 1233/65, and 1909/65, Meru Law Court (hereafter MLC).

3. Dr. Clive Irvine, Church of Scotland Mission, Chogoria, to H. E. Lambert, District Commissioner, Meru, October 10, 1939, quoted in Meru District, Annual Report, 1939, DC/MRU/4/5, KNA.

4. Meru District, Annual Report, 1939, DC/MRU/4/5, KNA.

5. KAC, CC Nos. 450/66 and 133/65, MLC.

6. Naaman M'Mwirichia, interview by author and Richard Kirimi, Makutano, North Imenti, September 18, 1995.

7. KAC, CC No. 397/64, MLC.

8. Job Kinoti, interview by author, Kaaga, North Imenti, June 28, 1995; James Laiboni, interview by author, Kangeta, Igembe, July 23, 1995.

9. E. Carey Francis, Principal, Alliance High School, Kenya, "Polygamy," July 3, 1942, African Foreign Mission Council Collection, NLS, Acc/7548/B404.

10. KAC, CC No. 1312/65, MLC.

11. Stephen Anampiu, Government Teacher Training Centre, Meru, to W. H. Laughton, Kagumo Government Teacher Training Centre, Nyeri, ca. 1957–1958, Miscellaneous Manuscripts, MSS/124/6, KNA.

12. The Meru-language reading primer for adults, *Kamincuria Metho* (The Little One That Opens Eyes), written by Methodist missionary E. Mary Holding, provides an example of a model letter. The example is a letter from a Meru wife to her husband, who is fighting as a soldier in Europe during World War II. *Kamincuria Metho* was first published by the East African Literature Bureau in 1951 and reprinted in 1956, 1966, and 1977. An earlier version (date unknown) that did not include the model letter was printed in Great Britain by Wyman & Sons Ltd., London, Reading, and Fakenham for the Methodist Mission, Meru.

13. KAC, CC No. 538/67, MLC. For other examples of letters sent as notification, see KAC, CC Nos. 776/64, 862/65, 2052/65, 206/66, and 518/67 and District Commissioner (hereafter DC) Civil Panel African Court, Case No. 147/65, both in MLC. For a case where the woman's father wrote a letter to the man's father notifying him of the pregnancy, see KAC, CC No. 1233/65, MLC.

14. DC Civil Panel African Court, Case No. 147/65, MLC.

15. KAC, CC No. 889/65, MLC. Also see, KAC, CC No. 766/64, MLC.

16. KAC, CC Nos. 1988/65 and 517/66, MLC.

17. KAC, CC No. 397/64, MLC.

18. KAC, CC No. 518/67, MLC. Also see KAC, CC No. 417/66, MLC.

19. Laiboni, interview by author, Kangeta, Igembe, July 23, 1995.

20. DC Civil Panel African Court, Case No. 123/65, MLC.

21. KAC, CC No. 1376/66, MLC.

22. KAC, CC No. 471/66, MLC.

23. KAC, CC No. 2052/65, MLC.

24. KAC, CC Nos. 1312/65 and 538/67, MLC.

25. In an interview with the author (Kangeta, Igembe, July 23, 1995), James Laiboni, a former headmaster who attended secondary school in Meru during the 1960s, similarly stated that the relevant sexual relations usually occurred during the holidays, while their repercussions were felt during the school term. Laiboni described how during the second month after each school holiday, he and his classmates would peer from classroom windows to see if the old man who worked at the local African Court was approaching the school office. If they saw the old man, they knew that one of them would soon be delivered a court summons, notifying him that a holiday tryst had resulted in a pregnancy-compensation suit.

26. DC Civil Panel African Court, Case No. 123/65 and KAC, CC No. 1376/66, MLC. "I am yours" ("*Ni ni waku*") was also the closing phrase used in the model letter in *Kamincuria Metho*.

27. KAC, CC No. 1376/66, MLC. On mail-screening at colonial mission boarding schools for girls, see L. Olive Owen, Church Missionary Society, Ng'iya, Kisumu, to Director of Medical Services, Nairobi, June 24, 1939, Health/BY/27/1, KNA.

28. For example, see DC Civil Panel African Court, Case No. 147/65, MLC.

29. The case records indicate that Sara had written letters to Thomas regarding her pregnancy at least twice before. Presumably, Sara's father did not submit these earlier letters as evidence because he either did not have copies of them or they did not contain the sort of statements—namely, references to the conception date—that he thought would be useful in court. While nowhere in the court records does Sara or anyone else mention that she received assistance in writing her letters, at least one Kenyan man who heard an earlier version of this chapter was quite convinced that Sara's Standard VII would not have allowed her to write such a fluid and fluent letter in English.

30. *Baraza* and *Taifa Weekly* sold 33,000 and 32,000 copies per week while *Taifa Leo* sold 23,000 copies each day. In comparison, the leading English weeklies, *East African Standard* (Friday) and *Sunday Nation,* had circulations of 44,000 and 31,000, while the leading English dailies, *East African Standard* and *Daily Nation,* had circulations of 28,000 and 17,000.

31. This formulation is very similar to Karin Barber's conception of a West African modernity: "a modernity defined not so much by the full insertion of plastic human activities and bodies into new disciplines of space and time . . . as by a partial and creative modification of these disciplines, which adopts them and yet subjects them to continual attack" (2000, 236).

REFERENCES

Abuoga, John Baptist, and Absalom Aggrey Mutere. 1988. *The History of the Press in Kenya*. Nairobi: African Council on Communication Education.

Appadurai, Arjun. 1991. "Global Ethnoscapes: Notes and Queries for a Transnational Anthropology." In *Recapturing Anthropology: Working in the Present*, ed. Robert Fox, 191–210. Santa Fe, N.M.: SAR Press.

Barber, Karin. 2000. *The Generation of Plays: Yorùbá Popular Life in Theater*. Bloomington: Indiana University Press.

Barlow, Tani E. 1997. *Formations of Colonial Modernity in East Asia*. Durham: Duke University Press.

Bledsoe, Caroline M., and Barney Cohen. 1993. "Education and Adolescent Fertility." In *Social Dynamics of Adolescent Fertility in Sub-Saharan Africa*, ed. Caroline M. Bledsoe and Barney Cohen, 89–115. Washington, D.C.: National Academy Press.

Chakrabarty, Dipesh. 1993. "The Difference-Differral of (A) Colonial Modernity: Public Debates on Domesticity in British Bengal." *History Workshop* 36 (Autumn): 1–34.

Comaroff, Jean, and John Comaroff, eds. 1993. *Modernity and Its Malcontents: Ritual and Power in Postcolonial Africa*. Chicago: University of Chicago Press.

Comaroff, John L., and Simon Roberts. 1977. "Marriage and Extra-Marital Sexuality: The Dialectics of Legal Change among the Kgatla." *Journal of African Law* 21, no. 1: 97–123.

Cotran, Eugene. 1968. *Restatement of African Law*. Vol. 1, *The Law of Marriage and Divorce*. London: Sweet and Maxwell.

Donham, Donald. 1999. *Marxist Modern: An Ethnographic History of the Ethiopian Revolution*. Berkeley and Los Angeles: University of California Press.

Eisenstadt, S. N. 2000. "Multiple Modernities." *Daedalus* 129, no. 1: 1–29.

Graubard, Stephen R. 2000. "Preface to the Issue 'Multiple Modernities.'" *Daedalus* 120, no. 1: v–xii.

Gupta, Akhil. 1997. *Postcolonial Developments: Agriculture in the Making of Modern India*. Durham: Duke University Press.

Hofmeyr, Isabel. 1993. *We Spend Our Years as a Tale That Is Told: Oral Historical Narrative in a South African Chiefdom*. Portsmouth, N.H.: Heinemann.

Holding, Mary E. 1951. *Kamincuria Metho* (The Little One That Opens Eyes). Nairobi: East African Literature Bureau.

Kitching, Gavin. 1980. *Class and Economic Change in Kenya: The Making of an African Petite Bourgeoisie*. New Haven: Yale University Press.

Larkin, Brian. 1997. "Indian Films & Nigerian Lovers: Media and the Creation of Parallel Modernities." *Africa* 67, no. 3: 406–440.

Leonard, David K. 1991. *African Successes: Four Public Managers of Kenyan Rural Development*. Berkeley and Los Angeles: University of California Press.

Leys, Colin. 1975. *Underdevelopment in Kenya: The Political Economy of Neo-Colonialism, 1964–1971*. Berkeley and Los Angeles: University of California Press.

Lonsdale, John. 1992. "The Moral Economy of Mau Mau: Wealth, Poverty, and Civic Virtue in Kikuyu Political Thought." In *Unhappy Valley: Conflict in Kenya and Africa*, ed. Bruce Berman and John Lonsdale, 265–504. Athens: Ohio University Press.

Mager, Ann Kelk Mager. 1999. *Gender and the Making of a South African: A Social History of the Ciskei, 1945–1959.* Portsmouth, N.H.: Heinemann.

Maxon, Robert M. 1995. "Social & Cultural Changes." In *Decolonization and Independence in Kenya, 1940–1993,* ed. B. A. Ogot and W. R. Ochieng, 110–147. London: James Currey.

Mbembe, Achille. 1992. "Provisional Notes on the Postcolony." *Africa* 62, no. 1: 3–37.

Newell, Stephanie. 2000. *Ghanaian Popular Fiction: "Thrilling Discoveries in Conjugal Life" and Other Tales.* Oxford: James Currey.

————. 2002. "Introduction." In *Readings in African Popular Fiction,* ed. Stephanie Newell, 1–10. Bloomington: Indiana University Press.

Niehaus, Isak. 2000. "Towards a Dubious Liberation: Masculinity, Sexuality and Power in South African Lowveld Schools, 1953–1999." *Journal of Southern African Studies* 26, no. 3: 387–407.

Penwill, D. J. 1951. *Kamba Customary Law: Notes Taken in the Machakos District of Kenya Colony.* London: Macmillan.

Puja, Grace Khwaya, and Tuli Kassimoto. 1994. "Girls in Education—and Pregnancy at School." In *Chelewa, Chelewa: The Dilemma of Teenage Girls,* ed. Zubeida Tumbo-Masabo and Rita Liljeström, 54–75. Östersund: Scandinavian Institute of African Studies.

Rofel, Lisa. 1999. *Other Modernities: Gendered Yearnings in China after Socialism.* Berkeley: University of California Press.

Rogo, K. O., L. Bohmer, and C. Ombaka. 1999. "Developing Community-Based Strategies to Decrease Maternal Morbidity and Mortality Due to Unsafe Abortion: Pre-Intervention Research Report." *East African Medical Journal* 76, no. 1 (Supplement): S1–S71.

Soja, Edward. 1968. *The Geography of Modernization in Kenya: A Spatial Analysis of Social, Economic, and Political Change.* Syracuse, N.Y.: Syracuse University Press.

Summers, Carol. 2002. *Colonial Lessons: Africans' Education in Southern Rhodesia, 1918–1940.* Portsmouth, N.H.: Heinemann.

Thomas, Lynn M. 2003. *Politics of the Womb: Women, Reproduction, and the State in Kenya.* Berkeley: University of California Press.

Vellenga, Dorothy Dee. 1974. "Arenas of Judgement." In *Domestic Rights and Duties in Southern Ghana,* ed. Christine Oppong, 77–101. Legon: Institute of African Studies, University of Ghana.

Waciuma, Charity. 1969. *Daughter of Mumbi.* Nairobi: East African Publishing House.

PART TWO

Reading Cultures, Publics, and the Press

ENTERING THE TERRITORY OF ELITES: LITERARY ACTIVITY IN COLONIAL GHANA

Stephanie Newell

8

Newspapers had columns devoted to our clubs. You were supposed to be civilized in those days if you talked literature. In other words, your horizons extended beyond the confines of your country. The people who joined literary and social clubs wanted to continue their education.
—*Henry Ofori, interview*

The 1920s and 1930s were characterized by intense literary activity in the Gold Coast (Ghana): during these decades new constituencies of readers emerged from the mission schools, set up literary and social clubs for the discussion of literature and culture, wrote reports on club activities for African-owned newspapers, and, by the late 1930s, produced essays and occasional novellas for publication by local and international presses.[1] In piecing together the available fragments of information about these primary-educated Africans and their clubs, this chapter explores the ways non-elite readerships launched themselves into printed debates in Ghana. Clubs provided the means for non-status-holding youths to assert the value of English literature and literacy, and through club debates and essays, newly educated readers could develop their own aesthetic rules for the reception of printed literature. In the process, club members inserted themselves into the expressive culture of the period as new literati, offering authoritative comments on social and cultural issues. They also became the authors of the earliest popular novels in the country.

Vital Literary Cultures: Literary and Debating Societies in Colonial Ghana

With the expansion of the colonial education system in the mid-1920s, young school-leavers—especially young men—set up "literary and social clubs" around their hometowns and in the areas where they worked as white-collar migrants. They selected patrons and chairmen from local elites, elected executive committees from members, and, in public demonstrations of their literacy, published schedules of lectures and transcripts of debates in African-owned newspapers. Club members themselves gave lectures, and they also invited prominent local professionals and administrators to give talks on various issues. Consistently between the 1920s and 1940s, literary clubs printed statements in the local press which emphasized their intention "to foster an intelligent interest in the community in all literary and social activities, to inculcate upon members the advantages derivable from literary and social pursuits, and to educate public minds . . . by means of public debates, lectures, talks and so forth" (*GCO,* May 22, 1942, 41). As this statement reveals, Ghana's literary clubs worked hard to form a local literary culture and they actively asserted a sense of cultural authority, or cultural citizenship, on behalf of newly educated social groups in the decades before national independence.

The promotion of education was the primary objective of most organizations: "We strive to arouse interest in education," declared the president of the Abbontiakoon Literary and Social Club in 1930:

> I think it is most necessary to secure the means for a scientific and recreative education; for a general understanding of the problems of social life and good fellowship. . . . It is of great importance, I think, to run the Club in a way that we can study the higher problems with the aid of good books; and in so doing every member would be able to speak in public without fear or hindrance. . . . [L]et us help ourselves by studying good things more and more, and in so doing we shall be equipping ourselves for the future. Yes, if we study hard to know the real meaning of every matter, we will soon find that it has opened to us a new world. (*GCT,* March 29, 1930, 4)

The club did not promote education for its own sake as an abstract acquisition, a "virtue" to enhance the individual's consciousness and literary sensitivities. Rather, education is presented as the tool to open "to us a new world," the means by which the group could gain access to "the higher problems," collectively insert itself into "the future," and, in so doing, develop its public visibility through speeches and articles on "the problems of social life."

As the repetition of the word "study" reveals in these manifestos, prospective members had to demonstrate that they were sufficiently literate to participate in the range of autodidactic activities promoted by clubs. Members were drawn from the geographically mobile groups of low-ranking civil servants who were transferred regularly between southern Ghanaian towns; the membership lists published in the newspapers reveal that clubs also included merchants' clerks and mining clerks, catechists, secretaries, cocoa-brokers, primary school teachers, and other members of the white-collar workforce. The criterion for club membership, as published in the local press, was educational rather than ethnic: candidates had to have obtained at least one or two years' secondary schooling. This stipulation excluded large numbers of primary-schooled Africans, especially women, but it included young men from diverse regional backgrounds who identified themselves as "literary aspirants" and potential members of the intelligentsia.

The clubs attended by this cross-section of educated Africans grew up wherever there was an urban development or an industrial enterprise that required clerical workers. One club, the Enthusiastic Literary and Social Club, was established in the large mining center of Aboso and attended by the "grandfather" of Ghanaian popular fiction, J. Benibengor Blay. Another club, the New Tafo Literary and Social Club, arose as a direct result of the establishment in 1937 of the Central Cocoa Research Station for West Africa and the consequent influx of African employees from diverse parts of the country (*GCO*, November 6–13, 1942, 400).

People joined the clubs for many reasons: Benibengor Blay joined his club to develop his reading skills and avoid falling into bad habits such as drinking alcohol and visiting the brothels around Aboso mines (see Blay 1970). In other cases, clubs provided a sphere of sociability to unmarried male migrants—products of Christian mission schools—who found themselves a long way from home. As Henry Ofori, founding member of the New Tafo Literary and Social Club, said in an interview, the club offered "relief from the tedium of that rural place, where you would be coming home to nothing at the end of the day" (Ofori 1999). Migrants' names often stand out prominently on the lists of club members that were printed in the regional newspapers. Clubs offered new bonds to these young men, who shared educational qualifications and were in search of "culture," companionship, and "the intellectual life."

None of the white-collar occupations listed above carried the social status or financial rewards possessed by members of the highly educated African elite, who worked as lawyers, newspaper editors, and political organizers in the southern coastal towns of the country. This elite group must have loomed large in the young men's consciousness of the effects of English literacy, for they figured prominently in politics and society. Few club members could afford to become such "big men," who enhanced their social status by investing in their home towns or sponsored the endeavors of other clubs and family members (see Nugent 1995).[2] However, what club members did share with

213

the educated elite was literacy in English and Christian values, and their literary societies expressed the increasing confidence of the so-called scholar, a much-derided figure in colonial documents in the early years of the century (see Newell 2002). The clubs offered a positive collective identity for aspiring intellectuals who had not yet entered the elite but who had, nevertheless, achieved the rare distinction of gaining a nominal secondary education and entering the salaried workforce in the 1920s and 1930s. Ghanaian newspapers in the colonial period provide abundant information about the activities and ambitions of this elusive, very mobile group.

The earliest literary clubs in Ghana were started by the politically active Cape Coast elite in the 1870s and 1880s. In 1877, an African correspondent bearing the pseudonym "A. Native" (probably James Hutton Brew) described the beginnings of this movement, writing at precisely the moment when highly educated commoners, contributing articles and letters to the newly established African newspapers, started to take an active interest in the production of African literature. Using a vocabulary which bears striking similarities to the self-help philosophy of Samuel Smiles, "A. Native" wrote, "I know three young men who banded themselves into a small private society for the purposes of study, and derived benefits therefrom which certainly cannot be despised" (*GCT,* December 5, 1877, 2).[3] This is one of the earliest recorded descriptions of what became, within fifty years, an influential social movement among Ghana's educated male population. "A. Native" continued:

> A library is to be procured where young men can meet and lecture and essay and discuss on various subjects. I need not dwell on the privilege that Cape Coast will have by possessing such a means of intercourse and mental improvement. . . . Let all come forward and help, let all prefer an enlightened mind to a bright coin in an ignorant pocket, and liberally subscribe towards purchasing the necessary books wherein we may peer into subjects that will readily interest and inform at the same time. (ibid.)

While this report reveals the need for patrons and sponsors, club members in these early years of literary activity were anything but the "men of the humblest rank" who formed Samuel Smiles's self-help groups in the 1850s (Smiles 1859/1997, iii). They were foreign-educated professionals and included future nationalist leaders and newspapermen such as J. E. Casely Hayford and J. P. Brown, who seem to have been among the original members of the Cape Coast Reading Club, established in 1882. In addition to literary discussions and public speeches, representatives of this club insisted that "extensive opportunities must also be allowed for political debates" (*GCT,* September 16, 1882, 2). Elite clubs maintained this political tradition for the next fifty years. The elite Nationalists Club in Accra, of which Dr. J. B. Danquah was a patron, hosted high-profile political speakers in the 1930s, and, as the club's name implies, members consciously embarked on the task of psychological decolonization many years before the achievement of national independence.

By contrast, the non-elite clubs which arose between the 1920s and 1940s studiously and explicitly avoided party politics. This demands explanation, for these decades marked a highly politicized period of anticolonial activism in Ghana (see Holmes 1972; Stone 1974). Club members declared their political neutrality with increasing vehemence in the 1920s and stormy 1930s, apparently to assert and defend their social and literary spaces against the nationalist activity around them. Indeed, most literary clubs were explicit in their view that "insubordination to the Government is forbidden, and members have given a restful good bye to all questions about the inclusion of politics" (*AMP*, September 3, 1938, 2). While better-educated nationalists and agitators such as Kobina Sekyi and I. T. A. Wallace-Johnson used the English-language newspapers to mount pressure on the colonial government for representation and constitutional change, members of the literary clubs used the same publications to describe how they took

> great care [to avoid] . . . the admission of youngmen whose minds are bent on politics. Any infusion of such members will eventually cause the collapse of the club. We have many instances on record where decent societies and clubs have been ruined through unwarranted introduction and unwholesome discussion of politics. (*GCT*, October 23, 1937, 7)

Club members seemed to be preserving the unity of their associations by circumventing party politics, thus avoiding trouble with the colonial government and local power elites. Perhaps this was the only policy available to young men who often came from a variety of occupations and ethnic groups but who nevertheless felt inspired to act together publicly as an intellectual class. The groups seemed to flicker perilously in the wind of political debate, and their statements of nonpolitical intent reveal the ways in which they avoided challenges to existing power groups, be they colonial officials, chiefs and elders, or members of the African elite, preferring instead to focus upon academic and cultural activities. In asserting an expressive space independent of party politics, club members in the 1930s united in an ivory tower from which they gained their cohesion and sustained their public authority as the "educated element": they seem to have been attempting to carve out a new space in the territory of existing elites, claiming for themselves the entitlement to comment on cultural issues.

Figure 8.1. Advertisement for the Gold Coast *Spectator*, published in the *African Morning Post*, July 7, 1938, p. 3.

Occasionally clubs were so politically neutral that they attracted criticism from newspaper editors and non-club members, especially during times of heightened political confrontation in the country. For instance, immediately after the cocoa "hold up" of 1938, when local farmers refused en masse to supply cocoa to monopolistic "combinations" of British firms, the *African Morning Post* carried the item reproduced in fig. 8.1, which was published for the Gold Coast *Spectator* and was entitled "Have the Literary Clubs in the Country Really Failed?"

This provocative bulletin is fascinating for what it presupposes about the readership of African newspapers and its mode of participating in printed debates. The column contains distinctive rabble-rousing qualities, particularly its quotation of past readers' strong views and its presumption that current readers would respond by producing their own "articles" and "candid opinions" on the subject of clubs. Letter-writers such as "Farmer's Son" were said to be "indignant," while "Agonaniba" "bewail[ed]" the situation. Rather than claiming to be a news-carrying organ that conveyed information to a relatively passive external audience, the *Spectator* promoted itself as a forum for debate among highly emotionally charged letter-writers. It set literate farmers against members of literary clubs on a battlefield the newspaper both refereed and manipulated. Large numbers of readers would have had opinions about the issues raised in the bulletin; others would have been members of the clubs which are criticized. In this way the bulletin seems designed to arouse the passions of the readership and inspire them to send in letters and follow the debate by purchasing subsequent issues of the newspaper.[4]

At less critical moments in the history of the Gold Coast, editors would lavish praise on the clubs for their literary pursuits and for taking the initiative to improve the social and intellectual environment of the country. "We are highly impressed by the insatiable avidity on the part of the literary clubs for intellectual enlightenment," the editor of the *African Morning Post* wrote in the months immediately before the escalation of the cocoa crisis, expressing particular pleasure to see "the youthful element of the educated communities . . . hand[ing] down to posterity the present-day culture and all that tends to sublimate the human nature" (*AMP*, October 21, 1937, 2). The full text of particularly informative or controversial lectures would be published in the newspapers, illustrating the manner in which one African readership—composed of club members—influenced the content of the newspapers and exported their own debates for continuation among the wider newspaper-reading publics in Ghana. Summaries of club debates would also be published in the press that would heap congratulations on particularly persuasive or eloquent speakers. Discussions of certain topics, such as "Is the Gold Coast a Nation?" would continue in editorials and letters pages for several days after a debate, as readers took up positions for or against the proposition and expressed their opinions as if they, too, were speaking from the podium to a hall filled with club members poised to vote (see e.g., *AMP*, January 29–February 1, 1938).

If clubs were not "political," then, it was only in the narrowest sense of the term: they might not have discussed party politics and colonial ordinances at their meetings, but they *did* discuss citizenship and government, social values, cultural issues, and the individual's civic duties. Lectures in the 1920s included topics such as "Elements of Nationalism" and "Patriotism" (*GCT*, February 16, 1929, 5); in the 1930s, lectures included "Indirect Taxation," "Self-Government," and "Is Mass Education Acceptable to the People?" (*AMP*, November–January 1937–1938).

Figure 8.2. Front-page report in *The African Morning Post* on a debate held by the Mfantsipim Old Boys' Association, January 14, 1938.

Similarly, club manifestos were riddled with governmental and bureaucratic language. Groups agreed upon constitutional laws, elected executive committees, carried the vote in debates, and wrote annual reports for the press. In addition to these governmental structures, at each debate, club members actively demonstrated their status as westernized democrats by replicating the Westminster debating model on a small scale. In 1938, for instance, a report on a debate about mass education held by the elite Mfantsipim Old Boys' Association describes how "in imitation of Parliament's Institutions the assembly was divided into two parties, Republicans and Democrats" (*AMP*, January 14, 1938, n.p.). In adopting such British and American structures, these club members displayed an apparent preference for western parliamentary models over indigenous systems based on rank and status. In this way, as the editor of the *African Morning Post* commented in 1954, "debating and literary societies, at the present stage of our struggle, will serve as preparatory grounds for the Legislative Assembly debates and will open up a wider horizon in the general outlook of the youth" (*AMP,* May 27, 1954, 2). Thus, the rhetoric and structures of party politics permeated club activities at all levels.

Gold Coast clubs published schedules of their lectures and debates in the local press, and it is surprising to see how central English literature was to their activities. Shakespeare's plays, Bacon's essays, and books by Ruskin would be read aloud in chunks at meetings or read in sections and discussed through the course of a year. Clubs held meetings entitled "Short quotations from the best English Authors with vivid explanations" or "Discussion on: Who would you rather be: Martin Chuzzlewit the Master, or Mark Tapley the Servant?" (*GCT,* September 21, 1929, 4). The clubs established small libraries that contained texts such as Ruskin's *Sesame and Lilies* and Dickens's *Martin Chuzzlewit* and *The Pickwick Papers,* which members would select for collective study, reenactment, or debate (see Newell 2002).

A distinctive assertion of status was taking place on the part of this educated class. They published details in the press of their eloquent debates about English classics, which were performed in English in the clubroom. Interestingly, their presence as a cultural force was almost entirely manifested through their production of texts for the press: numerous reports, minutes of meetings, schedules of work, and texts of debates appeared in the newspapers. For these young men, the press was the medium of visibility, providing the ink and the space for their public self-realization as intellectuals. It provided the forum for "scholars" to show off their erudition to the various groups who were most likely to have read the newspapers, which included colonial officials, the African elite, educators, civil servants, elders, members of other literary societies, and the business community. In this way, non-elite readers formed themselves into "literate constituencies" and sought public status as a direct result of their reading activities.

The vast amount of cross-referencing and literary quotation in the novelettes club members produced illustrates in a starkly visible manner the dynamic relationships between local readers and the English literary canon. To take just one example, the short final chapter of J. Abedi-Boafo's novella *And Only Mothers Know* (1938/1946) contains citations from Marie Corelli, the Bible, James Shirley, and Shakespeare. Novels such as this contain an extensive "library within": authors' quoting processes create a library shelf within each text. They showed—or showed off—the literary material that had been in circulation in previous years and revealed which books were picked up and absorbed when authors were students at mission schools and Sunday schools and members of literary clubs.

Figure 8.3. Comments on literary clubs in *The African Morning Post,* October 21, 1937, p. 2 (left) and *The Gold Coast Times,* October 23, 1937, p. 7 (right).

Like the artisans and clerks in eighteenth-century London who set up literary clubs, young Ghanaians established their organizations as "centres of public sociability" from which they took responsibility for defining cultural tastes and urban modernity (Clark 1986, 13; see also Rose 2001). Victorian metropolitan England was the primary reference point for clubs' cultural pursuits. Thus, in conjunction with their reading activities, some clubs held social events such as Ludo championships, dance competitions, "black tie" evenings, fancy-dress balls, and even the occasional croquet match. It is, however, important not to homogenize the clubs: different types of social events were arranged by the different types of club. Elite clubs held fancy-dress balls, concerts, dances, and croquet matches; non-elite clubs were more likely to hold interclub debates, essay-writing competitions, and Ludo championships. Between the 1920s and 1940s, these social occasions provided opportunities for the public display of "mental cultivation," for to have mastered Ludo or ballroom dancing was also to have mastered the cultural refinements many Europeans believed Africans lacked (see Cohen 1981).

Until the late 1930s and early 1940s, the majority of literary and debating societies in Ghana insisted that members speak English, wear three-piece suits, and respect Christian values. Failure to do so could result in expulsion from the club, as the following letter to the problem page of the *African Morning Post* reveals. A club member from Dunkwa asks: "Where is the rule of Literary Clubs that members should appear at meeting in complete dress? Should a member who appears at a meeting in cloth be expelled?" (*AMP*, December 4, 1937, 2). The editor's reply is surprisingly absolute:

> There is no excuse whatsoever for a member of any club to appear in a cloth or for that matter, in any dress other than that prescribed by the club regulations; what satisfactory reason could such a member possibly offer for what we regard as an affront to the dignity of the club concerned? Any delinquent who commits such a deliberate and unpardonable breach of the club's rules deserves to be expelled. (*AMP*, December 4, 1937, 2)

This condemnation lacks the respect often shown by African nationalists and editors toward African clothing and culture. Rather, it seems that a highly sensitive code of propriety has been violated regarding the English "dignity" promoted in literary clubs. The editor's response suggests that any public status achieved by the clubs is under a permanent threat of erasure and that the "gentlemanly" mystique expressed through the suit and tie can be preserved only if the outward appearance is kept up. These problems with social legitimacy are expressed cogently in the following month's *African Morning Post*. "What makes a gentleman?," asks J. W. Kuma Rottman. While "the polish of manners" and an "outwardly graceful manner" are important, the true gentleman has within himself "all the fine behaviour that springs naturally from a self-denying spirit" (*AMP*, January 10, 1938, 2). Thus, by not wearing his "outwardly graceful" clothing, the club member in Dunkwa has jeopardized the "gentlemanly" inner spirit on which many of the clubs were founded.

Despite the apparent mimicry of colonial cultural norms this example implies, the center-periphery model which has dominated postcolonial theory until recently is not appropriate to describe the public identities that were generated by Ghana's literary and social clubs as they utilized the newspapers in the colonial period. Club secretaries wrote regular reports for the Gold Coast newspapers, and at no point in these reports are club members represented as "provincial" or marginal to a political center located elsewhere, nor did club debates and lectures show any consciousness that members were situated on the "periphery" of the British Empire. A more complicated and intriguing political identity seems to be in formation, whereby the sense of a "national" identity in Ghana was expressed through the *locally targeted* activities of literary and social clubs. An example of this process can be found in the Accra Clubs Union (ACU), which was established in 1932 and was composed of nine literary societies from Accra, Christiansborg, and Labadi. In October and November 1937 this union of clubs became fully active and publicized its intention to petition the chiefs on the Ga State Council for reforms to Ga funeral customs. By way of preserving their nonpolitical role as mediators rather than activists, the young men issued a memorandum in which they emphasized their status as culturally "advanced" locals and expressed their wish to discuss "questions of social interest affecting the life of the community" (*AMP*, November 1, 1937, 6). "The ACU represents the intelligent and advanced youth of the community on whose behalf it claims to speak," they explained, and their document pleads that Ga funeral customs be discarded or "modified to suit the present-day conditions" (*AMP*, November 1, 1937, 6).

This request reveals much about the group's social status and aspirations, for they asked Ga State Council to place specific limits upon fees payable by male family members. The ACU's demands illustrate the ideological shifts in conceptions of value that had occurred since the late nineteenth century. These young Ga men considered "social investments" such as lavish funerals and the giving of gifts to be wasteful; instead, they wanted to accumulate personal capital (see Ekejiuba 1995). In not so many words, then, the petition expressed concerns that funeral expenditure within a customary system would deplete a young Ga-speaking man's personal savings and place him at an economic disadvantage in relation to less-burdened Fante and Asante men. In taking this action to transform the local community, the ideological underpinnings of this particular group of clubs are exposed, for their desire for "improvement" is centered on new notions of capital and investment (see Guyer 1995).

The Accra Clubs Union mobilized men from the more or less monoethnic literary clubs around Accra. In a similar vein, within a year of the ACU's campaign, another club, the Anum Improvement Society, set itself up as "a machinery against all internal disputes arising among the Anum people, and to improve the social and economic concerns of the Anum State" (*AMP,* September 3, 1938, 2). Operating within a "community of different elements," these young men described themselves in glowingly superior but socially integrated terms as "people of high intellectual faculties and great understanding, of varying shades of occupation and vocation, actuated by the spirit of patriotism, altruism and philanthropy to congregate for the stabilisation of mutual help and co-operation" (*AMP,* September 16, 1938, 2). Through organizations such as the ACU, young men in the stormy 1930s carved out a space for themselves in local political systems: they did so by asserting their authority as nonaligned arbiters for opposing power groups and by loudly declaring both their "patriotism" and their possession of "high intellectual faculties." Combining these with an insistence upon matters of social interest and culture, they disguised any ambitions to participate in local political systems under the banner of "culture."

The activities of the Anum Improvement Society and the Accra Clubs Union reveal the ways in which club members regarded western literacy— "book knowledge"—as a way to offer non-elite young men an array of new opportunities that allowed them to insinuate themselves into established structures of power in their communities. The members of Ghana's literary and social clubs used their literacy to create new public domains for themselves and launch themselves as a group who would "congregate for the stabilisation of mutual help and co-operation" (*AMP,* September 16, 1938, 2). They seem to have been generating a new social category for themselves, that of literati, through which they could influence affairs at both the local and the national levels. Thus, their apparent mimicry of western cultural and literary mores was complex and multidirectional, oriented not only toward the fashions and literature of the metropolitan center but also toward the debates taking place among the country's various elites on issues that affected the locality.

Clubs were not simply offshoots of the European presence in West Africa that offered windows into local imitations of western cultural values. Nor were they a unique phenomenon that appeared in the late nineteenth century without precedent. The history of clubs in Ghana is multilayered and complex, probably stretching back far beyond recorded memory and certainly existing well before colonial interventions in the region. The term "club" had accumulated several layers of meaning by the mid-twentieth century, some residual and archaic, others incipient and innovative. Included within its parameters were not only literary societies but also the plenitude of fraternities which sprang up in the early years of the century—all of which had uniforms and rulebooks—that included clerks' unions, singing bands, prayer groups, friendly associations, mutual benefit and funeral societies, miners' unions, farmers' associations, and societies initiated by and for "ladies" (see Casely-Hayford and Rathbone 1992). Such associations formulated "aims and objectives" which often meshed ideologically with the manifestos published by literary clubs. Hence, the Gomoa Mansu clerks' union, formed in October 1937, declared its aims in terms that were familiar to the literary associations, for it hoped "to foster unity among the local educated young men and to bring about needed improvements in the town. All educated citizens are invited to enrol for membership" (*AMP*, October 9, 1937, 5).

The clubs also contained residues of the far older tradition of *asafo* associations, in which regiments of commoners worked together on social projects in the community, wore uniforms, and militarized according to their age-grades (see Li 1995; Simensen 1975). As a mode of social organization, then, the literary and social clubs reverberated with meanings from the distant past and the recent past, from the colonial present, and from the wished-for future. If young men in the 1920s and 1930s burst forth with newfound confidence, empowered by their mission schooling, salaried jobs, and abilities in the English language, they also burst *from* a club ethos which had prevailed in the Gold Coast for generations.

In addition to these local initiatives, Ghanaian literary and social clubs displayed traces of the Boy Scout movement and the International Red Cross, both of which were active in the 1920s and recruited African schoolchildren into quasi-military units and sent them into surrounding villages to carry out "social welfare" work. Perhaps the most comparable social movement was the British "self-help" tradition, popularized by Samuel Smiles in the mid-nineteenth century. The philosophy of "self-help" generated hundreds of mutual improvement societies throughout Britain that were attended by dedicated scholars who studied the English literary classics, wrote essays, and engaged in aesthetic and philosophical debates (see Rose 2001, 58–87). However, there is insufficient archival material to demonstrate any definite connections between the British mutual improvement tradition and Ghana's literary and debating societies. Except for occasional acts of homage to Samuel Smiles—which included readings of *Self-Help* at club meetings and one instance in the 1950s of a child named "Sammy Smiles Opong"—no evidence can be found of the direct import of British associations into the Gold Coast by missionaries, educators, or administrators. The similarities are striking and pronounced, however, down to the clubs' shared preference for canonical English literature and their repeated insistence that "knowledge is power" (see Rose 2001, 26–35, 58–87).

The vernacular languages figured increasingly in the Gold Coast literary clubs' visions of national progress in the 1930s and 1940s as attention among colonial and missionary educationists turned toward African languages and as country-specific nationalisms started to supplant the transatlantic and pan–West African networks that had previously engaged the energies of African activists. The shift toward a distinctive anticolonial discourse was manifested in the Gold Coast by the emergence of a new type of literary society that broke away from the ethos of preceding decades in two respects. First, as with the earliest literary clubs in the 1870s and 1880s, the new organizations were initiated and led by the foreign-educated professional classes, including figures such as Kwame Nkrumah and S. R. Wood among their members. Second, unlike the non-elite clubs of the 1920s and 1930s with their English-language orientation, the new groups promoted vernacular literatures by sponsoring translations of secular material and commissioning histories and textbooks for classroom use, thus mounting a challenge to decades of missionary control over the production of vernacular material. In this reclamation of African languages, club members asserted African spaces within the dominant culture by politicizing the vernaculars and criticizing education policy to date (see Newell 2002).

In his autobiography, Kwame Nkrumah mentioned one such organization: "When I was not studying, my spare time was devoted to forming the Nzima Literature Society," he wrote, adding that "it was through this work that I met Mr S. R. Wood who was then secretary of the NCBWA [National Congress of British West Africa]. This rare character first introduced me to politics" (1957, 21). The intention of the Nzima Literature Society, which was founded in 1933 by Rev. S. E. Quarm with the support of local chiefs, elders, and the educated elite (it made no affiliations with non-elite clubs), was to unite "all educated Nzimas at home and abroad" in the retrieval of the Nzima language from the obscurity of unwrittenness (*GCT,* March 31, 1934, 5). Following in the footsteps of the earliest missionaries, who prioritized translations into African languages, but expanding the agenda to include a nationalist perspective on literacy, Rev. Quarm expressed great concern about the lack of Christian reading matter in the Nzima language and insisted that Nzima schoolchildren needed "better reading books in the mother tongue" (ibid., 5).

The striking feature of this African initiative is the similarity between the society's choice of genres for vernacular writing and the publications favored by Christian missionaries in the Gold Coast. "The production of school text-books and versions of the Holy Writ" took precedence over translations and original creative writing in Rev. Quarm's list of proposed publications (ibid.). Grammars, dictionaries, and primers dominated the agenda, closely followed by "oral," customary, and historical matters. This pattern was repeated in 1945, when another cultural organization, the GSRA,[5] launched an ambitious appeal for a Ga national library. The library was to be filled with original Ga writings alongside newly commissioned translations of "standard works on World History, Economics, Political Science, Psychology, Philosophy, Geography, Logic, Aesthetics, etc" ("Ga National Library," RG 3/1/315, April–May 1945, n.p., NAG). Although they noted the "good intentions" of the GSRA, education department officials rejected the scheme as "over-ambitious," proposing instead that a Ga section should be established in Accra's new municipal library (ibid.).

The Nzima Literature Society[6] and the GSRA exemplify the new model of identity to be found in the literary clubs of the 1940s, for in calling for vernacular textbooks, novels, and scriptures in a standardized Nzima script, club leaders voiced a clear belief that "God has better things in store for this . . . nation" (*GCT,* April 7, 1934, 12). The leaders of the Nzima Society insisted that their region's potential for social development and "progress" would be realized only when its dialect was given an orthography and thus rendered a fully recognized "national" language. "The Nzima language," wrote the vice-president of the society, "seems to have been looked upon both by missionaries and officials as either too difficult or barbarous. . . . They have led the Christian natives to learn other foreign languages with the result that the natives have been discarding their own mother tongue" (*GCT,* March 31, 1934, 5). As a result of this perception, "the educated element" in Nzimaland, with the patronage of local chiefs, set about "reducing the Nzima language into writing" and established a printing press for the publication of vernacular books by local authors (*AMP,* June 1, 1931, 6).

While it acknowledged the long, mission-led tradition of local language work in West Africa, the Nzima Literature Society publicly condemned the fact "that hitherto most of the vernacular literature in this country are the works of foreigners." The association embarked upon a plan for translation and vernacular creative writing, liaising with the Gold Coast Education Department for material and supervising the preparation of "books for use in schools and churches" (*AMP,* October 18, 1937, n.p.). An office was set up in Axim for the duration of the project and a club member—an experienced teacher—was seconded to it for six months by the executive (ibid.). By the late 1930s, the society had achieved a monopoly over Nzima writing; it controlled publications in much the same way that missionaries had controlled African-language material in previous decades, for the executive insisted upon vetting and approving any manuscript in the language and blocked the publication of "disapproved" material.

Despite their ultimate lack of success in launching large-scale literary production in the vernaculars, these bold local ventures provide evidence of a localized but increasingly nationalist mindset among literate groups in the Gold Coast. These pro-vernacular organizations reveal the critical connection between the writing down of mother tongues and the expression of nationalist sentiment. The interesting point, however, is the parallel and persistent belief among non-elite reading groups in the prestige conferred by the English language. The distinction between elite clubs and non-elite clubs is perhaps the most pronounced in relation to this issue of language.

Rev. Quarm and his successors voiced a kind of "parochial nationalism" which defied fears of the colonial government that ethnoregional fragmentation would occur in the absence of a unified script. Sponsoring grammars, folktales, and ethnohistories in their various vernaculars, the clubs used printed literature as the basis for the formation of mini-nations.[7] From these diverse platforms, they expressed support for the polyphonic new nation of Ghana; club members seemed to celebrate their standing on an equal footing alongside the speakers of vernaculars from other regions. As with many other African territories, Ghana emerged from the decolonization process as a nation-state composed of diverse linguistic jigsaw pieces; the new nation did not fall apart for the lack of a singular lingua franca. The vernacular clubs of the 1930s and 1940s illustrate the manner in which literate locals managed to steer a course through the difficult task of writing, in their numerous languages, what the GSRA proudly termed "the gospel of unity and constructive national effort without being chauvinistic" ("Ga National Library," RG 3/1/315, April–May 1945, n.p., NAG).

This indigenous vernacular enterprise is not echoed in non-elite literary and debating clubs until the 1950s. In 1952, schoolteacher and popular novelist J. Abedi-Boafo called for literature in the Dangme language, explaining that "all Dangme people now think and feel that the hidden virtues in their cultural heritage must be made known to the outside world" (*AMP*, November 15, 1952, 3). "We educated people in Dangmeland," he wrote in a subsequent article, "have inadvertantly [*sic*] created a vacuum of ignorance between us and our unfortunate aged people who are unlettered" (*AMP*, November 17, 1952, 4). To heal the rift between the privileged "educated" and the "unfortunate unlettered," Abedi-Boafo and his peers formed the Dangme Cultural Society in order to "discover and explore the hidden truths of fallacies in Dangme culture and to write books thereon for the benefit of posterity" (*AMP*, November 17, 1952, 4). Of course, in claiming the ability to use their literacy to distinguish between "hidden truths" and "fallacies," members of these literary societies were subtly inscribing their own readings into "tradition," producing it for posterity. Their aim, however, like that of the Nzima Literature Society in the 1930s, was to "uphold, preserve and improve the best things in our traditional culture and then to denounce, abolish or jettison all such things that might hinder the progress of the Adangme people" (*AMP*, November 17, 1952, 4). As with the Nzima Literature Society, Abedi-Boafo and his colleagues were embarking upon a process of "lettering" the local, thereby transforming it into a "national" script. Through these vernacular initiatives, Ghanaian literary clubs took upon themselves a role similar to that played by Christian missions in the previous century; they eschewed party politics but involved themselves in aspects of culture that were inherently civic and likely to stimulate local interest.

A full-blown sense of Ghana as either an "imagined community" or as a nation-state cannot be superimposed on the activities of these diverse literary clubs and associations. As the Accra Clubs Union and the vernacular clubs reveal, literary and debating societies were neither "traditionalist" nor "anti-chief": many of them worked assiduously for acceptance within local political frameworks. Club identities seem to bypass (or supersede) the connections scholars often make between print capitalism and the rise of nationalism (see Anderson 1983; Hastings 1997). Until the late 1940s, these ethnic and vernacular clubs confined their activities to their "visible communities," creating mini–mother countries or cultural centers from their immediate networks of language, culture, patronage, occupation, and kinship. National identities and the concept of patriotism were imagined from this local starting point.

The term "parochial" accurately describes the projects undertaken by literary and social clubs in Ghana: "parochial" need not be interpreted as a negative comment that implies an ethnocentric political consciousness in Ghana before independence. The primary connotation of parochial is "of a parish," closely followed by "denominational" and "confined to a narrow area" (*Oxford English Dictionary*). These three interconnected meanings are significant for the Ghanaian literary clubs that were connected by the vital threads of mission schooling, regional solidarity, and a shared local language. The cultural work undertaken by the Accra Clubs Union, the Nzima Literature Society and the Dangme Cultural Society illustrates the manner in which club members in a particular region would be "of a parish," coming together in the manner of Christian missionaries to develop the locality into a respectable part of the nation that possessed the civic virtues required of a "civilized," "enlightened" region.

Mission schoolrooms and church halls were often used as venues for club meetings, and large numbers of catechists and mission schoolteachers enrolled for membership. It is curious, however, that there are no references to any of the literary and social clubs in missionary or colonial archives. Perhaps club membership was so limited, and so politically unthreatening, that it had no noticeable impact on the colonial and missionary authorities. Perhaps the readings and writings that emerged from Ghana's clubs were ignored for their "unliterary" orientation. Club members belonged to precisely the group European commentators dismissed for having "remained in school only a year or two—long enough to acquire a scrappy English vocabulary" and for being "driven by ambition and a desire to imitate the white man" (Buell 1928). Such a blinkered view fails to recognize the autonomous literary enterprise that was taking place outside the formal school system, initiated by locals who were anything but simple "imitators of the white man."

The silence of colonial officials on matters literary and local is not matched by African political commentators at the time. Between the 1920s and 1950s, newspaper editors in the Gold Coast initiated regular discussions of club activities, and by the end of the period, they were lamenting the decline of the self-help ethos that had been so prominent in previous decades. In June 1947, J. B. Danquah coined the word "clubism" and expressed the common wish that such organizations could be jump-started back into life. He wrote, "I feel rather ashamed to think of it that under the recent administration clubism has been such a dismal failure both in Accra and Sekondi. . . . I feel strongly that there is wanting to-day in our national life a strong living and vital centrifugal force around which our national life should revolve" (1970, 31).

Given Danquah's nostalgia, it is ironic that the clubs' decline seems to be related to the rise of nationwide youth movements such as the Gold Coast Youth Conference, of which Danquah himself was general secretary in the 1930s and early 1940s. The youth conference aimed at achieving unity with chiefs on the provincial councils, working with the professional elite, and absorbing all clubs and associations into a large-scale movement which would prepare the country socially for decolonization. This process of absorption seems to have been amicable and noncoercive. Danquah warmly invited members of the country's clubs, as groups or individuals, to sign up to the youth conference and participate in the broad national movement toward independence (see *AMP*, December 3, 1937, 2).

The manner in which the youth conference assimilated the clubs took much of the initiative away from a section of the population which had only ever established itself as an aspirant or emergent social group and lacked the power and credentials to step onto the national stage as a "class." As the country moved toward full-scale general elections and independence, literary and social clubs dwindled into insignificance, becoming once again the preserve of the professional elite, as they had been in the nineteenth century. In 1954, the editor of the *African Morning Post* complained, "About three decades ago, the educated elements of this country took keen interest in literary matters and the sequel was the formation of first-rate debating and literary clubs. But in recent years, owing, perhaps, to the political agitation that has overwhelmed the country, literary life has received a serious setback" (*AMP*, May 27, 1954, 2). In another club obituary from the early 1950s, the editor of the *Spectator* wrote, "One hears practically nothing about literary clubs these days—the intellectual light of the country is growing dim" (January 24, 1953, 2).

Clearly in this postwar period African readerships were choosing to participate in other—perhaps more exciting—cultural events, such as highlife dances, "concert parties" and viewing Hollywood blockbusters instead of debating texts by Dickens, Ruskin, and Shakespeare in the clubroom. Cultural flows in Ghana had been steadily internationalized after the Second World War, and as a consequence, the "literary gent" with his three-piece suit, Ludo board, and love of the formal debating environment seems to have become an increasingly anachronistic figure that was irrelevant to educated young people's conceptions of what constituted a "modern" lifestyle. In addition, chapters of the People's Education Association, adult literacy units, and the Department of Education took over the localized self-help activities of the literary and social clubs on a mass, national scale. "Literary" knowledge lost some of its power, for the ability to read and write no longer marked out a small social group that could assert its status through its textual proficiency. Finally, the literary and social clubs lost their mouthpieces in the 1950s, when many of the local newspapers they had used to publish their reports and programs closed down, replaced by high-tech enterprises that reserved press space for national and international stories (see Jones-Quartey 1974).

The activities of Ghana's literary and debating societies demonstrate that attention to readers is vital in the study of the country's literary history. Of equal importance, the clubs' literary activities and assertions of "cultural citizenship" are inextricable from the rise of African-owned newspapers in the

230

colonial period. Club members' literary interpretations, their debates about the function of literature, and their production of printed material in response to current texts all took place through the African-owned newspapers that grew up in the colonial period. Newspapers provided the ideal public forum for club members to make themselves visible as the new literati: editors charged no fee for articles, invitations were regularly issued for new contributions, and the vast majority were published in the English language, allowing club members to display their English eloquence in a public space. As a result of this close interconnection, the newspapers reveal extraordinary details about the lifestyles and aspirations of club members; editors helped to co-produce and sustain the club culture described in their pages. Literacy meant different things to different social groups in Ghana, but it also created a meaningful shared reference point for the various fraternities of readers who jostled for positions in the modern state. The press acted as the loudhailer, transmitting literary material from the debating platform of the clubroom into the printed realm of the newspaper.

Readers Turned Writers: Ghana's First Popular Novelists

The multilayered connections between clubs, "scholars," and creative writing in the Gold Coast are revealed by the fact that many of the country's earliest popular novelists were also members of literary clubs. For example, J. Benibengor Blay joined the literary club at Aboso mines when he was a youth. In his autobiographical novel *Coconut Boy* (1970), Blay describes how club "debates centred around African intellectuals such as Dr Aggrey, Mensah Sarbah, Atto Ahumah [*sic*] and S. R. Wood" (24). In the club library, he studied the great masters of English literature, and his creative flame was "kindled" by the books he read. He started to compose journalistic pieces in the late 1930s, which were shortly followed by political booklets and love stories which were printed at a local newspaper press (ibid.). Club activities in the 1920s and 1930s had prepared the way for this local literary production.

Another club member who went on to become a popular Ghanaian author surfaces in a report on the Altruism Literary Club that was published in the *Times of West Africa* in December 1934 (*TWA*, December 29, 1934, 6). Speaking at a ceremony for a fellow club member who had achieved the remarkable feat of gaining an honors degree, "Mr J. E. Edu (critic)" quotes a poem and hails the graduate's success in "removing the stigma on the much maligned African" (ibid.).[8] In the 1950s, J. E. Edu published a number of novellas and pro-Nkrumah political pamphlets for distribution to local readerships.

Several other new popular novelists of the 1940s and 1950s were club members in the 1930s. Novelist J. Abedi-Boafo is described in the *African Morning Post* as the "Vice-President and Founder of Koforidua Study Circle," to which in 1938 he gave a lecture on "Our Priceless Legacy," a topic "entirely outside the region of politics and any religious denomination" (*AMP,* September 16, 1938, 2). The immensely successful author and publishing entrepreneur Gilbert A. Sam, who founded the Gilisam Press in the early 1950s, can be found at a Christmas dinner party in 1939 giving "a short, but impressive opening address" as club secretary of the Cherry Ocaa Literary and Social Club (*Spectator,* January 6, 1939, 4). After dinner, club members and their guests danced "merrily to the music of a gramophone" until 3.35 AM (ibid.). Literary and debating clubs thus helped to produce the country's first non-elite authors and offered an intellectual space in which young men could air their ideas and put pen to paper in the closed, receptive environment of peers.

Striking similarities can be found between the themes chosen for literary-club debates and the morally righteous but politically neutral content of locally produced novels. Such a coincidence is hardly surprising, given that many of the authors of popular texts were members of Ghana's literary clubs. These authors occupy a special position as readers turned writers; they responded to the books they read by producing their own texts and inviting readers to debate the issues raised. In so doing, they continued the dynamic dialogical relationship that existed between the text and the reader in Ghana's newspapers and literary clubs.

The extensive archive contained in Ghanaian newspapers allows us access to unique details about literary and social clubs as they developed and declined in the years before independence. Except for a few associations which were attended by the professional elite and lasted for twenty-plus years, the majority of clubs turned out to be what locals called "nine-day wonders." Lasting four or five years at most, they marked the struggle for social status of individuals without conventional or recognizable forms of authority. Taken together over a period of fifty years, the clubs can be seen as an influential local social movement that reveals the uses to which English literacy was put by self-determining, ambitious school-leavers, the very section of the population ignored by the nationalist politicians until the 1940s and bypassed or derided in colonial and missionary writings. The clubs provide evidence of a vital reading culture in Ghana, and the documentation club members produced for publication in the press constitutes the main public archive of this social group. It is to be hoped that the new anthropological interest in hidden histories and tin-trunk literacy will yield memoirs, letters, minute books from club meetings, essays, and diaries of club members that will enable future scholars to piece together a fuller social history of the new literati of the 1920s and 1930s.

NOTES

1. This material is considered in Newell (2002), which provides an account of Ghanaian literary and social clubs in relation to colonial policy and broader West African cultural networks.

2. For an analysis of emergent and established elites in Kwawu and Asante, see Miescher (in this volume, 2001a, 2001b) and Arhin (1986).

3. In *Self-Help* (1859/1997), Samuel Smiles wrote, "Two or three young men of the humblest rank resolved to meet in the winter evenings, for the purpose of improving themselves by exchanging knowledge with each other. . . . Those who knew a little taught those who knew less" (iii–iv).

4. Curiously, for the months immediately after July 1938, the *Spectator* contains no readers' letters, no articles, and no editorial comment on the political role of clubs. Perhaps readers failed to be inspired by this stage-managed debate and preferred to offer more-spontaneous responses to current affairs.

5. Documents in the National Archives of Ghana do not reveal the full name of this organization: my guess would be the "Ga State Reading Association" or the "Ga State Research Association."

6. The Nzima Literature Society was also known as the Nzima Literature Association. Its leaders used both names and finally settled upon Nzima Literature Association.

7. The word "nation" is often used in newspaper reports to describe particular ethnolinguistic groups, especially the Fante.

8. Many literary clubs had an elected "critic," usually the best-educated member, whose responsibility was to correct members' English grammar and pronunciation and to advise essayists on their prose style.

ABBREVIATIONS

AMP	African Morning Post (Accra)
GCO	Gold Coast Observer (Cape Coast)
GCT	Gold Coast Times (Cape Coast)
NAG	National Archives of Ghana

REFERENCES

Abedi-Boafo, J. 1983/1946. *And Only Mothers Know: A Thrilling Discovery in Conjugal Life*. Aburi: Mfantsiman Press.
Anderson, B. 1983. *Imagined Communities*. London: Verso.

Arhin, K. 1986. "A Note on the Asante *akonkofo:* A Non-Literate Sub-Elite, 1900–1930." *Africa* 56, no. 1: 25–31.

Blay, J. Benibengor. 1944. *Emelia's Promise.* Accra: Benibengor Book Agency.

———. 1945. *After the Wedding.* Accra: Benibengor Book Agency.

———. 1970. *Coconut Boy.* Accra: West African Publishing Co.

Buell, R. L. 1928. *The Native Problem in Africa.* Vol. 1. New York: Macmillan.

Casely-Hayford, A. C., and Rathbone, R. 1992. "Politics, Families and Freemasonry in the Colonial Gold Coast." In *People and Empires in African History: Essays in Memory of Michael Crowder,* ed. J. F. Ajayi and J. D. Y. Peel, 143–160. London: Longman.

Clark, P. 1986. *Sociability and Urbanity: Clubs and Societies in the Eighteenth Century City.* Leicester: Victorian Studies Centre, University of Leicester.

Cohen, A. 1981. *The Politics of Elite Culture: Explorations in the Dramaturgy of Power in a Modern African Society.* Berkeley: University of California Press.

Danquah, J. B. 1970. *Journey to Independence and After (J. B. Danquah's Letters), 1947–1965.* Vol. 1, *1947–1948.* Ed. H. K. Akyeampong. Accra: Waterville Publishing House.

Ekejiuba, F. 1995. "Currency Instability and Social Payments among the Igbo of Eastern Nigeria, 1890–1990." In *Money Matters: Instability, Values, and Social Payments in the Modern History of West African Communities,* ed. J. Guyer, 133–161. Portsmouth, N.H.: Heinemann; London: James Currey.

Guyer, J., ed. 1995. *Money Matters: Instability, Values and Social Payments in the Modern History of West African Communities.* Portsmouth, N.H.: Heinemann; London: James Currey.

Hastings, A. 1997. *The Construction of Nationhood: Ethnicity, Religion and Nationalism.* Cambridge: Cambridge University Press.

Holmes, A. B. 1972. "Economic and Political Organizations in the Gold Coast, 1920–1945." Ph.D. diss., University of Chicago.

Jones-Quartey, K. A. B. 1974. *A Summary History of the Ghana Press, 1822–1960.* Accra-Tema: Ghana Publishing Corp.

Li, A. 1995. "*Asafo* and Destoolment in Colonial Southern Ghana, 1900–1953." *International Journal of African Historical Studies* 28, no. 2: 327–357.

Miescher, S. 2001a. "The Making of Presbyterian Teachers: Masculinities and Programs of Education in Colonial Ghana." In *Men and Masculinities in Modern Africa,* ed. L. Lindsay and S. F. Miescher, 89–108. Portsmouth, N.H.: Heinemann.

———. 2001b. "The Life Histories of Boakye Yiadom (Akasease Kofi of Abetifi, Kwawu): Exploring the Subjectivity and 'Voices' of a Teacher-Catechist in Colonial Ghana." In *African Words, African Voices: Critical Practices in Oral History,* ed. L. White, S. Miescher, and D. W. Cohen, 162–193. Bloomington: Indiana University Press.

Newell, S. 2002. *Literary Culture in Colonial Ghana: "How to Play the Game of Life."* Manchester: Manchester University Press; Bloomington: Indiana University Press.

Nkrumah, K. 1957. *The Autobiography of Kwame Nkrumah.* Edinburgh: Thomas Nelson and Sons.

Nugent, P. 1995. *Big Men, Small Boys, and Politics in Ghana: Power, Ideology and the Burden of History, 1982–1994.* London: Pinter.

Ofori, H. 1999. Interview with S. Newell, Accra, September.

Rose, J. 2001. *The Intellectual Life of the British Working Classes.* New Haven: Yale University Press.

Simensen, J. 1975. "The *Asafo* of Kwahu, Ghana: A Mass Movement for Local Reform under Colonial Rule." *International Journal of African Historical Studies* 8, no. 3: 383–406.

Smiles, S. 1859/1997. *Self-Help; With Illustrations of Character and Conduct.* London: Routledge/Thoemmes Press.

Stone, R. L. 1974. "Colonial Administration and Rural Politics in South-Central Ghana, 1919–51." Ph.D. diss., University of Cambridge, Cambridge.

THE BANTU WORLD AND THE WORLD OF THE BOOK: READING, WRITING, AND "ENLIGHTENMENT"

Bhekizizwe Peterson

9

This chapter is an exploration of the complicated notions of reading and writing Africans in South Africa engaged with during the first half of the twentieth century. Ever mindful of the confluence between social context and cultural practice, I am interested in the myriad ways the African intelligentsia drew on the ideas of reading and writing to imagine, improvise, proclaim, and perform its senses of individual and group identity. Reading and writing were, in crucial ways, anything but the private, passively contemplative, and desk-bound activities that the citadels of bourgeois and missionary society propounded and that were desperately embraced by the African elite. On the contrary, reading and writing were enmeshed in a paraliterate landscape and in many of the daily, public, and social rituals of the emergent African intelligentsia in Johannesburg between 1920 and 1950. As was to be expected, the contradictions, complexities, and downright convoluted practices of reading and writing found sharp relief in the notion, circulation, and reception of texts. Texts encompassed everything from speeches to plays, advertisements to letters to the editor, biographies to obituaries, literary criticism to travel news, newspaper articles to books.[1] Texts were, on the one hand, reified as supreme markers of "civilization" and modernity. Yet, very often, texts were encountered not as printed pages between covers but rather as free-floating performative encounters that many a time were reduced to unaccredited, anonymous extracts and quotations that could find their moments of enunciation and elaboration in a diverse range of social spaces and occasions.[2]

Arguably, one of the most useful sites where one can examine the multiple literary, cultural, and social strategies that went into the class and nationalist consciousness of the African intelligentsia on the Witwatersrand would be the pages of the *Bantu World* newspaper, which was launched in Johannesburg in 1932. Newspapers and books formed part of a larger "world of the book" that encompassed important social spaces such as, in particular, the Bantu Men's Social Centre (BMSC), which was set up in 1929. The Bantu Men's Social Centre was to become the central place for a wide range of activities and projects, including the formation of a literary society and a library in the club.[3] From 1933, the library operated as one of the depots for the Carnegie Non-European Library Service.

The Melancholy of Enlightenment

The three decades that frame the period of my analysis mark a period of contending hopes and fears among the African elite on the Rand. Their experiences and thinking had to contend with and negotiate a series of difficult historical and political moments. There is, first, the founding of the modern, unified South African state in 1909, a state that was structured in racial dominance and that denied Africans any rights to citizenship and equality. Furthermore, the state's policy of segregation, in its rationalization of separate reserves for Africans, constructed novel forms of neotraditionalism that the African elite were expected to embrace in line with the government's policies of "separate but equal" polities. This foregrounded culture as an important dimension in the arguments both for and against segregation. Second, there is the development of an increasing awareness among the elite that they were an urban population and that there was a need to think through the implications of urbanity with regard to the issues of identity, culture, and politics.

It was within this overdetermined context that reading, writing, and performance were to play an important role in the self-awareness, self-projection, and self-actualization of the African intelligentsia. In the eighteenth century, the ideology of Enlightenment "claimed that the book was capable of reforming society, that educational popularisation could transform manners and customs, that an elite's products could, if they were sufficiently widespread, remodel a whole nation" (de Certeau 1988, 166). In the colonies, it was the African population as a whole that needed to be remolded. Of course, the educated African elites' first sustained engagement with the three R's was in mission schools, where the *Royal Readers* served as the preliminary preparation for the "great tradition." Those who were fortunate enough to acquire some level of tertiary education were familiarized with the canon of Shakespeare, Milton, Dickens, Bacon, and the Romantics, especially Wordsworth, Shelley, Keats, and Longfellow (see Couzens 1985, 51–52). English Literature, with a capital L, was valorized as the sourcepoint for the construction of a framework for moral orientation, the rockbed of character, and the ultimate measure of the level of "civilization" attained by a society. Missionaries and colonial authorities saw the "absence of literature" among Africans as a crucial mark of their primitivity and backwardness, which, in turn, justified either the total exclusion or separation of Africans from mainstream forms of governance and democracy.

No wonder, then, that the African elite, with the assistance of white missionaries and liberal philanthropists, became involved in the creation of a complex network of social and cultural institutions and practices where, among other things, they valorized the pursuit of art by Africans as both a mark of their progress and claims to modernity.[4] In the process, the emergent African elite tended to overstate their own break away from and transcendence of the limitations of their past, or, in the popular phrase of the time, "tradition." As "new" Africans, or "progressives," they kept reminding themselves, the elite had ostensibly jettisoned the superstitions, backwardness, and heathenism associated with traditional African societies and the chiefly classes that exercised authority in the reserves. In their stead, and very much against the tenets of the colonial oligarchy, the moral, social, and intellectual horizons of the Enlightenment, with their stress on reason, science, and individual rights, were now much-vaunted qualities in the rhetoric of civilization, together with the concern that the sovereignty of the state needed to be subject to the will and welfare of the "people" (à la Rousseau's social contract).[5]

However, a much-more-complicated picture emerges from a close study of the times, reading practices, and writings of the African elite. First, the past, however it was recast rather than transcended, continued to cast a strong shadow on the thinking and actions of the elite. Many of the ideas associated with tradition, even when they did nothing more than provide the "negative" impulses that had to be superseded, continued to provide the channels for thinking through the construction of modern identities.[6] Of course, the literary works of Solomon Plaatje, Thomas Mofolo, R. R. R. Dhlomo, H. I. E. Dhlomo, and Samuel Edward Krune Mqhayi, among others, offered profound narrativizations of the past. Students and other aspirant literati were not averse to engaging in similar thematic excavations that also served as renewals of indigenous genres and performance traditions. Students at Adams College held annual performances where plays, dances, and sketches were dedicated in honor of favorite icons such as Moshoeshoe and Shaka.[7]

Also, in Europe, the eclipsing of religious knowledge by the rise of the rationalist secularism of the Enlightenment led to the demise of the religious notion of regeneration that sought to negotiate the links between the dead and the yet-to-be-born. In their "secular transformation of fatality into continuity, contingency into meaning," the new nation-states also "always loom out of an immemorial past, and, still more important, glide into a limitless future. It is the magic of nationalism to turn chance into destiny" (Anderson 1983, 19). Or in the words of Magema Fuze, after using the allegory of a grasshopper laying its eggs before it dies, "We should remember that on death we do not come to an end, but by our progeny we renew ourselves to continue indefinitely, and so arise anew as if we were beginning at the beginning" (Fuze 1979, 147–148). Furthermore, many of the key tenets of the Enlightenment were denied to black South Africans. In fact, colonial discourses predicated their denial of the African intelligentsia's claims to modernity by foregrounding racist distortions of the African past—reducing it to a period without any history, subjects, or aesthetic value. For this intelligentsia, this not only reinscribed the African past as an important moment, it also compelled them to find and, paradoxically, highlight the "good" in the past that seemed to be invisible to colonial ideologues. In complex ways, this process laid the terrain where nationalist sensibilities increasingly returned and found succor.

The Bantu World

The launching of *The Bantu World,* the first national African newspaper, under the editorship of R. V. Selope-Thema in 1932 was an important acknowledgement of the rising rates of literacy among Africans as well as the continued importance of the African press in the affairs of the African elite. It has been estimated that "[l]iterate Africans constituted about 12.4 per cent of the adult African population by 1931 . . . and the number of registered African newspapers alone was nineteen in 1930—the highest in the history of South Africa's black press" (Switzer 1988, 351; see also L. and D. Switzer 1979, 6). The mainstay forms of employment for educated Africans were largely in the areas of teaching, journalism, and clerical work in institutions as diverse as churches, schools, industrial concerns, mines, and government departments. In spite of its increase in numbers, the African intelligentsia remained a small and politically vulnerable social group. Also, the class and social distinctions that separated it as a group from the African lower classes meant that the sociopolitical fragility of the African elite compelled it to make its major interventions not in the domains of mass and class struggles but in the sphere of ideology.[8]

The seminal role newspapers played in the instruction of the African elite, the development of a national consciousness, and the pursuit of literary and cultural activities among Africans has been emphasized by successive generations of the African intelligentsia (see Vilakazi 1933 and H. I. E. Dhlomo 1943). The African press, in combination with other social forces, created the templates for the emergence of a national consciousness through both their mediation of time and space and the narratives they proffered. Even in their anonymity, the stories created links between the worlds of their characters and the world outside, feelings of continuity and community among dispersed reading individuals and communities. Furthermore, even speakers of different languages could comprehend each other through the use of a common print language. Even though a substantial amount of material was written in African languages, English was the new language of power that reigned from the classroom to newspaper offices. At times, Africans had to remind themselves about the sociopolitical and cultural significance of African languages, as in the following headline: "Pride in Bantu Languages: Pride in Bantudom."[9]

Two editorials, "The Library Movement" and "The Book World," which were published in *The Bantu World* in 1938 and 1940, respectively, give a comprehensive and incisive analysis of the attitudes of the African elite toward reading and writing and the challenges and politics of literacy within a colonial context.

"The Library Movement" made three broad observations. First, it testified to the central role the "growth of the newspaper movement," especially the African press, played in the spread of literacy among blacks and as "a forerunner and a complement to the book-reading habit." Second, it emphasized the significance of literacy and education as both the conduit and the sign of "this slow awakening" of a "new and regenerated African." Last, literacy, seen as ritualized in the daily habit of reading literature (in the form of either newspapers or books) was also crucial in bridging the development from initially simply reading (or consuming) to ultimately writing (producing) texts emanating from African authors.

> The Library Movement will give impetus to the production of Bantu Literature. This is important. The African people must have their own authors who will express the feelings, aspirations, thoughts and visions of the race. And today there is a growing spirit of discontent among African authors who find channels of expression closed to them. A library, then, is like an extensive orchard where one may pick delicious gems and appease their hunger, gather fruit to sell to the world. . . . Therefore like the prophet we invite our thirsting people to "come and eat: yea, come, buy wine and without money and without price. Wherefore do ye spend money for that which is not bread? And you labour for that which satisfieth not?"[10]

Figure 9.1. *The Bantu World,* article on "The Library Movement," August 27, 1938.

The Bantu World

3 POLLY STREET

North of Bantu Sports Grounds.]

P. 4 Box 6663   JOHANNESBURG

SATURDAY, AUGUST 27, 1938

The Library Movement.

The growth of the newspaper movement, the migration into urban areas, the facilities for travel and contact, the development of the educational movement, the spread of the gospel, the intimacy of inter-racial contacts in commerce, industry and domestic service—these and other factors are creating a new and a regenerated African. One of the signs and results of this slow awakening is the steady growth of literacy.

The Carnegie non-European Library, established in 1931, and whose second report we publish elsewhere in this issue, stands to encourage this steady growth of literacy. At the present stage of their development, the African people need librarians who are also organisers and literary religionists ; men who can leave the four walls of the library, go out to the people, organise them in reading circles, and infect them with the love for literature. Unlike Europeans, the problem of African librarians is not only to find books for readers, but readers for books also. The task is to help in the schooling of a race. It is to create a literary urge and beget intellectual hunger among the people. The library is fortunate in having a committee of men who have constantly kept the vision of this great task before them. To encourage readers and stimulate interest, the library arranges for lectures by competent men, African and European, and we can think of no better sphere in which African graduates and leaders of thought can render real service.

The social significance of cultural movements cannot be over-emphasised. Crime, delinquency, vagrancy, corruption, ill-health and other social problems are diseases of ignorant society. They can and must be checked. But society cannot be cured of its diseases by one-sided process of treatment. Each need calls for a distinct prescription. Each must be met if we are to keep a healthy balance of life. Our urban African population, like any other urban group, is a complex whole made up of maintains balance and order. And what is tragedy but the disturbance of this balance. The Bantu Press, we hold, has played a vital role in this development. By its influence it has given birth to an awakening and a craving among the people—thus creating a market for commerce and industry, producing a literate, well-informed peasantry, creating healthy contacts between Black and White, and encouraging progress. The newspaper is both a forerunner and a complement to the book-reading habit. To the semi-illiterate masses it touches and fosters the habit to read books. In the cultured it is an indespensable current commentary on what they gather from the byways of literature. And "The Bantu World" can justly claim that it has played a leading part in this respect. The Library Movement will give impetus to the production of Bantu literature. This is important.

The African people must have their own authors who will express the feelings, aspirations, thoughts and visions of the race. And today there is a growing spirit of discontent among African authors who find channels of expression closed to them.

A library, then, is like an extensive orchard where one may pick delicious gems and appease their hunger, gather fruit to sell to the world. But this orchard cannot be kept without funds, and we hope the Reef municipalities and other urban centres in the Transvaal will support the good cause liberally. But the authorities will not give this support unless the Africans themselves show active interest in the work. Therefore like the prophet we invite our thirsting people to "come and eat; yea, come, buy wine and without money and without price. Wherefore do ye spend money for that which is not bread? And your labour for that which satisfieth not?"

The next major statement was written in response to the opening of the Winifred Holtby Memorial Native Library in Western Native Township, Sophiatown. In "The Book World," we are reminded that "In the beginning was the word, and the Word was with God" and that "If oral speech has played a vital role in human evolution, written speech has performed an even greater one because it is in the recorded and imperishable language of books where is enshrined all that is great and most valuable." This is why battling the forces of illiteracy was an urgent task, "for illiteracy is death."

> Before Africans can take their place in the league of progressive nations, our people must be taught to read; be provided with good books and these brought to them. That is where the Library Movement comes in. . . . A people who read become an articulate people. Reading makes a people rediscover themselves and the world round them, impels them not only to progress, but to expression—to live more abundantly. To contribute his share to S. Africa, the African . . . must interpret the fact and the meaning of Africa to the world, he must create works which breathe the beauty, the image and the soul of Africa. For culture is to produce men of genius in the creative arts and sciences.[11]

The two editorials clearly acknowledge the overdetermined environment in which the Manichaean battle for literacy is to take place. First, horizontal and vertical differentiations (local/global, rural/urban, illiterate/educated, black/white) are highlighted in this environment, but they are also erased if the desired united front is not only imagined but realized. Second, the environment is a paraliterate milieu where, in more than one sense, "in the beginning was the Word." Over and above its back-and-forward slides from oral to written speech, not everyone had the same access with regard to the social meaning and power of the "words" that are, can, and should be in circulation. Finally, the tensions (or the required journey) between darkness and light, being exploited and "exploiting oneself," between death and life are brokered through the appropriation of biblical tropes in order to emphasize the demands and rewards associated with reading and, later on, writing. Writers, librarians, and readers were all evangelists of sorts, faced with the transient temptations of the modern world and tasked with cultivating bodies and minds in order to reap fruits in "due season." What is also striking is the consistent conflation of the personal and the political, the desire "to live more abundantly" within the "self," the domestic sphere, and in the "larger home," the South African state. Also, literature is deployed in its much wider sense of referring to printed matter, in contrast to its later restrictive association with imaginative or fictional works (see Williams 1978, 45–51; Vilakazi 1945, 269). However, as evidenced in debates around what constitutes "good" liter-

PAGE FOUR

THE BANTU ❀ WORLD

Printed and Published by the Bantu World (Pty.) Ltd., at their offices, 14, Perth Road, Westdene, Johannesburg.

SATURDAY DECEMBER 7 1940

The Book World

One of the most significant and poetic passages in the Scriptures is the prologue to the gospel according to St. John: "In the beginning was the Word, and the Word was with God, and the Word was God. All things were made by Him. In Him was life; and the life was the light of men. And the light shineth in darkness."

It is no wonder the writer grew lyrical in speaking of the Word, for language—words—is one of those unique attributes of man which distinguish him from, and place him above, the rest of creation. If speech has played a vital role in human evolution, written speech has performed an even greater one because it is in the recorded and imperishable language of books where is enshrined all that is great and most valuable.

These thoughts are prompted by the announcement that to-morrow (Sunday) will be the official opening of the Winifred Holtby Memorial Native Library, Western Native Native Township, Sophiatown. How times have changed! Is itself this announcement is proof of Bantu progress and improvability, an indication of the new trend of official policy and public attitude towards interracial contacts, and a hope and a pointer to the future. The problem of illiteracy is universal and urgent. Everywhere leaders of thought and action—writers, reformers, businessmen, politicians—are fighting desperately in the battle between illiteracy and salvation, for illiteracy is death. H. G. Wells calls it the race between salvation and chaos.

It is clear that most of our ills and disasters spring from the existence of illiterate, blind, emotion-controlled masses who cannot read and reason for themselves and who are fertile ground for the doctrines of political demagogues and chauvinists, and the poisonous harangues of perverted agitators and dictators. An illiterate mind is pliable but easy-crumbling clay. If this is true of civilised countries it is even truer of Africa where 95 per cent of the people are still unable to read and write. This is both a challenge and an indictment to all educated black patriots. Our political liberation, our social status, our economical strength, our mental growth, and our spiritual wealth all depend on the extent of the literacy of our great numbers.

Before Africans can take their place in the league of progressive nations, our people must be taught to read; be provided with good books and these brought to them. That is where the Library Movement comes in. It solves the vexed problem of distribution which of late years has been found both in the sphere of social economies and that of intellectual progress, to be more urgent and difficult than that of production which scientific achievement has made easy.

The public library movement brings good books, free of charge, to the very door of the readers—but it is literacy that can take them to the head and heart. It only remains for us to prove that we are worthy of this new development by making use of the library facilities now so generously provided by the authorities. Figures speak louder than words, and it is the records of the reading we do that will count, therefore.

In this connection "let us now remember and praise famous men," who pioneered this movement in this country. First is the Carnegie Corporation of New York which initiated the movement by making large endowment funds available. Here it may be mentioned that Andrew Carnegie himself, the poor Scotch boy who rose from errand-runner to be multi-millionaire, he owed his unique success to books. In S. Africa we owe much to Senator J. D. Rheinallt Jones, Mr. M. M. Stirling (State Librarian) and to the late Dr. C. T. Loram who together helped launch the Carnegie non-European Library.

Through the efforts of Senator Jones, the Transvaal Council of Education rendered essential services in the early stages of the Movement. To the Carnegie non-European Library Organisation pioneers in this

Being part of a great chain of five newspapers which circulate all over the Union and Rhodesia, "The Bantu World" has achieved unique results and paved the way to more serious reading. This paper has shown also what genius in organisation can do to solve the problems of distribution, for to-day we have a chain of active agents throughout the country.

The growth of the Library movement has wide implications and will have far-reaching results. A people who read become an articulate people. Reading makes a people rediscover themselves and the world round them, impels them not only to progress but to expression—to live more abundantly. This aspect of the matter is fundamental and highest. To contribute his share to S. Africa, the African must learn not only to resist being exploited but to exploit himself, his position and abilities; he must interpret the fact and the meaning of Africa to the world. He must create works which breathe the beauty, the image and the soul of Africa. For culture is to produce men of genius in the creative arts and sciences.

This he can do by acquiring the skill not only to recognise words, but to name them; learning not only to read words but to see light and life in them; training not only to understand words, but to live them.

For words—books—are the Alpha and Omega of progress.

"In the beginning was the Word... All things were made by Him. In Him was life; and the life was the light of men."

Figure 9.2. *The Bantu World*, article on "The Book World," December 7, 1940.

ature, there were strong intimations of the tensions that flow from the different perceptions of what literature is.

What is also apparent is that in addition to reading strategies based on the appropriation of indigenous and biblical repertoires, an allegorical interpretation of the many challenges Africans faced and how African readers needed to understand the methods and demands of reading itself was frequently privileged. Between bondage and redemption, self-improvement and leadership lay a series of prerequisites whose profits might not be immediately obvious but would definitely be understood by those who grasped the resonance of the constant equation of reading with fields, cultivation, and reaping. In order to appreciate the challenges the altered states required, readers were often expected to use the journey motif as an interpretive device. The journey, apart from its structural and metaphoric uses, was in many narratives the quintessential representation of the themes of quest, pilgrimage, and self-realization on the personal and political levels. Finally, there is no doubt that whatever its benefits and pleasures, reading was presented as an active exercise or process that required dedication and "hard work."

As one reader emphasized to the editor in a letter tantalizingly headed "The Pleasures of Reading," "literature is this square field of human happiness" for the individual who was prepared to acquire "the habit of reading as his daily dinner" by entering into a "marriage with the daughter of 'Mr. And Mrs. Literature.'" Once the habit of regular reading has been achieved, "the home becomes a most good-tempered place because it undergoes a perfect stillness after every last repast of the day."[12] But then, as another reader cautioned under the title "A Plea for Literary Clubs," there were many who questioned why they "should read any papers at all—they see no value in reading—they say it is useless. Many also think it is only a waste of money on abstracts." Even among those who read, let us be clear, more than one type of reader walked the "world of the book." Some "read only to pass time," others "to show off that they are learned," and even "the few intelligent readers quickly lose what they have got—because they can seldom apply it quickly. Life's worries causes mind wandering and soon they forget what they have read, before they use it." Despite these obstacles, the letter-writer was unequivocal in his belief that the organization of libraries and literary clubs would "mark a turning point in the course of the progress of our people" and even invoked the following rallying cry: "*Let us be brave and bold for the cause of enlightenment. . . . Culture is the basis of all achievements.*"[13]

Similarly, it must be added, not just any kind of book was considered suitable for reading, or at least reading that was meant to "cultivate" "taste" and "discrimination." For instance, there were heated debates about "objectionable literature," especially the increasing popularity of "Detective Story Books and Love Novels," which were accused of dealing "with sex matters in the crudest manner." Although detective and love novels were also, admittedly, "books printed for reading, . . . in so far as students are concerned . . . these could do no better than deteriorate and warp minds with sordid propensities."[14]

Such debates indicate that the spread of literacy did more than expand the social aspirations, relationships, and horizons of the African intelligentsia; they also threw into sharp relief contending ideas about desirable texts and respectable conduct. The acceptance of the idea of history as moral progress meant that pronouncements were regularly made about respectability, progress, the need for moral character, and the dignity of labor. These attributes were, after all, regarded as part of the results of acquiring a sound education and were prerequisites for the leadership roles that awaited the African elite.

Furthermore, the African elite felt it crucial to celebrate inspirational and aspirational values and agendas; these were articulated in speeches and writings for individual and collective acceptance and action. The reports on the achievements of exemplary individuals in life and the depiction of model characters in fiction were all constantly held up as beacons for emulation.[15] The political continuities between past, present, and future were strongly intimated in headlines such as "Honour Where Honour Is Due—Our Illustrious Dead: How Can We Perpetuate Their Memory?"

> As it is the graves of most of them are obscure, unmarked, unhonoured, and we do not hear, when the birthday of these heroes come round, tributes from those who knew them or thanksgiving prayers for the lives of such noble characters. . . . We need a national memorial, something big enough to show our appreciation of the lives of these men and women—a standing tribute to their inestimable service to Bantudom. What form will it take?[16]

The significance of such interrogations is that they intimate a strategic desire that resonates beyond the imperatives of memory work. At the center of the dilemma of "how can we" is the realization of the importance of finding occasions when Africans, drawing on their own mnemonic symbols, can collectively rehearse and perform their senses of identity.

The Bantu World provided a wide range of social services not available or accessible elsewhere such as readers' forums and advice on issues ranging from the legal to the medical to personal matters. The newspaper also served as an important space and catalyst in the political affairs of black readers. The features and editorials focused on the burning issues of the day facing the community. Major political developments, such as the passing of the discriminatory Hertzog Bills in 1936 (which sought to remove Africans from the common voters' roll in the Cape), were detailed and criticized in the African press by black leaders and readers. *The Bantu World*, for instance, took a very critical stance against the bills, attacking them in editorials in English[17] and Zulu.[18] The editor opined in an editorial entitled "The Security of White Civilisation" that "there is an erroneous belief in certain quarters that the security of White civilisation lies in the repression of the Africans."[19] Readers intoned similar anger and, occasionally in apocalyptic tones, described the process of colonization and its endless acts of hypocrisy: "We gave the Europeans our land. Today they have extended their fences inch by inch, foot by foot, yard by yard, mile by mile until they have the whole country in their possession and have become our masters. They pacified us by giving us the Franchise which they are 'raping' today." Writer Isaac Ramadiba implored his fellow readers not to despair but to take comfort in providential justice: "God knows how to make yesterday's failure the secret of today's success and the sufferings of today the glory of tomorrow." In a telling stroke that drew on the power of "quotable texts," Ramadiba gave his letter the heading "The Fault Is Not In Our Stars" without any need for elaboration on or acknowledgement of the source.[20] Elsewhere, the works of Thomas Carlyle, Ralph Waldo Emerson, Booker T. Washington, W. E. B. Du Bois, and Langston Hughes, to mention a few, were frequently raided to support all sorts of historical, political, and social arguments the African elite wanted to advance. The Bible, Bunyan, Shakespeare, and the Romantics were not simply quoted but were recast and made to carry the imprints of the creativity and ideology of the African intelligentsia.[21]

The African elite was very adept at using quotations as a mode of discursive intervention. They were well versed and deeply steeped in the assumptions of Englishness, and their free-flowing use of quotation from the English canon was a testimony to their mastery of the great tradition and their assertion of their own claims as figures of moral authority and intellectual ability. It would be too simplistic to equate mastery with mimicry or total identification with the empire, for "to have . . . knowledge of . . . a thing is to dominate it, to have authority over it" (Said 1978, 36). As C. L. R. James observed, even though his generation "lived according the tenets of Matthew Arnold, spreading sweetness and light and the best that has been thought and said in the world," such mastery also set the scene for the possibilities of rupture and the emergence of dissident thoughts: "Here Mr. T.S. Eliot will help. In addition to what poetry gives, he is of special value to me in that in him I find more often than elsewhere, and beautifully and precisely stated, *things to which I am completely opposed*" (James 1994, 64, 59).[22]

The BMSC and the Carnegie Non-European Library

In fulfillment of its motto of "stronger in body, mind, spirit and character" the Bantu Men's Social Centre devised programs that would target and improve the physical and mental "health" of its members: "Having made the body fit for intellectual development then there is the question of how to develop the mind along right lines." Somewhat predictably, the answer was "that reading is one of the chief factors in the development of intellectual powers" and that, also, "there is the Gamma Sigma club, a debating and literary society within the Bantu Men's Social Centre, whose object is to improve the literary attainments of its members as well as to develop their debating powers."[23]

One of the areas in which members of the African intelligentsia often felt a daily and personal lack and reminder of their poverty was their inability to secure a room of their own, which they regarded as indispensable to reading and writing. In his advice to teachers, D. D. T. Jabavu, was unequivocal: "You need a room that you can regard as private to yourself for meditation and reading. . . . Move heaven and earth to get this" (Jabavu 1920, 77). B. W. Vilakazi, exasperated by "the lack of privacy . . . haunted constantly by disturbing elements and fear," was forced to conclude that "no Bantu Madonna will be painted in our locations, no Bantu Keats or Milton will come from them." The solution was that "municipalities should apportion certain places where people passing certain tests could live quietly and serenely and uphold the good they had gained from Western civilization."[24]

What is important about the inability to find spaces within the domestic sphere that allowed for the solitary development of oneself, whether through reading or study, is that it meant that members of the African elite had to come to terms with the fact that a large part of their reading and further education was to be of a communal rather than individual nature. Paradoxically, the African elite's poverty and their aspirations to be learned catapulted them into public spaces such as the BMSC which, unintentionally, become the quintessential space for the collective imagining and rehearsal of the intelligentsia's self-improvement and group identity. Peter Abrahams, unable to find "perfect stillness"[25] at home, was drawn to the BMSC because "the atmosphere there was more conducive to learning than at home." At the BMSC he met other students, got assistance when he needed it, and was enthralled by the range of discussions, debates, dances, and performances held there. As he acknowledged, "I wormed my way into these sessions and became a silent, unobtrusive listener" (Abrahams 1981, 198).

My point is that because of the lack of a "room of one's own," the difficulty of procuring books, whether because of their price or inadequate distribution, meant that reading (or rather learning) very often became an expansive process that involved much more than the desired but elusive private, silent, contemplative "moment" organized around the "mobility of the eye" (de Certeau 1988, 176). Instead, it called on other sensory abilities, other genres and cultural repertoires. The African intelligentsia had to assume the role of listeners, speakers, respondents, and performers at the frequent lectures, talks, or debates they attended at the BMSC and elsewhere. In such performative contexts, books escaped the confines of their covers and became one of many tools available to the intelligentsia in their marshalling of the various facets of orature. In this sense, books presented themselves as texts embodied in the speaker(s) who would discuss them, analyze them, recite poems from memory or the page, or read extracts or quotations from them, often as catalysts for a wide range of social and political discussions. I have argued elsewhere that on occasion, the meaning and political symbolism behind the performance of texts as "inappropriate" as *She Stoops to Conquer* and *Lady Windermere's Fan* lay, to a great extent, in the social processes the dramas were inscribed in. Key among these were the spirit of independence that informed the production process and, above all, the fact that once the actors were in costume and on stage, the performances erased the temporal and social distance between "new African" and Victorian ideals (see Peterson 2000, 152–154).

At any rate, the move to providing library facilities for blacks was partially in response to the perennial complaints from members of the African elite about the racist absurdity of not being allowed entry into the "whites only" state and municipal libraries. The decision of the Carnegie Corporation of New York to establish the Library Services for Non-Europeans followed the visit to South Africa in 1928 by two Carnegie visitors. Through its local representative, Dr. C. T. Loram (then the minister of education in Natal), the Carnegie Corporation was prepared to grant the sum of £1,000 each to libraries in the provinces of Natal, Cape Town, and Transvaal that would be "administered on precisely similar lines to the County Library Systems of Great Britain and the United States of America."[26] The grants were to be spent "solely on the purchase of books." The Transvaal project, which was based in Germiston, was officially launched in 1931 and was administered by the Carnegie Non-European Library Committee with Mr. M. M. Stirling as chairman. In 1932, the BMSC's library was inaugurated as a receiving depot of the Carnegie Non-European Library. By 1937, the Carnegie Library had a collection of 5,000 books at its headquarters, which it distributed to about sixty centers countrywide. Each center had a voluntary librarian and, in some cases, even library committees. By the end of 1940, 100 centers were in existence.[27]

In its assessment of the use of its facilities as well as the reading habits of its members, the *First Report of the Committee* observed: "From statistics kept, it has been found that school-children and students attending Training Institutions are the most ardent readers; they are followed closely by readers at centers such as the Bantu Men's Social Centre." In answer to the question "What Do Non-Europeans Read?" the report noted that "Indians will read anything that the European reads, and so will the better educated native and coloured person." However, "some natives will not read novels because they think it a waste of time; they are keen on improving their knowledge of the world and prefer to read books which give information rather than amusement." The report further noted that "in one location the best read book was James H. Breasted's 'History of the Ancient Egyptians.' Biography, especially of people connected with Africa; travel; history . . . and books well illustrated, of general interest, such as the 'wonder Books' and the 'National Geographic Magazine' are the most popular classes. All books dealing with Native life and South African affairs are well received."[28] Two anecdotal accounts are useful in illustrating the diverse opinions held on the challenges of promoting reading among Africans. In 1935, the secretary for the Carnegie Library, after addressing "natives who were attending a Course of Instruction for Scoutmasters" and "judging from the questions put to the speaker," felt that "a lot of work has yet to be done in providing elementary instruction in reading; and that an [*sic*] necessary preliminary to good reading on the part of natives is a verbal introduction to the written word."[29] Writer and journalist H. I. E. Dhlomo, for his part, "advised several school centres to introduce playreading" as "an aid to literary appreciation."[30]

One important development in the affairs of the library was the appointment of Dhlomo as librarian-organizer in February 1937. Dhlomo's appointment was hailed as a "welcome sign of the cultural advancement of the non-European people of the Union." The challenge, as *The Bantu World* had surmised, was that "unlike Europeans, the problem of African librarians is not only to find books for readers but readers for books also."[31] Dhlomo's duties

included "the organising of reading centres, the supply of books to them, lec-
turing and advising on reading matter . . . endeavouring to interest adults and
children in the benefits of self-education through reading."[32] His appointment was "heartily" received, with the exception of the one or two "jealousy
trumper[s]" who felt that "Mr. Dhlomo does not satisfy the requirements as
advertised."[33] Those who supported him felt that amid the apocalyptic headlines of Africans and criminality such as "The Knife is Finishing the Race"
and "The Judges Warning to Africans, etc.," Dhlomo's appointment felt "like
discovering an oasis in a desert, to read or hear about men and women who
are not sparing themselves in the great battle of paving the road for future
generations. . . . We are hoping and praying for a great majority in exemplary
achievements and a very small minority in criminals and 'I don't cares.'"[34]

Dhlomo wasted no time in arranging a talk on libraries for adults and
schools at the BMSC.[35] He arranged other talks and lectures, many of which
were led by distinguished local and international guests. In one week at the
BMSC, members had the privilege of hearing Mr. R. V. Selope give a wide-
ranging lecture on "Bantu Literature" which, *inter alia*, touched on a diverse
range of topics that would not be out of place at many present-day confer-
ences. With regard to the promotion and "future of Bantu Literature," Thema
explored "sources of inspiration" that included the Bible, "the reduction of the
Bantu languages to writing," the demands of translation, ideas about "the
problem of tribal as distinct from Bantu or national literature" and the "problem of a lingua franca, English vs. tribal mediums." Other topics that were
touched on included "publication houses, censorship and literature committees, the limited market of tribal literature, the danger and crippling effect of
writing books for school purposes only." Two days later the BMSC hosted a
Dr. A. W. White ("himself a Negro") who gave a lecture on "Negro Literature" from the days of slavery to contemporary times. Dr. White also "con-
tended that it was the Negro and not the white American that has given
America original and distinct artistic contributions" and he "mentioned . . .
[the] . . . names of several so-called European writers who were in fact Negroes."[36]

One of the conclusions that the newspaper article (or I should say
Dhlomo) drew from the two lectures is the assessment of Thema's presentation as "altogether a most vital lecture, touching on problems that must,
sooner or later, be faced and solved, not by European experts and linguists, but
the Africans themselves."[37] In addition to organizing talks, Dhlomo inaugurated arguably one of the earliest written documents of African literary criticism in South Africa, "The Reader's Companion." A remarkable aspect of

"The Reader's Companion" is that after dealing with the obligatory update on news and new acquisitions by the Carnegie Library, it presented a "series of brief biographical sketches on 'Some African Authors'" or "the foremost writers of the race," specifically, S. E. K. Mqhayi, Sol. T. Plaatje, and Thomas Mofolo.[38]

Dhlomo participated in the Bantu Author's Conference, described as a "conference on vernacular literature," which was held in October in Florida. Rheinalt Jones described the event as "a unique gathering" and reported that among other things, it considered the possibility of setting up "an academy of Bantu languages and literature" which would facilitate sessions where African authors could meet from time to time. The "Bantu Academy" would also attend to the "means of distributing literature among the African people."[39]

"Take paper and ink . . . load it . . . fire with your pen"[40]

As part of its commitment to the "betterment" of the "race" through its evocations of the "world of the book," *The Bantu World,* like other sectors of the African press, adopted a multipronged strategy that tried to look both ways at once. This meant acting as a catalyst in promoting the new habits of reading and serving as the forum for the publication of writings by Africans. On the other hand, it also meant initiating processes of cultural retrieval and reconstruction.

In the latter regard, in 1936, one Mr. Leo Hudson, the South African representative of the British company responsible for "the famous 'Ovaltine' Health Drink," sponsored a "Folk Lore Competition" in *The Bantu World* that offered readers "two guineas" for the best rendition of folklore.[41] As was the case with previous and subsequent interventions, the interest in and promotion of folklore was the result of a complex layering of concerns. These ranged, on the one hand, from the fascination with what was seen as African exotica—that is, "story-tellers" huddled "[a]round a fire at night" narrating stories to the young generation. On the other hand, some expressed anxiety about the "negative" consequences of modernity on "native life" and the practice of orature, including the shift toward the much-vaunted reading of books and newspapers: "The old story telling round the fire at night is a habit which is fast disappearing. Unless something is done, many of our folk lore stories will have been forgotten beyond recall." Often the romantic and anxious attitudes to African orature were, of course, part of the same continuum. The Ovaltine competition was billed as "An Opportunity to Preserve African Stories for Coming Generations" by recording the oral tales in books.[42]

Clearly, despite the stark dichotomy that is posited between orality and literature, the competitions were in themselves suggestive of the possible articulation between orature and literature. There are similar hesitancies with regard to the veracity and status of orature as historical knowledge. The more enlightened welcomed "folk-lore [as] now a well defined study side-by-side with history" and felt that it was an indispensable source of the history of societies still dependent on the "oral tradition."[43] The material deemed appropriate for collection as folklore included "family or tribal history, proverbs, plant names (with specimens), folk tales, descriptions of customs, 'praises', poetry, genealogies, [and] lists of regiments or age grades."[44]

African writers, for their part, felt that the "state of play" with regard to African literature was often simplified. D. D. T. Jabavu contested the idea "that the Bantu have no literature." He argued that because the literature is "far from being universally advertised . . . in public places" it "does not necessarily denote that it is little or non-existent." In support of his perspective, he reminded readers that "where a strong mission press has long existed," such as in Lesotho and in the Cape, "there is a considerable amount of published and manuscript literature."[45]

In 1935 the stakes were increased considerably with the inauguration of the May Ester Bedford prizes for Bantu literature, art, and music. The awards were intended to "encourage original works of distinctively African culture . . . in a Bantu language, with English translation."[46] The first recipients of the May Ester Bedford Prize were renowned Xhosa poet S. E. K. Mqhayi and artist Ernest Methuen Mancoba for his important sculpture *Future Africa* (1934).[47] Mqhayi was to repeat his feat in 1936 together with Rev. Jolobe in a year where it was felt that "the work submitted this year . . . [was] . . . considerably below the standard of work submitted last year."[48]

The African press was one of the most important sites for the first sustained publication of literary endeavors by Africans, especially poetry.[49] The promotion of literature—as an imaginative genre—was consistent with and complementary to the larger objectives of forming a pan-ethnic and -class community in pursuit of social status and liberation. In the words of one correspondent in an article entitled "Towards Our Own Literature," "We have no desire to foster any narrow national or racial spirit. But we want to intensify, through literature, our individual experience . . . to pool our emotions; to identify common aspirations. . . . We want to establish a brotherhood of the heart."[50] In a special feature on "Poetry and the African," *The Bantu World* boasted:

This week we publish some poems composed by African scholars (i.e. men of learning not school children!) as further proof of the fact that "the African mind is reaching out and grasping the knowledge of the West," to use the words of Peter Abrahams, the young African poet. Poetry is one of the most eloquent media of the soul—expression, and it comes naturally to almost all Africans. But when the African expresses himself in poetry and does it in a foreign tongue and does it well, that shows that there is a great Soul in the African people. *We are glad to say that on account of our regular encouragement of poetry, some of our readers have now tried their hand at poetry.* And, succeeded![51]

The poetry (in African languages and English) of Vilakazi, Abrahams, and Dhlomo, among others, was published in *The Bantu World*.[52] So too were reviews of books such as Vilakazi's *Noma Nini*[53] (reviewed by R. R. R. Dhlomo), H. I. E. Dhlomo's *Nongqause: The Liberator*[54] and *Valley of a Thousand Hills*,[55] and the works of R. R. R. Dhlomo.[56] The reviews were, in themselves, an elaboration of literary criticism by Africans and so too were essays such as H. I. E. Dhlomo's "Drama and the African."[57]

Conclusion

A perusal of *The Bantu World* indicates that the practice of reading and writing among the African intelligentsia formed part of a fairly extensive and expansive social environment. *The Bantu World*, together with institutions such as the BMSC and the myriad texts and ideas circulated between and among these entities, all of which were animated by the dedication, hopes, and aspirations of its readers, helped to create a "brotherhood of the heart." The texts, ultimately, provided a sense of a common background and experience and created social contacts (even if they were only networks of the imagination) that all, ultimately, facilitated a sense of community among dispersed and disparate individuals. Common to the fellowship of reading and writing were the prerogatives of self-improvement and, once the necessary mastery of literacy and a "progressive" consciousness was attained, engagement in activities that promoted social transformation.

It is important to underscore that the elite's nationalist sentiments must be understood as reflecting much more than an anticolonial stance. These sentiments also embodied the distinct aspirations of the middle classes, their embodiment of the changes they had wrought because of their turn away from tradition, and their acquisition of education and civilization. So together with the litanies and stories written and published, a wide range of great expectations were also being cultivated among readers. Even in the identification of the opportunities that they were being denied, the inverse was just as crucial; the elite foregrounded the opportunities they felt entitled to. Since in the period under discussion the African elite was relatively weak in most areas of social organization and power, it was largely on the level of ideology and cultural practice that they could will into being (even if just imaginatively) their hopes for a better life. That is why they accorded such significance to reading and writing in their search for redemption.

NOTES

1. For a discussion of letter-writing among Africans at the turn of the nineteenth century, see Vukile Khumalo's chapter in this volume.

2. I cannot resist using the following description of the range of activities organized by the Baumannville Cultural Society in Durban during its first year of existence: "All in all the club coordinated 46 events for its members. These were made up of 29 lectures, 5 musical nights, 1 banquet, 2 social evenings, 4 markets and 5 food meetings. All the events were attended by 213 participants. To start with the lectures, these included quite a diverse range of topics ranging from 'Nursing as a profession' by Miss E. Sililo, 'How to get about getting a life partner' by Mr. C. Matiwane, 'How to entertain guests' by K. E. Masinga (Head of the Zulu Programmes Department, SABC) to 'Etiquette' by Matiwane. Social and political addresses covered areas such as 'Communism' by Mr. Wilson Cele, 'African Workers and the Trade Union Movement' by Mr. E. Shanley, 'The struggle of the African women for freedom' by Miss J. Lax, 'American Negroes—with special reference to American Youth' by Mr. S. Ngcobo, M.A. B. Econ., and a series of talks on 'Native Customary Laws' by Mr. L. Mthimkulu. Literary matters were covered in '13 Among the odds'—a book review by Mr. C. Matiwane—with special reference to Paul Robeson, '13 against the odds'—a book review with special reference to Langston Hughes by Miss F. Zuma and 'The Bantu Press' by H. I. E. Dhlomo." See *Ilanga lase Natal,* July 6, 1946.

3. For an equivalent case study of the literary activities pursued by the emergent African elite in Ghana, see Stephanie Newell's chapter in this volume.

4. Not all sections of the white community were convinced that it was important to promote literacy among Africans. By 1940 the report of the Non-European Library Movement stated: "Nearly all local authorities are now adding thousands of pounds annually to their revenue by selling beer to Natives and profits on beer selling must be used solely for the benefit of the Native population. A number of towns are at present using this source of revenue to further many admirable prospects; but with only two exceptions (Johannesburg and Germiston) local authorities seem to consider the spread of civilisation through reading to be a matter of no importance, and consequently make no grants to this library, or else grant such small sums that very little work of lasting value can be done"; *Umteteli wa Bantu,* December 7, 1940.

5. See R. V. Selope-Thema's editorial "Chiefs and the Franchise" for an indication of the tightrope the elite had to walk between chiefs and colonial authorities; *Bantu World,* November 2, 1935.

6. Similar observations have been made with regard to the Enlightenment in eighteenth-century Europe. Scholars such as Charles Taylor (*Sources of the Self: The Making of the Modern Identity*) and Peter Gay (*The Enlightenment: An Interpretation*) draw attention to a number of continuities in terms of key assumptions between Christianity and the Enlightenment, especially the abiding moral horizons bequeathed by Christianity to modernity.

7. *The Bantu World,* October 24, 1936.

8. For a fuller treatment of this argument, see Peterson (2000, 15–19).

9. *The Bantu World,* June 27, 1936.

10. *The Bantu World,* August 27, 1938.

11. *The Bantu World,* December 7, 1940.

12. *The Bantu World,* August 3, 1935.

13. *The Bantu World,* August 7, 1937, emphasis added.

14. *The Bantu World,* October 2, 1937.

15. For a sample of tributes paid to African achievements, see *The Bantu World,* March 21, 1936, June 24, 1936, and July 25, 1936.

16. *Umteteli wa Bantu,* November 11, 1939.

17. *The Bantu World,* July 25, 1936.

18. *The Bantu World,* June 13, 1936.

19. *The Bantu World,* July 25, 1936.

20. *The Bantu World,* April 15, 1936.

21. For examples of quotations used in poetry, mostly published in the *Bantu World,* see E. C. Jali's "Despair," V. N. Plaatje's "What Is In a Name," R. R. R. Dhlomo's "The Wailings of Rolfes R. R. Dhlomo," Stanley Silwana's "I Sing of Africa," and Walter M. B. Nhlapo's "The Revolution Song," all in Couzens and Patel (1982, 68, 73, 64, 82, 86).

22. De Certeau has noted that colonized people have "often made of the rituals, representations, and laws imposed on them something quite different from what their conquerors had in mind; they subverted them not by rejecting or altering them, but by using them with respect to ends and references foreign to the system they had no choice but to accept. They were other within the very colonization that outwardly assimilated them; their use of the dominant social order deflected its power, which they lacked the means to challenge; they escaped it without leaving it" (de Certeau 1988, xiii).

23. *Umteteli was Bantu,* June 22, 1929.

24. *Umteteli wa Bantu,* June 12, 1937. For a response to Vilakazi's speech, see *Umteteli wa Bantu,* June 26, 1937.

25. *The Bantu World,* August 3, 1935.

26. See "Transvaal Carnegie Non-European Library Report for the Period Ending June 30, 1935," in AD 843 / B68.1.2, Historical and Literary Papers, South African Institute of Race Relations Collection (hereafter SAIRR), University of the Witwatersrand. For more extensive discussions of the Carnegie Library in South Africa, see Cobley 1997 and Rochester 1999.

27. See Non-European Circulating Library, Witwatersrand and Pretoria, "Minutes of a Meeting of the Temporary Committee held at the Bantu Men's Social Centre, Johannesburg, March 12th, 1930" in SAIRR Collection, AD 843/B68.1.3, Historical and Literary Papers, University of the Witwatersrand.

28. See "Transvaal Carnegie Non-European Library Report for the Period Ending June 30, 1935." A report from the BMSC notes that based on the books borrowed over a

six-month period, although "English fiction claims a high percentage of readers among the Europeans, the contrary is just the case with non-European readers. Of the 3,985 books borrowed 698 were English fiction, 276 children's books and 249 in the vernacular. Books on philosophy and religion numbered 319; those on education and sociology 797; while those on science and art and literature and language numbered 504 and 352 respectively. Books on history, travel and biography totalled 691." *The Bantu World,* April 27, 1940.

29. See Transvaal Carnegie Non-European Library, *The Honourable Secretary's Report. July–November, 1935,* AD 843/B68.1, Historical and Literary Papers, SAIRR, University of the Witwatersrand.

30. *Umteteli wa Bantu,* December 7, 1940.

31. *The Bantu World,* August 27, 1938.

32. *Umteteli wa Bantu,* February 20, 1937. See also *The Bantu World,* 20 February 1937.

33. See letter, *The Bantu World,* March 13, 1937.

34. See letter, *The Bantu World,* March 6, 1937.

35. *The Bantu World,* April 3, 1937.

36. For reports on other "literary socials" see *The Bantu World,* April 27, 1940, and *Umteteli wa Bantu,* December 7, 1940.

37. *The Bantu World,* July 30, 1938.

38. *The Bantu World,* July 16, 1938.

39. *The Bantu World,* November 21, 1936.

40. I. W. W. Citashe "Your Cattle Are Gone," in Couzens and Patel (1982).

41. *The Bantu World,* September 5, 1936.

42. *The Bantu World,* September 5, 1936.

43. *Umteteli wa Bantu,* March 18, 1922.

44. *Umteteli wa Bantu,* November 18, 1922.

45. *Umteteli wa Bantu,* May 26, 1922.

46. *The Bantu World,* March 19, 1935.

47. *The Bantu World,* December 28, 1935. "Eighteen manuscripts in all the four chief Bantu languages and of good quality were submitted." For an exemplary introduction to the works of the internationally celebrated Mancoba, see Miles (1994 and 1997, 136–143).

48. *The Bantu World,* December 26, 1936.

49. For an excellent and comprehensive anthology that also draws on poetry published in the African press, see Couzens and Patel (1982).

50. *Ilanga lase Natal,* December 21, 1923, cited in Couzens (1976, 71).

51. *The Bantu World,* December 12, 1936.

52. See for a sampling the editions of February 8, 1936, April 18, 1936, June 27, 1936, and June 15, 1940.

53. *The Bantu World,* June 13, 1936.

54. *The Bantu World,* October 31, 1936.

55. *The Bantu World,* November 15, 1941.

56. See "R. R. R. Dhlomo—Author and Journalist: The Man and His Works," *The Bantu World,* July 17, 1937; see also *The Bantu World,* October 23, 1937 for another review of Dhlomo.

57. *The Bantu World,* April 15, 1933, October 21, 1931, and May 12, 1944.

REFERENCES

Abrahams, Peter. 1981. *Tell Freedom.* London: Faber and Faber.

Anderson, Benedict. 1983. *Imagined Communities: Reflections on the Origin and Spread of Nationalism.* London: Verso.

Cobley, Alan G. 1997. "Literacy, Libraries, and Consciousness: The Provision of Library Services for Blacks in South Africa in the Pre-Apartheid Era." *Libraries & Culture* 32, no. 1: 57–80.

Couzens, Tim. 1976. "The Social Ethos of Black Writing in South Africa 1920–50." In *Aspects of South African Literature,* ed. Christopher Heywood. London: Heinemann.

————. 1985. *The New African: A Study of the Life and Work of H. I. E. Dhlomo.* Johannesburg: Ravan Press.

————, and Essop Patel, eds. 1982. *The Return of the Amasi Bird.* Johannesburg: Ravan Press.

de Certeau, Michel. 1988. *The Practice of Everyday Life.* Trans. Steven Rendall. Berkeley: University of California Press.

Dhlomo, H. I. 1943. "Influence and Power of African Press." *Ilanga lase Natal,* March 3.

Fuze, Magema M. 1979. *The Black People and Whence They Came.* Trans. H. C. Lugg. Pietermaritzburg: University of Natal Press.

Gay, Peter. *The Enlightenment, an Interpretation.* 2 vols. New York: Knopf, 1966, 1969.

Jabavu, D. D. T. 1920. *The Black Problem.* Lovedale: Lovedale Press.

James, C. L. R. 1994. *Beyond a Boundary.* London: Serpent's Tail.

Miles, Elza. 1994. *Ernest Mancoba: A Resource Book.* Johannesburg: Johannesburg Art Gallery.

————. 1997. *Land and Lives: A Story of Early Black Artists.* Johannesburg: Johannesburg Art Gallery; Cape Town: Human and Rousseau.

Peterson, Bhekizizwe. 2000. *Monarchs, Missionaries & African Intellectuals: African Theatre and the Unmaking of Colonial Marginality.* Johannesburg: University of the Witwatersrand Press.

Rochester, Maxine K. "The Carnegie Corporation and South Africa: Non-European Library Services." *Libraries & Culture* 32, no. 1: 27–51.

Said, Edward. 1978. *Orientalism.* London: Routledge.

Switzer, Les. 1988. "Bantu World and the Origins of a Captive African Commercial Press in South Africa." *Journal of Southern African Studies* 14, no. 3: 351–370.

Switzer, L., and D. Switzer. 1979. *Black Press in South Africa and Lesotho: A Descriptive Bibliographic Guide to African, Coloured, and Indian Newspapers, Newsletters, and Magazines, 1836–1976.* Boston: Hall.

Taylor, Charles. 1989. *Sources of the Self: The Making of the Modern Identity.* Cambridge, Mass.: Harvard University Press.

Vilakazi, Benedict. 1933. "What Writers Has This National Press?" *Ilanga lase Natal,* March 17.

————. 1945. "The Oral and Written Literature in Nguni." Ph.D. thesis, University of the Witwatersrand.

Williams, Raymond. 1978. *Marxism and Literature.* Oxford: Oxford University Press.

READING DEBATING/DEBATING READING: THE CASE OF THE LOVEDALE LITERARY SOCIETY, OR WHY MANDELA QUOTES SHAKESPEARE

Isabel Hofmeyr

10

As many commentators have noted, Nelson Mandela has a proclivity for quoting Shakespeare. At a gathering of South African business executives in 1990 he invoked *The Merchant of Venice* ("Hath not a Jew eyes?"; Mandela 1990). When addressing the English Parliament in 1996, he referred to *Coriolanus* ("We are accounted poor citizens"; Mandela 1996). For the 13th International AIDS Conference in Durban in 2000, he used *Julius Caesar* ("Cowards die many times before their deaths"; Mandela 2000). When the former South African president gives a speech, Shakespeare is more than likely to be present.

This interest in Shakespeare goes back to Mandela's school days at the Eastern Cape mission institutions, Clarkesbury and Healdtown, and to his short-lived career at the University of Fort Hare. It continued during his imprisonment on Robben Island, where one of Mandela's fellow inmates, Sonny Venkatrathnam, kept a secret copy of Shakespeare disguised with Indian religious pictures on the cover. The copy was passed around, and each prisoner signed their name next to their favorite lines. As Anthony Sampson notes in his biography of Mandela:

> Ahmed Kathrada chose Henry V's "Once more into the breach." Wilton Mkwayi chose Malvolio's "Some are born great," from *Twelfth Night*. Govan Mbeki

chose the opening lines of the same play: "If music be the food of love." Billy Nair chose Caliban's lines from *The Tempest:* "This island's mine, by Sycorax my mother." Sisulu chose Shylock's "Still have I borne it with a patient shrug, / For suff'rance is the badge of all our tribe." (Sampson 1999, 234)

Mandela chose as his signature "tune" the passage from *Julius Caesar* that he quoted to the AIDS conference delegates:

Cowards die many times before their deaths;
The valiant never taste of death but once.
Of all the wonders that I yet have heard,
It seems to me most strange that men should fear;
Seeing that death, a necessary end,
Will come when it will come. (ibid.)

This proclivity for quoting Shakespeare characterized senior African National Congress leadership as much inside prison as outside. Chris Hani, for example, was known for his love of the Shakespeare quotation (Taylor 1993). Thabo Mbeki too is an avid user of the Bard (Mbeki 2000).

This quoting behavior has generally been attributed to two factors. The first is the style of schooling this generation of leaders experienced in mission schools. These institutions taught English literature intensively, often requiring pupils to recall large passages by heart. Alexander Kerr, a lecturer at Fort Hare, is identified as the person responsible for Mandela's love of Shakespeare. Somewhat unusually for the time, Kerr taught "with a vividness which made Shakespeare seem totally relevant to contemporary Africa" (Sampson 1999, 23). A second explanation is that Shakespeare offered an allegorical resource through which to comment on the oppression of apartheid South Africa. In the forums of the black intelligentsia, in their writing, and then in prison discussion groups Shakespearean texts were reworked as commentaries on political oppression and injustice in South Africa (ibid., 233–234), often in opposition to the anodyne and avowedly apolitical teaching of literature that characterized most mission schools. As one commentator puts it: "Were they not wronged and deceived by a criminal ruler as had been Hamlet, the prince of Denmark? The subjects of a treacherous Macbeth, and like Macbeth was the South African regime not doomed to destruction? Or, were they not rightfully conspiring against a despotic Julius Caesar? Did not the future rest upon them?" (Hallengren 2001). Shakespeare, in short, became a way of talking about politics.

These various explanations are important and draw out the boundaries of how one might begin to explain the phenomenon of the "quoting politicians."

Schooling does throw considerable light on this widespread use of quotation which would not have been possible without years of classroom memorization. Literary quotation as a sign of erudition and eloquence was also probably found among the upper echelon of mission teachers, although as a rule, this class, particularly toward its less-elite reaches, tended toward biblical rather than secular literary citation. The "workshopping" of Shakespeare in the political forums of the black intelligentsia would in all likelihood have encouraged the practice of quotation by encouraging the use of the "clinching" quotation, like a trump card.

Yet however useful these explanations are, they are necessarily broad brush and hence raise more questions than they answer. From whence, for example, comes this view of literature as a compendium of mottos? In the case of the Robben Island Shakespeare volume, each selected text became a second signature or autograph. After Robben Island, these quotations continued to function as proxies or textual *cartes de visite* that were produced in a variety of public forums.

At work in such use of quotation is something more complex than simply the textual practices of the classroom overlaid by the interpretive procedures of resistance politics. This chapter attempts to delineate what the "something more" might be. It argues that one important forum for shaping the ideas of the mission-educated generation of leaders regarding the proper uses of literature was indeed the school. However, within this milieu, the agenda for such ideas was not simply dictated by teachers. Instead, mission schools themselves constituted complex "marketplaces" of contending groups, ideas, and intellectual traditions shaped by overlapping contours, within and beyond the school perimeter, of student/teacher, Christian/non-Christian, male/female, black/white, chief/commoner, settler/African. Each of these currents supported its own ideas regarding the proper function and uses of literature. One forum where these currents emerged most clearly was in the school debating society, where contenders had a license, albeit a curtailed one, to state their views. The records of school debating societies seldom survive. However, in the case of Southern Africa's most prominent mission school, Lovedale, detailed minutes of the Literary Society (which also included debating) for the period 1936–1948 survive. These provide us with an invaluable insight into what the contending definitions of literature and its functions were and how these were played out in the arena of a debating forum. As the chapter attempts to demonstrate, in this forum, African students (predominantly male students) attempted to redefine the Literary Society as a leadership forum in which they, through debating, could develop and practice the requisite rhetorical skills so as to take their place as scions of the African elite. In this configuration, literature came to be defined as a source of maxim and motto, a domain for fossicking quotation. By contrast, for most teachers, literature properly functioned as a secular evangelical force, a quasi-religious domain which would moralize leisure time, instill virtue, and uplift its readers. At times, the views of teachers and pupils cohabited peacefully. At other times, the contradictions between them surfaced. The Lovedale Literary Society provides a useful lens through which to capture these conversations.

* * *

In 1945, the secretary of the Lovedale Literary Society received a letter from the school's senate. It came in response to a letter of complaint the students in the society had sent off a few months earlier itemizing a slew of problems which ranged from the demand that the ban on discussing political topics in the meetings of the Literary Society be lifted to opposing the practice of imposing a subscription (Minutes of the Lovedale Literary Society [hereafter Minutes], June 9, 1945). The senate responded by turning down all of the requests. Part of its letter read: "In recent years the whole character of the Literary Society has changed. Formerly one of the great educative influences on the life of the students, it has become merely a debating society entirely dissociated from direction or guidance by members of staff. These are fatal defects which cannot be allowed to continue" (Minutes, September 12, 1945). Or, as another staff member had earlier noted: "Members seem to be interested mostly in debates but . . . the Literary Society is mainly meant for lectures, plays, etc" (Minutes, February 28, 1941).

The phrase "merely a debating society" captures one's attention. Why, one wonders, should any self-respecting mission school object to debating? Surely this would be considered an uplifting and moralizing pastime. Yet object the school authorities did, almost on an annual basis. Virtually every year, students would put through a request that the title of the society be changed from "the Lovedale Literary Society" to "the Lovedale Literary and Debating Society." Every year the request was turned down. What was it about these two words "literary" and "debating" that sparked such intense feeling?

One route to the answer to this question is a brief sketch of the history of the society. The brainchild of the first principal, William Govan, the society was inaugurated during his tenure (1841 to 1870; the exact date is unknown). Govan was deeply committed to an academic (as opposed to a technical) education and the society dovetailed with his educational philosophy and objectives (Shepherd n.d., 156–157). It met every Friday evening and its program included the reading of essays and stories, recitations, musical evenings, talks, lectures, spelling bees, and debates (which were generally held twice a year; Lovedale Missionary Institute 1873–1950). The society was one of the show-cases of the school and attracted an outside audience from the town of Alice, on the border of which the school lay (Lovedale Missionary Institute 1873, 12–13). The Literary Society hence provided a weekly forum in which ideals of civility and erudition could be enacted not only for those in the school but also for members of the public. As Rev. Wilkie, the principal, explained to students in a pep talk in February 1937, the function of the society was twofold: "to deal with the study of great literature and to discuss problems that affect the people as a whole." Students should "speak sincerely on a sub-ject that moulds us" (Minutes, February 19, 1923).

This stress on civility has led some commentators to see the Literary So-ciety as no more than a mini-forum for imperialism. A close look at the top-ics discussed, however, demonstrates a more complex scenario. In some cases, the topics did indeed look "imperial" and focused on English writers and themes of English history: for example, Henry VIII (December 1, 1882), Milton (October 3, 1884), Cromwell and Bunyan (October 30, 1874, and December 4, 1874), and Wordsworth (February 11, 1881). These topics were however sandwiched between others which cast a skeptical light on the ap-parently straightforward imperialness of these "English" themes. To begin with, Lovedale was a Scottish Presbyterian institution and, not surprisingly, themes of (or related to) Scottishness cropped up from time to time in topics such as "The Covenanters" (October 27, 1899) or "Was the massacre of Drogheda justified?" (March 26, 1897). The sense of world history that oper-ated at Lovedale was also not straightforwardly "English" and "imperial." Take, for instance, a topic such as "Is the late arbitration in regard to the Al-abama claims honourable to Great Britain?" which was discussed in 1873 (April 25, 1873). "The Alabama claims" referred to an episode that had been sparked by the sale of a ship (built, incidentally, on the Scottish dockyards) to the Confederate forces. The Union government and sections of the British public objected to this commerce with the slave-owning South. As the *Al-abama* roved around sinking the trading vessels of the North, this opposition mounted. Such a discussion could only have been pursued in the context of a robust discussion of slavery. Likewise, one wonders what transpired in a talk on "Were the English chiefly to blame in the Mutiny of 1857?" (November 21, 1873) or "Should Socialism be adopted?" (June 2, 1899).

A further complicating factor was the consistent presence of debates pertaining to pressing local issues of concern to an emerging African elite. These included debates on progressive farming methods ("Whether is stock or agricultural farming best for the Natives of this country?" [September 3, 1897] and "Is it justifiable to kill all cattle on a farm where there is Rinderpest?" [May 20, 1898]); changing gender roles (brideprice [November 18, 1881], monogamy versus polygamy [June 4, 1937], and whether women should enter the ministry [June 2, 1937]); the nature of education (should it be academic or technical? [October 10, 1897], in which language [September 27, 1878], compulsory or not [March 28, 1879], free or not [May 19, 1882], could it erase "superstition"? [October 13, 1876]); forms of government (chief/monarchy versus republic [October 28, 1882, and September 24, 1875]); and how to shape public opinion (through the pulpit or the press? [November 11, 1899]). Questions of what constituted "progress" and "civilization" were also common and appeared in topics such as "Has the time come for heathen custom to be put down by Act of Parliament?" (March 7, 1876) and "Does education remove superstition?" (November 13, 1897).

In literary terms, these subjects cast a querying shadow on the discussion of any canonical figures of British literature and history. Take, for example, a talk on Wordsworth, which was situated in the annual program between a lecture by a leading Lovedale figure, John Knox Bokwe, on the early African Christian, Ntsikana, and a debate on "Should Native marriages, as celebrated according to native custom, be recognized in colonial law courts?" (Mr. S. Mzimba arguing for the motion, Mr. J. Tengo-Jabavu, one of the region's most prominent intellectuals, arguing against it; November 2, 1881; August 5, 1881; November 18, 1881). Or consider the case of a talk on Oliver Goldsmith that was followed the next week by a debate on "whether the battle of Marathon, or the battle of Waterloo, has had more influence on the world" (April 30, 1875, and May 7, 1875). These were bracketed in turn by a talk on the "Kat River Settlement" (a colonially created "coloured" settlement established on Xhosa land) and "Whether the introduction of foreign labour will be beneficial to the Colony" (April 2, 1875, and June 4, 1875).

What these various strands demonstrate is that the nineteenth-century Lovedale Literary Society was animated by a range of different agendas. In such a forum, any topic was necessarily resituated in a gallery of competing ideas, discourses, and frames of reference. In addition, the cumulative programs for the society demonstrate a determined "reshelving" of imperial themes and writers on a locally assembled "bookshelf" of issues. As we shall see below, this pattern was to persist in the twentieth-century life of the organization.

Notable in these nineteenth-century programs of the society are the biannual debates. During this period at least, the idea of debating formed a staple of the society. What happened to change this accepted place for debating?

The first factor that appeared to change circumstances was a waning interest in debating among the European staff. The Lovedale Annual Report of 1926 noted, "Unfortunately perhaps as the European staff continues to grow, the tendency is more for the Europeans to keep to themselves, and attendance [at the Literary Society] . . . dwindles" (18). A year later, the annual report pleaded for more staff to attend the meetings of the society (Lovedale Missionary Institute 1927, 70). By 1934, the annual report lamented that it was impossible to keep a chairman (who had always been a staff member) interested for more than six months or a year (Lovedale Missionary Institute 1934, 36). As the war approached, several European men enlisted, eroding yet further the possibility of meaningful supervision by European staff.

Against this background, the society became a largely student-run affair. Under student leadership, the proportion of debates went up and the degree of literary talks declined. To complicate matters further, the war heralded a period of intense student militancy in Lovedale and indeed in most mission schools across the country. Increasingly starved for provincial funding and facing wartime inflation, most mission schools were in serious debt and had to cut back on resources. In addition, the students had been exposed to ever-hardening segregationist policies, both beyond the school and to a lesser, but nonetheless palpable, extent within it. Spurred on by militancy elsewhere in the country, students took the opportunity to make their views felt. During 1946, for example, a year of prolonged student revolt, Lovedale was in a state of near-insurrection (Hyslop 1990, 95–122).

In a climate of declining resources and rising nationalism, a series of teachers tried to win back control of the society. These included the grimly determined R. H. W. Shepherd and the more pliable J. W. Macquarrie, who held office for only a few months before departing on military service (Lovedale Missionary Institute 1940, 37). The teachers did have some success in stamping their authority on the society, but their control was brittle and always challenged. For example, the 1945 annual report noted: "Unfortunately as the year progressed some members sought the altering of the constitution so that the Senate might have little or no say on the Literary Society and that politics and racial subjects should have a larger place in its programme. The present constitution was adopted in 1930–40 [*sic;* 1939–1940] because of the level to which the Literary Society had sunk" (Lovedale Missionary Institute

1945, 32). By 1946, Macquarrie was back but because of the riots and disruption, the society's meetings were cancelled. By 1951, the Literary Society seems to have disappeared, at least from the annual reports. The final comment on the society read: "It is not appreciated that the function of any Literary Society is cultural rather than recreational" (Lovedale Missionary Institute 1950, 37).

Against this fraught and contested background, the terms "literary" and "debating" became part of a coded linguistic arsenal hurled between staff and students. For most staff, the term "literary" signaled the long history of the society with its performances of civility, erudite discussion, and learned debate which required the mustering of considerable historical and literary evidence. For staff, this was what a literary society should be. Indeed, they continued to draw up programs for the students that used debating topics that had been around for more than a century. One of these was "Which is more influential books or people" (Minutes, March 26, 1938; August 24, 1940), something of a favorite in colonial schools (Newell 2002, 44). The use of such "ancient" topics caused the students considerable annoyance (Minutes, November 13, 1948).

From the perspective of the staff, the society had lost "dignity and authority" (Lovedale Missionary Institute 1926, 18). Staff complained that it was student run and hence chaotic, characterized by poorly prepared and pompous speeches (Minutes, February 17, 1939; Lovedale Missionary Institute 1933, 42), it lacked all decorum or rigor (there was no longer a rulebook or a program, a fact that apparently bothered the staff; Minutes, March 8, 1940), topics were not advertised in advance (Minutes, January 9, 1945), and the disappearance of subscriptions had taken the elite edge off the society (for example, there were no longer ushers to take one to reserved seats; Minutes, March 8, 1940). Or, as the annual report noted: "Careless statements [are] sometimes made by pupils who speak with little knowledge of the bigger problems of life" (Lovedale Missionary Institute 1930, 31).

Debating always has a potentially radical edge to it, as those who have studied debating societies have shown. Debating draws together those in similar circumstances and allows them a chance to share and analyze their problems, refine their discourses, and sharpen their grievances. As Newell has shown in the case of the sub-elite urban classes in Ghana, as Thale (1995) has shown for the lower classes in eighteenth-century London, and as Glaser (1988) has shown for youth in Soweto in the 1970s, debating provided an effective forum for social organization, networking, and the intellectual refinement of a mutually created set of ideas.

Yet at the same time, it must be noted that debating was a standard practice in many colonial schools and when conducted in the relatively controlled environment of a school, some of its more dangerous edges were dampened. The objections of the Lovedale teachers were consequently not solely motivated by distaste for the political radicalism of their students. Their concern was equally motivated by the values they attached to the idea of "literature" and the literary. What were these ideas? What deeply held moral economies motivated the fierce defense of this concept?

This question takes us into the domain of mission understandings of literature. At present, this topic is generally only superficially understood and it is assumed that most missionaries held evangelical views or saw literature as a moralizing force. Such views, however, take little account of the extraordinary variation of the mission project. This could include, on the one hand, a small, poorly funded, nondenominational and fervently evangelical mission which eschewed virtually all secular literature and drew its recruits from the less-privileged reaches of European society. On the other, one could have a large well-funded denominational organization such as the Church Missionary Society (CMS), which was much less ardently evangelical and drew its recruits from the better-educated middle classes and supported the use of a surprisingly wide program of secular literature. Lovedale, with its massive library which rivaled that of a British public school or even a university, fell into the latter category, although its Scottish recruits generally came from less privileged backgrounds than CMS personnel.

For many Lovedale staff (several of whom were secular recruits), the term "literature" carried a particular meaning that was an amalgam of evangelical views of reading overlaid with notions derived from the emerging discipline of English literature; for them, literature was heavily moralized. On the one hand, it could "improve" its readers and "save" them from corrupting pastimes. On the other, like the literature of England, it could function as an index of nationality. Any nation worth its salt could adduce its nationalness by its literature. This was to become a particular project of Shepherd, who interested himself in what was then known as Bantu writing in both English and Xhosa. Shepherd frequently exhorted his pupils to aspire to produce an elevated literature in order to confer a sense of nationhood on their people (Shepherd 1942, 65–68). Students at the society consequently heard comments such as the "Bantu are not a leading people because they do not read" or the "Bantu must read more great literature whether in Latin, English or mother tongue . . . Such men as Lincoln rose to the rank of great orators only by reading great literature" (Minutes, September 13, 1941, and March 19, 1927).

But what did the term "literature" mean to the students? At some levels, of course, students subscribed to mission understandings of literature. Many came from prominent mission families which by the 1940s had been Christian for more than a century and would have wholeheartedly endorsed the idea of literature as a moralizing force. In addition, the strong moral messages of African oral literary forms dovetailed neatly with these moralizing views, a confluence strengthened by the long tradition of mission uses of such forms in school readers. The Lovedale variant of this trend took the shape of the famed Stewart readers in Xhosa and English which drew heavily on Xhosa oral forms.

Yet at the same time, in the context of the Literary Society, students evolved ideas about literature that were at odds with those of their teachers. As the history of the society demonstrates, for students, literature was less important than debating because debating provided training for leadership. Literature as a moral endeavor was subordinate to the need for these scions of the African elite to prepare themselves for such positions of authority as were open to them in a settler-dominated society. Indeed, "debating" came to acquire a wide ambit of associations that meant more than just standing up to defend an opinion. It was a shorthand term for a training in the performances of a new elite leadership. Such leadership included many levels and skills. Most obviously it was about learning eloquence and self-discipline, or, as one Lovedale alumnus told the society, "develop[ing] powers of speech to know how to oppose a person without offending him or her, self-control in speech, politeness and respect" (Minutes, June 4, 1937). Debating prepared students for this leadership: "Many a leader [has] been fashioned and modeled by this society" (Minutes, February 14, 1948). The society also forged networks for the future: "The Literary Society is the foundation of our future careers" (Minutes, January 8, 1948). (Indeed, it was not uncommon for some students to join the Society for "CV purposes" without becoming actively involved; Lovedale Missionary Institute 1948, 19.) One teacher, Mr. Bennett Mdledle (a Lovedale alumnus and also a staff member), informed his audience that the society prepared students for life after school and taught them how to be "cultured." "A cultured man is often distinguished not by his dress but by what he does and says, a man who faces the situation objectively with coolness, and he that gets into the truth first and gets heated afterwards" (Minutes, February 14, 1948).

Debating, then, offered an apprenticeship for leadership, and the Lovedale Literary Society provided a surprising number of opportunities in which to debate, albeit indirectly, the pressing issues of the day. Some topics (although surprisingly few) were "neutral" and apparently decontextualized ("A sense of humour is a handicap" [Minutes, April 14, 1946]; "Are uses of adversity sweet?" [Minutes, April 1, 1938]), but even these could with imagination be turned to address local circumstances. Other topics were specifically framed around an agenda of local issues that returned again and again to a cluster of themes. The first of these concerned education (unsurprisingly for a school, especially one whose student body would overwhelmingly go into teaching). Topics included "Time is ripe for native inspectors" (Minutes, November 6, 1936); "Education has triumphed over superstition" (Minutes, March 4, 1937); and "Is education a destructive force?" (Minutes, March 9, 1937). Students also debated whether education should be coeducational (Minutes, March 17, 1939) or compulsory (Minutes, April 12, 1940). They discussed which languages should be used to educate students (Minutes, August 9, 1940); whether education should be free (Minutes, November 1, 1940); whether it should be technical or academic (Minutes, March 7, 1941, and June 9, 1944); and whether it should be elite or popular (Minutes, April 24, 1944).

Closely linked to these debates on education were discussions regarding "progress" and "civilization." These topics included on the one hand more-abstract debates about the benefits or otherwise of science, technology, and progress ("Is competition injurious to the community or not?" [Minutes, ? 1936]; "Is the world growing better?" [Minutes, May 7, 1937]; "Is world peace possible?" [Minutes, July 25, 1937]; "Are we happier than our forefathers?" [Minutes, ? 1938]; "The advance of science spells the ruin of mankind" [Minutes, April 18, 1941]; "Science corrupts the world" [Minutes, November 3, 1944]). At times, these themes were cast in terms of national debates regarding competing ideas of progress and modernity: "Is westernization of the Bantu desirable?" (Minutes, October 24, 1941); "Though the Bantu are progressing, they are not progressing fast enough" (Minutes, February 27, 1942); "Has town life any future for the native?" (Minutes, August 6, 1937); "Can a rapid progress be better maintained by the segregation of the civilized from the uncivilized?" (Minutes, March 18, 1938); "Should the native develop on his own lines?" (Minutes, March 4, 1938).

These debates were buttressed further by a set of topics which grappled with issues closer to home. In September 1947, for example, students debated whether the Bunga (a governing structure of indirect rule peculiar to the Transkei, the region in which Lovedale fell) should be "the mouthpiece of Africans" (Minutes, September 27, 1947). They also discussed whether stock should be diminished (Minutes, July 28, 1939), a pressing issue in a cattle-keeping society, and whether kings, chiefs, or elected leaders made for the most effective governance (Minutes, ? 1945).

These were issues that stood at the heart of the kinds of choices the young men of the Eastern Cape elite faced. This group occupied a complex social position pinioned between traditional chiefs, white missionaries, and rabidly racist settlers. In relation to chiefs, the elite stressed their modernity; in relation to missionaries, their knowledge of African tradition; and in relation to settlers, the superior claims to "civilization." An additional issue for this modernizing stratum was questions of gender and these made up a recurrent strand in the deliberations of the society: Should divorce be allowed? (Minutes, August 9, 1938); Are men tyrants? (Minutes, October 28, 1939); Are women more clever than men? (Minutes, August 8, 1941); Do modern inventions make housewives lazy? (Minutes,? 1942); Should parents be consulted in matrimonial affairs? (Minutes, May 5, 1939); Should women [rather than men] pay *lobola*? (Minutes, October 23, 1942); Should women be doctors and ministers? (Minutes, April 2, 1943, and June 4, 1937).

Within this context, an increasingly militant group of men (and to a lesser extent women) saw themselves not as a sector in need of moralization and uplift but as an emerging nationalist leadership. Their views of literature were subordinated to this prerogative, and literature became a resource to buttress this political objective. In this capacity, it was deployed in three discernible ways. The first of these, as we have seen, emerged from the long-standing tradition of the Literary Society of inserting discussions of literature into the field of discussion about current events, be they local or international. Literature was hence seldom understood as a discrete field of intellectual activity and instead was seen as tightly woven into discussion about the affairs of the world. (This view was paralleled in some way by the view of missionary teachers, who likewise seldom saw literature as a separate field, except that for them, literature formed part of a religious rather than a political field. However, by the 1940s most teachers at Lovedale were secular and probably held a far more "modern" view of literature as a discrete intellectual field.)

Second, literature became a vehicle for exploring lessons of leadership. This strand emerged strongly in the popular dramatic meetings the society held from time to time. Most popular of all were the performances of Xhosa plays. These performances, which invariably drew the largest crowds, explored themes of dispute resolution and the political leadership skills it required. The minutes of one production of *Ityala lamawele* (The Case of the Twins) by the great Xhosa writer S. E. K. Mqhayi note that the function of the play "was two fold . . . it was for amusement as well as it brought to light, to those who did not know anything about pure African life, how complicated cases . . . used to be successfully and easily settled by consulting the old sages" (Minutes, May

24, 1945). The reference to those "who did not know anything about pure African life" was perhaps a dig at white teachers and missionaries. By contrast to this "ignorant" group, the new male elite apparently possessed such knowledge and could, on occasion, borrow the robes of chiefly power in order to position themselves critically vis-à-vis the white mission authorities. However, students could also satirize the power of chieftaincy as a way of asserting their authority. At another production of the same play, the minute-taker (who was somewhat perturbed by developments) noted:

> The opening scene was realistic and impressive. It was a true representation of rustic councilors who stayed at the great place as officials of justice. The play progressed and was good and interesting. The actors knew their parts well but they failed to preserve the dignity of the "Inkundla." They failed to observe the atmosphere of the play. Thus they spoiled good acting i.e. the Inkundla is not peopled by a noisy rabble but by dignified councilors. It therefore gives a wrong impression of rustic Bantu life in the days of yore. Some interjections, clowning, shouting and laughing by actors robbed the play of its reality. Thus it failed to be a true representation of how cases were solved. (Minutes, May 15, 1948)

The third use of literature in the context of debating was as a source of quotation, maxim, and motto. Quotations studded speeches and demonstrated erudition, eloquence, and the ability to clinch a rhetorical point. At times, these quotations were of a recognizable provenance and were drawn from writers such as Shakespeare, Dickens, and Scott. Others were of a more "do-it-yourself" variety. At times, these were epithet-like quotations "War is the mother of peace" or quasi-quotations "Change with the time and move with the tide" (Minutes, ? 1936). At other points, the quotations were "invented": "That that is is and that that is not is not"; "A disadvantage that has an advantage is no advantage" (Minutes, ? 1936).

For some staff, the practice of quotation was a source of irritation that demonstrated either "the tendency to misquote" or, even worse, the proclivity to deploy "the ill-digested catch phrase" (Lovedale Missionary Institute 1930, 31). These linguistic "vices" in turn formed part of the tendency to use "words of learned length and thundering sound" rather than "sincere" and "simple English" (Lovedale Missionary Institute 1927, 71).

*   *   *

The historiography of African literary studies has concerned itself with how the continent's multiple inheritances are mobilized and deployed by various writers. In attempting to understand such processes, it is critical to focus attention on the sites and institutions in which such inheritances are "work-shopped" and experimentally combined. This chapter has explored one such institution, the Lovedale Literary Society, which functioned as a complex and multidimensional interpretive community. Its legacies have been considerable. The first, and perhaps most obvious, concerns the idea of literature as an index of nationality, a key theme of many of the talks and debates at Lovedale. As Couzens and others have demonstrated, these ideas on literature and nation spread out from institutions such as Lovedale into a variety of public forums. From at least the turn of the century, debates concerning literature and nationality were taken up by a wide spectrum of commentators who discussed literature in African languages and English. These discussions on "creating a literature of our own" (quoted in Couzens 1985, 59) were pursued in newspapers, novels, poetry, pamphlets, and public debate and accelerated as debates in the political arena took on an increasingly nationalist tone. The question of literature and its relation to nationhood would eventually be taken up by virtually every leading black intellectual in South Africa. Their work established an agenda that stills shapes critical discussion around South African literary studies today.

A second legacy of the Lovedale Literary Society concerns its key genre, namely the speech. The form has been deployed by most black writers and intellectuals but has attracted little serious critical attention. In some respects, its prevalence is hardly surprising: most black South African intellectuals of necessity had to assume a political role for all or some part of their careers, and speech-making became something of a second nature. Many intellectuals subsequently published these speeches. Yet the prevalence of the speech as a genre equally reminds us of the apprenticeships most black intellectuals undertook in debating societies of the type established at Lovedale. Indeed, the debating society as an enabling mode of address becomes apparent in John Knox Bokwe's travelogue *Two Weeks' Trip to Cape Town: or, A Native's Impression of the Cape Industrial Exhibition.* The narrative was originally composed for, and delivered to, the Lovedale Literary Society in 1884. It appeared in the Lovedale journal *Christian Express* and then as a freestanding book. In similar vein, D. D. T. Jabavu, another Lovedale alumnus, published a collection of "papers and addresses" under the title *The Black Problem* (Jabavu 1920). As anthologies of African prose indicate (Blyden 1982; Pixley ka Seme 1982; Casely Hayford 1982; Mutloatse 1981), one could cite many other examples of the speech as an important medium. A genre learned and nurtured in the debating society, the speech is a form whose importance to the history of South African (and indeed African) literature has yet to be fully explored.

Within the stylistic weave of these speeches, we can detect a third legacy of the Lovedale Literary Society: a particular use of quotation. Again, this is an important but little-studied topic that would repay more-detailed investigation. My comments here must necessarily be brief and touch only on three strategies for using quotation that emerge in work of Lovedale alumni. The first, and most obvious, deployment of the device concerns the attributed quotation, used generally by way of summary and emphasis. D. D. T. Jabavu, for example, in addressing a gathering of teachers in 1920, concluded his address thus: "Emerson once said 'Hitch your wagon to a star', and it is very wise counsel, for if your aim at the stars you are not likely finish up too low in your efforts. Let your standard be a very high and excellent one and you will thus fortify yourself against falling into the ditch" (Jabavu 1982, 63–64). There are many other such examples where a quotation is used as a final flourish which epitomizes the key message of the speech (see J. T. Jabavu 1973; Tyamzashe 1973; D. D. T. Jabavu 1973, Bokwe 1973). One Lovedale alumnus, Dan Twala, observed in an interview with Tim Couzens that the Lovedale convention was to end one's speech with a quotation: "You became the hero of the school then. You just broke through with a quotation" (quoted in Couzens 1985, 51).

Yet in several instances, the use of quotation has further dimensions. Take, for example, the obituary of Samuel Edward Krune Mqhayi, the legendary Xhosa writer and poet, written by A C Jordan, an equally legendary writer. In discussing the life and work of Mqhayi, Jordan from time to time drops in a quotation but without however identifying its author. The first example emerges when Jordan, discussing Mqhayi's youth, notes how the young poet listened attentively to *izibongo* (praises) and "began to 'lisp in numbers,' praising famous oxen, other boys or himself" (Jordan 1973, 538). The quotation ("lisp in numbers") comes from Thomas Love Peacock's essay "The Four Ages of Poetry," in response to which Shelley wrote his "Defence of Poetry." A short while later Jordan makes use of two quotations, the first from Bunyan's *The Pilgrim's Progress* and the second from the Acts of the Apostles (Acts 26:24).

> Because [Mqhayi] was nurtured in Christian culture and in the primitive culture of his own people at the same time, Christianity was for him not an "escape from the City of Destruction," but a mode of life abundant that was not irreconcilable with his native culture. Small wonder then that Tiyo Soga's translation of *The Pilgrim's Progress* should have had such an appeal for him that at the age of thirteen he was able to recite its first chapter with such feeling and expression that many who listened to him at an elocution competition at the Station School at Lovedale feared that "much learning hath made him truly mad." (539)

A while later we encounter a quotation from Robert Browning's "Andrea del Sarto." In discussing Mqhayi's utopian novel *UDon Jadu*, Jordan portrays it as a brilliant but flawed work.

> *UDon Jadu* makes very interesting and thought-provoking reading. It is true that in constructing a "bridge" between our present South Africa and his Utopia, the author idealizes away a few hard facts, but—
> "its soul is right,
> He means right,—that, a child may understand."

The quotation comes from a dramatic monologue in which the Renaissance artist Andrea del Sarto sets out the contradiction of his life: he is an accomplished artist but it makes little difference to his wife, who does not love him. In addressing his wife, del Sarto comments in passing on a painting by Raphael. In del Sarto's opinion, some of its details are awry ("That arm is wrongly put" [line 111]) but the picture nonetheless possesses its own perfection and absolute clarity: "its soul is right, / He means right—that, a child may understand" (lines 113–114).

These quotations undertake multiple tasks. By being unattributed, they signify an ideal readership, namely one that will instantly recognize these quotations and where they come from (I incidentally fall outside this ideal readership and had to trace most of the quotations on the Internet). These ideal readers can instantly undertake the type of textual navigation and comparison that quotations ask us to make. In the case of Jordan's obituary, one is, for example, required to navigate between Peacock (and implicitly Shelley) while thinking about the position of Xhosa literature in a bigger world picture. Likewise, in the quotation from Browning, the reader's understanding must travel between the Italian Renaissance, Browning's depiction of it, and Mqhayi's novel while simultaneously pondering the relationship of artistic form and intellectual insight. Likewise, the quotation from Bunyan is a complex gloss on the ways in which the African elite in and around Lovedale reinterpreted *The Pilgrim's Progress*, a text intensively propagated at Lovedale in English and Xhosa and one that students would have encountered in the classroom, in dramatic reenactments, in extramural societies such as the Students' Christian Association, and in both English and Xhosa church services (Hofmeyr 2004). As a widely known and quoted text, *The Pilgrim's Progress* was used by the African elite as a source of shared religious and political references. The book became a type of portable landscape onto which various political journeys could be projected and experimented with. Jordan's use of the phrase from Bunyan accords with this type of practice. The quotation itself suggests that in becoming Christian,

ISABEL HOFMEYR

Mqhayi did not see his conversion as a simple journey from "heathendom," or the City of Destruction, to "salvation" and enlightenment. Instead, Jordan complicates this simplistic view and offers a reconfiguration between Christianity and existing African traditions in which the former becomes yet another framework of explanation added onto an existing repertoire of intellectual and spiritual practices. In some senses, then, to become Christian is to become more, rather than less, African.

The quotation from the Acts of Apostles functions in an analogous way. The quotation itself is drawn from the period when Paul is imprisoned and is called before a court of notables to be cross-questioned. Paul narrates his conversion experience, which causes one dignitary to comment that "much learning doth make thee mad" (Acts 26:24). Jordan's quotation aligns Paul and Mqhayi as leading Christian converts and asks us, as much writing from African Christians did, to compare the early Christian church with the early African church.

In these examples, the quotation becomes a way of linking and configuring different worlds. It functions as a membrane between Mqhayi's obituary and the world of the text he invokes. Through the quotation, this text is made portable.

This idea of portability is also captured in the third use of quotation, demonstrated in this instance from John Knox Bokwe's travelogue *Two Weeks' Trip to Cape Town*. Near the beginning of this text, Bokwe writes:

> It is hardly necessary to state that the journey we were about to take was the longest in the record of our life, and as such we felt it would require to be carefully provided for. Not the least necessary item of preparation was, we thought, that of *Travelling Companions*, whose aid and experience might be needful where difficulties arose. Consequently out of many good fellows who were arranged before us in all the shades of commendable qualities possessed by each, all willing to lead and guide us, we show four which we thought were the pick of the lot, the heart and marrow of them all. Their names were: *Bible, Civility, Discretion,* and *Humility*. (1884, 7–8)

This passage does not, of course, contain direct quotations, but in using the device of personified and allegorized characters, it "quotes" *The Pilgrim's Progress*. As Bokwe goes on to demonstrate, the point of such allusion or "quotation" is precisely to demonstrate how texts (or their parts) can be made portable and useful.

> *Bible* was to be a bosom friend, whose counsel was to guide us to that which is good. When an emergency arose, *Civility* for ever lovable, and *Discretion*, whose good common-sense always directs you to choose the right course, promised to

be always ready, if only I was willing to follow their advice. When in company, whether in the house or on the road these were to be at my disposal to do me service. And when I should be well-treated by those around and prospered in my journey, *Humility* engaged to be at my side, to counsel me not to forget her, and also not to forget myself. (8)

A text from the Bible can thus function as a friend if applied in a judicious way. Likewise, virtues such as civility, discretion, and humility can be employed by applying them in the correct circumstances. This idea of texts and quotations as portable messages or morals emerges clearly elsewhere in Bokwe's writing. On his train journey to Cape Town, Bokwe, an ardent teetotaler, encounters a drunkard, whom he tries to dissuade from alcohol. Bokwe concludes the episode thus:

I have dwelt at such length on this incident in order to draw a moral. "Beware of bad companions," "Evil communications corrupt good manners"—"Wine is a mocker, strong drink is raging, and whosoever is deceived thereby is not wise." "He that being often reproved hardeneth his neck, shall suddenly be destroyed and that without remedy." (11)

In this passage, the reader is invited to apply each of these maxims to the story of the unrepentant drunkard. Each axiom in turn highlights a different aspect of the episode and retrospectively creates a new story. As Barber has indicated in the case of the Yoruba traveling theater, the key to understanding such "maxim-driven" texts is to grasp the relationship between the narrative itself and axiom which it produces (2000, 267). Each story becomes an exemplification of the moral proposition attached to it. This message is "then 'picked' by the audience as a 'lesson' they can apply to their lives. When they apply it, it becomes re-concretized in a new context. It is the process of extracting and re-applying lessons that makes this discourse meaningful" (268). This method is clearly one that guides Bokwe, since he offers the reader a series of "takeaway" maxims which he expects them to ponder, take heed of, and apply to their lives.

It is a skill that Bokwe must in part have honed in the Lovedale Literary Society. As this chapter has suggested, this forum functioned as an interpretive textual community shaped by cooperation and conflict between teacher and pupil. Like all such communities, it was wrought in an environment determined by overlapping factors of age, race, religion, gender, and vocation (teacher, pastor, chief). When thrust into a national arena of rapidly mounting nationalist sentiment, the Lovedale Literary Society offered a forum in which pupils with aspirations of leadership could do an apprenticeship. One of the rhetorical qualifications required was an ability to pepper one's speeches with quotation. Such interpretive formations characterized most mission schools in the 1930s and 1940s. Lovedale was the most visible and well-resourced institution and the one that left the most comprehensive records. But there were similar arenas in other less-visible and less-well-resourced mission schools. These constituted crucial arenas of intellectual history which have left their mark on a generation of mission-school graduates such as Thabo Mbeki and Chris Hani (both of whom are Lovedale alumni). While Mandela never attended Lovedale, his experiences at Clarkesbury and Healdtown (both of which are close to Lovedale) provided him with his initial apprenticeships in becoming both a quoting and—subsequently—a quotable politician.

REFERENCES

Barber, Karin. 2000. *The Generation of Plays: Yorùbá Popular Life in Theater.* Bloomington: Indiana University Press.

Blyden, Edward Wilmot. 1982. "The African Must Advance by Methods of His Own." In *Two Centuries of African English,* ed. Lalage Bown, 47–50. London: Heinemann.

Bokwe, John Knox. 1884. *Two Weeks' Trip to Cape Town: or, A Native's Impression of the Cape Industrial Exhibition.* Lovedale: Lovedale Press.

Bokwe, R. T. 1973. "We Are Starving." In *Outlook on a Century: South Africa 1870–1970,* ed. Francis Wilson and Dominique Perrot, 427–429. Lovedale: Lovedale/Spro-cas.

Casely Hayford, J. E. 1982. "Casely Hayford Proposes a Toast." In *Two Centuries of African English,* ed. Lalage Bown, 52–56. London: Heinemann.

Couzens, Tim. 1985. *The New African: A Study of the Life and Work of H. I. E. Dhlomo* Johannesburg: Ravan.

Glaser, Clive. 1998. "'We Must Infiltrate the *Tsotsis*': School Politics and Youth Gangs in Soweto, 1968–1976." *Journal of Southern African Studies* 24, no. 2: 301–324.

Hallengren, Anders. 2001. "Nelson Mandela and the Rainbow of Culture." September 11. Available online at http://www.nobel.se/peace/articles/mandela.

Hofmeyr, Isabel. 2004. *The Portable Bunyan: A Transnational History of* The Pilgrim's Progress. Princeton, N.J.: Princeton University Press.

Hyslop, Jonathan. 1990. "Social Conflicts over African Education in South Africa from the 1940s to 1976." Ph.D. thesis, University of the Witwatersrand.

Jabavu, D. D. T. 1920. *The Black Problem: Papers and Addresses on Various Native Problems.* Lovedale: Book Depot.

———. 1973. "The Franchise." In *Outlook on a Century: South Africa 1870–1970,* ed. Francis Wilson and Dominique Perrot, 264–265. Lovedale: Lovedale/Spro-cas.

———. 1982. "Motive and Ambition in Life." In *Two Centuries of African English,* ed. Lalage Bown, 63–64. London: Heinemann.

Jabavu, John Tengo. 1973. "Our Suspicions Allayed." In *Outlook on a Century: South Africa 1870–1970,* ed. Francis Wilson and Dominique Perrot, 148–149. Lovedale: Lovedale/Spro-cas.

Jordan, A. C. 1973. "Samuel Edward Krune Mqhayi." In *Outlook on a Century: South Africa 1870–1970,* ed. Francis Wilson and Dominique Perrot, 537–544. Lovedale: Lovedale/Spro-cas.

Lovedale Missionary Institute. 1874–1951. *Reports.* Lovedale: Lovedale Press.

Mandela, Nelson. 1990. "Nelson Mandela's Address to South African Business Executives." May 23. Available online at http://www.anc.org.za/ancdocs/history/mandela/1990/sp900523.html.

———. 1996. "Address by President Mandela to UK Parliament." July 11. Available online at http://www.polity.org.za/html/govdocs/speeches/1996/sp0711.html.

———. 2000. "Closing Address by Former President Nelson Mandela." 13th International AIDS Conference. July 14. Available online at http://www.actupny.org/reports/durban-mandela.html.

Mbeki, Thabo. 2000. "Ou sont-ils, en ce moment—Where Are They Now?" Second National Institute for Economic Policy (NIEP) Oliver Tambo Lecture, August 11. Available online at http://www.anc.org.za/ancdocs/history/mbeki/2000/tm0811.html.

Minutes of the Lovedale Literary Society. 1936–1948. BRN 122325. Lovedale Archives, Cory Library, Rhodes University, Grahamstown.

Mutloatse, Mothobi, ed. 1981. *Reconstruction: 90 Years of Black Historical Literature.* Johannesburg, Ravan.

Newell, Stephanie. 2002. *Literary Culture in Colonial Ghana: "How to Play the Game of Life."* Manchester: Manchester University Press, 2002.

Sampson, Anthony. 1999. *Mandela: The Authorised Biography.* London: Harper Collins.

Seme, Pixley ka. 1982. "A Zulu Student's Prize Speech." In *Two Centuries of African English,* ed. Lalage Bown, 50–52. London: Heinemann.

Shepherd, Robert H. W. n.d. *Lovedale South Africa: The Story of a Century, 1841–1941.* Lovedale: Lovedale Press.

Shepherd, R. H. W. 1942. "Lovedale and Literature for the Bantu." Ph.D. thesis, University of the Witwatersrand.

Taylor, Paul. 1993. "Apartheid Foe Hani Slain in S. Africa." Washington Post Foreign Service, April 11. Available online at http://www.washingtonpost.com/wp-srv/inatl/longterm/s_africa/stories/hani041193.htm.

Thale, Mary. 1995. "Women in London Debating Societies in 1780." *Gender and History* 7, no. 1: 5–24.

Tyamzashe, H. D. 1973. "Why Have You Educated Me?" In *Outlook on a Century: South Africa 1870–1970,* ed. Francis Wilson and Dominique Perrot, 210–211. Lovedale: Lovedale/Spro-cas.

"THE PRESENT BATTLE IS THE BRAIN BATTLE": WRITING AND PUBLISHING A KIKUYU NEWSPAPER IN THE PRE–MAU MAU PERIOD IN KENYA

11

Bodil Folke Frederiksen

Introduction

Henry Muoria (1914–1997) was a particularly interesting Kenyan pioneer journalist and intellectual. He was the leading Kikuyu nationalist publicist during a crucial period in the anticolonial struggle—the years between the end of World War II and the declaration of the Emergency in 1952—and friend and political spokesman of Jomo Kenyatta. His commitment to Kikuyu and Kenyan African progress and self-rule prompted him to start a Kikuyu-language newspaper, *Mumenyereri*. He was the owner and the editor and wrote numerous articles in the paper, which came out regularly from May 1945 to October 1952. During this period he also wrote political pamphlets, didactic works on modern living, and translations into Kikuyu from Swahili and English. In 1952, Muoria left Kenya for Great Britain, where he stayed for the rest of his life. During his London exile, he continued to write autobiographical, historical, and philosophical manuscripts in English.

He was a "man of the new age" (Berman and Lonsdale 1992, 414), a representative of a rising "intermediate class" between professionals and peasants (Barber 2000, 2) who exploited both rural and urban opportunities and relied on hard work and merit more than on patronage. As a member of a land-owning clan in Kiambu, he was at the center of battles over key resources such as land, education, and enterprise being fought between classes, genders, and generations of Kikuyu and between Kikuyu and the colonial government. Though not formally educated, he exerted considerable influence as a self-appointed guardian of his people's wisdom and progress.[1]

The political picture in Kenya during the period when *Mumenyereri* was a central actor in the struggle, from 1945 to 1952, was characterized by the colonial government's efforts to get the postwar economy on its feet and re-store production, an improved economic climate that was beneficial to African enterprise, the need for an increasing labor force docile enough to ac-cept wildly unequal wages, rural and urban spatial segregation, inadequate ed-ucation and appalling housing conditions for Africans, colonial appointment of chiefs and a few African political representatives, social engineering and in-trusive welfare interventions, and, finally, harsh control in areas of successful African initiative such as trade, the cultivation of cash crops, the keeping of livestock, and the creation of political organizations. It was also the period in which class differentiation among rural Kikuyu led to bitter conflicts between tenants and landowners and between *mariika*—generations of men who had been initiated during the same year.[2] In spite of conflicts and disagreements, the (Kikuyu) nationalist opposition initiated and upheld a great variety and number of political activities—mass rallies, strikes, guerilla attacks on white farms, cattle-maiming, and political assassination that rendered parts of the country, including African areas of Nairobi, ungovernable. The government's attempts at social containment and political co-optation proved futile in the face of widespread clandestine oathing and rural and urban revolt—the be-ginnings of Mau Mau (Throup 1989, 171–196; Rosberg and Nottingham 1966, 272–276; Kershaw 1997, 218–227). Prominent members of the Kikuyu Central Association, the African Workers Federation, and the Kenya African Union were detained, jailed, and deported. Antagonism between Kikuyu col-laborating with the colonial regime and those resisting peaked with the assas-sination of Senior Chief Waruhiu, who was appointed by the government and was one of its most important supporters. This event provoked the declaration of the Emergency in October 1952 and directed the attention of the world to Britain's colonial crisis in Kenya.

The wide circulation of the nationalist press added to the fraught politi-cal atmosphere. The production of reading material as well as the very pro-cesses of reading and writing were highly politicized. Literacy was promoted by African nationalists, agents of government, and missions but was also con-trolled and interfered with.[3] Distribution of African newspapers was relatively effective, and demand generally exceeded supply in the case of *Mumenyereri* and other African-language papers.[4] Political issues were covered at length and debated with intensity. *Mumenyereri* was in the vanguard of the debate, as *Muigwithania* had been in the late 1920s. The newspaper covered key activi-ties, meetings, and speeches by members of government, settler representatives, and the opposition—not least those by Jomo Kenyatta—and created a political discourse grounded in the history and social values of the African population. The values expressed in *Mumenyereri* were close to those of the Kikuyu community, but the paper's ideology was flexible enough to encompass a broader nationalism and pan-African ideals and thus to suit nationalist leaders' ambitions for the nation of Kenya as a whole.

In this postwar period, which was characterized by high political tension, the government had to constitute the African population as a public and design effective ways of disseminating information and propaganda using modern technologies. Institutions and individuals representing the government, settlers, missions, African political parties, and ethnic organizations were engaged in a virtual battle over information, truth claims, and knowledge. When Muoria wrote in a headline that "the present battle is the brain battle" (*Mumenyereri*, November 24, 1947), he was addressing the contemporary propaganda wars in Kenya, in which government claims about the merits of gradualism and moderation were countered by nationalist demands for land and freedom. The weapons were films, radios, loudspeaker vans, pamphlets, and newspapers. He was also drawing on a discourse about replacing the spear with the pen that went back at least to *Muigwithania*, the newspaper Kenyatta had edited in the 1920s.[5]

Like other African-owned newspapers at the time, *Mumenyereri* was under scrutiny by the government. Muoria was well aware that he was writing not only for his Kikuyu readership but also for watchful bureaucrats in the offices of the attorney general, the chief native commissioner, and the director of intelligence and security; the latter made sure that translations of a broad selection of letters to the editor and articles were available. They are now housed in the Kenya National Archives. *Mumenyereri* was closed down as one of the measures of the Emergency that was declared in October 1952. After this event, it was dangerous to be found with a copy of the newspaper. As a consequence, the Kenya National Archives has only a few complete issues of *Mumenyereri*.

This chapter will sketch Muoria's antecedents and concentrate on his activities and journalistic output between 1945 and 1952, primarily *Mumenyereri*, in the context of the war of words in Kenya. It argues that as a self-taught intellectual who stood outside the educated African elite but was connected to a layer of small landowners and had close ties both to Kikuyu and nationalist politics, he was eminently well suited to publicly articulate an African resistance that reflected global and national politics as well as everyday concerns. Both grassroots political communities and government officials shaped the production of *Mumenyereri*; an everyday as well as official political discourse reached the printed page. From the evidence available, the chapter will characterize the political environment, the production process, Muoria's editorial practice, and the content and readership of the paper. Newspaper items that illustrate the role of readers in their interaction with the paper and reflect writers' engagement with Kenyan political and social realities are the sources for this analysis.[6]

Muoria: Life and Work

Henry Mwaniki Muoria's long and dramatic life played itself out in Kenya until the Mau Mau crisis in 1952 and thereafter, until his death in 1997, in exile in north London. He was a capitalist and a self-taught journalist. Words were the raw material of his main enterprise, although he also had sidelines in building and landownership, cultivation, and trade. He came out of a large southern Kikuyu family, and members of the Muoria *mbari* still own tracts of land in Kiambu, close to Nairobi. His parents Mwaniki wa Muoria and Wambui wa Mbari cultivated their land near the busy Wangige Market— a center of trade and politics. Muoria senior, Henry's grandfather, probably the original buyer of the land and founder of the *mbari*, had several wives, and land was scarce for sons and grandsons. Henry's father migrated on a daily basis to Nairobi to work as an electrician in a private company. Although illiterate, his skills sufficed to earn wages to supplement farm income. He embraced modernity in combining cultivation with migrant work. His son went farther along that same road by acquiring literacy, converting to Christianity, and setting up his own independent business.

His first job was to herd the family's goats and sheep. He had an active mind, and in "The British and My Kikuyu Tribe," an unpublished autobiographical manuscript written when he was an accomplished writer in his late fifties, Muoria described how he discovered the "magic" of reading and writing on the green slopes near his home (Muoria 1982, 7). While herding, he became friendly with two children who passed him on their way to and from school every day. They showed him their schoolbooks and informed him that the black dots on the pages embodied meaning. Muoria asked them, " 'Tell me, do you mean that learning how to write letters would enable you to write down such words as we are talking to each other, and then send that letter to someone who is not here . . . and that man will be able to know what we are saying to each other by reading that letter?' " When they affirmed that that was indeed the case, he realized that he would have to learn that skill. He described his excitement at the transformation of meaningless dots that made up the Kikuyu words *moko mwaka,* "my arms," to signs that duplicated an object in the real world (Muoria 1994, 41). He now started "respecting all those who were reputed to know how to read and write," because they "know something which others do not know." As a consequence, "Instead of indulging in his earlier habits of daydreaming, the writer formed a habit of picking every scrap of printed paper he found by the roadside and gazing at it" (Muoria 1982, 6–7). When his younger brother was old enough to take over herding, Muoria managed to get himself into a nearby mission school. While at school, he was circumcised with his age-mates but without the proper Kikuyu rituals, and a few years later he was baptized. Instead of becoming a *mundu mugo,* a traditional Kikuyu seer and wise man, as had been prophesied at his birth, he was "converted to Christianity . . . through his great desire to know how to read and write" (ibid., 8).

After an unhappy episode as an "artisan's mate" in the employ of a Nairobi plumbing firm, he entered the Railway Training School, where he trained as a telegrapher; when he completed his training, the British East African Railways employed him as a signalman and assistant stationmaster at remote country stations. He married a young Christian woman, Elizabeth Thogori, in 1933. Later, after further training, he was transferred to Eldoret in western Kenya, from where he worked as a guard on trains between Eldoret and Nakuru.

His first piece of writing for the public was a letter to the editor of the leading Kenyan newspaper, the *East African Standard,* in which he protested against the colonial policy which favored the settlers' demands on Kenya's land over those of Africans, to whom the land rightly belonged. His letter, signed "A young Gikuyu," led to further correspondence; when the paper rejected a second letter from his hand, he enrolled in a course in journalism in order to make it difficult for the authorities to "suppress African views" (Muoria 1994, 45). This was in the late 1930s. The lessons were sent to him in bulk from Britain and although the war prevented him from returning the assignments, he worked his way through the course. In 1945, he left his job with the railways to set up his newspaper. He did so on the strength of working capital earned from his published book, *Tungiika Atia Iiya Witu?* (What Should We Do for Our Sake?), a didactic and prophetic collection of essays addressed to his fellow Kikuyu. While as a young man he earned money for school fees by selling vegetables from his mother's *shamba* during weekends at Nairobi markets, popular writing made his mature career as a newspaper owner and editor possible.

Muoria's determination to start his own newspaper cost him his marriage. Thogori, his wife of more than twelve years, was completely against his decision. This is how he recalls the conflict: "When she learned that I was resigning from my secure job with the Railways . . . she was shocked to the extent of thinking that her husband had gone completely mad, and she told our neighbours so." She attributed his "madness" to witchcraft, a way of thinking Muoria thought his fellow Africans should discard. He noted, "With such an attitude, it was impossible for us to stay together since I had dedicated my life whole-heartedly to running my newspaper" (Muoria 1994, 48). His enterprise depended on family labor and networks of kin and community. He was already involved with a young primary school teacher, Judith Nyamurwa, and they were able to marry in 1945, since although "tribal custom does not recognize divorce . . . it does recognize second and further marriages by the husband" (ibid.). After the birth of their first son, they together wrote *Muturire wa Kiriu* (What It Takes to Live Sociably Today), a manual of family life, health, and cleanliness.[7]

Muoria was intensely active in the period from 1945 to 1952. In 1948 he married his third wife, Ruth Nuna, who was to follow him to London. He now had duties to three wives, who also supported him in a variety of ways, and he had to provide for a growing number of children and look after houses, rented offices, cars, and political and business networks in Kikuyuland and Nairobi. He supported, followed, and reported the activities of Jomo Kenyatta, who had returned from Britain in 1946. He fended off persecution by the government, and, most important, he brought out *Mumenyereri*, not every day, as he would have liked, but with increasing frequency.

In September 1952, Muoria left for London. One of his aims was to buy an automatic printing press. Meanwhile, Judith took over the production of the paper at a time of extreme political tension. She would travel to Nairobi, organize the printing of material that Muoria had sent her, and get the paper out. In October, the newspaper was banned under the emergency regulations, and her publishing activities were over. According to her co-wife, Ruth, Judith was arrested because of her involvement in the production of *Mumenyereri*: "They came and arrested her at home, because she was the one left with the newspaper to run."[8] She spent seven months in Kajiado detention camp with her youngest child. Before she left, she organized the transfer of the printing press used to produce *Mumenyereri* to Muoria's home in Kiambu.

Influential friends warned Muoria against returning to Kenya, as he would most certainly be arrested. The authorities refused to renew the license for his printing press, and he found himself "left in London to rot without

Figure 11.1. Henry Muoria and his wife Ruth Nuna Muoria, photographed in London, 1954.

money or help from any official" (Muoria 1994, 77). In 1954, Ruth Nuna joined him. Settled in London, he tried to pursue a writing career. He applied for jobs as a journalist, took further courses, now in fiction writing, and sent manuscripts to publishers. However, his efforts were in vain, and when he was offered a job as a guard with London Transport, the responsibility to the family he had left behind in Kenya and his growing family in London left him with no choice. He worked for the underground until he retired in 1975.

Audience: Between Kikuyu and African

The Kikuyu were the constituency of *Mumenyereri*. During Kenya's occupation by the British, they were the population group most affected by the settlement of white farmers and estate owners who appropriated what came to be known as the White Highlands—a huge area of pastoral and cultivated land that had previously been owned and used by the intermingled ethnicities of Maasai and Kikuyu. In Central Province and Rift Valley, a large proportion of men lived with their families in crowded reserves and worked for wages on white-owned farms, or whole families became squatters, dependent on increasingly oppressive labor contracts and limitations on their rights to keep stock. The state and white settlers interfered with the options of those who kept a precarious hold on land. Many men were employed by the government, and an increasing number of young men and women sought to fend for themselves in Kenya's growing towns as migrants or permanent city-dwellers (Furedi 1989, 13, 79–80; Atieno Odhiambo 1995, 28; Kershaw 1997, 86 ff.; Berman and Lonsdale 1992, 108 ff.).

The earliest newspaper addressed to the Kikuyu was the Kikuyu Central Association's famous *Muigwithania,* which at times was edited by the young Jomo Kenyatta. The paper played a key role in making it possible for Kikuyu to enter into conversation with colonial modernity on the basis of an emerging communal identity. In the words of John Lonsdale, *Muigwithania* "created . . . readers who could see that there was indeed a Kikuyu people, themselves" (1996, 11)—an echo of Rosberg and Nottingham's earlier formulation about the paper that "its riddles, proverb, and stories encouraged its readers to think of themselves still as Kikuyu" (1966, 101–102). The colonial authorities were vigilant about and skeptical of independent writing in Kikuyu from the beginning. In a letter to the secretary of state for the colonies (October 26, 1926) the governor of Kenya, Edward Grigg, noted the appearance of the "vernacular newspaper" and aired his worries: "The object of its publication is . . . avowedly that of unifying the Kikuyu people." This might in itself have been acceptable, but according to Grigg the paper had quickly come under the influence of the "proprietors of the 'Democrat,' the organ of Indian extremists," and a "sinister tone" of "emotional and semi-religious propaganda" harmful to the "excitable and ignorant natives" was noticeable. Grigg asked whether it was possible to "control" the newspaper, and it was finally banned under wartime emergency measures in 1940.[9]

After the banning and until the emergence of *Mumenyereri* in 1945, Kikuyu newspapers were at a low ebb. The few that existed published translations of news and articles from other papers but published little original material (Pugliese 2003, 99). Muoria's ambition was to continue the mission of *Muigwithania* by bringing truth and enlightenment and contributing to Kikuyu and African unity—one followed from the other in *Mumenyereri* discourse.[10] Its name, the "guardian," or the "observer," captures Muoria's double mission as a cultural nationalist and a journalist, but it does not capture his reforming zeal.

The first issues of *Mumenyereri* signaled a direct engagement with colonial modernity in that they were bilingual; the paper was printed in both English and Kikuyu. Soon, however, the paper was publishing in Kikuyu only. Apart from considerations of cultural nationalism and the desire to promote literacy in Kikuyu, Muoria had no choice about what language to use if his audience was to include the rural population and the urban poor. Only a small elite knew English enough to read a newspaper. In its seven years of publication, the paper went from monthly to biweekly publication and its print run rose from 1,000 to 11,000. The paper was influential and circulated widely—each issue was read by several people and in many cases groups listened as items were read aloud.[11] According to a "conservative estimate," *Mumenyereri* reached "some 60,000 of the Kikuyu people each week" at its height (Gadsden 1980, 526).

Muoria claimed to write "on behalf of all Kikuyu." Such a claim from a guardian of an imagined Kikuyu community was made possible by print media, among other factors, and was justified insofar as it was not contradicted by influential sections of the Kikuyu political establishment. Writing from the midst of his kin, Muoria was able to address not only the injustice of colonial rule but also the weaknesses and moral failings of his own people:

> We Kikuyu people are advanced, we have many Companies of various trades, hotels, buses, etc. At the formation of the Company the people are very strong and work very hard, but after a short period the company dies out. Why do our Companies die out? . . . Because we think and form an opinion, but to work out that opinion is very hard. Therefore stupidity is our hindrance and prevents the success of our Companies. . . . If we want our tribe to succeed and be equal with other races, we must teach our directors and leaders the correct way to run a business. Unless we do that and work very hard, we shall remain in slavery for ever. (*Mumenyereri*, June 21, 1948)

The topic discussed—the success or failure of Kikuyu businesses—was at the heart of political controversy in the late 1940s in Kenya's Central Province, where indigenous protocapitalists fought with each other, with appointed chiefs, and with the colonial administration over state patronage and economic opportunity (Throup 1987, 144–146). The opening words as well as the mixture of admonishment and confidence show an intimacy permissible within a family, where harshness is tempered with love. Kikuyu self-identification and an ensuing urgency about pushing for progress are unmistakable and are characteristic of Muoria's editorial voice.

Under the headline "The present battle is the brain battle," Muoria ex-

𝔐𝔲𝔪𝔢𝔫𝔶𝔢𝔯𝔢𝔯𝔦

NA MUGITIRI WA IGAI RIA ANDU AIRU

THE GIKUYU NATIONAL BI-WEEKLY (ESTD. 1945)
EDITOR & PUBLISHER HENRY MUORIA P. O. BOX 1956 NAIROBI

No. 451   Registered at the G.P.O. as a Newspaper   JUMAMOSI 20-9-52 KINYA JUMATATU 22-9-52   ni 20 CTS

Ati ona Thirikari ya guku Ruraya nimakitio ni Mau Mau

Ûhoro ûyû ûrehetwo nī Mwandīki wa ngathīti īno, e ītūrainī rīa angeretha London nake ekuga atīrī:—

Twakinya gūkū Rūraya Jumamosi ûhoro ûria twonire ngathīti-inī imwe yakuo īgwītwo Daily Mail na ûria wandīkitwo na ndemwa nene nī wa Kenya wa kuuga atī kīhuhūkanio kīria gīkuo nigūgūtūũirwo athuri koumā gūkū Rūrayo nī thirikari yakuo gīūke kūu kionenye kīhumo gīa kīhuhūkanio kīu. Igacoka ikoiga ati athūngū erī atongoria athirikari ya Kenya ūrīa CNC na Atorney General nimegūka gūkū rūraya materete na mwandīki mūnene wa mabūrūri ma ithamīro nīguo kūmenywo ūria gūgwīkwo ciiko cia kūnyihanyihi kiama kīu kīa riitho kīa Mau kīria atī kīrūmagīrirwo na thūrī iwa Agikūyū.

Athonī aitū nimūkūririkana atī thūngū cia Kenya niikoretwo igiciria kūhinga ūteti wa andū airū na watho wa kūhinga ūteti ūcio ūgathugundwo na ūkarehwo gūkū Kūraya wī kirūo tiairi nī Mwandīki ūcio mūnene wa mabūrūri ma ithamiro indi mwandiki ūcio arambā gūikara ta ategwītikira gwī kira mawatho macio thairi mawatho macio nimo maratū maga kiama kia Barūthi kira ririo na ihenya o hindi iria Mathu e gūkū rūraya. Na nī tagūkiuga atongoria acio a thirikari mokite gūkū niguo mahote gūtereta na mwandiki maamūringīririe ekire mawatho macio thairi mambiririe kūhūthirūo.

Ūhoro ūngi atī waheanitwo nī ngathīti iyo nī wa ūria mūbea erigite gūteng'erio ni andū a Mau-mau makienda kūmūraga. Ūhoro wa Kenya gūkū

ni ūrario na njira nene ya gicambanio na kigathi kinene.

Mūthuri ti Mathu na Mbiyū Koinange nī maari na Mūcemanio wa andiki a Magathīti marakana ūhoro ūcio wa Kenya ota ūria muonete. Indi ūhoro wao ndūnacabwo magathiti-inī ma gūkū. Ningi ngathiti iria itagwo The Times ya Jumatatū noī ikūheana ūhoro ūcio wa Kenya na ūria atī ūgūteretwo ni atongoria acio a thirikari ya Kenya na mwandiki ūcio mūne nei wa mabūrūri ma Ithamiro Gūkūgathiririo atī Barūthi ūria mwerū ūgūka Kenya oke narua niguo aheane hinya mūingi wa gwika ciiko. Gūkwīrūo atī ūhoro wa būrūri wa Kenya niūthūkite makiria.

Mwandiki riu me Ruraya. Thoma ūhoro wa rugendo rwao na hau kabere.

Barūthi ūria ūratūire Kenya

tene we aroigire atī ūhoro wa Kenya ti mūtnūku toria kūrerwo no atī ena mwihoko mūnene nī amu akirie gūcoka kuo na mūtumia wake atuike mūrimi.

— — —

Mwandiki ni mukinyu ruraya
RUGENDO RWAO

Twahaica ndege ithirii Alhamisi twina ngatho aria twombūkaga tondū woria mūingi wa Gikūyū na Mūmbi wenogirie ona gwakorūo kwarī rūcinī tene na Mūgīūka gūtugīra ūhoro mwina mothiū ma Gikeno tūkiugīrno ngema nī Nyakīnyua itū na tūkiburirūo hi. Ūndū ūria ūkirī meeiriainī maitū nī wa gīkeno wagūtūmenyithia atī nī inyuī mwatūtūmire toadū korūo ti inyuī mūtingiar.irūo nī heho mūgīūka gūtugīra ūhoro kwoguo ni tugucokia ngatho mūno.

Ekuga atīrī ūndū ūria ndaiguire ndahaicha ndege yarikia kūmbūka nī ta ūria mūndū aiguaga e mūcuhainī tūgīcoka tūkīheo mbamba twīkīre matu matigateo nī mūrurumo na theremende ciakūmumunya. Twoima Nairobi tondū kwari kīnundu ndege ya haicire igūrū wa kio igīthii igūrū wa mtu maria merū tūkonaga riua twi kūu igurū tuonaga mīgūnda na nyūmba ta ari tūria twakagwo ni twana tūgikururuga. Irīini twathiathia tūkimenyithio atī riu twihakuhī iria rīria ri githimo ritagwo L. Victoria na ati ihenya ria ndege riari mairo 185 gwa thaa imwe na atī kuuma thi nynmū i biti ngiri itbathatū na atī ndicereirūo nigukīnya Entebbe thaa iria yathīiruo. Nīguo twacokire tugikīnya iriaini riu warora miena no maī matberi mahana ta matu maria mairū. Na twarikia kuringa iria tugikinya gicukīro kia kia Entebbe Uganda hau tūgicuka na tugitonya mukawainī wa athungu uria wihe tugikira cai panded on the theme of Kikuyu and African versus European government and enterprise. The point of departure was a radio broadcast to Africans by the governor. In his address, Sir Philip Mitchell taunted Africans for not being able to make "roads, bridges or steam engines" and talked of them as "people who are braying like donkeys," according to the newspaper report. In his refutation, Muoria, following Kenyatta (Pugliese 2003, 100), urged Africans to use the brains that God had given them; if they did so, they would be the equals of Europeans. He argued that Europeans had brought misrule, jiggers [worms], and slavery and that Kikuyu used to "rule their people much better than they are being ruled now. . . . They were wise but they did not know how to write books," "they were not confused with many religions." Finally, the crowning argument was that "the Agikuyu work hard and they always bring riches to their homes, but they do not like to oppress others as European settlers do, that we may always be their servants." Muoria pointed out that "most of the Africans we have seen with motor cars and stone buildings, have not achieved their gains by the money earned from Europeans, but from their trading business and from their *shamba*" (*Mumenyereri*, November 28, 1947).[12] The sophisticated dialectics of this barbed attack on European complacency demonstrate the abilities that had made Muoria a respected spokesman of his people.

Contents of *Mumenyereri*

Thanks to Louis Leakey, the government's most trusted Kikuyu expert, and other translators, it is possible for non-Kikuyu speakers to get quite a good impression of the contents of *Mumenyereri*, although there is a limit to how representative the translations are.[13] The colonial files contain the material that was most controversial. Items that were omitted from these files include advertisements, announcements of meetings, and notices of missing persons; such items were for the immediate use of its readers and contributed to the paper's popularity and easygoing conversational tone. The translated articles in the archive, with their flow of uniform neutral English and cover notes from one bureaucrat to the other, are worlds apart from the pioneering, flawed materiality of the actual newspapers.

When Muoria wanted to start his newspaper in 1945 he was prevented by war regulations. His solution was to take over a defunct paper, *Muthithu*, the "treasure," and relaunch it.[14] The first issue of his paper was published in May 1945 under the combined name *Muthithu na Mumenyereri* (Muoria 1994, 47). The last issue, number 456, was dated October 8–9, 1952.

In the issue of September 20, 1952, one of the last to come out, the editor addressed his readers from London.[15] He had been in London for a week and had left the practicalities of printing and publishing the paper to Judith. Muoria's portrait accompanied his front-page report on the adventure of traveling by air from Nairobi to London: going up in the air is "like what a person feels when swinging in a swing." He wondered at the expanse and emptiness of the Sahara Desert—"Our Kikuyu, let me tell you that the desert is beyond one thousand kilometers wide"—and noted that it divides Africa from what is "abroad." Muoria, however, was out to make *connections* between Africa and abroad. He noted that people in the Sudan are dressed recognizably like Swahili or Indians in Kenya; that Malta, like Kenya, is ruled by the British; that mountains in France are "like the ones you pass at Taita on the way to Mombasa as you know"; and that the weather in England is like that of Limuru, Kereita, or Molo.

In another front-page article Muoria reported on the biased coverage of Mau Mau activities by the British press; as a result, prominent Kenyans in London had called a press conference to correct the negative image of Kenya. A letter to the editor from one Kinyungu Wanyoike demonstrates that readers shared Muoria's concern with what went on in the public sphere. Wanyoike opened his letter with a call to fellow readers: "Give your opinions to the printers of Mumenyereri." He shared his views on "how Kenya is now, how it was before and how it will be when the black people win." He noted the importance of memories, dreams, and thoughts—processes internal to a person that need to make their way to the outside world in order to be debated: "It is good for a person to let the public know what one is thinking. It helps the public." He described his dream visions of an independent Kenya, "I think again about freedom for the black people and I hear sounds of instruments playing good music," a sharp contrast to the fate of whites after a nationalist takeover: "I see them with a lot of grief and isolated along the roads where we will come rejoicing and raising the flag of KAU [Kenya Africa Union] just like we have seen in public meetings from all sides."

As in other issues, the last page was taken up by advertisements and announcements of "tea parties"—occasions for the sons and daughters of Kikuyu and Mumbi to get together to be entertained, talk politics, and collect money for community purposes. Kenyatta's new book, *Kenya the Land of Troubles*, printed by Mumenyereri Printing Press from its new location in Grogan Road, was announced, and customers were advised to hurry—"the early bird catches the worm."

The format of the last issues is no different from the eight-page issues of

April 2–3 and May 3–4, 1950.[16] All are organized in three-column pages and are typeset and printed by hand—letters skip and dance. The Kikuyu paragraphs are long and punctuation is scarce. Headlines and subheadings use different fonts and sizes and articles continue over several pages, giving the paper a disorganized but inviting appearance. The May issue carries the photograph of the well-known politician and age-group leader, Dedan Mugo, in the middle of the front page to illustrate the coverage of his early-morning arrest in Kiambu on suspicion of having administered an illegal oath. The other top story is about a meeting between the Kenya African Union and the East African Indian National Congress where a number of African grievances were discussed, including theft of land.

The May 27 and July 5 issues of the same year are different—they have been produced on a duplicator. They are four-page publications with the characteristic *Mumenyereri* heading in handsome Gothic letters, followed by "The Gikuyu national bi-weekly, est.d 1945," the editor's name and post-office address, a notification of registration, and the price—twenty cents. The feature articles and reports of meetings are as thorough and sharp as in the earlier issues, but there are fewer letters to the editor. One urges Kikuyu to drop the habit of giving their children English names such as John and Henry, Hanna and Grace. Keeping Kikuyu names meant upholding Kikuyu society—if people did not name their children properly, their grandchildren would forget the names of their forefathers. There were no good reasons for giving children Christian names: "No matter what we do a *nganga* [guinea fowl] will not change into a *ngware* [partridge]." The letter ends with *Thaai*, the traditional Kikuyu greeting (May 27, 1950).

Several items announce meetings, most commonly of business companies or age-set associations (*wariika*). One is signed by Muoria in his capacity of secretary of the *Ndege* (airplane) *riika*. In another notice, he urges his sales agents to pay him before they receive copies of the paper. An earlier issue of the paper had advertised the publication of Muoria's new pamphlet, *Our Mother Is Soil and Our Father Is Wisdom*, in which he demonstrated "how Africans were made slaves by Europeans; that soil is essential: how these things can be abolished by education." Readers were advised to "keep their money ready as there are very few copies" (June 7, 1948). Advertisements announce motorcar insurance, bicycle repair, and chickens for sale and recommend eating at the Nairobi Racecourse Restaurant—*the* place for traditional Kikuyu dishes. A missing-person notice tells of a wife who has disappeared and left her one-week-old baby behind. Her husband promises 100 shillings to the person who can bring news of her. A large advertisement for a film

called *Two Girls and a Sailor*, starring Van Johnson and June Allyson, features
a photograph of a group of gun-toting cowboys on horseback. The film shows
were to take place in Nairobi's two African community halls, one each in
Kaloleni and Pumwani.

In the eight-page typeset issues from the 1950s, signed letters from readers take up more than a third of the space. Most letters in the issues consulted
and in the government files are from Kikuyu correspondents, judging by the
names. Some are from women. One letter, signed by Mrs. Gathaku, related
women's issues to the larger questions of who deserves to rule. She made a
two-pronged attack on the ineffectiveness of Kenyatta's mere words and the
power of chiefs: although "women were told by Jomo Kenyatta not to dig ter-
races, the women are still digging." They have to, since "only a chief's wife can
get sugar without digging. . . . She stays at home, sitting in a chair, just like a
chief" (September 29, 1947). Wairimu, wife of Njoroge, directed her anger at
white people—they, and not African men, had turned Kikuyu women into
slaves. Women were strong and quite capable of carrying heavy loads without
losing their dignity, but they should not be deprived of their land and sent to
places such as Olenguruone, a settlement of Kikuyu who had been displaced
by the settlement of the White Highlands by British colonialists.

Semukula Mulumba may serve as an example of *Mumenyereri*'s broader
political constituency. He was a friend of the Kenyan African opposition, a
Ugandan political exile who was living at the time in Hampstead. A letter
signed by him demanded freedom now, reminded readers of the fate of black
people in South Africa, and urged them to support the Kenya African Union
(June 3, 1950).[17] A reader from Kikuyu, a village west of Nairobi, warned
against following Jesus Christ, who was white like those who oppress Kenya
Africans. Other correspondents complained that whites would not listen to
arguments, that missions had taken land away from people, that young men
slept in the bush for fear of being arrested, that people were forced to carry
kipande (passbooks), that it was impossible to receive visitors because people
were arrested without reason—in short, the "whites wish us to be slaves"
(ibid.).

Letters had diverse forms. James Muchendu shaped his as a dramatic dialogue between Kamau (K) and Njoroge (N), warning fellow Kikuyu against
unproductive labor. In what John Lonsdale has called the Kikuyu "labor theory," clearing the forest and making land productive for cultivation was what
made civilized life possible. Genders and generations needed to collaborate in
this endeavor (Berman and Lonsdale 1992, 381–388). Unity and productive
collaboration would "lead the clan of Mumbi to progress and not allow them

to be weed cutters and diggers." The opposite would lead to the collapse of the social and moral order and the ability of men to control their wives: "N: 'What do you think about our girls crowding into towns?' K: 'There is nothing else hurts me like that, my wife went away leaving a young baby whom I had to take to the hospital for feeding.' . . . N: 'Is that not the way to disgrace the clan of Mumbi?' K: 'Yes, but this is a tiny thing for the clan of Mumbi, if we have unity with all associations and unions'" (June 7, 1948). A fortnight later, G. N. Tharau added to the plea for an end to Kikuyu political infighting. He urged the leaders of prominent Kikuyu organizations to form a "powerful union" to which the various associations should send their requests regarding "land, education, trade and many other things" (June 21, 1948). Another reader asked "natives of Kiambu, Gatundu, Githunguri and Cura locations" to fight the following evils: three-card trick players, robbers, false accusers, people who sell liquor in homes "for it is not a Kikuyu custom," keeping prostitutes in reserves, and "loafers who are the sole promoters of things I have mentioned above" (February 2, 1948).

Mumenyereri covered gender relations, marriage, and male control of women's sexuality more broadly. As we have seen, women's morality was a key issue in both the countryside and urban areas. The ease of movement between one and the other was part of the problem—it facilitated women's access to trade and cash.[18] Letters urged men to keep close watch over women and stay away from prostitutes. The newspaper gave space to the president of the Kenya Houseboys' Association, who encouraged his members to protest if their wives were not allowed to stay with them in their urban lodgings: "Wives of African workers are sent away by Europeans and Government is feeling very bad about this. When wives of workers are evicted and go home, the houseboys go after prostitutes who infect them with venereal diseases then Europeans dismiss them from employment. The houseboy goes to hospital where he remains consuming medicine of Government for nothing" (July 5, 1948). Another letter quoted the address of a Kisii chief to Kikuyu proponents of tribal purity at a *baraza* (public meeting)—"We are feeling very bad because you are refusing us to marry your tall, beautiful and brown girls"—but warned against following the wishes of the chief: "These Kisii want us to follow their habits in order to marry our girls. Our children never wear strings on the neck, therefore we have refused to intermarry with Kisii" (July 21, 1948).

Strong voices argued for women's equality and progress: a lengthy article reported from a *riika* meeting at Githunguri in early 1948. This was the heartland of Kikuyu opposition to the government and the seat of Kenya Teachers

College, started by Mbiu Koinange in 1939 to train teachers for independent African schools. This institution was central in building up the power bases of Mbiu Koinange and Jomo Kenyatta and was being sustained by their efforts along with those of Muoria and other Kikuyu politicians. Part of this effort was the call to Kikuyu to pay the controversial "Kenyatta tax" (Berman and Lonsdale 1992, 410 ff.; Kershaw 1997, 218–219; Peterson 2004, 153–155). On this occasion a prominent young Kikuyu woman spoke—Wangoi, the daughter of Mbiu's father, Senior Chief Koinange Mbiu. She had returned to Kenya from South Africa, where she had been a student, and recommended that every time a young man was sent abroad to be educated a young woman should also be sent. Kenyatta introduced her, stressing that she represented not only Kikuyu "but other tribes of black race." This was probably intended to counteract Wangoi's style of Kikuyu nationalism, which was unacceptable to both Kenyatta and her father. She went on to speak of the dangers to the tribe that might follow from marrying outside it. To further stress that it was a nationalist and not a tribal meeting, the paper reported that her father got up afterward, although he was hesitant about speaking after "such a clever girl's speech," and emphasized that Githunguri College, though built by Kikuyu, belonged to "all . . . members of the black race," a claim that probably did not convince many among the audience (February 16, 1948). Muoria later helped Wangoi write a short book about South Africa that was based on her experiences there.

In her study of Kenya's African press of this period, Gadsden classifies *Mumenyereri* as belonging to the "radical populist press . . . which intended to politicize the poor for radical action and came to reject the moderate politics of the educated." Its counterparts were *Sauti Mwafrika*, the newspaper of the Kenya African Union, and *Radio Posta* and *Mwalimu*, whose editors, W. W. W. Awori and Francis Khamisi, were moderate nationalists with formal education and some training in journalism (Gadsden 1980, 516–518). In fact Muoria, who was more of a nationalist than a populist, was moderate. He demanded self-government, predicted that one day the governor of Kenya would be an African, and condemned the Mau Mau movement and its leadership. The paper did print letters demanding independence and supporting oaths. However, at this time oaths bound Kikuyu to "unity and moral constancy" rather than revolt.[19] One came from an independent Kikuyu school. It reminded Kikuyu leaders that they had taken the oath of the soil as babies, which made it a duty for them write in the paper and thus strengthen the case for Kikuyu nationalism: "Isn't it a good thing to follow this oath that we administered ourselves without the advice of anybody?" (July 12, 1948). The newspaper mostly supported gradualism. An example is Muoria's compliance with the request of the government's Information Office that he publish an article that would calm Kikuyu fears about the expansion of Nairobi in 1950. He did so under the heading, "The Nairobi Municipal Council is not going to take away Kikuyu lands" (April 12, 1950).

Mumenyereri in the "Battle of Brains"

The colonial government did not have legal mechanisms in place to prevent Henry Muoria from making his readily available newspaper a propaganda instrument. The newspaper was able to mobilize support for nationalism, for the antigovernment Githunguri College student body, and for Jomo Kenyatta's ideas and claims. In spite of government control and restrictions in most areas of Kenyan African civil life, there was considerable freedom of the press until 1950. The government was not entitled to censor pamphlets and newspapers before publication, but it did resort to warnings and persuading the judiciary to prosecute after the fact.[20] Before the amendment of the Penal Code that year, which made it possible for the state to seize the printing presses of newspapers convicted of sedition, editors were mostly fined, if they were convicted at all. Covering one of Muoria's appearances in court, the Indian-owned radical newspaper *Daily Chronicle* reported that his was "the sixth non-European court appearance in the last three years."[21] This fairly low number was an indication that the government did not have the instruments to quell the African press and needed to take new initiatives in the offensive against nationalist dominance of the public sphere.[22]

One government strategy was an intensification of the circulation of British-produced news, entertainment, and information. The Information Office handed out newssheets and propaganda on a large scale, and from 1939 the *East African Standard* published *Baraza,* a weekly paper in Swahili, created especially to take the wind out of the sails of the African opposition by serving as a forum for "African aspirations and grievances."[23] In the late 1940s a Kikuyu version of *Baraza* was started that was never very successful. By this time, African politicians, editors, and readers were skeptical of material written purposely for an African audience by officials, missionaries, or the white-owned so-called independent press. They had reason to be so. One reader of Muoria's paper reminded Europeans that they had declared that having translated "the Bible, Common Prayer Book and Hymn Book . . . they would never print anything else for us in the Kikuyu language." He wondered why they now "print papers and give them to Africans free" (*Mumenyereri,* June 10, 1950). In early 1948 the paper reported from a meeting called by the Kenya

African Union that Kenyatta, "holding a newspaper in his hand . . . warned all the newspaper correspondents that they should print news exactly as it was spoken" (May 31). Kenyatta was referring to misrepresentation in *Baraza* of his own and the Kenya African Union's stance on the right of Europeans to settle in Kenya. More generally, however, his comment addressed the changing roles and rules of oral and written communication in a growing public sphere. The fluidity and pleasures of words of mouth were risky and were increasingly replaced with the discipline of verbatim reportage.[24]

Six weeks later, Muoria summed up the nationalist position on European newspapers: "Some are given free and some are sold cheaply because they want the African to read just what they think the African should know and no more." However, "Africans are wide awake and will not buy papers which have no interesting news. . . . People are not goats, they cannot buy a worthless thing" (June 14, 1948). Had the colonial authorities listened, large quantities of paper, newsprint, and brainwork might have been saved that went into producing publications such as the East African Literature Bureau's "popular" magazine *Tazama*, or *Picha*, which was brought out by the Information Office.

Another government strategy was to simultaneously consolidate, curb, and co-opt the African press using a carrot-and-stick method. Officials tempered threats and prosecution with offers to editors of money, training, and printing presses. As part of the effort, a report by the press officer, H. C. E. Downes, analyzed the problem of the African press—"the gutter press of Kenya," as he called it.[25] One reason for what he saw as its dismal state was the easy passage into newspapers of uncensored letters—"correspondence is accepted and published without verification or comment." Furthermore, readers or correspondents with no formal connection to the paper occasionally covered political incidents, meetings, and petitions. Finally, he was disturbed by what he saw as the injudicious mixture of genres that African editors allowed: "In the world of the African Press the Editor *is* the newspaper. . . . The Editor[,] who usually possesses a very low standard of education, publishes what he feels, mixing news with Editorials and Editorials with news."

Downes's account of a meeting with African editors illustrates the Press Liaison Office's despair at what they saw as the lack of professionalism shown by African journalists. The purpose of the meeting was to persuade the newspapermen to accept a degree of government assistance and control. Downes was puzzled by the presence of what he called "an extraordinary crowd of khaki overcoated gentlement [*sic*] sitting in the background." The editors described them as "our correspondents." Downes wrote: "I realized . . . that they were the chief letter writers, but as no 'correspondent' entered into the conversation or understood a word of what we were discussing, they appeared to matter little."[26]

Reliance on writers who might be close to the ground but whose information was difficult to verify was a problem also for the editors and printers who were held responsible for the contents of the newspapers. If reputedly inaccurate reporting could be taken to be seditious, as in the case of *Mumenyereri*'s coverage of the shooting of workers by the police during a strike at Uplands Bacon Factory, the very existence of the papers was endangered.[27]

A letter from Mwangi Kahoro is an example of the genre that enraged officials. The writer reported on a visit and *baraza* by the district commissioner and the agricultural officer in Kiambu. Its topic was the red-hot issue of state interference with landownership and regulation of cultivation practices. The purpose of the visit, as it had been explained to Kiambu cultivators, was to persuade them to measure and parcel out land so that everyone would have enough to "cultivate, to keep cattle and to build a house." Then came the crux: the two officials had apparently declared that "the remaining or unoccupied land will remain in the hands of Government." Kahoro reported vigorous protests—"some were saying that they would prefer to be bombed" rather than allow the government to interfere with their land. He reminded readers that as a result of the Kikuyu fathers agreeing with the Europeans to have forest boundaries, "the forests are now the Europeans' property, whereas the Kikuyu are now strangers in this country" (*Mumenyereri*, July 5, 1950).[28] In a lengthy letter to the Nyeri provincial commissioner, the district commissioner explained that he had been misrepresented and that the purpose of the visit was an agricultural census. He argued that Kahoro's account of the incident and its background was yet another case of African editors encouraging misrepresentation of government motives and policies by giving space to irresponsible letter-writers. He urged the provincial commissioner to "take up the matter with the Attorney General" so that "when opportunity offers such pernicious people should be severely dealt with."[29] There is no trace in the files of prosecution in this case.

Mumenyereri's coverage of events in the faraway settlement of Olenguruone, where displaced Kikuyu settlers were threatened with yet another deportation, sparked an order to Muoria to visit the offices of the attorney general. Resistance in Olenguruone was closely connected to local politics in Kiambu, where many of the Kikuyu settlers originated and had owned land.[30] *Mumenyereri* reported that the attorney general had warned Muoria that if he persisted in writing in a manner which might "bring illfeeling between

Agikuyu and Europeans," he would be "put in prison or deported." Muoria made a vague promise that "I shall try to see that such news is not printed" and was free to walk away. The newspaper report ended with Muoria's ambivalent message: "You should, therefore, Mumbi[31] family, stick to the truth and right, leave all news that would cause illfeeling" (December 15, 1947).

Speaking with two tongues was a consequence of indirect censorship in a situation where the Kikuyu opposition carefully assessed action strategies and communication strategies. Muoria knew the dangers of political reporting, which, in his own words, made him "unpopular with both white officials and African tribal chiefs." As a political journalist, he chose to "sail as close to the wind as possible" in order to get his message across and contribute to the general and growing opposition against British-run colonial "slavery" (Muoria 1994, 69, 74). Reporting from close to the ferment of local-level politics was one prong of resistance; stating the principles and philosophy of a Kikuyu way of life and of nationalist opposition was another.

The Enterprise of Editors

Muoria was the sole editor of *Mumenyereri,* but he depended on a supportive environment in the complicated and mobile business of producing the paper. Initially, family labor was needed primarily to distribute the paper. Later, he relied on his second wife, Judith, and his third wife, Ruth, for assistance with the actual writing and production. Ruth might be sent to cover an important meeting and Judith would spend hours in the law courts, listening to cases to decide if anything merited reporting. Ruth contributed a fairy tale that narrated the victory of a selfless sister over a worldly brother with the help of a magic snake. C. Passfield, the astute director of intelligence and security, pointed out in the cover letter to the chief native commissioner that the writer was Muoria's wife and offered an instance of secret agent turned textual analyst: "It is assumed that the brother represents the European, the sister the African and the snake God."[32]

From 1947 to 1950, Muoria employed an assistant editor, John Gatu.[33] Together they wrote the larger part of the newspaper. Running the paper "took a lot of doing." In the 1940s Muoria did not have an office—he operated from his car or from the offices of his printers. Though he worked hard, he was not highly organized. He did not keep accounts—money "went into one pocket and out of the other." Nor did he type. He wrote everything by hand and gave it to the printers to do the typesetting, "one letter at a time." Gatu wrote on an old typewriter and also did the proofreading. The printer,

Mr. V. G. Patel, worked a treadle press, and "it used to take many hours to produce 11,000 copies" (Muoria 1994, 45). The political situation made production risky and unstable, and after both Patel and Muoria had been fined for printing seditious material, Patel refused to continue printing the paper. From early 1948, *Mumenyereri* was printed together with Achieng Oneko's popular Luo paper *Ramogi* and W. W. W. Awori's *Radio Posta* at Ramogi Press in Eastleigh, the African and Asian area of Nairobi.[34] Delays in bringing out the newspaper made Muoria return to Flash Printing Works, the firm of Patel, who was losing money and was willing to take him on again. However, shortly afterward, his printing works were devastated by a fire from which only one press was saved.

Muoria then decided to duplicate the paper, which would make him his own master. He got hold of a duplicator from his political associate, Mbiu Koinange, principal of Githunguri College; bought ink, stencils, and paper; and mobilized his family. This is how his widow Ruth remembers the production of the paper:

> He had to find a duplicator, from Githunguri College. They had a duplicator there. He hired the thing. We used to duplicate in Eastleigh. First we did it in my mother's place, but there was a kind of strike in Majengo, people were not allowed to strike, they were beaten, arrested. We knew that if they came and found it there they would take it away. We moved and did it at Kangemi, a friend of my husband called Mugo; he agreed we could stay in his place so the newspaper could come out in the morning. He used to type on the stencil. My job was to pin it together. The other son put it together. We would do it all night without sleeping. In the morning the newspaper was ready. The people would buy—so much. They used to fight for it. They used to wait in the street. . . . People loved the paper. That is how he got money.[35]

For the first time in his career as a newspaper owner, Muoria made a profit from his paper, and he bought Patel's surviving printing press in order to be in charge of production himself. He installed it in rented premises in Grogan Road in white Nairobi and produced the paper from there until he left for London.

Muoria was part of a group of struggling African editors and journalists. Some, like Francis Khamisi, were employed in the colonial media—radio, newspapers, magazines, and propaganda and information units. Others attempted at various times to strike out for themselves. The editors of what Gadsden called the "populist press" were part of a rising modern intermediate class. Although they were a labor aristocracy, they did not represent the African elite; rather, they represented those who has been displaced by colonial policies and had managed to escape from scratching the meager land in the reserves or exchanging their labor power for the use of insufficient pieces of land on European farms. They sought alternative livelihoods. Some were second-generation squatters who became traders or artisans and joined others in their exodus from rural Kikuyuland and the White Highlands region to towns and cities (Furedi 1989, 79–80). Gadsden listed the professions of Muoria's fellow African newspaper editors as follows: "one carpenter, a shoemaker, driver, sign writer and one bookbinder together with several clerks, traders and farmers" (Gadsden 1980, 518–519). This class of people was a key group in other parts of Africa as well. Karin Barber has attributed the success of modern Yoruba popular theater in Nigeria to the inventiveness, independence, and entrepreneurial spirit of members of a similar intermediate class. She gave the professions of central actors in the theater companies as "tailors, bricklayers, clerks, shoeshine boys, petty traders, taxi drivers" (Barber 2000, 2). The similarity between the two groups of wordsmiths, radically divided by space, is striking.

Harassment by authorities was of marginal concern to these editors. They were preoccupied with costs. Not being in possession of their means of production was a major setback. A letter-writer suggested in *Mumenyereri* that "all Kikuyu should buy their own printing presses" because Indians were "charging them exorbitant prices for their printings" (November 24, 1947). As it was, editors relied on their own labor to make a profit and were adept at getting by in situations fraught with obstacles.

The "artisanal" production process of the newspaper enabled mobility and flexibility. Contracts were done orally. When a printing press became insecure for political reasons, went bankrupt, or burned down, the production of newspapers moved to a different site. When owners of printing presses would no longer print their controversial newspapers, editors obtained duplicators and churned them out themselves. When a paper was prosecuted for not being licensed, it folded and reemerged under a different name. Editors who were warned in court for being inflammatory printed an apology in the next issue of their paper. Shortage of correspondents was remedied by family labor. And finally, running a newspaper was one of a string of entrepreneurial activities. Muoria owned land and was involved with his wives and children in cultivation, popular writing, and trade, among other activities. When he and his educated wife Judith had their first child, they wrote a book on modern living, spreading their knowledge of childcare. When he found out that the soil on his land could be used for bricks, he started producing them not only for sale but also for the didactic value of the project; in his pamphlets, he described the advantages of brick houses that let in the light. His enterprises reflected on each other and came together as one endeavor, creating structures of physical and moral enlightenment.

Although in the war of words the deck was stacked in favor of the colonialists, the African press was successful in reaching its desired audience, creating community and keeping colonial officials on their toes. Like the producers of Yoruba theater who did the creative as well as the manual, logistical, and administrative work, newspaper editors worked in an atmosphere of "inspired improvisation" (Barber 2000, 350). Spatial, political, and mental segregation meant, however, that although the African editors were firmly situated at the center of African politics and aspirations, they were simultaneously relegated to the interstices of society, dominated as it was by a powerful and aggressive colonial political culture that was more influenced by white settlers than by Whitehall.

Conclusion

In the large conversation between landless peasants, chiefs, settlers, British officials, and African politicians in the letters, features, and editorials of *Mumenyereri*, controversies were covered, debated, judged, and sometimes even settled. Letters and articles described the experiences of the poor and displaced as well as the well-off and landed, thus belying hierarchies of wealth, race, age, and gender and affirming writing as an institution of equality (Lonsdale 2002).

Muoria was a proponent of Kikuyu values—work, wealth, and wisdom— but he took care to inscribe them as African values. In the pages of *Mumenyereri*, "Kikuyu" and "African" were used interchangeably, creating a certain instability rather than an atmosphere of Kikuyu exclusiveness. Muoria needed both identifications to establish his credentials and the trust of his readers. His own thinking rather than his background drove him into public life. In his political pamphlets and in his dialogue with readers in his newspaper journalism, he invented new ways of living and accompanying discourses that simultaneously articulated values from versions of Kikuyu history, from an emerging nationalism, and from Christianity and enlightenment in its colonial entanglement. As a true cultural nationalist, he deliberately took up the "quasi-external position" that was necessary for his task of "cultural editing" (Barber 2000, 316). Muoria was a critical guardian of values who was in a position to edit not only his own lifeworld but also competing discourses on Kikuyuness and nationhood, including those by Kenyatta, in the meeting place of his newspaper. He found and strengthened an incipient nationalist public sphere that persisted until late 1952, when it was crushed by the government's extreme measures during the Emergency. His role as a spokesman, arbitrator, and popularizer was fashioned by the emergence of a semi-anonymous modern audience whose steps toward enlightenment matched his own. His critical engagement with the colonial order was open: "The Europeans, whether they like it or not, must be told the truth." Like his mentor Jomo Kenyatta, he believed that "we must select educated Africans to lead us." The only weapons of Africans were brains, truth, and honesty, and if they did not use them, "there will be calamity" (*Mumenyereri*, August 30, 1948). Muoria's life and work may be understood as an uphill struggle to spread that message for the benefit of his countrymen.

THE GUARDIAN
AND THE CARETAKER OF THE BLACK PEOPLES INHERITANCE

THE KIKUYU NATIONAL BI-WEEKLY   (ESTD. 1945)
EDITOR & PUBLISHER   HENRY MUORIA   P.O. BOX 1956 NAIRIOBI.

No.451 Registered at the G.P.O. as a Newspaper Saturday 20.9.52 to Monday 22.9.52 Price 20 Cts.

Even the government abroad is worried because of Mau Mau

This news is brought by the Editor of this newspaper, while he is in London the town of the British people. He says:-

When we arrived here abroad on Saturday, the news we saw in one of the newspapers of this place, called Daily Mail, and which was written with big letters was about Kenya, saying that because of the crises which are there the government is going to send some delegates from here to come there and find out the origin of these crises. Again it is written that two white leaders from the government of Kenya, one of them CNC together with the Attorney General are coming here abroad to discuss with the High Commissioner for colonial countries about which measures should be taken to stop the widespread influence of the secret organisation of Mau Mau which is followed by the Kikuyu tribe.

Our readers, do you remember that white people in Kenya have been thinking of prohibiting black politics? The laws for prohibiting black politics are already formulated and are brought here abroad to be signed by the Secretary for colonial countries, but it seems as if he does not want to sign these laws. These laws are the reason why the meeting for the commonwealth countries was quickly arranged while Mathu was still here in this foreign place. That means that those government leaders came here to be able to negotiate with the colonial Secretary in order to persuade him to sign these laws so that they can start enforcing them.

Another story in this newspaper was about how a person from Mbea was harassed by Mau-mau people who wanted to kill him. The news about Kenya are being talked about with a lot of contempt and malice here.

As you have seen, the elder Mathu and the Mbiyu Koinange had a press meeting with journalists of newspapers where they denied this news about Kenya. But their story was not published in the newspapers of here. Again, the newspaper called The Times for Monday will bring this news about Kenya and news about the outcome of the negotiations between the government leaders from Kenya and the Secretary for colonial countries here. There is pressure that the new Governor who is coming to Kenya comes soon so that he can empower a lot of force to actions. It is said that things in the country of Kenya have gone too far.

> [Henry Muorias Photo]
> The writer now they are abroad.
> Read their journey ahead.

The governor who was staying in Kenya ealier said that things in Kenya are not as bad as it is said that he has a lot of hope for the country because he is going back there together with his wife to become a farmer.

———   ———   ———

Figure 11.3. *Mumenyereri*, September 20–22, 1952, translated from the Kikuyu by Eunice Wandia Tonnesen.

302

The writer has arrived abroad
THEIR JOURNEY

When we went inside the plane on Thursday while flying we were very thankful because of how the people of Kikuyu and Mumbi had troubled themselves too early in the morning and came to say goodbye to us happily and singing. We were very happy when we came to realize that it was you who sent us, because if it was not you you would not have troubled yourselves in all that cold to come and say goodbye to us. Therefore we thank you very much.

The writer says what he experienced in the aeroplane when it got up in the air, is like what a person feels when swinging in a swing then we were given cottonwool to put in ears so that they would not be damaged by the noise from the aeroplane and we were given sweets to put in the mouth. When we left Nairobi because there was a lot of fog the aeroplane went high above the fog and above the white clouds where we could see the sun while up there. From up there the farms and the houses looked like the ones drawn by children. After flying for a while we were told that we were near the lake at Kisumu which is called L Victoria and that the speed of the aeroplane was 185 kilometers per hour and from the hard earth the height is six thousand feet and that the aeroplane was not late it will reach Entebbe the time it is supposed to be there. Then we came to that lake and looking from all sides it was only water which looked like the black clouds. When we got close to the lake we came to the stage of Entebbe in Uganda there we got out and went to a white hotel which was there and took tea.

After staying for 30 minutes we started the journey again at about 09.15 in the morning. This country of Ugandans is very fertile, it is more warm than the Kikuyu country and there are a lot of bananas.

A BIG FOREST WITHOUT A SOUL

When we left Entebbe we went to a place called Waliseigona in the country of Sudan. Sudan is between the country of Aganda people and Nubi people. The aeroplane flew very high so that the travellers could see the wild animals which are there and we saw a very big forest without any people at all. That place is very hot because the breeze from the big winds feels as if it is damp from hot water. After half an hour before flying too far we came to the sand desert called Sudan. Our Kikuyus, let me tell you that desert is beyond one thousand kilometers wide, and it goes to the boundary which divides Africa and abroad and there is not a single tree anywhere only sand and the heat which is there is big. From above this country looks like a country where the trees dry out and fall just by themselves because what l thought when l saw this land was this was a dead land because there was nothing at all and the big mountains you can see are eroded out and when you look far it was only red sand which looked like fog. When our aeroplane left there it went to a place called Wadi Halfa for the night in the country of Sudan far down in the valley of the Nile river. This river is very big because it carries ships to the harbour of Wadi Halfa from the land of sand. There are a lot of Nubi people who have built houses of brick and there is no soil erosion here. The women of Sudan wear only Ibuyabui (the black garment worn by arab women covering the whole body from head to toes) like the Swahili people and the men wear a white robe and a turban like those of Indians. They have donkeys which are not as big as other horses, and the men ride these donkeys while at the same time these donkeys are carrying luggage. It looks very funny to see a grown up man riding these donkeys because it looks as if the man is riding a calf. The 12.9.52 we started flying very early in the morning and we began crossing the desert and after flying about six hundred miles we stopped in Libya for petrol, then we started the journey again and within 15 minutes we came to the Mediterranian Sea and then to the island called Malta at about 04.30 p.m. local time but it was about 06.30 Kenyan time because when we arrived in Malta and when still in the aeroplane, we were told to set our watches two hours back. The people of the Island of Malta look like Italians but they have better houses. Here they still have donkey carts and we rode in one of them while some of the children were looking at us and some ran away and others were borrowing money from us, here it is as hot as in Mombasa. There are a lot of stones of many kinds and even some are white. They are ruled by the British people but the local people here are given big jobs in the government because even one of the local people is the Prime Minister and there are many Catholic churches here. This country is in Italy which is part of Europe. Where there are no buildings there are many gardens fenced with stones and many places look like empty rocks.

ARRIVAL ABROAD

The aeroplane we took was delayed two hours on Saturday while being repaired. When the aeroplane was fit for flying again, we flew high above the ocean and after many hours the first land of abroad which we saw is the one called Sicily in Italy, it is not a fertile country but it has a lot of farms. Then we came to France here we saw very many big rocky mountains like the ones at Taita on the way to Mombasa as you know, this is how this part of France looks like nothing can grow there but when you pass these mountains you come to fertile places with fenced farms but even the rich people here abroad do not have as big farms like the ones they have there at home they have farms just like the ones the Kikuyus have there at home. After flying 600 miles from Malta we landed in France and had lunch there. Then we continued the journey and came to the country of the English people. Here there are towns everywhere just like there some are big others small there are rivers mountains and valleys the only difference is their gardens because even if they are small they are tended with a lot of care and beauty. This country of the people who rule us is very fertile there are forests and their houses look like those of the mountains. Nairobi is not hot at all it is cold, here it is like Limuru or like Kereita or like Molo. We arrived in the evening at about 06.00 p.m. and then we took a Taxi which brought us to the town of London at about 08.00 p.m. in the evening . We found two white people members of the organisation called Moral Rearmament waiting for us. I was familiar with them because one of them is the one I escorted to Githunguri when they were in Kenya. Mr. Stephen Foot and the other one was David Sturdy. They told us that the governor had come to welcome us but he was told that our aeroplane was late and he said that he would come back in the following morning and that was what he did, he came as he had promised. When we arrived Kubai and us got a separate house together and Ndisi got his own house and they wanted us to go to Swizerland on Sunday but we told them that we would like to rest and go by train on Monday 15.9.52 direct to Switzerland. When I arrive there, I will send more news.

E. W. Mathu is coming today.

The elder, Hon. E. W. Mathu and his wife are landing at the airport today at about noon, therefore it is good if the people are already there to welcome him.

And the young man called J. Karuga who was going for study left the day before yesterday with the evening aeroplane at 06.00 p.m.

Mûcohi Gikonyo.

Travelling at night by Vehicles is going to be prohibited in order to reduce Crimes.

The Kenya police has announced that from Tuesday, they will start arresting all vehicles travelling at night from Nairobi town to Thika, Fort Hall and Nyeri, and again to Kiambu from Nairobi, and to Limuru, along the roads A and B. And even from Nairobi on your way to Ikamba, Kajiado, and from Thika heading for Ikamba to Machakos and Kitui, and again from Nairobi to Naivasha. They say that it is not allowed to travel on these roads from 07.00 p.m. to 04.00 a.m in the morning unless you have a permit from the police with explanation that you are allowed to travel during these hours and why ? They say that these permits are given from your nearby police station.

BEER FOR THE CHILD OF NDURURU

The elders Mwingi and Maina together with their women, humbly invite you to a beer gathering in favour of the child of Ndururu on 12.10.52 and the gathering will be held between Limuru and Uplands the village of Nyambari at Kinuku, s/o Gatimû. We ask all young and old to come early because a child's gathering has no age. Now, our house of Kikuyu and Mûmbi we kindly ask you to arrive early the 12.10.52. Come and see things at this gathering.

I am the district chairman for this gathering, on behalf of the owner,

Kinuku Gatimû.

ANNOUNCEMENT OF

The meeting of The African Traders & Farmers Co. Ltd will be held on 25.9.52 beginning at nine o`clock in the morning. Arrive early so that we discuss the matters of the forest and bring your contributions to the writer's home at Kamandura.

Yours John Mbûgua
P. O. Limuru

The laws are published

As you already know two whites, leaders of the laws one J. Whyatt and the other Davies have been abroad to meet with the secretary for colonial countries in order to sign laws to prevent crimes in Kenya. They have already met with him and these laws were published in yesterday's English newspaper here and it says that they will be negotiated by the organisation of Governors at a meeting which will be held this coming Thursday. These laws are combined of eight points and one of the points says that all public meetings should be registered with the government and their origin and purpose should be known. Another point says that the P.C. should enforce laws to jail anybody connected with the organisation of Mau mau and connected with religions of big men and connected with the religion of Mbojet. Another one is that all written songs, books and newpapers will be controlled. The fourth one was to increase the penalty for crimes, theft and for trespassing on private properties without permission and the fifth one was to allow personal witnesses in the court and if the accused has documents from a witness, who cannot come to the court but has given his witness before the day the case is going to the court, these documents have to be signed by the Chief Inspector of police. Their laws are not supported here, but the agreement was made between the two whites and the high commissioner for colonial countries even if there were a few adjustments. It is said that all members of the separate organisation of the colonial governors have been contacted by telephone and asked to prepare themselves because of this coming meeting. The government delegates who are abroad are coming back to Kenya today.

WHO HAS SEEN THE GIRL ??

A girl called Wagithi Gacemburi is missing from her home at Mukore the village of Gachiku with headman Gichina location of chief Muhindi while following her mother who was going to Karatina in the month of September 1951.

The girl is brown about 10 years and with jiggers in her feet. If you see her inform Gakara Book Service Box 3632 Nairobi.

Reward is Shs 50.

By Mwangi Mbeu

S Memia is at his home

The elder who is called Solomon Memia who was judged two years imprisonment some time ago was released the day before yesterday and now he is at his home resting at Gatundu

---

Matters about FORESTS IN TANZANIA
are going to be discussed in
the Organisation of UNO

The letter which was written by fifteen elders of Labour Party about forests of Meru people in Tanzania was brought by the news through cable yesterday saying that the matter about that letter is going to be presented to the organisation of all countries UNO which is called Trusteeship Council to be discussed.

It is good for a person to open his mind in public

Give your opinion to printers of Mumenyereri. Many times when I am sleeping, when I am walking along the road, when I am at work, I think a lot about how Kenya is now, how it was before and how it will be when the black people win. About all these things, I see them as one sees things asleep in a dream. And when I remember the KAU delegate I see as if I am sitting together with him and I see that he is going to win, secondly, I get a strange feeling in stomach every time I think about him. Again, when the laws which took the black land Crown Land Ordinance 1902 which was enforced in 1938 comes to my mind, I see that KAU is deeply involved in this matter. I think again about freedom for the black people and I hear sounds of instruments playing good music and I think it is soldiers of black people praising the freedom. At that time, I come to think of what will happen to the white people and white leaders and about what will become of them. I see them with a lot of grief and isolated along the roads where we will come rejoicing and raising the Flag of KAU just like how we have seen it in public meetings from all sides. I would like to ask our readers whether there are some who have thoughts like these. It is a good for a person to let the public know what one is thinking. It helps the public.

Kinyûngû Wanyoike,
Kamahindu School. Uplands

COLONIAL VULCANIZING WORKS
P.O Box 1572 (Telephone 3535)
Hardinge Street, Nairobi.

Repairs of used tyres to become just like new ones. We sell all kinds of tyres which have been repaired and are as good as new ones. You can buy tyres for lorries, cars and all sizes. Our prices are cheaper than all other prices in the whole of Nairobi. You can get your old tyres repaired very quickly, and you get them within 2 days. We are near Marfak Petrol Station Nairobi.

Come yourself to

STAR STUDIO near Kiburi House Grogan Road Nairobi. They take very good pictures and they develop them, produce them in big sizes and at the same time, they flame them. It is near the building of firewood and charcoal company on the southern side.

P.O Box 1720 Nairobi.

Charandas & Lajpatrai
RIVER ROAD & DESAI ROAD
P.O BOX 1493 NAIROBI

A new cloth shop and the prices are cheap. Our shop is the fifth one from Nairobi Tea Room. We sell all kinds of Khaki materials and prices are:

Khaki	Stockport pure	4.50 per yard
—	Wigan —	4.00 per yard
—	Hull —	5.00 per yard
—	Durban —	5.00 per yard

TEA FOR WEITHAGA IN FOUR
VILLAGES (MURANG'A)

To the house of Kikuyu and Mumbi from Ngong to Karimatura , we are happy to invite you to come to our tea party on 3.10.52 (Friday).

The reason for this tea gathering will be explained home matters are not for public there is a dispute that somebody saw him/her dance naked in public.

Preparation for this tea will start on Saturday early, the time goats leave home for grazing. Cooking will be at Kikuyu Club Pumwani. The best Kikuyu musicians led by the elder Kinuthia Mugia will entertain the people.

Peace Peace
Organisers are

B.N. Nyaga
Gichina Gatuna.
Kiragu Macharia.
Gathua Muruithia.

FORT HALL GENERAL STORE

This shop is on your left side on the way to D.O., you leave the first shop and go to the second one.

It is owned by Kikuyus who get their things overseas and they sell things much cheaper than the Indians.

First, ask all what you need here and we sell all kinds of newspapers sold in the whole of Murang'a.

THE BEST TEA COOKER IN THE
WHOLE OF NAIROBI
MACHARIA KIBICHO

If you want coffee which is very well cooked, come to Desai Memorial where buses to black villages stop.

KENYA THE COUNTRY OF TROUBLES
IS PUBLISHED.

We would like to let all our readers and others waiting for the book written by our brave man Kenyatta, called Kenya the country of cries is published and if you come to the printing house of Mumenyereri you can buy all the books you want before they are finished. The price is ksh. 1/50. each and if you want many the price is ksh.1 / 35 each.

PRINTING HAS MOVED

The other thing is that the printing of Mumenyereri has moved from where it was and is now at the east of Kiburi House heading east along Grogan Road where the shops of Kikuyus are, we are on the same side.

The sooner you come the better. The early bird catches the worm. If you are living far away send the money for the number of books you want by the Post Office and don't send stamps instead of money.

TEA TEA TEA

To all the peoples of the house of Kikuyu and Mumbi from Ngong to Karimatura, we kindly let you know that there will be a tea gathering for your son of the house of

Kikuyu and Mumbi who is called Njuguna Gakuo B.A. of Com. He came back from India with a debt. He comes from Murang'a North, number 12, location of Chief Joel Michuki.

Tea gathering will be in Kikuyu Club Pumwani, Nairobi on 28.9.53

Your humble servants in the house of Kikuyu and Mumbi.

Kimani Kamau
Maina Gathuo
Maina Buki

ATHLETIC GAMES AT KEREITA PRIMARY SCHOOL DATE 20 9 52

Our house of Kikuyu and Mumbi we kindly ask you with big respect to come to games of the children of Kikuyu and Mumbi. Many wonders and Kikuyu songs will be there. The organisers are the parents of KKEA Kereita.

WHO HAVE SEEN A MISSING BICYCLE ?

Announcement of a missing bicycle which was lost on 10.9.52. at the cars travelling to Limuru. The person who finds it, can send it to Kiburi House BSA no 342049 if you find it I will thank you with a reward of shs 20. Yours friendly with the tribe of Kikuyu and Mumbi

Kabû Wacira.

TEA ! FOR MATHIRA
Kikuyu Club Pumwani 21. 9. 52.

All the people of Kikuyu and Mumbi from Ngong'u to Karimatura, we would like to let you know that there will be a big tea gathering in order to finish the School for the children of Mûmbi and Kikuyu. Independent School at Matira in Mathira area Nyeri. Tea gathering will be held at Kikuyu Club Pumwani - Nairobi 21-9-52 on Sunday from 8.00 a.m to the evening.

The pupils of Matira School will play games and Kikuyu magicians from Mathira will come to show their magic and all other things done at tea gatherings according to modern arrangements of today will be done.

We are the generations of Kikuyu and Mumbi

Kabui wa Kamanja (Kikuyu)
Nyagiciru wa Njibo (Mumbi)

TEA FOR THE CABBAGE TRADERS

To all in our house of Kikuyu and Mumbi we kindly ask you to come to tea gathering in favour of cabbage traders here in Nairobi. This tea will be held at Kikuyu Club, date 5.10.52 on Sunday from morning to evening. The entertainer will be chiada gikombe.

There will be funny Kikuyu songs which are not heard elsewhere in these days. Therefore as you know about things in these days we ask you members of the house of Kikuyu and Mumbi to come to this tea with a good heart and you will hear for yourselves how we will be selling cabbages to you without arguments.

Come Come Come, and see for yourselves
Yours, the people from your own house
1. Gikonyo Kanyuira
2. Karanja Njuguna
3. Gatuthu Kanyore

Printed by Mumenyereri Printing Press and Published by Henry
Muoria P.O Box 3561 Nairobi.

Kikuyu newspaper "MUMENYERERI".
Translated from Kikuyu to English by Eunice Wandia Tonnesen.
September 2003. Denmark.

NOTES

1. This chapter has grown out of a collaborative project on the life and works of Henry Muoria, undertaken by Wangari Muoria, John Lonsdale, and myself. I am indebted to them for wisdom and insight. Any misrepresentation is mine. Henry Muoria's widow, Ruth Nuna Muoria, and other members of the Muoria family in Kenya and Britain have been generous with time, friendship, and knowledge. I thank them all. I am grateful also to Derek Peterson for his comments and added perspectives and to Karin Barber for suggestions and inspiration. I presented the project to colleagues at the Danish Centre for the Advanced Study of the Humanities. I am grateful to them all but particularly to Birgitte Possing for her interest and valuable response.

2. See Kershaw (1997, 98–106); Berman and Lonsdale (1992, 348–355); and Peterson (2001, 2004).

3. For an example of fateful controversy between literates and illiterates during the Mau Mau revolt, see Lonsdale (2003). For a deep history of Kikuyu oracy and literacy in the context of a discussion of *Muigwithania,* the first Kikuyu newspaper, see Lonsdale (1996) and Peterson (2004).

4. "The African Press have their own agents, both in towns and districts, who pay in advance for supplying newspapers to the public." Press Officer H. C. Downes to the Director of Information C. Y. Carstairs, Colonial Office, April 3, 1951, MAA 8/23 African Press, Kenya National Archives (hereafter KNA).

5. Thanks to Derek Peterson for pointing out the provenance of this notion of the power of writing. The title of Ngugi wa Thiong'o's essay collection, *Barrel of a Pen: Resistance to Repression in Neo-Colonial Kenya* (1983), indicates the afterlife of the idea in Kenyan radical nationalism. Concerning the battle over public space: the municipal African affairs officer, who was in close touch with African urban realities, noted that the "most popular . . . form of literature among Africans is the newspapers and they are almost entirely full of politics"; City Council Library, *Report of Native Affairs: 1946–47* (Nairobi: Government Printer, 1947), 124. General Sir George Erskine, who was in charge of the military quelling of the Mau Mau revolt, identified "the state of public opinion inside the

Kikuyu tribe" as one of the uprising's most effective weapons; *East African Standard,* September 4, 1953.

6. Sources for this chapter include seven issues of the paper from 1950 and 1952 and English translations of articles, editorials, and letters to the editor, housed in AG 5/23, Prosecution of Seditious Publications, "Mumenyereri"; MAA 8/106, Intelligence, Security Newspaper Reports, "Mumenyereri"; MAA 8/102, Intelligence and Security, Press Cuttings, Miscellaneous; MAA 8/32, African Press, all in KNA. Notes on *Mumenyereri* articles from KNA files by David Throup, kindly passed on to me by John Lonsdale, have been a valuable supplement. I thank them both. I have benefited from Muoria's memories and reflections in *I, the Gikuyu and the White Fury* (1994) and his unpublished autobiographical writings, most important among them "The British and My Kikuyu Tribe" (1982), and from interviews with his widow Ruth Nuna Muoria, his daughters, and his assistant editor. I owe my knowledge of the contents of the original issues of *Mumenyereri* to the translations by Peter Mutahi and Eunice Wandia Tonnesen. I am deeply indebted to them.

7. Interview with their daughter, Rosabell Mbure, Nairobi, November 2000. I have not been able to locate a copy of this publication. The translation of the title is by Derek Peterson.

8. Interview with Ruth Nuna Muoria, London, July 2000.

9. Letter from Governor Edward Grigg to the Right Honourable L.C.M.S. Amery, Secretary of State for the Colonies, October 26, 1926, CO 533/382/6, Public Record Office. On the banning, see Pugliese 2003, 97.

10. Pugliese's interpretation of Muoria as an ethnic chauvinist is not borne out by Muoria's newspaper writings (Pugliese 2003, 102). He used "Black" and "African" interchangeably with "Kikuyu." Kikuyu were clearly *Mumenyereri*'s primary audience, but the awareness of global issues in his contributions belies a parochial identification. See "The Europeans Still Plan to Oppress Africans"; "Kenya Laws Are Retarding Africans' Defence"; and "Let Us Demand Self Government for Africans in the Whole of East Africa," all in *Mumenyereri,* April 22, July 24, and September 4, 1950.

11. Children reading to grandparents was the situation most commonly described to me in interviews with Kenyans who remembered the newspaper.

12. One of several examples of slippage between "Kikuyu" and "African."

13. The services of Leakey are referred to in "Caution Olenguruone Case," *Mumenyereri,* December 15, 1947, and the *Daily Chronicle*'s account of Muoria's October appearance in court (October 17, 1947). His apology was read out "by the Kikuyu speaking curator of the Corydon Museum, Dr. Leakey." *Daily Chronicle,* October 17, 1947, MAA 8/109 Intelligence Security, Newspaper Reports, Daily Chronicle 1947–1949, KNA.

14. The paper had been edited by James Beauttah, a well-known Murang'a politician.

15. See translation of this issue appended to this chapter. This issue of the newspaper is held by Wangari Muoria. I thank her or having provided me with a copy, and Eunice Wandia Tonnesen for the translation.

16. I thank Peter Mutahi for translation of articles and items in these issues.

17. On Mulumba, see Muoria (1994, 70) and Throup (1989, 133).

18. The moral crisis over sexuality and class formation in northern Kikuyuland is treated fully in Peterson's article on "revival" and "wordy women"; see Peterson (2001).

19. Thanks to Derek Peterson for this formulation on the character of early oaths.

20. For annotated copies of controversial *Mumenyereri* articles, see MAA 8/106, Intelligence, Security, Newspaper Reports, "Mumenyereri," KNA. "Borderline" cases were sent on to the attorney general for advice or prosecution. In court, "seditious intention" had to be proved in order to convict editors or printers. See also Press Liaison Officer H. C. E. Downes to Attorney General K. K. O'Connor, January 18, 1951, asking the attorney general to be lenient in a sedition case against Victor Wokabi, editor of another Kikuyu newspaper, *Muthamaki*, whose collaboration the government needed. AG 5/24 Seditious Publications, "Muthamaki," KNA.

21. *Daily Chronicle*, October 16, 1949.

22. See, however, Ogot (2003, 25–27) on laws of sedition and the persecution of the radical Indian newspaper publisher and editor Girdhari Vidyarthi by colonial authorities.

23. Editor to the Secretariat, December 21, 1939, MAA 2/5/4 Administration, Propaganda, Native Newspapers, KNA. On information strategies and activities of colonial officials, see Frederiksen 1998.

24. See a related discussion on the dangers of talk and the virtues of writing in Peterson (2001, 489).

25. "A Scheme to Improve the African Press of Kenya," 1951, AG 5/24, Seditious Publications, "Muthamaki," KNA.

26. Ibid.

27. In this case the reporter was jailed for six months, while the printer and Muoria were fined. See Scotton (1975, 33–34) and Muoria (1994, 55) for differing accounts of the episode.

28. In writing thus, he followed up on an earlier correspondent, N. Nyaga, who had written, "Didn't our witch doctor Mugo s/o Kibiru prophesy that there will come some people whose skin is like a crab's and who will worry you?" (*Mumenyereri*, June 1, 1950)

29. *Mumenyereri*, July 17, 1950, AG 5/23, Prosecution of Seditious Publications, KNA.

30. On Olenguruone, see Throup (1989, 120–138) and Kanogo (1987, 105–116).

31. A reference to the mythical founder of the Kikuyu nation, the wife of Gikuyu.

32. "One who is despised by the people is not despised by God"; Director of Intelligence and Security C. Passfield to Chief Native Commissioner P. Wyn Harris, June 23, 1948 that included a clipping from *Mumenyereri*'s June 14, 1948, issue, MAA 8/102 Intelligence and Security, Press Cuttings, Miscellaneous, KNA.

33. After leaving the army, where he had been a wireless operator, Gatu took courses in journalism at the Bellman Institute in London. He returned to Kenya in 1946 and offered his services to Henry Muoria "because he was the editor of the most important nationalist paper." Gatu later entered the church and became the moderator of the Presbyterian Church of East Africa. He is now retired. Interview, Nairobi, November 2002.

34. Director of Intelligence and Security C. Passfield to Chief Native Commissioner P. Wyn Harris, February 2, 1948, MAA 8/102 Intelligence, Security, Press Cuttings, Miscellaneous, KNA. This firm, owned by Zablon Oti of the Luo Thrift and Trading Corporation, and not Mumenyereri Printing Press, as Pugliese writes (2003, 97), was probably the first African-owned printing firm in Kenya.

35. Interview with Ruth Nuna Muoria, London, July 2000.

REFERENCES

Atieno Odhiambo, E. S. 1995. "The Formative Years, 1945–55." In *Decolonization and Independence in Kenya 1943–93,* ed. B. A. Ogot and W. R. Ochieng, 25–47. London: James Currey.

Barber, K. 2000. *The Generation of Plays: Yorùbá Popular Life in Theater.* Bloomington: Indiana University Press.

Berman, B., and J. Lonsdale. 1992. *Unhappy Valley. Book Two: Violence and Ethnicity.* London: James Currey.

Frederiksen, B. F. 1995. "Making Popular Culture from Above: Leisure in Nairobi 1945–60." In "Collected Seminar Papers," ed. L. Gunner. London: Institute of Commonwealth Studies. Revised in 1998, unpublished typescript.

Furedi, F. 1989. *The Mau Mau War in Perspective.* London: James Currey.

Gadsden, F. 1980. "The African Press in Kenya, 1945–52." *Journal of African History* 21, no. 4: 515–535.

Kanogo, T. 1987. *Squatters and the Roots of Mau Mau, 1905–63.* London: James Currey.

Kershaw, G. 1997. *Mau Mau from Below.* Oxford: James Currey.

Lonsdale, J. 1996 "'Listen while I read': The Orality of Christian Literacy in the Young Kenyatta's Making of the Kikuyu." In *Ethnicity in Africa: Roots, Meanings and Implications,* ed. L. de la Gorgendière, K. King, and S. Vaughan, 201–254. Edinburgh: Centre of African Studies.

———. 2002. "Contests of Time: Kikuyu Historiography, Old and New." In *A Place in the World: New Local Historiographies from Africa and South Asia,* ed. A. Harneit-Sievers, 17–53. Leiden: Brill.

———. 2003. "Authority, Gender and Violence: The War within Mau Mau's Fight for Land and Freedom." In *Mau Mau & Nationhood,* ed. E. S. Atieno Odhiambo and J. Lonsdale, 46–75. Oxford: James Currey.

Muoria, H. 1982. "The British and My Kikuyu Tribe." Unpublished Manuscript.

———. 1994. *I, The Gikuyu and the White Fury.* Nairobi: East African Educational Publishers.

Ngugi wa Thiong'o. 1983. *Barrel of a Pen: Resistance to Repression in Neo-Colonial Kenya.* London: New Beacon.

Ogot, B. A. 2003. "Mau Mau and Nationhood. The Untold Story." In *Mau Mau & Nationhood,* ed. E. S. Atieno Odhiambo and J. Lonsdale, 8–36. Oxford: James Currey.

Peterson, D. R. 2001. "Wordy Women: Gender Trouble and the Oral Politics of the East African Revival in Northern Gikuyuland." *Journal of African History* 32, no. 3: 469–489.

———. 2004. *Creative Writing: Translation, Bookkeeping, and the Work of Imagination in Colonial Kenya.* Portsmouth, N.H.: Heinemann.

Pugliese, C. 2003. "Complementary or Contending Nationhoods? Kikuyu Pamphlets and Songs." In *Mau Mau & Nationhood,* ed. E. S. Atieno Odhiambo and J. Lonsdale, 97–120. Oxford: James Currey.

Rosberg, C. G., and J. Nottingham. 1966. *The Myth of "Mau Mau": Nationalism in Kenya.* Nairobi: East African Publishing House.

Scotton, J. F. 1975. "Kenya's Maligned African Press." *Journalism Quarterly* 52 (Spring): 30–36.

Throup, D. W. 1989. *Economic & Social Origins of Mau Mau, 1945–53.* London: James Currey.

PUBLIC BUT PRIVATE: A TRANSFORMATIONAL READING OF THE MEMOIRS AND NEWSPAPER WRITINGS OF MERCY FFOULKES-CRABBE

12

Audrey Gadzekpo

Introduction

On November 28, 1936, the *Gold Coast Times* launched the "Women's Corner," a column authored by a pseudonymous "Gloria." This popular column was carried regularly in the inside pages of the newspaper and functioned as most women's columns did—as the primary locus of the feminization of discourse and the most effective outlet for women's voices in the predominantly male space of the early Gold Coast periodical. The first four articles in the "Women's Corner" had no byline, but beginning December 26, 1936, and lasting until 1940, it was "Gloria" who presided over the column.

Recent research has revealed that the authorial voice behind "Gloria" was Mercy Kwarley Quartey-Papafio (later Ffoulkes-Crabbe), the first indigenous woman to head a school in the Gold Coast (Gadzekpo 2001). The *Gold Coast Times* on occasion carried the text of public lectures given by Ffoulkes-Crabbe, but it maintained secrecy about the identity of "Gloria." Until recently, not even members of Ffoulkes-Crabbe's close family knew she had been a newspaper columnist. That revelation came in 2001, when her daughter Dorothy was prompted to look through her mother's old suitcase, which contained scores of papers and books, minutes of meetings, letters, and notebooks, which had been left untouched since Ffoulkes-Crabbe's death on June 14, 1974, at the age of 80. Perhaps the most exciting legacy she left behind were three nondescript exercise books that had served as her personal journals; in these, she had made copious notes on different subjects. Most revealing of the three notebooks was one that contained an entry "outing" her more discreet vocation as a newspaper columnist. Written in the top margin of a page were the following words: "Mrs. Ffoulkes-Crabbe was for a time a columnist under the penname of 'Gloria,' of the Women's Corner of the *Gold Coast Times,* published at Cape Coast."

The discovery of Ffoulkes-Crabbe's unpublished autobiographical material not only unlocked a major mystery about the identity behind the column but, more important, provokes questions about the ways in which women in early-twentieth-century Gold Coast used their literacy.

These two varied genres of text, one public, the other private but produced by the same person, direct us to interrogate the agency and processes that may have informed the production of women's public texts (in newspapers, for example) and their more private unpublished writings. The aim of this chapter, therefore, is to gain an understanding of the gendered conditions of textual production in the Gold Coast: How and in which ways were women able to self-present and express their literary competence? What prohibitions hampered their participation in Gold Coast print culture?

A fair amount of speculation and reconstruction is required to achieve this. We cannot assume that the contents of the personal notebooks of the author of "Women's Corner" are pretexts for her newspaper columns; clearly they are not. Still, we can conceive of such private literary material as furnishing us with markers or guides to the agent responsible for the construction of the pseudonymous public texts.

Mercy Ffoulkes-Crabbe and the Gold Coast Elite

Christianity and western education were the two forces that shaped and restructured social relations in the Gold Coast during the period of colonization. These forces influenced and provided the colonized African—both male and female—with economic and social opportunities, standards of "appropriate" behavior, and susceptibility to new ideas and ways of life. They were also the most important markers of elite status. Although small in number, the Gold Coast elite had power, prestige, privileges, and responsibilities that legitimized their speaking on behalf of the rest of the majority population. This group embodied values prized by their societies and standards of behavior that were emulated by less-educated members of their communities (Lloyd 1966). Access to elite status was open to those who could acquire education, income, and modern skills, although the early elite tended to be from Fanti, Ga, and sometimes Ewe coastal towns, areas that were the first to be pene-

Figure 12.1. Mercy Ffoulkes-Crabbe as a girl.

trated by westernization. However, anyone could aspire to become a *krakye* (a westernized gentleman) or an *awura* (a westernized lady).

Cape Coast, the quintessential Fanti town, was not only the locus of "Gloria's" newspaper but Mercy Ffoulkes-Crabbe's home for thirty-seven years. Ffoulkes-Crabbe was an epitome of Gold Coast female elitism and a visible pillar of Cape Coast modern society. She was born into the influential Quartey-Papafio Ga family on January 6, 1894, at Royal Lane, Cape Coast, and was the daughter of Benjamin William Kwatekwei Quartey-Papafio, an Edinburgh-trained medical doctor, and Hannah Maria Ekua Duncan, who, though not very educated, hailed from a prominent Cape Coast/Elmina family. Hannah Duncan had three children by Quartey-Papafio, who also married an educated elite Ga woman, Elizabeth Sabina Myers, with whom he had six children.

Ffoulkes-Crabbe projected "civilized femininity." Elite women like her imitated the lifestyle of upper-class Europeans in dress and in the social and leisure activities they engaged in. They read the "right books," gave musical recitals in their homes or in the homes of other prominent elites, organized soirees and dances which were strictly by invitation, and organized, founded, or belonged to self-improvement clubs. Most lived in urban centers such as Cape Coast or Accra and shopped in England.[1] Adelaide Casely Hayford, the Sierra Leonean wife of Joseph E. Casely Hayford, described Cape Coast, where she lived between 1904 and 1914, as "by far the best spot for an educated woman on the Gold Coast" (Cromwell 1986, 88).

Socially well connected as a result of her teaching and high-profile social engagements, Ffoulkes-Crabbe interacted with members of the European community and formed personal friendships with them, even though as a general rule the European community maintained a social distance from the African community, including the elite. For example, she was invited to attend the reception at the Castle when the Prince of Wales visited the Gold Coast in 1925, and when her daughter Dorothy got married, she included on her guest list the former governor, Sir Gordon Guggisberg, and his wife Decima and the former colonial secretary, Mr. Selwyn Clarke.[2] This telegraphed the height of elitism.

Ffoulkes-Crabbe's carefully constructed unpublished memoir, complemented by interviews and conversations with her daughter Dorothy, have provided much of the information about her life and predilections. Written in the third person but in Ffoulkes-Crabbe's handwriting,[3] the memoir details her achievements, her career, and her social activism. It also reveals some of the transformational processes such texts undergo, as betrayed in this case by different-colored ink and deletions, corrections, revisions, and additions in certain portions of the memoir. She used the top margins to insert forgotten accomplishments; for example, she appeared to have added: "Latin was her forte and she had several prizes, competing with boys. Her intelligence was above average"; "At Accra she served on several educational committees, sometimes she and her father served on the same ed. com"; and "Enquiry into prisons and made recommendations, Mrs. Ffoulkes was member of the committee of flood relief fund."

The conclusion that she went back to read through her private writings is bolstered by the fact that she appears to have overlooked two empty pages in the memoir section of her notebook, which she later filled with information that was unrelated to the personal narrative she was constructing. The insert was a "special message from the President of the Federation of Ghana women

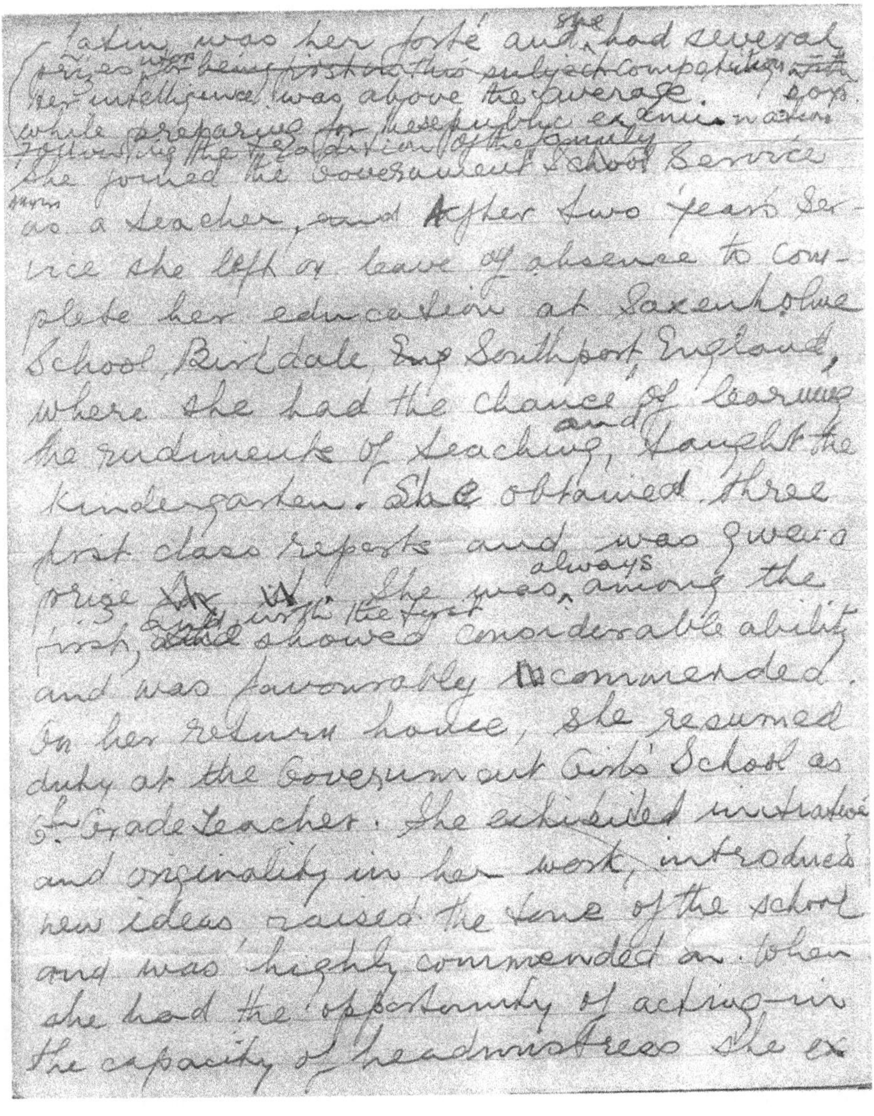
Latin was her forte and she had several
prizes won for being first in this subject competitions with
her intelligence was above the average.
while preparing for these public examinations
following the position of the family
She joined the Government School Service
as a teacher, and after two years service she left on leave of absence to complete her education at Saxenholme
School, Birkdale, Eng Southport, England,
where she had the chance of learning
the rudiments of teaching and taught the
kindergarten. She obtained three
first class reports and was given a
prize ... She was always among the
first, and with the first showed considerable ability
and was favourably commended.
On her return home, she resumed
duty at the Government Girls' School as
5th Grade teacher. She exhibited initiative
and originality in her work, introduced
new ideas, raised the tone of the school
and was highly commended ... When
she had the opportunity of acting in
the capacity of headmistress she ex

Figure 12.2. A page from Mercy Ffoulkes-Crabbe's journal.

in commemoration of the Birthday of the Prime Minister, Sept 21st 1958 to be published in a special souvenir by the Ghana press."[4] The ink used in drafting this speech was different from the ink used for the memoir but appears similar to the ink she used when she edited certain portions of her texts. The insertion itself indicates some disorder in her writing processes.

A transformational framework is helpful in understanding how and why Mercy's texts were constructed. All literary productions undergo transformations of one kind or another as part of the writing process. Therefore, every reading and writing practice in the disciplines of the humanities and social sciences is underpinned by transformational theory and strategy (Hodge 1990). Robert Hodge argues that literary texts have always been understood as transformations of reality or life in which the transformations reflect the biases or distortions of the agent or author. The question is What has changed to what? Who is doing the changing and why?

Because transformation theory is predicated on the belief that it is possible to discover the reasons and motives that exist in some form in the present and the past that shape the text, the edits in Ffoulkes-Crabbe's memoir are worthy of attention. They provide clues to the motives that may have informed their production and suggest that beyond the initial act of writing, Ffoulkes-Crabbe reviewed this privately constructed text and improved on it.

Opoku-Agyemang (1989, 5) describes autobiographical texts as the "literary embodiment of a person's way of seeing the world" and insists that "even the mistakes, lies, lapses in memory, ambiguities, confusions, disorderliness, missed ironies, conjectures, stupidities and perplexities . . . remain special and epiphanic." Clearly both her private memoirs and pseudonymous texts imply Ffoulkes-Crabbe's desire to self-represent and self-express. Their value lies not only in the information they provide but also in what was omitted, in the language of their telling, and in the secrecy surrounding their production. The fact that both the public and private forms of writing concealed her authorial identity (one through pseudonymity, the other by its very private nature and storage at the bottom of a suitcase) suggests the interplay between public and private texts, where the "public" persona is a kind of camouflage and the "private" memoir rehearses the public.

The language of their telling implies a self-consciousness of her public stature. As a prominent educator, Ffoulkes-Crabbe felt the need to go back at different times to read through what she had written, carefully editing for style, punctuation, and clarity as well as content. Perhaps she anticipated that a future reader might read her for didactic purposes or that a time might come when these private writings would become public; this latter reason may also explain the obvious exclusions in the text. There is no sense, and indeed no evidence to suggest, that in life Ffoulkes-Crabbe opened up her personal notebooks for public consumption. She had not treated her family to any readings from them, as some Gold Coast diarists tended to do,[5] and she does not appear to have even made them aware of their existence. Rather, she seems to have been largely successful in concealing her literary competence altogether. Yet the style of her private writings suggests that she secretly courted acknowledgement for her impressive public achievements. If we had to speculate on the motives that lay behind Ffoulkes-Crabbe's careful chronicle of accomplishments, it might be fair to say that she may simply have wanted to provide material for a well-informed obituary one day or wanted to remind her family of her public stature. On the other hand, her motives may have been more publicly directed: to serve as a role model for future generations of women or to sharpen her own and others' awareness of her communal role.

Her reticence in divulging only her public self in her private space may have been derived from a consciousness that she always had to maintain a respectable public persona and conform to etiquette, even in private moments. Perhaps "staying on message" also betrays an awareness that no matter how private, the act of writing itself is a public act, the purpose of which, even if ill-defined, attracts a public audience sooner or later.

Hodge likens exclusions in writing to etiquette that marks cultivated persons on formal occasions and maintains that these rules of politeness or etiquette exclude or displace many things that those concerned think and say and do. He insists that "polite people know exactly what isn't said or done in polite society, [even as] they continue to say and think such things in other more private domains" (Hodge 1999, 128). Etiquette forms part of the socialization process in all cultures. So, according to Hodge, etiquette acts as an example of the social control of behavior. In terms of transformational theory, polite behavior can be read into a transformed text whose meaning is derived partly from what it ostensibly represents and partly from the prior text from which it is transformationally derived. Transformed texts are ideological in prescribing "a version of society which is foregrounded on occasions of politeness" (129).

Ffoulkes-Crabbe conveys unwritten rules of etiquette in her memoir through the obvious exclusions in her accounts. The ideology inscribed in the politeness of her private text is partly conditioned by gender, partly by social status. The omissions in her text are not designed to deceive but rather to enable her, as a socially competent "civilized" lady, to remain in the domain of politeness. She maintains a zone of privacy in her public-style writings, marginalizing or excluding information that might have been considered too personal. These include her thoughts and feelings on such intimate matters as giving birth to a daughter at age 40 and her marriage to Edward Atkin Niven Ffoulkes-Crabbe,[6] a man eleven years her junior, nine years after the birth of their child.

Such juicy tidbits of information are not contained within the margins of any of her private texts. Her discretion is even more conspicuous when one reads two slightly different accounts of a twelve-day sea voyage she took to England on the *MV Accra* in December 1948 (which she recorded in two different notebooks). Although her descriptions of aspects of this journey are very detailed, she never once indicated that she was traveling with her fifteen-year-old daughter, even though the ostensible purpose of the trip was to take Dorothy to school in Falmouth, Cornwall.[7] The only clue perhaps is when she reports: "I turned down to my cabin fell on my knees and committed myself and my darling one into the hands of God who alone can protect us on the boundless ocean." Dorothy later explained that she was the "darling one."[8]

Rather than touching on her private life or the nationalist politics that formed an inescapable context of the times in which she lived, she selected for her memoir those aspects of her life which conformed to her public image as an efficient, apolitical civil servant in the field of education and an effective, indefatigable community organizer and social reformer. This is perhaps understandable; politics was a no-go area for well-bred women like her and thus an inappropriate subject for discussion, especially in a public space.

Ffoulkes-Crabbe notes that she started school at age 4 in Cape Coast but was sent to Accra to live with her father when she was 8 and attended both Government Girls' School and Accra Grammar, a school founded by her father and his family. She claimed that her "more than average" intelligence was discernable even then, for she obtained a third-class certificate from the College of Preceptors and the Junior Cambridge Certificate at the age of 16, the first girl in the whole of West Africa to hold this certificate. She started teaching in 1911, for which she was paid £25 a year. According to her daughter, at the height of her career as a headmistress, she would become one of the highest-paid women in the civil service, earning a princely annual salary of £600 before retiring in 1948.[9]

Ffoulkes-Crabbe's father was among the growing number of elite men who afforded their daughters some of the same facilities and privileges as their sons. She attended Saxenholme School in Birkdale, Southport, England (1913–1915) where, according to her memoir, "she had the chance of learning the rudiments of teaching, and taught kindergarten, obtained three first class reports and was given a prize." Teaching was considered the most appropriate employment for elite women then, so Dr. Quartey-Papafio channeled three of his daughters into that profession, where they excelled to become educators of note.[10] Dorothy said that her mother would have preferred to have studied medicine like her father but was never given the chance, a fact that remained a sore point throughout her life.

Education, particularly female education, became Ffoulkes-Crabbe's preoccupation. She regarded herself a pioneer in women's education in Ghana and highlighted in her memoir her role in transforming the Cape Coast Girls School, where she was headmistress from 1921 to 1948, into what she felt was an exemplary female educational facility. It is worth quoting extracts to illustrate how she perceived her contributions to educational development in Ghana. I have attempted to convey the transformational processes at work in her memoir. Strikeouts indicate that she crossed those words out; brackets {} are meant to signal that she amended the word or sentence after her original text was written. She also abbreviated certain words, using occasionally what appeared to be shorthand symbols: for example, "be-" for "became":

> At Cape Coast Government Girls' School she with consummate skill, foresight and considerable ability carried on the good work started by the former headmistress Miss Goring, a West Indian. She started morning classes for her teachers for the Teachers' External Examination, which they successfully passed. This work was continued for many years until Teachers Training College {for women} were established. Improvements went on rapidly . . .
>
> She introduced school uniforms {for the 1st time} for which were followed by other schools in Cape Coast. The press ~~was~~ viewed this new idea with disfavour (opining that ~~I~~ {she} was trying to turn the girls English). Eventually she was thanked by grateful parents. {Her} girls were taught the Maypole Dance for the 1st time. She held the 1st evening classes for women, which were going on successfully when the men kicked against the idea and it came to {an} end.
>
> The first Parent-Teacher Association was initiated by her and it be- a useful organ in promoting cooperation between the home and the school and helped considerably in carrying on the work in peaceful atmosphere. After several committee meetings of those in charge of girls' education she {was among those who} introduced for the first time domestic science into the school and helped greatly to popularise it. She first taught her teachers what was on the syllabus. A study of the condition of living of girls attending her school was extensively carried on in order to find out the real need of the girls and give practical lessons accordingly. Visits were made on several occasions to the homes, the market, etc, before drawing up syllabus and planning lessons.
>
> She introduced vernacular cards, charts ~~for~~ and pamphlets for use in her school when it was thought advisable to teach the mother tongue extensively in the primary schools. She had the school extended 3 times its usual size with separate new blocks for Domestic Science, a new playground for hockey and every facility any {modern} school could enjoy was provided. . . .

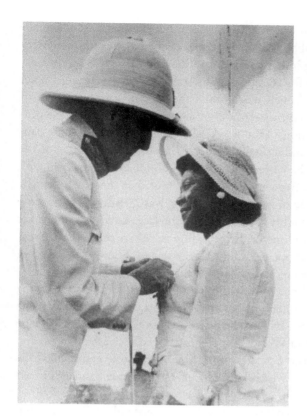

Figure 12.3. Mercy being decorated with a medal.

> Her school became a model school. She inculcated in her girls the princi-
> ples of Christianity and raised the moral tone of the school. Her teachers and
> girls always thanked her for this part of education.

Ffoulkes-Crabbe's memoir extends beyond the classroom, chronicling the
fact that she served on educational committees and boards, some of them in-
dicative of the pioneering role she played in her field. For example, she served
on the planning committee of Achimota School, a model coeducational institution established in 1927, and was on the board of governors of Adisadel College, a boys' secondary school first founded in 1910 by the Society for the
Propagation of the Gospel. When she retired after twenty-seven years as headmistress and more than thirty-five years as a teacher, she was awarded the
MBE (Member of the British Empire). She was also the recipient of the King
George V Jubilee Medal and the King George V Coronation Medal.

As a privileged woman who was conscious of her status as part of the talented tenth, Ffoulkes-Crabbe was very active socially and was intimately involved in effecting change in her community. She notes that she and her sisters formed the first club for young girls in Accra, called the Young Ladies Association, the object of which was to raise the tone of young women socially. The association staged concerts and other events and donated the proceeds to charitable institutions. Ffoulkes-Crabbe was also a Girl Guide captain and a commissioner and a member of the Executive Committee of the Girl Guide Association. She reorganized the Girl Guide unit connected with her school and added the Brownie Pack to that unit. For those services she was awarded the Certificate of Merit for Guiding, was mentioned in government dispatches, and was highly commended in the Legislative Assembly, her memoir notes. She was also one of the founding members of the Red Cross Society in Cape Coast and opened a unit in her school. She was involved in setting up the Young Women's Christian Association (YWCA) in Ghana.

She identified herself not only with charitable causes but also with the British war effort, noting in her writings that during the First World War she sent a pair of socks "knitted by herself for the 1st time," to Admiral Jellicoe and that during the Second World War she organized concerts, dances, and variety shows in aid of the Spitfire Fund. She was also a member of the Women's Voluntary Service, which knitted scarves and made bandages in aid of the war effort.

Ffoulkes-Crabbe was a civil servant and so was not politically active, but publicly she was engaged in Gold Coast sociopolitical life as a government nominee to the Cape Coast Town Council. After her retirement from the education service, her feminist activities became more political in tone. As national president of the Federation of Ghana Women, whose aims included the improvement of the economic and legal positions of women, she led two delegations to interview the southern Ghana chiefs at their joint provincial councils at Dodowah and the northern chiefs at their Northern Council as part of efforts to influence proposals regarding native customary marriages.

According to extensive notes she made in one of her notebooks (the same one containing the memoir), she represented the Federation of Ghana Women at the annual conference of the Commonwealth League for Women in London in 1954 and gave a speech that emphasized the federation's politicized social activism. She noted in her draft speech that since its inception the federation had, among other activities, called for teachers' strikes "when all attempts [at negotiation] had proved abortive" and mounted an attack on poor and inadequate housing which brought representatives of the federation onto a committee on housing. The federation also raised the issues of babies in prisons, overcrowding in mental hospitals, malnutrition, and the provision of school canteens; called for the lowering of school fees; was involved in the Marriage Ordinance Council and registration of native customary marriages; and helped run vocational training centers for girls.

The exercise book, which contained the accounts of Ffoulkes-Crabbe's life and achievements, also contained notes on other subjects and the drafts of some of her speeches and public lectures. Two other notebooks, one titled "articles and impressions," the other in such a tattered state it is difficult to determine if it too had a title, echoed some of these subjects. It is hard to tell when most of the writings took place. Except for a few articles, the author fails to date her entries. It can be surmised however, that most of the personal writings mentioned here probably occurred in the 1950s, when Ffoulkes-Crabbe had retired from the civil service and had the time and inclination to look back on her life. The draft of her speech to the Commonwealth League for Women in 1954 was written in pencil and preceded the memoir entry, which suggests that she may have written the memoir after that time.

These various fragments of writing reflect what she considered important and worthy of noting down—articles on education, women's employment, religion, marriage, social change, and social activism. Similar themes were generated by "Gloria" in the Women's Corner of the *Gold Coast Times*, indicating a continuation of discourses between Ffoulkes-Crabbe's private and public writings. It is reasonable to assume that these were also discussions that resonated with elite women in the period in which "Gloria" was writing and throughout the era in which Mercy Ffoulkes-Crabbe lived.

"Gloria" and Gold Coast Print Culture

"Gloria" was constructed as a religious, morally upright, articulate Ghanaian woman who possessed a sound education and was knowledgeable on a broad range of subjects. This positioning enabled her to instruct members of her sex on topics she considered important and to dutifully propagate the Victorian values she had imbibed to her kind and to other "sisters" who were aspiring to elite status. "Women's Corner" by "Gloria" is therefore revelatory of the normative role newspapers played in the lives of the women these columns targeted and the manner in which the privileged women who presided over them set the agenda and policed the boundaries of social discourse.

The *Gold Coast Times*, which provided the platform for Gloria's didactic messages to her fellow women, belongs to that generation of nationalistic newspapers that used the written word to chronicle and register dissatisfaction with colonial policies and actions and assert an emerging national identity. From the late nineteenth century right up to the period of independence in 1957, such newspapers were about the only platform available to the educated African for any kind of social debate or exchange of ideas on national issues. Launched in Cape Coast on February 3, 1923, the weekly *Gold Coast Times* became a very visible public space that hosted a heterogeneity of sociopolitical discourses, many of them authored by notable contributors. It was published and edited by Chief Sakyiama, a well-connected newspaper personality, until his death in August 1934. Following Sakyiama's death, the paper went through some difficulty and suspended publication for a few months. The introduction of the "Women's Corner" formed part of the paper's reorganization strategy and attempt to attract a wider readership.

It is difficult to get a true sense of "Gloria's" readership and, for that matter, the size of the Gold Coast textual community. However, the Gold Coast Colony *Blue Book* confirms suspicions that patronage was rather low for many newspapers. So although it claimed in advertisements in 1936 to circulate in Nigeria and Ivory Coast, and although it was by 1938 the only weekly in Cape Coast (the intellectual center and former administrative capital of the Gold Coast), the *Gold Coast Times* had a circulation of only 550 copies per print run.[11]

The ability to buy and read newspapers is, of course, tied to literacy and financial capability. At a time when the population of the Gold Coast was made up of 3,527,483 Africans and 3,182 non-Africans,[12] school attendance in 1938 was as follows: 42,995 males in primary school as against 14,534 females, 919 males in secondary school as against 27 females, and 378 males in teacher-training colleges as against 163 females (Crabtree 1950). Faced with such realities, newspapers struggled to keep afloat by being open and accommodating about contributions, recognizing that with such a small community of readers the distance between the producers of the text and the consumers of the text had to be bridged. They actively solicited readers and encouraged them to become contributors. The *Gold Coast Leader*, for example, encouraged all "classes" to cut out excuses of "can't write, don't have good grammar, etc." and to "just write and leave the correcting" to the paper.[13]

Typically, therefore, both the well-educated and those who aspired to that status could display their literacy through newspaper contributions, often in the form of letters to the editor. Judging from attribution, it would appear that few women did so, especially before the first half of the twentieth century.

This is understandable; women's low educational status compared with that of men was the likely reason they rarely engaged in press activity. Oyewumi (1997) argues that colonization had a negative impact on women and that women's inferiority largely resulted from their disadvantaged position in the educational system. Males were the targets of missionary education, while women's education was ancillary, aimed at producing mothers who would be the foundation of Christian families.

According to Oyewumi, the colonial process was "sex-differentiated insofar as the colonizers were male and used gender identity to determine policy" (122). The colonial hierarchy, which was based on race and gender relations, placed European men at the top, European women next, and then African men. At the bottom of that hierarchy was the African woman. African women were largely excluded from the newly created colonial public sphere.

Oyewumi identifies several spheres that operated during the colonial period: the gender-based division of males into a public sphere and females into a private sphere, which was in keeping with what largely pertained in Europe; the primordial public sphere based on existing groupings, sentiments, and activities; and the civic public sphere which was associated with the colonial administration and based on civil structures. The primordial realm existed orally and in social practice alongside, but subordinated to, the newer civic public realm.

It is within this civic public construct that the patriarchal nature of the colonial state was visibly manifested. The nature of this sphere largely contributed to the silencing of women within public discourses. Historically, women were absent from acts of public expression and self-representation. Cameron uses the idea of silence to underscore the fact that "even where it seems women could participate if they chose to, the conditions under which they are obliged to live their lives may make this a difficult or dangerous choice" (1998, 3). Silence, according to Cameron, could also mean imposed self-censoring because of "fear of being ridiculed, attacked or ignored"—perhaps another plausible reason for Ffoulkes-Crabbe's secrecy about her writing. In a 1929 article, Virginia Woolf alluded to the material and social constraints on women who might have aspired to write, even privileged and relatively well-educated women (Woolf 1998). Others (Easely 2000) have suggested that in the past and in certain cultures, such as Victorian England, women who wrote were considered transgressors because public writing, even the autobiographical, was considered beyond the scope of women and outside their purview. If we reflect on the status of female authorship in these other societies, therefore, we can understand why women generally, even elite women such as Ffoulkes-Crabbe, were reticent about publicly displaying their literary abilities.

In the space of the male-oriented newspaper especially, the only hospitable areas allotted women were the gendered spaces such as "Gloria's" "Women's Corner," which were largely constructed as an extension of the private sphere to which women had been relegated. Women's columns provided the female elite in the Gold Coast with opportunities to speak for themselves, share feminine experiences invested with the authority of their gender (Shevelow 1989), and grapple with some of the fundamental issues confronting them in a society undergoing transformation. In the Gold Coast, such columns were instrumental in forming a female reading audience organized around the representation of women as readers, writing subjects, and textual figures situated within a reformist discourse designed to instruct and entertain them (Beetham 1996). These feminized spaces engaged directly with readers on specific topics in their lives by offering to show them how to improve themselves. The tendency of Gold Coast newspapers, even those that were fiercely nationalistic, to hold up elite (Victorian, colonial) values as the hallmark of progressive, civilized people is manifest in the kinds of discourses that were found in women's columns. They articulated values to which Africans, including the less-educated, were expected to aspire. In this sense this was not a class-exclusive inward-looking discourse but a discourse marked by the expectation that it would filter into a wider and more popular public.

While women's columns provided an important and consistent discursive space for women, they also delineated the process of simultaneous liberation and restriction that marked women's engagement with print culture and with the colonially constituted public space. Conventions and constraints that guided such spaces were well established and were transported from Europe. The preferred articles for women's columns were those on fashion, female society, dancing, musical concerts, children and children's education, the home and the kitchen, literature, books, religion, marketing, dressmaking, and so forth; subjects "in which the cultured lady of fashion is interested" (*Times of West Africa*, March 12, 1934). Political articles were considered inappropriate unless they were "moderately toned in harmony with the polite taste of women" (ibid.).

Part of the purpose of the public writings of "highly cultured ladies"[14] such as Ffoulkes-Crabbe was to "instruct scholars to read";[15] this way, a "love for reading good and instructive books may be instilled in them."[16] "Gloria" exerted power over her readers by highlighting certain concerns and sidelining others. Her position as the author of a woman's column enabled her to confer status on some issues, recommend certain feminine interests, validate certain feminine experiences, advocate a particular course of action, and recommend ways that women could achieve prescribed aims and goals. Her articles were aspirational for non-elite women who hoped to aspire to elite status and confirmatory for elite women who already understood "the rules."

"Gloria" functioned as a one-woman debating team, often setting up gendered ethical or social dilemmas that allowed her to explore a range of social discourses. Her subject matter betrayed the attitudes of elite women toward transformations in Gold Coast society in the 1930s and 1940s. Typically, headlines in the "Women's Corner" would pose questions which set the agenda for the column's discourse: "Which is more suitable for the African woman, marriage according to the native or the English form?"[17] "Wealth and love: which is the bulwark of marriage?"[18] "Is the exposure of a lady's calf in a public street respectful?"[19] "What is the best profession for a woman?"[20] "Marriage and career which is preferred by the average young woman?"[21] "Can a woman smoke and drink?"[22] "Can a dancing woman make a good wife?"[23] "If women were rulers how would the world look like?"[24] "The place of our illiterate women in our native social life."[25] "Should our young women adopt the native dress in place of the frock?"[26] "Are higher mathematics a useful study for girls?"[27]

Some of these themes deserve close scrutiny, and the following sections examine the nature of these discourses in more detail, drawing similarities between them and the themes in the personal writings of Mercy Ffoulkes-Crabbe.

Discourse on Education and Literacy

We have already noted that elitism was predicated on acquiring a western education and upgrading literacy skills in order to achieve social status. Women's columns joined the crusade for education and initiated debate on the quality and type of education available in the colony. In the nineteenth to early twentieth centuries especially, newspapers advocated the kind of education which would prepare girls for a cultured companionate marriage and shape them to become good intelligent mothers and wives to the benefit of the nation. Ideally, a wife was to possess a sufficiently cultivated mind to be able to enter into agreeable and intelligent conversation with her husband so that he would find pleasure in being at home, but she should not be so educated as to have a mind and opinions of her own. Her education was to be geared toward a superficial cultivation, primarily of the arts, and not toward turning her into an expert or training her for a career (see Charvet 1982, 14).

Women were thus encouraged to draw their reading preferences from material that would cultivate and edify their minds—the Bible, classical literature, fashion magazines, and, if they could lay hands on them, British newspapers. Ffoulkes-Crabbe's references to texts were predictable for her generation—the Bible, English classics such as Shakespeare, *The Pilgrim's Progress*, and books by Marie Corelli, the best-selling British author whose spiritual and didactic novels were immensely popular among the newly formed literate group in the Gold Coast in the 1920s and 1930s (Newell 2002). These were the kinds of titles that made up her personal library and that informed "Gloria's" recommended literature. So, for example, in one of her columns titled "What books should a woman read?" "Gloria" argued that literature should be aimed at enriching the mind, improving the heart, and adding to a woman's happiness and the usefulness of her life. She instructed women to read *Aesop's Fables, Arabian Nights, Robinson Crusoe, Pilgrim's Progress, Don Quixote, The Vicar of Wakefield*, Shakespeare's plays, Milton's *Paradise Lost*, and Pope's *Essay on Man* alongside the Bible and histories of England, America, and the Gold Coast and other African countries.[28]

Reading was also for practical purposes, as reflected in an entry in one of Ffoulkes-Crabbe's notebooks:

> The farmer must read of new ideas about farming, the carpenter about carpentry, the housewife about housewifery. They must all read about their community and its government. They must read about the outside world too. [There must be] mass enlightenment of the public such as inculcating in them the necessity of preventing of disease and keeping healthy and teaching the truth about current affairs.

Commenting further on the need and growing desire for education in the Gold Coast in the second quarter of the twentieth century, she explained that "the masses wish to learn English because without English they cannot obtain their driving licenses or find jobs as cooks, steward boys, gardeners, messengers & so on. English has come to have economic value and importance for our people."

"Gloria" also adopted a functional approach to literacy, arguing that women should seek knowledge about food, water, air, plants, beasts, birds, insects, diet and hygiene, agriculture, and philosophy. The columnist also recommended narratives of real adventures in foreign lands, travel books, and stories of legends and voyages which, according to her, were bound to contain useful information. Her preference for histories, she revealed, was predicated on a belief that "the lives of eminent divines may be read with much profit" and because "it will give a desire to learn something about great men who fig-ure in history."[29] Might this desire to learn from the lives of great men (and women) have motivated Ffoulkes-Crabbe to write her memoir?

As the twentieth century wrought more social change, attitudes toward education for girls, a topic that had been viewed with considerable reservation in the past, began to change as well. Education was perceived as the means of improving both the social and economic status of women. In an address she delivered at her farewell party when she retired from the Government Girls' School in 1948, Ffoulkes-Crabbe noted that change, commenting that when she first started teaching, "education of women was then still looked upon with suspicion," but on the threshold of retirement, "what a wonderful change and vast improvement women have today made in education." She observed that women could now be found in almost every business, "trying to put their strength against men and claim their independence," and was glad she had been a part of that change.

In one of her columns, "Gloria" too remarked on how education had en-hanced the career opportunities of women in teaching, hospital nursing, mid-wifery, telephony, and dressmaking. "Gloria" went on to speculate on whether "our country [would] be proud of her professional women, journalists, au-thors, musicians, politicians, etc." if women were given the "advantage of higher education."[30]

Discourse on Religion

Christianity and colonialism came hand in hand, and for many of the early converts there was little differentiation between the Christian missions and the colonial power structures (Assimeng 1989). Christianity conspired with colonialism to destabilize traditional economic, social, and political hier-archies as it prescribed new values for the colonized convert. As an important marker of elitism, educated Ghanaians strove to lead good moral lives as di-rected by the strictures of the Christian religion. Mercy Ffoulkes-Crabbe was a devout Christian—an Anglican who later in life became a Christian Scien-tist and who very early on in life committed her life to God. She claimed in her private writings to have had a religious epiphany and to have waged a constant battle "with the world, the flesh and the devil." Her greatest struggle, according to her, was "with the Flesh. It is the ugliest of the three sins . . . of mankind."

It is clear from conversations with her daughter Dorothy and from the several drafts of sermons and lectures in her personal notebooks—for the fiftieth anniversary of the African Methodist Episcopal Zion Church in Cape Coast, at the harvest festival of the All Saints Church at Adabraka in Accra on October 1, 1950, to the women's fellowship of the Parish Church in Falmouth England, on March 31, 1949, and so forth—that she tried very hard to live her faith, even if there were moments when she fell off her religious and moral pedestal.

The pervasive influence of Christianity in her life is reflected not only in her personal writings but also in the discourses "Gloria" introduced into her column. She questioned why Christians were inconsistent in their lives[31] and preached a sermon on Christian living and what Christianity had done for women.[32] She pondered, "Why does the Bible appear contradictory?"[33] "Gloria's" discourses positioned women in the role ascribed them by Christian doctrine. She considered religion to be more natural to women and pronounced women to be more "Godlike" than men.[34] For this reason, she preached a Victorian notion of a woman's place in society, arguing that it was the woman who drew family to religion, "which is the crowning grace of motherhood," and that failure to grasp this "fundamental truth" meant that the world would be made poorer by women's existence. "In matter of moral and spiritual oversight," declared "Gloria," the woman "stands alone."[35] Not surprisingly, "Gloria" conceived of the home as a "woman's kingdom. She is queen, creator and cherisher of family without whom man degenerates."[36]

Marriage

Such views, of course, also influenced her notions of marriage. Christian prescriptions on marriage, coupled with colonial attempts to regulate marriage through ordinances, posed a serious challenge to traditional forms of contracting marriage. The churches expected and pressured their converts to adopt monogamy along with western ideas of companionate marriage and to reject polygyny as primitive, immoral, and denigrating to women. The Marriage Ordinance of 1884 attempted to define and codify legitimate forms of marriage and structure laws on inheritance, divorce, and adultery.

Especially because the lifestyles of the elite were predicated on the strictures of Christianity and colonialism, they, rather than the majority population, were caught up in the debates over such colonial policies as marriage. And as elite women continued to feel the pressure to contract marriages under the Marriage Ordinance, the "marriage question" became of paramount importance in their private and public discourses. Ffoulkes-Crabbe's notes suggest that she played an active part in structuring debates on marriage and in attempts to resolve the conflicts between traditional (or native) marriage and ordinance (or Christian) marriage.

"Gloria" also duly explored what was "more suitable for the African woman—marriage according to the native, or the English form?"[37] And while she leaves her readers to decide for themselves, she notes in relation to native marriage disadvantages such as the fact that the "wife rarely resides in the same home with her husband, but only carries food to him daily and ministers to his desires" and the fact that "the husband can contract other marriages, can divorce the wife on the ground of adultery, but the wife cannot enforce divorce or discontinue marriage on the ground of her husband's adultery or on his marrying more wives, though she has a right to the protection of her husband."[38]

Marriage narratives were also linked to discourses on education. Thus, in some of her columns "Gloria" pondered whether educated men ought to marry uneducated women in the first place and painted an apocalyptic picture of an illiterate woman "fortunate" enough to marry an educated man and live in a monogamous home:[39]

> Only in very exceptional cases can such a wife instinctively fill her place as homemaker. She cannot be a companion or real help mate of her husband whose ideas may be infinitely higher than hers may and whose outlook on life may be broad and comprehensive. . . . As a mother, she has harder problems to solve. Her children may be educated and have invariably imbibed notions that are quite foreign to her way of thinking; and as she may not see eye to eye with them, she concludes they are rebellious.

Her position on marriage and women was clinched in a column in which she staged one of her recognizable gender debates: "Would it be consistent with natural law for a woman to be independent of man?" Here she pronounced that "natural law condemns such a situation and no human being has courage enough to advance such views" because woman is supposed to be "helpmate" to man and "whatever civilisation can make a woman her dependence on man will remain unshaken! God has made it so."[40]

Transformations of Reality

Were such fixed positions submitted to in real life? Not necessarily. Extra-textual evidence suggests that far from abiding by the strict Victorian mores promoted in their public presentations, elite women subverted and quietly challenged the status quo in their personal lives without suffering much social opprobrium. For women such as Ffoulkes-Crabbe, the very fact of their public roles as social commentators and career women made them visible actors in the public domain, placed demands on their time, and made it difficult for them to play the role of the ideal companionate wife. Ffoulkes-Crabbe's memoir and other private writings attest to a very full public life of social activism and professional and administrative responsibilities, including that of town counsellor. And even if "Gloria" thought a woman's "dependence on man will remain unshaken," Ffoulkes-Crabbe took no steps to marry until she was 49 years old. More telling of the disconnect between the public script and the private reality was the fact that Ffoulkes-Crabbe was and remained an unwed mother for nine years, following the birth of her daughter on January 1, 1934. Dorothy was left in Accra to be nursed by her aunt a few weeks after she was born, while her mother went back to Cape Coast and pretended nothing had happened. It wasn't until she was eighteen months old that Dorothy, together with two young cousins, joined her mother in Cape Coast.[41]

On a certain level one can argue that Mercy was not unaccustomed to concealment. After all, she remained hidden as "Gloria" throughout her lifetime. But her secrecy about the birth of her daughter was also necessitated by colonial civil service rules prescribing morals and private behavior. Even when general orders governing the civil and public services were revised in the relatively more liberal 1950s, women's terms of employment within the service remained severely constrained by their gender. The rules stipulated, for example,

> A woman officer whose duties are concerned with or are liable to be concerned with teaching or inspection in primary, middle or secondary schools or training colleges, who is not married, or who has not reported her marriage, must, if she becomes pregnant, report her pregnancy. She will then be required by her Head of Department to resign, or to retire if she is eligible for a retiring award, unless her special qualifications or experience make it in the interests of the Service to retain her.[42]

Despite these strict regulations, Ffoulkes-Crabbe retained her job and her status in polite Gold Coast society. Colonial administrators appeared reluctant to fully investigate rumors that she was a single mother,[43] and she continued, despite the circumstances of her personal life, to enjoy respect as a role model for Gold Coast women. The explanation for this contradiction lies partly in the fact that the Gold Coast elite "faced two ways" (Gocking 1999). Mercy's father was a typical example. Notwithstanding his elite status as the first Ghanaian doctor in the Gold Coast civil service and his Christian religious beliefs, he lived a polygamous life, having never left his first wife, to whom he was traditionally married, before contracting an ordinance marriage with his more socially acceptable educated wife. With one foot firmly planted in conservative western society and the other still rooted in traditional society, therefore, it was possible for Mercy Ffoulkes-Crabbe to break from religious strictures and decouple motherhood from wifehood, at least for a while, because of the importance attached to procreation in the African cultural context. The Cape Coast traditional society to which she belonged would have frowned on her childlessness and would have insisted that contrary to her religious and Victorian western beliefs, at nearly 40 years of age, childbearing had to outweigh all other concerns. Such prevailing views, even among the educated elite, would have also undercut any stigma attached to having children outside the institution of marriage. For Ffoulkes-Crabbe, the question posed by "Gloria"—"a penniless woman with a child, a childless woman with money, who is happier?"[44]—was not just hypothetical.

In sum, given the realities of Ffoulkes-Crabbe's private life versus the ideologies inscribed in her literary agency, it would appear that a major function of both her public and private writings was to script and promote an image of Gold Coast womanhood within "the context of several particularly feminine characteristics and needs which required a regulatory and protective response" (to co-opt Shevelow 1989, 52). The script need not have mirrored reality. As adjudicator of a gendered space and the epitome of "civilized femininity" Ffoulkes-Crabbe's primary task, and therefore the motive behind her writings, was to offer her guidance as part of a larger agenda of improving women's social and educational status (ibid.). It was a mission she fulfilled in a manner that masked her self-presentation in both her public and private texts; an approach that undoubtedly conformed to the expectations of both elite and non-elite Ghanaians.

NOTES

1. Interview with Agnes Sampson (93 years old), February 6, 1999, Cape Coast; interview with Marion Odamtten (91 years old) January 31, 2001, Accra; interview with Dorothy Ffoulkes-Crabbe, February 3, 2001, Accra.

2. In conversations with Dorothy Ffoulkes-Crabbe, November and December 2002, she revealed that they attended her wedding.

3. Dorothy Ffoulkes-Crabbe confirmed that it was her mother's handwriting in an interview on February 3, 2001.

4. Mercy Ffoulkes-Crabbe was a founding member and president of the Federation of Ghana Women, which was formed in July 1953.

5. See Stephan Miescher's contribution in this book

6. He became the first African clerk of the Legislative Assembly.

7. Dorothy Ffoulkes-Crabbe confirms that she was on the journey.

8. Interview with Dorothy Ffoulkes-Crabbe, November 2002, Accra.

9. Ibid.

10. Two of Mercy's sisters, Grace and Ruby, were teachers of renown also. Ruby was decorated with the Grand Medal (Civil Division) in 1970 and awarded an honorary doctorate by the University of Cape Coast in 1974 in recognition of her contribution to educational development in Ghana (Vieta 1999, 342–344). Though she is at times referred to as the first Ghanaian headmistress, that distinction belongs to her sister Mercy.

11. Gold Coast, *Blue Book* (Accra: Government Printing Office, 1935).

12. Ibid.

13. *Gold Coast Leader*, July 5, 1902.

14. *Gold Coast Times*, September 18, 1937.

15. Ibid.

16. Ibid.

17. *Gold Coast Times*, January 30, 1937.

18. *Gold Coast Times*, January 29, 1938.

19. *Gold Coast Times*, June 6, 1937.

20. *Gold Coast Times*, June 12, 1937.

21. *Gold Coast Times*, January 16, 1937.

22. *Gold Coast Times*, January 15, 1938.

23. *Gold Coast Times*, July 9, 1938.

24. *Gold Coast Times*, March 6, 1937.

25. *Gold Coast Times*, March 13, 1937.

26. *Gold Coast Times*, March 20, 1937.

27. *Gold Coast Times*, April 3, 1937.

28. *Gold Coast Times*, January 6, 1940.

29. Ibid.

30. *Gold Coast Times*, November 28, 1936.

31. *Gold Coast Times*, December 3, 1938.

32. *Gold Coast Times*, December 4, 1937.

33. *Gold Coast Times*, December 23, 1938.

34. *Gold Coast Times*, May 15, 1937.

35. *Gold Coast Times*, December 12, 1936.

36. Ibid.

37. *Gold Coast Times*, January 30, 1937.

38. Ibid.

39. *Gold Coast Times*, March 13, 1937.

40. *Gold Coast Times*, April 17, 1937.

41. Conversations with Dorothy Ffoulkes-Crabbe, November 2002.

42. Gold Coast General Orders 265 (i).

43. Conversations with Dorothy Ffoulkes-Crabbe, February 2001 and November and December 2002, Accra.

44. *Gold Coast Times*, August 14, 1937.

BIBLIOGRAPHY

Assimeng, Max. 1989. *Religion and Social Change in West Africa.* Accra: Ghana Universities Press.

Beetham, Margaret. 1996. *A Magazine of Her Own? Domesticity and Desire in the Woman's Magazine: 1800–1914.* London: Routledge.

Cameron, Deborah. 1998. "Introduction." In *The Feminist Critique of Language: A Reader,* ed. Deborah Cameron. 2nd ed. London: Routledge.

Charvet, John. 1982. *Feminism: Modern Ideologies.* London: J. M. Dent & Sons Ltd.

Crabtree, Alice. 1950. "Marriage and Family Life among the Educated Africans in the Urban Areas of the Gold Coast." M.Sc. diss., University of London.

Cromwell, Adelaide. 1986. *An African Victorian Feminist: The Life and Times of Adelaide Smith Casely Hayford, 1868–1960.* London: Frank Cass & Co. Ltd.

Easley, Alexis. 2000. "Authorship, Gender and Power in Victorian Culture: Harriet Martineau and the Periodical Press." In *Nineteenth-Century Media and the Construction of Identities,* ed. Laurel Brake, Bill Bell, and David Finkelstein. Hampshire: Palgrave.

Gadzekpo, Audrey. 2001. "Women's Engagement with Gold Coast Print Culture: From 1857 to 1957." Ph.D. thesis, University of Birmingham.

Gocking, Roger. 1999. *Facing Two Ways: Ghana's Coastal Communities under Colonial Rule.* Lanham, Md.: University Press of America.

Hodge, Robert. 1990. *Literature as Discourse: Textual Strategies in English and History.* Cambridge: Polity Press.

Lloyd, P. C. 1966. "Introduction." In *The New Elites of Tropical Africa: Studies Presented and Discussed at the Sixth International African Seminar at the University of Ibadan, Nigeria, July 1964,* ed. P. C. Lloyd. London: Oxford University Press.

Newell, Stephanie. 2002. *Literary Culture in Colonial Ghana: "How to Play the Game of Life."* Manchester: Manchester University Press.

Opoku-Agyemang, Kwadwo. 1989. "African Autobiography and Literary Theory." *Asemka: A Literary Journal of the University of Cape Coast* 6 (September).

Oyewumi, Oyeronke. 1997. *The Invention of Women: Making an African Sense of Western Gender Discourses.* Minneapolis: University of Minnesota Press.

Shevelow, Kathryn. 1989. *Women and Print Culture: The Construction of Femininity in the Early Periodical.* London: Routledge.

Vieta, Kojo T. 1999. *The Flagbearers of Ghana: Profiles of One Hundred Distinguished Ghanaians.* Vol. 1. Accra: Ena Publications.

Woolf, Virginia. 1998. "Women and Fiction." In *The Feminist Critique of Language: A Reader,* ed. Deborah Cameron. 2nd ed. London: Routledge.

Innovation, Cultural Editing, and the Emergence of New Genres

PART THREE

Innovation, Cultural Editing, and the Emergence of New Genres

WRITING, READING, AND PRINTING DEATH: OBITUARIES AND COMMEMORATION IN ASANTE

13

T. C. McCaskie

"The fashion of making death notices"

In 1939, J. W. Tsiboe founded the Abura Printing Works in Kumasi to publish his newly launched *Ashanti Pioneer* newspaper.[1] He intended only to report news of the war against Hitler, but the newspaper was a success and it soon expanded and diversified. After 1945 it embraced the rising postwar demand for self-government. Tsiboe, his formidable wife, and his editorial staff were all supporters of accelerated decolonization.[2] Krobo Edusei, who was employed at the Abura Printing Works, emerged as the best-known anticolonial activist in Kumasi. In 1948, he led Asante participation in the Gold Coast "riots" against the British. These happenings shook the colonial administration, which decided that Tsiboe's business was a hotbed of agitation. Special Branch police officers searched his premises for subversive literature. They found nothing compromising, but the police made a full list of the contents of Tsiboe's warehouse and print shop. At the former, an outbuilding was found to contain upward of 200 reams of blank paper. Paper was still subject to wartime rationing, and the police asked Tsiboe to produce a government receipt showing his legal title to this stockpile. He could not and said he had acquired it piecemeal over the years. He was then asked what it was for, since cut paper was of no use for roll-printed newspapers. He claimed it was much in demand for mimeographing or printing multiple copies of single-sheet obituaries.

This reply perplexed the Chief Commissioner of Asante when he read the police report. He asked C. E. Osei of the Asantehene's administration for

341

elucidation. Osei stated that Tsiboe's claim was probably true and gave the following explanation.

> During the past ten years or thereabouts the fashion of making death notices has come into vogue in Kumasi as in every town all about Ashanti. No one who dies and is a member in good standing of e.g. Literary or Debating Society or other Association of any sort will pass over without the family and friends giving a notice of said sad event. A man who is a businessman such as contractor, lorry owner, cocoa buyer, storekeeper etc. will receive an equal tribute. Chiefs and Royal Families started this fashion in copying of Nana Prempeh [Asantehene Agyeman Prempeh] of blessed memory when he went to meet his Maker [in 1931]. Nana's life and times as also the grand funeral were put into the first death notice to be written down. You know how Ashanti people from up on high to low always think of making a grand funeral to impress everyone. Now people say they want to make the Wuhu Dawerebu [i.e., *owu ho dawurabo*, lit. "striking the gong-gong of death"; i.e., a death notice, an obituary] to tell everyone both near and far—"Come and look who we are burying today—it is Somebody and we too who are making the Funeral are also Somebody." Death notice is sent all around to show this thing. It is a big expense but a family of even a village man will do it if they are able.[3]

This chapter is about "the fashion of making death notices" in twentieth-century Asante. Elsewhere I have written extensively on colonial modernity in Asante, but let me begin by saying a little about my approach and intention here.[4] All sources on Asante's past and present show the importance of death and the commemorative rituals attendant upon it. Death was and is a social event, conceived of and observed as something that happens to an individual person, but only within the contexts of family (ancestry and posterity as well as the living) and community. In the Asante view, nobody should ever die alone: *owuo atwede wo ho yi se na bako nforo o* ("no one climbs up death's ladder on their own"). Thus, numerous social rituals were brought into being throughout historical time to mark Asante death—*ahoda da* (lying in state), *apese* (keeping wake), *afunsoa* (carrying the corpse), *owuasore* (funeral rites), *aye keseɛpa* (public mourning), *afunsie* (burial), *aseda* (thanksgiving), *nnawotwe da* (eight-day custom), *adaduanan* (forty-day custom), *afehyia* (one-year custom), and others. In the twentieth century, some of these were abandoned or otherwise fell into disuse, while others were adapted to meet changing (often Christian) circumstances. Be that as it may, ethnographers have reported an accelerated innovation and elaboration in twentieth-century Asante funeral customs. Driven onward by the historical imperative of "making a grand funeral to impress everyone," as described by Osei in 1948, Asante people today often spend themselves into massive debt on baroque obsequies so as to assert their status and that of their kin in comparison with others. This sort of competitive display (*mpoatwa*) has deep historical roots, but over the last 100 years capitalist modernity has supplied an ever-growing array of opportunities for people to substantiate comparative advantage. In brief, twentieth-century funerals have become the most important public arena for proclaiming such an advantage (or for pretending to it), by exhibiting a realized modernist selfhood on its own terms through extravagant displays of consumerist novelty, taste, and consumption. Such performances are directed at peers and neighbors and now exist at every level of Asante society. They also commonly reference history in order to make claims upon it. "Now many people inflate their ancestry by puffing themselves up at the funeral of one of their relatives," declared Butuakwa stool-holder Baffour Osei Akoto in 1998. "The deceased," he continued, "is overlooked while the living strut all about making a big thing of themselves and who they claim to be."[5]

As noted, ethnographers have had much to say about twentieth-century Asante funeral practices.[6] What they have not supplied thus far is a documented historical discussion of the origin, adoption, dissemination, and subsequent evolution of any of the funerary practices they report. Nor have they done much to relate such matters to other temporal shifts or changes within Asante society. Precise chronology is absent. Not that historians have done very much better, the present author included. Historical writing about death and funerary rituals has tended to concentrate on isolated cases of instance and event rather than on developing more elusive narratives of process and evolution.[7] In what follows, I try to redress this situation. My account of "the fashion of making death notices" in twentieth-century Asante seeks to establish chronological connectivities between questions of the origin, adoption, dissemination, and evolution of this practice. I pick up on clues left by C. E. Osei and many others in an attempt to show when, why, and how written obituaries—"death notices"—became widespread in Asante. Like any purposeful historical sociology, my analysis of "death notices" is interleaved with other narratives. Most salient among these is the history of writing and reading English and Twi in Asante, the values invested in literacy in a hitherto oral culture, the issues of authorship and audience, and the sheer potency of words set down on paper as a signifier that a participant belongs in modernity. Let me expand a little on this last point. Often in Asante I have been shown *afunsɛm* (funeral things): printed, mimeographed, photocopied, or handwritten "death notices"; valedictions; genealogies; biographies; burial programs; church notices; signed photographs; sympathy and visiting cards; and sometimes even inscribed commemorative plates. These were disclosed from carefully tied bundles produced from drawers, cupboards, chests, trunks, or, on one occasion, from underneath a bedstead that seemed to be perched atop a mountain of documents. This process has taught me that the medium and the message both possess significance. Such items are valued intrinsically as well as for whatever they might record and say. In both senses they are mnemonics of death, tokens of the still ambiguous place of writing in a historically oral culture, and above all, as noted, icons of aspiration to a transfigured belonging within modern Asante society.[8]

"A memorial of King Prempeh's remarkable life and funeral"

C. E. Osei dated the origin of written "death notices" to items produced when Asantehene Agyeman Prempeh died in 1931.[9] Informed contemporaries shared this view.[10] In 1945, Baffour Osei Akoto stated that Agyeman Prempeh was the subject of "the first obituary read throughout Ashanti."[11] Fifty years on I revisited this matter with him. He repeated his earlier opinion and amplified it, saying that Agyeman Prempeh's pioneering "death notice" had served as both authorization and inspiration for others to follow suit. Such obituaries soon became fashionable among "enlightened people" and thereafter spread throughout Asante society, even among those poorly equipped to read the texts they had commissioned. People wanted such things to show that their dead relative "had picked up the family torch and left a good name worthy of his predecessors." They also wanted them to "boast of successes" in acquiring money, educating children, building houses, and other things "needful to progress in the modern world." Obituaries placed the deceased at the hub of a list of kin, in reality a constellation of connections and influence. The reader (or listener) was exposed to a text that made claims on behalf of a family by making a record and inviting assent to it. Assessing the truth or otherwise of what was being said demanded knowledge of the formula and skill in deconstructing the wording, tropes, evasions, and silences of the text. It is therefore no surprise that Asante society has fostered a kind of connoisseurship among devotees of "death notices." Baffour Osei Akoto also disclosed that Asantehene Agyeman Prempeh's obituary was remembered almost as much for the controversy that surrounded its making as for its innovative reputation.[12]

Agyeman Prempeh was born in 1872, appointed Asantehene in 1888, exiled by the British in 1896, repatriated to colonial Asante in 1924, made "Kumasihene" in 1926, and died on May 12, 1931. His cycle of funeral obsequies ended with the "one-year custom," which was celebrated from May 21 to May

31, 1932. It was then that his successor Osei Agyeman Prempeh II asked for British support to compile, print, and distribute "a memorial of King Prempeh's remarkable life and funeral."[13] Chief Commissioner of Asante H. S. Newlands was enthusiastic, for Agyeman Prempeh had "turned himself into a modern ruler" under British tutelage.[14] It was agreed that J. W. K. Appiah, the chief clerk to Osei Agyeman Prempeh II and a Methodist-educated schoolteacher, would write an account of the "one-year custom," and F. W. Applegate, the District Commissioner of Kumasi and Newlands' deputy, would contribute a preface to Appiah's narrative in the form of a short biographical appreciation of Agyeman Prempeh. Newlands planned to have this composite text published in hundreds of copies by the government printer in Accra for circulation throughout Asante. Acting Gold Coast Governor G. A. S. Northcote agreed but insisted on seeing all drafts before they went to press.[15] At this stage, British officials in Kumasi and Accra were united in believing that the published text would be a notable milestone in Asante's march into colonial modernity. Appiah and Applegate set to work, completed their drafts in September 1932, and had them approved by Newlands and Osei Agyeman Prempeh II. The texts were then forwarded to Accra to be cleared for publication.

Northcote approved Appiah's text but rephrased Applegate's preface with a European rather than Asante readership in mind. He sent this revised version back to Kumasi. Newlands and Applegate were incensed at Accra's high-handedness and at the way Northcote's revisions contrived to turn Agyeman Prempeh into an exotic specimen for the titillation of British readers. But their fury paled into insignificance beside that of Osei Agyeman Prempeh II. He condemned all the rephrasing, but one passage in particular enraged him. Applegate had noted that Agyeman Prempeh had a typically "long Ashanti head"; Northcote rewrote this to read "his long narrow head furnished a good example of the artificial elongation of the infant skull practised by the Ashanti." Osei Agyeman Prempeh II protested that such a comment was "a forbidden thing" (*akyiwadeɔ*) and that "Ashanti Custom does not permit such a personal insulting statement about a member of the House of Agyeman" (i.e., the Asante royal family). He demanded that Northcote's "offending" text be scrapped and replaced by Applegate's original version, "which does not take the name of great Ashanti in vain."[16] Newlands conveyed these views to Accra, but Northcote replied that the completed text had already gone to press with his revised preface included under Applegate's name.[17] In due course, boxed copies of *Report on the Observance of the Funeral Custom of the late Kumasihene* (Accra: Government Printing Office, 1933) were sent to Kumasi for distribution. I have a published copy before me as I write, bound in green card, with Northcote's revised preface (over Applegate's name) followed by Appiah's nine-page description of Agyeman Prempeh's *afehyia* (the text is reproduced at the end of this chapter). It is the only published copy I have ever seen, for Osei Agyeman Prempeh II—supported by Newlands and Applegate—refused to let it be circulated in Asante. My copy was given to me by the late Meyer Fortes, who told me that Osei Agyeman Prempeh II had given it to him as a parting gift in 1946. It was a rare item even then, for almost all the copies sent to Asante had already been destroyed. Nevertheless, Manhyia Palace clerks were set to work typing multiple carbon copies of Appiah's account of the "one-year custom" as a stand-alone text. These typescripts were widely distributed, and many are still extant. But Osei Agyeman Prempeh II was still determined to produce a "death notice" of his predecessor to replace the mangled preface. Accra forbade the circulation of Applegate's text, so Osei Agyeman Prempeh II convened an all-Asante committee to compile a replacement.

The committee chairman was Henry (Kwadwo) Owusu Ansah, Osei Agyeman Prempeh II's cousin and intimate, and an authority on Asante history. The other members were I. K. Agyeman, J. W. K. Appiah, and C. E. Osei, all educated palace administrators with family links to traditional chiefship and modern business. The committee's mandate was to compose "a memorial worthy of late King Prempeh" to "hearten all loyal Ashanti youngmen in hearing of his life."[18] This seems transparent in its call to patriotism and pedagogy, but it was not. Osei Agyeman Prempeh II held his predecessor in low esteem, regarding him as an uneducated anachronism in modern colonial Asante.[19] The aim of the "death notice" was to use Agyeman Prempeh's life as a peg on which to hang a propagandist narrative in support of monarchy, hierarchy, and received order. Osei Agyeman Prempeh II loathed "youngmen" (*nkwankwaa*) and their demands for political participation and saw them (not without justification) as incorrigible conspirators against himself and the historic privileges of chiefship.[20] He wanted to use the planned obituary as a tract to call them back to their duty to himself. Owusu Ansah shared his cousin's views, and theirs was the spirit in which the committee set to work. I. K. Agyeman acted as recorder, and a completed draft was submitted to Osei Agyeman Prempeh II in mid-1934. Copies were made and distributed to chiefs and village heads throughout Asante. These recipients were instructed "to beat gong-gong to call all the people to assemble" to hear the text read out.[21] At Ofinso, where the chief's stool was unoccupied, royal servants (*nhenkwaa*) from Kumasi led by I. K. Agyeman were sent to perform this task. The occasion was witnessed by the Kumasi barrister T. D. Williams, who sent

an account of the proceedings to his business associate and legal client Osei
Agyeman Prempeh II.

> Mr. Agyemang called the Offinsu people to him to hear him. He told them he
> will read out for all to hear a Wonderful Eulogy of late Nana Prempeh to show
> the Great Things done by Ashanti Kings but anyone also capable to read En-
> glish can read it themselves. A hush of respect fell over all. Mr. A. read it out and
> told of late Nana's Life and Adventures and his Funeral. When he finished he
> said late Nana's Life was lesson to all being selfless to work for the good of
> Ashanti and now they had heard this was true. Late Nana as all the Ashanti
> Kings and Chiefs in the past and future were working for the good of all. This
> was how Progress came about and people must think to support their Natural
> Rulers in making Peace and Progress for the Country. At the close Mr. A. sent
> for the Eulogy to be stuck on to the Police post so all can see it. He gave a copy
> to the Methodist schoolteacher and said he must read it with the children. The
> occasion went off well.[22]

No complete copy of the 1934 "death notice" appears to have survived.
The longest fragment I have seen was shown to me by Asantehene Opoku
Ware II (1970–1999). It was a stained and torn foolscap page with faint
mauve carbon type, bearing the handwritten page number 5 in the top right-
hand corner. I read it, but it was far too fragile to photocopy and I was not
shown it in a situation where I could transcribe it by hand. The text described
Agyeman Prempeh's wisdom in overruling armed resistance to the British
when they abducted him from Kumasi in 1896, thereby sparing his people
much bloodshed. It went on to describe his dignified farewell and departure
into exile amid the wailing of his subjects. The page broke off as the royal
prisoner crossed the Pra River into the Gold Coast Colony. This narrative of
kingly self-sacrifice was repeated in Osei Agyeman Prempeh II's authorized
history of Asante compiled in the 1940s, and the "death notice" may have
been one of the numerous texts consulted during the making of that work.[23]
However, if we no longer have a complete copy of the 1934 "death notice,"
then we do have evidence about its impact, influence, and legacy.

"Now a notice of death is a thing to proclaim success in life"

E. C. Bobie-Ansah was one of those *nkwankwaa* so detested by Osei
Agyeman Prempeh II. He was also a licensed notary and letter-writer, a busy
job in a modernizing society where people's need for documents in English
still outstripped their capacity to write them. Between the world wars, such
men were key mediators in Asante society, and by the very nature of their occupation they were formidably well informed about what was going on.

Bobie-Ansah was an intelligent man—and an opponent of Asante kingship. In the early 1930s, he became a client of O. S. Agyeman, Osei Agyeman Prempeh II's chief critic and bitter enemy.[24] In November 1934, he wrote to his patron about the impact of Agyeman Prempeh's "death notice." It was "the talk of the town," and Osei Agyeman Prempeh II was satisfied that it had "improved the reputation of the Royals." It had also started a trend. The wealthy and prominent Asafu-Adjaye, Otchere, and Bandoh families were all "determined to have the same thing made at [their] funerals." Bobie-Ansah disapproved. "It is all a New Show for people to boast of nobility and money even when both are lacking," he said, and "now a notice of death is a thing to proclaim success in life."[25]

For the remainder of the 1930s, "death notices" were a near-monopoly of chiefs and the commercial elite, in practice often the same or closely related people. Kumasi Adontenhene Kwame Frimpon (ca. 1860–1937) was a senior colonial chief and one of the richest businessmen in Asante. He was a Methodist (baptized John) and was literate in English. He educated two of the Asafu-Adjaye brothers, his nephews, in England to become the first native-born Asante lawyer and doctor, respectively. He was an epitome of the modernizing colonial chief and in 1931 was honored as "an educated chief" with a "higher intellect" and a "comprehensive mind" in a series of "pen-pictures of Modern Africans and African Celebrities" published by a Gold Coast Fante in England.[26] George, the third of the Asafu-Adjaye brothers and his uncle's chosen successor as Adontenhene, was given responsibility for organizing Kwame Frimpon's funeral rites. Christina Asafu-Adjaye, the dead man's favorite daughter and George's wife, paid for a "death notice" to be produced by a Kumasi businessman named Sackey. We know this because there was a row about the contents and the bill. Christina and George argued over the biographical section of the text, the daughter wanting to emphasize her father's ascriptive (if controversial) descent, the nephew wishing to proclaim his uncle's achieved modernity and "go-ahead business acumen." Christina won this particular battle, for she was paying for the "death notice," but she lost an argument with Sackey about the cost of production. In the event, George read out the "death notice" to Kwame Frimpon's kin in Kumasi and Baaman during the funeral rites. This too caused problems, for George was widely disliked "by the family" and was constantly undermined by his forceful wife. Unfortunately, we only have George's version of these events. With hindsight, he admitted to having felt great strain at having to read out his wife's "pompous memorial" of her father, for it "strained credulity by claiming for him an association with all of the great figures in Ashanti history."[27]

Unlike his contemporary Kwame Frimpon, Kofi Sraha (ca. 1863–1936) was not a chief; rather, he was one of colonial Asante's most successful entrepreneurs and merchants. He was a leading light in the *akonkofoɔ kuo*, that association of businessmen that played a crucial part in embedding the new economic order while guarding against the resurrection of the old. Like his peers, he feared the return of royal fiscal imposts and so was secretive in all his commercial dealings. Illiterate himself, he educated his half-brother J. E. Bandoh to take care of the paperwork required by colonial business. In 1931, Bandoh persuaded him to have the first written will in Asante drawn up and notarized. When Kofi Sraha died five years later, Bandoh tried to take charge of the funeral rites so as to monopolize the position of estate executor and impose his own interpretation of the will. He had a "death notice" drawn up that was fulsome in its praise of Kofi Sraha's entrepreneurial virtues but that also contrived to situate himself as the dead man's closest friend, partner, and ally. This was a blatant attempt to stake claim to property that the traditionalist Kofi Sraha had left to his matrilineal kin at Abrepo and in Kumasi. Bandoh's gambit failed. His attempt to subvert the will was overturned, and while he forced a reading of his "death notice" at Kofi Sraha's Kumasi house, he was stopped from doing the same thing at Abrepo. Osei Agyeman Prempeh II commented on these proceedings in a note that chided Bandoh for "taking on too much" in "your no doubt heartfelt tribute to your brother."[28]

In the 1930s, "death notices" written in English were read out and passed around at a small if rising number of elite Asante funerals. They evidenced participation in or aspiration to modernity, but they also built upon a legacy of customary oral practice. At funeral rites before the twentieth century, it was common to eulogize (*yi ayɛ*) the dead in perorations that reviewed their lives in order to praise their virtues and achievements. A key element here, reflecting Asante social imperatives to ground belonging in kinship and increase the stock of human beings, was to list by name the deceased's ancestors, living relatives, and children. In 1925, analogous considerations underlay the meticulous listing of names written down and distributed by the returned Agyeman Prempeh to account for his stewardship of all those who had died or been born while sharing his 28-year exile.[29]

The practice of making funeral orations was reinforced by the spread of Christianity in early-twentieth-century Asante. Extolling (*kamfo*) the dead person's life was a component of the Christian burial service in Asante (as elsewhere), and it resonated with already-existing traditions of funeral oration. Indeed, in one vital respect, Christian tenets served to underline the performative tone and emphasis of Asante practice. Both traditions held that deeply felt emotions such as grief were unhealthy and injurious if repressed. Both esteemed the therapeutic powers of speech on shattering occasions such as death and funerals.[30]

If the sources of the written "death notice" are clear historically and in relation to modernity, then we are on less-well-documented ground when we consider matters of readership or audience. To begin with, as late as 1924 there were fewer than 7,000 pupils in Asante schools, and by 1939 literacy in English was still very much a minority attainment. Any more widespread fluency in reading or writing English was a post-1945 phenomenon, particularly among non-Kumasi villagers. Thus, we may surmise that few Asante were able to read for themselves the elite "death notices" produced between the world wars. This is why, in the cases documented above, the standard practice seems to have been to have someone assemble people together so as to read the text out loud to them. We can detect in this, perhaps, a transitional stage between the speech extemporized for those actually present at the traditional funeral and the text read at any time after the event by those interested, however remotely, in a particular funeral today. We must recall that "death notices" written in English originated as symbols of leading-edge modernity. As such, they were exclusive icons of elite identity, and those who first employed them saw no evidently good reason to worry about the fact that less-advantaged Asante could not read them and required mediators to comprehend them. Indeed, the very fact of having to read them aloud to the excluded mass reinforced the precious sense of privileged elite belonging in the forward march of progress. It also echoed pleasingly with earlier elite practices, when chiefs and office-holders gathered people together and hectored them. But such exclusivity could not be sustained indefinitely, for, however slowly, ever-larger numbers of Asante were learning English. Some of these, excluded from the elite of chiefship and business wealth, formed the nucleus of an emerging professional and commercial middle class of teachers, journalists, pastors, pharmacists, storekeepers, clerks, and all the rest. Such people also aspired to modernity within the colonial dispensation and for personal as well as political reasons emulated the tastes and coveted the trappings of those who declared themselves their betters. By the 1940s, a growing number of Asante were gaining access to and familiarity with ideas and practices that had been the property of a much more restricted elite only twenty years before.[31]

"Honourable Mr. Agyei is deserving to be remembered as any chief"

It was some among the *nkwankwaa*—often well-born men who felt un-justly excluded from rights to office, wealth, and political power—who spear-headed the emergence of an alternative, non-elite modernist identity in colo-nial Asante. I have written of such people at length elsewhere and repeat here only what is relevant to present concerns.[32] To the Asante elite of chiefship and commercial wealth, the *nkwankwaa* were the enemy—rancorous, liti-gious, conspiratorial men bent on inserting themselves into power by conspir-acy and subversion. Accordingly, after the British restored Osei Agyeman Prempeh II to the office and prerogatives of Asantehene in 1935, one of his first acts was to ban *nkwankwaa* organizations and clubs. But frustrated *nkwankwaa* rapidly found ways around this prohibition. Starting in the late 1930s, they began to form themselves into literary and debating societies in Kumasi and in other towns in Asante. Modeling themselves on comparable clubs in the Gold Coast Colony, they claimed educational and recreational purposes that met with the tacit approval of British administrators interested in civic improvement.[33] But from the outset, Asante *nkwankwaa* literary and debating societies were political meeting places, no matter what the ostensible subject of discussion placed before the membership. By their nature, these were fugitive organizations and showed sound political instincts in keeping few records. Thus, we have names of many such societies throughout Asante but little documentation generated by them. One exception is the Mampon Literary Club (MLC), founded in 1938. It kept a membership list, correspon-dence, and minutes of its meetings in 1938–1939, 1941–1944, and 1948–1951.[34] The MLC was known to be devoted to discussing politics, but it appears to have survived because its existence was condoned by the Mampon-hene simply because the Asantehene wanted it closed. That is, the MLC was an unwitting beneficiary of the historic rivalry between Mampon and Kumasi. Whatever the truth, some of the MLC's politics were notably in-flammatory. It was addressed on several occasions by Ata Mensa, an activist enemy of the Asantehene and later a stalwart of Nkrumah's Convention People's Party. At one such gathering, recorded in the minutes as being "at-tended by over sixty members," he proposed the abolition of chiefship, and this was "warmly received."[35]

The MLC minutes for the monthly meeting of March 1942 recorded the death at age 47 of Mr. Isaiah Afrifah Agyei, the club's official Public Orator. Agyei belonged to the Babiru branch of the Mampon royal family and was educated in Kumasi. Thereafter, he worked as a storekeeper and timber merchant before becoming an importer of Dodge trucks. In 1929, he set up a motor-hire business at New Asafo in Kumasi and rented his trucks out to people with bulk goods to move. Once this business was up and running, he retired to Mampon and built a family house. He funded the education of the children of both his sisters, campaigned for improvements in the town's dispensary, and gave generously to St. Monica's College. All these biographical details were supplied from the floor as tributes by his fellow MLC members in 1942. But if Agyei was a good citizen, he was also a political activist. MLC members remarked that he had petitioned more than once for the restoration of the banned office of Nkwankwaahene ("head of *nkwankwaa*") in Mampon and had been beaten by Native Authority Police for his presumption. They recalled that he had been arrested by the government and fined and jailed for his part in the 1933 riot against the incumbent Mamponhene. They said he had attended an *nkwankwaa* meeting in Kumasi at which a motion was passed condemning chiefs for their pride and avarice. In sum, Agyei was remembered as a man who had "with resolution set his face against the tyranny of Kings and Chiefs" and who had "supported the cause of the common man against the Powers That Be." The meeting then turned to the question of a fitting memorial for Agyei. Funeral plans were discussed, during which it was suggested that a "death notice" be "made up" and paid for by subscription, as "Honourable Mr. Agyei is deserving to be remembered as any chief." This proposal was approved by acclamation. MLC Treasurer Mr. Kwabena Amponsah was instructed to assess how much the project would cost. Vice-President Mr. Samuel Garbah was asked to write a letter to "the other clubs" in Kumasi, Nsuta, Agona, and Effiduase to tell them about Agyei's death and to explain what the MLC planned to do to mark his passing. "We are intending an Obituary Notice," Garbah wrote,

> as a fit and proper thing for Mr. Isaiah Agyei our departed friend to be remembered by this society. We are asking a subscription of 6d each raised from among the members here to have a suitable Memorial Tribute i.e. Obituary Notice written up and printed if the money is there. This can let many friends in this Town and in Kumasi etc. know that his Memory Will Be Ever Green by telling of his path through life. Mr. Isaiah Agyei triumphed over all trials and difficulties he was suffering in raising up of Ashanti people. He did good works all his days and eased troubles of Others as he was able. He was no friend to those who set themselves to Rule over us all as Petty Kings or Opressors [*sic*] because of making claims of their Ancient Right To Rule. He was a valiant Friend of Freedom. It is not to be borned [*sic*] then if that Chiefs or a rich man alone should reap the benefits after death to be sung Hymns of Praise by all around. We are singing the Praises of Mr. Isaiah Agyei.[36]

The MLC minutes of April–May 1942 are missing, so we do not know if Isaiah Agyei's "death notice" was ever brought into being. But his case has broader resonances. During the war years and beyond, British and Asante authorities were concerned, each for their own reasons, to intensify surveillance over unsanctioned writings that circulated in the public domain. The British war effort in Asante saw a heightening of intelligence-gathering, monitoring, and censorship, and when peace and then the Cold War came along these practices were maintained to watch over nationalist and communist politics.[37] For his part, the Asantehene was especially troubled by what he saw as the increasing insolence of *nkwankwaa* arising from their susceptibility to the speeches and writings of political demagogues. He blamed this on ill-conceived educational policies and on the emigration from the villages to Kumasi and other towns by unemployed and unemployable youth.[38] Men such as Agyei, Amponsah, and Garbah were legion, and they enraged and alarmed Osei Agyeman Prempeh II. Above all else, he wanted to stop or otherwise control their assembling together to exchange ideas, listen to speeches, read broadsheet tracts, or air grievances. Societies and clubs of such men were anathema to him, but so also was any kind of mass public gathering involving them. By the later 1940s, this included funerals.

"They must not say or write anything of the sort"

In 1945–1946, the Ashanti Social Survey devoted time and effort to the investigation of Asante funeral practices. In the orthodox British ethnographic manner of that time, fieldworkers sought to identify traditional burial customs and rituals and discover what changes, if any, were in the process of taking place. They identified a variety of modifications and innovations that they associated with colonial modernity and monetization. These shifts were also recognized by Asante commentators. In 1947, the Asantehene wrote privately to Atipinhene (soon to be Akyempemhene) Boakye Dankwa, a son of Agyeman Prempeh, asking him to look into the organization and cost of funerals. Osei Agyeman Prempeh II made it clear that he wanted a confidential response and asked particularly that Boakye Dankwa report on "riotous behaviour or disorder of a rebellious kind" observable at funerals.[39] The Atipinhene set to work and submitted his findings in a five-page report in November 1947. Like the Ashanti Social Survey, he concluded that funeral practices were changing and that competitive consumerism and "the desire to impress" were driving up costs to unsustainable levels and sharply increasing family debt. When he turned to the specific issue mentioned by the Asantehene, he had the following to say:

> Funeral gatherings in Jackson Park, Kejetia, Bantama High Street and other places where people gather in Kumasi now are big affairs. They attract crowds from outside the family when the deceased is well known to people and they think there is excitement to be had or even more so trouble. These funerals attract mobs of noisy youth. Mr. Ingham (Deputy Police Inspector) told me last year the police needed reinforcements to control the crowd when Yaw Assibey's procession was addressed by agitators. They tried to rush to Manhyia and when halted ran to Prempeh Hall to shout out about anythings they didn't like such as the Chiefs courts and tribunals, high cost of living, shortage of cooking oil etc. The police charged them seizing bottles, sticks etc. out from their ranks. Mr. Ingham told me that during Assibey's procession men were moving up and down among the crowds giving out to all and sundry their Obituary saying he Assibey was dead, but Long Live Assibey! and saying he and the rest were wrongly punished by beating at Ashantihene's Court when all denied charges of insulting Ashantihene the occupant of the Golden Stool. Crowds were standing to read this nonsense and as many are unable to read it it was read out to them. I think and Mr. Ingham is the same that this is mere Treason and Sedition. Funeral notices praising malcontents up to the skies excite the disrespectful attitudes on the part of the youngmen. But since notices are now the ordinary thing at a Kumasi funeral it is hard to quell them. The police have no means to search out where all this takes place or stop it as to printing or copying same is an easy matter. Such things notifying of death are put on the walls of Chiefs houses so it is said "to warn them" and at Kejetia, Adum etc. often are to be seen lying in the streets. Since however big funerals have ever been an Ashanti Custom it is impossible to prevent people meeting in celebrating them. Vigilance must be the motto together with the police.[40]

The trend of criticizing Asante royal and British colonial government in broadsides got up as short obituaries for distribution at funerals reached a peak in the increasingly politicized late 1940s. It is not overstating the case to see in this development echoes of the historic Asante custom of "setting at defiance" through role reversal and lampooning.[41] Chiefs and the wealthy had once made people listen respectfully to them as they spoke and later read aloud at funerals. Now the audience could hear its dissenting views articulated by orators drawn from its own ranks or read for itself its own critical opinions set down on paper in the context of a "death notice." In the 1980s, I. K. Agyeman showed me a mock obituary headed "Death and Funeral Rites of Ashanti Kingship." This one-page cyclostyled text reported the infamous episode in 1949 when the Asantehene was shot at in court and was then hurried out of the building without his sandals—an "abomination" in Asante custom.[42] The text recounted this in a pompously solemn style and went on to say that Osei Agyeman Prempeh II had escaped but that he had left the Asante monarchy dead on his courthouse floor. Mourners were respectfully invited to attend the funeral, to be conducted at Manhyia. The motto of the (anonymous) Funeral Committee was "Dry Your Eyes. A Better Day Is Dawning."[43] Lampooning in this style combined the political with the satirical.

In a similar vein, an obituary of the sacred lake Bosomtwe appeared on the streets of Kumasi when rumors circulated that the Asantehene was in negotiations to sell it off to a European company. The text has not survived, but we do have Osei Agyeman Prempeh II's reaction to it. "This lie," he wrote in 1950, "is repeated again and again and now it is being said I have sold the Lake to a German scientist. A. [A.Y.] K[yerematen] brought me a pamphlet that is going round the town. It shows me (not a good likeness) holding a bag of money and handing over Bosumtwi to some white men. The King has killed the Sacred Lake! The King is killing Ashanti! How can anyone believe this? They must not say or write anything of the sort."[44]

The proliferation of such "death notices," real and imaginary, in the late 1940s was encouraged into being by a dissenting politics that still lacked any formal means of expression. The moment could not and did not last, and its passing began with the inauguration of Nkrumah's Convention People's Party in June 1949. Simply put, the obituaries of the late 1940s disappeared when emerging party politics made them redundant. I have included all of the little I know about them in the preceding paragraphs. I imagine that precious few have survived. They were *pièces d'occasion*, fugitive texts produced in and for very particular circumstances. Why would people keep them? And if they did preserve copies of any such documents, for whatever reason, then flimsiness alone is sufficient to explain their vanishing. If copies were kept, then we can be sure they were hidden away in locked "tin trunks," wooden chests, or cupboards. To possess them in the 1940s was hazardous, and even today to bring them out into the open and show them around publicly would be inadvisable.

"It is there to remind all of our family history"

From the early 1950s, the *Ashanti Pioneer* began to publish growing numbers of "death notices" in the form of funeral announcements. They became formulaic, usually back-page boxed items with the deceased's name in bold print set off against necessary information about the funeral and an all-important list of family members. It seems likely that this formula was arrived at as a compromise between publishing conventions, modeled after Gold

Coast and English newspapers and clients' information requirements, which were rooted in Asante funerary norms. These "death notices" asserted status and conferred prestige. They were paid for, published, and written in English and so proclaimed membership in that burgeoning sector of Asante society that had access to some means and education. The formula was itself a symbol of that belonging, for its very repetition pointed readers to the community with which identification was sought. This was a democratic genre in that ordinary people made use of it. Little is known about cost, but I am told the newspaper sold box space in different sizes that had a maximum number of lines for each size. Here are three examples of the genre, drawn at random from 1952. As far as is possible, they are reproduced as they appeared in the *Ashanti Pioneer.*

FUNERAL ANNOUNCEMENT
Messrs Yaw Bediako, Kwabena Adu,
Kwabena Sakete, Kwaku Abebrese and
Madam Abena Dumfeh wish to inform
the general public that the funeral
obsequies of their late mother
AFUA FOFIE
which sad event took place at the Colo-
nial Hospital Kumasi on Sunday the
10th Feb. will be observed at Kumasi
Adum Street O.T.B. 200 on Thursday
The 14th February.
ALL ARE CORDIALLY INVITED
Chief Mourners

FUNERAL ANNOUNCEMENT
Mr. Cudjoe, the Manager of California
Bar, Adum and family wish to inform the
General public that the funeral obsequies
Of the late **MISS AIDOO** of the Methodist
Infant Junior School which sad
event took place at Kumasi by Electric
Shock will be held at Kumasi Naja Da-
vid House No. 1 on Saturday, 23rd Feb.
1952. Wake-keeping will be held on
Friday 22nd and Thanks-giving Service
on Sun. at the Methodist Church Ksi.
R.S.V.P. **J.E. MENSAH**, Methodist
Book Depot, Kumasi.

FUNERAL ANNOUNCEMENT
Chief Aboagye Ababio, Ama Nyarku,
Odikro Asumadu, Kweku Bewuah and

Family beg to announce that the funeral
obsequies of their beloved son Daniel
Kodjo Aboagye formerly Cocoa Grader
U.A.C. Atuakrom who passed from
time to eternity on the 24th March
1952 at Kumasi would be held at
Kumasi on Saturday 29th March 1952
House No. 00 127/8.
Wake-keeping on Friday 28th March
1952 in the same house.
Chief Mourners[45]

Thirty years ago, I used to sit with Joseph Agyeman-Duah, a Mampon Botaase royal and member of the Asantehene's administration, in Boateng's Bar at the foot of Manhyia hill by Kagyatia as he and his cronies read through, dissected, and talked over newspaper obituaries just like these. On a day when a "death notice" concerned a known family, and that was virtually every day, the entire bar joined in to trade opinions back and forth about the people involved. This was oral fieldwork in the richest sense of that term, as narrative and anecdote ranged far and wide, prompted by the bald facts set down on the page. Too much, too torrential, and too polyphonic to be written down in full, these discussions were nonetheless a free-flowing seminar in how to read Asante society. I listened, questioned, remembered, and endeavored to learn. Thus, the first of the 1952 obituaries set out above concerns people from north Asante, probably Sekyere, where the names "Sakete" and "Abebrese" are more common than they are in the south. I cannot say more about them, but my interlocutors in Boateng's probably could have. The second concerns a tragic death from electrocution, and I am sure this would have launched a spirited conversation about the inadequacies of the Asokwa sub-station, from where power lines ran to the Methodist Infant School; things today are more complex but not much improved, as the demand for electricity in a vastly larger city has led to power surges and failures and left the Asokwa outflow lines heavy with illegal power cables and looking like a nest of snakes. The third is about a chief's family, and any "death notice" of this kind would have produced heated disquisitions on particular genealogies and local histories. I have set things down in this way not to indulge a taste for reminiscence but rather to emphasize some important general points. Starting in the 1950s, "death notices" published in the newspapers came to occupy a central place in sparking Asante talk about all sorts of contingencies that stemmed from reading the name of the deceased, the names of his or her relatives, and their known, presumed, or supposed connections. Reading allowed the people who did it, and those who just listened to it being done, access to a published history of death. This might be revisited over and over again to serve as a trigger for memories, thoughts, and speculations. Thus, it is commonplace to see "death notices" clipped from newspapers, put in frames, and hung on Asante parlor walls. As an old lady in the Manwerehene's Ashanti New Town house in Kumasi once told me, "It is there to remind all of our family history." The newspapers reinforced the already-central significance of death and funerals in Asante life.

The heyday of the newspaper, when it was the unchallenged venue of choice for announcing death and recalling its victims, lasted from the 1950s until the 1990s. Over this period, published "death notices" became more elaborate. Full-page obituaries emerged in the 1960s, and photographs of the deceased became common during the 1970s. The same formula prevailed throughout, but those with money and status reasserted their claims to difference by paying for ever-grander "death notices." In 1978, for example, the notice of "Final Obsequies for the late Nana Amma Serwa Nyarko, Asantehemaa" was not only published as a page in the *Ashanti Pioneer*, complete with full-length photograph, but was also printed as a broadsheet with a run of some 3,000 copies. These were pasted on walls, fences, and hoardings across Kumasi and on road signs leading into the city. They were available as commemorative keepsakes to callers offering condolences at the Manhyia Palace. Such visitors were also handed an elaborate "Full Programme," far too big for a newspaper, in which rituals were described in detail, including the timing and observance of the mourning period of fasting (*abuada*), when the Asantehene would sit in state at Dwaberem, or when and how the mass farewell "firing of muskets" (*trae*) would take place. After the event, I discussed the published newspaper notice with some palace officials and servants (*nhenkwaa*). The "royal" nature of the "Final Obsequies" page was to be seen, so I was informed, in its layout as well as its size. Not only the photograph but also the amount of paper within the usual box that had been left blank to serve as margins or other design features marked this "death notice" as being of supreme quality. In further conversation, I was given to understand that "even today" historic sumptuary laws still obtained. No one would have the ill-breeding or bad manners to publish a "death notice" larger or more elaborate than those favored by the Kumasi royal family. And even if someone did perpetrate such a solecism, the newspapers would refuse to print it.

In the first twenty years or so after independence from the British in

1957, the inherited model of the "Ashanti gentleman" that had been fashioned in the era of colonial modernity still exercised a potent sway over aristocratic and wealthy middle-class lifestyles and representations. Such persons were educated (school and the networks it created being of signal importance), Christian (in public observance above all), liberal (in a legalist, constitutionalist manner), progressive (as Westminster-style nationalists), and leisured (in the sense of being rentiers with land and buildings). If they shared one other characteristic, it was an interest in Asante history and customs. Perhaps the doyen of the type was Henry Owusu Ansah, that cousin to the Asantehene Osei Agyeman Prempeh II we have already met as a committee man in the 1930s. It is said that he wrote, and then severally rewrote, his own obituary over many years. There was a question in all this of tone, of the mot juste, and of touching the right buttons for his audience of like-minded peers (many of whom were engaged in a similar writing exercise). The object was a "death notice" of a very particular kind—brief, lapidary, exclusive, and designed to be kept by the like-minded as a memento mori. When Owusu Ansah did die in the 1970s, his drafts were used as a basis for a "death notice" in the *Ashanti Pioneer* that was also printed as a one-page memorial. As intended, the resulting text is an epitome of the "Ashanti gentleman." "Bemah Owusu-Ansah," it reads,

> was the son of Nana Ama Mansah, daughter of Nana Yaa Achiaa, Asantehemaa, mother of King Prempeh I of blessed memory. His father was the late Baffour Kwabena Sarfo, Anantahene of Kumasi.
>
> The late Bemah Kwadwo Owusu-Ansah had his primary education at the then Kumasi Wesleyan Missionary School and continued at the Richmond College, now Mfantsipim School. He was the second Ashanti to enter the Richmond College. He left Richmond College and worked with the Commercial firms in Ashanti.
>
> On the repatriation of his uncle in 1924, he resigned and took up appointment with his uncle as his first Private Secretary.
>
> He later retired and confined himself to the researches of Ashanti Customs and History.
>
> Until his death, he was a member of the National Cultural Centre and served on several cultural affairs committees.
>
> Many cultural and historical research students have passed through his hands.[46]

A copy of this document serves as a pasted-up preface to the typescript "History of Oyoko Family of Ashanti," which Owusu Ansah worked on from the 1940s until his death.[47]

"Video is a better memory than reading and writing"

Over the past ten to fifteen years, print culture in Asante has been over-taken by rapid change. Thus, in 1970, the death of Asantehene Osei Agye-man Prempeh II was marked by newspaper obituaries and a restricted number of commemorative pamphlets. All these were authorized or sanctioned by the Kumasi royal family. The main funeral report was drafted but never pub-lished. Two printers in succession were awarded the contract, but both were unable to do the work because of shortages of imported paper and machine parts in the Ghanaian economy. Furthermore, those items that did make it into print looked as if they might have been produced at any time in the thirty years prior to 1970. Newspaper obituaries were of the formulaic box type. Other publications were short, with no visible design agenda. Print and pho-tographs were muddy, typography was haphazard, text was poorly set out, margins were ungenerous, and paper was of low quality. No colors were used, and everything was black on white. The author of one such commemorative pamphlet told me of the huge difficulties he encountered in printing, proof-ing, publishing, and distribution. He blamed this on Ghana's economic cir-cumstances, specifically on the moribund state of publishing. Thirty years after the event, a man inspecting a copy of this very same pamphlet in the Manhyia Palace Museum bookshop told me with a laugh that it was "colo," old-fashioned (der. "colonial").[48] In 1999, the succeeding Asantehene Opoku Ware II died. Immediately, something happened that was completely un-precedented. The Kumasi royal family first lost control over reporting the death and funeral and then struggled to reassert its monopoly rights. One of the key developments that made this situation possible was a huge revolution in print culture. In the 1990s, word processing, color printing, desktop pub-lishing, digitization, and all the rest brought about the biggest opportunity in Asante publishing since the inception of literacy and printing. This change was democratic, at least in the sense that it hugely multiplied publishing re-sources. Everyone could and did have their say. With hindsight, we can see that a "battle of the books" took place around Opoku Ware II's death. It would be impossible here even to list the flood of published "death notices," pamphlets, newspaper columns, editorials, opinion pieces, letters, broad-sheets, and, in due course, books that reported the death, burial, and funeral rites of the Asantehene. The "battle" that underpinned all this verbiage was between the Kumasi dynasty and the media over who should report events and in what ways. In striking contrast to 1970, publications on both sides were lengthy and often expertly designed. Print and photographs were crisp, typography was ambitiously varied, text was clearly set out, margins and spacing were generous, and paper was plentiful and of generally good quality. Color printing was extensively used (as were numerous color photographs), and some texts had pages with color-washed, motif-enriched backgrounds to contrast with the typography. Furthermore, print runs of everything from souvenir newspaper supplements to individually produced pamphlets were plentiful everywhere in Asante.[49]

On the surface, then, it would appear that the writing and publishing economy surrounding "death notices" has entered a triumphant new technological age. It is certainly true that families continue to circulate "death notices" and newspapers continue to print them. Paradoxically, however, just as print culture has achieved revolutionary new levels of sophistication and availability, the reporting and commemorating of death in that medium is no longer at the leading edge in Asante. Literacy and reading in a sustainedly attentive way are yesterday's fashion, increasingly associated with the vanished modernity of the colonial era. There are many reasons for this, including a depleted education system and the long-term downgrading of teaching, public service, and some professions as the sovereign roads to individual economic advancement. Like the rest of Ghana, Asante is now exhorted to take part in an officially proclaimed and supported "golden age of business." Economic well-being is associated with entrepreneurship and is oriented toward globalization. A supposed key to this, as elsewhere, is evolving electronic technologies. Culturally, Asante people now associate modernity with all such breakthrough developments and increasingly regard the printed page as a tool from a receding and discardable past. Death and funerals, such central features of Asante life, are inevitably subject to the same currents of change and innovation. In Kumasi a couple of years ago, I saw advertising for a company called Oteng Photos and Video Production, which is located in the Oforikrom area. One notice said, "Video is a better memory than reading and writing" and offered a "full service" in video-recording funerals.

Video films, some of them very long, are now the leading-edge technology used to record Asante funeral rituals and commemorate death. In parallel with the "battle of the books" in 1999, numerous videos were made of various stages of Asantehene Opoku Ware II's funeral. Some of these were "official," and were advertised as such, for all manner of illicit and pirated tapes were also in circulation. Even the video of the royal burial rites approved by the Manhyia Palace was available for purchase in cut-price copies (of admittedly variable quality) around Kumasi on the day of its official release.[50] In fact, anybody in Asante with the means now has a video made of family funerals, and the cost of doing this is coming down all the time as the technology itself becomes cheaper and more widely available. In 2000, I talked over these developments with Manfred Okyere of MOST Video Inc. in Kumasi Adum. I asked specifically about funerals, video, and the future of written "death notices."

> Video is now part of the "funeral services" in Kumasi and it is being done in other towns like Edweso, Konongo, Dwaaso, Bekwai and elsewhere. Everyone wants a recording to be made of the funeral done for loved ones. It is a record of what happened that will last for all time. Copies are made and sent to relatives in the U.S.A., U.K., Germany, or wherever. I think people want it because it is the modern thing to do and they can watch it again and again. If you do not have a video some people will say you have cheated in not spending enough money. You will be ashamed of what you have done and other people will talk of you. [Laughs.] It is still done to make "funeral announcement" in the newspaper or make a "Funeral Programme" to tell people the venue, date, or what is happening when. But this is not enough. It is shameful "to bury the old woman" only with pieces of paper. You can tell more of her life by making [a] video than writing can do. In the future people might go on making notices in newspapers, but only old men read newspapers. [Laughs.][51]

Another informant, who asked to remain anonymous, told me that written obituaries in Asante had begun when chiefs and other wealthy people wanted to show they were up to date as well as being important. He pointed to the Manhyia Palace and said that "the people in there started it" but that times had changed and few now wanted to hear or read about the history of chiefs and their doings.

What is the future in Asante for the print culture that generated the "death notices" discussed in this chapter? I am no prophet, but I would hazard two opinions. First, Kumasi and (some) other towns are now locked into globalized, consumerist modernity, an arrangement reinforced and renewed by the increased mobility of diasporic Asante bringing new ideas and products from the developed world. In the rites surrounding urban death and funerals, this traffic is being translated into an extravagant escalation in the objects of consumption and their cost. Asante funerals have always been sharply competitive affairs in which outdoing the neighbors to the renown of one's own kin is crucial. In the precolonial past, such displays were the jealously guarded prerogative of kings and chiefs. During the British period and the first decades of independence, one-upmanship was linked to the leading-edge features of colonial modernity, notably participation and belonging in cultures of education, reading, and literacy. In the present globalized "golden age of business," technology and consumption count above all else. The written word is in danger of being buried under accelerating materialism. It is also under threat from the shortened attention spans encouraged by the electronic age of mobile phones and the Internet. Leading-edge urban funerals today are riots of borrowing and spending, frequently into bankruptcy, in which what counts is recording the public display rather than reading the printed word. This juggernaut is driven onward by the wealthy, but large numbers of urban-ites aspire to, emulate, or envy it, and the "Asante funeral business" has be-come an object of concern to government and the butt of moralists and satirists.[52] Second, in increasingly depopulated Asante agricultural villages, depleted by emigration to the towns, funerals today have a different set of meanings and resonances. Here the culture of writing and reading, of insert-ing a "death notice" in a newspaper, of circulating a modestly printed memo-rial, was always a minority pursuit. Thirty, even twenty, years ago, all villagers aspired to some participation in these practices, but this no longer seems to be true. Village funerals today are about restating interpersonal values and com-mitments in a notably uncertain social and economic environment and a rap-idly changing world. They are "a time-out from daily practice," and this may or may not include commissioning a printed "death notice."[53]

Report on the Observance
of the Funeral Custom of
the late Kumasihene.

———

GOLD COAST :
Printed by the Government Printer
Accra.
—
1933.

Figure 13.1. *Report on the Observance of the Funeral Custom of the late Kumasihene,* 1933.

PREFACE.

The history of the late Nana Edward Agyeman Prempeh I, Kumasihene, is well known to students of African history. The important years of his remarkable life are 1888 when he came to the Golden Stool of Ashanti, his banishment by the British Government to the Seychelles Islands in 1896, his repatriation by the same authority to Ashanti in 1924 and his election as Kumasihene in 1926. His death took place on 12th May, 1931. The following account of the great funeral " custom " or ceremony in his honour and memory marks the anniversary of his death.

Prempeh, as his name indicates, was of stout build, less than medium height: and with his long narrow head furnished a good example of the artificial elongation of the infant skull practised by the Ashanti. Withal he was dignified as befitted a king, of forceful personality and great charm of manner: a born ruler whose powers years of exile had not weakened. With obvious sincerity he would often say that his time in the Seychelles was not all loss, for he had used those years to educate himself and so be ready for such time as the British Government should call him again to live among his people, perhaps to assume their leadership.

With astonishing adaptability Nana Prempeh fitted himself into the new order of things. He came back to find a modern well-planned and well-built town where he had left a huge crowded African village: to sit on a Town Council at whose table he was as much at home in European dress as perhaps but an hour before he might have been fully arrayed in crown ornaments and Ashanti robes while presiding at a Tribunal or heading some national pageant. His notable ability to adapt himself to the new, dual existence took its rise from no mere shrewd gift of " savoir faire ". It inspired him because he was utterly informed by the desire to serve the real interests of the Ashanti and the British Crown whose rule over his fellow countrymen he recognized as being to their advantage both immediately and ultimately.

His untimely and regretted death was an occasion of great public sorrow; the lying-in-state and burial attended by thousands of his subjects was a time of national mourning. Indeed there was witnessed the passing of a king and the end to a life of drama, sorrow and, finally, happiness the last arising from the fruition of a cherished hope that his bones should lie in Ashanti soil side by side with the past rulers of his nation.

F. W. APPLEGATE,
Assistant Chief Commissioner of Ashanti

GLOSSARY OF THE TERMS USED IN THE REPORT.

Abusua Kuruwa ...	Family Statue.
Ahinfie	King's Palace.
Ahenemma	Princes and Princesses.
Ahinkwa P. Nhinkwa	Servants.
Akwamuhene	War Captain.
Akyempimhene	Head of King's bodyguard.
Ankobiahene	Head of King's personal attendants.
Asante Kotoko Society	A Society composed of educated Ashantis; Kotoko = porcupine, the emblem of Ashanti.
Atenehene	Chief of Torch bearers.
Ayitam	Mourning apparel.
Ayokofuo	The Royal Family of Ashanti.
Batakare-Kesie	War dress worn by Ashanti Kings.
Bogyawi	A meeting place near the King's Palace.
Buro	The ceremony which precedes the commencement of a funeral custom.
Dako Yokofuo	A branch of the Royal Family who live at Nsuta in the Mampong District.
Dareboase	Sacred grove.
Fontomfrom	State drums.
Etumpan	Talking drums.
Gyasehene	Master of King's Household.
Kete	Drums.
Kobini	Mourning cloths.
Krontehene	Commander of Asante Army.
Kuntunkuni	Mourning cloths.
Manhyia ...	Central meeting place of the Ashantis.
Nkodwasuafohene ...	Head Stool carrier.
Nsaa	Hausa blanket.
Nsebe	Talisman.
Ntanu	£16.
Ntansa	£24.
Odumakuma-Abrafuo ...	Executioners who in the olden days functioned on the death of a King.
Ohene	Chief.
Omanhene	Head Chief.
Oyokoman	A costly cloth worn originally only by the King of Ashanti.
Pata	Hut.
Summe	A reed botanically called Palisota Tayrsi Flora Benth.
Sura	The obsequies observed towards the close of a funeral custom for an Ashanti King.
Wirempi	Electors—Principal Elders of the State.

REPORT ON THE GREAT FUNERAL CUSTOM OF THE LATE NANA EDWARD AGYEMAN PREMPEH I, KUMASIHENE.

The observance of the ceremonial rites in connection with the passing away to his eternal rest on the 12th day of May, 1931, of the late Nana Edward Agyeman Prempeh I, was commenced on the night of Saturday the 21st of May, 1932, at 8 o'clock at the Kumasi-hene's palace. This preliminary is termed " Buro " and was confined only to the members of the Royal Family and a privileged few. The Kete players provided the music for this Buro and many were moved by the sweet and solemn music, so much so that they danced unceasingly.

The Buro continued throughout the night until the early hours of Sunday morning—the 22nd of May. Drinks were freely served to those who were in attendance. On the morning of Sunday the 22nd and at about 8 o'clock the Kumasihene accompanied by his Chiefs and Elders and his attendants paraded in palanquin throughout the town—all wearing " Kuntunkuni " and " Kobini " cloths showing that they were mourning. Returning to Manhyia at about 1.30 p.m., the Kumasihene and his people continued the preliminary ceremony in connection with the Funeral Custom which was to take place on the following Monday—the 23rd of May; this was continued throughout the night under the radiant lights supplied by the electric lights installed at the Ahinfie purposely for the ceremony.

State Firing.

Monday the 23rd of May saw the firing in State of the Kumasihene, the Amanhene and the Ahenfu as a customary sign of honour and respect for their great Hero and most lamented Nana Agyeman who dearly loved them so that he elected to go into banishment rather than plunge them into a bloody conflict with the British Army in 1896. This State firing marked the beginning of the Funeral Custom. Every Omanhene and every Ohene of note in Ashanti was in attendance. The only Omanhene who could not attend the ceremony owing to his confinement in hospital consequent upon ill-health was the Juabenhene. He was, however, represented by his Krontihene and his Ankobiahene and other Elders who contributed their quota towards the firing and the other events that followed. In connection with the State Firing, two special stands were erected on the firing place near the New Zongo under the supervision of a Mr. S. T. A. Affainie who gave up his services free of charge and to whom the thanks of the Kumasihene are due. The clearing and levelling of the grounds were undertaken by the Kumasi Public Health Board through the kind offices of Doctor William Chisholm, the Senior Health Officer, and the Town Engineer, Mr. Tindall. To these officers also the Kumasihene owes a great debt of gratitude.

One of the stands was for His Honour the Chief Commissioner and suite and other Europeans, and the other stand was for the African community. Both of these stands were beautifully decorated and provided with chairs. The chair provided for the Chief Commissioner was covered with a very costly native cloth known as " Oyokoman ".

Arrival of His Honour.

On his arrival on the grounds at 9 o'clock a.m., His Honour the Chief Commissioner was received by the Queen Mother, Nana Kwarduo Yeadom, and Mr. James Prempeh—Secretary to the Kumasihene. It is worthy of record that His Honour attended the ceremony in his uniform and represented the Government of Ashanti, thus expressing the sympathy of the Government to the nation for the great loss it had sustained. It must be mentioned at this juncture that it was not possible for the Kumasihene personally to receive His Honour on his arrival on the ground, owing to his being at the rear of the interminable long procession which was winding its way through the Kingsway to the place of firing via the Antoa Road. To avoid cars and lorries interfering with the procession, it was arranged for those going by cars and lorries to witness the firing to go by the Zongo Road, and the pedestrians also by the Antoa Road. The firing was commenced no sooner than His Honour's arrival on the ground. All the Amanhene, and some of the important Chiefs (Kumasi and district) were presented to His Honour who shook hands with them before their people started firing. The Kumasihene, on his entry into the field, dressed in a majestic manner (Batakare-Kesie containing the talismans of the famous Asantehene Nana Osei Tutu) and befitting the occupant of Osei and Poku Stool shook hands with His Honour and, as a sign of respect, fired one shot in front of His Honour. His dress was adorned with gold and silver nsebe. The Amanhene and Chiefs also were in their war dresses which were reminiscent of the days gone by when the Ashantis indulged in internecine wars. The firing continued from 9 a.m. until in the neighbourhood of 3 o'clock in the afternoon when the last clan fired and the gathering repaired to Dwabraim where they were served with drinks by the Kumasihene. The Chief Commissioner and suite and the other Europeans left the field before the firing came to an end.

It is gratifying to record that notwithstanding the myriads of people who attended the ceremony, everything went on in an orderly manner and smoothly, so much so that nothing untoward arose to mar the function and tarnish the fair name of Ashanti. In this connection the thanks of the nation are due to the Senior Commissioner of Police, Mr. de Carteret and his able Lieutenant, Mr. Penno, and the officers and members of the Asante-Kotoko Society who took charge of the firing.

TUESDAY, 24TH MAY.

According to the way the Ashantis reckon their weeks and years the anniversary of the passing away of the late Kumasihene synchronized

3

with this day. And, consequently, the Kumasihene and the members of the Royal Family and the Oman commemorated the event by sitting in state at Dwabraim and playing " Fontomfrom," " Kete " and " Etumpan " from 9 a.m. until 4.30 p.m. when the gathering dispersed. It may be mentioned that it was found expedient to close each day's event at 4.30 p.m. so as to give the sympathizers and the mourners opportunity of returning home before dusk so as to avoid any mishap.

His Honour, accompanied by Mr. E. A. T. Taylor, Deputy Chief Commissioner, and His Honour's Secretary, Mr. Caruth, returned greetings to the Amanhene on this date—thus conforming to usage. Doubtless, His Honour must have been impressed with the seating arrangements of the Amanhene and the Chiefs. This was how they sat when they came to Kumasi in the days of old when Ashanti had one head.

EMPIRE DAY.

Owing to the celebration of this day clashing with the Funeral Custom, the Kumasihene and the Queen Mother were unable to accept the District Commissioner's invitation to attend the parade.

WEDNESDAY, 25TH MAY.

The Kumasihene sat in state and, surrounded on the right hand by the Ayokofuo consisting of Juabenhene's proxy, Bekwaihene, and Kokofuhene, and on the left hand side by Dako-Ayokofuo consisting of Nsutahene, Kuntanasihene, Akokofehene and Ayadwasihene, he received donations of the Amanhene and the Ahinfu from the districts to defray the cost of the funeral.

THURSDAY, 26TH MAY.

Similar sitting as on the previous day, but this day was devoted to the receipt of donations of the Kumasi Chiefs and their people and other well-wishers.

FRIDAY, 27TH MAY.

There was nothing worthy of record done in the morning of this day; except that a gong-gong was beaten beseeching the Oman, the Amanhene and the Ahinfu " to bathe " and take food as hitherto they have been fasting according to custom. They were supplied with sheep and venison individually by the Kumasihene for their food.

In the afternoon, the Kumasihene, the Queen Mother and the members of the Royal Family congregated at Bogyawi and basked (hata) under the scorching sun signifying that they were drying the ayitam (mourning cloths). Palm wine was poured on the site where a pata (hut) was to be erected for the Sura on the following Saturday. The pata was then erected under the personal supervision of the Queen Mother. One peculiarity about this pata is that according to custom it is to be started and finished within a day. It is built with wooden sticks and summe stems are put across them in a rectangular form; and it is built by only the ahenemma of Ashanti, and it is their duty to provide the necessary materials for its erection.

4

Before the Sura took place on the following afternoon, all but one of the four wooden sticks supporting the pata were removed before dawn, and the space covered by the pata was surrounded with nsaa (Hausa blankets) and the odumakuma-abrafuo were set to watch the place throughout the night so as to prevent people from trespassing. After the drying of the ayitam, the Kumasi Clan Chiefs who constitute the Wirempifuo left the town in the afternoon of Friday (27th May), for Wirempi about one and a half miles from Manhyia. At this time, the Kumasihene was deprived of his nhinkwa as well as the stool paraphernalia and other important things which went to make him Kumasihene, and in consequence he became melancholy. Chief Kojo Poku (Gyasiwahene) also left here on the same day for a place called Abuakwa on the Nkawie road to fetch the Abusua Kuruwa, i.e. the statue of the late Kumasihene. (It is at Abuakwa where the makers of the Abusua-Kuruwa live.) When this was brought in the dead of night it was kept in a second pata erected near the Queen Mother's house, whence it was removed and placed under the remaining wooden stick in the first pata in the early hours of Saturday morning.

Road Clearing.

At the break of Saturday morning, all the ahenemma (male and female) of Ashanti, headed by the Akyempimhene under whom they serve and with him as their master of ceremony, went on the Bremen road and cleared the foot-path leading to the place set apart for the storage of the family statues. On their return from the road, they were given ntanu (£16) by the Kumasihene to satisfy custom.

Shaving of Heads and Paring of Nails.

When the Abusua-Kuruwa was brought and placed in the first pata, all the members of the Royal Family of Ashanti shaved their heads and pared their finger and toe nails and put them into a special receptacle under the Abusua-Kuruwa. To this rule, the Kumasihene, Juabenhene, Bekwaihene, Kokofuhene and Nsutahene and other Ayoko Ahenfu were no exception. Other Amanhene, Ahenfu and other persons also shaved their heads and pared their nails, but as they are not members of the Royal or Oyoko Family, their hairs and nails were not included. The significance of this is that the surviving members of the family have purged themselves of the impurity which the demise of one of their number has brought upon them. It is very strange to remark that native custom does not allow the Kumasihene to see the sight of the Abusua-Kuruwa.

Wirempi.

The following clans: Kronte, Akwamu, Ankobia-Atene, and the stool carriers who composed the Wirempifuo went two days before the sura and quartered at about one and a half miles from Manhyia with all the stools including the Golden Stool and all the nhinkwa and the paraphernalia of the stools. At Wirempi, a new stool was created for the perpetuation of the memory of the late Kumasihene, and the

5

necessary ceremony connected therewith was performed—shewing that the late Kumasihene was no longer among the living. It was believed until this time that the late Kumasihene was still in possession of the stools and their regalia and other paraphernalia attached to them, and to enable the Wirempifuo to dispossess him of these things for the benefit of the Kumasihene as his successor, the stool was created. This along with the old stools was brought by the Wirempifuo who paraded through the town with all the stools and the Golden Stool displaying them to the public. At about 3 p.m. the Kumasihene, the Amanhene, the Ahenfu, the Asafohene, Adikro and Peninfuo (Kumasi and other divisions), the members of the Royal Family and other people assembled by the Sura pata and awaited patiently the return of the Wirempifuo with the newly created stool, the old stools, the Golden Stool and their paraphernalia. Before they left the Wirempi for the town with the national properties, they claimed from the Kumasihene a customary fee of ntansa ($£24$), plus two cases of gin and one sheep, and $£4$ plus one piece of cloth also for the Nkodwasuafohene (Head Stool-carrier). After parading the town with the stools, the Wirempifuo returned to Manhyia at about 5 p.m., when the important Chiefs such as the Krontehene, Akwamuhene, Wenkyihene (Omanhene), and others greeted the Kumasihene who shook hands with them and congratulated them upon returning the stools safely and handing them over to him. When the Head Stool-carrier and his subordinates neared the Kumasihene with the stools the carrier of the newly made stool as also the carrier of the Golden Stool placed them respectively on the Kumasihene's laps thrice, symbolizing the fact that he had succeeded the late Kumasihene who had been dispossessed of the stools and their paraphernalia and thenceforth he (Kumasihene) was in possession of the stools and the Golden Stool, and all the regalia and other paraphernalia attached to them, and that he was privileged and entitled to sit upon the Golden Stool when he would be ready to stand the necessary initiation. It might be mentioned here that the Wirempifuo were privileged by custom in the olden days to take foodstuffs free and catch domestic animals that crossed their path on their way to Wirempi and while there—on these they used to live during their sojourn there.

In the afternoon of the Sura day, everybody, irrespective of rank, dressed in white—those who chose to adorn themselves with gold ornaments did so. Palm wine having been poured on the ground as a libation on this occasion too, a supply of palm wine to the Amanhene and Chiefs then followed. The reason why everybody appeared in white on this occasion was and is that all impure things had been carried away by the late Kumasihene, and that the advent of the new Kumasihene had brought in its train hope for the future; in other words old things had passed yielding place to new. After the drinking of the palm wine supplied to the assembled Ahenfu, the Kumasihene, the Amanhene, the Ahinfu and the spectators repaired to their respective homes, leaving the Queen Mother and the female members of the Royal Family on the scene.

6

The Carriage of the Abusua=Kuruwa to New Dareboase.

At about 8.30 o'clock p.m., the Abusua-Kuruwa was carried to Dareboase on the Breman road and placed alongside the other Abusua-Nkuruwa of the past Ashanti Kings. Custom does not allow any commoner other than a blood relative of the deceased monarch to carry the Abusua-Kuruwa. This one was carried by Nana Amah Akyia who was the niece of the late Kumasihene. The procession to Dareboase was accompanied by all kinds of African music. Meanwhile, the Kumasihene, surrounded by Kronte, Akwamu, and Ankobia Clans, continued playing Kete which played sentimental songs narrating the great deeds of the past Ashanti Kings. This continued until 1 a.m. when the Queen Mother and her large retinue returned to Manhyia from Dareboase before the gathering dispersed.

SUNDAY, 29TH MAY.

There was no ceremony performed on this day—it having been kept as a day of rest.

MONDAY, 30TH MAY.

On the invitation of the Kumasihene, all the Amanhene, the Ahinfu, and others assembled on the grounds at Manhyia Dwabraim and the Kumasihene, the Queen Mother and the Royal Family returned thanks to them for attending the ceremonies and shewing their practical sympathy with them.

TUESDAY, 31ST MAY.

This day saw the termination of the series of events that took place in connection with the Funeral Custom.

WEDNESDAY, 1ST JUNE.

Those District Amanhene and Ahinfu who elected to return to their towns and villages were granted leave by the Kumasihene to do so. They, however, left their Linguists behind to represent them on the following day when the funeral expenses and the total donations received would be made public. As the presence of Juabenhene's representative, Bekwaihene, Kokofuhene and Nsutahene and their Queen Mothers was essential at the Thursday's gathering, they being close relatives of the deceased, they did not leave on the previous day.

THURSDAY, 2ND JUNE.

At 9 a.m. on this day, the remaining Amanhene and Ahinfu met at the Ahinfie as notified on Monday the 30th May, by the Kumasihene, and after customary salutations, the Funeral Committee through Mr. Appiah—Kumasihene's Chief Clerk—read the total expenses incurred in connection with the funeral and also the amount of donations received. It was observed that the expenditure exceeded the donations received by over one thousand pounds. Undoubtedly, the hearts of the Gyasis and Ankobias who are responsible according to native custom for the payment of this huge debt, must have burned within them when the debit balance was announced by Mr. Appiah. Despite the fact that the expenditure exceeded the donations, over two hundred pounds were doled out of the donations to the Amanhene, Ahinfu, the Ayoko Family, the Kumasi Chiefs and the Royal Family in accordance with custom. This augmented the debit balance. And one could read from the faces of the Gyasis and the Ankobias that they were still uneasy in their minds about this huge debit balance which they would be called upon to pay, but it is gratifying to place on record that the Kumasihene instead of putting to his own use the amount of donations given him personally, and saddling the Gyasis and the Ankobias as any other Omanhene would have done, he elected to forgo his personal donations and supplement them with his own money in order to liquidate the huge debit balance which had put the Gyasis and the Ankobias into stupor and free his subjects from the heavy burden of taxation. The Gyasis and the Ankobias having been transported as it were on a magic carpet to the realm of joy and gladness, jumped on their legs and expressed their deep sense of gratitude to the Kumasihene for his indescribably kind act. The Oman also congratulated him upon the unprecedented act of his. From this kind act, one can safely infer that money would appear to be no object to the Kumasihene.

LONG MAY HE RULE OVER US.

Distribution of Sheep and Venison.

On the days following, sheep and venison were again distributed to the Amanhene, Ahinfu and all other persons who contributed financially towards the great event. It is pleasing to remark that the heads of the various churches in Kumasi were not forgotten in the distribution of the sheep to the Oman.

Presence of Europeans at the Sura.

One remarkable feature about the observance of the Sura was the large number of Europeans (ladies and gentlemen), including His Honour the Chief Commissioner of Ashanti, the Assistant Chief Commissioner, the Acting District Commissioner, and the Assistant District Commissioner who were in attendance. It is believed that this was the first occasion in the annals of Ashanti when Europeans had had the privilege and pleasure of witnessing the Sura.

Closing Remarks.

This report would not be complete if the great and excellent services rendered by Mr. de Carteret—Senior Commissioner of Police, and Mr. Penno, Commissioner of Police, were not placed on record. They have the congratulations of the Oman. The thanks of the nation are also due to the Political Officers, most especially His Honour the Chief Commissioner of Ashanti and the Assistant Chief Commissioner, who by advice and other means at their disposal helped to make possible the huge success that crowned the series of events that took place in connection with the observance of the Funeral Custom of Nana Agyeman.

AND MAY HE REST IN PEACE.

8

Finally, God be thanked that during the period covered by the Funeral Custom nothing untoward arose to mar the various events and thus tarnish the fine reputation that Ashanti has won in the eyes of the Government, as a result of mutual prayers offered on behalf of the Funeral Custom by the local churches at the request of the Kumasihene.

Prepared by

J. W. K. APPIAH,
Chief Clerk to Kumasihene.

9

LIST OF AMANHENE AND OTHER AHINFU WHO ATTENDED THE FUNERAL CUSTOM FROM THE DISTRICTS.

Mampong Division.
(Nifahene of Ashanti)
Mamponhene
Ohene of Effiduasi
Ohene of Jamasi
Ohene of Asokori
Ohene of Biposu
Ohene of Ejura.

Juaben Division.
Juabenhene represented by :
  Krontehene
Ankobiahene
Ohene of Juaso.

Bekwai Division.
Bekwaihene
Ohene of Esumengya
(Benkumhene of Ashanti)
Ohene of Abodom
Ohene of Amoaful
Ohene of Pekyi
Ohene of Adankrangya.

Kokofu Division.
Kokofuhene
Ohene of Asaman
Ohene of Sekyire.

Nsuta Division.
Nsutahene
Ohene of Asaman
Ohene of Ntonsu
Ohene of Benka.

Kumawu Division.
Kumawuhene
Ohene of Bodomasi.

Offinsu Division.
Offinsuhene
Ohene of Kikansu.

Ejisu Division.
Ejisuhene
Ohene of Asutwi
Ohene of Bonwere.

Denyasi Division.
Denyasihene.

Agona Division.
Agonahene
Ohene of Bipoah
Ohene of Wiamoasi
Asiniehene.

Ashanti Akyim Division.
Boguhene.

Mansu-Nkwanta Division.
Mansu-Nkwantahene
Ohene of Esuowin
Ohene of Adubiah
Ohene of Mpatuam
Ohene of Mbem.

Wenkyi Division.
Wenkyihene.

Prepared by

J. W. K. APPIAH,
Chief Clerk to Kumasihene.

375

Figure 13.2. Excerpts from Baffour Osei Akoto's 70-page commemorative pamphlet, 2002.

T

R

I

B

U

T

E

S

THE SECRETARY-GENERAL

TRIBUTE TO NANA BAAFOUR OSEI AKOTO
<u>October 2002</u>

I was deeply saddened to learn of the passing away of Nana Baafour Osei Akoto, a close friend I had the pleasure to visit in Kumasi only a few weeks ago.

His death robs Asanteman of one of its greatest sons, a leader who has been for so many decades not only a priceless repository of Asanta history, culture and traditions, but also a tireless advocate for the office and status of the Asantehene.

By his unfailing devotion to the preservation of the vitality of Asanteman, Nana gave us all an extraordinary example of courage and commitment. He had a strong sense of his roots and identity; showed total dedication to a cause larger than himself, and inspired others to do the same. His many contributions earned him great respect, and ensure that he will be long remembered.

I extend my deepest condolences and best wishes to the bereaved family, to Asantemen as a whole, and to all others touched by this loss. The greatest tribute we can pay to his memory is for each and every one of us to do all we can to preserve for posterity, as he did, the best in our traditions, cultures and societies, thereby enriching all humankind.

Kofi A. Annan

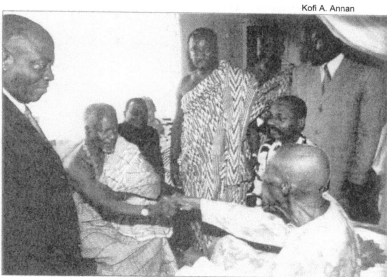

*The last photograph of Baafour before his........with His Excellencies
Kofi Annan and Vice President Aliu Mahama
and other Dignitaries at his bedside at his Asokwa residency, 17th August, 2002*

377

T. C. MCCASKIE

A group picture of Baafour, his family and children after a
Thanksgiving service at the St. Pauls cathedral, Kumasi in 1966

Papa, your radio went silent and with it, your spirit.

It was with a deep sense of loss, that we received news of your end, though you kept telling us that your time was up.

Paa, you fought a good fight and finished the race.

Yours was the lone voice crying out when all others had been cowed into silence.

You were maligned, slandered, imprisoned and even disowned by your very own, but you stood your ground and laid the foundations for a democratic Ghana.

The seeds you sowed have ripened, borne fruit and blossomed today.

Paa, your labor has not been in vain.

The vacuum created by your departure can never be filled. While, we mourn our loss, we give thanks to the Lord for your life and the long years he gave you to guide us into maturity and adulthood.

We will miss you dearly, particularly your humor-filled rich laughter. We shall keep you in our hearts and never forget you, passing on your legacy from generation to generation.

May the good Lord keep you safely and restfully in his arms till we meet again.

Osabarima, Agya Pa, Obaatanpa, da yie.

Onyame nfa wo nsie. Amen.

TRIBUTE TO BAAFOUR OSEI AKOTO

BY MRS. KOJO THOMPSON, WIFE OF THE LATE LAWYER KOJO THOMPSON

MY MOST PLEASANT RECOLLECTION OF BAAFOUR AKOTO IN KUMASI IN THE EARLY 1930'S

T

R It is indeed an exceptional privilege, and rare honour in the affairs of Asanteman for a 95 year old, Nigerian by birth, and a Ghanaian by both naturalization and marriage to write a tribute in memory of one of the greatest sons of the Ashanti and Ghana in modern times, and to take the opportunity to explain some social and political interactions in the ruling houses between Nigeria and Ghana.

I My contact with Okyeame Akoto at Manhyia Palace was not fortuitous but by Royal Patronage at the highest level. I was a Nigerian citizen at the time of our acquaintance and my background was known to the late Prempeh I. By treaty my grandfather King Akitoye of Lagos had established Lagos colony with the help of Her Majesty's government in 1852. My father settled in the Gold Coast in 1891 and

B was a key player in the cocoa trade across the colony. It was against this background that the late Prempeh I requested Sir Hugh Clifford to release my late sister and I from our teaching contract at the Accra Government Girls School to proceed to the Kumasi Government Girls School in 1929. Okyeame Akoto was highly religious, intelligent and dashing young man actively involved behind the scenes at the court at Manhyia Palace. As a matter of fact, his whole soul was inextricable linked to the palace. As a devoted Courtier, Okyeame Akoto helped organized most of the Akwasidae

U celebrations during the reign of Prempeh I with pomp and pageantry.

In spite of his many responsibilities, Okyeame Akoto always found time to watch my late sister and I

T play tennis at the palace in the company of Prempeh II and Prince James, son of Prempeh I. Time without number Okyeame Akoto welcomed us in English with all the courtesies accorded ladies whenever we played tennis at the pleasure of the King.

E Okyeame Akoto was an articulate and powerful young man who made an impression on any visitor who came to Manhyia Palace. He was indeed a socialite par excellence. He lent instinctive support to the organization of the funeral of Otumfuo Prempeh I which was superbly organized by Dasebre Kwaku Duah, Mamponghene at that time. I can vividly recall Okyeame Akoto in his black batakari (war dress) in the company of the late Cobina Kesse and his late Uncle I K Agyemang in the funeral procession.

S By his death, his family, the Ashanti nation and Ghana at large have lost a great son. May Okyeame Akoto rest in peace.

NOTES

1. I thank Dr. Wilhelmina Donkoh and the Abura Printing Works staff for information about the history of Tsiboe's enterprise.

2. Asst. Chief Commissioner of Asante (CCA) to CCA, Kumasi, April 5, 1948, Civil Disturbances in Kumasi 1948, ARG 1/1/25/1–6, Public Records and Archives Administration Department (PRAAD), Kumasi.

3. C. E. Osei to CCA, Manhyia, May 3, 1948, Correspondence and Papers of Asantehene Osei Agyeman Prempeh II (1931–1970), Manhyia Palace, Kumasi. This is a file copy. The original sent to the CCA has not come to light. I thank Ernest Sarhene, Chief of Protocol, Manhyia Palace, and his staff for all their help.

4. McCaskie (2000).

5. Interviews with Baffour Osei Akoto, Kumasi, July 1998. Baffour Osei Akoto was himself the subject of a lavish 70-page commemorative pamphlet that was produced by his family and the Funeral Committee when he died at age 98 in 2002. Sample pages of this document, *State Burial Service in Cherished Memory of the Late Baffour Osei Akoto on Wednesday 13th to Sunday 24th November 2002* (Kumasi: Buck Press Ltd., 2002), are reproduced at the end of this chapter. For autobiographical materials on his life and times, see also Baffour Osei Akoto (1992) and Donkoh and Britwum (2000).

6. Recent examples include Arhin (1994), Manuh (1995), and de Witte (2001).

7. See McCaskie (1989).

8. Compare McKenzie (1999); see Yankah (1998) for current views of orality and literacy in Ghana; and see McCaskie (1999) for the complexities attendant upon literacy in the context of Asante legal documents.

9. For Agyeman Prempeh see Adu Boahen et al. (2003).

10. See Yaw Opoku (J. R. Poku) to Asantehene Osei Agyeman Prempeh II, Nsuase, March 11, 1934, ARG 1/2/1/149, Request for the Removal of Chief Akwasi Nuamah from his Post as Head Linguist, PRAAD Kumasi; and Testimony of Adontenhene Kwame Frimpon, Kumasi, December 5, 1934, Records of the Adontenhene's Tribunal 1927–35, Case 17/33, Antoa Lands, Manhyia Record Office, Kumasi.

11. M. Fortes, "Conversations with Bafuor Akoto and C.E. Osei," Kumasi, December 1945–January 1946, Ashanti Social Survey Papers, Birmingham.

12. Interviews with Baffour Osei Akoto, Kumasi, July 1998. In 1979, the late I. K. Agyeman (1894–1986) treated me to his reading of the "Burial and Funeral Notice" of *abusuapanin* Kwasi Adusei (d. June 20, 1978), the titular head of the Antoa stool royal family. He gave an opinion on the persons and lives of many of the 50-plus "chief mourners" listed in the text, ranging from petty traders to lawyers living in the United States. This deeply informed analysis ranged through past and present and included everything from traditional history to (often-scurrilous) comments about individuals. For I. K. Agyeman's own family, see McCaskie (1998).

13. Agyeman Prempeh II to CCA H. S. Newlands and District Commissioner (Kumasi) F. W. Applegate, Kumasi, May 27, 1932, Correspondence and Papers of Asantehene Osei Agyeman Prempeh II (1931–1970), Manhyia Palace, Kumasi.

14. CCA H. S. Newlands to Osei Agyeman Prempeh II, Kumasi, June 11, 1932, Correspondence and Papers of Asantehene Osei Agyeman Prempeh II (1931–1970), Manhyia Palace, Kumasi. For Newlands as Chief Commissioner of Asante, see Wilks (2000).

15. Northcote was Acting Governor from April 5 to November 30, 1932, after which Shenton Thomas arrived on the Gold Coast and assumed the governorship. Northcote then reverted to his substantive appointment as Colonial Secretary to the Governor.

16. Osei Agyeman Prempeh II to Assistant CCA F. W. Applegate, Kumasi, May 11 and 23, 1933, Correspondence and Papers of Asantehene Osei Agyeman Prempeh II (1931–1970), Manhyia Palace, Kumasi.

17. Assistant CCA F. W. Applegate to CCA H. S. Newlands, Kumasi, May 29, 1933; CCA H. S. Newlands to Secretary for Native Affairs G. S. Northcote, Kumasi, May 31, 1933; and Secretary for Native Affairs G. S. Northcote to CCA H. S. Newlands, Accra, June 13, 1933. All in D.656, National Archives of Ghana, Kumasi. I am grateful to Dr. Wilhelmina Donkoh for copies of this correspondence. The National Archives of Ghana was reorganized as the Public Records and Archives Administration Department in the 1990s, but thus far I have been unable to locate D.656 in the revised ARG classification system.

18. Osei Agyeman Prempeh II to Committee per I. K. Agyeman, Manhyia, November 14, 1933, Correspondence and Papers of Asantehene Osei Agyeman Prempeh II (1931–1970), Manhyia Palace, Kumasi.

19. M. Fortes, "Interview with Ashantihene, 2 March 1945," Ashanti Social Survey Papers, Birmingham.

20. See McCaskie (1998).

21. Osei Agyeman Prempeh II to Edwesohene Kwabena Wusu, Manhyia, July 7, 1934, Correspondence and Papers of Asantehene Osei Agyeman Prempeh II (1931–1970), Manhyia Palace, Kumasi.

22. T. D. Williams to Osei Agyeman Prempeh II, New Asafu Chambers, Kumasi, August 4, 1934, Correspondence and Papers of Asantehene Osei Agyeman Prempeh II (1931–1970), Manhyia Palace, Kumasi. Williams handled mining share certificates and income for Osei Agyeman Prempeh II and represented him as a nominee in land dealings in Asokwa.

23. See Adu Boahen et al. (2003, 19).

24. See McCaskie (1998) for both O. S. Agyeman and E. C. Bobie-Ansah.

25. E. C. Bobie-Ansah to O. S. Agyeman, Kumasi, December 12, 1934, Mss. Deposited by the Executors of J. Asafu Buachi (Lawyer, Me Dan Nyami Nadum Chambers, Box 370, Kumasi Adum), Manhyia Record Office, Kumasi.

26. Hutchison (1931, 1:93). This tribute is headed "Worthiness" and takes the form of eight stanzas of blank verse.

27. M. Fortes, "Conversations with George Asafu-Adjaye," 1945–1946, Ashanti Social Survey Papers, Birmingham. Fortes talked a lot with all three Asafu-Adjaye brothers—lawyer Edward, doctor Isaac, and George—and was especially close to George. George unburdened himself to Fortes about his turbulent marriage to Christina, which had been arranged by Kwame Frimpon in 1932. The couple separated for a time but were reunited at Kwame Frimpon's insistence. Fortes thought the brothers were trapped by their obligation to their uncle and that George was dependent upon Christina, for she was her father's principal legatee and inherited much of his property. She was educated by her father at Wesley Girls' High School in Cape Coast.

28. Osei Agyeman Prempeh II to J. E. Bandoh, Manhyia, October 19, 1936, Correspondence and Papers of Asantehene Osei Agyeman Prempeh II (1931–1970), Manhyia Palace, Kumasi. See also McCaskie (1999).

29. See Adu Boahen et al. (2003, 175–182).

30. Compare Yankah (1998, 20).

31. See McCaskie (2000) for some discussion of these trends in the 1940s.

32. See McCaskie (1998).

33. For such societies and clubs in the Gold Coast Colony see Newell (2002).

34. Mampon Literary Club (MLC) Mss., Curator's Archive, Manhyia Palace Museum, Kumasi. These papers were assembled by the late A. B. Nyantakyi, MLC Secretary (1939–1945).

35. MLC Minutes, June 1949, Curator's Archive, Manhyia Palace Museum, Kumasi.

36. MLC Minutes, March 1942, and S. Garbah to Agona Youngmens' Improvement Society, Kumasi, April 9, 1942, MLC Mss. MLC members often used the approving term "Friend of Freedom." This might be because some of them had taken part in the Friends of Ashanti Freedom Society (FAFS) when that body opposed the restoration of the Asantehene in 1934–1935. The FAFS was active in Mampon, where it was led by the educated royal *akwankwaa* W. B. Agyeman. See Tordoff (1965, 406–407).

37. On the war years, see Lawler (2002). See also Intelligence Reports from the Superintendent 1941–1948, ARG 1/20/8/2, PRAAD, Kumasi, and "Screening of Correspondence, Subversive Matter and Communist Propaganda [Top Secret]," n.d.

38. See for example "Asantehene Talks of 'Youngmen,'" n.d. [1946], 8.63, Fortes Papers, Cambridge University Library.

39. Osei Agyeman Prempeh II, Manhyia, March 28, 1947, Manhyia Palace, Kumasi. Correspondence and Papers of Asantehene Osei Agyeman Prempeh II (1931–1970), In part this letter was a reply to, and perhaps inspired by, Atipinhene to Asantehene, Manhyia, February 16, 1946, which bemoaned the rising expense of funerals. See *Minutes of the Eighth Session of the Ashanti Confederacy Council held at the Prempeh Assembly Hall, Kumasi, on 21st and 25th February and 4th, 5th, 6th, 7th and 11th March 1946* [1954], Appendix J, 104–106, Manhyia Record Office, Kumasi.

40. Boakye Dankwa to Asantehene, "Report on Funeral Customs [Secret]," Kumasi, November 2, 1947, Correspondence and Papers of Asantehene Osei Agyeman Prempeh II (1931–1970), Manhyia Palace, Kumasi.

41. Compare McCaskie (1995, 212–217).

42. For the political context, see McCaskie (2000, 226).

43. I. K. Agyeman died in 1986. This document is presumably still in his extensive archive, now in the care of one of his sons.

44. Osei Agyeman Prempeh II to E. O. Asafu-Adjaye, Manhyia, January 20, 1950, Correspondence and Papers of Asantehene Osei Agyeman Prempeh II (1931–1970), Manhyia Palace, Kumasi. See also "Present Political Discontents," ms. prepared by J. W. K. Appiah, July 1950.

45. *Ashanti Pioneer* (Kumasi), February 14 and 21 and March 26, 1952.

46. The copy cited is in Curator's Archive, Manhyia Palace Museum, Kumasi. For "Owusu Ansah of Asante" at Mfantsipim School (Richmond College), see Adu Boahen (1996, 168). This book conveys the continuing importance of Mfantsipim in shaping the lives of the Asante and broader Ghanaian elite.

47. I understand that this typescript is now with the unclassified papers left by the late Asantehene Opoku Ware II.

48. The commemorative pamphlet is by Kyerematen [n.d.]. See too "Report of the Funeral Committee (Burial Service and Last Rites of Otumfuo the Ashantihene Sir Osei Agyeman Prempeh II)" n.d. [early 1970s], Correspondence and Papers of Asantehene Osei Agyeman Prempeh II [1931–1970], Manhyia Palace, Kumasi.

49. I thank Emily Asiedu and Dr. Audrey Gadzekpo for their sterling work in supplying me with publications about the death and funeral of Asantehene Opoku Ware II.

50. I have an authorized copy of *Burial Rites of the Late Asantehene Otumfuo Opoku Ware II on Sun. March 21, 1999 to Thurs. March 25, 1999*, which I bought in a sealed cassette box. I also have a number of pirated copies. One of these is spliced with what seems to be downloaded TV footage. Another was presented to me as a gift by the manager of a Kumasi hotel because I seemed "interested" in Asante culture. The videotape *Born to Lose*, a Nigerian-made horror film available in Ghana, has spliced-in footage from the Asantehene's funeral as part of its mise-en-scène.

51. Interview with M. A. Okyere, Accra, July 2000.

52. See G. A. Asare, "Funerals: The New Business in Kumasi," *Daily Graphic*, Accra, January 2, 2003.

53. De Witte (2001, 190).

REFERENCES

All primary sources are cited in full in the endnotes.

Adu Boahen, A. 1996. *Mfantsipim and the Making of Ghana: A Centenary History, 1876–1976*. Accra: Sankofa Educational Publishers.

———, E. Akyeampong, N. Lawler, T. C. McCaskie, and I. Wilks, eds. 2003. *"The History of Ashanti Kings and the Whole Country Itself" and Other Writings by Otumfuo, Nana Agyeman Prempeh I*. Oxford: Oxford University Press for the British Academy.

Arhin, K. 1994. "The Economic Implications of Transformations in Akan Funeral Rites." *Africa* 64, no. 3: 307–322.

Baffour Osei Akoto. 1992. *Struggle against Dictatorship: Autobiography of Baffour Osei Akoto*. Kumasi: Payless Printing Press.

Donkoh, W. J., and K. A. Britwum. 2000. *Baafour Osei Akoto: A Biographical Sketch*. Kumasi: MBK Printing Press.

Hutchison, C. F. 1931. *The Pen-Pictures of Modern Africans and African Celebrities*. 2 vols. London: Africana Library Press.

Kyerematen, A. A. Y. n.d. *Daasebre Osei Tutu Agyeman Prempeh II, Asantehene: A Distinguished Traditional Ruler of Contemporary Ghana*. Kumasi: Abura Printing Works.

Lawler, N. E. 2002. *Soldiers, Airmen, Spies, and Whisperers: The Gold Coast in World War II*. Athens: Ohio University Press.

Manuh, T. 1995. "Changes in Marriage and Funeral Exchanges in Asante: A Case Study from Kona, Afigya-Kwabre." In *Money Matters: Instability, Values, and Social Payments in the Modern History of West African Communities*, ed. J. I. Guyer, 188–201. Portsmouth, N.H.: Heinemann; London: James Currey.

McCaskie, T. C. 1989. "Death and the *Asantehene*: A Historical Meditation." *Journal of African History* 30, no. 3: 417–444.

———. 1995. *State and Society in Pre-Colonial Asante*. Cambridge: Cambridge University Press.

———. 1998. "*Akwankwaa*: Owusu Sekyere Agyeman in His Life and Times." *Ghana Studies* 1: 91–122.

———. 1999. "The Last Will and Testament of Kofi Sraha: A Note on Accumulation and Inheritance in Colonial Asante." *Ghana Studies* 2: 171–181.

———. 2000. *Asante Identities: History and Modernity in an African Village 1850–1950.* Edinburgh: Edinburgh University Press for the IAI; Bloomington: Indiana University Press.

McKenzie, D. F. 1999. *Bibliography and the Sociology of Texts.* Cambridge: Cambridge University Press.

Newell, S. 2002. *Literary Culture in Colonial Ghana: "How to Play the Game of Life."* Manchester: Manchester University Press.

Tordoff, W. 1965. *Ashanti under the Prempehs, 1888–1935.* Oxford: Oxford University Press.

Wilks, I. 2000. "Asante Nationhood and Colonial Administrators, 1896–1935." In *Ethnicity in Ghana: The Limits of Invention,* ed. C. Lentz and P. Nugent, 68–96. London: Macmillan; New York: St. Martin's Press.

Witte, M. de. 2001. *Long Live the Dead! Changing Funeral Celebrations in Asante, Ghana.* Amsterdam: Aksant Academic Publishers.

Yankah, K. 1998. *Free Speech in Traditional Society: the Cultural Foundations of Communication in Contemporary Ghana.* Accra: Ghana Universities Press.

WRITING, GENRE, AND A SCHOOLMASTER'S INVENTIONS IN THE YORUBA PROVINCES

14

Karin Barber

In the obscure sphere of tin-trunk literacy, individuals and groups experiment quite recklessly with available conventions of expression and communication, and from this we may be able to learn something about the conditions in which genres are established and mutate and thus how cultural innovation occurs in the very matrix of convention.

Here is a case of an inventor whose new ideas were not taken up but simply disappeared from the record. It provides a glimpse into what people at the time saw as possibilities that existed or could be created. It is testimony to the scope and range of inventiveness of obscure individuals and to the loneliness of their chosen sphere.

Adenle's Life

I came across S. A. Adenle because of two pamphlets, published in the 1930s and reprinted in the 1940s, which were included in the Bascom collection of Yoruba texts.[1] From them, it was possible to deduce that the author had been the headmaster of a school in Oṣogbo in western Nigeria and had later become the Ataọja (king) of the town. The shorter pamphlet, forty-six pages long, is entitled *Iwe Aiye Toto Fun* (The Book of "Beware of the World"). The front page states that the first edition was printed in 1934, the second edition in 1944 and a reprint in 1947. The longer one, a booklet of 124 pages, is entitled *Iwe Iwa Rere L'Oṣo Enia* (The Book of "Good Behavior Is the Best Adornment"). No date is given, but the Bascom collection documentation suggests that it was published after *Iwe Aiye Toto Fun*.

These two pamphlets are curious literary efforts that make use of unusual elaborate poetic and narrative strategies—*Iwe Iwa Rere L'Oṣo Enia* in particular being unlike anything which has been published in Yoruba before or since. On a recent visit to Nigeria, therefore, I tried to find out more about this author and the literary climate in which he worked. His son, Victor Adenle, was most helpful in supplying details of Adenle's life story. Another person who had known Adenle well was Chief Ọladunjoye Omigbọdun, now in his nineties: he was a junior colleague and protégé of Adenle's, who became the first principal of Oṣogbo Grammar School when it opened in 1950. Mr. D. B. Adegoke, a much younger man, was a pupil of Adenle's who later also became a secondary school principal in Oṣogbo. For the purposes of this discussion, I will draw selectively on these sources, taking Victor Adenle's narrative as the central one; in a future study I hope to be able to explore the nature of these narratives and the implications of the overlaps and contrasts between them.[2]

All the accounts agreed that this was the story of a man who began life at a disadvantage but who was exceptionally determined, inventive, and astute. Born in 1900, Samuel Adelẹyẹ Adenle lost his father while still a baby and was brought up by other relatives. One of these, a convert of the Church Missionary Society mission (which had been established in Oṣogbo in the year of Adenle's birth), ensured that Adenle attended the Anglican primary school up to Standard VI, from 1908 to 1916. After that he supported himself until 1922, when he gained admission to St Andrews College Ọyọ, the country's premier teacher-training college. In those days St Andrews was, as Mr. Adegoke put it, "like our university—it was our highest institution of learning." Admission depended on merit, and once accepted, students paid virtually nothing. This made it possible for an impoverished young man to put himself through the most advanced education available. Adenle was an able student, completing the four-year program in three years through "accelerated progression" and gaining an "upper credit" in mathematics. In 1925, he qualified as a teacher, joining the minuscule group known in Oṣogbo as "Tọyọbọ"— those who have returned from (St Andrews College) Ọyọ. Adenle was immediately posted to an Anglican primary school in Benin City, and within three years he was promoted to headmaster there. Education, which had given him his first chance, remained a central preoccupation throughout his life, as we shall see. However, during his years in Benin, another engine of his advancement started up: he had an extraordinary flair for trade. Chief Omigbọdun recounted that "as he was working as a teacher, he was wondering, 'What is it that the people of Benin like a lot?' He began to investigate the question, and found that the Benin City people liked chickens." So Adenle began to import chickens from Oṣogbo to sell at a handsome profit in Benin. Mr. Adegoke told another version of the story, which stressed the unforeseen, and in this case felicitous, results of letter-writing: Adenle had decided that what the Benin people lacked was Yoruba tie-dyed indigo cloth (aṣọ adirẹ), so he wrote a letter to his mother asking her to send some. "But he didn't write 'aṣọ adirẹ,' he just wrote 'adirẹ,' and they misread it here, as hens—'adiẹ.' They bought a lot of hens—wondering what on earth he wanted them for over there—and packed them in a coop and sent them. That's how he stumbled on the fowl business. A hen that doesn't cost more than a shilling here can be sold for ten shillings there."

The trade in both chickens and indigo-dyed cloth expanded until Adenle was employing many people and was so lucrative that when he was posted back home to Oṣogbo in 1933 he was able to raise enough capital to establish a school of his own, which he called the Adenle Primary-Secondary School.[3] This was a daring venture and a source of prestige. Mr. Adegoke judged that "Adenle's most important action was establishing that school." There were few primary schools and not a single secondary school in the Oṣogbo area at the time (the first government-supported grammar school was not opened until seventeen years later, partly as a result of Adenle's campaigning). Many people mocked him, saying, "Do you think you are a European? Only Europeans open schools." It was difficult to recruit staff and pay them, and Adenle had to do most of the teaching himself. But he managed to keep the primary section of the school going for nearly a decade, and when he eventually relinquished it, it was taken over and continued by the government. Meanwhile, however, the other side of his career was developing rapidly. He became a highly successful cloth salesman for the European importing companies which had opened offices in Oṣogbo—Patterson Zochonis, CFAO, UAC, and John Holt. Unlike most agents, who hung on to the cloth in the hope of selling it for the highest possible profit, Adenle sold his allocations quickly at cheap prices, making a small profit and constantly going back to the suppliers for more. This efficiency impressed some of the importing companies so much that they made him their sole distributor. Then, between 1941 and 1943 there was a wartime salt shortage and the European firms made him the sole distributor for salt, too. It was in the salt trade, according to Chief Omigbọdun, that Adenle first made owo yanturu—loads of money. He became such an important agent for these firms that he found it necessary to build a large private warehouse to which they could deliver their goods in bulk.

Adenle had grown up in the Oluawo Ṣangoṣọwọ branch of the royal family of Oṣogbo, and by the early 1940s it was becoming apparent that there might soon be a vacancy in the kingship. Adenle now focused both his

educational and his trading activities on the pursuit of high office. He cultivated the kingmakers, offering them free places for their children at his
school, and providing them with bags of salt to trade with on their own account. He also stockpiled his own wealth. Though his eligibility for the
throne was in doubt, for his biological father was believed not to be of royal
descent—and perhaps not even a Yoruba[4]—he used his education and his
entrepreneurial flair so astutely that he beat his main rival and gained the
throne of Oṣogbo in 1944.

According to one version of the story of the contest for the kingship, the
family council had initially selected Adenle's main rival—an older and extremely wealthy and influential prince—as the obvious and natural successor
to the throne. They asked Adenle, as the family's most educated member, to
act as the secretary of the family meeting and sent him to Ibadan to inform
the colonial authorities of their choice. The district officer in Ibadan questioned Adenle closely about the nominated successor: "So this is the person
you have chosen? Is he enlightened?" Adenle said no, the candidate hadn't
been to school. "An old man, and one that doesn't understand English and is
not educated! Then you had better reconsider. In the modern world, it is important to have an enlightened person there. Otherwise they will cheat you."[5]
So Adenle returned home and proposed himself as a more suitable candidate.
The head of the household, his adoptive father, asked if he had enough money
to match the ostentatiously lavish expenditure of his rival. Adenle's wealth
was less obvious: "He never changed his cloth—no one knew whether he had
any money or not." But he was able to "put down" a substantial sum (one account said it was "a capful of shillings") and from then on had the backing of
the family head. Thereafter, he had a long reign as a dynamic and "enlightened" ọba who promoted education, adult literacy, and cultural activities in
Oṣogbo and helped to turn the town into a center of artistic and theatrical innovation.

What stands out vividly in these accounts of Adenle's life is his brilliantly
astute and opportunistic exploitation of his two major assets: his flair for trading and his education. Both assets were aspects of Adenle's equipment as a
new man, though he used them to attain the most traditional of prestigious
roles. His ability to spot market opportunities—discovering the Benin
people's demand for chickens and indigo-dyed cloth, for example—was no
doubt part of the ancient entrepreneurial culture of the Yoruba, but the commerce in which he made his fortune was a new form of trade brought to Oṣogbo by the colonial railway line after 1905. He outsmarted his rivals and secured a monopoly in various lines of imports because he was quicker than

them to understand how to exploit the European trading system. Victor was deeply impressed by this: "He somehow or other discovered, or read about, the principle of small returns, rapid turnover—I don't know how he hit upon this idea or where he got it from," he said, "but it made his fortune." Education, similarly, was a novel avenue to influence which Adenle had the foresight to pursue single-mindedly. When Adenle began attending All Saints' School in 1908, it was the only school in Oṣogbo and had been in existence only three years (Bamisaiye 1995). Many Oṣogbo people, according to popular memory, were initially resistant to missionary education, refusing to let their children attend or withdrawing them after a few years.[6] Adenle, unlike many of his fellow pupils, moved without a hitch through the nine-year program, a success he repeated and surpassed when he attended St Andrews. He was thus one of the very first cohorts to qualify as a teacher in Oṣogbo. This education, as Adenle correctly grasped, could displace and override even hallowed traditions of royalty when it came to dealing with the colonial government. Though there were petitions and protests about his selection as *ọba*, Adenle triumphed through his astute deployment of his wealth and his education.

Adenle's Inventions

Adenle was remembered and applauded for his wealth, his establishment of a school, and his progressive initiatives as *ọba*. He was also the subject of more critical comments from those who resented his method of gaining, and subsequently enjoying, the ọbaship. But among his colleagues, pupils, friends, and children, he was also remembered for his inventions.

It was in the 1930s, according to Victor Adenle, that he did most of his creative work. Chief Omigbodun remembered Adenle above all as a highly intelligent person, "a man full of wisdom," who had "made a machine, a machine for grinding cassava." Victor Adenle was able to give a clearer picture of what was involved: in 1937, Adenle invented not a grinding machine but a mechanical loom, using a bicycle wheel which was wound by hand and connected by cogs to the shuttle. To produce this machine, Adenle drew on his knowledge of the principles of mechanics learned at St Andrew's College, but he also visited local weavers to study their techniques. He used imported silk as the thread and he got his wives to wind the handle. The loom worked. According to Victor, "I myself have worn clothes made of cloth woven on that machine." Some of the cloth was used at home and the rest was sold. But the invention was a nine-days' wonder. No one copied it, and after his accession, during a crisis in the palace, someone stole the machine and it has not been seen since.

In the same period, after he had come home from Benin but before he embarked on the project of contesting for the kingship, Adenle undertook his experiments in writing. He wrote the two pamphlets that have survived and possibly others that were never published. The first pamphlet, *Iwe Aiye Toto Fun*, was composed in the early 1930s. It took Adenle some time to find a printer. Eventually Tani-mẹhin-ọla Press, based in Ijẹbu-Ode but with a branch in Oṣogbo, took it on and printed it, initially in a small run, from Adenle's handwritten manuscript. Soon afterward—around 1939, Victor said—he published *Iwe Iwa Rere L'Ọṣọ Enia*. Later, after his accession, he had both books reprinted on a very large scale—according to Victor, he had two 10' × 10' rooms filled with copies, "thousands of them." It is unclear how many of them he managed to sell. On the one hand, both Victor and Mr. Adegoke stated that they were widely used in schools at the time[7] and that Adenle employed a sales manager to distribute them across the Yoruba-speaking area.[8] On the other hand, Victor said that Adenle managed to sell only about 10 percent of what he had printed and that the stacks of unsold copies were not valued or preserved by the family: Adenle's wives "used them as firewood."

In their comments on Adenle's mechanical and literary inventions, Chief Omigbọdun and Victor Adenle stressed two points. The first was that Adenle's wide and often unhappy experience of the world was what shaped him and inspired his work. He had suffered from losing his father in infancy; he had been passed from one relative to another and was treated as a houseboy in their households. This early suffering, according to Victor, formed Adenle's character, filling him with a determination to succeed in life so that his own children would not have to undergo the same experience. His extraordinarily energetic and pioneering drive to succeed and create was attributed to his need to overcome painful origins. Chief Omigbọdun thought that Adenle's literary works were inspired by bitter experience. As a teacher and a trader,

> He must have come across some disappointments, as a human being, and that was what led him to write the books. And anybody who has to have dealings with a lot of people, there's bound to be some quarrelling: "People are difficult." *"Beware of the world!"* That's to say, "The world cannot be trusted," "People are not all that reliable," that's the meaning of *"Beware of the world."* . . . His experience arose from dealings he had, not just with pupils but also with their parents, and then when he was trading, dealing in chickens, making *adire*, selling salt, he met all kinds of people. And he would have had all kinds of experiences which he used in writing [or which led him to write] his books.

The second point that Victor in particular stressed was Adenle's isolation. He may have been immersed in activity in the world, but he was also lonely.

> There was a large intellectual gap between himself and his wives, and they didn't understand what he was doing. He would shut himself away in his room at night to write. They (and other people too) thought he was in a cult and that the spirits would come at the dead of night to discuss with him. They thought he was writing all those things at the behest of the spirits. They thought that instead of writing those things he should have been making money. It was the same when he was inventing the weaving machine: he shut himself in his room to think, and they thought he was mad.

He had few people to talk to. He assembled a library: "bookshelves in his room where he kept his favourite books," which apparently included Aristotle, Socrates, Shakespeare, and George Bernard Shaw as well as the Yoruba Bible, which "he must have read a thousand times." He constantly read and reread his books, and he "liked to talk about them to his children and wives, but they were not interested." Victor himself—today a devotee of inspirational and speculative literature—ruefully remarked that as a boy he was only interested in physics and mechanical engineering and could very rarely be prevailed upon to discuss philosophy with his father.

Adenle married while still a schoolteacher in Benin, and he went on marrying: according to Victor, he had six wives by the time he became Ataoja in 1944 and thereafter added another sixteen. He had many children, of whom 120 survived and many more died. In the tradition of the old-style Yoruba big man, he built up an establishment of "people" which functioned both as a source and as a demonstration of wealth. But he also tried to modernize this traditional household: "He was much disturbed that his people could not read," said Victor. He established adult education in the palace, employing teachers to instruct his wives and other adults who could not attend primary school because of their age or social position. In private, he himself taught his wives and children. He sent all his children at least to secondary school and in some cases beyond. Victor saw this enlightened policy as the outgrowth of Adenle's loneliness—he wished to surround himself with people nearer to his own educational level.

This goal, however, he was unable to attain. His most original creations were never appreciated. Victor portrays him as a man who bore his cares alone, turning to Christian texts for consolation and encouragement.

> He loved English hymns, and loved singing them, especially the old English hymns in the Anglican hymnbook, and the Methodist and Baptist hymn books

in Yoruba translation. His favourite hymn was no. 555 in the Anglican Yoruba hymnbook,[9] and his favourite psalm was no. 46.[10] The reason he loved them was that both conveyed the same philosophical message—that a troubled mind finds solace in the abundant love of the Almighty. He said this himself. After a day's work—after being misunderstood, castigated and mistreated—to get solace he would sing that hymn. It would give him strength to continue to lead his people.

Loneliness and Enlightenment in Oṣogbo

This stress on Adenle's early suffering and his loneliness needs to be understood in the context of the environment in which a provincial trader-schoolmaster operated in the 1920s–1940s. From the beginning of the twentieth century, Oṣogbo was a thriving, dynamic commercial city with a rapidly increasing population and a strong artisanal tradition. But it was predominantly pagan and Muslim, and the tiny educated Christian elite, though salient and influential in local affairs, did not have the strong institutional base they enjoyed in Lagos. They lacked a local press, bookshops, literary societies, reading circles, and the other amenities that enabled the literary culture of Lagos to flourish in the 1920s. As new literates in a predominantly oral culture, and as a Christian minority, educated people in Oṣogbo had to construct their own intellectual resources. Personal libraries, diaries, and collections of valued documents were the characteristic focus of their mental lives. Both Chief Omigbọdun and Mr. Adegoke assembled their own libraries of school textbooks, which they preserved carefully over many years. Mr. Adegoke also monitored his own educational progress in a diary which he maintained over a number of years. Adenle himself had several "iron boxes" (the Nigerian term for tin trunks) which he kept under his bed and in which he stored his treasured papers. After his accession, according to Victor,

> His wife kept his clothes, beads and paraphernalia for him, but he kept his own special documents in the iron boxes. In those days, people without the means to buy iron boxes, which were expensive, would use wooden ones. They would keep any publications wrapped among clothes to protect them from termites. They would treasure everything they got in print.

As a private man, Victor said, Adenle probably kept a diary too, but after his accession he did not continue, "because a diary is supposed to be private. As an ọba you are a public person and cannot keep a private record." Instead, he kept a "to do" list which he checked from day to day, crossing things off as they were accomplished—but even this was written in a secret code.

In their reminiscences, both Chief Omigbọdun and Mr. Adegoke evoked a network of fellow teachers and fellow pupils. Chief Omigbọdun several times alluded to Adenle's and his own former pupils who later became famous. One became a senior chief in Benin; two others became prominent lawyers. He recalled their full names, their nicknames, and their titles. He recalled the name of the examiner who came from Ibadan to conduct the Standard V examination in 1926 and the exact dates of his own, Adenle's, and the novelist D. O. Fagunwa's years at St Andrews. The loneliness of the educated man (and all these reminiscences revolved exclusively around men) conferred a kind of salience and a kind of company too. By being isolated from their families and fellow townspeople, they became permanent, vivid landmarks in the mental terrain of their educated peers. As late as the 1950s and 1960s, the Tọyọbọ, or "Andreans," who all knew each other, were virtually the only educated people in Oṣogbo: people educated elsewhere (at other teacher-training colleges and at Ibadan University, which opened in 1948) "were not up to ten in number," according to Mr. Adegoke. The educated set was not necessarily the wealthiest or of the highest social status: "There were only two cars in Oṣogbo at that time, the car of *ọba* Adenle and the car of the manager of GBO, Chief Adedipẹ a native of Akurẹ. . . . Rich people among the uneducated elders would ride horses, all the big heads of households, horses, the wealthy people, horses; the small clerks and literate people, bicycles." If this little group of literates was highly conscious of its own distinctiveness and its own progressive mission, it also tended to be dispersed, for graduates of St Andrews usually became teachers and were posted around the country by the government.

As *ọba*, Adenle's bitter experience of "the world" and his sense of himself as a rarity were transposed into a new key. Although solitary activities such as mechanical invention and creative writing and private activities such as keeping a diary had to be abandoned when he took the throne, his new status gave him a vastly expanded scope for the development of public projects that promoted "enlightenment" and for the projection of his own progressive persona. He was answerable day and night to the demands of the mass of his people; yet he now had unprecedented opportunity to advance the causes of the educated minority. He lent his full support to the campaign for Oṣogbo's first grammar school. He welcomed missionary organizations that sought to establish schools, allocating them as much land as they wanted: "He would take them to the bush and tell them to throw a stone—wherever it landed was theirs to build on, as extensively as they liked." He pioneered adult literacy classes. He instigated or supported the creation of a free public library for schoolchildren, the installation of which Chief Omigbọdun supervised during his period as chair of the town council. He welcomed visitors such as Ulli

Beier and Suzanne Wenger, encouraging them to stay and supporting their role as catalysts of visual, musical, and theatrical arts in Oṣogbo.[11] And he used his new resources to produce new editions of his two pamphlets. The new title pages named him as "Mr S.A. Adenle, Former Principal, Oshogbo Grammar School,[12] now H.H. Adenle I, The Ataoja of Oshogbo," thus retaining his status as a senior schoolmaster while simultaneously proclaiming his royal identity as the father of the whole town. The reprinting of the two books on a large scale after his accession transposed his lonely, private, and experimental literary endeavors into a public affirmation of the value of literacy and the importance of having an "enlightened" *oba*.

The Texts

Both *Iwe Aiye Toto Fun* and *Iwe Iwa Rere L'Oṣo Enia* are moral or philosophical statements—or sermons, as one commentator put it[13]—presented through a narrative framework. In *Iwe Aiye Toto Fun*, Adenle's first published pamphlet,[14] a schoolgirl wants to find out the nature of life on earth. She goes from one acquaintance to another and each delivers a lengthy poetic commentary, some saying the world is sweet but most affirming that it is a vale of tears. The poetry is freestyle, sonorous, and proverbial, with biblical reverberations. It is constructed largely of long strings of parallel formulations:

> *Aiye ti o kọ otọ, Aiye ọrẹ eke, ọta ododo*
> *Aiye ọrẹ okukun, ọta imọlẹ*
> *Aiye ọrẹ ẹni mẹdọgbọn, Aiye a gbọ eyi sọ eyi*
> *Ma gbe ara le wọn.*
> *Aiye to to, ẹru aiye ma mba mi ẹ jare, aiye to to fun* (p.3)

> The World that rejects truth, the World, friend of deceit, enemy of honesty
> The World, friend of darkness, enemy of light
> The World, friend of twenty-five people at once, the World which hears one thing and reports another
> Don't trust them [i.e. people that make up "the World"]
> Beware of the World, sure I'm scared of the world, beware of the world.

These strings are divided into numbered sections of variable length, many of them ending with the rather haunting and songlike refrain "*Aiye to to, ẹru aiye ma mba mi ẹ jare, aiye to to fun*" (Beware of the World, sure I'm scared of the world, beware of the world). In the end the girl asks her father if there is another world beyond this one and he teaches her about heaven. It was this pamphlet that our informants remembered best. Its numbered stanzas and its sonorous, sententious proverbial and biblical language have some affinity with the pamphlets of A. K. Ajiṣafẹ which were published in Lagos in the 1920s, in particular *Aiye Akamara* (The Vicissitudes of the World, 1921)—a homily addressed to schoolchildren in which the warning *"Aiye toto fun"* (Beware of the world) actually occurs several times.

Iwe Iwa Rere L'Ọṣọ Enia, the second book, is much longer and has a more complex structure. As far as I know, from a formal point of view it has no clear precedent in Yoruba published literature. It is a highly elaborate compilation of nested narratives told entirely in unrhymed verse, most of it organized in regular stanzas. The scaffolding of the narrative is the story of an arrogant *ọba* who boasts that he is the wisest, handsomest, strongest, most independent, and most contented ruler in the world. He challenges his servants to find examples of others who can match him. One by one, the seven servants tell him edifying stories which rebut each of his claims in turn, either by producing examples of people who outshine the *ọba* or by demonstrating that his boast is misconceived in the first place. In some cases these stories feature long set-piece speeches, dialogues, or moral disquisitions—all in verse form—or have further stories nested within them. Finally the *ọba* repudiates all this advice, rashly engages in a war with a neighboring town, and ends up losing his throne to a slave who though not royal is wise, modest, and good to his people.

What is most remarkable about this text is the systematic attempt at meter. The stanzas occur in sets. In each set, every stanza has the same number of lines, and each line has the same number of syllables. For each set of stanzas, the number of syllables per line is indicated at the top of the set, much in the manner of the Baptist hymnbook.[15] The shortest is six syllables, the longest sixteen. In some more ambitious sets, two different line lengths alternate regularly throughout each stanza. There are also headings to show who is speaking to whom or to link episodes. The lines are rigorously syllable-counted throughout the entire text. This is a remarkable feat in a tonal, unstressed language whose orature is entirely nonmetrical. The fact that it is an artifact of writing can be seen in the way Adenle counts syllables, following orthography rather than phonology, and producing grammatical overhangs (e.g. ending a line with *tí*, "who" or *àti*, "and") that would be impossible in orature, where lineation (i.e., breath group) is coterminous with the syntactic unit. The results are often awkward. The overweening *ọba* is introduced thus:

> *O l'okiki pupọ, bẹni ko s'ogun ti i lọ ti ki i ṣe*
> *Ṣugbọn o fẹran afẹ ṣiṣe pupọ o si ni inu*
> *Didun si ẹnikẹni t'o ba le ṣe afẹ ati ti*
> *O ba si fẹran ogo asan aiye yi bi tirẹ gan* (pp. 1–2)

> He had great renown, and likewise there was no war he went to which he did
>   not win
> But he liked finery and pomp a lot, and he would be well-
> Disposed towards anyone who could display finery and who
> Also liked the vain pomp of this world as much as he did.

This is a peculiar form indeed: as the novelist Ọladẹjọ Okediji put it, "It's not Yoruba poetry, and it isn't like the poetry we know about in any other place either. It's got its own form. The division of the poetry into stanzas is artificial, it is a complete invention, there's no one else who divides it like that. And," he added, "it's not so good that anyone else would want to copy it."

The rigorous artificiality of Adenle's chosen prosodic form is echoed in the larger structure of the text. The challenge that supplies the framework of the narrative is a discursive one: the *ọba* invites his servants to bring evidence, to demonstrate if they can the existence of something the *ọba* does not believe in—that is, people superior to himself. The text is all talk. Only at the end of the story, when the recalcitrant *ọba* spurns all his servants' wise words—which have made up the bulk of the text—and decides to make war on his neighbor, does anything actually happen. Not only this, but the servants' stories themselves are often framed as puzzles, set by one character to be solved by another, or as exercises in exposition, in which one character shows another character something which demonstrates a propositional truth. Thus, for example, the first servant's story begins with a challenge from an *ọba* who is a personification of Wisdom to two of his subjects to explain the meaning of their names. One is called "Ṣebiotimọ" (Moderation, "Act within your limits") and the other "Alaṣeju" (Over-doer, "One who goes too far"). In their very manner of answering the *ọba*'s summons to the palace, they enact the meaning of their names, Ṣebiotimọ proceeding quietly and modestly while Alaṣeju, attended in all pomp and circumstance by throngs of unsavory hangers-on, is almost disgraced even before he gets there when the crimes of his associates (Trouble, Anger, and Disgrace) are exposed along the way. But enacting the meaning of their names is not enough. The discursivity of the story is intensified by the addition of an "ẹni airi," an Unseen Person who intervenes to warn Alaṣeju about the consequences of excess. Alaṣeju answers back, and they hold a formal debate in the middle of the road before Alaṣeju reaches the palace. Then a child who sees the sad end of Alaṣeju's drunken and promiscuous companions (some fall into a pit and die, others get sick with sexually transmitted diseases) runs to its mother to report that though they set off in splendor, Alaṣeju and his followers have arrived at the palace in disgrace. The mother explains that this is because Alaṣeju despised Ṣebiotimọ and preferred vainglorious worldly display to godly behavior. "My child, remember that if you / Act excessively, you too will be disgraced." Alaṣeju himself spells out the lesson after he has been found guilty and condemned to death, and Ṣebiotimọ winds the story up with six nine-line stanzas of moral summary headed "The lesson that Ṣebiotimọ taught the world." Thus, the narrative functions as a clotheshorse to carry layers of didactic discursive garments—in different stanzaic formats and put into the mouths of different characters, but all elaborating the same moral strictures. It is as if the text fills a space rather than rushes toward an objective. It's staged; it's set up so that everything demonstrates a proposition, a proposition whose truth is known from the beginning and which is also enunciated repeatedly at every juncture of the narrative.

This artificiality may be the secret of the book's constitution as a text and can be understood in terms of Adenle's loneliness—the fact that he or his literary activity inhabited a kind of vacuum. It was a vacuum that spelled freedom to invent but also a precarious absence of points of reference. This led to a peculiarly insistent yet fragile style characterized by a house-of-cards piling up of repetitious, because homologous, themes and forms. This is the suggestion I want to explore in the rest of this chapter.

Adenle's Discursive Environment

The relationship between Adenle's intellectual isolation and the artifice of his writing becomes clearer by comparison with the cultural situation of his counterparts and contemporaries in Lagos.[16]

By the 1930s, Lagos literary culture was at least three generations old. Though small in relation to the indigenous Lagosian population, the Lagos elite (the backbone of which was Christianized Yoruba recaptives who were repatriated from Sierra Leone and nicknamed the "Saro") was a well-established, much-intermarried, influential, and confident group. They controlled a flourishing local press which had been producing Lagos newspapers since the 1860s and generated a lively cultural life involving music, theater, social events, and public discussion. Yoruba-language writing had been significant since the 1880s, as is evident from the growing number of local histories, studies of Yoruba culture, religious works, and books of poetry in Yoruba. In the 1920s, there was an explosion of Yoruba-language weekly newspapers, which contributed to a public culture in which political and cultural issues were vigorously debated (see Barber 2005).[17]

At this period, partly because of a long-running conflict with the colonial government over the Lagos kingship, the Saro elite moved to widen its public platform and draw in the less-elite literates. A kind of populism entered their discourses, while at the same time they retained the atmosphere of a comfortable club in which everyone knew everyone else. It was a highly interactive culture: large portions of the newspapers were constituted out of readers' letters and amateur contributions in epistolary form. In this discursive environment, literary innovations could be tried out and would receive instant response from readers, critics, and rival writers. The first Yoruba novels appeared as serials in the weekly papers—a natural outgrowth of the sociable world of newspaper communication—and the most famous of them, *Itan Emi Ṣẹgilọla* (The Story of Me, Ṣẹgilọla) was actually in the form of letters to the editor that were so lifelike that many readers thought they were real.[18] Readers in turn contributed to the conversation when they responded to the narrative with moral commentaries, supplementary narratives, and questions about "Ṣẹgilọla" in their own letters to the editor. There was an equally lively conversation among the writers themselves, who copied each other's styles and commented on each other's experiments with form and voice—for example, a poem published in the newspaper *Eleti Ọfẹ* in 1924 announced itself as being "in the voice of" Ṣọbọ Arobiodu, the noted Ẹgba poet. Not only this, but the domain of writing was sustained by a live culture of performance and discussion. The earliest historical essays were commissioned by cultural associations and were discussed in their meetings; sermons and public lectures were published in full; poetry was recited at "concerts" and appeared in every issue of most papers.

That by the 1920s a new, written, Yoruba literary tradition was in formation is suggested not just by the proliferation of written texts and responses to them but by the care with which valued past productions, whether oral or written, were retrieved and published or republished in the newspapers—as for example when *Akede Eko* republished, in response to readers' requests, a mixed English-Yoruba poem that had first been printed in *Iwe Irohin Eko* in 1889. This suggests that successful innovations became part of an active tradition.

This new literary tradition was fed by several different currents. It was in contact with English-language literature, and poems by Lagos authors were often published simultaneously in English and Yoruba in the bilingual newspapers. It was also in touch with Yoruba oral traditions which flourished among the indigenous population in Lagos and the hinterland, and the press sometimes featured texts of praise poetry and articles on proverbs. Some poets drew heavily on oral style while purveying a literate's view of the world; some attempted a style modeled on conventional stanzaic English poetry, even to the extent of trying to produce rhyme; others eventually found a voice which evoked speech intonations while exploiting the abstract and generalized address made possible by print.[19] Most of the columns, stories, and poems published in newspapers are characterized by an easy and confident mode of address to the reader, who is assumed to share the same local references and preoccupations as the writer—for although national issues were sometimes alluded to in passing, the overwhelming preoccupation was with internal Lagos affairs which the literate public knew firsthand.

In short, there was a discursive environment in Lagos that made it possible to think of Yoruba-language literary production as constituting a tradition, with the usual backwaters, dead ends, and periodic surges in innovative productivity. It was very different in Oṣogbo. Victor felt that apart from the Yoruba Bible, "there was no other Yoruba literature available to Adenle, or known to him." Chief Omigbodun said "There weren't a lot of books available then, as there are now—the only thing we had was what we call 'text-books', books that we used in class." Adenle, as we have seen, did not lack possible models of Yoruba-language writing: in addition to the Bible, there was the Protestant hymn book, the CMS reader, *The Pilgrim's Progress* (one of the earliest books to be widely available in Yoruba), and very possibly A. K. Ajiṣafẹ's pamphlets as well.[20] But Adenle did not participate in a sustaining discursive environment. His only educational equals were fellow students from St Andrews, who were few and scattered and most of whom in any case only read school textbooks and standard devotional works. The concentration of doctors, lawyers, civil servants, teachers, clergy, and literate businessmen that was found in Lagos had no parallel in the hinterland. Nor was Adenle cosmopolitan: at any rate there was no mention of friendships outside the town or of correspondence with fellow writers in Lagos, Abẹokuta, or Ibadan. On the contrary, he appears to have been wholly immersed in local business and politics.

Like the astute businessman he was, Adenle may have seen this vacancy as an opportunity to market a product. If there was not yet an adult literate public in Oṣogbo, there was a future public in the making—the growing population of primary school pupils, who were literate in Yoruba but much less so in English and had little to read. His first pamphlet, *Iwe Aiye Toto Fun*, is built around the figure of a schoolgirl who is seeking wisdom from her age-mates and elders. Although the message imparted may seem very adult in its extreme world-weariness, the style was relatively accessible and the theme was that of a child in the act of learning. It is this text that Adenle's colleagues and pupils spontaneously remembered and commented on fifty years later, and it may be that this obviously didactic and relatively readable pamphlet was the only one to be widely distributed in schools. Certainly the absence of the second, longer, and more complex text *Iwe Iwa Rere L'Ọṣọ Enia* from Ogunsheye's recent bibliography suggests that it was less well known (Ogunsheye 2001). But even in *Iwe Aiye Toto Fun,* there is a reticence, a closed-in quality, which contrasts strongly with the poem's possible inspiration, Ajiṣafẹ's *Aiye Akamara.* Ajiṣafẹ addresses the schoolchild-reader directly throughout and offers a string of useful lessons. "*Iwọ ọdọmọde ọrẹ mi / Ti o ndagba bọ / Jọwọ fiyedenu / Gbọ ọrọ ti ngo sọ fun ọ yi*" (You young child, my friend / Who are just beginning to grow up / Please, be patient / Listen to what I am going to tell you). The advice he offers is intended to help the child succeed in life by working hard, being trustworthy, and avoiding bad friends and deceivers. The style is conversational, informal, and persuasive, full of the confidence of an experienced elder taking his young protégés in hand. Adenle's pamphlet, by contrast, does not address the reader at all, except in the preface; it is constructed as a series of internal dialogues between Moji and her age-mates and elders. The reader is merely a witness, and what he or she witnesses is an unequivocal rejection of the world as a nest of cruelty, vice, deception, and folly—a message which, one imagines, it would be hard for a schoolchild-reader to appropriate as a "moral lesson" to be used in their own lives. The second and more ambitious pamphlet, *Iwe Iwa Rere L'Ọṣọ Enia,* as we shall see, retreats even further from dialogic engagement with an imagined reader.

Adenle was not wholly insulated from larger currents of thought. In the first place, the influence of 1930s and 1940s nationalism in its most general mode—for the liberation of Africa as a whole, rather than the progress of Nigeria or the cultural affirmation of the Yoruba—is announced in the very first stanzas of *Iwe Iwa Rere L'Ọṣọ Enia* with an exhortatory poem lamenting Africa's ignominious darkness and calling on all "children of Afrik" to do their part to bring progress, unity, and freedom to the continent. This theme is muted thereafter but does occasionally surface, for example when a narrative of a poor woman who chases her escaped chicken through thick and thin is revealed as an allegory of Africa pursuing its independence. It is not, however, enriched by the kind of Yoruba cultural nationalism that had been pioneered and vigorously developed by the Lagos intelligentsia over the preceding fifty years. Adenle's chosen metrical system rules out the incorporation or recreation of oral poetic genres, and his themes and motifs are more reminiscent of the eclectic textual assemblage of the CMS Yoruba readers (*Iwe Kika* I–V) than of the living orature that flourished all around him. Like the *Iwe Kika* series, Adenle's text draws on fables (which could have come ultimately from *The Arabian Nights* or *Aesop's Fables*), on Victorian sentimental didacticism, on allegorical and personified forms of representation that seem reminiscent of Bunyan, and on recensions of Yoruba history. At one point he produces a striking Yoruba recreation of Henry V's speech before the Battle of Agincourt, and the closing poem seems, beautifully if somewhat incongruously, to be inspired by "Twinkle, Twinkle, Little Star." If an address to his readers as bearers of Yoruba culture is intended, it is at an abstract level, an affirmation which, rather than appealing to a shared indigenous heritage, sets out to construct a new entity: a literary monument parallel to, and comparable with, the English literature he studied at college.

Second, by addressing the implied reader *as* a reader rather than as a listener, the text affirms certain modernizing, supralocal values. In *Iwe Iwa Rere L'Ọṣọ Enia* especially, literariness itself is foregrounded: by adopting a metrical system that is not only nonexistent but downright inconceivable in Yoruba orature, the text announces its own writtenness. Adenle creates a form which cannot be read aloud without discomfort, the remarkable and intricate construction of which can only be appreciated on the page. The narrative, set in a folkloric and fabular world, does not overtly preach the virtues of schooling, but it is clearly a self-conscious exercise in the exploitation of the possibilities of written text. The sheer scale of the effort involved suggests that the implied reader is being earnestly appealed to as a fellow member of an educated minority—a public characterized by its translocal affiliations. To Adenle, however, this educated public seems to have been an abstract ideal rather than an imagined community in which he felt himself to be engaged with other participants.

The appeal to literariness notwithstanding, Adenle's poems have a populist streak, for running through them—and especially through the second and longer work, *Iwe Iwa Rere L'Ọṣọ Enia*—is the theme of the virtue and deservingness of the common man. Throughout the poem, an opposition and oscillation echoes between two categories, the rich and the poor, the king and the slave, the privileged and the unfortunate, and these change places as a result of their moral condition. The framework narrative of the book is a reversal in which the virtuous slave replaces the arrogant *ọba* on the throne. Many of the encapsulated narratives tell of similar reversals. The first servant brings a madman into the court and announces that even this man is better than the *ọba* because at least he knows he is worthless. The second servant shows a modest man being rewarded while the flamboyant overreacher is executed; the fourth portrays the impoverished woman recapturing her escaped chicken through the sheer determination of her pursuit; the fifth tells of a war between a good king and an overweeningly arrogant king, in which the latter is defeated and enslaved; in the seventh, a chief greedy for power rises and rises until he goes too far and tries to outdo God, when he loses everything. The language echoes with the contrast:

Ranti pe ọlọrọ ndi talaka
Talaka ndi ọlọrọ ni aiye
Ọba ilu ndi talaka l'aiye
Talaka a si ma di ọba nla (p. 7)

Remember that the wealthy person often becomes poor
The poor person often becomes wealthy in this world
The king of a town becomes poor in this world
And the poor person may become a mighty king.

The poor are associated with virtue, the rich with the lack of it—hence the necessity for reversals. When *ọba*s search for good character, "They search for you, but they don't find you / You have gone to hide with / The poor and wretched."

This association of positive values with poverty is uncommon in Yoruba popular culture—the normal view is that poverty in itself is either the result of laziness or an unfortunate temporary state unrelated to the person's moral condition—but was clearly articulated in Lagosian elite literary culture. One of the most popular poems of the time sentimentally evoked "a beggar's cry at Lagos." Ajiṣafẹ's *Aiye Akamara,* in its opening verse, urges its youthful readers to learn from the experience of orphans, the destitute, people who have been rejected by their parents—for these are the ones who can teach us wisdom about the world (1921, 6). In this respect, then, Adenle can be seen to be participating in a new and partly alien culture influenced by a sentimental Victorian Christianity and perhaps also by Islamic asceticism. It is worth noting that this moral inflection may also reveal something of Adenle's personal aspirations and sense of entitlement. A personally advantageous project is not otherwise apparent in the text: it is not a lineage or town history which could be mobilized in local political maneuvers; it is not openly autobiographical, glorifying its writer; it is not personal poetry, in the manner of D. A. Ọbasa or Ṣọbọ Arobiodu, sounding off, commenting, establishing a public speaking persona that the audience will recognize. The extraordinary constraints of Adenle's chosen verse form impart to the text an impersonal style which excludes the effect of an individual speaking voice. Yet the text of *Iwe Iwa Rere L'Oṣọ Enia* clearly announces, years before the Oṣogbo throne became vacant, that the most unlikely candidate—the disadvantaged orphan of impoverished parentage—is also, by reason of his virtue, the most eligible.

Thus, although Adenle did participate in wider currents of thought, he remained a curiously involuted and isolated figure. What I wish to suggest is that the vacancy in which Adenle operated was existential as much as practical. Without feedback or fellow writers—without a local press in which to make experiments and solicit responses; without a debating society, a reading circle, or a cultural association; and without successors to imitate and preserve his experiments—Adenle could not be said to belong to a living literary tradition.[21] His writing had no afterlife—of the people who knew him, only his son Victor had a copy of the pamphlets. All the people I spoke to remarked that it had been a long time ago, that no copies were now in circulation, and that they had lost their own copies. Other, officially recommended textbooks have long displaced the resourceful headmaster's efforts. But more important, at the time of its production, his writing seems to have had no context of reception beyond the classroom. This seems to me to explain key features of its style and construction.

Artifice and Vacancy

Adenle, then, was constructing a text that would occupy space in a social vacuum where he could not assume a readership with whom he shared references, common concerns, recent experiences, or expressive conventions. It was impossible for him to write easily, comfortably, and colloquially in Yoruba about contemporary events, as his counterparts in Lagos and Abeokuta were beginning to do. It was impossible for him to sound off, to produce short forms or serials which would engage in an unfolding dialogue with readers and other writers. Adenle had to create a compendious, atemporal, self-sufficient text, a text which contained its own dialogue and its own reception within it. His textual mode, especially in *Iwe Iwa Rere L'Oso Enia*, is a mode of assemblage, of filling in and filling out, erecting a flimsy framework (the succession of servants responding to their master's question) to support a collection of flimsy narratives revolving around conundrums, puzzles, and explanations. Nothing just happens: everything is a demonstration of something else, an illustration of a lesson. It is precariously extended, but even if it had been far larger it could not have filled the space, for the space has no edges. The text has no sounding board and presumes no interlocutor. Instead, it attempts to be self-sustaining by creating its own multiply-layered internal audience.

The *oba* in the framing narrative, who challenges his servants to produce stories of people who outshine him, thereafter becomes the internal audience to all that is said. It is striking that he is the most hostile and unresponsive listener one could well imagine.[22] He periodically reacts to his servants' disquisitions by brushing them aside and launching a fresh claim and fresh challenge, to which the next servant rises. The other audiences within the text are usually ignorant, innocent, or very young people whose only role is to be instructed. Many of the stories have internal preceptors who expound the meaning of the action as it proceeds and respond to questions from their listeners.

Take the story of the third servant, intended to show the folly of the *ọba*'s claim to be the handsomest person in the world. The lesson is summed up in advance in the well-known proverb, "*Ìwà lẹwà*" (Beauty lies in [good] character). The sequence opens with twenty-eight verses in praise of good character and an additional four verses exalting the only kind of beauty worth wishing for—the imperishable beauty of God and his angels. Then follows the story of how a wise father taught his eager son about the difference between character and beauty. The father announces to his son that he is going to take him to see the Iyalode (the principal woman chief) to taste her soup. He explains that her soup looks very beautiful, with palm oil floating on the surface, but it has no salt and is therefore tasteless. The boy is surprised—he thought it was palm oil alone that made soup tasty. Not at all, replies the father: without salt, the soup is no good. They go to the Iyalode's house and "the boy's lesson begins." They see constant streams of customers coming in, but once they taste the soup they all abandon it, and no one who has been once ever comes back again. The boy asks to try it and finds that indeed it has no taste at all. He thanks his father for the lesson. The father says he wants the boy to add a further lesson to the one he has already learned: beauty is like the palm oil, good character is like the salt; God gives the world beauty, but it is up to us to supply the good character. They then thank the Iyalode for the lesson she has taught them—and advise her to put salt in her soup in future so that her customers will not run away from her![23]

This curious (and, I must admit, extremely tedious) narrative has no forward motion whatsoever—it has nowhere to go. It's not just that we know from the outset what lesson the story will impart—it's that the story is a byproduct of the lesson rather than the other way round. The act of imparting—the didactic father transmitting a message to the receptive son—is all the action there is. The Iyalode seems to exist in perpetually frozen motion, making the same mistake forever—a mistake that teaches others but from which she herself appears unable to learn. She is not an agent in a narrative but an image in a tableau, existing in order to be expounded by father and construed by son. Such pictorial and allegorical modes of representation might have been suggested to Adenle by *The Pilgrim's Progress*. But the enormous power and memorability of Bunyan's story lie in its construction as a one-way journey to salvation. The journey is the *point* of the story as well as its structural spine, and it is all forward movement. Adenle brought off the opposite feat. He constructed a series of episodes that not only have no narrative motion from one to the next—each existing in a purely contiguous and additive relation to the others, as another example expounded by another royal servant—but also often have no internal narrative thrust either.[24] As in the story of the Iyalode's soup, the exemplificatory mode can be taken to the point where the episode virtually ceases to function as a story and becomes a discursive object lesson instead. The representation of nested layers of speakers and listeners, teachers and learners, expounders and questioners engrosses the whole text.

And it is significant that in all this represented discursivity, there is almost never a dialogue between equals for mutual pleasure. Respondents are either hostile, like the *ọba*, or blank slates, like the boy taken to taste the Iyalode's soup. As if this one-way communication were insufficiently authoritative, the "ẹni airi kan," an Unseen Person of divine attributes, is brought in from time to time to underwrite it. In the absence of endorsement from a real reading public of adult interlocutors, Adenle may have been trying to install an incontrovertible authorization of his message *within* the text.

However one judges Adenle's text artistically, it is witness to the way obscure writers in the colonial provinces could test the limits of the space they found themselves in. As I have suggested, this space was an arena, but it was also a vacuum. Adenle was an inventor who established something in that vacuum that had not previously been thought of. The lack of a close and responsive discursive community meant that there was freedom to invent and carry out projects of an extreme kind. His dogged thoroughness, his determination to erect an enormous structure of his own invention, is witness to that. His case raises questions for other studies of the obscure practitioners of tin-trunk literacy: questions about how and in what circumstances a tradition is constituted, how texts can exist without a tradition, how textual innovation takes place, and how we can conceptualize the history of some of the more isolated and sporadic private inventions. One thing this preliminary study may suggest is that innovation is not the problem. The problem is how to make innovations stick; in other words, how to constitute and sustain an enduring textual environment.

24.

28. Iwa ẹni n' ipa ẹni,
Iwa ẹni l, ogbọn ẹni,
Iwa ẹni l' ayọ ẹni,
Iwa ẹni l' adun ẹni,
Iwa ẹni l' ọrọ ẹni
Iwa rẹ. l' onidajọ ẹni
Bi o ṣe re, b'o ṣe rere,
Iyin rẹ mbẹ l' ẹnu aiye.

TỌLANI KỌ ORIN YI FUN ỌBA:

1. Ewa kan wa ti kì bajẹ   *8 Syl.*
Ewa ti ogo rẹ ki ti
Ewa kan si wa ti ki ga
Ewa na ti Ọlọrun ni.
Ni ọdọ Rẹ l' awọn mimọ
Atẹ'adẹ nwọn mimọ, mimọ
Ju gbogbo ogo aiye lọ.
Gbe nkọ mimọ, mimọ mimọ.

2. Ewa nwọn l' ogo ju t'orun,
Irawọ ati oṣupa
Ati gbogbo ogo aiye.
Ti ma ran, ti si ma wọkun,
Ti ma ti, ti si ma bajẹ.
Ko n' oru ninu ẹwa nwọn,
Ko si 'tanjẹ n'nu, ẹwa wọn,
Ewa wọn n' iwa mimọ nwọn:

3. Ewa wọn kò dabi t'aiye
Nibi ti aniyan 'aiye,
Gbe nba ẹwa aiye jẹ,
Oran ododo l' ẹwa nwọn,
Ibugbe ati ẹwa nwọn,
Kun fun mimọ, mimọ, mimọ,
Nwọn nkọ mimọ, mimọ mimọ,
Ayọ nwọn n' iwa mimọ nwọn.

4. Oluwa wa, mẹtalọkan,
Ṣugbọn Ọlọrun kanṣoṣo,

25.

Eni mimọ, mimọ, julọ,
Jọ fun wa ni iwa mimọ,
Ma jẹki a fi iwa wa,
ti'ẹwa iwa mimọ rẹ jẹ,
K'alẹ l'awọn angeli kọ,
Mimọ, mimọ, l'oke ọrun. Amin,

TỌLANI TUN SỌ FUN ỌBA WIPE....10 Syl.

"Emi y'o tun sọ itan kan fun ọ,
Wo mi, ani, emi y'o sọ itan,
Iyalode at' ọbẹ rẹ fun ọ,
Ki ọba at' awọn ijoye rẹ,
Ki o le mọ dajudaju wipe,
Iwa rere ni ọṣọ enia,
Atẹ l'ọbẹ ti ko ni iyọ ninu
Bẹ si ni atẹ at'oba l'ẹwa
L'aisi iwa rere ninu ẹ."

ẸKỌ TI ỌBẸ IYALODE KỌ AIYE ATI ẸDA INU RẸ

1. Baba ti o kun fun ọgbọn,   *8 Syl.*
L' ọjọ kan, o dan ọgbọn wo
O si fẹ fi ẹkọ kan kọ
Ọmọ rẹ t'o fẹ kọ ẹkọ,
T' o nnaga lati ri ọlọ
Ti mbẹ n'nu iwa at' ẹwa
l'awo l'ayọ ọmọ na to
N' igba ti baba rẹ wi pe.

2. "Ọmọ mi, ba mi de ọdọ
Iyalode, ki a le ba
Tọ ọbẹ rẹ wo ni oni,
Nitori mo gbọ bayi pe
Ọbẹ rẹ ni epo l'oju,
O fa ni mọra l'akere.
Ṣugbọn atẹ ni ọbẹ rẹ,
L' aisi iyọ ko si dun.

26.

3. Baba ki l'a npe ni iyọ?
L'aisi iyọ, nje ọbẹ
Iya mi ko le l' adun bi?
Mo ro wipe epo nikan
Ni ninu ọbẹ iya mi dun!
Baba mi tun jẹ ọba,
Emi 'ba jẹ iyọ, pupọ
Ni ọbẹ ju ẹgbẹ mi lọ

4. A! ọmọ mi, bẹkọ rara,
N' idahun baba rere yi
Ọmọ mi, gbọ jẹ k'o ye ọ,
Atẹ l'ọbẹ ti ko n'iyọ,
A ki fi ọla jẹ iyọ
Iye iyọ ti talaka
Yio jẹ n'nu ọbẹ kan,
Iye rẹ na l'oba y'o jẹ

5. Ọmọ mi mu aarn diẹ
Sara ma ni' baba iwa
Maṣe kanju ju Ọlọrun lọ,
Maṣe foya, maṣe lẹru,
Ọwọ rẹ fẹ tẹ ifẹ rẹ,
Awa ko ni pe de ọdọ
Iyalode lati kẹkọ
Iwa rere l' ọṣọ ẹda

6. Nitori mo mọ gbangba pe
Idahun ibere rẹ wa
Ninu ọbẹ Iyalode
Baba ati ọmọ rẹ de
Ọdọ Iyalode nitọtọ
Pẹlu adun ati ayọ
Ni nwọn fi ri Iyalode
Pẹlu ọbẹ ati iwa rẹ

7 Ekọ ọmọ na si bẹrẹ.
Bawo l'ayọ rẹ ha ti to,
Ni igati Iyalode
Yara ko iṣasun ọbẹ rẹ

27.

S'ode pẹlu orin ayọ
T'ero ati ta ọbẹ na
Si gba ọkan Iyalode
Alepo l'ọbẹ ma n' iyọ

8. Ifojusilẹ ọmọ yi
Ni a ko jọ ninu ina
Bi iyangbo at' irawe,
Bẹ l'oye at' ọgbọn rẹ l'on
Ti ro ni agbẹdẹ dada,
Bi doje ti o mu banhan
Ti ọlọgbọn fi nrẹ oyin
Ti y'o fi adun t'ẹkan rẹ,

9. Bẹni ọmọde rere na
Nfi oye kọ ẹkọ tirẹ,
O nfi imọ kun imọ, rẹ
O ulo ọgbọn at' oye rẹ
Lati fi iyọ silẹ pe
Bi ọṣọ ero ti nyawa
Lati ra ọbẹ Iyalode,
Bẹni nwọn nkọ aiye l' ẹkọ

10 Ti nwọn si nkọ ghogbo ọbẹ
Ti nwọn ra s' ilẹ l' aijẹ,
Ati pe ẹniti o ba
Ti ra ọbẹ Iyalode
L' ẹkan, ani l' ẹkan ọọjọ,
Ko jẹ tande ọdọ rẹ mọ
Lati ra tabi lati ta,
Tabi lati gba ti ọbun.

11. Ọmọ yi dan ẹkọ rẹ wo,
O tun t' imọ kn imọ rẹ.
Pẹlu iyaun at' ọgbọn.
Ọmọde na duan wipe
"Baba mi at' oluko mi,
Mo kiyesi dada wipe
Awọn araiye nwa ntọtọ
Lati ra ọbẹ Iyalode.

Figure 14.1. Excerpt from S. A. Adenle's *Iwe Iwa Rere L'Ọṣọ enia*.

28

12. Ko si igba kan ti ẹṣe
Nda ni ọdọ Iyalode;
Ii' ọkan ti nlọ bẹ l' omi nde,
Sugbọn ohun ti o 'ya mi
Ni ẹnu ni eyi 'wipe
B' awọn ero wọnyi ti nwa
Iẹni nwọn si npada lọ gan
Nwọn ko jẹ ọbẹ ti nwọn ra pa.

13. Baba da ọmọ rẹ l' ohun
Pe, "Ọmọ mi yi, mu suru,
Iwọ y'o ri ẹkọ kọ si
Ninu ọbẹ Iyalode
Ati l' ọdọ awọn ti nrạ,
"Tori pe nwọn nnạ owo nwọn
Si nkan ti ko ni iyọ
Sugbọn ti o fa ni mọra."

14. Ọmọ kekere yi sọ pe,
"iya ọlọbẹ gbogbo aiye,
Jẹ, ta ọbẹ diẹ fun wa
Fun itẹlọrun ife wa
K' ebi k' o maa ba pa wa mọ,
K' ongbẹ k' o ma si gbẹ wa mọ
K'awa ki o le di ọrẹ
A'talabara rẹ titi.

15. Iyalode ta ọbẹ rẹ
Fun baba ati ọmọ yi
Baba ati ọmọde na
Tọ ọbẹ Iyalode wo.
Ọbẹ na ni epo l'oju
Sugbọn ko ni adun rara,
Nitorina ọmọ yi ati baba rẹ
Kọ ọbẹ na silẹ l'aiyẹ.

16. "Baba mo dupe lọwọ re
Fun ẹkọ ti o kọ mi yi,"
L'omọ na wi fun baba rẹ,
"Nisisiyi ni mo ti mọ pe

29

Atẹ l'ọbẹ ti ko n'iyọ,
Ati pe a ko gbọdọ ra
Ikan ti ko ni adun
Bi o ti wu k'o l'ẹwa to"

17. Mo dupe l'ọwọ rẹ pupọ,
Ọmọ rere at' ọlọgbọn.
Mo tun fẹ kọ l' ẹkọ kan si,
So nwọn mọ okan aya rẹ,
Lo ẹkọ na ni igba ti
Inu rẹ ba bajẹ l'aiye,
Jẹ ki ẹkọ na ki o jẹ
Olori ayọ rẹ gbogbo.

18. Ọmọ ranti, jẹ ki o ya ọ
Lati oni lọ titi pa-
Atẹ l'ọbẹ ti ko n'iyọ
Aki fi ọla jẹ iyọ.
Bi ọbẹ Iyelode yi
Ti jẹ atẹ l'aisi iyọ,
Bẹ l'ẹwa ọda aiye ri
L'aisi iwa rere mbẹ.

19. Ewa ni epo fun aiye,
Iwa rere n'iyọ aiye
Ewa ti o'lepo dada
Ti o si ni iyọ dada
Ni ẹwa ti opo dada,
Ewa l'Ẹlẹda ṣe a'aiye
Iwa ku si ọwọ ẹda.
Lati nu ẹwa aiye dun.

20. Aiye at' ogbọn inu rẹ.
Ki Iyalode bayi pe,
"Iyalode ọlọbẹ wa,
A dupe l'ọwọ rẹ l'oni.
Fun ẹkọ ti a ri kọ yi
Ni inu ọbẹ rẹ wọnyi
Jọwọ, maṣai fi iyọ
Si ọbẹ rẹ l' ọjọ miran.

30

21. K' aiye ma ba ṣa fun ọ mọ,
K' ẹwa rẹ le l' alafia.
Maje k' iwa rẹ k'o tẹ ọ.
F' iwa ṣe iyọ ẹwa rẹ.
Fi Olorun ṣe ẹwa rẹ,
Fi iwa gbogbo rẹ gbá,
Ni ogbọn at' aiye dara,
Lọwọ baba rere na pe.

22. "Baba, oluṣọ wa rere,
A dupe l' ọwọ re l' oni,
Fun ẹkọ ti o kọ wa yi.
Jọ, kọ 'wa t'a ti hu iwa
Ki ẹwa wa ko ma ba le
Alafia wa l'ọdọ wa.
Jọ, tun ma kọ aiye l'ẹkọ
"Iwa rere l'ẹwa ẹda"

Okan Adooye lọ si o tun wi fun ẹmẹwa kẹrin pe
Bi o ba jẹ pe emi ki ẹni ti o l'ẹwa ju l'aiye
Sugbọn emi ni ẹni ti o l'agbara ju l'aiye yi.
Idowu ti ṣe ẹmẹwa kẹrin da ọba lohun pe,
"Jọ, fi eti si itan ti emi yio sọ yi, ọba.
Iwọ yio si mọ ẹniti o l'agbara ju l' aiye."
Ọba dahun pe, "Idowu, yara sọ itan na ki ngbọ"
Idowu pẹlu ayọ nla-nla bẹrẹ si sọ itan ti

OBINRIN ALAPỌN ATI IROMỌ-ADIẸ RẸ. 16 Syl

1. Apọn kọ si iṣẹ pẹlu igboya nla bayi wipe
Wa ni ihin, tete yara wa wo aladiẹ kan
Obinrin ti o ṣe arẹwa ni aladiẹ na jẹ
Apọn ati iforiti rẹ ni a ti danwo dada
Ni igbehin, ifẹ rẹ ni a si de l'ade iṣẹgun

2. Ki ni o ba nṣe obinrin ati adiẹ rẹ na bẹ ?
Eini, obinrin ati adiẹ rẹ nwa kiri bayi ?
Idanu ki ni o ba obinrin 'at' adiẹ rẹ bayi ?
Iru ogbọn wo l'obinrin at' adiẹ rẹ y'o kọ wa ?
Nkan yi ni iṣẹ bere l'ọwọ Apọn at' Iforiti ?

31

3. Pẹlu ẹrin ati ogbọn ni Apọn daun bayi pe,
"Wo, adiẹ Ebun yi silẹ on si fẹ nạ lati lo o
Sugbọn o ṣe, o ma ṣe o, ọwọ Ebun ko tete tẹ ẹ
O mura, o tun nghiyanju siwaju ati siwaju,
N'gbakugba ni ma ku diẹ k'ọwọ rẹ k'o tẹ ifẹ rẹ

4. Ni ikẹhin Ọgbọn kọ obinrin yi l'ogbọn dada kan
Oye tun fi imọ kan ti o dara han a kiakia
Eyi-ti on yara gba pẹlu ọpẹ, ayọ at'ifẹ.
O bẹrẹ si ṣe iṣẹ rẹ pẹlu ogbọn ati oye
O si nwa ọna ti ọwọ on yio fi tẹ ifẹ rẹ

5. L'ọwọ obinrin yi ni agbado diẹ wa nisiyi
Lati lo ogbọn ẹwọ kan lati fi mu adiẹ yi
Lati fi bi agbara npọn at'iforiti ti to han,
"Sugbọn bi iwọ papa ba wa ni ihẹ ni ọjọ na"
Ni obinrin rere yi na ma wi ikẹhin aiye rẹ,

6. " Iwọ iba'da emi ni are, o ba si sọ wipe
Obinrin yi ja ija iforiti ati ti apọn.
Ki on ki o to ri ifẹ, ayọ ati iṣẹgun rẹ
On si ti fi suru ṣẹgun ogun nla kan ti o n'iyi
Ju ti akin ati ti alagbara kan lọ l'aiye yi,

7. N'gbakugba ti Ebun ba yin agbado diẹ silẹ,
Ni adiẹ kekere yi nwa lati jẹ agbado na.
N'gbakugba ti Ebun ba na ọwọ rẹ tan lati fi mu,
Adiẹ yi, ni Ebun ati adiẹ rẹ nkọ wa pe,
Suru apọn at' iforiti ni ma mu iṣẹgun wa.

8. O maṣe o adiẹ na ko t'ara balẹ fun Ebun to
Ni 'igba kan, na ku diẹ kiun ki o mu adiẹ na,
Nigbamiran adiẹ na a yọ ọrẹ kuro l'ọdọ rẹ
N'gbamiran adiẹ na a suru ṣẹṣẹ siwaju
N'gbamiran adiẹ na a fo piriri lọ siwaju rere

9. Sugbọn bi obinrin yi ti nbẹrẹ kiri gbogbo ilu
Ti o si npa kuku kẹkẹ ni chin adiẹ rẹ yi
Ati bi adiẹ yi ti ngbe e sure kiri bi were

THE LESSON THAT THE IYALODE'S SOUP TAUGHT THE WORLD AND ITS INHABITANTS

1.   A father who was full of wisdom,
        One day tried out his wisdom
        And he wanted to impart a certain lesson
        To his child, who was eager to learn,
        Who was straining to perceive the truth
        About character and beauty
        How happy the child was
        When his father said

2.   "My child, come with me to the
        Iyalode's place, so that we can
        Taste her soup today,
        Because I hear that
        Her soup has palm oil floating on the surface
        It attracts one from a distance.
        But her soup is tasteless
        Without any salt, and it is not sweet.

3.   Father, what is it we call salt?
        Is it the case that without salt, the soup
        Of my mother would not be tasty?
        I thought it was only the palm oil
        That made my mother's soup tasty!
        If my father were the ọba,
        I would eat a lot of salt
        In my soup, more than my fellows.

4.   Ah! my child, it is not so at all,
        Was the reply of this good father,
        My child, listen, try to understand,
        A soup without salt is flavorless
        But we never take advantage of our position to eat [excessive] salt
        The amount of salt that a poor man
        Will eat in a soup
        Is the same amount that the ọba will eat.

5.   My child, be a little patient
        Patience is the father of all virtues
        Don't be in greater haste than God
        Don't be alarmed, don't be afraid
        What you desire is almost in your grasp,
        We will soon arrive at the
        Iyalode's in order to learn the lesson
        That good behavior is humankind's adornment.

Figure 14.2. Translation by Karin Barber of passage reproduced in figure 14.1.

6.   Because I know for certain that
       The answer to your question is
       In the soup of the Iyalode
       The father and his child arrived
       At the Iyalode's indeed
       With pleasure and joy
       They saw the Iyalode
       With her soup and her behavior

7.   And the child's lesson began.
       How happy he was
       When the Iyalode
       Quickly brought her soup pot
       Out, with a merry song
       And the intention of selling that soup
       Seized the heart of the Iyalode
       It was a soup with palm oil but no salt

8.   The attention of this child
       Was purified [as if] with fire[1]
       Like brushwood and dead leaves
       And his intelligence and wisdom he
       Had forged in the smithy very well
       Like a razor-sharp blade
       That a clever person uses to skim honey
       Whose sweetness will gladden his/her heart,

9.   In the same way this good child
       Was using his intelligence to learn a lesson
       He was adding to his knowledge
       He was using his wisdom and intelligence
       In order to observe
       The way in which many customers were flocking in
       To buy the Iyalode's soup,
       And in this way were teaching the world a lesson

10   Because they were refusing all the soup
       That they had ordered, and leaving it uneaten
       And [he observed] that anyone who happened
       To have bought the Iyalode's soup
       Once, I repeat, just once,
       Would never come back to her place again

---

[1] This and the following line are somewhat puzzling. I am grateful to Dr Akin Oyetade for suggesting that the image of fire is an allusion to Psalm 12:6, "The words of the Lord are pure words, like silver tested in a furnace of earth, purified seven times," perhaps implying metaphorically that the child's attention was sharpened by the experience of observing the strange scene before him.

Either to buy or to sell,
Or to receive it as a gift.

11.   This child tested the lesson
He again added more to his knowledge.
With astonishment and wisdom.
The young person spoke up, saying
"My father and my teacher,
I observed quite clearly that
The people of the world are indeed coming
To buy the Iyalode's soup.

12.   There is never a time when the feet [of visitors]
Cease to sound in the Iyalode's place:
As one departs another arrives,
But the thing that has filled me with
Amazement is this, that
As these customers are coming
So they are departing
They don't eat any of the soup they have bought.

13.   The father answeréd his child
Saying "My child, be patient
You will learn still more
From the Iyalode's soup
And from the people who buy it.
Because they are spending their money
On something which has no salt
But which is attractive to look at."

14.   This little child said
"Soup-seller to all the world,
Please, sell us a little soup
To satisfy our desire
So that we can assuage our hunger
And so that we can slake our thirst
That we may become your friend
And your customer for a long time to come."

15.   The Iyalode sold her soup
To this father and child
The father and the child
Tasted the Iyalode's soup.
The soup had palm oil floating on the surface
But it had no taste at all,
And so this child and his father
Left the soup uneaten.

16. "Father, I am grateful to you
     For this lesson that you have taught me"
     The child said to his father,
     "Now I have come to understand that
     Soup that has no salt is flavorless,
     And that we should not buy
     Something that has no taste
     However beautiful it may be."

17. Thank you very much
     Good and wise child
     I want you to learn one more lesson
     Keep them [the lessons] safe in your heart
     Use those lessons when
     You are unhappy in the world
     Let the lesson be
     The chief of all your joys.

18. Child remember, make sure you understand
     From today onward, that
     Soup without salt has no flavor
     We never take advantage of our position to eat salt to excess.
     Just as this soup of the Iyalode
     Was flavorless in the absence of salt
     So too is the beauty of human beings
     In the absence of good character.

19. Beauty is the palm oil of the world
     Good character is the salt of the world
     Boiled beans that have plenty of palm oil
     And that have plenty of salt as well
     Are boiled beans that are complete.[2]
     Beauty is sent to the world by the Creator
     Character is for us humans to add.
     To make the beauty of the world sweet.

20. The world and the wisdom in it
     Greeted the Iyalode thus,
     "Iyalode, our soup-seller
     We give thanks to you today
     For this lesson that we have learned
     From these soups of yours
     Please, don't fail to add salt
     To your soup in future.

---

[2] It seems that in this verse Adenle is making a pun on the words *ẹwà* (beauty) and *ẹ̀wà* (boiled beans), differentiated by the tone of the first syllable.

21.   So that the world will no longer shun you
If you want your beauty to thrive
Don't let your character disgrace you.
Season your beauty with good character.
Leave your beauty to God."
After all this
Wisdom and the world gave thanks
To the good father, thus

22.   "Father, our good teacher,
We give thanks to you today
For this lesson that you have taught us.
Please, teach us how to behave
So that our beauty doesn't drive
Our well-being away from us.
Please, keep on teaching the world the lesson—
'Good character is the beauty of humankind.' "

NOTES

1. During research trips to western Nigeria, William and Berta Bascom assembled a substantial library of Yoruba-language texts—mostly locally published pamphlets—which was placed in the Bancroft Library, University of California at Berkeley, and later made available to other libraries on microfiche. The microfiche version is catalogued as "The Yoruba Collection of William and Berta Bascom" (1993), edited and published by Norman Ross Publishing Inc, New York. Norman A. Ross also published a guide to the microfiche edition in 1994.

2. Interviews were conducted in and around Oṣogbo in July 2002. With my colleagues the late Chief Adebayọ Ogundijọ and Dr. Paulo Farias, I paid several visits to Victor Adenle. We are grateful to him not only for his time and enthusiasm but also for allowing us to photocopy his original copies of S. A. Adenle's two pamphlets. We also visited Chief Ọladunjoye Omigbọdun in Oṣogbo and Mr. D. B. Adegoke in Ọkinni and are grateful to both for their very helpful and expansive responses. Our thanks also to Mr. Gboyega Ajayi of Ọbafẹmi Awolọwọ University and to participants at a seminar at the Institute of Cultural Studies, Ọbafẹmi Awolọwọ University, for additional comments on Adenle's history. We thank the Centre of West African Studies, University of Birmingham for a small grant to support the field work.

3. The secondary section of the school was also referred to as Adenle Grammar School.

4. Not surprisingly, this was an issue on which narratives from different sources diverged radically. It is not necessary to go into the details here. For a published version, see Falade (2000).

5. The force of this argument would have been increased by the fact that the Ataọja who had just died, Ọba Samuel Latọna, had himself been a literate Christian convert, indeed a graduate of St Andrew's College (Falade 2000, 105). Thus, to choose an illiterate successor, however wealthy, would have been regarded as a retrogressive step. However, the story of the messenger who goes to the district officer and turns the tables on a rival candidate seems to be a popular motif: a similar story was told about Ọba Oyekunle of Okuku (see Barber 1991, 223).

6. This early resistance to the CMS school in Oṣogbo is commemorated in a play created in 1961 by the popular Oṣogbo actor-dramatist Oyin Adejọbi; see Barber (2000, 321–326).

7. According to Mr. Adegoke, "all Anglican schools used them." According to Victor, they were used in schools of all denominations in Oṣogbo, including All Saints' School, the Methodist Primary School, St Benedict's (RC) Primary School, and the Baptists' Primary School as well as Adenle Grammar School. He said they were also used in a few primary schools in neighboring towns where Adenle's former classmates were working as teachers.

8. This manager was dismissed when Adenle discovered that he was cheating him. Thereafter Adenle relied on his wives to do the distribution and the printer also sold copies direct to customers.

9. In the 1923 edition of the CMS Yoruba hymnbook, hymn 555 begins *"N'nu gbogbo ayida aiye / N'nu wahala, 'gba mo kepe / Iyin Ọlọrun mi y'o ma / Wa l'ẹnu mi titi"* (In the midst of all the perturbations of this world / In the midst of trouble, when I cry out / The worship of God will always be / On my lips forever).

10. "God is our refuge and strength / A very present help in trouble." This Psalm appears to have been a favorite in colonial Oṣogbo. Verse 9 ("He maketh wars to cease unto the end of the earth; He breaketh the bow, and cutteth the spear in sunder") became the basis for one of the "Opening Glee" songs performed by the Oyin Adejọbi Theatre Company and stayed in their repertoire for at least thirty years.

11. For a favorable assessment of Adenle's cultural influence in Oṣogbo, see Beier (1960).

12. Strictly speaking, this should have read "Adenle Primary-Secondary School," or "Adenle Grammar School," as the Oṣogbo Grammar School was not opened until 1950, six years after his accession to the throne. Adenle must have decided to bestow this title on his own, by then defunct, secondary school (only the primary section of his school continued after the early 1940s) pending the establishment of the new grammar school.

13. Mr. Ọladẹjọ Okediji, the well-known Yoruba novelist, read and discussed these texts with me in July 2002. He described both texts as "*iwaaṣu iwa huhu fun awọn onkawe rẹ*" (sermons/preaching about how to behave for his readers).

14. As far as we know. However, in verse 30 of this text, page 7, there is an allusion to "*orin ti mo kọ nijọsi nipa Aiye*" (the song I sang/wrote some time ago about the World.) The four-line verse which is then quoted could be a hymn or devotional song written separately, perhaps for a special church service. It seems likely that Adenle expects his readers to remember this song and recognize it as a quotation of his own previous work. Whether it was previously published is a question to be investigated.

15. Thanks to Ben Knighton for pointing out this as a probable source.

16. Ibadan also had a considerable cultural life, with the Ẹgbẹ Agba-o-tan (Association of "Elders Still Exist"), and its publication *The Yoruba News*, edited by the poet D. Ọbasa. Abẹokuta was a center of poetic and other kinds of Yoruba-language writing and the home of the pioneering poet Ṣobọ Arobiodu. However, there is no doubt that Lagos was the most important focus of Yoruba literary and cultural activity throughout the colonial period.

17. Several of these papers gave the addresses of their distributors in major inland cities, suggesting that they were quite widely available, but more research would be needed to discover the extent to which these papers were actually read outside Lagos. There is no evidence that Adenle subscribed to any of them, and the only periodical Mr. Omigbọdun mentioned in the course of his reminiscences was the *Reader's Digest*!

18. *Itan Emi Ṣegilọla* appeared in 1929–1930 as a serial; it was published in 1930 as a book.

19. For an illuminating discussion of early Yoruba print poets' experiments with style and voice, see Nnodim (2002).

20. Ajayi Kọlawọle Ajiṣafẹ, previously known as Emmanuel Olympus Moore, was a Lagosian of Ẹgba origin who published more than fifty books and pamphlets in a lifetime of involvement in public affairs (Falola 1999, 13). Among his most notable publications were his *History of Abẹokuta* (n.d.), later published in a Yoruba version, and his moralizing pamphlets *Aiye Akamara, Tan' t'Ọlọrun?* and *Enia Ṣoro*; all three were published in 1921.

21. I am grateful to Stephanie Newell for helping me formulate this question about the relationship of individual tin-trunk writers to larger textual traditions.

22. I am grateful to Paulo Farias for pointing this out.

23. The original text of this episode is reproduced at the end of this chapter, together with my translation.

24. The Arabian Nights might also have been one model for the episodic narrative structure. But again, note the remarkable differences. In the Arabian Nights, the whole point of the narration is to maintain suspense and forward motion by imbricating each story in the next. If the tension of expectation is lost, the narrator will die. The framework of the Arabian Nights is a powerful sexual challenge and triumphant response, very different from the cold, empty, and essentially autistic challenge issued by the *ọba*.

REFERENCES

Adenle, S. A. 1934. *Iwe Aiye Toto Fun.* Ijẹbu-Ode: Tanimẹhin-Ọla Press.

———. *Iwe Iwa Rere L'Ọṣọ Enia.* Ijẹbu-Ode: Tanimẹhin-Ọla Press.

Ajiṣafẹ, A. K. 1921. *Aiye Akamara.* Lagos, Nigeria: Ifẹ-Olu Printing Works.

———. 1921. *Enia ṣoro.* Bungay, Suffolk: Richard Clay.

———. 1921. *Tan' t'Ọlọrun?* Bungay, Suffolk: Richard Clay.

Bamisaiye, Rẹmi. 1995. "Sociological Influences of Western Education in Oṣogbo." In *Oṣ-ogbo: Model of Growing African Towns,* ed. C. O. Adepegba, 52–70. Ibadan: Institute of African Studies, University of Ibadan.

Barber, Karin. 1991. *I Could Speak Until Tomorrow: Oriki, Women and the Past in a Yoruba Town.* Edinburgh: Edinburgh University Press for the IAI.

———. 2000. *The Generation of Plays: Yorùbá Popular Life in Theater.* Bloomington: Indiana University Press.

———. 2005. "Translation, Publics and the Vernacular Press in 1920s Lagos." In *Christianity and Social Change in Africa: Essays in Honor of J. D. Y. Peel,* ed. Toyin Falola, 187–208. Durham, N.C.: Carolina Academic Press.

Beier, Ulli. 1960. "Oshogbo." *Nigeria Magazine* 64 (special issue *Nigeria 1960*): 94–102.

Falade, S. A. 2000. *The Comprehensive History of Oṣogbo.* Ibadan: 'Tunji Owolabi Commercial Printers.

Falọla, Toyin. 1999. *Yoruba Gurus: Indigenous Production of Knowledge in Africa.* Trenton, N.J.: Africa World Press.

Nnodim, Rita. 2002. "Ewi—Yoruba Neotraditional Media Poetry: The Poetics of a Genre." Ph.D. thesis, University of Birmingham.

Ogunsheye, F. Adetowun. 2001. *Bibliographic Survey of Sources for Early Yoruba Language and Literature Studies, 1820–1970.* Ibadan: Ibadan University Press.

Thomas, I. B. 1930. *Itan igbesi aiye emi "Ṣegilọla, ẹleyinju ẹgẹ" ẹlẹgbẹrun ọkọ l'aiye.* Lagos: CMS Bookshops.

INNOVATION AND PERSISTENCE: LITERARY CIRCLES, NEW OPPORTUNITIES, AND CONTINUING DEBATES IN HAUSA LITERARY PRODUCTION

15

Graham Furniss

Introduction

Literary production would appear to require nothing more, at the bare minimum, than paper and a pen and a sentient being who has acquired literacy. Yet of course the social contexts in which people put pen to paper are infinitely various. That primary act may be a lonely one, but the perpetrator is embedded in a network of social relations that impact upon the continuing process of literary production. From the hidden private accumulation of texts to the organized industrial production of newsprint, a variety of social formations are deployed in support of text-writing. Looking at aspects of Northern Nigerian cultural history, I trace here the persistence of one particular idea, the notion of a circle of writers and discussants. This organizational form is rooted in precolonial intellectual movements, appears in the colonial period as both literary and debating forums that go on to become nascent political organizations, reemerges in poetry circles in newly independent Nigeria, and most recently is manifest in writers' clubs that respond to the decline of formal publishing by going it alone in the production of a whole new world of Hausa popular fiction. The writers' club or circle has been a locus for debates about the value, or lack of value, of such cultural production judged against two cross-cutting evaluative frameworks, "Hausa customs" and "Islamic values."

During the early 1930s, at the height of colonial power in Northern Nigeria, a colonial official, Rupert East, was grappling with a serious long-term issue in his attempt to engender a new literary form in Hausa (East 1943). There was no tradition of imaginative prose-writing in Hausa. In his efforts to establish such a form and provide Hausa speakers with material that would be, as he viewed it, enjoyable, educative, and interesting, East wanted to use government money to subsidize the production of books through the Literature Bureau (later the Gaskiya Corporation) but did not have a commercially viable market of readers who could or would buy the books. A popular market for his kind of printed book did not exist. The market for the crop of Hausa novellas that were produced in the 1930s, 1940s, and 1950s was primarily western (rather than Qur'anic) schools. The colonial and postcolonial curriculum provided the guarantee of sales for Hausa novellas up until the early 1980s. Sixty years after East was faced with his early conundrum, an explosion did take place in the production of Hausa printed books—romances, crime stories, social realism, fantasies, morality tales—and that explosion saw a new popular readership snapping up books from markets, corner stores, and new bookshops. In recent years the same people involved in book production have moved into the more lucrative production and sale of Hausa video films, which are often derived from Hausa novels.

This chapter traces some of the issues that have been involved in the cultural transition from the situation of the 1930s to the explosion of the 1990s, focusing on the role of literary circles as forms of intellectual social organization that provided a mechanism for literary and other cultural production and took advantage of technological change while they often were part of broader sociopolitical movements. Innovation in genre, style, and subject matter is complemented by persistence in a debate about morality and legitimacy.

Hausa is spoken as a first language by about 25 million people in the northern and northwestern states of Nigeria and along the southern borderlands of Niger. Approximately 25 million other people speak it as a second or third language in Nigeria and Niger, in northern Ghana, and in trading communities from Senegal to Sudan. While I am aware of the broader linguistic community, the bulk of my comments below relate to the northern states of Nigeria, Kano in particular. Since at least the jihad of the early nineteenth century, Hausa has been written in the Arabic script (known as *ajami*), and literacy in Arabic and *ajami* was widespread among the cleric class of Islamic scholars in the towns and cities of northern Nigeria from before the nineteenth century. It is important to be aware that communities of literate people were a well-established phenomenon in this part of the world at the beginning of the twentieth century. They debated the nature, norms, and prospects of the society in which they lived, and they wrote for each other about such issues. At the same time, their Islamic education system produced teachers with established reputations for knowledge and understanding of particular Islamic texts who gathered around themselves students, all at various stages of learning, who copied out texts while learning how to interpret them. People would study with one scholar and then move to study with another, sometimes living for years in various parts of Nigeria or Niger while pursuing their studies. The copying and sale of manuscripts, particularly Korans, was a widespread, painstaking, and time-consuming activity. The notion of a group, sometimes a self-sustaining community, who came together to talk, write, copy, and study was familiar to both urban and rural Hausa-speaking people both prior to and during the nineteenth century.

The writing of Hausa in roman script was an innovation of the late nineteenth century and one which came into use in Nigeria with the British colonial administration after 1900. When Rupert East looked to engender Hausa imaginative prose-writing in the early 1930s it was because his Translation Bureau had been translating colonial "public enlightenment" pamphlets on hygiene, disease control, and agriculture into roman-script Hausa and the colonial education department needed "more interesting" materials if it was to get anywhere with its adult literacy campaigns, or so it seemed. East's problems of simultaneously engendering book production and a reading public related to roman-script Hausa, not *ajami* Hausa, which continued along its own track. However, a number of the changes in technology were to impact equally on *ajami* writing and writers, as we shall see.

Technologies

Access to "media outlets" has been a recurring stimulus to the formation of groups of writers, whether they are working in the long-established tradition of written poetry or in the field of prose-writing. The technology of pen and ink required sustained labor by individuals working within the Islamic education system. For the development of roman-script materials, the introduction of government and Christian-mission presses allowed, naturally, for the automated production of print runs but required a literate printer to typeset the pages, whether they were in roman script or Arabic script (the early government press in Kano set type in both scripts). Early Hausa prose produced for the Translation Bureau was printed on Christian-mission presses in Jos. The later establishment of the Gaskiya Corporation in Zaria brought together a community of Nigerian and British editors, typesetters, illustrators, and production and distribution agents into a community housed in Tudun Wada with all the technology of 1940s book production.

A technological innovation from around 1960 transformed the prospects of literary production, particularly for producers of *ajami* manuscripts. The photo-offset printing system allowed a printer who could not even read the script to produce a print run of a text in whatever script, as long as he knew the pagination and which way up to print the pages. Many businesses were established in the commercial districts of northern cities that provided printing services for commercial firms and anyone needing stationery. Such businesses were very often owned, from 1960 onward, by Igbo or Yoruba residents of such cities. This meant that Hausa-speaking Islamic scholars could take a manuscript to a southern printer unfamiliar with the script and yet arrange for unlimited reproduction of the manuscript.

A major stimulus to the formation of literary circles was the introduction of radio and television stations that drew upon local Northern Nigerian sources for a proportion of their programming. In addition to international stations that broadcast in Hausa, the national radio (Broadcasting Corporation of Nigeria), which worked mostly in English, was complemented by the northern-based Broadcasting Corporation of Northern Nigeria (BCNN) in 1962, which drew heavily upon Hausa musicians for material and instituted some of the early radio dramas and poetry recitations. Local stations such as Radio Kano were open to local poets and singers and indeed to a number of poetry-writing circles that were established and flourished in the 1960s and 1970s. The introduction of television provided further stimulus to Hausa drama (often humorous drama) and to popular singers. By the boom years of the 1970s and early 1980s, recordings of popular singers, preachers, poets, and comedians were also circulating as commercial products on cassette tape, thereby providing a livelihood for a new kind of dealer, even if the original artist saw little if any of the proceeds. The growth in the ownership of radios and televisions was astonishing throughout these same boom years. M. Abdulkadir (2000, 130) reports a BBC survey in 1993 indicating that 93 percent of urban households in Nigeria owned a radio set and 52 percent a television set.

The most recent, and culturally most radical, shift in technology has been the extension of television into videocassette recording. The survey in 1993 referred to above indicated that 11 percent of households also owned a VCR.

The fact that a handheld video camera, a group of friends, and some editing facilities are all that are required to make a video version of an action- and dialogue-packed novella has led to an explosion in the production of Hausa-language videos that are increasingly done more and more professionally. These can be watched by young and old, particularly women and girls in the privacy of their own homes (in contrast to the public space of the cinema).

The final technological change I wish to outline is not the opportunity provided by a new technology but the Nigerian response to a collapse in the economy of a technology, one which goes back to the early colonial period, namely printing and publishing. If the answer to Rupert East's conundrum in relation to achieving "take-off" was the simultaneous appearance of a critical mass of interested literate readers and a group of productive writers, all in an economic environment in which books were a profitable commodity, then 1979 should have been about it. At that time it looked as if a mass readership was on its way, a relatively large number of publishers were operating in the Nigerian market, manuscripts were piling up (or so I was led to believe by the editor of the Northern Nigerian Publishing Company at the time), and the economy was booming such that ordinary people had money in their pockets with which to buy books.

By the mid-1980s, however, "structural adjustment" had put the Nigerian economy into sharp decline. Publishers were shutting up shop, and the buying power of both the middle classes and the young was dropping rapidly.

Sociopolitical Organization and Literary Production

The stimulus for the formation and activity of literary circles is of course not provided solely by the technological opportunities that arise. Broader political and intellectual currents constitute the contexts in which people are moved to articulate their ideas, imaginings, and experiences. The earliest known context in which a group of intellectuals came together to articulate in written Hausa their political and religious views was the jihad of 1804. That Islamic reform movement of the early nineteenth century was centered around a veritable intellectual hive of debate and discussion on Islam and society in which a woman, Nana Asma'u, daughter of the Shehu Usman dan Fodio, was centrally involved. That reform movement set the imprimatur of didacticism upon the genre of written poetry for over 100 years and has been a model of reforming zeal for religious and political movements ever since. The outpouring of Islamic religious writing that accompanied the jihad was embedded in the technology of pen and ink. Within the world of Islamic religious organization that developed through the nineteenth and twentieth centuries was a series of international movements that had their counterparts in Northern Nigeria. The most important for this part of Northern Nigeria was the Sufi brotherhoods, particularly the Qadiriyya and the Tijaniyya, but also anti-Sufi movements such as the Izala and umbrella organizations such as the Jama'atu Nasril Islam. In the 1950s and 1960s these two Sufi brotherhoods transformed themselves into mass organizations with a public presence at prayer, in leadership structures, and in extensive networks able to raise finance, look after members, deploy property, and, most important from our point of view, distribute brotherhood literature. The advent of offset printing allowed poets and scholars within the brotherhood to reproduce large quantities of their literature and distribute it through the *zawiya* organization (see Paden 1973). The writers producing the poetry and religious treatises were often the local leaders of the brotherhoods, who debated among themselves as the leaders of the jihad had done 150 years earlier.

A second stimulus to the process of writing and collaborating with others in writing was the growth of formal politics and political parties in post–World War II Nigeria, both before and after independence in 1960. The products of the only western secondary school for many years, Katsina College, were a select group of young men who went on to become the political and intellectual leaders of the north. With a foot in both western education and Islamic education, they provided the political leadership of both the conservative party (Nigerian Peoples' Congress, NPC) and the reformist party (Northern Elements Progressive Union, NEPU), they rose to the top of the new independent Nigerian civil service, and they were the writers of roman-script Hausa literature. From among their number came the first Hausa editor of the Hausa-language newspaper, Abubakar Imam. The precursors of these political parties were "discussion circles" and "literary circles," arenas in which these men discussed their political aspirations for their part of Nigeria. The more radical of them would make demands through local traditional rulers or sometimes directly to the British colonial officers who kept a close eye on such organizations. Time and again, both before independence but even more in independent Nigeria, the appearance of poetry in print would be linked to political rivalry between proponents of the NPC and the NEPU. Very quickly it became the norm for political parties to deploy not only their poets but also their musicians and singers in praise of their leadership and in vilification of their opponents. Interestingly, writers of prose fiction who had followed the models of the picaresque, the fantastical, and the ribald derived from the early novellas of the 1930s would break the mold only to engage in politically committed depictions of corruption, abuse of power, and social alienation in the early 1980s—a recent move prompted by their reading of English-language materials as much as by an awareness of earlier Hausa novellas. Political and social protest was, until recently, much more closely associated with poetry and song than it was with prose-writing, perhaps an effect of the earlier association of the poetic form with the didacticism of jihadist Islam.

Intellectual Organizational Mechanisms: The Colonial Period

The communities of Islamic scholars, the intellectual leadership of the brotherhoods, and the structure of the Islamic education system were all conducive to the notion of groups of people working to produce written literature, often poetry, that promoted and explained the practice and beliefs of Islam to the people at large. During the colonial period, however, a number of cultural and literary societies emerged which have primarily been seen as the precursors of political parties but which—I would argue—are also models which persisted into the postcolonial era—mechanisms whereby people could come together to assist each other and to talk, write, and debate about the nature of northern society, Hausa and Islam. Two of the central figures in the production of published poetry and prose in the 1940s and 1950s were Sa'adu Zungur and Abubakar Imam. They became, respectively, key figures in the more radical and more conservative political parties of the era. Sa'adu Zungur was the founding figure in the short-lived Zaria Literary Society, founded in 1939 (D. Abdulkadir 1974, 10) and a participant in the more significant Bauchi Discussion Circle (BDC). (There is some uncertainty about dates and nomenclature; Imam [1989, 158] indicates that Sa'adu Zungur was the prime mover behind the founding of the Zaria Friendly Society in 1940, presumably a variant version of the Zaria Literary Society.)

The Bauchi Discussion Circle and the Bauchi General Improvement Union

Yakubu (1999, 35–36) describes the situation in Bauchi in 1943 as follows:

> By sheer coincidence, the Bauchi of 1943 had a sizeable number of Western educated Northerners. In the Middle School were the future Prime Minister of Nigeria, Abubakar Tafawa Balewa, as well as Yahaya Gusau and Aminu Kano with Muhammadu Baba-Halla at the NA [Native Authority] Veterinary De-

partment. There was also a large number of enthusiastic NA employees as well as a sizeable number of others, among them southern Nigerians employed mainly as clerks in the Railway Corporation and the Post and Telegraph Department. Having invalided him from service, the colonial administration lost its leverage on Sa'adu [Zungur] and his activities and should he try to organise a forum, as he had done in Zaria, to advance the views he expressed in [a] letter to the DO . . . there was a willing intelligentsia which would not only listen sympathetically but was also potentially capable of carrying these views forward. Since Sa'adu's major grouse was the lack of freedom of expression, the Administration sought to create the enabling platform for a controlled expression of opinion through an officially-sponsored and officially-managed weekly forum. Through the Bauchi Emir's Council as well as a direct contact between Aminu Kano and the Senior DO, A.J. Knott, the Administration sponsored the formation in February 1944 of *Majalisar Taskar Hikima* (Local Brains Trust) which became popularly known as *Majalisar Tadi ta Bauchi[,]* or the Bauchi Discussion Circle.

Yakubu goes on to describe a series of sometimes-heated discussions led by Sa'adu Zungur that ended in the closing down of the Bauchi Discussion Circle by the administration and the independent establishment of another forum, the Bauchi General Improvement Union (BGIU), which was banned from using government property for its meetings and which was one of the precursors to the emergence of political parties in Northern Nigeria.

Writers of political histories of Northern Nigeria have focused upon such literary and cultural organizations in terms of the emergence of political parties and opposition to the colonial state. Another aspect of such organizations, whether they were nascent political parties or not, is their role in generating texts, and it is that side of their activities I wish to address.

In the quotation above, Yakubu makes mention of a letter from Sa'adu Zungur to the district officer, and it is clear that a large number of entreaties, cases of complaint, treatises, and written replies were produced by members of these discussion circles, including Sa'adu, Aminu Kano, Tafawa Balewa, and others. Sometimes they were directed at the colonial administrators and their client officials and at other times they were debating among themselves. The eloquence and strength of Sa'adu Zungur's English writing can be gleaned from the example that Yakubu quotes. Sa'adu, who was suffering from tuberculosis and had been invalided out of government service in 1943, wrote to the district officer as follows:

> I have tried NOT to write this letter. I have tried to absorb myself in my condition of chronic ill-health. I have tried to put the thoughts of the destiny of Northern Nigeria behind me and tend to my own immediate personal affairs. And I cannot. I go to bed with these thoughts; I get up with them. They are

there when I experience ghastly attacks of my neurotic conditions. The same thoughts are there when I say my prayers, or sit and converse with a friend or to read a local "daily." . . .

I am again, speaking as a Hausaman, an ignorant and weak Hausaman, if you will, emotional, impulsive, illogical, conservative, dreaming, impractical, over-enthusiastic or any of the common vices you care to pin on me. I write knowing that all these vices cannot help but be used to undermine anything I say. I write knowing fully that I may be laughed at again, brushed aside with the new broom so handy to masterful administr-*ators and modern critics, that facile condemnation of the amateur intruding into a field he knows little about. We have been denied such *reasonable* freedom of thought and speech as would enable us to enlighten public opinion and to help in guiding or directing the enlightenment and culture of the masses. But we have been exposed to attacks far more insidious and hurtful than bodily blows. The very air we breathe is heavy with impalpable fears, and we are harassed by oppressive shadows of insecurity. (Yakubu 1999, 34–35)

Yakubu goes on to make the following remark about the meetings of the Bauchi Discussion Circle: "However, there was no doubt about the individual who dominated each proceeding whether he was proposing, opposing, or contributing to general discussions. Sa'adu's role was so pivotal and his choice of words so captivating that many people attended the forum essentially in order to listen to him" (37–38).

Letters, treatises, and complaints constituted an important component of the textual output of Sa'adu Zungur and his colleagues in the BDC and later the BGIU. Another equally significant component was the production of poetry. Sa'adu Zungur was a fine poet, and his published and unpublished Hausa poetry was very influential. But he was not alone. Among the young followers of his friend and colleague Aminu Kano was the poet Mudi Sipikin, who went on to play a crucial role, thirty years later in independent Nigeria, in the foundation of a new generation of literary circles.

Two years before his untimely death at the age of 43 in January 1958, Sa'adu Zungur wrote a letter to his colleague Aminu Kano which encapsulates the importance of poetic literary production within the framework of the politics of Northern Nigeria (the letter is quoted both in Yakubu 1999, 366–368 and in Paden 1973, 296–297). It addresses the significance of literacy in roman and Arabic script, the problems of printing and circulation, and the power of performance and group activity, with a final poignant reference to treatment for his illness. In this version, Paden inserts Hausa original terms in square brackets and he indicates original English phrases in quotation marks. Paden provides a footnote (not given here) dating the letter as May 16, 1956, and thanks Aminu Kano for permission to quote:

Malam Aminu Kano, President General of NEPU [Northern Elements Progressive Union], may it please your leadership. I write this letter in order to introduce this emissary of mine, Mallam Hassan Kosasshe, a tailor from Bauchi, who is accompanying his father, Mallam Ahmadu, to Kano to see you and acquaint you with my message—a letter. Mallam Ahmadu, the father, has come in order to prepare for the pilgrimage—to be inoculated. Mallam Hassan is coming to pay you a visit and to carry my message to you. I hope that the people in the Kano branch of NEPU will receive him as a real brother [*dan uwa*] and treat him with dignity. Under the umbrella of your leadership [*girmanka*] and your excellence [*martaba*], he is a bona fide NEPU man of tireless effort. I am particularly glad that he is going to Kano for he will be able to explain properly to you the situation here in Bauchi. He carries with him a NEPU poem from Bauchi, and I hope you will make it possible for him to sing it in front of an important gathering of the Kano NEPU branch so that real cooperation will emerge in the production of poems in our struggle [*jihad*] for dignity and freedom [*sawaba*]. I hope this poem will impress our brothers in the gathering of NEPU at Kano. We are hoping that he will be given the full opportunity to read it from beginning to end. We also hope that the Kano branch will provide him with a chorus of about twelve youths, for that is how we do it here. I implore our brethren in Kano to be tolerant of our differences [between the Kano and the Bauchi branches of NEPU], which are manifest in the poem, and also to be tolerant of the voice in which Mallam Hassan will sing it. I hope on the strength of your reverence and position Mallam will be entertained and will be shown solidarity. He cannot use roman script [*ajamin turawa*], but writes in the Arabic script. All the same he is a fully enlightened man.

We are also asking for another favor besides that of allowing Mallam Hassan to read his poem. We want help in rendering two copies of this poem: one in roman script and the other in the proper script [Arabic]. We hope that the copy in roman script will be printed in about 5,000 copies. This printing we shall count as an act of comradeship and we hope that [Hassan] will bring us the bill. This poem is majestic [*haiba*] and impressive [*kwarjini*]. It is the first in a series of poems that we intend to compose as an aid to our struggle for freedom. The north is at the stage where it is extremely receptive to the message of serious political songs.

This is only one of the poems that are in our possession, but we are in such a hurry to take it to you that we have not made more copies apart from "the corrected draft." Please help us with the services of those who are really proficient in writing Hausa, so that the copying will be done immediately before this one is destroyed, since it had started to deteriorate before he left Bauchi. The poem has about three hundred lines. Choose the easiest method of "printing," we are not particular. It can be arranged in a single or in double lines, as follows:

Oh God, Oh single King, / Lead the north out of danger
[*Ya Allah ya Sarki witiri / ka fitar da arewa cikin hadari*].

In addition, there are many things we have decided on at the Bauchi NEPU divisional conference. Because he [Hassan] was in a hurry we did not obtain "typed copies" of the deliberations on the provincial constitution [of NEPU]. However, here are the English and Hausa copies of *Sawaba Creed* which we have prepared and are working with. We hope you will review it properly and if you agree with it, please help us in getting headquarters to accept it and print thousands of copies and distribute or sell it. We have no rights with regard to that. Ours is only to produce. Again, here is the copy of a "circular letter" which is being sent out inviting all political parties in Bauchi Province dedicated to the achievement of freedom. We shall later make available to headquarters [in Kano] a full report on the conference and all that was decided upon there.

P.S. "Please sir," I reiterate my appeal to you or the party to help us with: one hundred tablets of Sonalgin; two hundred tablets of APC codine; 400 ("very small tablets") of isonicotinic acid (not isoniacid): I am extremely grateful,
  "Yours fraternally," [Signed] Sa'ad Zungur. (Paden 1973, 296–297)

The literary activities of Sa'adu Zungur and Aminu Kano, and later disciples of theirs such as Mudi Sipikin, Akilu Aliyu, and others, were part of the range of activities outside the framework of colonial government organizations and constituted elements within new and oppositional political movements. At the same time, other looser networks of intellectual and literary production occurred within the heart of organizations that were established by the colonial administration itself.

The Literature Bureau

Abubakar Imam was the central figure alongside Rupert East in the Literature Bureau, later to become the Gaskiya Corporation. As editor of the Hausa-language newspaper and major early author of Hausa imaginative prose he was a key figure in the establishment of a northern cultural association in Zaria (Jam'iyyar Mutanen Arewa) in 1948 which later became the NPC, the dominant political party in immediate post-independence northern Nigeria (Imam 1989, 167–168). The Literature Bureau had assembled a number of young recruits from all over Northern Nigeria to work in journalism and book production. One of them, Abubakar Tunau, wrote that "the recruitment drive was continued for some time until Gaskiya Village was adequately populated with Gaskiya Corporation Junior and Intermediate Staff" (Tunau 1989, 272). Not only did these staff members constitute the group that worked together on book and newspaper production, they also met regularly to discuss literary production with people from across the north, as Alhaji Baba Ahmed describes: "Many malams also used to attend meetings at the Literature Bureau, from all over the Hausa states. . . . One day the *alkalin* Zango, Malam Muhammadu, visited me with two gentlemen from Kano and Katsina. During the course of our discussion, they said they would like to translate some Arabic books into Hausa therefore they would like me to teach them how to use an Arabic dictionary" (Ahmed 1989, 257). Haliru Binji indicated that meetings and discussions took place both within the Literature Bureau and at the houses of the Hausa staff: "Abubakar Imam, more often than not, initiated discussions at his house on controversial or not very clear Islamic topics, with a view to finding their logical conclusions. We might call such a friendly gathering of learned men a *Qiyas* or a symposium, where they compared notes and gave analogical reasoning with regard to the teaching of the Qur'an" (Binji 1989, 263). Such meetings were the spur not only to literary production but also to political activity, as Abubakar Imam himself described:

> In September 1948 . . . we in Zaria were making efforts to form an organisation stronger than the Zaria Friendly Society, which had existed only in name. . . . On a Saturday evening in October 1948, Dr R A B Dikko invited a group of friends for a discussion at his house. Eleven of us accepted the invitation including Malam Ali the Turaki of Zaria and Malam Umaru Agaie. After the usual exchange of greetings, Dr Dikko disclosed the reason for his invitation which was in connection with the founding of an organisation to be called *Jam'iyyar Mutanen Arewa* meaning an association of the Northern People. After deliberation we all unanimously approved the idea and the proposed name for the organisation. (Imam 1989, 167)

The model of the discussion circle that produced poetry, polemics, letters to the editor, representations to authorities, political tracts, and literary texts was one which persisted into the postcolonial era.

Intellectual Organizational Mechanisms after Independence, 1960–1980

In the northern Nigeria of the late 1960s and early 1970s a number of literary societies emerged alongside cultural organizations that championed the Hausa language and "Hausa customs." A member of the NEPU, the northern opposition party, who had been a young supporter of Aminu Kano in the 1950s emerged as a popular poet and political figure. Mudi Sipikin had access to Kano radio and in 1963 founded the Hikima Kulob (Wisdom Club) as a poetry circle to facilitate access to a wider audience through a half-hour program every Thursday during which poets would recite their poetry on air (Furniss 1995, 25–40). By 1974, the club had about twenty-three active members who met on Sundays at Mudi Sipikin's office in order to read aloud and discuss their poetry and determine who would recite on radio the following

Thursday. A collected volume of their poetry was published by Oxford University Press in 1973. The conventions of the poetry circle, as articulated by its leader, encouraged writing that was serious, hortatory, and didactic and that addressed public issues. The frivolous, personal, or scurrilous was to be eschewed. Nevertheless, the poetry was no longer confined to religious topics; a broad range of secular issues constituted the subject matter of such poetry, and politics was a part of the mix. The Hikima Kulob was not alone. A rival poetry circle was active during the same period, headed by another well-respected poet, Akilu Aliyu, and called Hausa Fasaha (Hausa Skill). Both societies were based in Kano. Other organizations and groups were subsequently involved in the promotion of both the study and production of Hausa literary forms. The growth of Hausa studies in the universities of the northern states, particularly Bayero University in Kano and Ahmadu Bello University in Zaria, gave rise to cultural events such as "Hausa Week," during which students, writers, poets, and academics came together to perform and discuss, and out of this ferment of Hausa cultural nationalism grew a Society for the Study of Hausa (Kungiyar Nazarin Hausa), which was mostly made up of academics and was founded in 1973; a Society of Writers and Students of Hausa Song and Poetry (Kungiyar Marubuta da Manazarta Wakokin Hausa), which was established in 1981 in Sokoto; and a Society of Hausa Authors (Kungiyar Mawallafa Hausa), which was also founded in 1981. For further discussion in Hausa of these organizations, see Yahaya (1988, 195–198).

Intellectual Organizational Mechanisms in a Collapsing Economy: 1980–2000

The crash in the Nigerian economy of the mid-1980s dealt a considerable blow to formal publishing. Nevertheless, the introduction of Universal Primary Education in 1976 had produced a situation where a new generation of young people who had been, say, 12 years old in 1976, were now, by the end of the 1980s, in their early and mid-twenties and were literate in both English and Hausa. They faced all the rigors and hardship that the economic collapse had wrought. A desire to express their frustrations, hopes, and expectations was seemingly blocked by the attendant collapse of formal publishing. A number of budding writers decided that in spite of all the difficulties they faced they would nevertheless do it themselves. Using the model of the writer's circle to support each other and provide a way of passing on information about how to do it, they set about creating their own literature and their own commercial commodities—new kinds of books.

Aminu Hassan Yakasai,

Alh. Hamisu Bature,

Aminu Abdu Na'inna,

Hajiya Balaraba Ramat.

Dan'Azim Baba,

Ado Ahmad,

wasu daga cikin shugabannin kungiyar marubuta litattafan Hausa ta Raina Kama (Kano)

Figure 15.1. Photograph of Raina Kama members as printed in their early books.

The founders of the writers' circle known as Raina Kama (Deceptive Appearances) were five men and one woman, and their circle rapidly gained new members from 1987 onward as they produced a growing number of new and popular titles. Seldom more than 100 pages, these books had hand-drawn covers and contained a list of titles by other members of the circle that were either already out or would shortly appear. Miniature photocopies of the covers of other books in the series would also appear printed in the back of the book. By this means, members of the group created a public presence for the body of their work and an identity as a group marked by logos on their books. Raina Kama was quickly followed by other groups of writers such as Kukan Kurciya (The Cry of the Dove), which was also based in Kano, and Dan Hakin da Ka Raina (The Splinter You Ignore), which was based in Kaduna.

The names of these literary circles were taken from proverbs, as indeed

Figure 15.2. Book-cover logos for Raina Kama, Kukan Kurciya, and Dan Hakin Da Ka Raina.

were the titles of many of their books. In more recent years a wider world of writers has emerged and the nurturing framework of the literary circle has been overtaken by commercial relationships, particularly between bookshop owners and fledgling writers. Using academics from the universities to endorse their works and to help with correcting orthography, these young writers are addressing the many current issues that impinge upon their lives: love unrequited, love thwarted, love fulfilled, unemployment, poverty, criminality, violence, corruption, and the pressures of family and responsibility. Influenced by the morality and romance of popular Indian films (see Larkin 1997, 2000), English-language romances, and thrillers on television and in print, they branched out into ways of writing which were very unfamiliar to those who had grown up with earlier types of Hausa imaginative prose-writing. While this literature was first given the sobriquet of Soyayya Books ("Love Stories"), the subject matter covered a wider range of topics. Nevertheless, an avid and growing readership emerged among school-age young people in particular, many of whom were female. As the literature has grown and developed, more and more women have become involved as authors as well as readers.

The scale of this explosion of cultural production that took place between about 1987 and 2000 is not yet clear. No definitive listing is available of the books that were produced. The partial collection in this author's possession runs to 1,300 volumes in Hausa (in 2004), and there are clearly gaps in that collection. In the latter part of the 1990s, fewer and fewer books were produced that were specifically marked as being associated with a literary circle. Nevertheless, the name Raina Kama, among others, emerged in a new context as certain writers began to move into a new production medium, namely the video film. Raina Kama became RK Studios as Dan Azumi Baba Chediyar 'Yan Gurasa took the name with him into films; the woman author who had also been a founder member of the Raina Kama literary circle, Balaraba Ramat Yakubu, became Ramat Productions; and Ado Ahmad Gidan Dabino

Figure 15.3. Street sign for Silhouette Readers' Club, Kano.

became a prime mover in Gidan Dabino Video Productions. The Nigerian National Film and Video Censors' Board indicated in 2002 that they had issued classification certificates to 616 Hausa-language video films between 1997 and 2001, and the industry has grown even more since that time.

The cultural significance of the rise of the video film in the last fifteen years cannot be overestimated, as it has provided a wholesale revolution both in entertainment and in the notion of what is appropriate for public presence and discussion, from the depiction of love, violence, and antisocial behavior to the emergence of women as film stars within the Hausa cultural firmament.

A further manifestation of the long tradition of discussion and debate that has surrounded the development of literature and other forms of cultural production in Hausa has been the emergence in very recent years of literary, film, and cultural magazines in Hausa that both print gossip about the actors and the writers and debate the cultural value of such material (for further discussion see Y. Adamu 1998, 2002 and A. U. Adamu 1999).

431

Persistent Issues: Debates about Morality and Debates about Cultural and Religious Legitimacy

Since the appearance of the first popular novellas in the late 1980s, a debate has raged, first in academic circles and subsequently in English- and Hausa-language newspapers and magazines and on radio and television, about the worth of this literature. A number of intellectuals took the position that this literature was essentially trashy. They felt that it was badly written and that the topics were either frivolous or inappropriate. Such critics were swiftly countered by others who held that the novellas were a cry from the heart by a younger generation faced with the dislocation of Nigerian society and struggling with the constraints and problems of love, family, unemployment, and rising crime, among other things. They proposed that "all the flowers should be allowed to bloom" and that in due course good writers and writing would emerge. The debate became wider and more visible as video films burst onto the market and cultural magazines were founded to capitalize on the burgeoning interest in films and books and in all the people involved in these industries.

Although novellas and video films were criticized on many grounds, the general yardsticks against which they were measured are the same yardsticks that were deployed in the poetry circle that I worked with in the early 1970s and that some people applied to the early production of imaginative prose in the 1930s and 1940s. The first and most important yardstick is whether the work can be judged to be consistent with, or supportive of, the moral and behavioral norms that are held to be prescribed by Islam. These are, of course, matters for discussion and interpretation by religious authorities and the subject of daily discourse among ordinary people—particularly since the extension of Shari'a law into areas of public life that had hitherto been the preserve of criminal law or where certain religious prohibitions on public behavior had hitherto not been applied. The accusation that a video film or book is inimical to Islam is a serious one. The second yardstick against which novels and video films are being judged is whether they portray accurately, are supportive of, or undermine "Hausa customs." The construction of a notion of a premodern Hausa way of life, unencumbered by western artifacts and western-derived ills and separate from the cultural mores of other linguistic groups, has been a theme that has motivated some politicians and intellectuals over the last half-century. These novellas and films have often been both defended and attacked in terms of whether they portray, uphold, and defend the notion of a Hausa identity and culture.

Whether the attack or defense is made in terms of Islam or "Hausa customs," the current debates share with the poetry circles of the 1970s, the literary/discussion circles of the 1940s, and the jihadist writers of the 1800s a general consensus that literature is about the "message". The didacticism of the jihad writers is mirrored in the insistence that literature should have a message one hears in the present-day debates around video film. Yet even that is now changing. While that voice can still be heard, the commercial demand for novellas and video film is leading to the growth of notions of entertainment, of thrill, of spectacle, of the pleasure of music and dance as justifications for the appearance of a book or a video film. It remains to be seen whether the public mood that endorses the advance of Shari'a law in parts of the Hausa-speaking world will suppress entirely the cultural tendencies that have produced the growth of these new cultural forms in public life.

Conclusion

The discussion circle, poetry club, literary society, or writers' association has been an enduring feature of Hausa cultural production over the years. Whether it was taking advantage of new technologies or resisting the collapse of old ones, the cooperative principle has allowed generations of writers to debate and articulate in print their assessments of society, religion, and politics. Sharing an evaluative purpose, their activities have produced new forms of writing, covered new types of subject matter, and made new evaluations of perennial human relationships and their problems. Looking back to the religious writers of the early nineteenth century and comparing their cooperative ventures with the recent explosion of popular literature and video film, it is clear that an earlier "restricted literacy" that nevertheless had a profound impact on Hausa society has been matched by an unprecedented upsurge of popular literacy and popular cultural production that has had an impact on society at large. In all of this, a debate has continued about how to measure the value and worth of these various kinds of cultural production—do they conform to and reinforce Islam and do they accord with and support "Hausa customs"? How to define "Islamic values" and "Hausa values" remains an enduring issue for each generation of writers and readers. Time and again the literary circle has been the organizational form in which such debate has taken place.

REFERENCES

Abdulkadir, Dandatti. 1974. *The Poetry, Life and Opinions of Sa'adu Zungur.* Zaria: Northern Nigerian Publishing Co.

Abdulkadir, Mansur. 2000. "Popular Culture in Advertising: Nigerian Hausa Radio." In *African Broadcast Culture: Radio in Transition,* ed. Richard Fardon and Graham Furniss, 128–143. Oxford: James Currey.

Adamu, Abdalla Uba. 1999. "Idols of the Marketplace: Literary History, Literary Criticism and the Contemporary Hausa Novel." *New Nigerian Weekly,* June 12.

Adamu, Yusufu M. 1998. "Hausa Novels: Beyond the Great Debate." *New Nigerian Weekly,* July 18.

———. 2002. "Between the Word and the Screen: A Historical Perspective on the Hausa Literary Movement and the Home Video Invasion." *Journal of African Cultural Studies* 15, no. 2: 195–207.

Ahmed, Baba. 1989. "Malam Abubakar Imam as I Knew Him (1939–1981)." In *The Abubakar Imam Memoirs,* ed. Abdurrahman Mora, 256–261. Zaria: Northern Nigerian Publishing Co.

Binji, Haliru. 1989. "A Short Biography of Alhaji Abubakar Imam." In *The Abubakar Imam Memoirs,* ed. Abdurrahman Mora, 262–271. Zaria: Northern Nigerian Publishing Co.

East, R. M. 1943. "Recent Activities of the Literature Bureau, Zaria, Northern Nigeria." *Africa* 14, no. 1: 71–77.

Furniss, G. 1995. *Ideology in Practice: Hausa Poetry as Exposition of Values and Viewpoints.* Koln: Rudiger Koeppe.

Imam, Abubakar. 1989. "First Political Leaders." In *The Abubakar Imam Memoirs,* ed. Abdurrahman Mora, 152–171. Zaria: Northern Nigerian Publishing Co.

Larkin, B. 1997. "Indian Films and Nigerian Lovers: Media and the Creation of Parallel Modernities." *Africa* 67, no. 3: 406–439.

———. 2000. "Hausa Dramas and the Rise of Video Culture in Nigeria." In *Nigerian Video Films,* ed. Jonathan Haynes, 209–241. Athens: Ohio University Press.

Paden, John. 1973. *Religion and Political Culture in Kano.* Berkeley: University of California Press.

Tunau, Abubakar. 1989. "I Served under Abubakar Imam." In *The Abubakar Imam Memoirs,* ed. Abdurrahman Mora, 272–275. Zaria: Northern Nigerian Publishing Co.

Yahaya, Ibrahim Yaro. 1988. *Hausa a Rubuce: Tarihin Rubuce-Rubuce Cikin Hausa* (Written Hausa: A History of Writing in Hausa). Zaria: Northern Nigerian Publishing Co.

Yakubu, A. M. 1999. *Sa'adu Zungur: An Anthology of the Social and Political Writings of a Nigerian Nationalist.* Kaduna: Nigerian Defence Academy Press.

Contributors

KARIN BARBER is Professor of African Cultural Anthropology at the University of Birmingham. Her books include *I Could Speak Until Tomorrow: Oriki, Women and the Past in a Yoruba Town* and *The Generation of Plays*, which won the Herskovits Award.

KEITH BRECKENRIDGE teaches in the History and Internet Studies programs at the University of KwaZulu-Natal. He is currently preparing a manuscript on the effort to erase insurgent literacy through the use of biometrics in South Africa.

CATHERINE BURNS teaches history, gender studies, law, and health at the University of KwaZulu-Natal. She has published articles on the history of health, healing, women's lives, and changing gender relations in South Africa.

BODIL FOLKE FREDERIKSEN is Associate Professor of International Development Studies at Roskilde University. She has published articles on media, literature, urban leisure, and the localization of global popular culture in East Africa.

GRAHAM FURNISS is Professor of African Language Literature at the School of Oriental and African Studies, University of London. He is author of *Poetry, Prose, and Popular Culture in Hausa* and *Orality: The Power of the Spoken Word.* He co-edited (with Richard Fardon) *African Languages, Development, and the State* and *African Broadcast Cultures: Radio in Transition* and (with Liz Gunner) *Power, Marginality, and African Oral Literature.*

AUDREY GADZEKPO is Senior Lecturer at the School of Communication Studies at the University of Ghana. She is co-author of *What Is Fit to Print: The Language of the Press in Ghana* and *Selected Writings of a Pioneer West African Feminist: Mabel Dove.*

LIZ GUNNER is Research Associate at WISER (Wits Institute of Social and Economic Research), University of Witwatersrand. She recently edited and translated *The Man of Heaven and the Beautiful Ones of God: Isaiah Shembe and the Nazareth Church*.

ISABEL HOFMEYR is Professor of African Literature at the University of the Witwatersrand in Johannesburg. She is author of *The Portable Bunyan: A Transnational History of* The Pilgrim's Progress.

VUKILE KHUMALO teaches African History in the School of Anthropology, Gender and Historical Studies at the University of KwaZulu-Natal in South Africa.

T. C. MCCASKIE is Professor of Asante History, Centre of West African Studies, University of Birmingham, U.K. He is author of *State and Society in Precolonial Asante* and *Asante Identities: History and Modernity in an African Village, 1850–1950*. He co-edited *"The History of Ashanti Kings and the Whole Country Itself" and Other Writings, by Otumfuo, Nana Agyeman Prempeh I*.

STEPHAN F. MIESCHER is Associate Professor of History at the University of California in Santa Barbara. He is author of *Making Men in Ghana*. He co-edited (with Lisa A. Lindsay) *Men and Masculinities in Modern Africa*, and (with Luise White and David William Cohen) *African Words, African Voices: Critical Practices in Oral History*.

STEPHANIE NEWELL lectures in postcolonial literatures at the University of Sussex. She is author of *Ghanaian Popular Literature* and *Literary Culture in Colonial Ghana*.

BHEKIZIZWE PETERSON is Associate Professor of African Literature at the University of the Witwatersrand. He is author of *Monarchs, Missionaries & African Intellectuals: African Theatre and the Unmaking of Colonial Marginality* and the co-writer and co-producer of the feature films *Fools* and *Zulu Love Letter*.

LYNN M. THOMAS is Associate Professor of History and Adjunct Associate Professor of Women Studies at the University of Washington in Seattle. She is author of *Politics of the Womb: Women, Reproduction, and the State in Kenya*.

RUTH WATSON is a Senior Lecturer in the School of History, Classics and Archaeology at Birkbeck, University of London. She is author of *"Civil Disorder Is the Disease of Ibadan": Chieftaincy and Civic Culture in a Yoruba City* (2003).

Index

Index

Index

litical involvement, 14, 214–20, 223, 228, 230, 261, 264–69, 416; performance of "civilized" values through, 262, 265; and popular novellas, 211, 219, 227–28, 231–32; pre-colonial history of, 223–24; "progress" debated in, 263, 268; radical potential of, 265–66; reasons for joining, 213; in schools, 2, 13; and self-constitution, 223, 232, 244; as a social movement, 232; in South Africa, 247; Victorian models for, 220–21; and youth movements, 229–30. *See also* debating societies; literary circles

literature: in African languages, 266, 269, 271, 273, 395–98; canon of English classics, 97, 219, 230, 237, 246, 258–59, 262–63, 270, 272–73, 317, 330, 391; cultural infrastructure for, 392; emergence as academic discipline, 266; and evangelism, 266–67; and interactive culture, 398; letter-writing and, 126–27; manuscript copying, 418, 420; map of black writing, 158; message of, 433; and nationalism, 266, 271; newspapers and, 240, 252, 271; printing of, 419, 421, 424–25; production of, 417–20, 424, 426, 430; readership for, 249–50, 255n28; and oral tradition, 267, 398; and socio-political organization, 420–22, 424; as source of quotations, 261, 270, 272–76; women writers, 17; world of the book, 236–54; Yoruba, 395–98. *See also various genres and forms of writing*

local presses: Abura Printing Works, 341; Adenle, S. A. and, 390, 392, 403; and advice literature, 96; and "battle of the books," 360; and book publishing, 289; and innovation, 3; Ekukhanyeni mission press, 118, 129; Fuze, Magema and, 129, 157; in Lagos, 397; and literary clubs, 213, 219, 226–30; Lovedale College press, 96; mission-run, 58, 96, 118, 129, 418; newspapers, 15, 67, 278–309; and Nzima Literary Society, 226; and obituaries, 341–42, 360; and popular novellas, 17, 232; and proliferation of written texts, 1; and the public sphere, 157; Salami Agbaje's printing press, 67, 75n42; Tani-mẹhin-ọla Press, 390; treadle press, 298; and vernacular languages, 226–28; and reading circles, 3, 17; and self-constitution, 157

Longfellow, H. W., 237
Lonsdale, John, 182, 285, 291
Loram, C. T., 248
Lovedale College, 13, 252, 258–76; Literary Society, 258–76
Lugard, Lord, 65, 68

Luo people, 181, 193–94, 298
Lutheran Church, 31

Maasai people, 285
Maclock family, 91–92
Macquarrie, J. W., 264–65
Made, Mrs., 155, 160, 162
Magwaza, Magema. *See* Fuze, Magema
Maine, Kas, 148, 160
Makerere College, 180, 184, 191, 196
Mallett, L. T., 128
Maluleke family (migrant workers), 147
Mamdani, Mahmood, 14
Mampon Literary Club (MLC), 351–52
Mampon people, 351, 357
Mancobe, Ernest Methuen, 252
Mandela, Nelson, 88, 258–59, 276
MaNdlovu (Nazareth Church deaconess), 174
Maphumulo, Lazarus, 11
marabi musical culture, 158
marital advice, 1, 30, 166, 332–33
marketplace literature, 417
Marks, Shula, 97, 128
marriage, Christian monogamy, 34–39, 41–42, 185–86, 332–35; and class mobility, 185–86, 190–91; concubinage, 34–39, 41–42; compensation for pregnancy (as alternative to marriage), 188, 193–94, 205n25; customary, 34–39, 41–42, 332–35; marriage market, 190–94; and modernity, 191–95; negotiations for, 188, 192; polygyny, 34–39, 41–42, 156, 186, 332–35; pre-marital pregnancies, 180–203
Masuku, N. J. N., 129
Masuku family, 157
Mathonsi, Mrs., 155
Mau Mau Emergency, 2, 15, 278–81, 289, 293, 301–302, 306
Mayer, Philip and Iona, 144
Mbeki, Govan, 258–59
Mbeki, Thabo, 143, 148, 152, 259, 276
Mbiu, Senior Chief Koinange, 293
Mbiu, Wangoi, 293
Mbuzeni (of Ekukhanyeni mission station), 123
Mdala, Kenneth, 21n1
Mdledle, Bennett, 267
media, 280, 298
Meintjes, Sheila, 157, 169
memoirs, 1, 314–35; exemplary lives in, 331; of Ffoulkes-Crabbe, Mary, 314–35; and ideology, 322; and public etiquette, 320–21; public-private dynamic in, 319–21; transformational analysis of, 319, 322, 333–35
Mensa, Ata, 351
Meru language, 188–90
Mfantsipim Old Boys' Association, 218

Index

Mfengu people, 90, 93, 108n35
Mickson, E. K., 17
Miescher, Stephan, 62
migrant workers, 1, 4, 6, 9, 46, 80, 83, 115, 124, 143–52, 166, 169, 184, 191, 212–13, 281, 285
Milner, Lord, 145, 147
Milton, John, 237, 262, 330
Mini, Stephanus, 161
ministers/preachers, 28, 47, 115, 164, 399
missions, and African languages, 225–27; African culture rejected by, 236–38; Basel Mission, 10, 31–32, 45; Church Missionary Society, 56, 58–60, 65, 386, 389, 399; and colonial state, 116–18, 331–32; and debating societies, 258–76; and diaries, 31–32; Ekukhanyeni Mission, 2, 4, 6, 113–38, 139n8, 157; and female initiation, 181–83; and land, 291; and letter-writing, 113–38, 144–45; and literacy, 2, 4, 6–7, 10–11, 16–17, 20, 31–32, 55–60, 65, 72, 97, 156, 159, 211, 219, 224, 236–37, 259–61, 279, 389, 393; and literary clubs, 228–29; as literary sphere, 118–20; and Mandela, Nelson, 258; Nazarene, 147; as political sphere, 116–18; and printing presses, 58, 96, 118, 129, 157, 252, 418–19; Scottish Mission, 32; and Shakespeare, 258–59. *See also* Presbyterian church
Mitchell, James A., 94
Mitchell, Sir Philip, 288
Mkize, Ida Nokuphila, 170
Mkwayi, Wilton, 278
M'Mwirichia, Naaman, 184
modernity, 3, 182, 191–97, 205n31, 220, 236, 238, 251, 269, 281, 285–86, 342–43, 348–51, 353, 359, 361–62, 391
Mofolo, Thomas, 238, 251
Molapi, Chief David, 104
Moral Rearmament movement, 304
morality tale, 96
Moshoeshoe, King, 238
Mostert, A. M., 145
Mozambique, 144, 147, 151
Mpande, King, 126–27
Mphephanduku, Lahlekile, 149
Mpondo people, 90, 150
Mqhayi, S. E. K., 238, 251–52, 269, 272–74
Mseleka, William, 158
Msimang family, 161
Mthimkhulu, Nceke, 123
Muchendu, James, 291
Mugo, Dedan, 290
Mulumba, Semukula, 291
Muoria, Henry, 2, 15–17, 278–309, *284;* in London, 283–84, 289, 291; "The British

and My Kikuyu Tribe," 281; *Kenya, the Land of Troubles,* 289; Mbari, Wambui wa (mother) Muoria, Mwaniki wa (father), 281; Nuna, Ruth (third wife), 283, *284,* 297–98; Nyamurwa, Judith (second wife), 2, 16, 283, 289, 297, 299; *Our Mother Is Soil and Our Father Is Wisdom,* 290; Thogori, Elizabeth (first wife), 282–83; *What It Takes to Live Sociably Today,* 283; *What Should We Do for Our Sake?,* 282;
music, 158, 394, 397, 419, 421
Mvemve, Louisa, 1, 11–12, 78–106, 148; *A Woman's Advice,* 96
Mwangi, Thomas, 180–81, 191–94
Myers, Elizabeth Sabina, 316
Mzayifani, Jones, 145
Mzimba, S., 263

Nair, Billy, 259
Nairobi. *See* Kenya
National Congress of British West Africa (NCBWA), 66, 225
National Geographic, 249
nationalism, 13, 15, 114–15, 214–15, 217, 221, 225–28, 236, 239, 253, 264, 266, 269, 271, 275, 278–80, 285, 293–94, 297, 300, 321, 326, 353, 359, 400
Nationalists Club, 215
Native Affairs Department (NAD), South Africa, 11–12, 78–106
Nazarene Mission, 147
Nazareth church, 2, 11, 155, 167, 172–73
Ndabuko, Chief, 121, 133–35
Ndiyana (of Ekukhanyeni mission station), 126
Negro Literary Society, 67
"new African," 238, 240
New Tafo Literary and Social Club, 213
Newell, Stephanie, 265
Newlands, H. S., 345
newspapers: *Abantu Batho,* 94; advertisements in, 94, 290, 307–10; *Africa and Orient Review,* 66–67; African languages and, 182, 193–94, 240, 278–309, 397; *African Morning Post,* 216–21, 230, 232; *Akede Eko,* 398; *Ashanti Pioneer,* 341, 355, 358; *Bantu World,* 236–54; *Baraza,* 193, 294–95; and book-reading, 240, 244; censorship and, 280, 285, 294; *Christian Express,* 271; and civil society, 15; as collaborative texts, 16; and cultural interaction, 398; *Daily Chronicle,* 294; *Democrat,* 285; *East African Standard,* 282, 294; and economic opportunity, 286, 290; and the educated elite, 214; *Eleti Ofe,* 398; English language, in 215, 240, 286, 356; and exemplary individuals, 245; *Gold Coast Times,* 220, 314, 325; and the

Index

Ibadan circle of Akinpẹlu Obiṣẹsan, 58, 66–69, 73; *Ibadan Weekly Review,* 67–68; *Ilanga lase Natal,* 94, 127, 140n40; *Imvo Zabantsundu,* 94; industrial production of, 416; *Inkanyise Yase Natali,* 119; *Iwe Irohin,* 58, 68; *Iwe Irohin Eko,* 398; Kikuyu-language, 278–309; in Lagos, 397; *Lagos Weekly Record,* 67–69; and letter-writing, 119–21, 127–28, 398, 427; and literacy, 167–68, 182, 193–94, 196, 212, 231, 236–54, 326; and literary clubs, 211–12, 214, 216–22, 229–32; and literary endeavor, 252, 271; and modernity, 286; *Muigwithania,* 279–80, 285, 310n3; *Mumenyereri,* 15, 278–309; *Muthithu,* 288; *Mwalimu,* 293; and nationalism, 280, 285–86, 293–94, 297, 300, 326; *Negro World,* 66; obituaries in, 355–60; and pan-Africanism, 280; poetry in, 252–53, 398; and political consciousness, 119–21, 127–28, 216–17, 239–40; popular novellas in, 398; and populism, 293, 298; as public space, 326; *Radio Posta,* 293, 298; and public/private dynamic, 319–20, 326; *Ramogi,* 298; *Sauti Mwafika,* 293; and self-constitution, 182, 193–94; *Spectator* (Gold Coast), *216, 217,* 230, 232; Swahili-language, 182, 193–94, 294; *Taifa Leo,* 193; *Taifa Weekly,* 193; *Tazama* magazine, 295; *Times of Nigeria,* 68; *Times of West Africa,* 231; *Umteteli Wa Bantu,* 94; *Weekly Dispatch,* 67; women's column, 314–16, 319, 325–35; and writing, 240, 252; *Yoruba News,* 58, 67, 414n16;Yoruba-language, 397

Ngidi, Jonathan, 117
Ngidi, William, 117–19, 126
Ngubane, Harriette, 169
Ngubane, Phumalani, 155, 160
Niger, 417
Nigeria: Abẹku, 61; Abẹokuta, 58, 60, 399, 403, 414n16; Akurẹ, 393; Bauchi, 422–25; Benin City, 386, 391, 393; Elekurọ, 70; Ibadan, 2, 20, 55–56, 59, 61, 64–73, 388, 393, 399, 414n16; Ijẹbu, 56, 61; Ijẹbu-Ode, 390; Inuodi, 61; Jos, 419; Kaduna, 429; Kano, 417–19, 425–26, 428–29; Katsina, 426; Lagos, 20, 56, 59, 392, 395, 397–99, 402–403, 414n16; northern, 4, 21, 416–33; Oṣogbo, 4, 385–92, 399; Ọyọ, 56, 61, 65, 386; southern, 423; Tudun Wada, 419; western, 385; Zaria, 419, 422–23, 426–28
Nigerian Cocoa Board, 53
Nigerian National Film and Video Censors' Board, 431
Nigerian Peoples' Congress (NPC), 421, 426

Nkrumah, Kwame, 29, 39, 43, 46, 225, 231, 351
Nondela (of Ekukhanyeni mission station), 125
Nondenisa, Mubi, 123, 125, 129, 132, 140n33
Nongqawuse, 173
Northcote, G. A. S., 345–46
Northern Elements Progressive Union (NEPU), 421, 425, 427
Northern Nigerian Publishing Company, 420
notebooks: biblical language in, 167; as chronicle, 167; exemplary lives in, 331; financial transactions in, 164; and ideology, 320; healing in, 156, 167, 169, 171–72; hymns in, 159–61, 163–64, 167; "illumination" effect in, 163; imprint of the sacred in, 160; Nazareth Church's "shared memorialization" in, 159–60; notebook-diary continuity, 160–62; and oral tradition, 163; and psychological illness, 158, 164, 168–75; and public etiquette, 320–21; public-private dynamic in, 319–21; and self-documentation, 1; and self-management, 1; specimen pages, *165–66, 318;* transformational analysis of, 319, 322, 333–35. *See also* diaries
Nottingham, J., 285
Ntsikana, 263
nurses, 83, 86, 105
Nyarko, Nana Amma Serwa, 358
Nzima Literary Society, 225–28
Nzima people/language, 225–27

Ọbasa, D. A., 66–67, 402
Obiṣẹsan, Akinpẹlu, 2, 5, 9–10, 52–73, *58;* and Abọdunrin (brother), 63–64; and Akinloye, Akanbi (friend), 61; and Aperin, Obiṣẹsan (father), 56, 65, 72; and Atunwa (wife), 62–63; and Ayọka (wife), 52; and Bamgbade (acquaintance), 70; and Bọlarinwa (brother), 63; and Dada, Rev. (acquaintance), 69; and Fadairo (brother), 63; and Laluwoye (friend), 70; and Lapade (son), 53; and Larewaju (wife), 63; and Motosho (cousin), 71; and Obasa, Daniel (friend), 66–67; and Ogunjọbi, *Mogaji* (family head), 72; and Ogunlana (brother), 63; and Okunyiga (son Ojo's teacher), 69; and Olugbode, Adedeji (enemy), 64; and Ricketts (mercantile agent), 69, 71
obituary notices: audience of, 343, 350; authorship of, 343, 345, 359; and "battle of the books," 360; and Christianity, 349–50; and class competition, 4; and the decline of print culture, 361–63; English language and, 347, 349; and funeral customs, 342–43, 349–50, 353–54, 356, 362; local demand for, 1; as long-term aspiration, 9, 320, 359; memories trig-

Index

Index

social networks, 6, 40, 42, 46, 62, 69, 82, 104, 113–38, 197, 228, 238, 253, 344, 359, 393, 426
Socrates, 391
Soga, Tiyo, 272
Sogoni, David, 150
Sohlathi, Ngilambi, 145
Ṣọlaja, Fọlarin, 57, 70–71
South Africa, 291, 293; Acornhoek, 147; Alice 85, 93, 262; Benoni, 78, 80–81, 84–85, 89, 92, 98, 102; Bishopstowe, 117, 139n11, 156–57; Boksburg, 159; Brakpan, 80–81, 85, 89, 98, 102, 104; Butterworth, 85, 103; Caluza, 161; Cape Colony, 116, 145, 252; Cape Town, 93, 103, 117, 123, 248, 271, 274–75; Clarkesbury, 258, 276; Durban, 147–49, 151, 155, 162; Eastern Cape, 1, 80, 84, 86, 90–91, 93, 96–98, 102, 104, 120, 144, 148, 156, 258, 269; East Rand, 81, 92, 105, 148; Edendale, 129, 155–58, 160–61, 169, 172, 175; Ekuphakameni, 155–56, 159–61, 163–64, 166–67, 172; Empangeni, 167; Eshowe, 129, 157; Florida, 251; Gingindlovu, 165; Grahamstown, 85, 89–90, 93, 101–104; Healdtown, 258, 276; Health Act (1928), 83, 102–103; Hertzog Bills, (1936) 246; Idutywa, 143; Inanda, 159, 161; Johannesburg, 13, 78–79, 85, 102, 105, 120, 127, 157, 165, 236–37; Judea, 165; Kingwilliamstown, 85, 89, 101; Komgha, 91; Lovedale, 96, 252; Mbewuleni, 143; Melmoth, 137; Mphumuzo, 162; Natal, 2, 9, 82, 94, 99, 113–38, 144, 151, 159, 161, 248; National Convention (1908), 114; Ndwedwe, 155; Nhlangakazi mountain, 155; Peddie, 85, 93; Pietermaritzburg, 85, 116, 128–29, 131, 156, 158–59, 167; Port Alfred, 90–91; Pretoria, 86, 95; Reef (Witwatersrand), 1, 99–100, 102–104, 125, 148–49, 236–37; Robben Island, 258; Siyamu, 156–57, 161; Sophiatown, 242; Transkei, 80, 84–86, 93, 98, 103–104, 143, 268; Transvaal, 80, 124, 248; Umtata, 85, 93, 103; Urban Acts (1920s), 83, 102–103; Valley of a Thousand Hills, 116, 155; West Rand, 145; West Transvaal, 148; Western Native Township, 242; Wizieshoek, 85; Zululand, 151, 159, 161, 165
South African Native National Congress (SANNC), 91, 113–15
Soviet Union, 30
Soyayya books, 430
spirit possession, 159, 161, 168–75
Sraha, Kofi, 349

St. Alban's College, 129
St. Andrew's College Oyo, 386, 389, 393, 399
St. Helena, 118, 120–23, 125, 129–30, 132–35
St. John of the Cross, 173
Stirling, M. M., 249
storytelling, 45–46, 251
Stowe, Harriet Beecher, 97
Sudan, 303, 417
Swahili language, 182, 278, 294
Swartkop location, 157

teachers: as diarists, 27–47, 60; discursive environment of, 399; in educated elite, 239, 321–23; and educational reform and development, 322–23, 325–27, 329–31, 387–88, 391, 393; fame through pupils, 393; gendered world of, 393; headmasters, 385; hoarded "shrines to literacy" of, 27, 29–30; Islamic, 418; as link in cultural communication, 347; and literary clubs, 30, 213, 229; loneliness and enlightenment of, 391–94; memory structures of, 393; as migrants, 46; and modernity, 388; and newspapers, 219; in non-elite intermediary class, 10, 28–29, 47, 83, 350; and popular novellas, 227; quality of, 120; and schoolgirl pregnancies, 182–83, 190; social networks of, 42, 46, 69, 393; teacher-catechists, 27–47; as writers, 27–47, 345, 385–412
Tengo-Jabavu, J., 263
Thale, Mary, 265
Tharau, G. N., 292
theater, 275, 299–300, 394, 397, 419
Thembu people, 90
Thimbler family, 104
Tiger Remedies, 87–88, 100, 107n24
Tippett (South African government official), 91
Townsend, Henry, 58, 68
traders, 1–2, 29, 31, 37, 40, 47, 52–73, 213, 281, 288–89, 352, 386–88, 392, 399, 417; Muslim, 57, 70
transformational analysis, 319, 322, 333–35
travel accounts, 39–42
Tshingana, 121, 133–35
Tsiboe, J. W., 341–42
Tswana people, 145
Tunan, Abubakar, 426
Twala, Dan, 272
Twala, R., 122–23, 127, 136
Twi language, 10, 30, 34, 44, 343
Tyler, Miss Susie, 127
Tyler, Rev. Josiah, 127

UAC trading company, 387
ufufunyane, 169–70, 175
Uganda, 291, 303
ukuthwasa, 169

450